World Economic and Financial Surveys

WORLD ECONOMIC OUTLOOK
April 2006

Globalization and Inflation

International Monetary Fund

Production: IMF Multimedia Services Division
Cover and Design: Luisa Menjivar-Macdonald
Figures: Theodore F. Peters, Jr.
Typesetting: Choon Lee

World economic outlook (International Monetary Fund)
World economic outlook: a survey by the staff of the International
Monetary Fund.—1980– —Washington, D.C.: The Fund, 1980–

  v.; 28 cm.—(1981–84: Occasional paper/International Monetary
Fund ISSN 0251-6365)
    Annual.
    Has occasional updates, 1984–
    ISSN 0258-7440 = World economic and financial surveys
    ISSN 0256-6877 = World economic outlook (Washington)
    1. Economic history—1971– —Periodicals. I. International
Monetary Fund. II. Series: Occasional paper (International
Monetary Fund)

HC10.W7979   84-640155

                                338.5'443'09048—dc19
                                        AACR 2 MARC-S

Library of Congress   8507

    Published biannually.
ISBN 1-58906-549-2

Price: US$49.00
(US$46.00 to full-time faculty members and
students at universities and colleges)

Please send orders to:
International Monetary Fund, Publication Services
700 19th Street, N.W., Washington, D.C. 20431, U.S.A.
Tel.: (202) 623-7430   Telefax: (202) 623-7201
E-mail: publications@imf.org
Internet: http://www.imf.org

recycled paper

CONTENTS

Tables

Figures

ASSUMPTIONS AND CONVENTIONS

A number of assumptions have been adopted for the projections presented in the *World Economic Outlook*. It has been assumed that real effective exchange rates will remain constant at their average levels during February 9–March 9, 2006, except for the currencies participating in the European exchange rate mechanism II (ERM II), which are assumed to remain constant in nominal terms relative to the euro; that established policies of national authorities will be maintained (for specific assumptions about fiscal and monetary policies in industrial countries, see Box A1); that the average price of oil will be $61.25 a barrel in 2006 and $63.00 a barrel in 2007, and remain unchanged in real terms over the medium term; that the six-month London interbank offered rate (LIBOR) on U.S. dollar deposits will average 5.0 percent in 2006 and 5.1 percent in 2007; that the three-month euro deposits rate will average 3.0 percent in 2006 and 3.4 percent in 2007; and that the six-month Japanese yen deposit rate will yield an average of 0.3 percent in 2006 and of 0.9 percent in 2007. These are, of course, working hypotheses rather than forecasts, and the uncertainties surrounding them add to the margin of error that would in any event be involved in the projections. The estimates and projections are based on statistical information available through early April 2006.

The following conventions have been used throughout the *World Economic Outlook:*

   . . .   to indicate that data are not available or not applicable;

   —   to indicate that the figure is zero or negligible;

   –   between years or months (for example, 2004–05 or January–June) to indicate the years or months covered, including the beginning and ending years or months;

   /   between years or months (for example, 2004/05) to indicate a fiscal or financial year.

"Billion" means a thousand million; "trillion" means a thousand billion.

"Basis points" refer to hundredths of 1 percentage point (for example, 25 basis points are equivalent to ¼ of 1 percent point).

In figures and tables, shaded areas indicate IMF staff projections.

Minor discrepancies between sums of constituent figures and totals shown are due to rounding.

As used in this report, the term "country" does not in all cases refer to a territorial entity that is a state as understood by international law and practice. As used here, the term also covers some territorial entities that are not states but for which statistical data are maintained on a separate and independent basis.

FURTHER INFORMATION AND DATA

This report on the *World Economic Outlook* is available in full on the IMF's Internet site, www.imf.org. Accompanying it on the website is a larger compilation of data from the WEO database than in the report itself, consisting of files containing the series most frequently requested by readers. These files may be downloaded for use in a variety of software packages.

Inquiries about the content of the *World Economic Outlook* and the WEO database should be sent by mail, electronic mail, or telefax (telephone inquiries cannot be accepted) to:

World Economic Studies Division
Research Department
International Monetary Fund
700 19th Street, N.W.
Washington, D.C. 20431, U.S.A.
E-mail: weo@imf.org   Telefax: (202) 623-6343

PREFACE

The analysis and projections contained in the *World Economic Outlook* are integral elements of the IMF's surveillance of economic developments and policies in its member countries, of developments in international financial markets, and of the global economic system. The survey of prospects and policies is the product of a comprehensive interdepartmental review of world economic developments, which draws primarily on information the IMF staff gathers through its consultations with member countries. These consultations are carried out in particular by the IMF's area departments together with the Policy Development and Review Department, the International Capital Markets Department, the Monetary and Financial Systems Department, and the Fiscal Affairs Department.

The analysis in this report has been coordinated in the Research Department under the general direction of Raghuram Rajan, Economic Counsellor and Director of Research. The project has been directed by David Robinson, Deputy Director of the Research Department, together with Tim Callen, Division Chief, Research Department.

The primary contributors to this report are Thomas Helbling, Subir Lall, Kalpana Kochhar, Sandy Mackenzie, Gian Maria Milesi-Ferretti, S. Hossein Samiei, Roberto Cardarelli, To-Nhu Dao, Selim Elekdag, Toh Kuan, Florence Jaumotte, Valerie Mercer-Blackman, Paul Nicholson, Alessandro Rebucci, Martin Sommer, Nikola Spatafora, and Johannes Wiegand. Christian de Guzman, Stephanie Denis, Angela Espiritu, Bennett Sutton, and Ercument Tulun provided research assistance. Mahnaz Hemmati, Laurent Meister, and Casper Meyer managed the database and the computer systems. Sylvia Brescia, Celia Burns, and Seetha Milton were responsible for word processing. Other contributors include Laurence Ball, Nicoletta Batini, Pelin Berkmen, Michael Bordo, James Boughton, Luis Catão, Jean Pierre Chauffour, Li Cui, Daniel Hardy, Lutz Kilian, Laura Kodres, Kornélia Krajnyák, Suchitra Kumarapathy, Doug Laxton, Vojislav Maksimovic, Sam Ouliaris, Lars Pedersen, M. Hashem Pesaran, Miguel Segoviano, Marco Terrones, Kenichi Ueda, and Frank Warnock. Jeff Hayden of the External Relations Department edited the manuscript and coordinated the production of the publication.

The analysis has benefited from comments and suggestions by staff from other IMF departments, as well as by Executive Directors following their discussion of the report on March 29 and 31, 2006. However, both projections and policy considerations are those of the IMF staff and should not be attributed to Executive Directors or to their national authorities.

FOREWORD

The *World Economic Outlook* is a cooperative effort. A few members of the Research Department put it together, but in doing so they rely heavily on staff from around the Fund. I thank Tim Callen, members of the World Economic Studies Division, and all the IMF staff from other divisions and departments who worked together to bring this *World Economic Outlook* to you. I am especially grateful to David Robinson, who has supervised an impressive series of high-quality *Outlooks* over the last six years, and will now be moving on to a different position in the Fund.

The world economy is in the midst of an extraordinary purple patch, with what looks like a third year of significantly above-trend growth. Growth is also becoming more balanced with Japan picking up strongly, and the euro area showing advance signs of steadier growth. Perhaps the best reflection of the times is that sub-Saharan Africa is headed for its best growth performance in over 30 years.

As past *Outlooks* have documented, an important reason for this good performance has been greater flows of goods, services, and capital across the world, a phenomenon known colloquially as globalization. The chapters in this *Outlook* all try to make sense of this phenomenon.

Chapter III, "How Has Globalization Affected Inflation?," finds that globalization has at times had an important impact on inflation over the past decade. IMF staff estimates suggest that through non-oil import prices, globalization has reduced inflation by an average of a ¼ of a percentage point a year in the advanced economies, with a larger effect of a ½ percentage point a year in the United States. At times when global spare capacity has been plentiful, as for instance after the 1997–98 crises in emerging markets, these direct effects have been even larger, shaving more than 1 percentage point off actual inflation in some advanced economies over one- to two-year periods. More generally, globalization has contributed to reducing the sensitivity of inflation to domestic capacity constraints, while increasing the sensitivity to global constraints. It has also restrained wage increases in industries most open to global competition, and even lowered the sensitivity of wages to productivity increases.

For globalization to have a substantial lasting impact on inflation, however, it must change the overarching objectives of monetary policy—such as the central bank's inflation target—which, over the medium term, determines inflation. After all, with such a target, downward pressure from abroad on the domestic price index would only allow central bankers more room to be accommodative. In my view, however, the true impact of globalization has been in contributing to wage and price restraint at a time when central bankers were establishing their inflation-fighting credibility, thus allowing them to achieve targets and gain credibility without the need to tighten to politically difficult levels.

Despite being helpful in the past, globalization may not continue to be a crutch for central bankers. Spare capacity is decreasing worldwide, especially in the United States, the United Kingdom, and Canada. International competition helps less in restraining prices when there are global supply constraints. Tight domestic labor markets can also attenuate the effects of global competition on wages—in the United States, wage pressures are beginning to come to the fore. Central bankers must therefore remain vigilant for signs of a pickup in inflation in the period ahead.

Another aspect of globalization is an integrated market for world savings and borrowing. What is particularly interesting here is that the identity of the savers and borrowers has shifted in the last few years. Corporations are usually net borrowers. In 2003 and 2004, though, total corporate excess savings (undistributed profit less capital expenditure) in the G-7 countries amounted to $1.3 trillion, which was more than twice the combined current account surpluses of emerging market and developing countries over the same period.

This increase in corporate savings can be decomposed into two main components. First, there has been a substantial increase in corporate profits in the G-7 since about 2000. In general, this has *not* been because of better operating profits, but because taxes and interest rates have come down so that profits after interest and taxes have gone up—in other words, profitability is largely due to accommodative monetary and fiscal policy rather than, as commonly believed, productive efficiency. The second and arguably more important component is falling capital spending. It accounted for as much as three-quarters of the total increase in corporate excess savings since 2000. One reason for lower capital spending is that the real price of capital goods has declined sharply, so less has to be invested to increase the real capital stock by a given amount. Another reason is a drop in *real* capital spending. Here there is no uniform pattern across all seven countries—the United States and Germany are responsible for much of the decline.

Taken together, Chapters III and IV suggest an extraordinary confluence of global forces have kept the world economy going in the last few years. As investment slowed following the overcapacity built up by excess investment in the late 1990s and early 2000s, excess corporate savings contributed to the global savings pool to push down long-term interest rates. Consumption picked up—driven more by accommodative policy and its effects on house prices and household wealth than by improved job prospects. Quiescent inflation, partly because of a significant global output gap, allowed monetary policy to be very accommodative. Now as the global output gap narrows, monetary accommodation is being withdrawn. Also real corporate investment is likely to pick up. Both will tend to reduce corporate excess savings and push up long-term interest rates. This will slow asset price growth, but consumption may continue to be supported, this time by improved job prospects.

Such a scenario would be the proverbial soft landing. There are less benign possibilities. For instance, consumption growth may fall more rapidly than anticipated as the froth comes out of house prices, and this may have knock-on effects on confidence and investment. Our overall assessment, taking a variety of risks into consideration, is that surrounding the central scenario of robust growth, the risks are weighted to the downside.

Even as the internal transition of savings from corporations to households and governments takes place within some countries, we also need a shift in aggregate demand across countries. Chapter II explains how the oil price shock—itself a result of past underinvestment in the industry—will widen existing global current account imbalances and prolong them. Because the inflationary consequences of oil prices have been limited—partly a result of globalization—and because financing conditions have been benign, oil consumers have not had to adjust as much as they did in the past. Oil producers are rightfully being more circumspect about spending, mindful of past waste. As a result, oil-price-induced imbalances are likely to be with us for some time.

Should this be a concern? More generally, should we worry about the size of the global current account imbalances, given that they have been financed so long? I think we should. For one, the benign global financing conditions appear to be turning so the past need not say much about the future. More important, the imbalances are unsustainable at their current level—even with increasing economic integration, there is a limit to how much a country can depend on the outside world. Deficit countries have to start thinking about weaning themselves of reliance on global savings while surplus countries have to find ways to depend less on external demand. Since adjustment is inevitable, would it not be better to commit to a medium-term policy framework today so that public policy can support private sector adjustment and ensure the process is smooth?

A set of such frameworks for all the major players would have two additional effects. First, it would indicate that the imbalances are a shared responsibility and help prevent concerns about imbalances degenerating into protectionism. Second, it would reassure financial markets that a policy framework for supporting adjustment is in place, thus limiting the risk of an abrupt and costly, market-induced, adjustment.

Unfortunately, the rapidity with which globalization is advancing seems to worry citizens. Some governments see their role increasingly as slowing globalization, extracting political mileage by pandering to vociferous interest groups obstructing change, rather than educating citizens to accept it. Even as linkages between economies grow, far too many governments are putting the slightest domestic constraint above any international interest. Others are reviving beggar-thy-neighbor policies, except they are now on the capital account—shielding large swathes of their own economy from corporate takeovers while encouraging their own companies to take advantage of the continued openness of others. Multilateralism is in retreat everywhere.

These are the best of times but they are also the most dangerous of times. We need to strengthen the process of multilateral dialogue, else globalization could prompt a backlash that might reverse much that has been gained over the last few decades. An important test of the resolve of economic policymakers is whether they will take serious steps to monitor each other (through organizations like the Fund) and force a narrowing of the imbalances over time, or whether they will take their chances with the market and protectionist politics. I hope good sense will prevail.

Raghuram Rajan
Economic Counsellor and Director, Research Department

CHAPTER I

ECONOMIC PROSPECTS AND POLICY ISSUES

Notwithstanding higher oil prices and natural disasters, global growth has continued to exceed expectations, aided by benign financial market conditions and continued accommodative macroeconomic policies. Looking forward, the baseline forecast is for continued strong growth, although—as illustrated in Figure 1.1— risks remain slanted to the downside, the more so since key vulnerabilities—notably the global imbalances— continue to increase. With the risks associated with inaction rising with time, the principal challenge for global policymakers is to take advantage of the unusually favorable conjuncture to address these vulnerabilities. In particular, an orderly resolution of global imbalances will require measures to facilitate a rebalancing of demand across countries and a realignment of exchange rates over the medium term, with the U.S. dollar needing to depreciate significantly from current levels, and currencies in surplus countries— including in parts of Asia and among oil producers— to appreciate.

The momentum and resilience of the global economy in 2005 continued to exceed expectations (Table 1.1 and Figure 1.2). Despite higher oil prices and natural disasters, activity in the second half of 2005 was stronger than earlier projected, particularly among emerging market countries; accounting also for statistical revisions in China,[1] global GDP growth is estimated at 4.8 percent, 0.5 percentage point higher than projected last September. At the same time, incoming data have been generally positive. Global industrial production has picked up markedly from mid-2005; the services sector

Figure 1.1. Prospects for World GDP Growth[1]
(Percent)

Global growth is projected to remain about 4¾ percent in 2006 and 2007, but the risks are slanted to the downside, the more so as time progresses (see text for a detailed discussion).

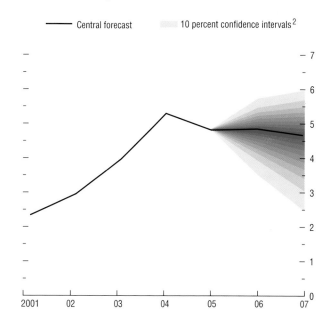

Source: IMF staff estimates.
[1]This so-called fan chart shows the uncertainty around the *World Economic Outlook* central forecast with the 90 percent probability interval. See Box 1.3 for details.
[2]Shaded areas of the same gradient above and below the central forecast add up to 10 percent.

---

[1]Following recent revisions to Chinese national accounts data, its share of global GDP (measured on a purchasing power parity, or PPP, basis) increased by 1½ percentage points to 15.4 percent. Since China's growth has been relatively high, this has raised global GDP growth by 0.1 percentage point in almost every year since 1992 (see Box 1.6).

Table 1.1. Overview of the *World Economic Outlook* Projections
(Annual percent change unless otherwise noted)

	2004	2005	Current Projections 2006	Current Projections 2007	Difference from September 2005 Projections 2006	Difference from September 2005 Projections 2007
World output	**5.3**	**4.8**	**4.9**	**4.7**	**0.6**	**0.3**
Advanced economies	3.3	2.7	3.0	2.8	0.2	−0.2
United States	4.2	3.5	3.4	3.3	0.2	−0.3
Euro area	2.1	1.3	2.0	1.9	0.2	−0.3
Germany	1.6	0.9	1.3	1.0	0.1	−0.5
France	2.1	1.4	2.0	2.1	0.3	−0.4
Italy	0.9	0.1	1.2	1.4	−0.2	−0.3
Spain	3.1	3.4	3.3	3.2	0.3	0.2
Japan	2.3	2.7	2.8	2.1	0.8	0.5
United Kingdom	3.1	1.8	2.5	2.7	0.3	−0.1
Canada	2.9	2.9	3.1	3.0	−0.2	−0.2
Other advanced economies	4.6	3.7	4.1	3.7	0.2	−0.3
Newly industrialized Asian economies	5.8	4.6	5.2	4.5	0.5	−0.6
Other emerging market and developing countries	7.6	7.2	6.9	6.6	0.8	0.7
Africa	5.5	5.2	5.7	5.5	−0.1	0.6
Sub-Sahara	5.6	5.5	5.8	5.7	−0.1	0.5
Central and eastern Europe	6.5	5.3	5.2	4.8	0.7	0.2
Commonwealth of Independent States	8.4	6.5	6.0	6.1	0.3	0.6
Russia	7.2	6.4	6.0	5.8	0.8	0.8
Excluding Russia	11.1	6.7	6.0	6.6	−0.8	−0.1
Developing Asia	8.8	8.6	8.2	8.0	1.0	0.8
China	10.1	9.9	9.5	9.0	1.3	1.0
India	8.1	8.3	7.3	7.0	1.0	0.5
ASEAN-4	5.8	5.2	5.1	5.7	−0.4	−0.1
Middle East	5.4	5.9	5.7	5.4	0.6	0.6
Western Hemisphere	5.6	4.3	4.3	3.6	0.5	0.1
Brazil	4.9	2.3	3.5	3.5	—	—
Mexico	4.2	3.0	3.5	3.1	—	—
Memorandum						
European Union	2.5	1.8	2.4	2.3	0.2	−0.2
World growth based on market exchange rates	4.0	3.4	3.6	3.4	0.4	0.1
World trade volume (goods and services)	**10.4**	**7.3**	**8.0**	**7.5**	**0.6**	**0.5**
Imports						
Advanced economies	8.9	5.8	6.2	5.6	0.4	−0.1
Other emerging market and developing countries	15.8	12.4	12.9	11.9	1.0	1.3
Exports						
Advanced economies	8.5	5.3	6.6	6.1	0.3	0.2
Other emerging market and developing countries	14.6	11.5	10.9	10.3	0.6	1.0
Commodity prices (U.S. dollars)						
Oil[1]	30.7	41.3	14.8	2.9	0.9	5.7
Nonfuel (average based on world commodity export weights)	18.5	10.3	10.2	−5.5	12.3	−1.1
Consumer prices						
Advanced economies	2.0	2.3	2.3	2.1	0.3	0.1
Other emerging market and developing countries	5.7	5.4	5.4	4.8	−0.4	−0.4
London interbank offered rate (percent)[2]						
On U.S. dollar deposits	1.8	3.8	5.0	5.1	0.5	0.5
On euro deposits	2.1	2.2	3.0	3.4	0.6	0.7
On Japanese yen deposits	0.1	0.1	0.3	0.9	0.1	0.4

Note: Real effective exchange rates are assumed to remain constant at the levels prevailing during February 9–March 9, 2006. See Statistical Appendix for details and groups and methodologies.

[1]Simple average of spot prices of U.K. Brent, Dubai, and West Texas Intermediate crude oil. The average price of oil in U.S. dollars a barrel was $53.35 in 2005; the assumed price is $61.25 in 2006, and $63.00 in 2007.

[2]Six-month rate for the United States and Japan. Three-month rate for the euro area.

remains resilient; global trade growth is close to double-digit levels; consumer confidence and labor market conditions are strengthening; and forward-looking indicators, notably business confidence, have risen (Figure 1.3).

From a regional perspective, the expansion is becoming more broadly based. Among industrial countries, despite a weak fourth quarter, the United States remains the main engine of growth, but the Japanese expansion is well established, and there are signs of a more sustained recovery in the euro area, although domestic demand growth remains subdued. Growth in most emerging and developing countries remains solid, with the buoyancy of activity in China, India, and Russia—which together accounted for two-thirds of the upward revision to global growth in 2005 relative to that expected at the time of the September 2005 *World Economic Outlook*—being particularly striking. Consistent with the strength of corporate profits and improved balance sheets, investment in major industrial countries appears to be picking up, although—with some exceptions, most importantly China—less so in emerging market countries, including many in Asia.

Oil prices remain high and volatile. After easing from Katrina-related highs, crude oil prices fluctuated in the range of $60–66 per barrel[2] over the past three months, with comfortable inventory levels—particularly in the United States—counterbalancing rising geopolitical uncertainties in the Islamic Republic of Iran and in Iraq and threats to oil production in Nigeria. With crude oil consumption somewhat lower than expected in 2005, prices are being increasingly driven by concerns about future supply, with the International Energy Agency assessing both upstream and downstream investment to be significantly below desirable levels (see Appendix 1.1); futures markets suggest prices will remain close to current levels for the fore-

[2]The oil price used in the *World Economic Outlook* is a simple average of the spot prices for West Texas Intermediate, U.K. Brent, and Dubai crudes.

Figure 1.2. Global Indicators[1]
(Annual percent change unless otherwise noted)

Global growth remains noticeably above the historical trend, while inflation and long-run interest rates are unusually low.

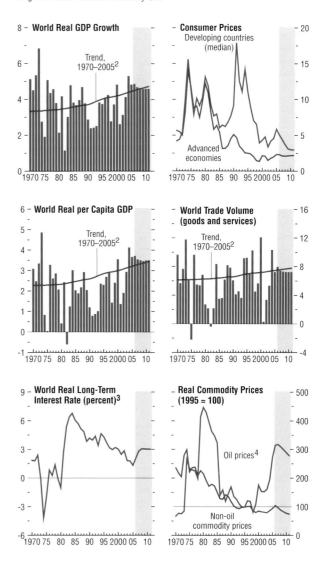

[1]Shaded areas indicate IMF staff projections. Aggregates are computed on the basis of purchasing-power-parity (PPP) weights unless otherwise noted.
[2]Average growth rates for individual countries, aggregated using PPP weights; the aggregates shift over time in favor of faster-growing countries, giving the line an upward trend.
[3]GDP-weighted average of the 10-year (or nearest maturity) government bond yields less inflation rates for the United States, Japan, Germany, France, Italy, the United Kingdom, and Canada. Excluding Italy prior to 1972.
[4]Simple average of spot prices of U.K. Brent, Dubai Fateh, and West Texas Intermediate crude oil.

Figure 1.3. Current and Forward-Looking Indicators

(Percent change from a year ago unless otherwise noted)

Global industrial production has turned up, while business and consumer confidence are generally improving.

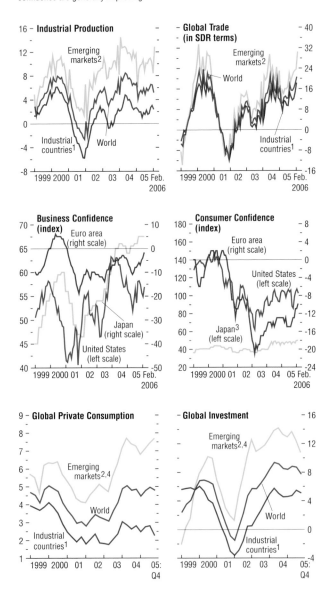

Sources: Business confidence for the United States, the Institute for Supply Management; for the euro area, the European Commission; and for Japan, Bank of Japan. Consumer confidence for the United States, the Conference Board; for the euro area, the European Commission; and for Japan, Cabinet Office; all others, Haver Analytics.

[1] Australia, Canada, Denmark, euro area, Japan, New Zealand, Norway, Sweden, Switzerland, the United Kingdom, and the United States.

[2] Argentina, Brazil, Bulgaria, Chile, China, Colombia, Czech Republic, Estonia, Hong Kong SAR, Hungary, India, Indonesia, Israel, Korea, Latvia, Lithuania, Malaysia, Mexico, Pakistan, Peru, the Philippines, Poland, Romania, Russia, Singapore, Slovak Republic, Slovenia, South Africa, Taiwan Province of China, Thailand, Turkey, Ukraine, and Venezuela.

[3] Japan's consumer confidence data are based on a diffusion index, where values greater than 50 indicate improving confidence.

[4] Data for China, India, Pakistan, and Russia are interpolated.

seeable future. Nonfuel commodity prices—particularly metals—rose strongly in 2005, reflecting both cyclical and supply-side factors, but are projected to moderate in 2006–07 as supply responds to higher prices. The semiconductor cycle has also turned up, particularly in Asia, and while forward-looking indicators are mixed and prices continue to decline, industry analysts expect some pickup in revenue growth in 2006.

Global financial market conditions remain very favorable, characterized by unusually low risk premiums and volatility.[3] Global short-term interest rates have continued to rise, led by the United States. With tightening cycles in the euro area and Japan less advanced or yet to begin, short-term interest rate differentials have widened considerably (Figure 1.4). Despite some recent increase, long-run interest rates remain below average, and the yield curve has flattened, the more so in the most cyclically advanced countries. Interest rate spreads—in both industrial countries and emerging markets—remain close to historic lows (Figure 1.5), reflecting both improved fundamentals but also a search for yield in an environment of easy liquidity, accompanied by buoyant inflows to emerging markets (Table 1.2), with many having already prefinanced their borrowing needs for 2006. Given this favorable environment, equity prices have risen significantly, particularly outside the United States, with some markets looking increasingly richly valued; property prices have been more diverse, although signs of a slowdown have increased in some cyclically advanced countries, notably the United States.

The flattening of the yield curve has raised questions about the durability of the current expansion, particularly in the United States. Certainly, there is a considerable body of evidence supporting the view that a flatter yield curve is a leading indicator of an economic slowdown, although the relationship has weakened

---

[3]See the April 2006 *Global Financial Stability Report* for a detailed discussion.

noticeably since the 1980s. However, the yield curve is only one such indicator, and others—such as equity markets and credit spreads—do not suggest a slowdown (indeed, the OECD's aggregate measure of leading indicators, which includes the yield curve slope, is rising both in the United States and elsewhere). More generally, the interpretation of the flattening of the yield curve is clearly related to the factors causing the unusually low level of long-run interest rates (see Box 1.1, p. 20), and how they will evolve over time. In this regard, as discussed below, the future behavior of the corporate sector, which is presently accumulating record net savings, appears of particular importance.

Within this favorable environment, beyond the continuing strength of oil prices, three features are particularly striking:

- *The U.S. current account deficit has continued to rise, matched by large surpluses in oil exporters, China and Japan, a number of small industrial countries, and other parts of emerging Asia.* That said, partly reflecting favorable short-run interest rate differentials, as well as high net savings in corporates, oil exporters, and much of Asia, financing has not been a problem; indeed, the U.S. dollar appreciated somewhat in trade-weighted terms during 2005, with depreciations against many emerging market currencies offset by appreciations against the euro and yen (Figure 1.6). Despite the record current account deficit, initial estimates suggest that the U.S. net investment position deteriorated only moderately as—for the fourth year in succession—the United States benefited from favorable valuation changes. In contrast to previous years, these stemmed not from U.S. dollar depreciation, but rather the relatively low rate of price increase of U.S. equities relative to the rest of the world.

- *Inflationary pressures remain surprisingly modest.* Global headline inflation has picked up in response to higher oil prices, but core inflation has been little affected (Figure 1.7) and inflationary expectations remain well grounded. This has raised questions as to whether low inflation reflects deflationary

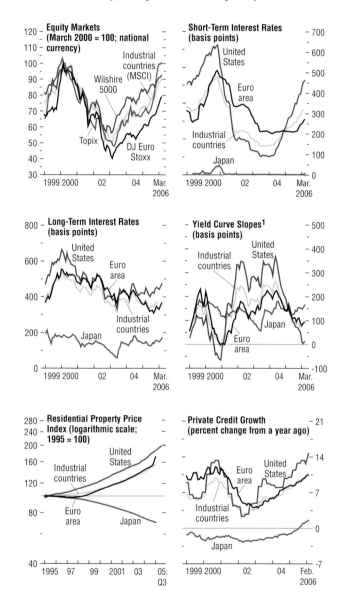

Figure 1.4. Developments in Mature Financial Markets

While short-term interest rates have generally risen, long-run interest rates have increased more modestly, resulting in a marked flattening of the yield curve.

Sources: Bloomberg Financial Markets, LP; OECD; national authorities; and IMF staff calculations.
[1]Ten-year government bond minus three-month treasury bill rate.

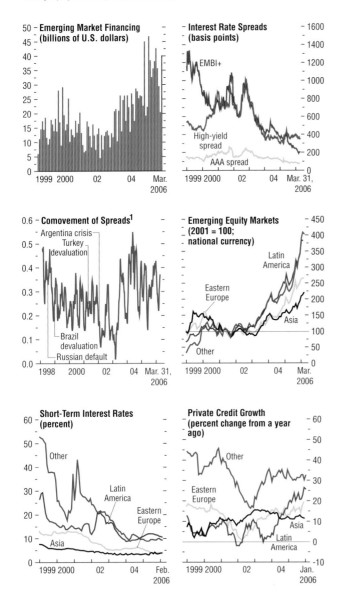

Figure 1.5. Emerging Market Financial Conditions

Emerging market spreads—and borrowing costs—remain unusually low, accompanied by buoyant capital inflows. In some regions, rapid credit growth and soaring equity markets pose potential risks.

Sources: Bloomberg Financial Markets, LP; Capital Data; and IMF staff calculations.
[1]Average of 30-day rolling cross-correlation of emerging market debt spreads.

pressures from other sources, notably globalization—the theme of this issue of the *World Economic Outlook*—or whether there is a danger that the inflationary impact has simply been postponed. The analysis in Chapter III, "How Has Globalization Affected Inflation?" concludes that while globalization has reduced the sensitivity of inflation to domestic capacity constraints, the direct impact of globalization on inflation has generally been quite small, except in several periods of excess global capacity when import prices suddenly plunged. In the current environment of strong global growth and diminishing excess capacity, the restraining effect of declining import prices has faded. Indeed, a cyclical upturn in import prices could contribute to stronger inflation pressures going forward, which monetary policymakers will need to remain vigilant against.

• *Emerging markets and corporations remain—highly unusually—large net savers, contributing to low long-term interest rates.* In the emerging markets, as discussed in the last *World Economic Outlook*, this primarily reflects a combination of low investment and—increasingly—buoyant oil revenues. Chapter IV of this *World Economic Outlook*, "Awash With Cash: Why Are Corporate Savings So High?," finds that record Group of Seven (G-7) corporate surpluses reflect a combination of lower tax and interest payments and low nominal investment; surprisingly, underlying profitability has barely changed. This surplus has been partly used to buy back equities, restructure debt, and build up liquid assets. While it is commonly argued that this mainly reflects a reaction to the high debt and excess investment in the late 1990s, Chapter IV argues that the underlying reasons are considerably more diverse. With some of these clearly temporary in nature, the current situation is unlikely to be sustained, suggesting that changing corporate behavior will start to put upward pressure on interest rates going forward.

Against this background, global GDP growth is projected at 4.9 percent in 2006, 0.6 percentage point higher than expected last September,

Table 1.2. Emerging Market and Developing Countries: Net Capital Flows[1]

(Billions of U.S. dollars)

	1995–97	1998	1999	2000	2001	2002	2003	2004	2005	2006	2007
Total											
Private capital flows, net[2]	204.8	66.2	80.8	74.3	75.6	97.3	160.4	230.6	254.0	178.8	153.8
Private direct investment, net	120.3	159.0	177.6	167.5	180.3	149.5	157.5	184.3	212.3	220.6	217.5
Private portfolio flows, net	71.0	42.9	72.7	17.6	−70.6	−78.6	−3.7	34.5	38.5	−4.7	−3.2
Other private capital flows, net	13.5	−135.7	−169.5	−110.8	−34.1	26.5	6.6	11.8	3.2	−37.1	−60.5
Official flows, net	6.8	52.3	26.4	−46.0	−0.1	9.0	−61.5	−81.5	−138.6	−161.3	−163.6
Change in reserves[3]	−103.9	−29.5	−101.3	−128.3	−128.1	−194.7	−351.6	−515.4	−580.2	−584.2	−562.3
Memorandum											
Current account[4]	−88.3	−49.6	42.9	128.6	90.5	138.5	229.4	310.5	511.2	576.5	569.8
Africa											
Private capital flows, net[2]	4.1	7.6	9.0	—	5.7	4.9	4.6	13.0	30.4	16.6	21.1
Private direct investment, net	4.3	6.3	8.6	7.6	23.0	13.3	14.9	15.1	23.2	21.5	21.3
Private portfolio flows, net	4.8	4.3	9.1	−1.8	−7.6	−0.9	0.1	5.5	4.5	5.3	5.4
Other private capital flows, net	−4.9	−3.0	−8.7	−5.8	−9.6	−7.5	−10.4	−7.7	2.7	−10.2	−5.6
Official flows, net	0.3	5.3	3.8	2.7	−0.5	4.3	3.7	1.8	−6.6	3.2	4.2
Change in reserves[3]	−6.3	3.6	−0.4	−12.8	−9.8	−5.7	−11.4	−33.0	−42.1	−46.3	−54.7
Central and eastern Europe											
Private capital flows, net[2]	27.1	27.2	37.0	39.7	11.6	53.5	52.3	71.0	108.2	94.7	84.4
Private direct investment, net	11.7	19.3	22.8	24.2	24.2	25.6	16.6	34.0	41.3	41.3	39.7
Private portfolio flows, net	4.5	−1.3	5.7	3.2	0.5	1.8	6.1	27.4	28.8	27.2	25.0
Other private capital flows, net	10.9	9.1	8.6	12.3	−13.1	26.1	29.5	9.7	38.1	26.2	19.7
Official flows, net	0.3	1.0	−2.6	1.8	5.9	−7.7	−5.3	−6.8	−8.5	−2.7	−2.6
Change in reserves[3]	−15.6	−9.3	−11.9	−6.6	−4.4	−20.3	−12.4	−14.3	−41.0	−25.5	−12.7
Commonwealth of Independent States[5]											
Private capital flows, net[2]	14.4	−1.5	−13.1	−27.3	6.3	16.1	16.7	8.0	24.9	−13.7	−21.3
Private direct investment, net	4.6	5.6	4.7	2.3	5.0	5.2	5.4	13.7	5.2	2.8	3.5
Private portfolio flows, net	16.9	7.8	−0.9	−10.0	−1.2	0.4	−0.5	5.7	1.0	−5.1	−5.3
Other private capital flows, net	−7.1	−14.9	−16.9	−19.7	2.4	10.6	11.8	−11.4	18.7	−11.4	−19.6
Official flows, net	−1.1	1.7	−2.1	−6.3	−5.2	−10.7	−8.6	−7.7	−15.5	−3.7	−4.6
Change in reserves[3]	−1.3	12.7	−6.2	−20.4	−12.9	−16.2	−31.7	−56.0	−75.2	−88.0	−76.8
Emerging Asia[6]											
Private capital flows, net[2,7]	90.1	−53.8	3.1	6.5	19.6	20.8	63.5	120.3	53.8	55.2	51.6
Private direct investment, net	54.0	56.8	71.6	59.0	51.6	50.7	67.9	60.0	71.8	76.5	78.7
Private portfolio flows, net	20.6	8.8	56.9	20.2	−51.2	−59.9	4.4	3.8	−31.1	−24.5	−27.0
Other private capital flows, net[7]	15.4	−119.4	−125.4	−72.8	19.1	30.0	−8.8	56.4	13.1	3.3	−0.1
Official flows, net	−2.3	19.6	1.8	−11.7	−11.7	4.6	−17.6	1.8	5.0	−0.2	−10.4
Change in reserves[3]	−41.7	−53.1	−88.2	−53.7	−90.2	−148.8	−226.5	−340.1	−281.9	−302.2	−306.0

easing to 4.7 percent in 2007 (Figure 1.8). Continued headwinds from high oil prices are expected to be offset by a gradual pickup in investment, as increasing capacity constraints encourage corporates to reduce their net savings; very favorable financial market conditions; and continued accommodative macroeconomic policies (Figure 1.9). Looking across key countries and regions:

• In *industrial countries*, GDP growth in the United States is expected to moderate to 3.4 percent in 2006, still the highest among G-7 countries. Despite the surprisingly weak growth in the fourth quarter of 2005, incom-

ing data suggest a relatively strong start to 2006, with a more abrupt slowdown in the housing market the most significant risk (see Box 1.2, p. 22). In *Japan*, activity picked up strongly in the fourth quarter while deflationary pressures continue to ease; risks are to the upside, especially if private consumption gains momentum in response to improving labor market conditions. Despite slowing fourth quarter growth, the expansion in the *euro area* also seems to be gaining some traction, although—with consumption remaining weak—it remains vulnerable to domestic and external shocks.

7

Table 1.2 *(concluded)*

	1995–97	1998	1999	2000	2001	2002	2003	2004	2005	2006	2007
Middle East[8]											
Private capital flows, net[2]	4.0	15.6	0.2	5.5	9.2	4.1	7.9	12.2	11.4	−8.7	−10.1
Private direct investment, net	5.0	9.5	4.1	4.7	9.6	9.8	17.6	13.3	19.6	24.5	23.6
Private portfolio flows, net	−2.8	−2.3	0.7	3.3	−3.5	−5.1	−5.4	6.0	7.6	−11.5	−6.1
Other private capital flows, net	1.8	8.4	−4.6	−2.6	3.1	−0.6	−4.3	−7.1	−15.8	−21.7	−27.6
Official flows, net	4.3	10.5	19.0	−27.4	−14.9	—	−39.7	−63.6	−87.9	−148.8	−148.8
Change in reserves[3]	−13.9	8.3	−2.5	−32.1	−12.5	−1.4	−34.1	−47.7	−108.4	−72.9	−77.4
Western Hemisphere											
Private capital flows, net[2]	65.2	71.2	44.7	49.9	23.1	−2.1	15.5	6.0	25.2	34.6	28.1
Private direct investment, net	40.6	61.5	65.9	69.6	66.8	45.0	35.1	48.1	51.2	54.0	50.6
Private portfolio flows, net	27.2	25.6	1.3	2.6	−7.6	−14.9	−8.4	−13.9	27.6	3.9	4.8
Other private capital flows, net	−2.6	−15.9	−22.5	−22.3	−36.1	−32.2	−11.2	−28.1	−53.6	−23.4	−27.3
Official flows, net	5.2	14.2	6.4	−5.2	26.3	18.5	6.1	−7.1	−25.2	−9.2	−1.5
Change in reserves[3]	−25.2	8.4	7.9	−2.8	1.9	−2.2	−35.5	−24.3	−31.6	−49.2	−34.7
Memorandum											
Fuel exporters											
Private capital flows, net[2]	5.8	9.7	−23.2	−42.9	−1.3	10.7	12.9	5.4	4.9	−52.8	−60.6
Nonfuel exporters											
Private capital flows, net[2]	199.0	56.5	104.0	117.1	76.9	86.7	147.5	225.2	249.1	231.6	214.4

[1]Net capital flows comprise net direct investment, net portfolio investment, and other long- and short-term net investment flows, including official and private borrowing. In this table, Hong Kong SAR, Israel, Korea, Singapore, and Taiwan Province of China are included.

[2]Because of data limitations, "other private capital flows, net" may include some official flows.

[3]A minus sign indicates an increase.

[4]The sum of the current account balance, net private capital flows, net official flows, and the change in reserves equals, with the opposite sign, the sum of the capital account and errors and omissions. For regional current account balances, see Table 25 of the Statistical Appendix.

[5]Historical data have been revised, reflecting cumulative data revisions for Russia and the resolution of a number of data interpretation issues.

[6]Consists of developing Asia and the newly industrialized Asian economies.

[7]Excluding the effects of the recapitalization of two large commercial banks in China with foreign reserves of the Bank of China (US$45 billion), net private capital flows to emerging Asia in 2003 were US$108.5 billion while other private capital flows net to the region amounted to US$36.2 billion.

[8]Includes Israel.

- Activity in *emerging market and developing countries* remains very strong, with forecasts revised upwards in most countries and regions. In *emerging Asia*, GDP growth in both China and India has continued to surprise on the upside, driven by strong domestic demand and—in China—a rapidly rising current account surplus. Along with the recovery in information technology (IT), this has supported an acceleration in activity in the rest of the region, although investment growth has yet to pick up substantially. In *Latin America*, notwithstanding the slower pace of growth in larger economies, GDP growth remains solid, aided by booming commodity prices. While this has aided a notable reduction in debt ratios, political uncertainty remains a concern, and many countries remain vulnerable to an abrupt deterioration in the external environment. In the *Middle East* and *Commonwealth of Indepen-*

dent States, rising oil prices continue to boost fiscal and external current accounts, with spending behavior generally more cautious than in past episodes of rising prices (see Chapter II, Box 2.1, "How Rapidly Are Oil Exporters Spending Their Revenue Gains?"). Inflationary pressures—while generally manageable—need to be carefully watched, and in some cases sharply rising asset prices pose risks. Elsewhere, GDP growth in *Emerging Europe* has proved resilient to higher oil prices, but high current account deficits and rapid credit growth in many countries remain central vulnerabilities.

- In the *poorest countries*, GDP growth in sub-Saharan Africa is estimated at 5.5 percent in 2005, rising to 5.8 percent in 2006—the highest in over three decades. Within this, the pickup owes much to surging growth in oil-producing countries as new capacity comes on stream. Perhaps surprisingly, GDP growth in oil importers has slowed only modestly, reflecting both improved macroeconomic and structural policies and the offset from higher nonfuel commodity prices—particularly in metals producers—but also more limited energy price pass-through in 2005, as well as rising external aid. Notwithstanding the tendency for past IMF GDP growth forecasts for Africa to be overoptimistic (see Box 1.3, p. 24, on the accuracy of WEO forecasts), the upward trend in growth is encouraging, although achievement of the Millennium Development Goals remains far off. Donors now need to fully deliver on commitments for higher aid and debt relief, including ensuring that additional resources are indeed additional, and not offset by reductions in other forms of assistance; African countries must continue to strengthen policies and institutions to ensure that those resources—as well as those coming from higher oil and other commodities—are well used.

Looking forward, notwithstanding the greater-than-expected momentum in the global economy, a number of uncertainties remain. On the upside, corporates could run down their surpluses more rapidly than presently expected, either through higher investment or increased wages or dividends, although the impact would be partly offset by higher long-run interest rates. It is also possible that growth in some emerging market countries could continue to exceed expectations (although, particularly in China, this would also increase the risk of a more abrupt slowdown later on). But, overall, the balance of risks remains slanted to the downside, the more so as time progresses (Figure 1.1 and Box 1.3). There are four primary concerns, two of which are uncertainties related to the current conjuncture and two of which are of lower probability but potentially high-cost:

- *High and volatile oil prices.* To date, the impact of higher oil prices on the global economy has been more moderate than generally expected, in part because inflationary expectations have remained well anchored,

Figure 1.6. Global Exchange Rate Developments

The U.S. dollar appreciated moderately over the last year, with appreciations in emerging market currencies—especially Latin America and parts of emerging Asia—offset by depreciations of the yen and European currencies.

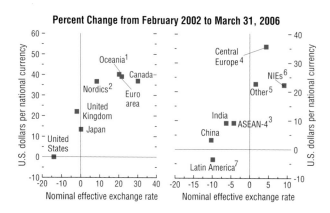

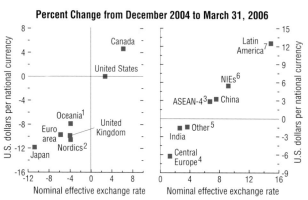

Sources: Bloomberg Financial Markets, LP; and IMF staff calculations.
[1] Australia and New Zealand.
[2] Denmark, Norway, and Sweden.
[3] Indonesia, Malaysia, the Philippines, and Thailand.
[4] Czech Republic, Hungary, and Poland.
[5] Russia, South Africa, and Turkey.
[6] Hong Kong SAR, Korea, Singapore, and Taiwan Province of China.
[7] Argentina, Brazil, Chile, Colombia, Mexico, Peru, and Venezuela.

Figure 1.7. Global Inflation
(Annualized percent change of three-month moving average over previous three-month average)

While headline inflation has increased with higher oil prices, core inflation has changed little.

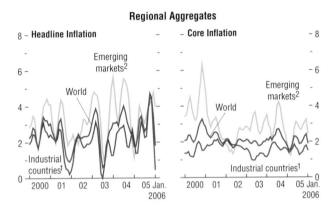

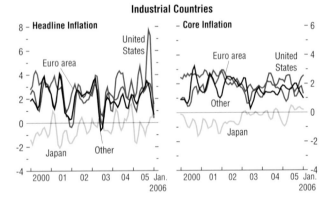

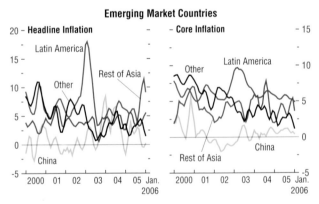

Sources: Haver Analytics; and IMF staff calculations.
[1]Australia, Canada, Denmark, euro area, Japan, New Zealand, Norway, Sweden, the United Kingdom, and the United States.
[2]Brazil, Bulgaria, Chile, China, Estonia, India, Indonesia, Hong Kong SAR, Hungary, Korea, Malaysia, Mexico, Poland, Singapore, South Africa, Taiwan Province of China, and Thailand.

and the shock has been driven by strong global demand.[4] Looking forward, however, there are three reasons for concern. First, the full effects of the recent shock may not yet have been felt, especially if producers and consumers are still treating it as temporary, rather than largely permanent in nature. Second, with excess capacity still very low, the market remains vulnerable to shocks—indeed, with the recent increase in geopolitical uncertainties in the Middle East, options market data suggest risks are slanted to the upside, with a 15 percent probability of oil prices spiking above $80 per barrel by mid-2006. Third, with prices increasingly driven by supply-side concerns, the adverse impact is likely to be greater than in the recent past, especially if feed-through to core inflation increased. This would be of particular concern for oil-importing developing countries, which would not in these circumstances benefit from an offsetting rise in nonfuel commodity prices. This underscores the need for progress in improving the medium-term supply-demand balance in oil markets, including through eliminating obstacles to upstream and downstream investment; ensuring full pass-through to domestic oil prices accompanied by a suitable safety net for the poorest; strengthening conservation efforts; and last—but not least—improving oil market data. Such measures would also help reduce price volatility in the short term, by making markets less vulnerable to shocks.

• *A tightening in financial market conditions.* Current benign financial market conditions are partly due to strengthening fundamentals, but also reflect more temporary factors, including very easy monetary conditions and, related to that, the continuing search for yield. Over the coming two years, global short-term interest rates will rise further,

[4]See the September 2004 *World Economic Outlook*, pp. 64–65 for a detailed discussion.

accompanied by significant changes in short-run interest differentials, as the tightening cycle in the United States reaches completion while those in the euro area—and, recently, Japan—become more advanced (see relevant country sections below); long-run interest rates are likely to rise further; and volatility and risk premiums may pick up. If the implications of the transition to more normal financial conditions are fully anticipated, its impact is likely to be moderate; if not, the effect could be considerably greater. As discussed in the April 2006 *Global Financial Stability Report*, financial institutions and markets seem relatively well placed to manage these changes, especially given the marked strengthening in their balance sheets in recent years; emerging market countries have also taken advantage of current conditions to improve debt structures, although some remain vulnerable to a deterioration in financing conditions. The greatest risks appear to lie in the household sector, particularly in countries where housing markets are elevated, especially since recent house price slowdowns have led to a noticeable slowing in private consumption and residential investment.

- *Rising global imbalances.* With the U.S. current account deficit being financed with little difficulty, and exchange rate movements relatively benign, there may be a temptation to put this issue on the back burner. But the fundamental arithmetic—that the U.S. current account deficit must ultimately fall substantially to stabilize its net investment position, while surpluses in other countries must fall—has not changed; and—as discussed in Chapter II, "Oil Prices and Global Imbalances"—higher oil prices are complicating the adjustment process. Looking forward, as described in detail in Box 1.4, p. 28, adjustment in the imbalances will in all circumstances require both a significant rebalancing of demand across countries, and a further substantial depreciation of the U.S. dollar and appreciations in surplus countries, notably in parts of Asia and oil producers; the issue is when and

Figure 1.8. Global Outlook
(Real GDP; percent change from four quarters earlier)

Following some slowing in the first half of 2005, global growth is expected to stabilize around 4¾ percent in 2006–07.

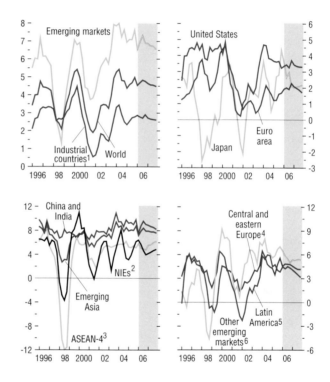

Sources: Haver Analytics; and IMF staff estimates.
[1]Australia, Canada, Denmark, euro area, Japan, New Zealand, Norway, Sweden, Switzerland, the United Kingdom, and the United States.
[2]Hong Kong SAR, Korea, Singapore, and Taiwan Province of China.
[3]Indonesia, Malaysia, the Philippines, and Thailand.
[4]Czech Republic, Estonia, Hungary, Latvia, and Poland.
[5]Argentina, Brazil, Chile, Colombia, Mexico, Peru, and Venezuela.
[6]Israel, Russia, South Africa, and Turkey.

Figure 1.9. Fiscal and Monetary Policies in the Major Advanced Economies

Real short-term interest rates are generally expected to rise in 2006–07, but—outside Germany and the United Kingdom—underlying fiscal positions show little improvement.

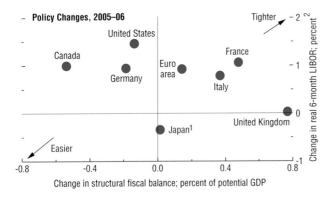

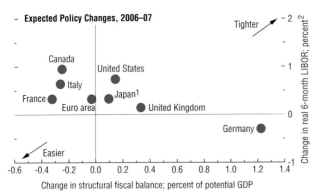

Source: IMF staff estimates.
[1]For Japan, excludes social security.
[2]Three-month rate for euro area countries.

how those adjustments occur.[5] While an important part of the adjustment will need to take place in the private sector, a purely market-driven adjustment will succeed only if foreigners are willing to increase their net holdings of U.S. assets substantially in the face of substantial capital losses from future dollar depreciation—which do not appear to be priced into yields on U.S. dollar assets at present—and if protectionist pressures can be held in check. If not, as illustrated in Figure 1.10, there is a risk of a much more abrupt and disorderly adjustment, accompanied by substantial exchange rate overshooting, a large increase in interest rates, and a sharp slowdown in growth worldwide.

- *An avian flu pandemic.* While both the probability and potential risks are impossible to assess with any certainty, a worse-case scenario could have extremely high human and economic costs, particularly in developing countries (see Appendix 1.2 on the avian flu pandemic). This underscores the importance of moving ahead with necessary public health precautions and providing the necessary assistance to developing countries to do so; measures to ensure that essential economic infrastructure—particularly payments systems—can continue to operate should also be a priority. In particular, all major financial institutions need to have a contingency plan that addresses the consequences of the loss of key personnel.

Looking forward, policymakers face three main challenges:

- *Making more rapid progress in addressing global imbalances.* As the *World Economic Outlook* has argued for some time, a coordinated package of policies across major regions—including measures to reduce the budget deficit and spur private savings in the United States; structural and other reforms to boost domes-

---

[5]See "How Will Global Imbalances Adjust?" Appendix 1.2, *World Economic Outlook*, September 2005, for a detailed discussion.

Figure 1.10. How Will Global Imbalances Adjust?[1]

In the absence of policy adjustment, an orderly adjustment may take place, but only if investors are willing to hold substantially higher levels of U.S. assets (despite large capital losses) and if protectionist pressures are avoided. If these conditions are not met, there is a clear risk of a disruptive adjustment and a global recession. However, strengthened policies—along the lines described in the text—would sharply reduce imbalances, with a modest short-term slowdown offset by stronger medium-term growth.

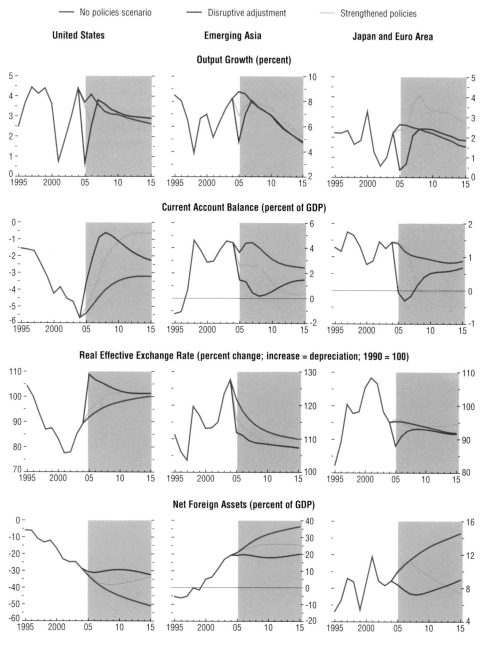

Source: IMF staff estimates.

[1]See Appendix 1.2, September 2005 *World Economic Outlook* for a detailed discussion of these projections. Since the no policies baseline includes significant short-term real appreciation in Asia through higher inflation, it may overestimate the adjustment in current accounts in the initial period.

tic demand in surplus countries; and greater exchange rate flexibility in China and some other countries to allow necessary appreciations to take place—could significantly reduce risks (see Box 1.4 for a detailed description). To date, however, only modest progress has been made in implementing these policies. As shown in the "strengthened policies" scenario in Figure 1.10, such a package would lead to a significantly earlier adjustment in imbalances, correspondingly reducing the risk of a more abrupt adjustment; while GDP growth would slow somewhat in the short term, over the medium term it would be both stronger and better balanced. Given the strong global conjuncture, and that these policies are in the national as well as the international interest, the cost of such insurance against a disorderly adjustment appears relatively modest.

• *Ensuring sustainable medium-term fiscal positions,* not least among many major industrial countries where—outside of Canada and Japan— underlying fiscal positions have improved only modestly since 2003 and—except in Germany and the United Kingdom—IMF staff projections suggest little further improvement over the next two years (Table 1.3). This is of particular concern since, despite some progress in Europe and Japan, pension and health systems across the globe remain unsustainable, with the difficulties associated with implementing even modest reforms being well illustrated by recent experience in the United States. A failure to accelerate progress will increasingly limit the scope for a fiscal response to future shocks, put upward pressures on long-run interest rates, and—over the longer term— pose risks to macroeconomic stability.

• *Putting in place the preconditions to take advantage of globalization and support global growth in the future.* At the multilateral level, the most important issues are to resist protectionist pressures—which have been on the increase in a number of countries—and ensure an ambitious outcome to the Doha Round. While the World Trade Organization (WTO) Ministerial Meetings in Hong Kong SAR made

some progress (Box 1.5, p. 32), wide differences in country positions remain; given the limited flexibility so far displayed, the risks that the very tight negotiating schedule will not be met are high. An unambitious outcome—or failure—of the Doha Round would have major costs both for the global economy and the multilateral trading system. The challenge at the national level is to advance the structural reform agenda, which in some areas appears to be in retreat—for instance on cross-border takeovers. While the priorities vary across countries, as described below, common themes included the need for greater labor market flexibility in the face of rapid technological change and global competition; improvements to the business climate and increased competition in emerging markets; and the strengthening of financial systems.

With the global economy set for its fourth consecutive year of 4 percent plus GDP growth, the current conjuncture is the strongest for many years. Current policymakers can take considerable credit for this outcome; past policymakers can perhaps take even more. The global economy would not have been so resilient to recent shocks without the strengthening of monetary frameworks since the 1980s, which helped anchor inflationary expectations, and the improvements in fiscal positions in the 1990s, which allowed room for policy easing in 2001–02; nor would global growth and trade be as strong as they are without the successful completion of the Uruguay Round in 1994. But behind today's rather favorable short-term conjuncture lie major risks and challenges that have yet to be fully addressed. From an economic viewpoint, there is unlikely to be a more favorable environment in which to tackle them; if progress cannot be made now, it will surely be even more difficult later on. In those circumstances, the risks of adverse shocks will rise, and the scope to react to them will decline, making the prospects of achieving the sustained medium-term global growth envisaged in the *World Economic Outlook* baseline increasingly remote. From that perspective, 2006 may

Table 1.3. Major Advanced Economies: General Government Fiscal Balances and Debt[1]

(Percent of GDP)

	1990–99	2000	2001	2002	2003	2004	2005	2006	2007	2011
Major advanced economies										
Actual balance	−3.4	−0.4	−1.9	−4.1	−4.9	−4.4	−3.9	−3.9	−3.7	−2.7
Output gap[2]	0.3	2.1	0.6	−0.8	−1.5	−1.0	−0.9	−0.7	−0.6	—
Structural balance[2]	−3.4	−1.4	−2.1	−3.8	−4.2	−4.0	−3.6	−3.6	−3.4	−2.7
United States										
Actual balance	−3.0	1.3	−0.7	−4.0	−5.0	−4.7	−4.1	−4.3	−4.0	−2.8
Output gap[2]	0.6	3.5	0.9	−0.9	−1.5	−0.8	−0.6	−0.5	−0.4	—
Structural balance[2]	−3.3	0.1	−1.1	−3.7	−4.4	−4.4	−3.9	−4.0	−3.9	−2.8
Net debt	53.7	39.4	38.3	41.0	43.8	45.3	46.0	47.7	49.3	52.4
Gross debt	69.5	57.1	56.6	58.9	61.8	62.5	62.9	64.2	65.9	69.1
Euro area										
Actual balance	...	−1.0	−1.9	−2.6	−3.0	−2.7	−2.3	−2.3	−2.1	−1.5
Output gap[2]	...	1.9	1.5	0.3	−1.1	−1.0	−1.5	−1.4	−1.3	—
Structural balance[2]	...	−1.6	−2.3	−2.6	−2.5	−2.2	−1.8	−1.7	−1.5	−1.5
Net debt	...	57.6	57.4	57.4	59.1	59.8	60.7	60.5	60.1	57.4
Gross debt	...	69.9	68.6	68.5	69.8	70.2	71.2	70.8	70.1	66.7
Germany[3]										
Actual balance	−2.6	1.3	−2.8	−3.7	−4.0	−3.7	−3.3	−3.3	−2.4	−2.0
Output gap[2]	1.2	1.7	1.5	0.2	−1.3	−1.0	−1.5	−1.5	−1.9	—
Structural balance[2,4]	−2.5	−1.2	−2.7	−3.2	−3.0	−3.2	−2.6	−2.8	−1.6	−2.0
Net debt	40.5	51.5	52.1	54.3	57.7	59.9	62.4	64.1	64.4	64.1
Gross debt	50.7	58.7	57.9	59.6	62.8	64.5	67.5	69.0	68.7	67.9
France										
Actual balance	−3.8	−1.5	−1.5	−3.1	−4.2	−3.7	−2.9	−2.9	−3.0	−1.4
Output gap[2]	−1.3	1.2	1.0	—	−1.4	−1.4	−2.0	−1.8	−1.6	—
Structural balance[2,4]	−2.8	−2.1	−2.1	−3.1	−3.4	−2.7	−2.1	−1.6	−1.9	−1.4
Net debt	39.7	47.0	48.2	48.5	53.0	55.3	57.7	57.3	57.3	54.2
Gross debt	48.9	56.6	56.1	58.1	62.7	65.0	67.3	67.0	67.0	63.8
Italy										
Actual balance	−7.6	−0.8	−3.1	−2.7	−3.4	−3.4	−4.1	−4.0	−4.3	−3.9
Output gap[2]	0.2	2.1	1.9	0.4	−0.8	−1.1	−2.2	−2.2	−2.0	—
Structural balance[2,4]	−7.5	−2.8	−3.9	−3.4	−2.9	−3.2	−3.3	−3.1	−3.3	−3.9
Net debt	108.5	105.6	103.0	100.4	100.4	100.2	102.5	103.0	103.8	105.4
Gross debt	114.7	111.3	108.2	105.4	104.0	103.9	106.3	106.9	107.6	109.4
Japan										
Actual balance	−2.9	−7.7	−6.4	−8.2	−8.1	−6.6	−5.8	−5.7	−5.4	−4.2
Excluding social security	−4.9	−8.2	−6.5	−7.9	−8.2	−6.9	−5.7	−5.5	−5.3	−4.4
Output gap[2]	—	−1.0	−1.6	−3.0	−2.8	−2.1	−1.1	—	0.3	0.1
Structural balance[2]	−2.9	−7.2	−5.6	−6.9	−7.0	−5.8	−5.4	−5.6	−5.5	−4.2
Excluding social security	−4.9	−8.0	−6.1	−7.2	−7.6	−6.5	−5.5	−5.5	−5.4	−4.4
Net debt	27.6	60.6	65.7	72.8	77.2	82.9	87.6	90.9	94.1	101.2
Gross debt	92.9	142.2	151.6	161.2	167.1	172.1	175.5	176.2	177.2	175.2
United Kingdom										
Actual balance	−3.7	1.5	0.9	−1.5	−3.2	−3.2	−3.6	−3.1	−2.8	−2.0
Output gap[2]	−0.7	1.1	0.7	—	−0.1	0.5	−0.3	−0.3	−0.1	—
Structural balance[2]	−3.3	1.3	0.3	−1.8	−3.2	−3.4	−3.7	−3.0	−2.6	−2.0
Net debt	32.9	34.2	32.7	32.7	34.6	36.5	38.5	39.4	40.4	41.6
Gross debt	38.4	41.6	38.4	37.9	39.4	41.2	43.3	44.1	45.1	46.0
Canada										
Actual balance	−4.5	2.9	0.7	−0.1	—	0.7	1.7	1.3	1.1	0.6
Output gap[2]	−0.6	1.9	0.3	0.3	−0.5	−0.4	−0.3	−0.1	—	—
Structural balance[2]	−4.0	2.0	0.4	−0.2	0.3	0.9	1.9	1.3	1.1	0.6
Net debt	80.5	65.3	60.2	57.9	51.4	46.8	41.9	38.2	35.4	27.0
Gross debt	112.7	101.5	100.3	97.4	91.9	87.9	85.0	78.8	74.2	59.1

Note: The methodology and specific assumptions for each country are discussed in Box A1 in the Statistical Appendix.

[1]Debt data refer to end of year. Debt data are not always comparable across countries. For example, the Canadian data include the unfunded component of government employee pension liabilities, which amounted to nearly 18 percent of GDP in 2001.

[2]Percent of potential GDP.

[3]Beginning in 1995, the debt and debt-service obligations of the Treuhandanstalt (and of various other agencies) were taken over by general government. This debt is equivalent to 8 percent of GDP, and the associated debt service, to 1/2 to 1 percent of GDP.

[4]Excludes one-off receipts from the sale of mobile telephone licenses (the equivalent of 2.5 percent of GDP in 2000 for Germany, 0.1 percent of GDP in 2001 and 2002 for France, and 1.2 percent of GDP in 2000 for Italy). Also excludes one-off receipts from sizable asset transactions, in particular 0.5 percent of GDP for France in 2005.

Table 1.4. Advanced Economies: Real GDP, Consumer Prices, and Unemployment
(Annual percent change and percent of labor force)

	Real GDP				Consumer Prices				Unemployment			
	2004	2005	2006	2007	2004	2005	2006	2007	2004	2005	2006	2007
Advanced economies	**3.3**	**2.7**	**3.0**	**2.8**	**2.0**	**2.3**	**2.3**	**2.1**	**6.3**	**6.0**	**5.8**	**5.8**
United States	4.2	3.5	3.4	3.3	2.7	3.4	3.2	2.5	5.5	5.1	4.9	5.1
Euro area[1]	2.1	1.3	2.0	1.9	2.1	2.2	2.1	2.2	8.9	8.6	8.3	8.1
Germany	1.6	0.9	1.3	1.0	1.8	1.9	1.8	2.5	9.2	9.1	8.7	8.8
France	2.1	1.4	2.0	2.1	2.3	1.9	1.7	1.8	9.5	9.6	9.6	9.1
Italy	0.9	0.1	1.2	1.4	2.3	2.3	2.5	2.1	8.3	8.1	7.8	7.6
Spain	3.1	3.4	3.3	3.2	3.1	3.4	3.4	3.1	11.0	9.2	8.6	8.5
Netherlands	1.7	1.1	2.5	2.4	1.4	1.5	1.5	1.6	4.6	4.9	4.5	4.3
Belgium	2.4	1.5	2.1	2.4	1.9	2.5	2.4	1.8	8.4	8.4	8.3	8.2
Austria	2.4	1.9	2.2	2.1	2.0	2.1	1.8	1.7	4.8	5.2	4.8	4.5
Finland	3.6	2.1	3.5	2.7	0.1	0.9	1.1	1.3	8.8	8.4	7.9	7.8
Greece	4.7	3.7	3.3	3.2	3.0	3.5	3.3	3.0	10.5	9.9	9.5	9.5
Portugal	1.1	0.3	0.8	1.5	2.5	2.1	2.1	2.1	6.7	7.6	7.7	7.6
Ireland	4.5	4.7	5.0	5.2	2.3	2.2	2.3	2.5	4.5	4.3	4.1	4.0
Luxembourg	4.5	4.3	4.0	3.8	2.2	2.5	2.3	2.2	3.9	4.2	4.5	4.7
Japan	2.3	2.7	2.8	2.1	—	-0.3	0.3	0.6	4.7	4.4	4.1	4.0
United Kingdom[1]	3.1	1.8	2.5	2.7	1.3	2.1	1.9	1.9	4.8	4.8	4.9	4.8
Canada	2.9	2.9	3.1	3.0	1.8	2.2	1.8	2.0	7.2	6.8	6.6	6.6
Korea	4.6	4.0	5.5	4.5	3.6	2.7	2.5	3.0	3.7	3.7	3.5	3.3
Australia	3.6	2.5	2.9	3.2	2.3	2.7	2.8	2.7	5.5	5.1	5.2	5.2
Taiwan Province of China	6.1	4.1	4.5	4.5	1.6	2.3	1.8	1.5	4.4	4.1	4.0	3.9
Sweden	3.7	2.7	3.5	2.4	1.1	0.8	1.5	1.8	5.5	5.6	4.5	4.2
Switzerland	2.1	1.8	2.2	1.7	0.8	1.2	1.0	1.2	3.5	3.4	3.3	3.3
Hong Kong SAR	8.6	7.3	5.5	4.5	-0.4	1.1	1.8	2.1	6.9	5.7	4.5	4.5
Denmark	1.9	3.4	2.7	2.3	1.2	1.8	1.8	2.0	6.4	5.7	5.1	5.3
Norway	3.1	2.3	2.2	2.6	0.4	1.6	2.1	2.3	4.5	4.6	4.1	4.0
Israel	4.4	5.2	4.2	4.2	-0.4	1.3	2.4	2.0	10.3	9.0	8.5	8.2
Singapore	8.7	6.4	5.5	4.5	1.7	0.5	2.0	1.9	3.4	3.0	2.9	2.9
New Zealand[2]	4.4	2.2	0.9	2.1	2.3	3.0	3.1	2.8	3.9	3.7	4.1	4.6
Cyprus	3.9	3.7	4.0	4.0	2.3	2.6	2.0	2.0	3.6	3.3	3.0	3.0
Iceland	8.2	5.5	5.5	2.3	3.2	4.0	4.0	3.5	3.1	2.1	1.9	2.0
Memorandum												
Major advanced economies	3.1	2.6	2.8	2.6	2.0	2.3	2.3	2.1	6.3	6.0	5.9	5.8
Newly industrialized Asian economies	5.8	4.6	5.2	4.5	2.4	2.2	2.2	2.3	4.2	4.0	3.7	3.5

[1]Based on Eurostat's harmonized index of consumer prices.
[2]Consumer prices excluding interest rate components.

prove a watershed year, both in terms of the outlook for the global economy itself, and the legacy that today's policymakers pass to their successors.

United States and Canada: Robust Growth Set to Continue, but the U.S. Housing Market Is a Key Uncertainty

The U.S. economy slowed sharply in the fourth quarter of 2005, growing at its slowest rate since early 2003. Private consumption was weak—largely due to a sharp drop in auto sales as buyer incentive programs ended and gasoline prices surged in the aftermath of Hurricane Katrina—corporate fixed investment was subdued, and net exports exerted a substantial drag on growth. Monthly indicators, however, suggest that this weakness was concentrated early in the quarter and that the economy has subsequently bounced back. In particular, industrial production has strengthened, capital goods orders are firm, nonfarm payrolls increased by an average of 220,000 a month during November–March, and consumer confidence has rebounded from its post-Katrina slump.

Consequently, real GDP growth is expected to rebound in the first quarter of 2006 and to average 3.4 percent for the year as a whole (Table 1.4). Strong corporate profits and comfortable financing conditions imply a positive outlook for business investment. Further, a pickup in growth in trading partners should mean that the external sector is less of a drag on growth, while in the near term there is likely to be higher government spending associated with rebuilding in the aftermath of Hurricane Katrina. Consumption growth, however, is expected to slow this year—by about ¾ percentage point—as a cooling housing market and elevated energy prices more than offset any acceleration in disposable incomes from employment and wage growth. With corporate profits expanding robustly and balance sheets in good shape, business investment and employment growth could be stronger than expected, but overall risks to the outlook are slanted to the downside. Specifically, the large current account deficit—6.4 percent of GDP last year (Table 1.5)—makes the United States vulnerable to a swing in investor sentiment that could put downward pressure on the dollar and see a spike in long-run interest rates. Even more importantly, against a background of low household saving and high energy prices, a weaker housing market could trigger a more abrupt withdrawal of consumer demand than anticipated.

Indeed, the future course of the housing market is a key uncertainty for the U.S. economy. House prices have grown strongly in recent years, providing a boost to economic activity through their effect on consumption, residential investment, and employment. But house prices are now looking more richly valued—see Box 1.2—and as affordability has declined, buyers have increasingly resorted to interest-only and negative amortization loans to gain access to the market. These nontraditional mortgage products accounted for over 40 percent of mortgage loans for purchase during 2005 (Figure 1.11).[6] And there are now indications that the housing market is cooling—mortgage applications have

Table 1.5. Advanced Economies: Current Account Positions
(Percent of GDP)

	2004	2005	2006	2007
Advanced economies	**-0.9**	**-1.5**	**-1.7**	**-1.7**
United States	-5.7	-6.4	-6.5	-6.5
Euro area[1]	0.8	—	-0.2	—
Germany	3.7	4.1	3.6	4.3
France	-0.4	-1.3	-1.9	-2.1
Italy	-0.9	-1.5	-1.1	-0.7
Spain	-5.3	-7.6	-8.1	-8.5
Netherlands	8.9	6.4	6.9	7.9
Belgium	3.3	4.5	4.8	4.8
Austria	0.2	0.7	0.9	0.9
Finland	5.0	2.4	2.8	2.7
Greece	-6.3	-7.9	-7.9	-7.9
Portugal	-7.3	-9.2	-9.5	-9.4
Ireland	-0.8	-1.9	-2.9	-3.3
Luxembourg	11.1	7.9	7.3	7.3
Japan	3.8	3.6	3.2	2.9
United Kingdom	-2.0	-2.6	-2.7	-2.8
Canada	2.2	2.2	3.1	2.9
Korea	4.1	2.1	1.8	1.7
Australia	-6.3	-6.0	-5.6	-5.5
Taiwan Province of China	5.7	4.7	5.4	5.5
Sweden	6.8	6.1	5.1	4.5
Switzerland	14.6	13.8	13.7	13.1
Hong Kong SAR	9.6	10.7	10.1	10.1
Denmark	2.1	2.4	2.4	2.6
Norway	13.6	16.8	18.6	19.9
Israel	1.6	1.9	1.0	2.1
Singapore	24.5	28.5	26.7	26.3
New Zealand	-6.6	-8.8	-8.9	-7.6
Cyprus	-5.7	-5.1	-5.6	-4.6
Iceland	-9.4	-16.6	-13.8	-8.6
Memorandum				
Major advanced economies	-1.7	-2.3	-2.5	-2.5
Euro area[2]	0.6	-0.3	—	0.2
Newly industrialized Asian economies	7.0	6.0	5.7	5.6

[1]Calculated as the sum of the balances of individual euro area countries.
[2]Corrected for reporting discrepancies in intra-area transactions.

declined, the supply of homes on the market is rising, and confidence among homebuilders has slipped.

Through the impact on wealth accumulation, a slowdown in real house price appreciation from last year's pace of around 10 percent (year-on-year) to zero would usually be expected to reduce consumption growth by 0.5–1 percentage point after one year. In present circumstances,

[6]Data from LoanPerformance MBS/ABS database.

Figure 1.11. United States: The Housing Market and Growth

The strong housing market has supported growth and employment in the United States in recent years. There are increasing signs, however, that housing activity is slowing, and a key question is how the economy would react to a period of slower house price appreciation.

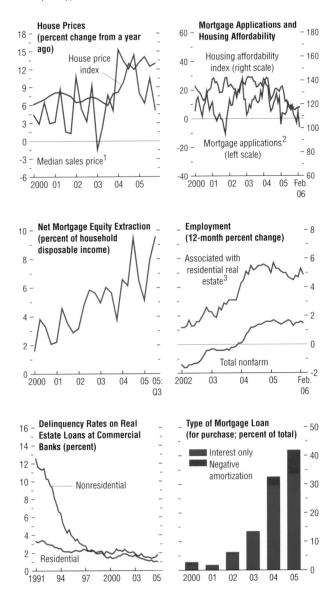

Sources: Haver Analytics; CEIC Non-Asia Database; Greenspan and Kennedy (2005); LoanPerformance MBS/ABS database (Period: 204, December 2005); and IMF staff calculations.

[1] Median sales price for new single family homes.

[2] For the purchase of homes. Index: March 16, 1990 = 100, percent change from a year earlier.

[3] The sum of employment in the following sectors: residential building construction, residential specialty trade contractor, furniture and home, furnishing stores, building material and garden supply stores, and real estate.

however, the wealth effect could be larger. The withdrawal of equity from the housing market—which amounted to 7.5 percent of household disposable income in the first three quarters of 2005—has provided a convenient way of borrowing, which has helped boost consumption in recent years. If house price appreciation were to slow sharply, equity withdrawal would likely fall. Further, real estate and related sectors have been important sources of job creation, and a slowing housing market could adversely affect employment in these sectors.[7] These factors could induce a more severe slowdown in consumption and overall GDP growth (see Box 1.2).

Inflationary pressures have remained muted, helped by ongoing productivity gains and by strong competitive pressures—including from overseas—that are limiting the ability of producers to pass on cost increases. Consequently, while headline CPI inflation jumped as gasoline prices soared—reaching a peak of around 4.5 percent in September, although it has eased in recent months—there has been little pass-through into core inflation, which is running around 2 percent. Nevertheless, with rising resource utilization, the Federal Reserve has continued to tighten monetary policy in recent months. Looking forward, the financial markets now expect one or two more 25-basis-point rate hikes in the coming months before the Fed ends this tightening cycle. With spare capacity in the economy nearly exhausted, however, inflationary pressures could strengthen more than anticipated, necessitating a stronger-than-expected monetary policy response. In particular, a tightening labor market—the unemployment rate has declined to 4.7 percent and initial claims for unemployment benefits have fallen in recent months—may lead to upward pressures on wages, and, with productivity growth easing, unit labor costs.

[7]Default rates on residential mortgage loans have been low historically. Together with securitization of the mortgage market, this suggests that the impact of a slowing housing market on the financial sector is likely to be limited (see the April 2006 *Global Financial Stability Report*).

Despite the substantial increase in short-term interest rates during this tightening cycle, long-term yields have risen only modestly, and the yield curve has at times been slightly inverted in recent months. In the past, an inverted yield curve has been a reliable leading indicator of a slowdown in the U.S. economy (predicting all but one of the postwar recessions). Nevertheless, with real short-term interest rates still low, the correlation between consumption growth and the yield curve having largely disappeared since the 1990s, and structural factors, including pension fund asset reallocation and demand from oil exporters boosting desired holdings of long-dated U.S. securities, it appears unlikely that the current shape of the yield curve is portending an imminent slowing of growth (see the April 2006 *Global Financial Stability Report*).

Turning to fiscal policy, the federal budget deficit improved markedly in FY2005, declining by 1 percentage point of GDP to 2.6 percent of GDP, due to strong revenue growth. In particular, corporate income tax receipts surged with strong profits and the expiration of provisions that allowed additional depreciation deductions for investment. The deficit, however, is expected to widen in FY2006 to around 3 percent of GDP as revenue growth slows and the costs of rebuilding in the Gulf coast area, ongoing military operations in Iraq and Afghanistan, and the introduction of the recent new prescription drug benefit scheme boost expenditures. Over the medium term, the U.S. administration's plan to cut the budget deficit in half by FY2009 is unambitious. It is also fraught with risks, given the reliance on an unprecedented compression of discretionary nondefense spending, ongoing pressure for Alternative Minimum Tax (AMT) relief, and the U.S. administration's push to extend the tax cuts of 2001 and 2003 beyond 2010. As discussed in the September 2005 *World Economic Outlook*, a bolder fiscal adjustment effort is needed with the aim of achieving broad budget balance (excluding social security) in the medium term. This more ambitious fiscal goal would put the budget in a stronger position to respond to unexpected future developments and absorb upcoming pressures from population aging, as well as contribute to the resolution of global current account imbalances.

In Canada, the economy continues to perform strongly, benefiting from the improvement in the terms of trade caused by high energy and other commodity prices. Private consumption is growing strongly, supported by rising employment and asset prices, while healthy corporate profits have underpinned a pickup in business investment. Growth is projected at 3.1 percent this year, with most of the risks to the outlook stemming from possible external developments—in particular, the Canadian economy is vulnerable to any slowdown in the United States, an abrupt depreciation of the U.S. dollar, or a worsening of the terms of trade caused by weaker global commodity prices. Inflation remains well contained but, with the output gap closing, further interest rate increases will likely be needed in the coming months. The fiscal outlook remains favorable. The new government has some fiscal room to maneuver in achieving its objective of lowering the tax burden and slowing spending growth, while maintaining fiscal surpluses and keeping government debt on a firm downward path. As in most other industrial countries, however, rising health care costs present a long-term challenge to fiscal sustainability, and reforms to the public health system will be needed to contain costs.

Western Europe: Is the Expansion Finally Gaining Traction?

The recovery in Europe appears to be strengthening, notwithstanding some slowdown in growth during the final quarter of 2005. Underscoring the vulnerability of activity to external factors, notably oil prices and world demand, growth slowed during the fourth quarter due to falling household consumption and weaker net exports. Importantly, however, investment appears to have remained resilient. Also, recent high-frequency indicators—for example, the German Ifo index which is at its highest level since early 1991—continue to point to healthy

Box 1.1. Long-Term Interest Rates from a Historical Perspective

By the standards of the last two decades of the twentieth century, long-term interest rates, whether measured in real or nominal terms, are currently very low. The British gilts market is a case in point: in January–March of 2006, the rate on ultra-long indexed gilts averaged about 70 basis points. But real long-term rates on unindexed government bonds are also low in the United States and Europe. In the same period, the interest rate on 10-year treasuries, deflated by the expected rate of inflation 10 years ahead, was about 2 percent.

When viewed from a historical perspective, however, the recent behavior of real government bond rates does not appear so unusual. Consider the behavior of rates in the period from 1870 to the start of the World War I. From 1870–95, nominal long-term rates, which were trending downward, averaged 3½ percent (see the figure) for the average of a group of eight countries (Australia, Canada, France, Germany, Italy, Japan, the United Kingdom, and the United States).[1] However, because the early part of this period witnessed marked deflation, which bondholders would not likely have foreseen, realized ex post real rates of return averaged 4½ percent, above what might be inferred to be their expected rate. Average real rates declined to 2.2 percent in 1895–1914, a period of prosperity and rising prices that ended with the outbreak of war. The variance of real long-term rates also declined in this period. A somewhat similar pattern is evident in the 20 years between the

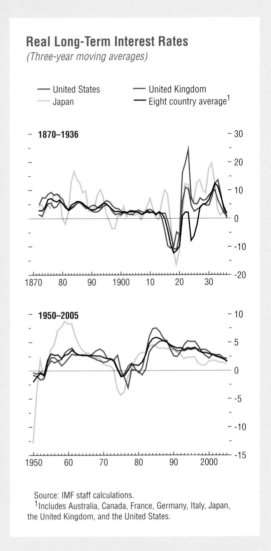

Real Long-Term Interest Rates
(Three-year moving averages)

—— United States   —— United Kingdom
—— Japan   —— Eight country average[1]

Source: IMF staff calculations.
[1]Includes Australia, Canada, France, Germany, Italy, Japan, the United Kingdom, and the United States.

Note: The principal authors of this box are Luis Catão and Sandy Mackenzie.

[1]This figure was computed by deflating the nominal long bond rate by the current rate of inflation in each country and obtaining a global rate as a GDP-weighted average of the real rates thus measured in the eight countries in the sample. The median of the annual global real rates over the entire 1870–95 period is reported. Deflating the nominal rate by the 10-year-ahead inflation rate, rather than by current inflation, yields essentially the same estimate of the average real interest rate for this period.

wars, with average realized real rates comparatively low during the 1920s, and higher during the Depression. In both the 1920s and the 1930s, however, variance was high, which reflected the well known economic instability of the period.

During most of the period since 1945, real long-term interest rates have been comparatively low, although real rates have fluctuated substantially in some subperiods. During the Bretton Woods era, from 1946 to 1971, real global long-term rates averaged 2½ percent.[2] In the case of treasuries, after a period of comparative stability from 1956 to 1973 when the real rate averaged about 2 percent, the real rate dropped precipitously to well below zero because of the unexpected inflationary impact of the first oil shock. During the disinflation of the 1980s, the opposite occurred. During the 1990s, the average rate of inflation and its variance declined, and real rates trended down. A similar if less pronounced pattern was evident in other markets during these decades.

In general, when inflation has been both low and stable, real long-term interest rates will tend to be low and stable as well. Conversely, when inflation is high and volatile, real interest rates will be volatile, and the premium investors demand for holding fixed-interest securities will rise.

Theoretically speaking, long-run interest rates are expected to be no lower than the trend growth rate of an economy. However, the historical experience clearly shows that this general rule can be broken. In about half of the years since the 1870s (excluding the war years), the growth rate exceeded the rate of interest for the eight-country average. Moreover, the rate of

growth has exceeded the rate of interest for as many as 20 years at a stretch. As discussed in previous issues of the *World Economic Outlook*, the outlook for long-run interest rates depends critically on economic fundamentals—notably, the extent to which the desired level of savings continues to exceed desired investment, as well as on such factors as the impact of regulatory change and aging on the demand of financial institutions for long-term assets—but other developments such as commodity price shocks, especially oil price shocks, also play a role (for econometric evidence on this point, see Catão and Mackenzie, 2006).

Should low real long-term interest rates persist, the relative positions of borrowers and lenders may be significantly affected. Governments will find it easier to attain or maintain financial stability, because the primary surplus they need to target to maintain a given debt-to-GDP ratio will decline. Lower rates of interest can also reduce the incentive to undertake needed but politically difficult fiscal consolidation. Investors, however, may need to revisit their assumptions regarding target rates of return on their portfolios. In particular, households, which in many countries are shouldering more of the risks associated with saving for retirement, may have to retire later, or increase the savings they planned to make during their working lives.

---

[2]This measure is obtained as explained in footnote 1. For alternative measures using estimates of inflationary expectations, but telling essentially the same story, see Catão and Mackenzie (2006).

---

activity, unlike during previous episodes of stalling growth; while some uncertainties remain, the fourth-quarter slowdown is projected to prove temporary.

Looking forward, the expansion will continue to depend on strong global demand, with an increasing contribution from business investment, supported by last year's depreciation of the euro and the continuation of supportive financing conditions. Household consumption—which is particularly weak in Germany—is expected to remain more subdued until labor market conditions improve and the effect of oil

prices on real disposable incomes tails off; the proposed increase in the value added tax (VAT) rate in Germany, scheduled for January 2007, is however expected to boost consumption spending in late 2006 at the expense of spending in early 2007. Against this backdrop, overall growth in the euro area is expected to strengthen to potential, or about 2 percent, in 2006, compared to 1.3 percent last year. Nevertheless, there are a number of downside risks, including an appreciation of the euro against the backdrop of large global imbalances or a renewed spike in oil prices. Further, elevated house prices in Spain

Box 1.2. The Impact of Recent Housing Market Adjustments in Industrial Countries

House prices in many industrial countries have been increasing at unprecedented rates in recent years, providing a boost to economic growth. An analysis in the September 2004 *World Economic Outlook*, however, found that this increase in house prices had significantly exceeded the amount justified by fundamentals—such as population and income growth and interest rates—in a number of countries, raising the prospect that house prices would need to adjust in the period ahead. Further, the analysis also found that the correlation of house prices across countries was surprisingly high—particularly given that housing is a nontraded asset—raising the possibility that such a weakening in prices could be synchronized across countries, magnifying the impact on global growth.

Over the past year, house price growth has slowed in many countries, consistent with the historical cross-country synchronization in these prices. In Australia and the United Kingdom, house price inflation has declined from 20 percent a year in late 2003 (middle of 2004 for the United Kingdom) to zero to 5 percent currently, while in Ireland prices slowed through mid-2005, but appear to have accelerated more recently. In France, Spain, and the United States, house price appreciation has also slowed to some degree, although it remains in double digits on a year-on-year basis. In the Netherlands, the downturn in the housing market started much earlier—in 2000—than in other industrial countries, and price appreciation has remained subdued in recent years. The slowing in price appreciation in Australia, Ireland, and the United Kingdom has brought house prices in these countries closer to current estimates of fundamental value, although the United Kingdom still appears quite richly valued (first figure). On the other hand, house prices in the United States and Spain appear to have moved further away from estimated fundamentals over the past year.

Note: The main authors of this box are Tim Callen and Marco Terrones.

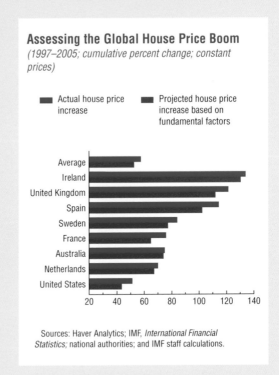

Assessing the Global House Price Boom
(1997–2005; cumulative percent change; constant prices)

■ Actual house price increase   ■ Projected house price increase based on fundamental factors

Sources: Haver Analytics; IMF, *International Financial Statistics;* national authorities; and IMF staff calculations.

There are now growing signs that housing activity in the United States has peaked. A key question for both the United States and the global economy is to what extent slowing house price appreciation will affect growth going forward. There are several channels through which house price movements affect aggregate demand and output. First, house prices affect households' net wealth and capacity to borrow and spend. Bayoumi and Edison (2003), for example, find that a dollar increase in housing wealth in industrial countries raises consumption by around 5 cents, with the impact being larger in countries with market-based financial systems (such as Australia, the Netherlands, the United Kingdom, and the United States) than in those with bank-based financial systems (such as France and Spain). As discussed in the main text, this would suggest that a 10 percentage point slowing in real house price appreciation would reduce consumption growth in the United States by some ½–1 percentage point in the first year. Second, house prices alter the incentives for residential construction, although this relationship has been hard to pin down empirically. Lastly, strong housing markets generate employment in the real estate and related sectors, boosting incomes and consumption. Combining these effects and allowing for the cross-country comovement of house prices, estimates for the United States by Otrok and Terrones (forthcoming) suggest that a 10 percent slowing in the rate of real house price appreciation could slow real GDP growth by as much as 2 percentage points after one year in that country. The recent experiences in the Netherlands, Australia, and the United Kingdom also suggest that a sharp slowing in the pace of house price appreciation could put a significant dent in the growth of private consumption, residential investment, and real GDP in the United States (see the second figure).

A more abrupt adjustment in house prices would of course have more serious consequences for growth. The April 2003 *World Economic Outlook* found that 40 percent of house price booms ended in busts, and that these "busts"—defined as a peak-to-trough decline in real house prices that falls into the top quartile of all such price declines—are associated with a substantial slowing in real GDP growth (for the average "bust" episode, real GDP growth was 3 percent before the "bust," but modestly negative two years after).[1] Nearly all such "bust" episodes were preceded by a significant monetary policy tightening (generally short-term interest rates increased by 400 to 500 basis points). A key question for housing markets going forward, therefore, is the extent to which interest rates increase in the period ahead.

A slowing U.S housing market would have important implications for the world economy given that the U.S. economy has been a key engine of global growth in recent years. Should

[1]The analysis in the September 2005 *World Economic Outlook* suggested that at least 18 states, accounting for more than 40 percent of U.S. GDP, are currently experiencing housing booms.

The Recent Slowdown in Housing Prices
(Percent change from a year earlier, constant prices; x-axis in quarters where zero denotes the quarter in which housing price growth reached its highest level)

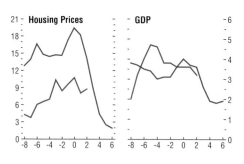

Sources: Haver Analytics; Bank for International Settlements; national authorities; and IMF staff calculations.
[1]Simple average of Australia's, the Netherlands', and the United Kingdom's recent booms and subsequent slowdowns.

U.S. growth and imports slow, trading partners—particularly significant exporters of consumption goods to the United States—would be adversely affected (over the past 25 years, the correlation between output growth in the United States and the rest of the world has been 0.5). Through its likely impact on household saving and residential investment, a slowing in the rate of house price appreciation in the United States would, however, contribute to a needed rebalancing of global growth and a reduction in existing current account imbalances.

Box 1.3. How Accurate Are the Forecasts in the *World Economic Outlook?*

A recent report commissioned by the IMF's Research Department evaluated the accuracy of the forecasts published in the *World Economic Outlook* (WEO), and made a number of recommendations for improving forecasting at the IMF (see Timmermann, 2006). The report—written by Allan Timmermann of the University of California, San Diego—is the fourth in a series of such evaluations (following Artis, 1997; Barrionuevo, 1993; and Artis, 1988).[1] This box discusses the findings of the report and the steps that are being taken to implement the report's recommendations.

Assessing the WEO Forecasts

As a first step, the report looked at the forecasting performance for five key variables—real GDP growth, inflation, the current account balance, and import and export volume growth—for 178 countries in seven economic regions (Africa, central and eastern Europe, the Commonwealth of Independent States (CIS) and Mongolia, Developing Asia, Middle East, Western Hemisphere, and Advanced Economies) since 1990. The analysis considered current-year and next-year forecasts published in the April and September issues of the *World Economic Outlook* (e.g., the April and September 2005 issues of the WEO have projections for 2005—current year—and 2006—next year). Overall, the report found that the *World Economic Outlook* forecasts for variables in many countries meet the basic forecasting quality standards in some, if not all, dimensions.[2] The report, however, also raised important issues that are discussed below on a variable-by-variable basis.

Note: The main authors of this box are Nicoletta Batini, Tim Callen, and Thomas Helbling.
[1]Other studies of the *World Economic Outlook* forecasts include Batchelor (2001), Beach, Schavey, and Isidro (1999), and U.S. GAO (2003).
[2]These dimensions are that the forecast should be unbiased and serially uncorrelated, that no current information should be able to predict future forecast errors, and that the variance of forecast errors should decline as more information becomes available.

- *Real GDP growth.* WEO forecasts for real GDP growth display a tendency for systematic overprediction. Looking at the G-7 countries, WEO forecasts systematically and significantly overpredicted economic growth for the European and Japanese economies during 1991–2003. In contrast, U.S. growth was underpredicted after 1990, although the bias was not statistically significant. In Africa, central and eastern Europe, the CIS, and the Middle East, growth in individual countries is, on average, overpredicted by more than 1 percentage point in both current- and next-year forecasts. That said, more than four-fifths of these biases are not statistically significant, which largely reflects the high volatility in the underlying growth series. For IMF program countries, growth was, on average, overestimated by about 0.9 percentage point in April current-year forecasts and by 1½ percentage points in April next-year forecasts, often significantly so.
- *Inflation.* The report found a bias toward underprediction of inflation, with these biases significant in the next-year forecasts in the case of many African, central and eastern European, and Western Hemisphere countries. The bias tends to be smaller in the current-year forecasts.
- *External current account balances.* Fewer problems were found in the forecasts for current account balances, except that in some cases the April next-year forecast errors were significantly biased or serially correlated.

As well as assessing the performance of the WEO projections against standard benchmarks of forecast performance, the report also compared them to the Consensus Forecasts, a widely used source that compiles the forecasts of economists working in the private sector. The analysis covered the G-7 economies, seven Latin American economies, and nine Asian economies. Overall, the performance of the WEO forecasts was similar to the Consensus Forecasts—for example, the current year WEO forecasts of GDP growth in the G-7 economies were generally less biased than the Consensus Forecasts, but the bias in the next-year forecasts was stronger in the WEO than in the Consensus.

Recommendations

The report made a number of recommendations to improve the WEO forecasting process. These included: (1) WEO growth forecasts for some countries could be improved if more attention were paid to important international linkages, particularly with the United States; (2) the accuracy of the forecasts should be assessed on an ongoing basis by instituting a set of real-time forecasting performance indicators; (3) IMF forecasters should more carefully consider the historical forecast "biases" when making their forecasts; and (4) the forecast process should be broadened to more explicitly consider the risks around the key central projections. Internally, the IMF has begun taking steps to implement the first three recommendations. The rest of this box discusses the fourth recommendation—forecast risks—and how these can be incorporated in the WEO process.

The increased use of policy targets for key macroeconomic variables—especially inflation—that are not fully under the control of policymakers and advances in econometric methodology have led to a more intense scrutiny of forecast uncertainty in recent years. For example, the Bank of England uses "fan charts" to illustrate the bank's view about the uncertainty around its central forecast path for inflation. Similarly, the Congressional Budget Office in the United States has started using fan charts to illustrate the uncertainty in its projection of the budget deficit. These fan charts are diagrams that represent forecasts of the probability distributions of variables of interest. The aim of such charts is to depict in a practical way the uncertainty that exists about future economic outcomes.

The fan chart in Figure 1.1 shows the IMF staff's assessment of the range of uncertainty around the central WEO projection for global real GDP growth in 2006–07. Specifically, it shows the 90 percent probability interval for growth outcomes in 2006–07. Past forecast performance and judgment about the current balance of risks,[3] as discussed in the main text, provide the inputs for the construction of the fan chart. In addition to uncertainty about the future course of oil prices, the U.S. housing market, corporate investment, and the future resilience of emerging market growth, two low probability, but high cost, events—an avian flu pandemic and the disorderly unwinding of current account balances—are also considered. The fan chart builds on the two-piece normal distribution used by the Bank of England in its inflation forecast. This distribution, unlike the standard normal distribution widely used in forecasting, allows for asymmetric probabilities below and above the central forecast.[4] In the case of the balance of risk being tilted to the downside—which is the view of IMF staff at this juncture—the expected probability of outcomes being below the central forecast exceeds 50 percent. As shown in Figure 1.1, the downside risks are expected to increase somewhat over time, in part reflecting the gradually increasing probability of a disorderly adjustment in global imbalances in the absence of policy action.

[3]Recent current-year and next-year forecast errors provide important information about the extent of forecast uncertainty.
[4]See Britton, Fisher, and Whitley (1998); and Wallis (2004).

and Ireland could pose downside risks to consumption in a rising interest rate environment.

While higher energy prices have kept headline inflation above 2 percent, core inflation in the euro area has remained subdued, reflecting sluggish wages and domestic demand. Underlying inflation is expected to remain contained going forward, although higher energy and administrative prices and the expected VAT increase in Germany are likely to keep headline inflation more elevated. Prompted by the persistence of headline inflation above 2 percent and perceived upside risks, the European Central Bank (ECB) raised its policy rate by 25 basis points in both December and March, and the market expects further moves over the course of the year. Nevertheless, with underlying inflationary pressures contained and domestic demand still fragile, there appears to be no need to rush to normalize rates.

Turning to fiscal policy, little progress was made in reducing the area-wide budget deficit last year, as policies, particularly in the larger countries, remained insufficiently ambitious. While a number of countries made efforts to meet their commitments under the rules of the Stability and Growth Pact (SGP), the fiscal deficit rose sharply in Italy and Portugal during 2005 and also—while meeting the SGP criteria—in Austria and Luxembourg. The euro area deficit of 2.3 percent of GDP in 2005 is expected to be maintained in 2006 as fiscal consolidation, as projected by IMF staff based on current policy plans, is again expected to fall short of the SGP requirements, particularly in the larger economies. Concrete plans announced by the German government are expected to bring the deficit below 3 percent in 2007, and the recent announcement of a 1 percent cut in real government expenditures in 2007 in France is welcome, although the measures to achieve this still need to be specified. In general, more ambitious fiscal consolidation of about ½ percent of GDP per year on average will be needed to attain balance by the end of the decade in line with the SGP and to meet upcoming demographic challenges.

Despite greater near-term optimism, Europe faces the fundamental issue of how to raise its low potential growth rate of output and increase employment in line with the Lisbon Agenda. As past issues of the *World Economic Outlook* have detailed, there is wide agreement that this requires fundamental reforms, particularly of labor markets. Achieving a public consensus for implementing reforms has, however, proven more difficult, as recent events in France underscore. As the Single Market reaches increasingly sensitive areas, resistance to reform has

increased, reflected in the watering down of the Services Directive and in government opposition to foreign takeovers in a number of countries (including France, Luxembourg, Poland, and Spain). More generally, there has been increasing debate about the nature of European social models, and the appropriate trade-offs between economic and social outcomes. In contrast to what is commonly perceived, European social systems display more diversity than uniformity, with differences within Europe often greater than those with other advanced economies (Figure 1.12). The Anglo-Saxon model has delivered the best outcome for productivity growth, while the Nordic and Continental models have been the most effective in reducing income inequality and poverty. The Mediterranean model appears to have performed less well than the others in reducing inequality and providing incentives for labor market participation. One key challenge for policymakers is to draw lessons from the examples of success within Europe in balancing the need for labor market flexibility with effective social safety nets, for example. While the appropriate approach in individual countries will vary, a combination of low employment protection, generous but short-duration unemployment benefits, and active labor market policies have in some cases been effective. Greater education levels also appear to reduce the probability of poverty by promoting higher levels of human capital, suggesting that this may be a more effective use of fiscal resources than redistributive policies alone.

Turning to other countries, growth in the United Kingdom slowed to 1.8 percent in 2005, driven by a slowdown in consumption in response to the cooling of the housing market, earlier monetary policy tightening, and higher energy prices, while business investment and export growth have remained steady. Looking forward, as the factors that dampened activity in 2005 wane, growth is expected to pick up to 2.5 percent in 2006 and 2.7 percent in 2007. The main risks to the outlook are—on the upside—favorable supply effects from immigrants joining the workforce and—on the downside—a renewed weakening of house price growth. With no signs of second-round effects from energy prices and a projected closing of the output gap, CPI inflation is expected to remain at about 2 percent. The Bank of England's response to the simultaneous slowing of aggregate demand and the rise in energy prices in 2005 was appropriate, including the ¼ percentage point cut in interest rates in August. Looking forward, monetary policy will need to focus on averting second-round effects of higher energy prices and ensuring that the recovery of demand is sustained. On the fiscal front, expenditure restraint and the announced rise in energy company taxes are expected to help support the stabilization of public debt at about 40 percent of GDP, but this depends on specifying concrete measures to contain spending after 2008. Greater consolidation efforts would be required to meet the authorities' more ambitious fiscal projections over the medium term. Reforms of the pension system will be needed to address the inadequate level of private saving for retirement; the Pensions Commission's recommendations are a key first step in developing a consensus on the extent of the problem and the required policy measures.

Economic performance in the Nordic countries has remained robust, fueled by domestic demand, although the pace of growth has moderated in Norway and Sweden. With inflation edging up, monetary conditions have begun to be tightened in both Norway and Sweden, and in Norway the government needs to continue its policy of resisting pressures for excessive increases in government spending following the surge in oil revenues. In Iceland, financial market concerns over the resolution of large macroeconomic imbalances built up during a three-year economic boom have led to downward pressure on the exchange rate and widening credit spreads for banks. In Switzerland, growth is expected to improve in 2006 in line with demand from the euro area. Monetary policy has been appropriately expansionary and the move toward a more neutral stance should be gradual. Credible medium-term fiscal adjust-

Figure 1.12. Western Europe: Social Policy Indicators and Outcomes
(U.S. average = 100)

Social policy models within Europe exhibit significant variations in design and in their impact on economic efficiency and equity. The examples of success within Europe can help guide reform of the models in line with the Lisbon Agenda.

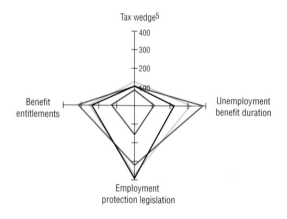

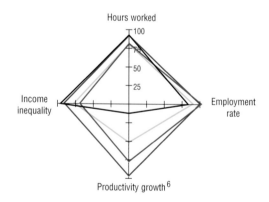

Sources: Eurostat, ESSPROS; Haver Analytics; Klenow and Rodriguez-Clare (2004); OECD, *Economic Outlook;* OECD, *Employment Outlook 2005;* and IMF staff calculations.
[1] Denmark, Finland, the Netherlands, and Sweden.
[2] Ireland and the United Kingdom.
[3] Austria, Belgium, France, Germany, and Luxembourg.
[4] Greece, Italy, Spain, and Portugal.
[5] Income tax plus employee and employer contributions less cash benefits (as a percent of labor costs) in a two-earner family with two children, one at 100 percent average earnings, and the other at 33 percent.
[6] Total factor productivity growth.

Box 1.4. How Much Progress Has Been Made in Addressing Global Imbalances?

This box updates the analysis of global imbalances and policy actions designed to facilitate their resolution presented in the September 2005 *World Economic Outlook*. Since then there has been no significant shift in the trend of external imbalances: the U.S. current account deficit is estimated to have reached the record level of 6.4 percent of GDP in 2005, and—at current exchange rates—is projected to remain at record levels in subsequent years (see the first figure). Capital flows to the United States remain strong, with an increase in purchases of U.S. bonds by the private sector offsetting a decline in official flows. As has been the case for the past four years, the deterioration of the U.S. net external position in 2005 has once again been contained by sizable net capital gains on its external portfolio despite the real appreciation of the dollar, thanks to the stronger performance of non-U.S. stock markets relative to the U.S. market.

As a matter of simple arithmetic, the global imbalances remain on an unsustainable trend over the long run, as—unless returns on U.S.-issued financial instruments continue to substantially underperform those issued in other countries, thus generating large further capital gains for the United States—they would lead to an ever-accumulating stock of emerging Asian and oil exporters' assets and U.S. external liabilities.[1] Therefore, the issue is not whether but

Note: The author of this box is Gian Maria Milesi-Ferretti.
[1]Hausmann and Sturzenegger (2006) have recently argued that since U.S. net investment income is still positive and changed little over the past 25 years, the "effective" net external position of the United States must also have changed little, and as of end-2004 the U.S. must still have been a net creditor. The main flaw in this argument is the assumption that all investments should earn the same rate of return (even though the risk characteristics of the U.S. asset and liability portfolio are very different). Allowing for this, there is no reason why net investment income cannot be positive even when a country is a net debtor (see "Why Is the U.S. International Income Account Still in the Black, and Will this Last?" Box 1.2, *World Economic Outlook*, September 2005).

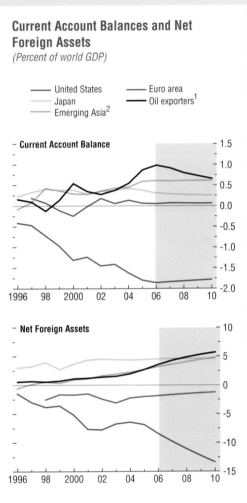

Current Account Balances and Net Foreign Assets
(Percent of world GDP)

Sources: Lane and Milesi-Ferretti (2006); and IMF staff estimates.
[1]Algeria, Angola, Azerbaijan, Bahrain, Republic of Congo, Ecuador, Equatorial Guinea, Gabon, I.R. of Iran, Kuwait, Libya, Nigeria, Norway, Oman, Qatar, Russia, Saudi Arabia, Syrian Arab Republic, Turkmenistan, United Arab Emirates, Venezuela, and the Republic of Yemen.
[2]China, Hong Kong SAR, Indonesia, Korea, Malaysia, the Philippines, Singapore, Taiwan Province of China, and Thailand.

how and when they adjust. As described in Appendix 1.2 of the September 2005 *World Economic Outlook*, the current configuration of external imbalances arises from a combination of shocks and economic trends across several countries and regions, with both the public and private sector contributing. It is possible that there will be an orderly private-sector led adjustment in imbalances even without policy action, with U.S. private savings rising gradually as interest rates increase and the housing market slows, accompanied by substantial real exchange rate adjustment, including through rising inflation in Asia (see Figure 1.10). This benign scenario assumes that foreigners will continue to purchase U.S. assets (with no significant interest rate premium, notwithstanding the risk of large capital losses) and that protectionist pressures can be avoided. If this does not happen, the figure also illustrates the implications of a much more abrupt and disorderly adjustment, characterized by a substantial overshooting of exchange rates; a large increase in interest rates; and a sharp contraction of global activity.

The question then becomes how public policy can best assist an orderly rebalancing. The *World Economic Outlook* has long argued that the key actions in this regard include measures to increase savings in the United States; exchange rate appreciation in the context of greater exchange rate flexibility, along with measures to boost domestic demand in emerging Asia; structural reform to boost domestic demand and growth in the euro area and Japan; and measures to increase demand in oil exporters (see Box 1.6 in the September 2005 *World Economic Outlook* for a detailed description of these policies). As shown in the "strengthened policies" scenario in Figure 1.10, this would essentially bring forward adjustment, but in an orderly way. Net external positions would be stabilized earlier, thus reducing the risk of abrupt and disruptive adjustment, and world growth would be more balanced. In addition, the proposed policies are advisable on domestic policy considerations, being in each country's and region's best interest.

Over the last year, how much progress has been made in implementing these policies?

- *In the United States, there are modest signs of an improvement in savings* (see the second figure), with the general government deficit falling to 4.1 percent in 2005. However, IMF staff projections suggest little improvement thereafter,

Global Imbalances: Macroeconomic Indicators
(Percent of GDP, unless otherwise indicated)

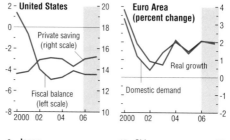

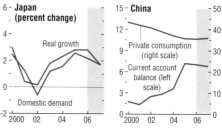

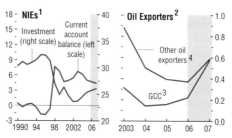

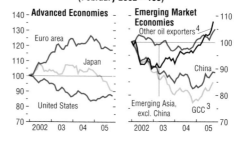

Source: IMF staff estimates.
[1]Newly industrialized Asian economies (NIEs) refers to Hong Kong SAR, Korea, Singapore, and Taiwan Province of China.
[2]Marginal propensity to import out of oil revenues (See Chapter II, Box 2.1 for details).
[3]Cooperation Council of the Arab States of the Gulf (GCC): Bahrain, Kuwait, Oman, Qatar, Saudi Arabia, and United Arab Emirates.
[4]See footnote 1 in previous figure excluding GCC countries.

Box 1.4 *(concluded)*

with the deficit remaining above 4 percent of GDP in 2006–07 and close to 3 percent of GDP over the medium term, substantially higher than the broad balance envisaged in the adjustment scenario. Recent budget proposals envisage only modest fiscal improvements and are based on an ambitious compression in nondefense discretionary spending. A more determined fiscal retrenchment, which would help prepare for the inevitable aging-related increases in spending, is likely to require revenue-enhancing measures, such as eliminating tax exemptions; raising energy taxes; or introducing a federal VAT or sales tax. The private savings rate would remain relatively stable, as a higher household savings ratio—partly reflecting a slowdown in the housing market—would be offset by a fall in the (currently very high) savings rate of firms.

- *In Asia, exchange rate adjustment remains limited, although there are some signs of a strengthening in domestic demand.* More specifically:

  On exchange rates, China's July 2005 exchange rate reform was a welcome step, and the authorities have taken further measures to liberalize and develop the foreign exchange market, including an increase in the number of financial institutions licensed to participate in the interbank foreign exchange market (including foreign banks), and the introduction of over-the-counter (OTC) trading of spot foreign exchange with 13 banks designated as market makers. However, the renminbi continues to move closely with the U.S. dollar, and the additional flexibility the reform permits needs to be used more aggressively to allow the renminbi to respond to market pressures and appreciate. Elsewhere in Asia, current account surpluses have declined in some countries, under the weight of higher oil prices, while currencies have generally appreciated, most notably in Korea and Thailand. Nevertheless, surpluses remain large in a number of countries, suggesting that further exchange rate appreciation would be required over the medium term.

  On the demand side, priorities differ across countries. In China, where investment is already high, the key is to strengthen private consumption. IMF staff projections suggest a stabilization but very little increase in the share of private consumption to GDP over the next two years, despite measures to boost rural incomes. Allowing for higher consumption over the medium term will require a number of structural reforms, including strengthening the financial sector, requiring state-owned enterprises to pay dividends to the state, rebalancing public expenditure toward higher spending on health and education, and reforming the pension system. Elsewhere in Asia, there are some signs of a pickup in investment since 2003, as corporate restructuring has advanced, bankruptcy rates have fallen, and debt levels have declined below pre-crisis levels in many countries. Nevertheless, further reforms are necessary to improve the investment climate, including financial sector reforms that deepen capital markets and thereby broaden the sources of corporate financing.

- *In Japan, where the expansion is now well grounded, the current account surplus has begun to narrow against the backdrop of strengthening domestic demand, and is set to decline further from its current high level over the medium term.* With fiscal policy needing to tighten significantly, boosting productivity in the nontradable sector is key. Further reforms can be pursued to improve labor market flexibility, as well as to enhance competition—especially in retail, agriculture, and other domestically oriented sectors. Such steps can promote more robust domestic demand that, along with population aging, will work to narrow the external imbalance over the medium term. Over time an appreciation of the yen is likely to make a contribution as well.

- *In the euro area, the key contribution—in some ways similar to Japan—is through measures to boost growth and domestic demand.* While there are signs that the recovery—primarily in investment—is becoming better grounded, further progress is needed on structural reforms at the national and European level. In recent months, the EU Services Directive has been approved by the European parliament, but in a much weaker form. In Germany, the recent package—while containing welcome measures in other areas—was relatively weak on product market reform and further labor market deregulation. For the area as a whole, past structural reform efforts have increased wage flexibility and strengthened employment resiliency, but have not delivered sufficient job creation, productivity, and output growth. Thus, comprehensive strategies to foster product market and financial sector competition, as well as a better integration of labor, product, and financial market reforms remain key priorities.

- *In oil exporters, adjustment is—understandably given the size of additional revenues relative to domestic economies—relatively gradual.*

  In oil exporters, scope remains for boosting expenditures in areas where social returns are high (education and health; infrastructure; private sector employment; and strengthened social protection schemes). To date, oil-exporting countries have, on average, spent 30–40 percent of their additional oil revenues

on imports, with relatively significant variation across countries—see Box 2.1 for details.

Exchange rates have appreciated noticeably in real terms in a number of oil exporters and more modestly in Cooperation Council of the Arab States of the Gulf (GCC) countries, whose exchange rates remain tied to the dollar in the runup to GCC monetary union. In these latter countries, real effective appreciation can only take place through inflation as spending adjusts.

Finally, it is important to stress that adjustment will require both a rebalancing of demand and exchange rate adjustment, with currency depreciation in several deficit countries and currency appreciation in several surplus countries—there is not a choice between one or the other. The longer adjustment is delayed, the larger these exchange rate adjustments will ultimately need to be, and the greater the risk of overshooting. Policymakers and private sector decision makers need to recognize that—although the timing is difficult to predict—exchange rate adjustment will eventually take place and to ensure that national economies, financial institutions, and corporations are as resilient to it as possible.

ment will need to be undertaken to contain the expansion in public spending and the rising tax burden. Raising productivity and labor utilization remain important challenges, and structural policies need to focus on competition in product markets and reform of the electricity and agricultural sectors.

Japan and Other Industrial Countries in Asia: Managing Three Major Transitions in Japan

Despite an inevitable slowdown from the 5 percent GDP growth rate in the first half of 2005, Japan's expansion remains solidly on track. With incoming data generally exceeding expectations, GDP growth for 2005 is now estimated at

2.7 percent, some 0.7 percent higher than projected last September. While export growth has been supported by strong demand in the United States and China and a depreciation of the yen, the expansion is increasingly being driven by final domestic demand, underpinned by rising employment, buoyant corporate profits, and a turnaround in bank credit growth (now positive, excluding write-offs). Partly reflecting this improved outlook, the Nikkei has risen by some 40 percent since mid-2005, by far the most rapid among the G-7 countries.

Looking forward, GDP growth in 2006 is projected at 2.8 percent, again driven by solid domestic demand. At this point, the risks are to the upside, especially if private consumption gains momentum in response to rising employ-

Box 1.5. The Doha Round After the Hong Kong SAR Meetings

The World Trade Organization (WTO) Ministerial Conference, held in Hong Kong SAR during December 13–18, 2005, was the second such conference since the Doha Round of multilateral trade negotiations was launched in the Qatari capital in 2001. In contrast to the failed Cancún Ministerial Conference in September 2003, the Hong Kong SAR meeting largely met its objectives—though these were disappointingly modest—and succeeded in instilling the Doha Round with some renewed political momentum. Ministers in Hong Kong SAR focused heavily on agriculture and development—the two most politically sensitive issues under discussion—largely leaving aside negotiations on nonagricultural market access (NAMA), services and rules.

In agriculture, the most tangible outcome of the Hong Kong SAR Ministerial Conference was an agreement to end all forms of export subsidies in agriculture by 2013, with an accelerated end date of 2006 for cotton. This was a welcome achievement, given the highly distortionary nature of export subsidies in OECD countries. Only marginal progress was achieved in the other dimensions of the agriculture negotiations, namely the need to discipline or eliminate trade-distorting domestic support and to increase market access in agricultural products.

On development issues, ministers outlined a "package" of trade and aid for least-developed countries (LDCs) and other poor developing countries in the form of market access privileges, less stringent disciplines ("special and differential treatment"), and assistance in trade-related capacity building. In particular, industrial and developing countries that declared themselves in a position to do so, agreed to provide duty- and quota-free market access for at least 97 percent of export items originating from LDCs by 2008. However, the 3 percent exception will allow highly protected products of significant export interest to LDCs to be exempted.

Although the Doha Round was dubbed the Doha Development Agenda (DDA), the "development dimension" of the Round has remained controversial. In Hong Kong SAR, there was a tendency to equate "development" with "policy space"—that is, the right to exemptions from global commitments and disciplines. Yet this understanding is at odds with the experience of successful development, which suggests that active trade integration offers the best hopes for spurring economic growth. Weak commitments may also reduce developing country leverage in achieving desired outcomes in their own areas of interest.

The conference set specific deadlines for intermediate steps in the negotiations, but made no headway on several central issues, and much uncertainty remains as to whether an ambitious outcome can be reached. Work subsequent to the Davos World Economic Forum has seen a serious engagement at the technical level and a cooling of the political rhetoric that had been encumbering the negotiations. The key parameters for liberalizing agriculture and nonagricultural trade are to be agreed by April 30, 2006, and final draft schedules of commitments in services are to be submitted by October 31, 2006. The aim is to conclude the Round by the end of 2006.

These timelines appear very ambitious in view of the remaining differences and the pace of the negotiations so far, but they may help focus decision makers' attention on the Round. A successful outcome to the negotiations is needed to strengthen the multilateral trading system and provide impetus to global economic growth.

Note: The author of this box is Jean-Pierre Chauffour.

ment and labor income. Most encouragingly, with underlying deflationary pressures easing, there is an increasing prospect of an end to eight consecutive years of declining prices. Core

CPI inflation—which includes oil prices and, therefore, results in some upward bias at present—has turned positive for four consecutive months, and unit labor costs are picking up as labor market conditions tighten. Correspondingly, CPI inflation is projected to turn slightly positive in 2006, although—given the margins of error—it is still too early to conclude that deflation is conclusively defeated.[8]

In the period ahead, the Japanese economy faces three key transitions.

- *The shift to a new monetary framework.* In early March, the Bank of Japan ended the quantitative easing policy, and reverted to targeting the overnight call rate. Given the uncertainties noted above, and the large costs of a deflationary relapse, the monetary policy stance is appropriately expected to be kept highly accommodative for the time being; the timing of interest rate increases will depend on the extent that incoming data confirm that deflation is decisively beaten and inflationary expectations are solidly established. The Bank of Japan also announced a new monetary framework, including clarification of its view that medium-term price stability entails inflation in the range of 0–2 percent, and greater transparency about the current view on monetary policy in its semi-annual report.

- *The restoration of budget sustainability,* in an environment of growing pressures from the rapidly aging population. Over the past two years, the general government deficit has been reduced from 8.1 percent of GDP to 5.8 percent of GDP in 2005, somewhat faster than earlier thought, although only modest further progress is expected in 2006. Further substantial adjustment will be needed in the future—indeed, IMF staff projections suggest that the primary balance excluding social security will need to improve by some 6 percent of GDP over the next 10 years even to stabilize net debt at 105 percent of GDP. The strengthening economy provides an opportunity to make more rapid progress; in this regard, the authorities' projection that the objective of primary balance excluding social security could be achieved in FY2011, one year earlier

than expected, is encouraging. It will be important to lay out a more detailed plan to achieve this target, through further curtailing expenditures, including limiting growth in health care costs; broadening the tax base, including by reducing exemptions; and over time raising the consumption tax rate, which is low by international standards.

- *Reviving productivity growth.* After a period of very rapid convergence in the 1970s and 1980s, Japan's per capita income fell sharply relative to the United States during the 1990s, and has since stabilized at broadly the European level (Figure 1.13). Given already high labor utilization rates and deteriorating demographics, further convergence toward U.S. per capita income levels will depend critically on raising productivity, which is well below both U.S. and European levels, particularly in the services sector. This underscores the need to complete the remaining agenda for financial and corporate sector restructuring (specifically regarding regional banks and some inefficient domestic sectors), and to press ahead with measures to improve labor market flexibility, downsize government financial institutions, enhance domestic competition and reduce regulation and trade restrictions, including in agriculture.

To a considerable extent, policies in these areas—particularly fiscal adjustment and productivity growth—are linked. In particular, higher productivity would help directly to improve fiscal sustainability (underscoring the importance of designing tax and expenditure measures to minimize adverse effects on growth). In addition, sustained higher productivity growth in Japan would have important benefits from a multilateral perspective. With the rise of China, the East Asian region has become relatively less reliant on Japan, but linkages still remain important; a 1 percentage point increase in productivity growth could increase GDP growth in the rest of the region by ¼ percent in the short run. More

---

[8]Based on the IMF staff's past forecasting history, there would still be a one-third chance of a further decline in the CPI in 2006.

Figure 1.13. Japan: Reversing the Relative Decline in Per Capita GDP Growth

After a rapid increase in the 1970s and 1980s, Japan's per capita income has since fallen sharply relative to the United States. With labor inputs already high, a reversal of this trend will require measures to raise productivity, which is low by international standards.

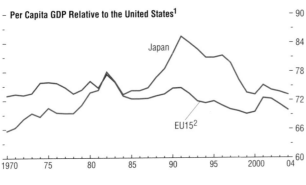

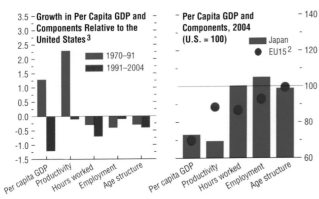

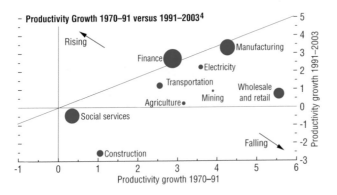

Sources: OECD, *Economic Outlook;* and IMF staff calculations.
[1]Ratio of per capita GDP in 2000 purchasing-power-parity (PPP) dollars in Europe and Japan to the United States.
[2]Austria, Belgium, Denmark, Finland, France, Germany, Greece, Ireland, Italy, Luxembourg, the Netherlands, Portugal, Spain, Sweden, and the United Kingdom.
[3]Employment ratio defined as employed persons as a percent of population of working age.
[4]Value added per person. Size of bubble represents the share of sector in 1991–2003.

generally, higher productivity growth could—through its impact on domestic demand—contribute to reducing global imbalances, especially if it is concentrated in the non-tradeables sector (where, as shown in Figure 1.13, it has weakened noticeably in recent years).

In Australia and New Zealand, real GDP growth slowed in 2005. Private consumption growth weakened in Australia in the face of the slowing housing market and high gasoline prices. Exchange rate appreciation hurt net exports in both countries, particularly in New Zealand. Growth is expected to pick up to 2.9 percent in Australia this year as investment strengthens further in response to capacity constraints and high commodity prices. In New Zealand, by contrast, growth is expected to moderate to 0.9 percent, given that domestic demand has begun to slow and there are signs that the housing market is cooling. The current account deficit remains high in both countries, although it has deteriorated more substantially in New Zealand—reaching 8.8 percent of GDP—and the exchange rate has depreciated substantially in recent months. While headline CPI inflation has risen in both countries, a wait-and-see approach to further monetary tightening is appropriate given the slowdown in activity and the associated decline in inflation risks. Both countries continue to demonstrate enviable records of fiscal prudence, with budgets remaining in surplus and public debt ratios on a firm downward track. In Australia, recent reforms to the industrial relations system and changes to the tax and benefit systems will improve work incentives, and should set the stage for continued strong employment growth.

Emerging Asia: Strong Growth Expected to Continue

Growth in emerging Asia eased slightly to 8.2 percent in 2005 (Table 1.6). This slowdown, however, was concentrated in the early part of the year, and growth accelerated in the second half as exports were boosted by a pickup in corporate investment in industrial countries, which

Table 1.6. Selected Asian Economies: Real GDP, Consumer Prices, and Current Account Balance
(Annual percent change unless otherwise noted)

	Real GDP				Consumer Prices[1]				Current Account Balance[2]			
	2004	2005	2006	2007	2004	2005	2006	2007	2004	2005	2006	2007
Emerging Asia[3]	**8.4**	**8.2**	**7.9**	**7.6**	**4.0**	**3.5**	**3.8**	**3.4**	**3.9**	**4.5**	**4.1**	**4.0**
China	10.1	9.9	9.5	9.0	3.9	1.8	2.0	2.2	3.6	7.1	6.9	6.7
South Asia[4]	**7.7**	**7.9**	**7.1**	**6.9**	**4.3**	**5.0**	**5.3**	**5.2**	**0.1**	**−2.3**	**−3.0**	**−3.0**
India	8.1	8.3	7.3	7.0	3.8	4.2	4.8	4.9	0.2	−2.5	−3.1	−3.1
Pakistan	7.1	7.0	6.4	6.3	7.4	9.1	8.4	6.9	0.2	−2.4	−3.2	−3.0
Bangladesh	5.9	5.8	6.0	6.3	6.1	7.0	6.1	5.6	−0.3	−0.9	−1.0	−1.1
ASEAN-4	**5.8**	**5.2**	**5.1**	**5.7**	**4.6**	**7.5**	**8.8**	**4.6**	**4.4**	**3.3**	**2.8**	**2.5**
Indonesia	5.1	5.6	5.0	6.0	6.1	10.5	14.2	6.6	1.2	1.1	0.4	—
Thailand	6.2	4.4	5.0	5.4	2.8	4.5	3.6	2.2	4.2	−2.3	−2.0	−2.1
Philippines	6.0	5.1	5.0	5.6	6.0	7.6	7.4	4.7	2.7	3.0	2.1	1.6
Malaysia	7.1	5.3	5.5	5.8	1.4	3.0	3.1	2.7	12.6	15.6	14.9	14.7
Newly industrialized Asian economies	**5.8**	**4.6**	**5.2**	**4.5**	**2.4**	**2.2**	**2.2**	**2.3**	**7.0**	**6.0**	**5.7**	**5.6**
Korea	4.6	4.0	5.5	4.5	3.6	2.7	2.5	3.0	4.1	2.1	1.8	1.7
Taiwan Province of China	6.1	4.1	4.5	4.5	1.6	2.3	1.8	1.5	5.7	4.7	5.4	5.5
Hong Kong SAR	8.6	7.3	5.5	4.5	−0.4	1.1	1.8	2.1	9.6	10.7	10.1	10.1
Singapore	8.7	6.4	5.5	4.5	1.7	0.5	2.0	1.9	24.5	28.5	26.7	26.3

[1]In accordance with standard practice in the *World Economic Outlook*, movements in consumer prices are indicated as annual averages rather than as December/December changes, as is the practice in some countries.
[2]Percent of GDP.
[3]Consists of developing Asia, the newly industrialized Asian economies, and Mongolia.
[4]The country composition of this regional group is set out in Table F in the Statistical Appendix.

offset a weakening in domestic investment. With global economic conditions expected to remain favorable—the ongoing domestic demand recovery in Japan is particularly helpful—this growth momentum is expected to continue in 2006, and real GDP in the region is projected to expand by 7.9 percent (a full percentage point higher than in the September 2005 *World Economic Outlook*, largely due to upward revisions in China and India, see below). The risks to the outlook are broadly balanced. On the upside, a stronger-than-expected rebound in corporate investment in industrial countries and recent equity and property price increases could underpin stronger growth. On the downside, avian flu is a significant, if difficult to quantify, risk (see Appendix 1.2). Other risks stem from a renewed rise in oil prices, an increase in protectionist sentiment in advanced economies, and the possible need for further monetary tightening if inflationary pressures do not abate.

Headline CPI inflation has risen over the past year in most countries, largely due to higher energy prices, although core inflation has also picked up sharply in Indonesia, the Philippines, and to a lesser extent in Thailand. Asset prices have continued to rise strongly, with equity markets posting record highs and property prices continuing to surge. Against this background, many central banks have moved to raise interest rates, although real rates remain low and short-term interest rate differentials have generally moved in favor of the U.S. dollar over the past year, one factor behind the moderation of non-FDI capital inflows into the region. Looking forward, monetary policy may need to be tightened further in countries where inflationary pressures have yet to retreat (India, Malaysia, and Thailand). On fiscal policy, the favorable outlook provides an opportunity for countries with high public debt (particularly India, Indonesia, Pakistan, and the Philippines) to take steps to put their public finances on a sustainable medium-term footing.

The current account surplus in emerging Asia has shown surprising resilience to the sharp hike in oil prices. Despite a deterioration in the oil balance of 2½ percent of GDP, the overall cur-

Figure 1.14. Emerging Asia: Understanding Recent Developments in the Current Account

Despite the rise in oil prices, the current account surplus in emerging Asia remains large. A redistribution of these surpluses, however, has taken place, with those countries where the real exchange rate has depreciated and/or domestic demand growth has weakened generally seeing an increasing surplus and others a deteriorating current account position.

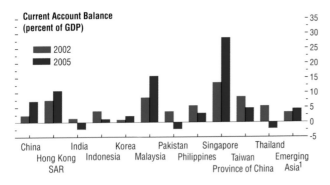

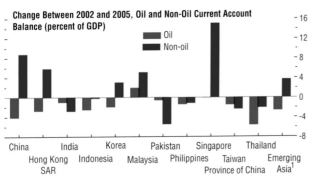

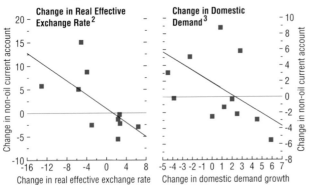

Source: IMF staff calculations.
[1]Consists of developing Asia, the newly industrialized Asian economies, and Mongolia.
[2]Fitted line excludes Korea.
[3]Fitted line excludes Singapore. For China, real GDP growth is used because of a large discrepancy between overall growth and the expenditure side components in the national account statistics.

rent account surplus in 2005, at 4.5 percent of GDP, was higher than in 2002 (Figure 1.14). A redistribution of surpluses within the region, however, has taken place. The surplus in China has risen substantially since 2002 and is estimated at 7.1 percent of GDP in 2005—and now accounts for two-thirds of the regional surplus, compared to around one-quarter in 2002—while surpluses have also risen in Malaysia, Hong Kong SAR, Singapore (and to a lesser extent Korea). On the other hand, the current account has weakened in other countries, moving into deficit in India, Pakistan, and Thailand in 2005. These disparate movements are due to the non-oil balance, which has generally declined in countries where domestic demand growth has accelerated and/or where the real effective exchange rate has appreciated.

Looking forward, with emerging Asia remaining central to the current constellation of global imbalances, the region will need to play a central and proactive role in managing the risks associated with these imbalances. This will require achieving a better balance between externally and domestically led growth in countries with current account surpluses. Reforms to domestic financial systems will need to be at the center of efforts to boost domestic demand. Exchange rate appreciation will also be necessary.[9] While a number of regional exchange rates have appreciated over the past year (notably the Korean won, Indian rupee, and Thai baht), there has been little change in exchange rate behavior in either China or Malaysia despite the reforms introduced last July (although the real effective exchange rate has appreciated given the upward movement of the dollar). In turn, this is likely constraining other countries from allowing greater upward exchange rate movement given regional interdependencies and concerns about competitiveness losses.

[9]Simulations of the IMF's Global Economic Model (GEM) suggest that more flexible exchange rates in emerging Asia that allowed for real appreciation would contribute to a reduction in global imbalances (Appendix 1.2, September 2005 *World Economic Outlook*).

Box 1.6. China's GDP Revision: What Does It Mean for China and the Global Economy?

China recently revised its production-side GDP estimates, showing higher nominal and real GDP growth rates over 1993–2004. This revision is based on the data collected from a recent economic census, which showed much larger output from the services sector than previously estimated; nominal GDP in 2004 is now about 16.8 percent higher than before. The highlights of the revision are:

- The services sector's share of GDP rose 5 percentage points on average and reached around 41 percent of GDP in 2004, largely offset by a lower share of GDP of the manufacturing sector. The rise in the share reflected better statistical recording of private businesses, especially in new areas such as computer and Internet services, and logistics support to the manufacturing and construction sectors. It should be noted that the economic census only covered 2004, and the historical data were backfilled by applying a statistical method that assumes a smooth path of the increase in services. Thus, the revision does not provide any information regarding when the newly uncovered activities emerged and expanded.

- As a result of the revision, the annual average real growth during 1993–2004 climbed to close to 10 percent, about ½ percentage point higher than before (see the figure). Annual growth rates of GDP deflators are also higher in the revised data, reflecting both the upward revision of services deflator and the larger share of services in GDP.

The 2005 nominal GDP under the new methodology has recently been released. It makes China the fourth-largest economy in the world in U.S. dollar terms, and the second-largest in PPP adjusted terms. Nevertheless, China's per capita income (US$7,204, PPP adjusted) remains very low. The revision has also added about 0.1 percentage point to global GDP growth estimates in recent years.

Note: The main author of this box is Li Cui.

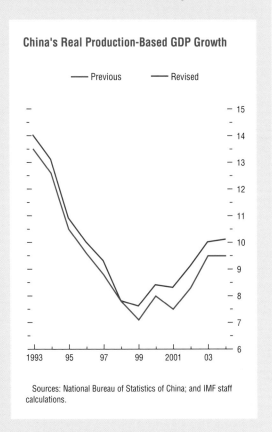

China's Real Production-Based GDP Growth

— Previous   — Revised

Sources: National Bureau of Statistics of China; and IMF staff calculations.

The nominal expenditure side GDP was also revised for 2004, bringing the expenditure side estimate for this year very close to its revised pro-

China: GDP and Components

	2004	
	Previous	Revised
GDP: Production based (RMB bln)	13,688	15,988
GDP: Expenditure based (RMB bln)	14,239	16,028
	Percent of GDP[1]	
Consumption	53	54
Private	41	40
Public	12	14
Investment	44	43
Net exports	3	3
Statistical discrepancies	0	0
Current account surplus	4.0	3.5

Sources: National Bureau of Statistics of China; and IMF staff calculations.
[1]Ratios based on expenditure side GDP data.

Box 1.6 *(concluded)*

duction-side counterpart. The new data imply shares of consumption and investment in GDP very similar to those prior to the revision, belying the speculation that the upward revision of the services sector would lead to a significantly higher share of consumption in GDP. In fact, private consumption as a share of GDP declined,

while the share of government consumption rose, which could reflect better reclassification of government spending between consumption and capital goods. While a fully revised historical series from the expenditure side has not yet been published, the basic assessment of China's economic situation remains unchanged.

Turning to individual countries, real GDP growth in China remains very strong—and recent data revisions indicate that it has been even stronger in recent years than previously thought (see Box 1.6)—with investment growth running at a high rate and the contribution of net exports increasing significantly. The pace of expansion is projected to slow modestly this year to 9.5 percent, from 9.9 percent in 2005, as the contribution from external demand falls and the government is assumed to act to slow investment growth (which is particularly needed in sectors facing the prospect of future overcapacity). The risks to this projection in the near term are on the upside given that without further tightening measures the ample liquidity in the banking system could underpin a rebound in lending and investment. Inflation pressures, however, remain limited due to continuing downward pressures on prices in some sectors due to excess capacity. The external position has continued to strengthen, and foreign exchange reserves increased by over $200 billion in 2005. Given the current favorable environment, the authorities have an ideal opportunity to utilize fully the flexibility available following the exchange rate reform last July which should lead to an appreciation of the renminbi. Greater exchange rate flexibility would allow monetary policy to be geared toward the needs of the domestic economy, and would aid in the development of the foreign exchange market. Exchange rate appreciation would also bolster households' purchasing power, which together with reforms to the pen-

sion, health, and education systems, and the financial sector, would boost consumption.

After a weak start to 2005, growth in the Newly Industrialized Economies (NIEs) has rebounded as exports have benefited from a stronger global IT sector (and demand for pharmaceuticals and oil rigs in Singapore). Looking forward, growth is expected to be supported by the favorable global outlook. With inflation pressures contained and public debt low, macroeconomic policies—outside of Singapore—can remain accommodative until the recovery is fully established. Turning to the ASEAN-4 countries, the Thai economy has rebounded from the tsunami-related contraction in early 2005, while growth in the Philippines is being supported by surging remittance inflows. Generally robust growth, however, has fallen slightly short of expectations in Malaysia and Indonesia, the latter due to high interest rates, the adverse confidence effects of financial market volatility last summer, and increases in domestic fuel prices. Policy priorities include containing inflation (all four countries), reducing public debt (Indonesia, the Philippines), and greater exchange rate flexibility (Malaysia).

In India, growth remains rapid, with strong momentum in the manufacturing and services sectors, and projections have been revised up for both 2006 and 2007. Exports have continued to grow robustly, but the current account has moved into deficit as strong domestic demand and high oil prices resulted in a surge in imports. Inflationary pressures have picked up, prompting the Reserve Bank of India to tighten

Table 1.7. Selected Western Hemisphere Countries: Real GDP, Consumer Prices, and Current Account Balance

(Annual percent change unless otherwise noted)

	Real GDP				Consumer Prices[1]				Current Account Balance[2]			
	2004	2005	2006	2007	2004	2005	2006	2007	2004	2005	2006	2007
Western Hemisphere	**5.6**	**4.3**	**4.3**	**3.6**	**6.5**	**6.3**	**5.8**	**5.6**	**0.9**	**1.2**	**0.8**	**0.2**
Mercosur[3]	**6.0**	**4.2**	**4.5**	**3.8**	**5.6**	**7.1**	**6.6**	**6.6**	**1.9**	**1.5**	**0.9**	**0.1**
Argentina	9.0	9.2	7.3	4.0	4.4	9.6	12.9	15.0	2.2	1.8	1.2	0.5
Brazil	4.9	2.3	3.5	3.5	6.6	6.9	4.9	4.4	1.9	1.8	1.0	0.2
Chile	6.1	6.3	5.5	5.2	1.1	3.1	3.8	3.0	1.5	−0.4	0.5	−1.2
Uruguay	12.3	6.0	4.0	3.5	7.6	5.9	5.5	4.9	−0.7	−2.4	−5.8	−2.5
Andean region	**7.8**	**6.3**	**4.8**	**3.8**	**8.4**	**6.4**	**5.7**	**6.5**	**4.1**	**6.5**	**5.1**	**4.2**
Colombia	4.8	5.1	4.5	4.0	5.9	5.0	4.7	4.2	−1.0	−1.7	−1.6	−2.7
Ecuador	6.9	3.3	3.0	2.2	2.7	2.4	3.4	3.0	−1.1	−0.9	0.2	0.4
Peru	4.8	6.7	5.0	4.5	3.7	1.6	2.7	2.2	—	1.3	1.4	0.3
Venezuela	17.9	9.3	6.0	3.0	21.7	15.9	11.7	17.3	12.5	19.1	14.1	13.4
Mexico, Central America, and Caribbean	**4.0**	**3.4**	**3.7**	**3.3**	**7.1**	**4.9**	**4.5**	**3.6**	**−1.4**	**−1.2**	**−1.1**	**−1.2**
Mexico	4.2	3.0	3.5	3.1	4.7	4.0	3.5	3.0	−1.1	−0.7	−0.6	−0.8
Central America[3]	3.9	3.8	3.9	3.8	7.4	8.6	7.4	5.8	−5.7	−4.9	−4.9	−4.8
The Caribbean[3]	2.3	5.9	5.3	4.5	27.2	6.9	8.3	5.8	1.3	−1.1	−1.0	−1.4

[1]In accordance with standard practice in the *World Economic Outlook,* movements in consumer prices are indicated as annual averages rather than as December/December changes, as is the practice in some countries. The December/December changes in the CPI for 2004, 2005, 2006, and 2007 are, respectively, for Brazil (7.6, 5.7, 4.5, and 4.5); Mexico (5.2, 3.3, 3.1, and 3.0); Peru (3.5, 1.5, 2.5, and 2.5) and Uruguay (7.6, 6.5, 5.5, and 4.5).

[2]Percent of GDP.

[3]The country composition of this regional group is set out in Table F in the Statistical Appendix.

monetary policy. Nevertheless, with monetary conditions still accommodative and credit expanding strongly, further interest rate increases will likely be needed. After three years of fiscal consolidation, the general government deficit remained broadly unchanged in FY2005/06. The draft budget for FY2006/07 aims to resume fiscal consolidation on the back of modest base broadening (primarily of the services tax) and the tight control of current expenditures, and it is important that this objective is achieved. The full pass-through of higher international energy prices into domestic prices (with adequate compensation mechanisms for the poor) is needed to curb the rising quasi-fiscal costs of petroleum subsidies and encourage improvements in energy efficiency. As the government recognizes, the reform agenda also needs to be accelerated in other areas, including infrastructure development, the power sector, and the liberalization of labor laws, while the decision to draw up a roadmap for moving to full capital account convertibility is welcome. In

Bangladesh and Pakistan, growth has remained robust despite headwinds from higher oil prices, devastating natural disasters, and the elimination of international textile trade quotas. In both countries, inflation has picked up, and a further tightening of monetary conditions is needed, supported by continued prudent fiscal policies. Regarding structural policies, priorities include energy sector reforms in Pakistan, and bank restructuring, trade reforms, and the full pass-through of higher oil prices into domestic fuel prices in Bangladesh.

Latin America: Improving the Business Climate Key to Raising Long-Term Growth

Robust economic expansion continued in Latin America in 2005 with overall growth of 4.3 percent (Table 1.7). Within this, many countries benefited from the strong global demand for commodities—in particular, fuels and metals (Chile and the Andean region) and agriculture

(Argentina and Uruguay). In contrast, growth slowed in Brazil, owing to weak domestic demand—investment in particular—and in Mexico as a result of the weaker performance of the agricultural and manufacturing sectors. Buoyant exports, sustained by improvements in the terms of trade, underpinned a third consecutive year of current account surpluses for the region and, combined with higher private capital inflows, resulted in substantial reserve accumulation. Correspondingly, regional exchange rates appreciated markedly, although taking account of their weak levels in 2001–02, competitiveness remains generally adequate. Reflecting their stronger external positions, Brazil and Argentina have repaid all outstanding IMF obligations ($15.5 billion and $9.6 billion, respectively).

Turning to 2006, regional growth is projected at 4.3 percent, some 0.5 percentage points stronger than projected in the last *World Economic Outlook*, mainly on account of higher than previously anticipated growth in Argentina and Venezuela. Recent interest rate cuts in some countries should support domestic demand going forward, although external demand will remain important. There are, however, a few notable downside risks to the outlook. A softening in global demand for the region's primary and manufacturing exports could weaken the contribution to growth from the external sector in many countries, while a deterioration in the global financial environment also poses risks given the still high level of public debt in the region. The region as a whole also faces a busy electoral schedule, underscoring the importance of maintaining sound economic policies and defending the hard-earned credibility among domestic and foreign investors during political transitions.

A major achievement in the region has been the decline in public debt on account of impressive fiscal discipline and the recent strong growth performance. Nevertheless, in many countries public debt still remains above the 25–50 percent of GDP range identified as safe in the September 2003 *World Economic Outlook*

(Figure 1.15). Indeed, in the case of Latin America, the current structure of debt—including the presence of interest indexation, short average maturity, or foreign exchange exposure—argues for debt ratios closer to the lower end of this range. Sustaining recent efforts to maintain the downward trajectory of debt is a key challenge facing policymakers. Continued expenditure restraint and tax reforms are essential to the improvement of public finances over the medium term. However, lasting reductions in public debt also require high and stable rates of economic growth that are much less dependent on the global commodity cycle. This, in turn, requires structural reforms to raise investment levels closer to emerging market averages. In this context, improving the business climate—which lags other regions along many dimensions, including as a destination for foreign investment—is a key priority. While the reform agenda varies by country, some common factors that would support higher private sector investment are a well-developed financial system for channeling savings toward productive investment; reforms to strengthen property rights; reforms of the judiciary and speedy enforcement of contractual obligations; and greater transparency and stability in rules and regulations governing private investment.

An important challenge for the region will be to achieve an appropriately balanced response to the likelihood of further upward pressures on exchange rates if the global environment remains supportive of continued strong external performance by Latin America. In this context, further tightening of fiscal policies would help to provide scope for monetary easing that could help diminish incentives for capital inflows, while maintaining the commitment to entrenching the gains against inflation and a flexible approach to exchange rates. Favorable external conditions also offer opportunities for strengthening public debt management to reduce long-standing balance sheet vulnerabilities. In this connection a number of country authorities are moving to increase reliance on domestic local currency issues, while implementing external debt buyback programs (e.g. Brazil, Colombia, Mexico, Peru). Lastly, structural reforms that boost productivity growth would also help maintain external competitiveness in the face of currency appreciation.

Turning to developments in individual countries, Argentina's economic expansion remains strong and broad-based, bolstered by buoyant domestic demand and robust export growth. Looking ahead, however, with capacity constraints likely to become increasingly evident, and inflation beginning to erode competitiveness, growth is expected to moderate. Fiscal policy in 2005 performed better than budgeted, as strong revenue growth offset a significant increase in government spending. Going forward, a combination of larger-than-budgeted fiscal surpluses, higher interest rates, and greater exchange rate flexibility will be needed to manage domestic demand pressures and contain accelerating inflation, projected to average around 13 percent this year. The authorities will need to introduce reforms in the utility sector, including the liberalization of prices, and raise investment in infrastructure, to avoid the emergence of supply bottlenecks and pave the way for higher medium-term growth. In Uruguay, growth remains robust against the backdrop of subdued inflationary pressures and buoyant exports. While the economy's short-term public debt vulnerabilities have declined, continued fiscal discipline will be necessary to ensure debt sustainability, complemented with reforms of the pension and financial systems.

In Brazil, activity slowed sharply last year. Domestic demand has been subdued, due primarily to inventory adjustments and some softening in investment following the earlier tightening of monetary policy, although private consumption has remained robust, underpinned by rising employment and real incomes. There are recent signs of a pickup in activity, such as in retail sales and industrial production, and growth is expected to strengthen in 2006, as lower interest rates spur a recovery in investment. With inflationary pressures moderating further and inflation expectations well

Figure 1.15. Latin America: Public Debt Ratios and Investment
(Purchasing-power-parity weighted averages unless noted otherwise)

Public debt ratios have benefited from disciplined fiscal policies and recent high growth. Sustaining recent progress will require increasing private sector investment to support stable long-term growth.

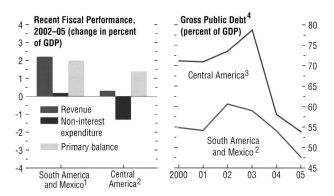

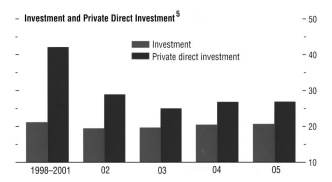

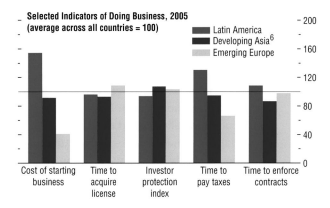

Sources: World Bank, *Doing Business Database;* and IMF staff calculations.
[1]Consists of Argentina, Bolivia, Brazil, Chile, Colombia, Ecuador, Mexico, Paraguay, Peru, Uruguay, and Venezuela.
[2]Consists of Costa Rica, El Salvador, Honduras, Nicaragua, and Panama.
[3]Excluding Argentina.
[4]Simple average.
[5]Latin America's gross capital formation in percent of GDP and private direct investment as a share of total emerging market and developing countries.
[6]Consists of China, India, Malaysia, Papua New Guinea, the Philippines, Sri Lanka, Thailand, and Vietnam.

grounded, there is room to continue the gradual reduction of policy interest rates initiated in September 2005. Reflecting a strong revenue effort, the consolidated primary surplus reached 4.8 percent of GDP in 2005, well above the 4.25 percent target. To continue the progress made in reducing public debt, it will be important to resist pressures for fiscal easing to sustain high primary surpluses, and to raise medium-term growth through reform efforts, including by improving the quality of fiscal policy and the business climate. In Chile, economic activity has remained robust and—despite some slowdown in the third quarter of 2005—is expected to remain buoyant going forward, supported by higher disposable incomes and solid consumer confidence. Efforts to boost underlying productivity will be essential to reduce the economy's dependence on copper prices. In this regard, greater labor market flexibility and increased investment in research and development would support greater expansion of the manufacturing sector.

Real GDP in the Andean region expanded by 6.3 percent in 2005, with activity strengthening in Colombia and Peru—as rising domestic demand broadened the recovery beyond exports—and growth in Venezuela remaining strong as high oil prices underpinned increased government spending. In Colombia and Peru, strong macroeconomic policies have supported low inflation, although monetary policy needs to remain vigilant to emerging capacity constraints (Colombia) and the possible effect of recent currency depreciation (Peru). In Venezuela, macroeconomic policies need to be tightened substantially to rein in double-digit inflation, while liberalizing the economy and improving the business climate will be important to boost private investment. Growth in Ecuador slowed as oil output stagnated, while a strong expansion in public spending and bank credit contributed to rising inflationary pressures in the second half of the year. Activity in Bolivia has benefited from favorable energy prices, but maintaining macroeconomic stability and deepening structural reforms are the key challenges for the new

administration in order to strengthen growth prospects.

In Mexico, growth slowed to 3 percent in 2005 due to weakness in the agricultural sector and to the slowdown in global manufacturing in the first half of the year. Looking ahead, the strength of the global manufacturing cycle and the continuing recovery of domestic investment are expected to underpin somewhat stronger growth of 3.5 percent in 2006. The decline in inflation over the past year, with core inflation having converged to the 3 percent target, has allowed an unwinding of earlier monetary tightening. Although the higher energy revenues of the last three years have led to some fiscal consolidation, the fiscal windfall from higher world prices of oil has been dampened by the long-standing policy of smoothing the domestic price of gasoline. Looking ahead, the recently approved fiscal responsibility law calls for an ongoing balanced budget and establishes a rule for allocating unbudgeted oil revenues. It will be important also to diversify the revenue base to reduce reliance on high oil prices, while ensuring that fiscal policymaking focuses on medium-term objectives. In the face of longer-term challenges from globalization, particularly given the importance of the manufacturing sector, enhancing the competitiveness of the economy through reforms in the energy and telecommunication sectors, the labor market, and the regulatory and business environment remains a priority.

Growth in Central American economies remained around 4 percent in 2005, despite the dampening effect of high oil prices on disposable incomes. Activity was supported by elevated prices of export commodities and a continued rise in remittances. Prospects for the region going forward would be boosted by the prompt implementation of the Central American Free Trade Agreement (CAFTA), which has been delayed beyond the original January 1 target. In the Caribbean, growth is expected to remain strong at 5.3 percent in 2006, supported by high tourism receipts and a construction boom ahead of the 2007 Cricket World Cup in several countries of the region. Important fiscal reforms—in

Table 1.8. Emerging Europe: Real GDP, Consumer Prices, and Current Account Balance
(Annual percent change unless otherwise noted)

	Real GDP				Consumer Prices[1]				Current Account Balance[2]			
	2004	2005	2006	2007	2004	2005	2006	2007	2004	2005	2006	2007
Emerging Europe	**6.6**	**5.4**	**5.3**	**4.8**	**6.2**	**4.9**	**4.2**	**3.4**	**−5.7**	**−5.2**	**−5.4**	**−5.3**
Turkey	8.9	7.4	6.0	5.0	8.6	8.2	6.5	4.4	−5.2	−6.3	−6.5	−6.1
Excluding Turkey	5.7	4.5	5.0	4.7	5.3	3.5	3.2	3.0	−6.0	−4.7	−4.9	−4.9
Baltics	**7.6**	**8.7**	**7.5**	**6.5**	**3.1**	**4.1**	**4.2**	**3.6**	**−10.4**	**−9.7**	**−9.8**	**−9.3**
Estonia	7.8	9.8	7.9	7.1	3.0	4.1	3.6	3.2	−12.7	−10.5	−10.1	−9.6
Latvia	8.5	10.2	9.0	7.0	6.3	6.7	6.4	5.5	−12.9	−12.5	−12.8	−12.0
Lithuania	7.0	7.3	6.5	6.0	1.2	2.6	3.2	2.7	−7.7	−7.5	−7.5	−7.3
Central Europe	**5.0**	**4.1**	**4.6**	**4.3**	**4.3**	**2.4**	**2.0**	**2.5**	**−5.2**	**−3.2**	**−3.6**	**−3.7**
Czech Republic	4.7	6.0	5.5	4.5	2.8	1.8	2.8	3.0	−6.0	−2.1	−2.3	−2.3
Hungary	4.6	4.1	4.4	4.2	6.7	3.5	2.0	2.7	−8.8	−7.9	−8.2	−7.5
Poland	5.3	3.2	4.2	3.8	3.5	2.1	1.3	2.3	−4.1	−1.6	−2.5	−3.1
Slovak Republic	5.5	6.0	6.3	6.7	7.5	2.8	3.6	2.5	−3.5	−7.2	−6.4	−5.5
Slovenia	4.2	3.9	4.0	4.0	3.6	2.5	2.4	2.4	−2.1	−0.9	−0.3	0.1
Southern and south-eastern Europe	**6.9**	**4.3**	**5.0**	**5.4**	**8.7**	**7.0**	**6.8**	**4.2**	**−7.3**	**−8.5**	**−8.0**	**−7.8**
Bulgaria	5.7	5.5	5.6	5.8	6.1	5.0	7.2	4.1	−5.8	−11.8	−10.2	−9.1
Croatia	3.8	4.1	4.1	4.5	2.1	3.3	3.2	2.5	−5.6	−6.0	−5.9	−5.9
Malta	1.0	1.0	1.3	1.5	2.7	3.1	2.8	2.4	−10.4	−6.7	−6.5	−6.3
Romania	8.4	4.1	5.2	5.6	11.9	9.0	7.9	4.8	−8.4	−8.7	−8.3	−8.1

[1]In accordance with standard practice in the *World Economic Outlook*, movements in consumer prices are indicated as annual averages rather than as December/December changes, as is the practice in some countries.
[2]Percent of GDP.

particular, the introduction of the VAT—are under way in many countries. These moves will serve to strengthen fiscal balances over the medium term. However, decisive steps need to be taken to reduce the very high public debt ratios and adapt to the erosion of EU trade preferences in bananas and sugar.

Emerging Europe: Addressing Rising Current Account Deficits

In emerging Europe, regional GDP growth has moderated to 5.4 percent from the exceptional level in 2004 (Table 1.8), and is projected to remain close to this level in 2006, underpinned by generally strong domestic demand and—despite appreciating exchange rates—solid export growth, buoyed by continued solid import growth in trading partners. Headline inflation remains generally moderate, with higher oil prices offset in many cases by rising currencies, although overheating pressures are a concern in parts of southern Europe and the Baltics. Looking forward, the key risks to the out-

look remain the strength of the recovery in euro area domestic demand; the large regional current account deficits; and rapid credit growth—especially for real estate lending—in a number of countries in the region, much of which is denominated in foreign currencies.

The regional current account deficit fell modestly to 5.2 percent of GDP in 2005, and is projected to remain at broadly that level in 2006 and 2007. Within that, developments differ widely across the region. In southeastern Europe, external deficits have increased—particularly in Bulgaria and to a lesser extent Turkey—driven by varying combinations of soaring private domestic demand and credit growth, higher oil prices, and buoyant capital inflows often accompanied by appreciating exchange rates. Elsewhere—particularly in the Czech Republic and Poland—deficits have been on a declining trend, although they remain high in the Baltics, Hungary, and, more recently, the Slovak Republic. On the financing side, the share of debt financing (particularly short-term) has been gradually rising—it is expected to finance

Figure 1.16. Emerging Europe: Current Account Deficits Remain High

Over the medium term, current account deficits will need to be significantly reduced—in general primary balances will need to turn positive—to stabilize net investment positions. The corresponding real exchange rate adjustment will be less the more open the economy, and the more investment has been directed to the tradeables sector.

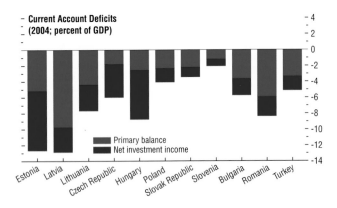

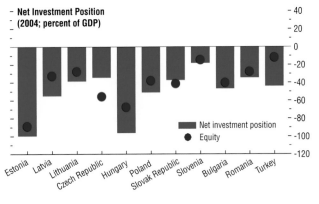

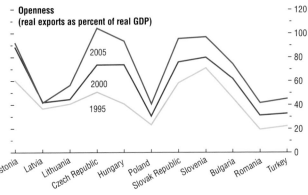

Source: IMF staff calculations.

about half of the regional current account deficit in 2006—and is particularly significant in Turkey, Hungary, and the Baltics.

As discussed in previous issues of the *World Economic Outlook*, the nature of and risks associated with these deficits vary widely. In central Europe, external deficits are closely associated with fiscal imbalances; in the Baltics and southeastern Europe they primarily reflect private sector behavior. Correspondingly, the risks and remedy in central Europe are relatively clear; in the Baltics and southeastern Europe, both are more complex, although—especially given the increasing resort to debt financing—there is an increasing case for policies to lean against the wind to reduce potential risks. Over the medium term, as a matter of arithmetic, current accounts in most countries will need to adjust substantially to stabilize net investment positions (Figure 1.16). That adjustment is likely to be smoother—and involve less real exchange rate adjustment—the more open the economy, the more past inflows have been invested in the tradables sector, and the more flexible domestic markets. Managing this adjustment will be of particular importance in those countries that have or plan shortly to move to fixed exchange rate regimes, including to avoid potential deflationary pressures.

In Poland, GDP growth slowed to 3.2 percent in 2005, noticeably below potential, reflecting flagging domestic demand in the aftermath of the 2004 EU accession boom, weak labor market conditions, and higher oil prices. Looking forward, GDP growth is expected to pick up to 4.2 percent in 2006, with consumption growth boosted by higher pension payments. Much depends, however, on external developments—notably in German growth—and the strength of investment in light of the complicated post-election political situation. With inflation projected to remain at or below the 2.5 percent target in 2006 and 2007, policy interest rates have been steadily reduced since early 2005. A key challenge remains to reduce the large general government deficit—which, barring adjustment measures, is likely to settle at about 5 percent of

GDP over the medium term—to stabilize public debt below 50 percent of GDP. With unemployment at 18 percent, and the investment-to-GDP ratio the lowest in the region, measures to improve the functioning of the labor market and to strengthen the investment climate are also priorities.

In Hungary, GDP growth remains close to potential, underpinned by strengthening exports, the recovery in Western Europe, and investment related to motorway construction. Despite higher oil prices, inflationary expectations remain under control and core inflation is at an historic low; after steady reductions in the policy rate through much of 2005, the easing cycle ended in October and rates remain relatively high in real terms. The very large external current account and fiscal deficits—both around 7½ percent of GDP in 2005—are significant risks; moreover, given recent tax cuts and continued high public expenditure commitments, little improvement in either is in prospect for 2006. While the situation is complicated by upcoming elections, signs of weakening market sentiment underscore the need for decisive fiscal consolidation. Substantial foreign exchange borrowing by households is also a risk, increasing vulnerability to a further depreciation of the forint. Slovenia continues to enjoy solid growth and a stable macroeconomic performance; with inflation falling back to 2.5 percent, it now meets all Maastricht requirements, and is well placed to adopt the euro in January 2007 as scheduled.

GDP growth in the Czech Republic rose to 6 percent in 2005, with slowing domestic demand growth offset by buoyant net export growth as past foreign-financed investment comes on stream, and is expected to moderate somewhat in 2006. The central bank has begun to reverse earlier policy easing, although with inflationary expectations securely anchored below the inflation target of 3 percent, further moves should await incoming data on the strength of the pickup in domestic demand, which remains fragile. While the general government deficit was reduced to 2.6 percent of GDP in 2005, over 2 percent of GDP below target, the draft 2006 budget more than reverses these gains, underscoring the need for additional consolidation efforts, especially given the pressures from aging, substantial outstanding public sector guarantees, and the limited scope for further privatization revenues. In the Slovak Republic, the macroeconomic outlook remains strong, although unemployment—while declining—is very high. Following the entry into ERM–2 in late 2005, a key challenge will be to reduce inflation to meet the Maastricht criterion while avoiding undue nominal currency appreciation, a task that would be facilitated by a tighter fiscal stance than currently planned.

In the Baltic countries, GDP growth has remained robust, underpinned by generally sound macroeconomic policies and wide-ranging structural reforms. However, with domestic demand fueled by rapid private credit growth, overheating concerns have risen, reflected in wide current account deficits; rapidly rising equity and real estate prices; and—to a lesser extent—upward pressures on prices, making it unlikely that any country will meet the Maastricht inflation criterion this year. While priorities among countries differ, measures to moderate credit growth are important, especially for mortgage lending (the recent tightening of prudential regulations in Estonia being a welcome step), along with strengthened financial supervision; fiscal policy—while generally very prudent—should also seek to dampen demand pressures.

In Bulgaria and Romania, domestic demand has substantially exceeded expectations, spurred by rapid credit growth, large-scale wage increases, a tax cut in January 2005 (Romania), and continued strong investment growth (Bulgaria). Correspondingly, inflationary pressures have picked up—in Romania, despite a substantial appreciation of the leu—and external current account deficits have widened sharply—in Bulgaria to 11.8 percent of GDP, one of the highest in the region. While external deficits are primarily driven by the private sector, they are an increasing source of vulnerability, underscoring the need to restrain credit growth, especially to

Table 1.9. Commonwealth of Independent States: Real GDP, Consumer Prices, and Current Account Balance
(Annual percent change unless otherwise noted)

	Real GDP				Consumer Prices[1]				Current Account Balance[2]			
	2004	2005	2006	2007	2004	2005	2006	2007	2004	2005	2006	2007
Commonwealth of Independent States	**8.4**	**6.5**	**6.0**	**6.1**	**10.3**	**12.3**	**10.4**	**9.7**	**8.1**	**9.1**	**9.6**	**8.1**
Russia	7.2	6.4	6.0	5.8	10.9	12.6	10.4	9.5	9.9	11.3	11.8	9.5
Ukraine	12.1	2.6	2.3	4.3	9.0	13.5	13.0	12.5	10.5	2.7	1.2	−2.1
Kazakhstan	9.6	9.4	8.0	8.3	6.9	7.6	7.5	7.5	1.2	1.8	2.3	2.4
Belarus	11.4	9.2	5.5	4.0	18.1	10.3	10.4	13.3	−5.3	1.2	−0.8	−2.0
Turkmenistan	17.2	9.6	6.5	6.0	5.9	10.8	7.9	5.0	0.6	2.8	1.4	1.1
Low-income CIS countries	**8.4**	**11.7**	**12.7**	**11.4**	**7.5**	**11.9**	**8.4**	**7.6**	**−7.1**	**−1.0**	**6.9**	**17.6**
Armenia	10.1	13.9	7.5	6.0	7.0	0.6	3.0	3.0	−4.6	−3.3	−3.9	−4.3
Azerbaijan	10.2	24.3	26.2	22.9	6.7	9.7	8.6	11.8	−30.0	−5.2	17.7	40.0
Georgia	6.2	7.7	6.4	5.0	5.7	8.3	5.3	4.0	−8.3	−7.4	−7.1	−5.5
Kyrgyz Republic	7.0	−0.6	5.0	5.5	4.1	4.3	5.7	4.5	−3.4	−8.1	−6.8	−5.6
Moldova	7.3	7.0	6.0	5.0	12.5	11.9	9.4	8.7	−2.7	−5.5	−5.2	−5.3
Tajikistan	10.6	6.7	8.0	6.0	7.1	7.1	7.8	5.0	−4.0	−3.4	−4.2	−4.8
Uzbekistan	7.4	7.0	7.2	5.0	8.8	21.0	11.3	6.5	10.0	10.8	9.6	9.2
Memorandum												
Net energy exporters[3]	7.6	7.1	6.7	6.5	10.4	12.3	10.1	9.2	8.6	10.3	11.0	9.6
Net energy importers[4]	11.5	4.2	3.3	4.4	10.2	12.1	11.7	11.6	4.6	1.2	−0.2	−2.5

[1]In accordance with standard practice in the *World Economic Outlook*, movements in consumer prices are indicated as annual averages rather than as December/December changes, as is the practice in some countries.
[2]Percent of GDP.
[3]Includes Azerbaijan, Kazakhstan, Russia, Turkmenistan, and Uzbekistan.
[4]Includes Armenia, Belarus, Georgia, Kyrgyz Republic, Moldova, Tajikistan, and Ukraine.

households; tighten fiscal positions; and, in Romania, increase wage restraint. Structural reforms are key to invigorate the supply side, including greater labor market flexibility, advancing privatization (Romania) and improving the business climate (Bulgaria).

Following the exceptionally rapid expansion through 2005, GDP growth in Turkey is expected to moderate to 6 percent in 2006, with the main risk facing the economy relating to the large current account deficit. In contrast to expectations, GDP growth has become increasingly reliant on domestic demand, particularly investment; the external current account has continued to deteriorate, driven mainly by higher oil prices and by surging capital inflows—in part reflecting ample global liquidity and Turkey's improving fundamentals—accompanied by a further real appreciation of the lira. While the composition of capital inflows has improved markedly—with the share of short-term inflows (including errors and omissions) nearly halving to 37 percent in 2005—Turkey

remains vulnerable to changes in investor sentiment. The 2006 budget appropriately provides for a modest tightening of fiscal policy, which should allow room for gradual monetary easing and an additional buildup of reserves. Further structural reforms, including early passage of the pension law, strengthening social security collection, income tax reform, and continued improvements in bank supervision—the more so given very rapid private credit growth—remain key to sustaining the strong economic performance to date and increasing resilience to a reversal in currently benign external conditions.

Commonwealth of Independent States: A Rebalancing of Growth Is Needed to Sustain the Expansion

Real GDP growth slowed significantly in the Commonwealth of Independent States (CIS) during 2005, to 6.5 percent from 8.4 percent in 2004 (Table 1.9). A particularly sharp slowdown in Ukraine accounted for much of this, although the pace of expansion also moderated in other key countries in the region. Lower output growth in the energy sector (Russia, Kazakhstan), political and economic uncertainties that undermined investment (Ukraine, Kyrgyz Republic), and an increasingly negative contribution from the external sector (Ukraine, Russia) all contributed to this weaker growth.

At the same time as growth has slowed, the composition of demand has been very unbalanced, raising concerns about the sustainability of growth going forward. Investment has remained weak, averaging just under 21 percent of GDP in 2005, the lowest of any emerging market and developing country region (Figure 1.17). Consumption, on the other hand, has expanded strongly, particularly in Russia, Ukraine, and Kazakhstan, underpinned by large hikes in wages and public pensions and increased access to credit. Indeed, credit has grown extremely strongly in a number of countries in the region, and in Ukraine and Kazakhstan has increasingly been directed at households and a significant share is denominated in foreign currency. While the ongoing process of financial deepening in the region is welcome—the ratio of bank credit-to-GDP is still low in many countries—rapid credit growth poses a risk to financial stability given banks' generally weak abilities to assess borrower creditworthiness and the increasing reliance by banks in some countries on financing from abroad.

This combination of strong consumption growth and weak investment has led to increasing capacity constraints in some countries and sectors and, together with higher food and energy prices (although pass-through to domestic prices has not been complete), contributed to a sharp increase in inflationary pressures in the first half of 2005 that have moderated only slightly in recent months. The current account, however, remains in large surplus at the regional level, although there is increasing differentiation across countries. In energy exporters as a group, higher oil prices underpinned a further increase in the surplus during 2005, but in energy-importing countries the surplus declined due

Figure 1.17. Commonwealth of Independent States: Unbalanced Growth Raises Concerns About the Outlook

Consumption has grown strongly in a number of countries, supported by wage and pension increases and rapid credit growth. Investment, however, remains relatively weak, raising concerns about the sustainability of current growth rates.

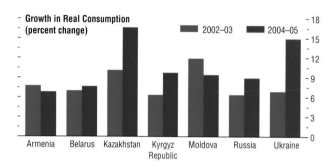

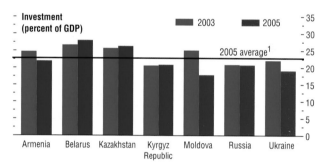

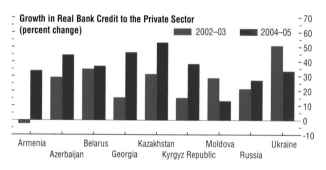

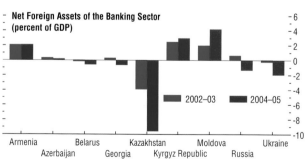

Sources: IMF, *International Financial Statistics;* and IMF staff calculations.
[1]Emerging market and developing countries excluding China.

both to higher oil imports and an increase in non-oil import volumes.

Looking forward, growth is projected to slow further to 6 percent in 2006, although decisive policy actions will be needed to lock in this pace of expansion. Monetary policy will increasingly need to focus on reducing or containing inflation, with the authorities correspondingly allowing nominal exchange rates to appreciate as necessary. And while countries that are benefiting from higher oil revenues have scope to raise productive government spending, such increases will need to be carefully managed in line with cyclical considerations to ensure they are consistent with overall macroeconomic policy objectives. To encourage investment spending, a more hospitable business climate needs to be created by reducing uncertainties about government intervention in the economy and moving to strengthen the institutional structures necessary for vibrant market-based economies to flourish. Structural reforms are also needed to boost productivity in the noncommodity sectors to improve competitiveness in the face of upward pressures on exchange rates. In terms of the financial sector, progress has been made in banking reform, but it has lagged that in countries in central and eastern Europe. Regulatory and supervisory systems, in particular, need to be upgraded in line with the growing importance of the financial sector.

Turning to individual countries, after a weak start to 2005, real GDP growth in Russia has accelerated, and the economy is expected to expand by 6 percent in 2006 (0.8 percentage points higher than projected in the September 2005 *World Economic Outlook*). The expansion is being driven by private consumption, while export growth has fallen. Investment, despite a recent pickup, is relatively subdued, and concerns remain that the economy may begin to run into capacity constraints. Real wages are rising faster than productivity, imports are surging, and CPI inflation is running at over 11 percent. Against this background, fiscal policy should not be relaxed until cyclical pressures have eased, and monetary policy needs to be tightened.

Without allowing for greater nominal exchange rate appreciation, it is unlikely the central bank will be able to meet its end-2006 inflation target of 8.5 percent. Turning to the financial sector, credit growth remains rapid, and it is important that prudential practices are strengthened under the new deposit insurance scheme to ensure that risks in the sector are appropriately managed.

In Ukraine, real GDP growth has slowed sharply, reflecting a less favorable external environment and political and policy uncertainties that have undermined investment. Growth is expected to slow further this year—to 2.3 percent—as continued political uncertainties and a significant hike in import prices for natural gas weigh on activity. Inflation has fallen from a peak of 15 percent in mid-2005, but remains over 10 percent, while credit growth remains strong. Reflecting uncertainties about the economic and political situation, spreads on Ukrainian external bonds have widened somewhat and the central bank conducted substantial foreign exchange interventions to maintain the official hryvina-U.S. dollar exchange rate. The authorities need to tighten monetary policy to reduce inflation, support this with fiscal restraint, and implement reforms to create a positive investment climate. In Kazakhstan, growth remains strong, underpinned by high oil prices. Inflationary pressures, however, have risen, and the central bank has raised interest rates, although further tightening is still required. WTO accession negotiations are proceeding, but progress with other structural reforms has been slow.

Growth in the low-income CIS countries remains very strong, although there are considerable differences across countries. In Azerbaijan (oil production), Armenia (remittance inflows and a good harvest), and Georgia (agricultural recovery), growth has picked up, but in the Kyrgyz Republic and Tajikistan it has slowed. The central challenge for the region remains to put in place the policies that will maintain the strong growth needed to reduce poverty going forward. To achieve this, the

Table 1.10. Selected African Countries: Real GDP, Consumer Prices, and Current Account Balance
(Annual percent change unless otherwise noted)

	Real GDP				Consumer Prices[1]				Current Account Balance[2]			
	2004	2005	2006	2007	2004	2005	2006	2007	2004	2005	2006	2007
Africa	**5.5**	**5.2**	**5.7**	**5.5**	**8.1**	**8.5**	**9.1**	**7.3**	**0.1**	**1.9**	**2.6**	**2.7**
Maghreb	**5.1**	**4.1**	**5.2**	**5.0**	**2.9**	**1.5**	**3.7**	**3.8**	**7.1**	**11.8**	**10.5**	**9.1**
Algeria	5.2	5.3	4.9	5.0	3.6	1.6	5.0	5.5	13.1	21.3	18.9	16.5
Morocco	4.2	1.8	5.4	4.4	1.5	1.0	2.0	2.0	2.2	0.9	−0.8	−0.9
Tunisia	6.0	4.2	5.8	6.0	3.6	2.0	3.0	2.0	−2.0	−1.3	−1.4	−1.1
Sub-Sahara	**5.6**	**5.5**	**5.8**	**5.7**	**9.7**	**10.6**	**10.7**	**8.3**	**−2.1**	**−1.1**	**0.3**	**0.8**
Horn of Africa[3]	**8.1**	**8.3**	**9.9**	**8.5**	**8.4**	**7.8**	**8.7**	**5.3**	**−5.8**	**−10.1**	**−7.0**	**−5.2**
Ethiopia	12.3	8.7	5.3	5.7	8.6	6.8	10.8	6.0	−5.1	−9.1	−7.5	−4.3
Sudan	5.2	8.0	13.0	10.3	8.4	8.5	7.5	5.0	−6.3	−10.7	−6.9	−5.4
Great Lakes[3]	**5.6**	**5.6**	**5.4**	**6.1**	**6.9**	**11.6**	**8.2**	**4.5**	**−2.7**	**−4.7**	**−5.1**	**−5.8**
Congo, Dem. Rep. of	6.9	6.5	7.0	7.2	4.0	21.4	9.3	6.4	−5.7	−4.8	−2.6	−2.1
Kenya	4.3	4.7	3.3	4.9	11.6	10.3	11.5	2.8	−2.5	−7.6	−4.4	−5.9
Tanzania	6.7	6.9	5.8	7.0	4.3	4.6	5.2	5.0	−1.6	−2.6	−7.6	−8.7
Uganda	5.6	5.6	6.2	6.1	5.0	8.0	6.5	4.0	−1.7	−1.2	−3.9	−4.2
Southern Africa[3]	**4.8**	**5.2**	**9.2**	**8.2**	**47.6**	**33.2**	**46.7**	**34.0**	**0.3**	**0.3**	**3.2**	**3.2**
Angola	11.1	15.7	26.0	20.2	43.6	23.0	13.0	8.3	4.2	8.2	11.3	12.0
Zimbabwe	−3.8	−6.5	−4.7	−4.1	350.0	237.8	850.4	584.2	−8.3	−11.1	1.7	−15.0
West and Central Africa[3]	**6.6**	**5.4**	**5.1**	**5.3**	**7.9**	**11.6**	**6.7**	**4.8**	**−0.4**	**4.6**	**6.7**	**7.4**
Ghana	5.8	5.8	6.0	6.0	12.6	15.1	8.8	7.1	−2.7	−6.6	−7.8	−5.3
Nigeria	6.0	6.9	6.2	5.2	15.0	17.9	9.4	6.5	4.6	12.6	14.2	15.3
CFA franc zone[3]	**7.7**	**4.1**	**3.4**	**4.8**	**0.2**	**4.2**	**2.4**	**2.3**	**−3.4**	**−1.3**	**0.1**	**0.0**
Cameroon	3.6	2.6	4.2	4.3	0.3	2.0	2.6	1.0	−3.4	−1.5	−1.6	−1.8
Côte d'Ivoire	1.8	0.5	2.4	2.6	1.5	3.9	2.8	3.0	2.7	0.7	1.9	1.9
South Africa	**4.5**	**4.9**	**4.3**	**4.1**	**1.4**	**3.4**	**4.5**	**4.9**	**−3.4**	**−4.2**	**−3.9**	**−3.6**
Memorandum												
Oil importers	4.8	4.4	4.6	4.7	7.5	8.3	10.0	8.0	−2.5	−3.7	−3.7	−3.6
Oil exporters[4]	7.2	7.0	8.2	7.5	9.7	9.1	7.2	5.8	5.8	12.0	12.7	12.3

[1]In accordance with standard practice in the *World Economic Outlook*, movements in consumer prices are indicated as annual averages rather than as December/December changes, as is the practice in some countries.
[2]Percent of GDP.
[3]The country composition of this regional group is set out in Table F in the Statistical Appendix.
[4]Includes Chad and Mauritania in this table.

sources of growth need to be diversified, particularly by improving the business climate to encourage investment in the noncommodity sectors, liberalizing trade regimes, and reducing high external debt levels.

Africa: Sustaining the Recent Growth Acceleration

Economic activity in sub-Saharan Africa continued to expand robustly at 5.5 percent in 2005 (Table 1.10). Among oil exporters, growth picked up in Nigeria, but slowed in some other countries—particularly Chad and Equatorial Guinea—following strong increases over the previous two years. Among oil importers, higher metal prices have supported growth in countries such as South Africa and Zambia, while growth in excess of 7 percent in Ethiopia, Mozambique, and Sierra Leone reflects the continuing positive effects of earlier reforms. The moderation in food and agricultural raw material prices, however, along with weather-related food production shortfalls, affected growth in the Sahel region and parts of eastern and southern Africa, while weakness in cotton markets hurt the CFA franc countries. The removal of textile quotas has also adversely affected a number of African countries. Output continued to decline in Côte d'Ivoire, Zimbabwe, and the Seychelles.

Figure 1.18. Sub-Saharan Africa: Growth, Investment, and Economic Transitions

Economic reforms have supported greater investment and improved growth performance in recent years. Sustaining progress on structural reforms will be important to maintain higher levels of long-term growth.

— Sub-Saharan Africa
— Oil-producing countries [1]
— Non-oil-producing countries [2]

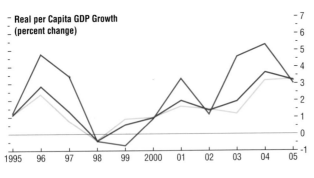

Real per Capita GDP Growth
(percent change)

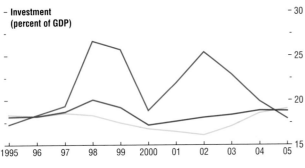

Investment
(percent of GDP)

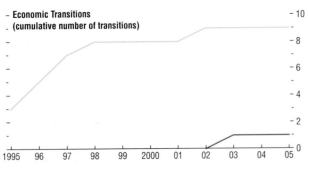

Economic Transitions
(cumulative number of transitions)

Source: IMF staff calculations.
[1] Angola, Cameroon, Chad, Republic of Congo, Côte d'Ivoire, Equatorial Guinea, Gabon, Nigeria, and São Tomé and Príncipe.
[2] Benin, Botswana, Burkina Faso, Burundi, Cape Verde, Central African Republic, Comoros, Democratic Republic of Congo, Ethiopia, Gambia, Ghana, Guinea, Guinea-Bissau, Kenya, Lesotho, Madagascar, Malawi, Mali, Mauritius, Mozambique, Namibia, Niger, Rwanda, Senegal, Seychelles, Sierra Leone, South Africa, Swaziland, Tanzania, Togo, Uganda, Zambia, and Zimbabwe.

Despite the increase in international oil prices, inflationary pressures have remained generally well contained, reflecting in part a lower degree of pass-through to domestic fuel prices in 2005 relative to previous years. This has, however, adversely affected fiscal and current account balances in a number of oil-importing countries, which was partially alleviated by external grants.

The economic outlook in sub-Saharan Africa remains positive, with growth of 5.8 percent projected this year—the highest rate in over 30 years—underpinned by high commodity prices, improved macroeconomic policies, and structural reforms in some countries. This acceleration in growth is largely due to the oil-producing countries, where capacity increases in Angola and the Republic of Congo and new production in Mauritania are expected to drive a substantial pickup in activity. Growth in non-oil producers is also expected to pick up, supported by continued, albeit slower, growth in non-oil commodity prices, a recovery in agricultural production, and stronger investment. While the outlook for the region's oil exporters is importantly tied to oil prices, for non-oil-producing countries, a softening in the global demand for non-oil commodities, higher energy prices, and weather-related factors are key risks. For the CFA franc countries, a weakening in the U.S. dollar against the euro would adversely affect competitiveness.

The strong projected expansion this year follows a period where growth in sub-Saharan Africa has clearly risen above its historical trend (Figure 1.18). Growth in both oil- and non-oil-producing countries has strengthened, the former spurred by the coming on stream of new capacity in recent years. In non-oil producers, reforms implemented in the second half of the 1990s in a number of countries have clearly started to pay dividends, with investment ratios importantly reversing their previous downward trend. Sustaining and further strengthening the recent economic performance are critical to making a lasting impact on poverty reduction. In this regard, continued fiscal discipline and low inflation are essential anchors for sustaining growth accelerations, but further improvements in economic institutions—where there have been few new transitions in recent years—will help secure stable long-term growth going forward.[10]

Lessons from the last *World Economic Outlook* suggest that the current favorable economic environment is particularly conducive to implementing necessary reforms to strengthen economic institutions. In particular, the reduction of trade restrictions and multilateral progress in trade liberalization in the Doha Round can be expected to support efforts to strengthen institutions. Under the Multilateral Debt Relief Initiative (MDRI), the IMF has granted debt relief amounting to $2.5 billion to 13 countries in Africa. Countries should take advantage of the opportunities offered by the MDRI to reorient spending to priority areas, including health and education, to raise the level of human capital and long-term growth. The New Partnership for Africa's Development (NEPAD) offers an important opportunity that needs to be fully grasped for strengthening cooperation at the regional level, with potentially large benefits from the improvement in institutional quality in the immediate neighborhood of countries. Finally, reforms to improve the business environment, including streamlining of regulations and improved governance, will help increase investment and employment.

Turning to individual countries, economic activity in South Africa was strong in 2005, driven by domestic demand and increasingly supported by exports. Consumer and investment spending have strengthened, while manufacturing growth began picking up at end-2005 in response to domestic and external demand. Looking ahead, growth is expected to moderate as output approaches potential. While higher oil prices and strong domestic demand have led to some widening in the current account deficit,

inflation has remained well contained and the recent appreciation of the rand has improved the inflation outlook. Nevertheless, the continued strength of domestic demand, high money and credit growth, and developments in international oil and food prices present potential upside risks to inflation. Following persistently strong fiscal performance and prudent levels of public debt, the government is appropriately planning to increase further social spending and infrastructure investment to help address social needs and supply bottlenecks. On structural policies, the authorities are focusing on skills development, improving efficiency in state-owned enterprises, and on measures to improve competition in domestic markets. The positive impact of these initiatives on growth could be enhanced by labor market reforms.

In Nigeria, growth strengthened in 2005 due to robust expansion in both the oil- and non-oil sectors, but is expected to slow in 2006. Following insufficient sterilization of oil-related inflows and low interest rates during much of last year, monetary policy has begun to be tightened and inflation is expected to decline from last year's 18 percent. Reflecting strong oil revenues and lower capital expenditures, the overall fiscal surplus reached nearly 10 percent of GDP in 2005, although the non-oil fiscal balance continued to deteriorate. Management of oil revenues remains a key challenge for policymakers, underscoring the need for lasting institutional reforms to ensure these revenues are used prudently to pave the way for stable long-term growth. Budgetary plans that place higher priorities on identifying allocations for key reforms, poverty reducing programs and infrastructure, and explicitly identifying domestic fuel subsidies are welcome, and need to be implemented going forward. Risks to the overall outlook stem mainly from developments in international oil prices as well as from any disruptions to oil production facilities.

---

[10]A transition is defined as the first year of a sustained improvement in the quality of the underlying economic institutions. The quality of institutions is assessed using an overall index composed of indicators encompassing the size of government, legal structure and property rights, access to sound money, the freedom to trade internationally, and regulation of credit, labor, and business. See Chapter III of the September 2005 *World Economic Outlook* for further details.

Table 1.11. Selected Middle Eastern Countries: Real GDP, Consumer Prices, and Current Account Balance
(Annual percent change unless otherwise noted)

	Real GDP				Consumer Prices[1]				Current Account Balance[2]			
	2004	2005	2006	2007	2004	2005	2006	2007	2004	2005	2006	2007
Middle East	**5.4**	**5.9**	**5.7**	**5.4**	**8.4**	**8.4**	**8.7**	**8.5**	**12.4**	**19.1**	**20.4**	**18.1**
Oil exporters[3]	**5.7**	**6.2**	**5.8**	**5.5**	**8.2**	**8.1**	**9.8**	**9.6**	**14.4**	**22.1**	**23.6**	**21.2**
Iran, I.R. of	5.6	5.9	5.3	5.0	15.2	13.0	17.0	17.0	2.5	7.5	7.6	6.2
Saudi Arabia	5.2	6.5	6.3	6.4	0.3	0.4	1.0	1.0	20.5	28.3	28.3	23.9
Kuwait	6.2	8.5	6.2	4.7	1.3	3.9	3.5	3.0	31.1	43.3	49.9	48.7
Mashreq	**4.2**	**4.7**	**4.8**	**4.8**	**8.4**	**9.5**	**4.9**	**4.5**	**−0.8**	**−2.5**	**−3.4**	**−4.4**
Egypt	4.1	5.0	5.2	5.2	10.3	11.4	4.4	4.5	4.3	2.8	1.3	−0.4
Syrian Arab Republic	2.5	3.5	3.6	3.6	4.6	7.2	7.2	5.0	−2.0	−5.5	−7.3	−8.6
Jordan	7.7	7.2	5.0	5.0	3.4	3.5	6.9	5.8	−0.2	−17.8	−16.0	−14.4
Lebanon	6.0	1.0	3.0	3.4	3.0	0.3	2.5	2.0	−18.2	−12.7	−12.9	−12.1
Memorandum												
Israel	4.4	5.2	4.2	4.2	−0.4	1.3	2.4	2.0	1.6	1.9	1.0	2.1

[1]In accordance with standard practice in the *World Economic Outlook,* movements in consumer prices are indicated as annual averages rather than as December/December changes during the year, as is the practice in some countries.
[2]Percent of GDP.
[3]Includes Bahrain, I.R. of Iran, Iraq, Kuwait, Libya, Oman, Qatar, Saudi Arabia, Syrian Arab Republic, United Arab Emirates, and Yemen.

In the Maghreb region, increased oil exports and sustained activity in the services and construction sectors have underpinned strong growth in Algeria, although inflation has eased due to a drop in food prices. Public spending—largely investment—increased by some 4 percent of nonhydrocarbon GDP, but rising hydrocarbon revenues have generated very large fiscal and current account surpluses. Against the backdrop of high energy prices, the outlook for growth remains strong, although absorptive capacity may be limited in the short term. Growth above 5 percent is projected for both Morocco and Tunisia, with the expiration of textile quotas having had only a modest impact on overall growth. Both countries, however, remain vulnerable to further oil price increases and possible delayed adverse effects on the textile sectors. Policies to attract investment and diversify the manufacturing base of the economy remain key policy priorities.

Middle East: Booming Asset Prices Across the Region

Oil-exporting countries in the Middle East enjoyed a third consecutive year of substantially higher export earnings, fueling average growth of 5.9 percent in the region and a current account surplus of 19 percent of GDP (Table 1.11). While a large proportion of the increase in oil revenues has been saved in most oil-exporting countries, domestic demand growth has strengthened considerably, although inflation has remained subdued. Growth in non-oil-producing countries in the region has benefited from the expansion in oil exporters and domestic reforms in some countries. With oil production near capacity, strong but moderating growth is expected in 2006, while current account surpluses in oil exporters reach 25 percent of GDP. The main risks to the outlook are closely related to the prospects for oil prices, although rising geopolitical uncertainty and developments in asset markets (see below) pose additional risks to the region.

The current oil cycle has been accompanied by a significant rise in money and credit growth, which has contributed to surging property and equity prices, with the latter also benefiting from increased profitability of petrochemical companies (Figure 1.19). During 2005, Middle Eastern stock indices were among the best performing in the world, and regional market capitalization at nearly $1.3 trillion in early 2006 exceeded that of emerging Europe and Latin

America. Many stock markets in the region, however, experienced significant corrections in the first quarter of 2006, although valuations still remain well above long-term averages. Indirect evidence from the performance of real estate and construction shares supports other evidence that real estate prices are also near record levels.

A key challenge in the region is to channel liquidity into productive investment in both the oil and non-oil sectors, given the need to raise potential growth and provide increased employment opportunities for the growing working-age population. In particular, financial sector reforms that support the development of deeper capital markets would allow new and smaller firms to tap into the pool of available liquidity to fund their investment plans. An increased role for managed funds could also allow investment by small investors in diversified portfolios, reducing portfolio volatility and facilitating greater flexibility in their spending decisions. More generally, however, recent developments have increased the exposure of bank balance sheets to any downturn in asset markets—possibly resulting from an unexpected drop in oil prices or increased geopolitical uncertainty—and supervisory authorities will need to carefully monitor these risks, particularly in terms of lending to the construction sector.

Turning to developments in individual countries, the growth outlook for the Islamic Republic of Iran remains favorable, supported by high oil revenues, the recovery in agriculture, and a strong performance of the manufacturing sector. Inflation, however, still remains in double digits, underscoring the need for fiscal restraint and greater exchange rate flexibility. Prudent macroeconomic policies, reforms of the financial sector and the public subsidy system, and increased private sector participation in the economy are essential preconditions if higher oil revenues are to be successfully used to foster growth and employment.

In Saudi Arabia, activity expanded by 6.5 percent in 2005, supported by both the oil and non-oil sectors, with substantial current account and

Figure 1.19. Middle East: Surging Asset Markets

Oil-related revenues have fueled growth in bank credit and asset prices. Regional equity markets have grown similar in size to other emerging market regions.

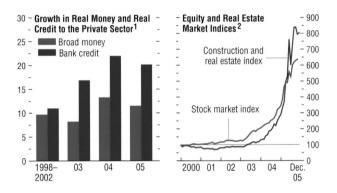

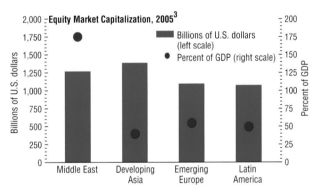

Sources: SHUAA Capital; IMF, *International Financial Statistics;* and IMF staff calculations.
[1] Oil exporters: Bahrain, I.R. of Iran, Kuwait, Libya, Oman, Qatar, Saudi Arabia, Syrian Arab Republic, Republic of Yemen, and United Arab Emirates.
[2] Indices represent the Arab composite with January 1, 2000 base year.
[3] Emerging Europe includes Russia and Ukraine; Developing Asia excludes Taiwan Province of China, Korea, Singapore, and Hong Kong SAR; and the Middle East includes the countries of the Cooperation Council of the Arab States of the Gulf (GCC) plus Egypt, Jordan, and Lebanon.

fiscal surpluses and subdued inflation. With oil export volumes not expected to increase substantially in the short term, growth is projected to remain broadly unchanged during 2006–07, with the current account surplus anticipated to remain high based on current oil price forecasts. The government's plans for substantial investment in the oil sector and infrastructure, accompanied by further structural reforms aimed at greater private sector participation, should help sustain strong growth and reduce unemployment. The substantial strengthening of the fiscal position and reduction of public debt will also create room for additional social spending in the areas of health and education.

Despite the very difficult security environment, Iraq has managed to maintain overall macroeconomic stability. Growth of 10 percent is projected in 2006, although the outlook is subject to considerable risks. The fiscal position has improved on account of higher oil revenues and the undershooting of some expenditure due to project implementation difficulties. The approval of the Stand-By Arrangement with the IMF in December paves the way for further debt reduction by Paris Club creditors which, along with the successful $14 billion debt exchange with private creditors, is expected to reduce debt obligations to a more sustainable level. Planned expansion of the oil sector, reform of public subsidies, and improved administrative capacity remain key challenges in the period ahead.

Economic activity picked up momentum in Egypt in 2005, with strengthening domestic demand broadening the expansion and boosting the prospects for robust growth this year. Inflation has declined impressively to below 5 percent, aided by the appreciation of the pound in early 2005. While the current account surplus has narrowed—with still buoyant export growth and rising remittances offset by higher imports of oil and capital goods—strong private capital inflows against the backdrop of recent nominal exchange rate stability poses challenges for monetary policy. Looking forward, a key macroeconomic challenge is to steadily reduce government deficits and public debt, both to

reduce vulnerabilities and create space for more productive public spending and higher private investment, the latter a key to raising growth and reducing high and rising unemployment. The recent momentum in privatization is welcome and efforts to resolve nonperforming loans in state-owned banks should be stepped up.

Elsewhere in the Mashreq, Jordan has successfully adjusted to higher oil prices and a sharp decline in external grants through a significant reduction in fuel subsidies and expenditure restraint, and growth, while slowing, is projected to remain robust in 2006. Activity in Lebanon is expected to rebound in 2006 following the stabilization of the political situation. Public debt—already extremely high—remains on an upward trajectory, and sustained measures to raise the primary surplus will be critical to reducing the debt burden and risks to the financial system.

Economic activity in Israel expanded by 5.2 percent in 2005, underpinned by robust private consumption and tourism revenues. The strength of domestic demand and wages has increased inflationary risks, prompting the Bank of Israel to raise interest rates in October and November. Looking ahead, growth prospects are favorable, although political and security risks remain. The government will need to outline specific spending plans to meet the medium-term budget deficit target of 3 percent of GDP and put high public debt—over 100 percent of GDP—on a firm downward path.

Appendix 1.1. Recent Developments in Commodity Markets

The authors of this appendix are Valerie Mercer-Blackman, To-Nhu Dao, Paul Nicholson, and Hossein Samiei.

The IMF commodities and energy price index increased by over 29 percent in dollar terms (30 percent in special drawing right, or SDR, terms) in 2005, on surging fuel and base metals prices. Energy prices rose by 39 percent, owing to significant increases in oil and natural gas prices.

Prices of nonfuel commodities rose by 10 percent during 2005, reaching record highs in nominal terms. Most metal prices experienced significant increases in 2005. Robust economic activity and limited supply response have been the main drivers of higher energy and metal prices. Looking ahead, limited excess capacity in the oil sector is likely to persist well beyond 2006, and prices will continue to be susceptible to geopolitical events. In contrast, metal prices are projected to weaken somewhat as capacity comes on stream by end-2006.

Crude Oil and Other Petroleum Products

The energy market has remained tight and increasingly susceptible to short-term events, reflecting concerns about future supply in the face of limited excess capacity among members of the Organization of the Petroleum Exporting Countries (OPEC).

Price Developments

The average petroleum spot price (APSP)[11] rose by another 41 percent in 2005. Prices spiked sharply in early September, peaking at $66 per barrel in the wake of Hurricane Katrina. Coordinated action by the International Energy Agency (IEA) and the U.S. government to provide additional supplies from strategic reserves, as well as OPEC's accommodative supply stance, temporarily calmed the market, and by November crude oil prices dropped back to pre-Katrina levels. Prices bounced back, however, in January 2006 and have fluctuated mostly in the $60–66 range, owing to renewed geopolitical concerns in the Islamic Republic of Iran, Iraq, and Nigeria. These countries together account for about 11 percent of world production, well above the current OPEC spare capacity of 2–3 percent of world production. Prices of refined products followed a similar trend up until December 2005 (Figure 1.20).

[11]The IMF average petroleum spot price is an equally weighted average of the West Texas Intermediate, Brent, and Dubai crude oil prices. Unless otherwise noted, all subsequent references to the oil price are to the APSP.

Figure 1.20. Crude Oil Prices, Futures, and Petroleum Product Prices

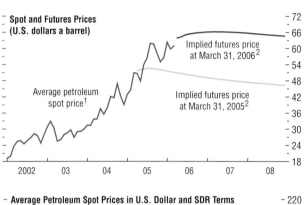

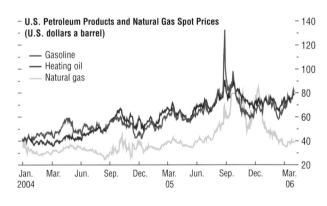

Sources: Bloomberg Financial Markets, LP; and IMF staff calculations.
[1]Average unweighted petroleum spot price of West Texas Intermediate, U.K. Brent, and Dubai Fateh crude.
[2]Five-day weighted average of NYMEX Light Sweet Crude, IPE Dated Brent, and implied Dubai Fateh.

Table 1.12. Global Oil Demand by Region
(Millions of barrels a day)

| | Demand | | Annual Change | | |
| | | | 2005 | | 2004 |
	2005	2004	Million barrels a day	Percent	Percent
North America	25.43	25.34	0.09	0.4	3.3
Europe	16.30	16.33	−0.03	−0.2	1.3
OECD Pacific	8.63	8.53	0.10	1.2	−1.8
China	6.59	6.43	0.16	2.5	15.2
Other Asia	8.72	8.56	0.16	1.9	6.3
Former Soviet Union	3.80	3.76	0.04	1.1	4.7
Middle East	5.91	5.62	0.29	5.2	6.6
Africa	2.90	2.81	0.09	3.2	2.9
Latin America	4.99	4.86	0.13	2.7	4.1
World	83.25	82.23	1.02	1.2	3.8

Source: International Energy Agency, *Oil Market Report*, March 2006.

Following a gasoline price spike in the aftermath of the hurricane, the result of bottlenecks in refinery capacity, prices fell to pre-Katrina levels by November. Unlike crude oil, they remained fairly stable, as relatively warm winter weather in January kept inventories at comfortable levels, but increased in March owing to strong demand in the United States.

U.S. natural gas prices almost doubled in 2005, peaking at $15 per MMBTU (million British thermal units), following the hurricanes in the Gulf of Mexico. Prices have eased below $10 recently, but remain above their five-year average. As of early February, about 16 percent of natural gas production in the Gulf of Mexico was still shut in. Prices in Europe, which have been lower than in the United States, also spiked in January owing to price disputes between Russia and Ukraine.[12]

Oil Consumption

Global oil consumption in 2005 rose by 1.1 million barrels a day (mbd)—well below the 3 mbd increase in 2004 and somewhat lower than initial projections by the IEA—mostly on account of lower consumption growth in China

and the United States (Table 1.12). Record-high prices—particularly of gasoline—may have begun to play a role in slowing consumption, but the evidence is limited and consumption growth still remains near the average of the past two decades. Other key factors include hurricane-related disruptions in the United States and developments in China—in particular, the apparent resolution in 2005 of shortage of coal-powered electricity generation, which had in 2004 increased demand for stand-alone diesel power generators; and policies in 2005 aimed at controlling domestic product prices, which encouraged local refineries to export abroad and repressed domestic consumption.

Oil Production

To satisfy growing demand in the face of flat non-OPEC supply in 2005, OPEC production (including natural gas liquids and condensates) increased by 1 mbd, to 34 mbd. Production levels in most OPEC countries (excluding Iraq) are close to their quotas, but Iraq's production has been disappointing. At 1.6 mbd in December, Iraq's production was 20 percent below 2004—and well below its capacity of 2.5 mbd—reflecting inadequate storage capacity and delivery bottlenecks, as well as sabotage attacks on production infrastructure. OPEC's spare capacity (excluding Iraq) stood at 1.25 mbd at end-2005 (Figure 1.21).

Non-OPEC supply in 2005, at 50.1 mbd, was almost unchanged relative to 2004, largely owing to production shortfalls in Russia (in part resulting from the production slowdown in former Yukos fields); and the United States (mainly due to infrastructure damage in the aftermath of the hurricanes, with production in the Gulf of Mexico still 430,000 barrels a day below pre-Katrina levels). Production also fell slightly in other oil-producing OECD countries, while some production gains occurred in non-OPEC Africa.

---

[12]Prices of natural gas in the three main markets (Asia, Europe, and the United States) can vary significantly owing to the difficulty of transporting natural gas.

Early indications are that global oil production is somewhat below expectations so far in 2006, mainly due to attacks on oil installations in Nigeria, weather-related disruptions in the North Sea and the former Soviet Union, and ongoing security-related disruptions in Iraq.

Inventories

The behavior of inventories is the most telling sign of a shift in the oil market balance in 2005 as, despite high prices, OECD commercial crude inventories have risen to their highest level in the past five years. Government-controlled inventories have also risen in both levels and days of forward cover. This contrasts markedly with the typically negative relationship between prices and inventories observed in the past, suggesting that concerns about future supply have likely led to precautionary accumulation of stocks on the part of consumers and governments. The fundamental negative relationship between inventories and the spread between spot and long-dated futures prices still holds (Figure 1.22).

Short-Term Prospects and Risks

Going forward, while mild winter weather in the United States may have provided some breathing space, the oil market is likely to be characterized by robust consumption growth and production uncertainties, in the context of buoyant global activity and limited spare capacity. The IEA projects global oil consumption growth of 1.5 mbd in 2006, broadly in line with other analysts' projections. Consumption in China is projected to pick up by 0.4 mbd to 7 mbd. Many analysts are becoming increasingly bullish about prices. Based on the futures market, prices are expected to remain at $61.25 per barrel on average in 2006 and increase slightly to $63 in 2007.

Supply-side risks remain significant, including in Nigeria (unrest in the oil-producing region); Iraq (security situation); and the Islamic Republic of Iran (the nuclear standoff). Recent attempts to attack oil facilities in Saudi Arabia have further increased risks of disruptions. Prospects for non-OPEC supply are also uncertain, given that out-

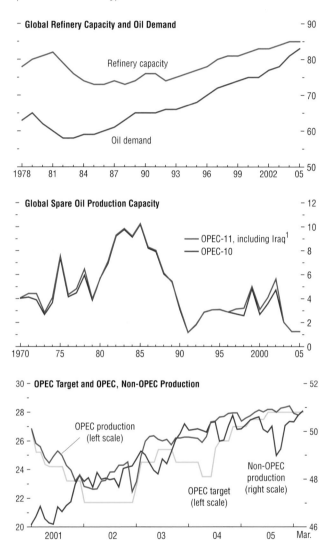

Figure 1.21. World Refinery Capacity, Spare Capacity, and Production

(Millions of barrels a day)

Sources: Bloomberg Financial, LP; British Petroleum Statistical Review; International Energy Agency; U.S. Department of Energy; and IMF staff calculations.
[1] OPEC-11 spare capacity refers to production capacity that can be brought online within 30 days and sustained for 90 days.

Figure 1.22. Commercial Oil Inventories, Spot and Futures Prices

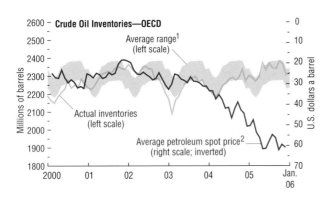

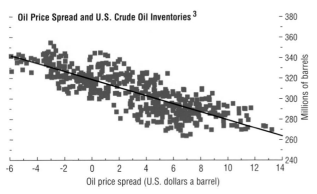

Sources: Bloomberg Financial, LP; International Energy Agency; U.S. Department of Energy; and IMF staff calculations.
[1]Average of each calendar month during 1992–2004, plus a 40 percent confidence interval based on past deviations.
[2]Average petroleum spot price of West Texas Intermediate, U.K. Brent, and Dubai Fateh crude.
[3]All prices are derived from NYMEX contract prices. Spread is the spot price minus the 24-month forward futures price.

put was virtually flat in 2005 compared with earlier expectations of an increase of over 1 mbd. In addition, concerns have increased regarding Russia's reliability as an oil and gas supplier, following its decision to briefly cut off gas supplies to Ukraine and Georgia in early January (which in one case affected supplies to western Europe). In this context, like many analysts (including the U.S. Department of Energy), IMF staff believes that the IEA's and OPEC's projections in the 1.2 mbd range for non-OPEC supply growth in 2006 may be optimistic. Even if OPEC's capacity increases by a projected 1 mbd, spare capacity will likely continue to remain low, and consist mostly of the heavy grades, for which refining capacity is limited.

Medium-Term Prospects and Policies

In light of the current tightness in the oil market and risks going forward, the key issue is how investors and consumers are responding to higher prices and supply-demand imbalances. The IEA estimates that investment in the oil sector is probably 20 percent below what is needed to meet projected demand over the medium to long term. In contrast, oil-exporting countries and major oil companies argue that they are investing as rapidly as is appropriate. Against this background, this section discusses prospects for investment and demand adjustment in the oil market.

Is Investment Forthcoming?

Many analysts argue that international oil companies have followed overly conservative investment strategies and have been slow to respond to higher oil prices, despite demand growth surpassing capacity growth for at least three years. This may have resulted from the persistence of the cost-cutting mentality of the 1990s. For their part, company managers argue that short-term price movements can only be a small factor in their planning decisions because of the long time horizons in the industry, and the importance of longer-term fundamentals, shareholder preferences, and business strategy.

Given past experience, they stress the need to wait and assess the permanence of higher prices before making investment decisions. To date, oil corporations appear to have used a large part of their profits to distribute to shareholders, buy back shares, accumulate cash reserves, or acquire other companies.[13]

Nevertheless, recent evidence does suggest that investment has increased significantly in nominal terms. A biannual survey by Lehman Brothers and Citigroup of 316 oil companies suggests that spending in 2005 was 20 percent higher than the previous year, and it could grow by 14–15 percent in 2006. Moreover, major oil countries such as Norway, Saudi Arabia, the United Arab Emirates, Mexico, and Brazil have markedly increased their capital expenditure, in some cases by over 50 percent in 2005, and have announced ambitious investment plans for 2006.

Of course, these investments may not affect output in the short to medium term, because the average time between initial exploration of a field and near-full-capacity upstream production is at least five years.

However, new investment, while significant in nominal terms, may not be large in real terms. Surveys suggest that the industry is facing increasing costs and a given dollar of investment will produce less quantity of oil than in the past. First, as it is becoming more difficult to find large oil fields where the oil is relatively easy to extract, production is moving increasingly into higher cost and riskier areas. Some company surveys show that the share of investment in exploration has increased, reflecting smaller average size of fields and more complex technologies necessary to extract the oil. Second, costs are increasing in part as a result of a lack of skilled and experienced personnel and petroleum engineers in the industry—reflecting the leaner

operations during the low oil price period of the 1980s and 1990s—and limited supply of drilling rigs, tankers, and related equipment. These additions to costs may be cyclical in nature but are affecting the real value of investments.[14]

Other factors contributing to higher production costs and limited investment of international oil companies are impediments to foreign investment in some oil-rich countries, either in the form of increases in royalty and export taxes, or restrictions on ownership and licensing. Many non-OECD oil-producing countries only allow foreign companies to enter as subsidiaries or contractors, which is much less attractive for international oil companies than ownership contracts. Saudi Arabia and Kuwait are effectively closed to foreign direct investment, as they are concerned that the international oil companies tend to extract oil too rapidly, thus reducing the ultimate recovery rate. Of course, this trend may not necessarily translate into less investment everywhere: some national oil companies, in particular Saudi Aramco, have major investment plans and have access to the latest technology. The recent general backlash against privatization that has occurred in emerging and transition economies has also affected the oil industry (e.g., the case of Yukos in Russia, and recent trends in Argentina, Bolivia, Ecuador, and Venezuela). While oil-exporting countries may be justified in requiring larger payments for the sale of their national assets, higher export and royalty taxes have become an increasing share of overall foreign investment costs in the industry.

Demand Adjustment: Substitution and the Role of Taxes and Subsidies

The delayed adjustment in some important consumer countries in part reflects the time it takes for consumers and governments to assess the permanence of the price increase so as to

---

[13]National oil companies in India and China are also purchasing shares in oil fields, on the belief that this will increase their domestic energy security.

[14]Downstream investment has also been plagued by uncertainty about the mix of grades, loss of know-how in refinery building, and excessive regulations in many OECD countries. Global refinery capacity has increased only 7 percent since 1980, while capacity in the OECD countries has actually declined by 10 percent.

Figure 1.23. Energy Prices, Taxes, and Fuel Subsidies

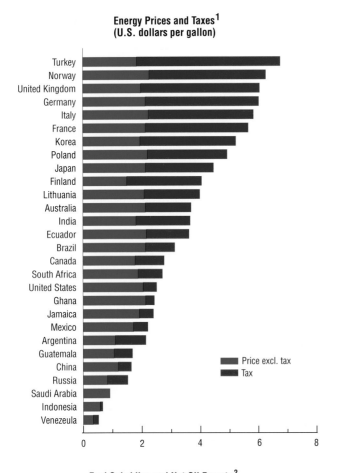

Energy Prices and Taxes[1]
(U.S. dollars per gallon)

Turkey
Norway
United Kingdom
Germany
Italy
France
Korea
Poland
Japan
Finland
Lithuania
Australia
India
Ecuador
Brazil
Canada
South Africa
United States
Ghana
Jamaica
Mexico
Argentina
Guatemala
China
Russia
Saudi Arabia
Indonesia
Venezuela

■ Price excl. tax
■ Tax

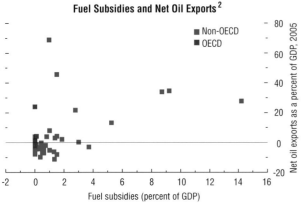

Fuel Subsidies and Net Oil Exports[2]

■ Non-OECD
■ OECD

Net oil exports as a percent of GDP, 2005

Fuel subsidies (percent of GDP)

Sources: Energy Détente; International Energy Agency; and IMF staff calculations.
[1]Latest 2005 observations.
[2]Fifty-three countries are represented. Fuel subsidies refer to implicit and explicit costs borne by the public sector. Estimates may not always be directly comparable.

readjust budgets accordingly. Over the longer term, the speed of adjustment of demand will depend markedly on government policies and on the viability of alternative technologies.

Many alternative energy sources that were not economically and technologically feasible during the high oil price episode of the 1970s are now viable. The most salient close substitutes to petroleum-based fuels are sugar-based ethanol, which can now be used in some gasoline-powered vehicles, and biodiesel (a substitute for petro-diesel). In Brazil, for example, over 60 percent of new cars can use ethanol. Both ethanol and biodiesel now receive fiscal incentives in many countries, justified by their generally lower greenhouse gas emissions compared to petroleum-based fuels. Mandatory mix requirements may also help spur their demand.[15] Nonetheless, markets for these fuel technologies are still in their infancy, and in most cases a speedy switch by consumers is unlikely because it requires a high sunk cost (such as, for example, switching to a different type of vehicle). Governments will also need to encourage the adoption of suitable infrastructure for the new technologies.[16]

Improved taxation policies would also help energy demand adjustment. While pre-tax gasoline prices are similar across many countries (Figure 1.23), retail taxes vary significantly. There is, for example, scope for higher gasoline consumption taxes in the United States—which consumes a quarter of the world's oil—so as to reduce excessive consumption. On the other hand, some European countries have very high taxes, in part aimed at encouraging conservation and correcting pollution externalities. A better taxation policy to be considered over the

[15]The implementation of emission-reduction schemes under the Kyoto agreement, such as the EU Carbon Trading Scheme, should further encourage the adoption of these and other carbon-reducing alternatives in the years ahead.
[16]In the United States, for example, plans to offer gasoline-powered cars that run 85 percent on ethanol will only be attractive to a wide number of consumers if there are sufficient fuel stations that offer the right fuel mix.

medium term would be to decouple externality charges from fuel prices by targeting the externality directly, for example through congestion charges (as in the United Kingdom) or producer emissions fees on all energy sources.

Many developing countries maintain general implicit and explicit subsidies for diesel, kerosene, and gasoline at substantial fiscal costs. These countries need to take steps to reduce subsidies (especially for diesel and gasoline where most of the benefits go to the rich) to allow price signals to work. A set of well-publicized targeted compensation schemes can be designed to mitigate the impact on the poor—for example, through direct or indirect government grants—lowering taxes that bear more heavily on the poor whenever it is feasible, or two-tier pricing systems. Such schemes can be financed by savings made from lower subsidies. Demand adjustment by developing country oil producers, in particular, where even gasoline is subsidized heavily (Figure 1.23), will be crucial to maintaining the oil supply-demand balance in the medium term. At the extremes, a gallon of gasoline in Venezuela costs $0.15 and in the Islamic Republic of Iran $0.34, compared to an average of $4.95 in OECD countries. The implied fiscal costs are very large, seriously hampering government's ability to allocate resources to more productive social expenditures. The IEA estimates that, under current policies, the share of global demand coming from developing countries will increase from about one-third in 2004 to almost one-half in 2030, with demand from the largest exporters in the Middle East and North Africa growing by 73 percent, and demand from China more than doubling (compared to the 17 percent increase in the OECD).

Nonenergy Commodities

The IMF nonfuel commodity price index rose by 10 percent in 2005, picking up strongly in the second half of the year and reaching a nominal record high in December 2005—and its highest level in real terms since 1997—on surging metal prices (Table 1.13). The recent period contrasts

Table 1.13. Nonenergy Commodity Prices
(Percent change for 2005)

	U.S. Dollar Terms	Contribution[1]	SDR Terms
Food	−0.3	32.8	−0.2
Beverages	21.0	10.8	21.3
Agricultural raw materials	1.8	7.7	2.00
Metals	26.4	48.7	26.9
Overall nonenergy	10.3	100.0	10.6

Sources: IMF, Primary Commodity Price Database; and IMF staff estimates.

[1]Contributions to change in overall nonenergy price index in U.S. dollar terms, in percent. Contributions to change in SDR terms are similar.

strikingly with the general downward trend observed in real nonfuel commodities prices over many years, in part reflecting substantial efficiency gains in agriculture and resource extraction technologies, in particular in the 1980s and 1990s.

A number of factors are contributing to the current upsurge: (1) strong demand from Asian emerging markets, in particular China; (2) high energy prices, which have contributed to higher prices for many nonfuel commodities—for example, energy-intensive aluminum and steel, some agricultural commodities (through higher fertilizer prices), sugar and edible oils (which are inputs in alternative fuels, demand for which has increased), and natural rubber (a substitute for petroleum-based synthetic rubber); and (3) increased financial investment in commodity markets as investors seek diversification from traditional stocks and bonds, as well as protection against potential inflation or changes in the value of the dollar.

Price performance across commodities also reflects inherent differences in their production conditions, in particular between base metals and other nonfuel commodities (Figure 1.24). The base metals markets are in some ways closer to the oil market, although supply response tends to be speedier—in particular for copper and zinc. In the case of the food and beverages market, in contrast, global supply can respond very quickly. In addition, the regularity of the cycle around the trend is somewhat more uniform for base metals because the demand move-

Figure 1.24. Nonenergy Commodities

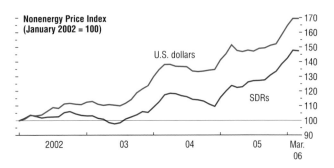

Nonenergy Price Index
(January 2002 = 100)

U.S. dollars

SDRs

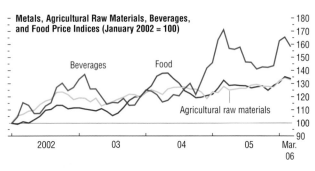

Metals, Agricultural Raw Materials, Beverages,
and Food Price Indices (January 2002 = 100)

Beverages   Food

Agricultural raw materials

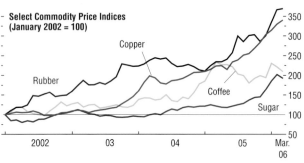

Select Commodity Price Indices
(January 2002 = 100)

Copper

Rubber

Coffee

Sugar

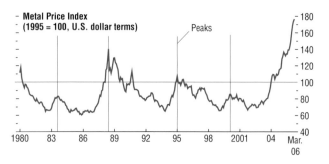

Metal Price Index
(1995 = 100, U.S. dollar terms)

Peaks

Source: IMF staff calculations.

ments among metals tend to coincide more closely, and their supply is not affected by unpredictable weather changes.

Recent Developments and Prospects

The IMF metal price index rose by 26 percent in 2005, defying analysts' expectations that prices would dampen as capacity came on stream. Higher prices reflect robust demand owing to strong industrial production growth and construction activities in China and the United States, as well as a series of supply shocks, including labor strikes in the United States and Chile in the copper industry and delays in Chinese zinc mine expansion projects planned for 2005. Higher energy prices forced closure of some aluminum processing plants, thus pushing up prices, while increased demand for uranium for nuclear energy caused a further significant increase in prices. Looking ahead, metal prices are expected to increase by 7 percent in 2006 on the continued strength of copper, zinc, aluminum, and uranium. Production is expected to catch up toward the end of the year.

The food price index remained almost unchanged in 2005 relative to 2004. Sugar was the strongest component of the index, rising to 24-year highs, as Brazil and Europe reduced exports: Brazil's sugar cane crop has been increasingly used for the production of ethanol, and EU exports have been limited by a WTO ruling and subsequent legislation. Oilseed prices fell, owing to large harvests and multi-year high inventories of soybeans, and offset a demand-driven gain in seafood prices. Overall beverage prices rose by 21 percent in 2005 on the strength of Robusta coffee prices reflecting weather-related supply disruptions in Vietnam, the world's largest producer. Looking forward, food prices are expected to rise slightly in 2006, as strong growth in sugar prices is offset by a small decline in the prices of other foods.

The agricultural raw material price index rose 2 percent in 2005, after falling in the first half of the year. Natural rubber prices rose on robust demand, as higher oil prices pushed up the prices of synthetic rubber, its substitute. Sawnwood prices showed strong recovery in the second half of 2005, owing to robust construction activity in China and new demand from the United States for the reconstruction of the hurricane-affected areas. In contrast, cotton prices declined in 2005 owing to good global harvests.

Semiconductors

Worldwide semiconductor sales revenue grew 6.8 percent in 2005 to reach record levels, after growing 28 percent in 2004 (Figure 1.25). Strong growth in unit sales more than offset falling prices, which resulted from a capacity overhang. Consumer interest in electronics was the primary cause of higher quantity demanded, as prices fell on cutting edge technologies and new products were introduced. Business purchases have been slow, owing to uncertainty regarding inflation, interest rates, and higher energy costs. In Asia (excluding Japan), consumption of semiconductors grew 16 percent in 2005.

Global capital spending by semiconductor producers increased slightly in 2005. In general, increasing tightness in existing capacity is expected to increase capital spending in 2006. Capacity utilization in the fourth quarter of 2005 was reported 91.8 percent, with leading-edge capacity at 98.4 percent. The global book-to-bill ratio for semiconductor equipment sales stood at 1.24 in February.

China's exports of electronics grew over 30 percent in 2005, while exports of other Asian countries grew more slowly. Over the medium term, regional and technological factors may shift production within Asia. For example, the increasing replacement of hard drive memory by flash memory will benefit Japan, Korea, and Taiwan Province of China over ASEAN-4 countries, which are heavily geared toward producing hard drives. And China's emergence as an important location for electronics manufacturing will likely attract new semiconductor investment to the country.

Figure 1.25. Semiconductor Market
(Seasonally adjusted; quarterly percent change of three-month moving average)

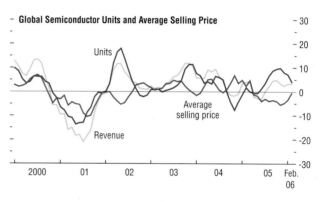

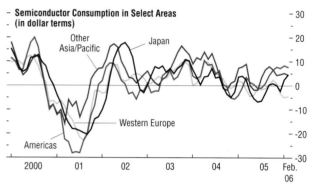

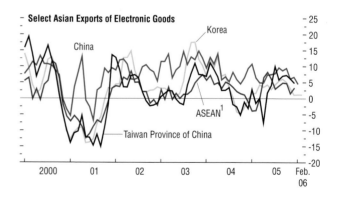

Sources: World Semiconductor Trade Statistics; and IMF staff calculations.
[1]Consists of Indonesia, Singapore, Malaysia, the Philippines, and Thailand.

Most analysts are optimistic about sales revenues in 2006. The semiconductor Industry Association (SIA) forecasts growth in sales revenues of 7.9 percent in 2006. Strong sales of consumer products are projected to continue as prices fall on higher-end products and more new product releases are scheduled. Business purchases are expected to grow, owing to expected new software releases, which may force a replacement cycle.

Appendix 1.2. The Global Implications of an Avian Flu Pandemic

The main authors of this appendix are Sandy Mackenzie, Johannes Wiegand, and Selim Elekdag.

Avian flu—or "A-strain flu"—refers to a type of influenza virus that is endemic in aquatic birds but can, in certain circumstances, be transmitted to human beings. When avian flu viruses merge and swap genetic material—a process called "antigenic shift"—new flu strains emerge that differ from both parent viruses. Antigenic shift can cause *human* epidemics if the new virus is easily transmitted between humans. The current H5N1 virus has not yet mutated into so deadly a form, but it has mutated rapidly in its avian hosts, and it has jumped the species barrier from birds to human beings.

The first documented human outbreak of the H5N1 virus occurred in 1997 in Hong Kong SAR. It infected 18 people, killing six of them. The virus resurfaced in December 2003 in poultry in Korea and spread to other east Asian countries. It reached southeastern Europe in August 2005, probably transmitted by migratory birds, and West Africa, as well as southern and central Europe, in February 2006. As of April 4, the World Health Organization (WHO) reported 191 human cases and 108 deaths since 2003.

The cost of a deadly epidemic in human terms is beyond any reckoning. However, an epidemic's impact on the health of a population is normally characterized by its attack rate—that is, the share of the population that contracts the illness—and the case mortality rate—the share of

the ill who succumb to the illness. There have been three avian influenza epidemics in the twentieth century. Although they are thought to have had similar attack rates, their case mortality rates have differed greatly. The Spanish flu pandemic of 1918–19 was by far the most lethal (see Box 1.7), and is thought to have claimed the lives of 40–50 million people worldwide.

It is next to impossible to predict what the case mortality rate of a future pandemic would be. This appendix discusses possible effects of a severe outbreak, with attack and case mortality rates similar to those observed in the United States during the 1918 pandemic—specifically, an attack rate of about 25 percent and a case mortality rate of 2.5 percent, implying overall mortality of 0.6 percent. It should be emphasized that such a scenario is not the most likely— as mentioned above, other influenza epidemics in the twentieth century have been far less virulent, and the probability of an epidemic with human-to-human transmission is still considered low at this juncture.

For simplicity, the appendix assumes that attack and case fatality rates would be the same in all countries. However, in 1918 substantially higher mortality rates than those observed in the United States were reported from other areas of the world. It appears plausible that in some developing countries, limited availability of medical care, overburdened public health facilities, and lack of sanitary infrastructure could cause higher mortality rates than would occur in advanced economies today.

Apart from the attack and the case mortality rates, the key parameters that determine the impact of an epidemic include its length and the average duration and number of periods of infection (i.e., periods when the virus has not returned to dormancy). Flu-like illnesses tend to last several weeks. It is not possible to be categorical about average periods of infection. The estimates of this appendix are based on the assumption that there would be one period of infection lasting six weeks. This is in line with the American experience in 1918—although there were three waves of contagion—in that a

Box 1.7. The Spanish Flu of 1918–19

The Spanish flu of 1918–19 was by far the most lethal influenza pandemic of the twentieth century. It infected about one-fourth of the global population and took the lives of 40–50 million people. This renders the Spanish flu the third most deadly pandemic on record, surpassed only by the plague pandemics of the sixth and fourteenth centuries. One unusual feature of the Spanish flu was that it killed not only the very young and the very old, but also adults in their prime years with above-average frequency, creating a "W-shaped" mortality pattern (Noymer and Garenne, 2000).

Despite its name, the first outbreak of Spanish flu was recorded in early 1918 in army camps in the United States. The pandemic came in three waves, with the second wave—beginning in August 1918 simultaneously in Brest/France; Freetown/Sierra Leone; and Boston/Massachusetts—being the most deadly. Mortality rates varied greatly between countries, ranging from an estimated 0.6 percent of the population in the United States to 5 percent in India and 20 percent on some Pacific islands, such as Fiji or Western Samoa. For many countries, the mortality figures have a large margin of error, which explains why estimates on the global death toll vary greatly.

Although data on the U.S. economy in 1918 are better than most, they are not good enough to allow the drawing of firm conclusions regarding the economic impact of the Spanish flu. In particular, there are no comprehensive national accounts or household survey data. Higher-frequency indicators show that both U.S. industrial production and the business activity index dipped in October 1918—that is, at the height of the epidemic—but then promptly rebounded. Factory payroll numbers behaved in a similar fashion, although data on the labor force as a whole are lacking. There were also temporary and modest reductions in passenger rail transport and retail sales. A recent study by the Canadian Department of Finance estimates that the overall impact on annual GDP was only 0.4 percent. However, it appears implausible that an outbreak of similar virulence today would have comparably limited effects (see the main text). In late 1918, the United States was still on a war footing, and there may have been considerable social as well as economic pressure to stay on the job.

A study by Brainerd and Siegler (2003) concentrates on the *aftermath* of the pandemic, studying U.S. economic growth across states between 1919–21 and 1930. The authors find that there was a *positive* relationship between the mortality rate and growth: one more death per thousand resulted in an *increase* of per capita growth over the next 10 years of at least 0.15 percent per year, which would point to a sustained period of catching up after a short and sharp shock. However, this result seems at odds with the observation that the pandemic's immediate impact on economic activity was only moderate.

There are only a few pieces of analysis that shed light on the economic impact of the Spanish flu in other countries. In a study on India—where mortality was particularly high—Schultz (1964) estimates that agricultural production fell by 3.3 percent during the pandemic, compared to a reduction in the agricultural workforce by 8 percent. However, more recent work by Bloom and Mahal (1997) finds no link between the population and the production loss.

Note: The main authors of this box are Sandy Mackenzie and Johannes Wiegand.

very large share of flu-related deaths occurred in one month—October. A further assumption is that the disease assails all countries within a matter of weeks.

The appendix draw parallels with the 1918 pandemic wherever possible. History can only provide very limited guidance to the economic impact of a pandemic, however, given the huge changes in economic organization and the progress in medicine and public health since then. The recent SARS (Severe Acute Respiratory Syndrome) epidemic is another possible model—better in some respects, given the improvements in economic statistics and the greater comparability of economic and medical institutions—but its relevance is limited by the virus's low infectiousness and mortality.

The next section analyzes the channels through which an avian flu pandemic would affect the aggregate output of an economy before turning to the impact on the budget and financial institutions. The final section summarizes the overall impact and considers the major policy conclusions.

Channels of Transmission

The following section examines the effects an avian flu outbreak would have on the supply side and demand side, including the impact on external demand.

Supply of Labor and Capital

The principal supply-side effect of an avian flu pandemic would be on labor force numbers and average hours worked. Given the stated assumptions, deaths caused by the pandemic could reduce the global labor force by about 20 million people, with three-quarters of the loss in developing countries. While the pandemic raged, large numbers of workers would be ill and unable to work. Others would be asked to stay at home, or would choose to do so to avoid infection or to care for a sick relative. The temporary impact of illness and absenteeism on total hours worked would be much larger than the immediate impact of mortality. In some sectors of advanced economies, telecommuting might compensate for a small part of the impact of absenteeism.

Once the pandemic had run its course, average hours worked should recover quickly to their normal level. They might even rise above it, as industry increased production to accommodate a bounce-back in demand (see below). The *working age population* would probably be permanently reduced, although this effect would be at least partly offset by an increase in the labor force participation rates of the survivors.

A pandemic would depress investment, at least temporarily, if it caused investment projects to be deferred until capacity utilization rates had recovered. Once the pandemic had subsided, however, it is likely that previously postponed investment would proceed. Hence, it is unlikely that the capital stock would be permanently affected.

Supply of Energy, Transportation, and Other Key Inputs

Shortages of key inputs like energy, water, and transportation would affect factor productivity. In the short run, the extent of disruptions would depend on the impact of the pandemic on labor, especially skilled labor, and on whether absent employees could be replaced (the impact on air, maritime, and road transport being possibly of greatest concern). The widespread adoption of just-in-time inventory management techniques is another possible source of disruption. Once the pandemic had run its course, production ought to recover quickly.

Overall Effects on Aggregate Supply

Overall, the most likely scenario is a short, but possibly sharp, decline in aggregate supply. A purely illustrative estimation of its magnitude can be derived from assumptions about the size and duration of the decline in hours worked and the parameters of an aggregate production function. Specifically, if 25 percent of the work force falls sick, stays home, or is sent home for six weeks and if 0.6 percent of the work force dies, aggregate labor input would decline by about 13 percent for one quarter, or about 3 percent for a year. A Cobb-Douglas production function with a coefficient on labor input of 0.6 then implies a drop in aggregate supply in the quarter of about 8 percent or a drop in terms of annual GDP of about 2 percent. This fall is likely to be reinforced by a temporary decline in factor productivity.

The American experience of 1918 is not easy to interpret, but it points to a much smaller decline. This suggests that absenteeism may not have been particularly great, possibly because of social pressures on workers to stay at work and the absence of a social safety net to cushion any declines in earned income. A 1918-scale pandemic in contemporary circumstances could well lead to a much larger decline in labor input.

Domestic Consumption and Investment

The impact of the pandemic on consumption would come through two main channels. First, with large numbers of people unable to work, incomes and, therefore, spending would decline, particularly for households that have limited savings or that receive limited sick pay. Second, during the contagious period, the demand for consumer goods—especially postponable durable and semi-durable consumer goods—would decline, as households shunned physical contacts in malls, market places, and other retail establishments or household members convalesced. The former effect would likely dominate in low-income countries, where consumer durables account for a smaller share of total consumption; the latter in more advanced economies. Provided that income levels were maintained or picked up sharply once the pandemic had ended, demand for consumer goods could be expected to recover quickly (and in advanced economies a significant rebound in purchases of durables could be expected). As mentioned above, investment postponed during the pandemic could be expected to recover once the pandemic had passed.

External Demand

Given the global decline in supply and demand, the volume of global trade would drop sharply for a period. Countries specializing in exports of investment goods, consumer durables or travel-related services, such as tourism, could suffer a particularly sharp decline in export earnings and a deterioration in external current accounts. SARS reduced airline passenger arrivals in Hong Kong SAR by nearly two-thirds in the month following the month of the peak of the outbreak, although it recovered to its pre-SARS level four months later. Commodity

exporters would probably experience a temporary terms-of-trade loss. Trade might also be affected by more restrictive inspection of goods in transit. Restrictions imposed on public health grounds could be a cloak for protectionist measures in some countries. Once the pandemic had ended, however, there is no reason why global trade should not recover fully.

Financial Institutions and Financial Systems

A pandemic could disrupt payments, clearing, settlement, and trading systems significantly. The source of vulnerability is basically the same as for utilities—reliance on specialized workers who must work together. The key to minimizing the risk of a serious slowdown or systemic failure is to implement contingency plans that provide for an adequate number of replacements, and perhaps alternative operating and backup systems. The more successful these efforts, the less likely would be a general panic entailing a massive and destabilizing flight to quality that could trigger major problems with creditor and counterparty risk (see the IMF's *Global Financial Stability Report*, April 2006, for a detailed discussion of these and related issues). One key issue is how disruptions of the financial system in one country would affect others. Serious problems in major financial centers could have a destabilizing knock-on effect. Disruptions in small countries would be less serious, but could nonetheless trigger contagion. Avoiding serious disruption to financial systems will also speed the recovery of countries from the pandemic.

Even if the core financial system continued to function adequately, some outflow of capital from emerging market countries would still be expected. Some emerging market countries would be more at risk than others; for example, countries whose current accounts would be worsened by the pandemic, or countries already deemed vulnerable to capital flight. However, basically stable countries would be unlikely to be pushed into crisis if the economic impact of the pandemic would be short-lived and the crisis well managed.

The Overall Effect and Policy Implications

If a global avian flu pandemic were to break out, the costs in terms of death and human suffering, of course, would be beyond calculation. From a narrow economic perspective, affected countries could be expected to suffer a sharp temporary decline in output. While the size is impossible to assess with any degree of certainty, the illustrative estimate of an 8 percent drop in GDP in one quarter from reduced labor input alone—equivalent to a 2 percent drop in annual GDP—is not outlandish. This could prove to be a significant underestimate if the fall in demand and effects from disruptions of physical and infrastructure services were large.[17] Some countries could be particularly vulnerable, in particular economies that depend heavily on exports of durable goods and services, countries that were vulnerable to a capital account crisis already before the pandemic, and developing countries with a weak public health infrastructure and relatively low institutional and financial capacity to deal with the outbreak. Once infrastructure services had been restored, economic activity could be expected to rebound relatively quickly, and the long-run economic impact of the pandemic would be modest.

As described above, the pandemic would lead to substantial reductions in both supply and demand. In principle, if demand dropped more than supply as many expect,[18] the overall impact would be deflationary and monetary policy should be eased; if the reverse, policy should be tightened. In practice, it will be very difficult to know which effect is dominating, and for how long the resulting supply-demand imbalance will last. In such circumstances, and given the likely adverse impact on confidence and probable strong demand for liquidity, monetary policies should err on the accommodative side. There may also be a need for temporary regulatory forbearance, particularly if asset values suffered a sharp decline.

On the fiscal side, a pandemic would temporarily worsen the budgetary balance. Revenues—particularly sales and VAT receipts and payroll taxes—would fall sharply, the more so if tax collection was disrupted; expenditures on medical and income support programs would also rise significantly. Given the one-off nature of these expenditures, the temporary widening of budget deficits should be accepted, wherever this would not pose serious risks to fiscal or external sustainability. Moreover, budgetary procedures would need to be flexible enough to reallocate public expenditures quickly across spending categories. At the present juncture, the key issue is to ensure sufficient funding of preventive measures, to reduce the risk that a pandemic takes hold and the costs if it does. Given the public good characteristic of measures to fight infectious disease, rich countries should fully subsidize the costs of such programs in poor countries. Extensive technical assistance with public health issues may also be needed.

As will be evident from the discussion above, the impact of a pandemic will depend critically on adequate contingency planning to ensure that the financial and physical infrastructure

---

[17]Several studies have attempted to simulate the effect of a human H5N1 pandemic on GDP. The results depend typically on the assumptions made about mortality and about the relative size of demand-side effects. One of the most sophisticated studies is McKibbin and Sidorenko (2006). The authors use a model with 20 countries/regions to simulate epidemic outbreaks that differ by the degree of severity. The model allows for differing mortality rates across countries—they vary with a proxy for the availability and quality of health care—and country risk premiums, which vary with mortality rates. With these assumptions, some emerging market economies are hit very hard by the pandemic. Canada, the United States, and the euro area are the least affected.

[18]A recent study of the hypothetical effects of a pandemic on the U.S. economy concluded that the demand-side would be greater than the supply-side impact, on the assumption the demand for certain services entailing congregations or crowds would drop to zero for a time (Congressional Budget Office, 2005). The recent SARS experience—where most of the economic damage was caused by demand-side effects—provides only limited guidance, as SARS had a minimal impact on labor market participation and other supply parameters.

continue to function. Given extensive global financial market linkages, countries that already have well-designed business continuity plans for their central bank and financial institutions have an interest in seeing that others achieve a similar standard. At the present stage, preparations appear well advanced in a few countries, particularly those affected by the 2003 SARS outbreak. However, in general the level of preparedness and awareness is still low.

References

Artis, Michael J., 1988, "How Accurate Is the World Economic Outlook? A Postmortem on Short-term Forecasting at the International Monetary Fund," in *Staff Studies for the World Economic Outlook* (Washington: International Monetary Fund).

———, 1997, "How Accurate Are the IMF's Short-Term Forecasts? Another Examination of the World Economic Outlook," in *Staff Studies for the World Economic Outlook* (Washington: International Monetary Fund).

Barrionuevo, Jose M., 1993, "How Accurate Are the World Economic Outlook Projections?" in *Staff Studies for the World Economic Outlook* (Washington: International Monetary Fund).

Batchelor, Roy, 2001, "How Useful Are the Forecasts of Intergovernmental Agencies? The IMF and OECD versus the Consensus" *Applied Economics*, Vol. 33, No. 2 (February), pp. 224–35.

Bayoumi, Tam, and Hali Edison, 2003, "Is Wealth Increasingly Driving Consumption?" DNB Staff Report No. 101/2003 (Amsterdam: Nederlandsche Bank).

Beach, William W., Aaron B. Schavey, and Isabel Isidro, 1999, "How Reliable Are IMF Economic Forecasts?" A Report of the Heritage Center for Data Analysis (Washington: The Heritage Foundation).

Bloom, David E., and Ajay S. Mahal, 1997, "AIDS, Flu, and the Black Death: Impacts on Economic Growth and Well-Being" in *The Economics of HIV and AIDS: The Case of South and South East Asia*, ed. by David E. Bloom and Peter Goodwin (Delhi; New York: Oxford University Press).

Brainerd, Elizabeth, and Mark V. Siegler, 2003, "The Economic Effects of the 1918 Influenza Pandemic," CEPR Discussion Paper No. 3791 (London: Centre for Economic Policy Research).

Britton, Erik, Paul Fisher, and John Whitley, 1998, "The *Inflation Report* Projections: Understanding the Fan Chart," *Quarterly Bulletin*, Bank of England, February.

Catão, Luis, and G.A. (Sandy) Mackenzie, 2006, "Perspectives on Low Global Interest Rates," IMF Working Paper 06/76 (Washington: International Monetary Fund).

Congressional Budget Office, 2005, "*A Potential Influenza Pandemic: Possible Macroeconomic Effects and Policy Issues*" (Washington: Congressional Budget Office). Available via the Internet: http://www.cbo.gov/ftpdocs/69xx/doc6946/12–08-BirdFlu.pdf.

Greenspan, Alan, and James Kennedy, 2005, "Estimates of Home Mortgage Originations, Repayments, and Debt on One-to-Four-Family Residences," Federal Reserve Board Finance and Economics Discussion Series No. 2005-41 (Washington: Federal Reserve Board).

Hausmann, Ricardo, and Federico Sturzenegger, 2006 "Global Imbalances or Bad Accounting? The Missing Dark Matter in the Wealth of Nations," Harvard University CID Working Paper No. 124 (Cambridge, Massachusetts: Harvard University).

Klenow, Peter J., and Andrés Rodriguez-Clare, 2004, "Externalities and Growth," NBER Working Paper No. 11009 (Cambridge, Massachusetts: National Bureau of Economic Research).

Lane, Philip R., and Gian Maria Milesi-Ferretti, 2006, "The External Wealth of Nations Mark II: Revised and Extended Estimates of Foreign Assets and Liabilities, 1970–2004," IMF Working Paper 06/69 (Washington: International Monetary Fund).

McKibbin, Warwick J., and Alexandra Sidorenko, 2006, "Global Macroeconomic Consequences of Pandemic Influenza" (Sydney, Australia: Lowy Institute for International Policy). Available via the Internet: http://apps49.brookings.edu/dybdocroot/views/papers/mckibbin/200602.pdf.

Noymer, Andrew, and Michel Garenne, 2000, "The 1918 Influenza Epidemic's Effects on Sex Differentials in Mortality in the United States," *Population and Development Review*, Vol. 26 (September), pp. 565–81.

Otrok, Christopher, and Marco E. Terrones, forthcoming, "House Prices, Interest Rates, and Macroeconomic Fluctuations: International Evidence," IMF Working Paper (Washington: International Monetary Fund)

Schultz, Theodore William, 1964, *Transforming Traditional Agriculture* (New Haven: Yale University Press).

Timmermann, Allan, 2006, "An Evaluation of the World Economic Outlook Forecasts," IMF Working Paper 06/59 (Washington: International Monetary Fund).

United States General Accounting Office, 2003, "International Financial Crises. Challenges Remain in IMF's Ability to Anticipate, Prevent, and Resolve Financial Crises." Report to the Chairman, Committee on Financial Services, and to the Vice Chairman, Joint Economic Committee, House of Representatives (Washington: United States General Accounting Office).

Wallis, Kenneth F., 2004, "An Assessment of Bank of England and National Institute Inflation Forecast Uncertainties," *National Institute Economic Review*, Vol. 189 (July), pp. 64–71.

OIL PRICES AND GLOBAL IMBALANCES

Two developments have dominated the international economic landscape over the past several years. First, large global external imbalances have persisted, including a large current account deficit in the United States matched by surpluses in other advanced economies, in emerging Asia and—more recently—in fuel-exporting countries (Figure 2.1). These imbalances have been matched by corresponding shifts in net foreign asset positions, although—particularly for the United States—this has been partly offset by valuation changes, reflecting exchange rate movements in conjunction with changes in the relative price of U.S. financial assets. Second, energy prices have risen sharply since 2003 (Figure 2.2), driven both by strengthening global demand and most recently by concerns about future supply.[1] With limited excess capacity, the medium-term supply-demand balance is expected to remain very tight, and oil prices will persist near current levels.

This chapter seeks to examine the implications of the rise in oil prices for global imbalances and how these imbalances may evolve, focusing on three main questions:[2]

• What has been the impact of higher oil prices on global imbalances, and what are the key channels of transmission?

The main authors of this chapter are Alessandro Rebucci and Nikola Spatafora, with support from Lutz Kilian, Doug Laxton, Lars Pedersen, and M. Hashem Pesaran. Christian de Guzman and Ben Sutton provided research assistance.

[1]See the April 2005 *World Economic Outlook*, Chapter IV, as well as Hamilton (2005); and Kilian (2006).

[2]See previous issues of the *World Economic Outlook*, including in particular the April and September 2005 issues, for a detailed discussion of how and why global imbalances have emerged, the associated risks, and the appropriate policy response.

Figure 2.1. Current Account Balances and Net Foreign Asset Positions
(Percent of world GDP)

Large global external imbalances emerged starting around 1996. In particular, the United States is now running an unprecedented current account deficit, with fuel exporters emerging as the main counterparts. Also, the United States is by far the world's largest net debtor. As a group, other advanced economies remain the largest creditors; fuel exporters' net foreign assets, while growing, remain relatively small.

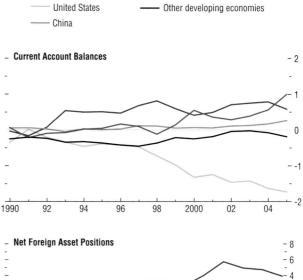

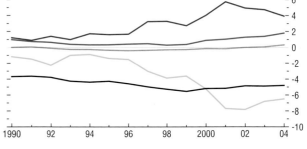

Sources: IMF staff calculations; and Lane and Milesi-Ferretti (2006).

- How has the recycling of oil export revenues, or "petrodollars," affected global and regional financial markets?
- How do policy responses—in particular the pace at which oil exporters spend additional revenues, and the extent to which oil importers allow pass-through of energy prices into core inflation—affect global and regional saving and investment, and hence the evolution of external imbalances?

Specifically, the next section documents key facts about the energy market, external imbalances, and their financing, contrasting the current oil price shock with previous episodes. The chapter then analyzes the likely impact of the current shock on imbalances and how the imbalances may evolve over time. In particular, it offers an econometric analysis of the historical impact of oil prices on external positions, the channels of transmission, and the associated adjustment process. It also investigates through simulations the impact of factors such as the speed with which oil exporters spend their additional revenues, and the extent to which oil prices are allowed to feed through into core inflation.

How Does the Current Oil Price Shock Compare with Previous Episodes?

As a result of the almost $30 per barrel increase in oil prices during 2002–05—and, to a much lesser extent, rising production—global oil exports have boomed. For a broad sample of fuel exporters,[3] the value of oil exports more

Figure 2.2. Real Oil Prices and Net Oil Exports

Energy prices started to increase in 1999, with a sharp rise since 2003. This upsurge is to a large extent driven by growing demand in advanced and emerging economies, as well as by expectations of future market tightness. However, current and expected future real oil prices are still significantly below their value in the late 1970s and early 1980s.

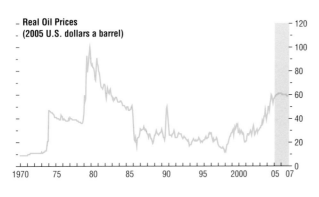

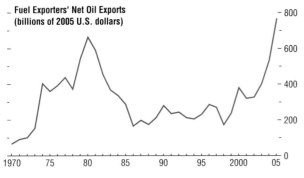

Sources: IMF, *International Financial Statistics;* and IMF staff estimates.

[3]This sample consists of Algeria, Angola, Azerbaijan, Bahrain, Brunei Darussalam, Republic of Congo, Equatorial Guinea, Gabon, Islamic Republic of Iran, Iraq, Kazakhstan, Kuwait, Libya, Nigeria, Norway, Oman, Qatar, Russia, Saudi Arabia, Sudan, Syrian Arab Republic, Trinidad and Tobago, Turkmenistan, United Arab Emirates, Venezuela, and Yemen. The sample includes all the countries in the *World Economic Outlook* "Fuel Exporters" analytical group as of February 2005, with the addition of Kazakhstan and Norway. The main criteria for selection were that, over the past five years, the average share of fuel exports in total exports exceeds 40 percent;

Table 2.1. Increase in Fuel Exporters' Net Oil Exports[1]
(Billions of constant 2005 U.S. dollars, unless otherwise noted)

	CPI-Deflated	Trade-Price-Deflated[2]	Percent of World GDP[3]	Percent of Own GDP[3]	Percent of World Private Capital Flows[3]	Percent of World Stock Market Capitalization[3]
1973–81	436	289	1.9	48.9	78.6	7.6
1973–76	239	139	1.1	27.8	58.4	5.5
1978–81	218	174	0.8	14.5	39.3	4.5
2002–05	437	382	1.2	33.2	37.3	1.6

Sources: IMF staff calculations, *World Economic Outlook, International Financial Statistics;* and World Bank, Financial Structure and Economic Development Database.

[1]All values deflated by the U.S. CPI, except where otherwise noted.

[2]Trade-price-deflated figure is calculated using a trade-weighted average of the G-7 non-oil export-price deflator.

[3]World GDP, own GDP, private capital flows, and stock market capitalization are all computed for the first year of the relevant period (except for private capital flows and stock market capitalization during 1973–76 and 1973–81, when the final year of the relevant period was used instead, reflecting limited data availability). Private capital flows are defined as the sum of net direct investment, portfolio investment, and other investment, from the balance of payments. Russia is excluded from all calculations in the "Percent of Own GDP" column, since it was not a market economy during 1973–81.

than doubled to nearly $800 billion in 2005 and in real terms is now well above the previous 1980 peak (Figure 2.2). For fuel exporters, the current shock is in real terms comparable to (or indeed slightly larger than) the shocks of the 1970s, although as a share of their GDP it is not quite as large (Table 2.1). Rising exports by fuel producers have, of course, been matched by rising imports elsewhere. The increase in the oil-import bill between 2002 and 2005 amounted to almost 4 percent of GDP for China, and over 1 percent of GDP for the United States, other advanced economies, and other developing countries (Table 2.2). From the perspective of the global economy, nevertheless, the current shock is smaller than in the 1970s, whether measured relative to world GDP, private capital flows, or the size of financial markets (Table 2.1). It is also worth noting that external imbalances were apparent well before oil prices started to edge upwards in 1999, and certainly before oil prices reached their current peaks (Figure 2.3). That said, over the past two years higher oil prices account for one-half of the

deterioration in the U.S. current account deficit.

Since 2002, fuel exporters have spent a somewhat smaller share of their additional revenues than after the first oil price shock. Their imports over the past few years have remained broadly constant as a share of GDP; even in absolute terms, the increase in imports accounts for little more than one-half of the additional revenues (as opposed to the three-quarters share observed in the early 1970s). A more formal statistical analysis (see Box 2.1, "How Rapidly Are Oil Exporters Spending Their Revenue Gains?") confirms these broad conclusions, while finding

Table 2.2. Change in Net Oil Exports, 2002–05

	Billions of Constant 2005 U.S. Dollars[1]	Percent of World GDP[2]	Percent of Own GDP[2]
Fuel exporters[3]	437	1.24	33.2
United States	−124	−0.35	−1.1
Other advanced economies[4]	−198	−0.56	−1.3
China	−53	−0.15	−3.8
Other developing countries[5]	−53	−0.15	−1.2

Source: IMF staff calculations.

[1]All values deflated by the U.S. CPI.

[2]Both world GDP and own GDP are computed for 2002.

[3]Includes all the countries in the *World Economic Outlook* group of fuel exporters, with the addition of Kazakhstan and Norway.

[4]Includes all the countries in the *World Economic Outlook* group of advanced economies, except for the United States.

[5]Includes all other countries.

and the average value of fuel exports exceeds $500 million. Kazakhstan was included even though data were not available to gauge whether the first criterion was met. The sample excludes large oil producers for which oil is not a key export earner, such as Canada, Ecuador, Mexico, and the United Kingdom.

Figure 2.3. Fuel Exporters' Cumulative Current Account Balances and Capital Flows
(Billions of 2005 U.S. dollars, cumulative)

Current account surpluses in the 1970s were associated with significant increases in official reserves and bank deposits. During the past few years, there has been relatively little accumulation of bank deposits, while portfolio investment flows have been sizable.

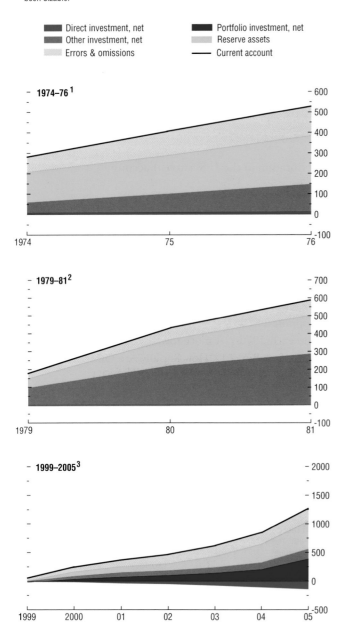

Source: IMF staff calculations.
[1] Cumulative, starting from 1974.
[2] Cumulative, starting from 1979.
[3] Cumulative, starting from 1999.

significant differences across countries (spending rates are relatively low in Cooperation Council of the Arab States of the Gulf, or GCC, countries, but considerably higher in the Islamic Republic of Iran). In particular, the public sector has been cautious about rapidly ramping up spending: between 2002 and 2005, government budget surpluses in fuel exporters increased on average by 11 percentage points of GDP. This appears to reflect concerns, fueled by past experience, about whether such large amounts can be spent effectively within a short period, and whether the current oil price shock may prove transitory (see also IMF, 2005).

Will the shock in fact persist? From a historical perspective, about one-half of the 1973–74 oil price shock proved enduring, while the 1979–81 shock was eventually completely reversed. While any long-run oil price forecast is subject to enormous uncertainty, both market expectations and an assessment of medium-term oil market fundamentals suggest that a considerable proportion of the recent shock will be permanent in nature (see Chapter IV of the April 2005 *World Economic Outlook*). Examining this issue from a different perspective, the shock has changed not just current income, but also wealth: the value of fuel exporters' petroleum reserves increased by more than $40 trillion between 1999 and 2005 (Table 2.3). If two-thirds of this were to prove permanent in nature, broadly consistent with the estimates in the April 2005 *World Economic Outlook*, it would imply an $850 billion increase in permanent income,[4] almost three times the observed increase in aggregate imports to date. That said, the increase in wealth has been spread very unevenly across fuel exporters; in some, such as Norway and Bahrain, the value of total petroleum reserves is equivalent to current GDP or less.

Fuel exporters' spending patterns are likely to affect the relative demand for goods from

[4] Assuming a U.S. long-term real interest rate of 3 percent, roughly the average value observed over the past 30 years.

Table 2.3. Petroleum Reserves

	Percent of World Reserves	Value of Reserves in Percent of 2005 GDP[1]	Change in Value of Reserves, 1999–2005		Percent of World Crude Oil Production
			Percent of 2005 GDP	Percent of 2005 world GDP	
Sample of selected fuel exporters	**88.2**	**2,156**	**1,763**	**98.3**	**62.4**
Kuwait	8.3	8,178	6,708	10.5	3.0
Libya	3.3	5,847	5,034	4.3	2.0
Saudi Arabia	22.1	4,722	3,856	27.6	13.2
Kazakhstan	3.3	4,145	3,663	4.5	1.6
United Arab Emirates	8.2	4,129	3,368	10.3	3.3
Iran, I. R. of	11.1	3,679	3,199	14.8	5.1
Venezuela	6.5	3,329	2,724	8.1	3.7
Azerbaijan	0.6	3,276	2,672	0.7	0.4
Qatar	1.3	2,244	2,143	1.9	1.2
Nigeria	3.0	2,111	1,862	4.0	3.1
Angola	0.7	1,826	1,672	1.0	1.2
Congo, Rep. of	0.2	1,729	1,425	0.2	0.3
Gabon	0.2	1,416	1,123	0.2	0.3
Sudan	0.5	1,290	1,280	0.8	0.4
Equatorial Guinea	0.1	1,133	1,042	0.2	0.4
Oman	0.5	1,033	849	0.6	1.0
Yemen	0.2	1,010	995	0.4	0.5
Brunei Darussalam	0.1	927	761	0.1	0.3
Syrian Arab Republic	0.3	661	572	0.4	0.7
Algeria	1.0	635	522	1.3	2.4
Russia	6.0	529	454	8.0	11.6
Trinidad and Tobago	0.1	399	354	0.1	0.2
Norway	0.8	185	144	1.0	4.0
Turkmenistan	—	175	142	0.1	0.3
Bahrain	—	53	36	—	0.1
Iraq[2]	9.7	—	—	12.1	2.5
OPEC	**74.9**	**3,601**	**2,997**	**95.3**	**41.0**
World	**100.0**	**153**	**128**	**128.0**	**100.0**

Sources: BP, *Statistical Review of World Energy 2005;* Energy Information Administration; and IMF staff calculations.
Note: Estimates of reserves refer to end-2004 and of crude oil production to 2004 (except for Bahrain, where production estimates refer to 2003).
[1]Total value of stock of reserves calculated using average petroleum spot price for December 2005.
[2]No GDP data available.

different regions. In particular, fuel exporters are importing fewer goods, measured as a share of their total merchandise imports, from the United States today than they were in the 1970s. In terms of market share of imports, the United States ranks well below either advanced economies or most developing economies (Table 2.4).[5] Hence, as the shock redistributes income from advanced economies and other developing countries toward fuel exporters, relative demand for U.S. goods declines. Even assuming that fuel exporters spend all their incremental revenues, this "third-country" effect would still act to increase the U.S. current account deficit by a further $25 billion, or 0.2 percent of GDP.

For now, however, oil exporters are saving a considerable share of their income. This raises the question of how the surplus funds are being recycled and how they are affecting global financing conditions, including the extent to which they are contributing to low global interest rates. At a broad level, the current account surpluses of the 1970s and early 1980s were

[5]As a caveat, the data reflect the composition of merchandise trade alone. However, there is anecdotal evidence that fuel exporters may be relatively large consumers of U.S. financial services.

Table 2.4. Composition of Merchandise Imports
(Percent of imports of given importing region sourced from given exporting region)

	Exporting Region					
	Fuel exporters[1]	United States	Other advanced economies[2]	China	Other developing countries[3]	Total
Importing Region—2004						
Fuel exporters[1]	—	8.4	59.0	7.6	25.0	100
United States	8.3	—	54.0	13.8	23.9	100
Other advanced economies[2]	19.5	25.8	—	21.3	33.4	100
China	9.2	8.6	65.3	—	17.0	100
Other developing countries[3]	13.3	19.5	59.3	8.0	—	100
Importing Region—Change Between 1981 and 2004[4]						
Fuel exporters[1]	—	−5.7	−9.0	6.6	8.0	...
United States	−11.4	—	−4.9	13.0	3.2	...
Other advanced economies[2]	−19.6	−8.7	—	18.1	10.1	...
China	8.5	2.6	−14.7	—	3.6	...
Other developing countries[3]	−9.2	−4.8	7.8	6.3	—	...

Source: IMF, *Direction of Trade Statistics.*
[1]This group is as defined in the text.
[2]This group included all the countries in the *World Economic Outlook* group of advanced economies, except for the United States.
[3]This group includes all other countries.
[4]Percentage point difference in the share of imports between 1981 and 2004 (i.e., a positive number indicates an increase since 1981). The year 1981 is the earliest date available with data coverage comparable to 2004.

almost entirely associated with increases in official reserves and bank deposits (Figure 2.4); much of this was on-lent to emerging market countries, particularly in Latin America, setting the stage for the 1981–82 debt crisis (see Box 2.2, "Recycling Petrodollars in the 1970s"). During the past few years, in contrast, there has been relatively little accumulation of bank deposits, whereas portfolio investment flows have been sizable. However, given the limitations of published data, it is difficult to be more precise regarding the current allocation of oil money by asset, currency, or region. Fuel exporters' recorded deposits in BIS-reporting banks, together with their identified purchases of U.S. securities, amount to less than one-third of the cumulative current account surpluses (Figure 2.5; see also BIS, 2005). In some countries, prepayment of external debt accounts for an important share of the difference.[6] Anecdotal evidence also suggests other possible explanations. Purchases of U.S. securities may be booked largely through intermediaries based

in London or offshore financial centers. Again, fuel exporters may be investing in more diversified portfolios—for instance, real estate, private equity, and hedge funds. They may also be investing relatively more in non-U.S. and, perhaps, non-G-7 securities, not least because of the reporting requirements of the post-9/11 Patriot Act. For instance, some of the savings may have been invested in regional equity and real estate, whose price is booming throughout the Middle East, and in emerging markets more generally. However, IMF staff estimates of the currency composition of fuel exporters' official reserves indicate that the share held in dollar-denominated assets, at about 60 percent of all identified assets, has not changed significantly since 2002.[7]

Given the limited hard data available, any impact of the recycling of oil revenues on financial market conditions must be estimated indirectly. To the extent that petrodollars are currently being recycled through market-based instruments, rather than bank-based lending,

[6]IMF staff estimates indicate that as much as 10 percent of fuel exporters' total 2005 hydrocarbon revenues were allocated to debt prepayments.
[7]See IMF (2006), Box 1.6, for a more detailed discussion.

any effect on financing should be concentrated on market-based financial systems and on traded assets. Box 2.3 ("The Impact of Petrodollars on U.S. and Emerging Market Bond Yields") analyzes whether the recycling of petrodollars has helped lower either U.S. long-term interest rates or emerging market spreads. There is indeed strong evidence that capital inflows from abroad have helped reduce yields on U.S. bonds. The precise impact of oil-related flows is more difficult to disentangle, although its magnitude is likely to be relatively modest (at most a ⅓ percentage point reduction in U.S. nominal yields in 2005), possibly reflecting the diminished importance of fuel exporters in the international financial system.[8]

Finally, it is worth underscoring that the current increase in oil prices is taking place in a very different global environment from the past. In particular, the pattern of external imbalances has changed markedly since the 1970s. Then, large external deficits were concentrated in oil-importing developing countries (Figure 2.3). Now, it is the United States that is running a large external deficit, aggravated by high oil prices; given the central role of the United States in the world economy, this must heighten concerns. Set against this, the nature of the international financial system has been transformed over time, with bank-based lending being largely replaced by intermediation through financial markets. Now that the recycling of petrodollars is market-based and less driven by a few large intermediaries, it may well prove more sustainable than in earlier episodes.

How Will the Current Oil Price Shock Affect Global Imbalances?

The previous section sought to place the recent oil shock in context. This section looks in

Figure 2.4. Fuel Exporters' Cumulative Current Account Balances and Identified Asset Purchases
(Billions of U.S. dollars, cumulative since 1999)

In contrast to the 1970s, tracking the precise assets and countries into which oil revenues have been invested over the past few years is difficult. Identified purchases only account for a small share of current account surpluses.

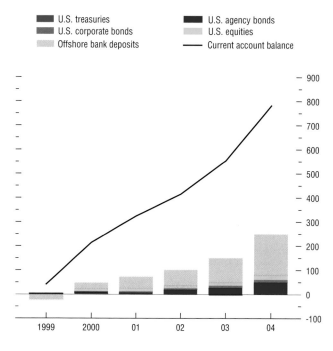

Sources: Bank for International Settlements; Treasury International Capital System; and IMF staff calculations.

---

[8]Their gross external assets as of end-2004 accounted for less than 4 percent of the world total, while their share of official reserves was about 10 percent.

Figure 2.5. Current Account and Oil Trade Balances
(Percent of GDP)

In the 1970s, large external deficits, financed by the recycling of petrodollars, were concentrated in oil-importing developing countries. In recent years, the oil price shock has instead contributed to a widening U.S. current account deficit and has redistributed current account surpluses from other advanced economies and emerging Asia toward fuel exporters.

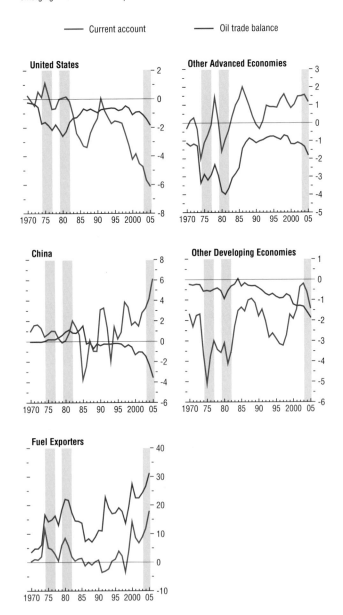

Source: IMF staff calculations.

more detail at how the global economy—and particularly global imbalances—are likely to adjust. Following the initial oil price shock, adjustment takes place broadly as follows.[9]

- In *fuel importers*, the rise in world oil prices worsens the trade balance, leading to a higher current account deficit and a deteriorating net foreign asset position. At the same time, higher oil prices tend to decrease private disposable income and corporate profitability, reducing domestic demand; along with a depreciation of the exchange rate, this acts to bring the current account back into equilibrium over time. The speed and output cost of adjustment depends on factors such as the degree of trade openness, structural flexibility,[10] and central bank credibility, as well as the shock's expected persistence and the speed with which it is allowed to feed through into domestic fuel prices. Among other things, these determine the extent to which rising oil prices raise inflationary pressures, necessitating a monetary tightening that could lead to a more pronounced slowing in growth.

- In *fuel exporters*, the process works broadly in reverse: trade surpluses are offset by stronger growth and, over time, real exchange rate appreciation. One important difference, however, is that fuel exporters may take longer than fuel importers to adjust to the increase in fuel prices.[11] Hence, their savings may remain at high levels for extended periods.

- Consequently, *aggregate global demand* is likely to fall. In turn, this sets in train a process of multilateral adjustment, driven by interest and exchange rate changes, as well as growth

---

[9]See Ostry and Reinhart (1992) and Cashin and McDermott (2003) for a detailed discussion of the international transmission of terms-of-trade shocks.

[10]See the April 2005 *World Economic Outlook*, Chapter III.

[11]The rise in oil exporters' revenues is often very large as a share of own GDP, and cyclical and/or structural and institutional constraints can make it very difficult to expand demand quickly and efficiently. In contrast, no such constraints prevent demand from rapidly adjusting downward in fuel importers.

Box 2.1. How Rapidly Are Oil Exporters Spending Their Revenue Gains?

Oil-exporting countries' export revenues have increased significantly over the past two years, with Organization of the Petroleum Exporting Countries (OPEC) revenues estimated at about $500 billion in 2005, twice that in 2003, but lower as a share of world GDP (1.1 percent) than both in 1974 and in 1979 (around 2 percent). Oil exporters' response to higher revenues has an important bearing on the evolution of global imbalances, as well as their domestic economic developments. This box assesses the response of major oil-exporting countries' imports to higher oil revenues and compares it with their past behavior, in particular with the 1970s' episodes of sharp increases in oil prices. To this end, it augments the use of the simple marginal propensities to import by a more formal estimation of import functions.

One might expect that after years of low oil prices and limited social expenditures in many oil-exporting countries, spending would adjust rapidly to higher prices, especially in countries with large populations (relative to their oil income) and sizable development needs. In the 1970s, however, oil exporters took time to respond to higher revenues, but once spending took off, it gradually rose to unsustainable levels, with the average propensity to import surpassing one by the late 1980s—reflecting in large part badly planned or wasteful projects and declining oil prices. Spending was finally curtailed (with the average propensity to import falling below one) by the mid-1990s, after years of low oil prices, suggesting that oil exporters must have initially assumed a higher permanent component in the price hikes than was justified ex post. The experience with the resulting fiscal deficits, therefore, could result in a more cautious use of higher oil revenues this time around, especially in countries where the ability to absorb the increased revenues is limited.

Note: The main authors of this box are Pelin Berkmen and Hossein Samiei.

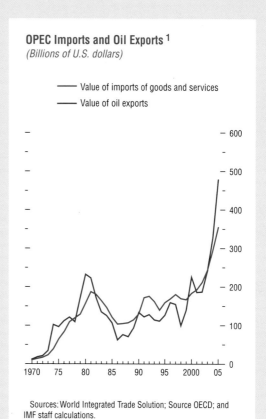

OPEC Imports and Oil Exports[1]
(Billions of U.S. dollars)

— Value of imports of goods and services
— Value of oil exports

Sources: World Integrated Trade Solution; Source OECD; and IMF staff calculations.
[1]OPEC-9, excluding Iraq and Indonesia; data for United Arab Emirates start from 1971.

A quantitative analysis and comparison of spending patterns across the three episodes is not straightforward in part because much depends on the time periods used and definitions of spending out of oil revenues. For example, a casual examination of the first figure—which depicts nominal imports and oil exports of OPEC countries—suggests that spending out of oil revenues has been larger in the current episode than in the past. Specifically, in 2004 imports constituted about 90 percent of oil exports, in contrast to 38 percent in 1974 and 75 percent in 1979.

However, more meaningful than these simple ratios is the behavior of the marginal propensity to import out of oil revenues over the shock periods. There is no single correct way of defining this propensity. One possible definition is

Box 2.1 *(concluded)*

Marginal Propensity to Import Out of Oil Revenues[1]

	1973–1974	1973–1975	1978–1980	1978–1981	2003–2005
GCC[2]	0.08	0.34	0.18	0.25	0.15
OPEC[3]	0.14	0.52	0.24	0.42	0.24
Iran, I.R. of	0.17	0.68	0.35	0.24	0.37
Saudi Arabia	0.01	0.32	0.27	0.39	0.26
Venezuela	0.18	0.65	–0.15	0.01	0.46
Major non-OPEC[4]	...	...	...	...	0.31
Russia	0.77	1.37	0.76	1.08	0.20
Norway	...	...	0.18	–0.30	–0.13
Mexico	...	...	...	...	0.78

Sources: World Integrated Trade Solution; OECD; *World Economic Outlook*; and IMF staff calculations.

[1]Defined as (change in imports net of non-oil exports, investment income, and transfers)/(change in oil exports).

[2]The Cooperation Council of the Arab States of the Gulf (GCC) includes Bahrain, Kuwait, Oman, Qatar, Saudi Arabia, and the United Arab Emirates.

[3]OPEC-9, excluding Iraq and Indonesia. Data for the United Arab Emirates start from 1971.

[4]Major non-OPEC includes Angola, Canada, Kazakhstan, Mexico, Norway, Oman, and Russia.

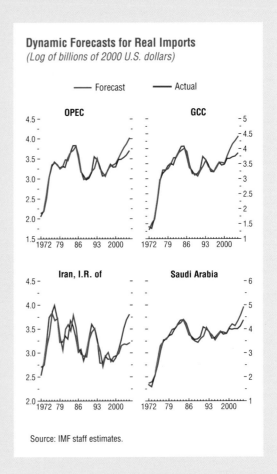

Dynamic Forecasts for Real Imports
(Log of billions of 2000 U.S. dollars)

Source: IMF staff estimates.

one minus the change in the current account over the change in oil revenues.[1] The results, shown in the table, suggest that OPEC is currently spending 24 percent of its additional oil revenues on imports. The figure is 31 percent for major non-OPEC countries and 15 percent for the Cooperation Council of the Arab States of the Gulf (GCC). The latter group also appears to be spending less rapidly than in most past episodes, while for OPEC the picture is less clear-cut. These results, however, could underestimate spending propensities if, in particular, additions to non-oil export revenues are also mostly oil-related (e.g., natural gas and oil products—as in many OPEC countries), although the extent that this may be the case is difficult to know given data deficiencies. If the above definition is modified to incorporate the change in non-oil revenues too, then the marginal propensity to spend in the recent period will be higher

[1]Or equivalently: (change in imports net of non-oil exports, investment income, and transfers)/(change in oil exports). This definition assumes that the increase in oil income is the only "shock" to external revenues and that additions to other revenues are fully spent on imports.

(and less different from past episodes). The figure for the GCC (34 percent) is also now close to that for OPEC (36 percent). These aggregate trends also mask important differences across countries. In particular, countries with larger populations and/or expenditure needs, such as the Islamic Republic of Iran, Mexico, and Venezuela have higher propensities to import than Saudi Arabia and most other GCC members.

The above analysis, while informative, does not capture the impact of other variables on imports. As an alternative—and more formal—statistical analysis, we estimate import functions for the 1970–2001 period and examine the out-of-sample forecasts for the recent period. This procedure does not distinguish shock episodes from other periods and focuses on testing whether current performance is similar to the average of the past. We use an error-correction formulation, with real GDP and the terms of trade as explanatory variables.[2] The estimation is done for oil-exporting countries individually, the GCC, and OPEC (for which comparison with the past is possible). The results (second figure) suggest that OPEC's spending is only slightly lower than that implied by its past behavior while the GCC's spending behavior is clearly

[2]The logarithmic change in real imports is regressed on its lagged values, current and lagged values of logarithmic changes in GDP and the terms of trade, and an error correction term. The estimation is carried out using an autoregressive distributed lag model, and employs the Schwarz-Bayesian criterion for lag selection.

more conservative. Most of the individual countries' responses (e.g., the Islamic Republic of Iran and Saudi Arabia) are also consistent with their spending needs and with the trends in the marginal propensity to import discussed above.

On balance, these findings suggest that average spending so far has been gradual, especially for most GCC exporters. But expenditure needs are great in many countries and, based on the 1970s experience, it is not at all certain that the current trend will continue. The outcome will also depend on perceptions about the magnitude of the permanent component in higher prices. Higher spending, when prudent and on projects with high returns, would help promote domestic growth in these countries and contribute to reducing global imbalances.

differentials. The incipient excess of global saving over investment puts downward pressure on real interest rates, which supports investment demand in fuel importers and weakens incentives to save in fuel exporters. At the same time, exchange rate changes and growth differentials shift aggregate demand from importers to exporters.

• Adjustment is also influenced importantly by *financial market developments*. Higher oil prices will tend to reduce asset prices—including equities and exchange rates[12]—in oil-importing countries and to raise them in oil-exporting countries. This will tend to reinforce the adjustment process, particularly in countries—such as the United States—where wealth effects are large. In addition, changes in asset prices have important valuation effects.[13] For example, if oil exporters hold equities or

bonds in oil-importing countries, their gains from higher oil prices may be partly offset by capital losses on their asset holdings, as stock markets in oil importers fall or their exchange rates depreciate.

To investigate the adjustment process in more detail, IMF staff used two separate but consistent vector autoregressions (VARs).[14] The first of these, a standard VAR, investigates the link between real oil prices and external positions (measured using both current accounts and net foreign assets) in the United States and in selected other country groups. The second, a Global VAR (GVAR),[15] looks in more detail at the link between oil prices, growth, inflation, and asset prices, to shed more light on how the adjustment takes place. Starting with the broad implications of oil prices for external positions, the VARs suggest that:

[12]Bond prices will also fall, as long as *nominal* interest rates increase.

[13]See the April 2005 *World Economic Outlook*, Chapter III, for a detailed discussion of valuation effects.

[14]Adopting two separate but consistent models allows for more parsimonious specifications. The results are consistent with those obtained combining the two models within a single GVAR.

[15]As estimated by Dees and others (forthcoming); see Appendix 2.1 for details.

Figure 2.6. Impact of Oil Price Shocks on External Imbalances, 1972–2004[1]

(Percent of GDP, x-axis in years)

In the short term, oil price shocks lead to external imbalances. However, the impact on net foreign assets has historically proved transitory.

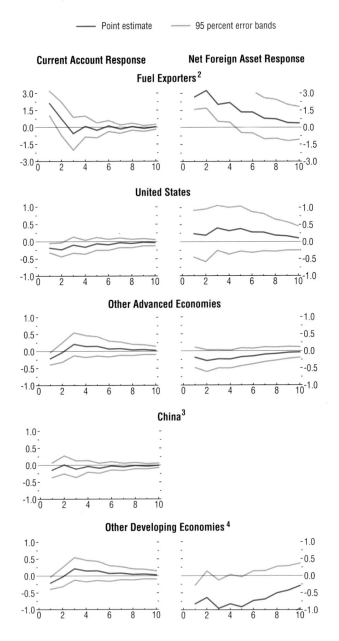

—— Point estimate —— 95 percent error bands

Current Account Response **Net Foreign Asset Response**
Fuel Exporters[2]

United States

Other Advanced Economies

China[3]

Other Developing Economies[4]

Source: IMF staff calculations.
[1]Response to a permanent $10 a barrel annual average increase in oil prices (measured in constant 2005 U.S. dollars).
[2]Fuel exporters' response presented on a wider scale.
[3]Net foreign asset data available only after 1980.
[4]Error bands partially out of scale.

• Oil price shocks have a marked but relatively short-lived impact on current accounts (Figure 2.6).[16] A permanent increase in real oil prices of $10 per barrel was on average associated with an increase in fuel exporters' current account surplus of about 2 percent of own GDP, with the effect dying out within three years. This was matched by higher deficits in the United States (about ¼ percent of GDP), other advanced economies, and developing economies other than China.[17] Among these, the impact on the United States was statistically the most significant as well as persistent (with a half-life of about three years).

• Oil price shocks also have a noticeable—and predictable—effect on the net foreign asset position of all regions, except the United States (see Figure 2.6). A permanent $10 per barrel oil price shock boosts the net foreign asset position of oil exporters by about 2 percent of GDP, in line with the increase in the current account; the increase has a half-life of about five years. More surprisingly, the estimated change in U.S. net foreign assets was positive (although statistically insignificant), while other countries experienced a larger and more persistent reduction in net foreign assets than implied by the (cumulative) impact on the current account.[18] This may reflect the valuation effects described above, with declines in asset prices in the United States reducing wealth in the rest of the world.

Against this background, how does the underlying adjustment to an oil shock occur, and are there significant differences across countries and regions? Figure 2.7 compares the adjustment process across regions in response to a perma-

[16]See Appendix 2.1 for a fuller discussion of the identification and interpretation of the oil price shock.
[17]China was a net oil exporter during the first half of the sample period.
[18]For many fuel exporters, complete data on foreign asset positions are not available. This may explain the similarity between the cumulative current account response and the estimated change in net foreign assets.

Figure 2.7. Adjustment to Oil Price Shocks, 1979:Q2–2003:Q4[1]

(Percent unless otherwise indicated, x-axis in quarters)

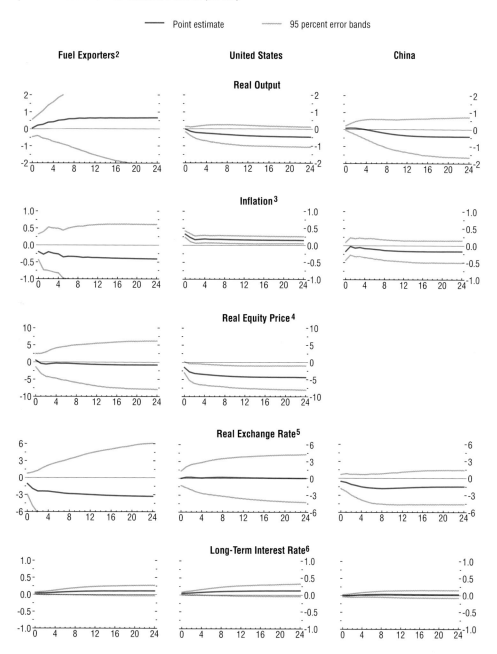

Source: IMF staff calculations, based on Dees and others (forthcoming).
[1]Response to a permanent $10 a barrel annual average increase in oil prices (measured in constant 2005 U.S. dollars).
[2]Groups described in Appendix 2.1.
[3]Y-axis in percentage points at a quarterly rate. For other developing countries, error bands out of scale.
[4]For fuel exporters, data only available for Canada, Norway, and the United Kingdom. For other developing countries, confidence intervals partially out of scale. For China, insufficient data available.
[5]Error bands partially out of scale. For the United States, real effective exchange rate vis-à-vis other groups shown. For all other groups, CPI-based real bilateral exchange rate vis-à-vis the United States shown.
[6]Y-axis in percentage points at a quarterly rate; multiply by four to annualize. For other developing countries, only Korea and South Africa shown. For China, short-term interest rates shown.

Figure 2.7 *(concluded)*[1]

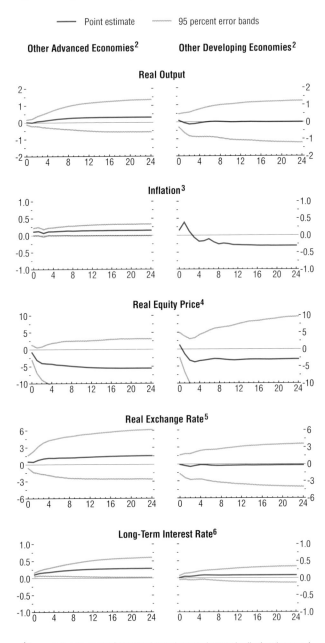

— Point estimate — 95 percent error bands

Other Advanced Economies[2]   **Other Developing Economies[2]**

Real Output

Inflation[3]

Real Equity Price[4]

Real Exchange Rate[5]

Long-Term Interest Rate[6]

[1]Response to a permanent $10 a barrel annual average increase in oil prices (measured in constant 2005 U.S. dollars).

[2]Groups described in Appendix 2.1.

[3]Y-axis in percentage points at a quarterly rate. For other developing countries, error bands out of scale.

[4]For fuel exporters, data only available for Canada, Norway, and the United Kingdom. For other developing countries, confidence intervals partially out of scale. For China, insufficient data available.

[5]Error bands partially out of scale. For the United States, real effective exchange rate vis-à-vis other groups shown. For all other groups, CPI-based real bilateral exchange rate vis-à-vis the United States shown.

[6]Y-axis in percentage points at a quarterly rate; multiply by four to annualize. For other developing countries, only Korea and South Africa shown. For China, short-term interest rates shown.

nent oil price shock (again, of $10 per barrel).[19] The key points are as follows.

- The basic adjustment channels work broadly as described above, with slowing growth and real depreciation supporting the trade adjustment in oil importers, while fuel exporters experience real appreciation and output growth. In particular, in the United States, the real effective exchange rate depreciates, and output declines by up to ½ percent, although this decrease is statistically weak. In other advanced economies, the exchange rate also depreciates, but any output declines are smaller than in the United States (especially in Japan).[20]

- Inflation in advanced economies rises after one year by an annualized ¾ percentage point in the United States, and somewhat less elsewhere.[21] This has historically been accompanied by an increase in both short- and long-term nominal interest rates. Long-term real rates, however, fall temporarily in response to the shock. This helps support demand in fuel importers and maintain the global saving-investment balance, until exchange rate changes and growth differentials work their way through the adjustment process. In developing countries, the response of inflation cannot be estimated precisely, reflecting strong heterogeneity within this group.[22]

[19]These results are based on the estimates of Dees and others (forthcoming). For this exercise, both the sample period (1979:Q2–2003:Q4) and the list of countries included (see Appendix 2.1) are slightly different from what was previously used. This reflects the limited availability of the quarterly data needed to estimate the underlying GVAR model.

[20]In Japan, there is a marked depreciation. In the euro area, in contrast, the real exchange rate does not respond (see Appendix 2.1).

[21]For this sample, which includes the second oil price shock and the associated delayed policy response, the hypothesis that inflation is affected even in the long run cannot be rejected.

[22]These results, while based on a different methodology, are broadly consistent with earlier IMF staff estimates of the impact of an oil price shock. For instance, the calculations in IMF (2000) suggest that a $10 per barrel increase in oil prices would reduce real GDP in the United States and euro area by about ½ percent, and increase inflation after one year by 1 percentage point.

Box 2.2. Recycling Petrodollars in the 1970s

The first "oil shock" began in the fall of 1973. The sudden tripling of world oil prices resulted in a large windfall gain for oil-exporting countries at the expense of oil importers. It also led to a major financial shock, since most exporting countries spent only a small portion of the increased revenues. In 1974, the first full year after the initial shock, the aggregate current account surplus of major oil-exporting countries amounted to $68 billion (one-third of their GDP). The major counterparts were the deficits of industrial countries ($31 billion, 0.8 percent of GDP) and of oil-importing developing countries, or OIDC ($34 billion, 10½ percent of GDP). Although these shifts moderated over time as oil exporters adjusted to the new market situation with increased spending, the general pattern persisted through the rest of the decade.[1]

Oil exporters faced the question of how to use their sizable current account surplus. Data on identified investments, which account for almost the entire surplus, indicate that most of the money was channeled into a few well-established

markets. In 1974, more than half was placed in bank deposits and money market instruments (including short-term treasury securities) in advanced economies (see the first table). Of the liquid investments in the United States, treasury securities accounted for less than a sixth of the total, with the rest placed mostly with commercial banks. About $25 billion was channeled into long-term investments, such as loans to national governments and international agencies, as well as government bonds in the United States and the United Kingdom. Broadly speaking, the pattern persisted throughout the rest of the 1970s.

The financial shock from the oil price increases of the 1970s came at a time when the potential for large private international capital flows was just beginning to be realized. The first relevant development, which began in the late 1960s, was the deregulation and consequent innovative evolution of Eurocurrency markets. The oil shock of 1973–74 reinforced this development, providing new fuel for these markets by making large sums of liquid assets available for investment. By then, banks in Europe and in less regulated "offshore" financial centers were much better prepared than they would have been even a few years earlier to accept and invest dollar-denominated deposits and other liquid liabilities. A third factor was weak aggre-

Note: The main authors of this box are James M. Boughton and Suchitra Kumarapathy.

[1]The current account balance of industrial countries swung from a cumulative surplus of $23 billion in 1968–73 to a deficit of $44 billion in 1974–79, while the cumulative deficit of OIDC doubled to $139 billion.

Fuel Exporters' Deployment of Current Account Surpluses
(Billions of U.S. dollars; by type of financial investment)

	1974	1975	1976	1977	1978	1979
Bank deposits and money market investments						
Dollar deposits in the United States	1.9	1.1	1.8	0.4	0.8	4.9
Sterling deposits in the United Kingdom	1.7	0.2	−1.4	0.3	0.2	1.4
Deposits in foreign currency markets	22.8	9.1	12.1	10.6	3.0	31.2
Treasury bills in the United Kingdom and the United States	4.8	0.6	−1.0	−1.1	−0.8	3.4
Total	**31.2**	**11.0**	**11.5**	**10.2**	**3.2**	**40.9**
Long-term investments						
Special bilateral arrangements	11.9	12.4	12.2	12.7	8.7	11.8
Loans to international agencies	3.5	4.0	2.0	0.3	0.1	−0.4
Government securities in the United Kingdom and the United States	1.1	2.2	4.1	4.5	−1.8	−0.9
Other[1]	9.7	6.1	8.5	5.8	3.3	2.4
Total	**25.1**	**24.7**	**26.8**	**23.3**	**10.3**	**12.9**
Total new investments	**56.3**	**35.7**	**38.3**	**33.5**	**13.5**	**53.8**

Source: Bank for International Settlements.
[1]Including equity and property investments in the United Kingdom and the United States, and foreign currency lending.

Box 2.2 *(concluded)*

gate demand in industrial countries, which meant that banks in those countries had to find other profitable outlets for the "petrodollars" that oil exporters were investing with them. For many banks, meeting this challenge meant moving into new markets where loan demand was stronger, including Latin America and other developing countries.

A large part of the initial response to the oil shocks took the form of official "recycling" of petrodollars, in which the IMF and other official creditors provided fast-disbursing loans to OIDC. The main vehicle for the IMF was an "Oil Facility," newly established in 1974, through which $2.4 billion were lent to 45 developing countries from 1974 to 1976. Because the shock was thought to be temporary, this financing was provided with only token conditionality. Overall, in 1974–76, official recycling from multilateral and bilateral creditors and donors amounted to $48 billion, two-thirds of which was bilateral.

Over time, international private banks took over much of the financing role. In 1975, long-term official loans and grants to OIDC amounted to about $18 billion, and private financing was estimated at roughly the same amount, most of it channeled through commercial banks. But cross-border private flows, especially through banks, then increased sharply. For instance, the external foreign currency assets reported by banks in eight European countries, Canada, Japan, the United States, and offshore branches of U.S. banks quadrupled to almost $1 trillion between 1973 and 1980.[2] The

---

[2]Since the lion's share of the recycling in the 1970s passed through the banking systems or securities markets of industrial countries, the Bank for International Settlements (BIS) was able to estimate the composition and direction of financial flows, using data obtained largely from its participating central banks. Subsequently, financial markets continued to globalize and diversify into new and more complex instruments, and a variety of nonbank financial institutions became major intermediaries for cross-border flows. Since the mid-1990s the BIS has ceased reporting cross-border banking claims on a basis comparable to earlier years, and tracking the course of overall flows has become much more difficult.

Financial Inflows for Selected OECD Economies in 1974
(Billions of U.S. dollars)

	Financial Inflows			
	Traditional capital inflows	Compensatory foreign borrowing[1]	Official inflows[2]	Total
United Kingdom	2.2	4.1[3]	3.2[4]	9.5
Italy	1.0	2.1	5.3	8.4
France	3.8	1.7	0.5	6.0

Source: OECD, *Economic Outlook*, 1975.
[1]Official or semi-official borrowing from foreign private institutions.
[2]Private and official borrowing from foreign official institutions.
[3]Of which, $2.6 billion representing foreign currency borrowing by the public sector under the exchange cover scheme, and $1.5 billion drawing on the government Euro-loan.
[4]Including an increase of $5.3 billion in sterling-denominated exchange reserves by oil-exporting countries.

Eurobond market also expanded considerably, with the total value of international and foreign bond issues growing from $12 billion in 1974 to $38 billion in 1980.

A portion of the recycled funds went to industrial countries with large current account deficits, including France, Italy, and the United Kingdom, which relied on a combination of official and private external financing (see the second table). In 1974, for instance, the United Kingdom financed its $7.5 billion current account deficit by means of compensatory foreign borrowing and direct inflows of funds from oil-exporting countries (at the time, the United Kingdom was still developing the North Sea oil fields and was a major oil importer). The IMF also provided financing to several industrial countries, including large Stand-By Arrangements for Italy and the United Kingdom, in part because of the failure of these countries to adjust policies and aggregate demand fully to the oil shock.

An even greater share of the recycled petrodollars went to developing countries, many of which had initially faced difficulties financing their increased current account deficits. Weak overall aggregate demand and a big unanticipated jump in price inflation kept world interest rates low in nominal terms and substantially negative in real terms throughout the 1970s, encouraging developing countries to take on loans. For many developing countries that were exporters of primary commodities, a commodity-price boom in the mid-1970s made their borrowing terms look even more attractive. For instance, in 1973–78 low-income countries as a group paid an average nominal interest rate of

just over 3 percent on their external debt, while their export prices—measured in the depreciating U.S. dollar—rose at an average annual rate of 18 percent. Latin America emerged as the largest borrowing region, accounting for two-thirds of total credits issued by reporting banks to OIDC—a development that laid the basis for the debt crises of the 1980s.

- There also appears to be an active valuation channel. Equity prices fall by 2–4 percentage points in major advanced economies, which—along with the depreciation of the U.S. dollar—results in a wealth transfer to the United States from other economies.

The analysis so far describes the average impact of oil price shocks in the past. However, the effects of the current shock, including the speed and nature of the future adjustment process, may be different, and in particular will depend on two policy-related factors. First, as noted above, oil producers appear to be increasing their spending in response to higher revenues more slowly than in the past. In addition, as discussed in Chapter I, the impact of oil prices on core inflation to date has been surprisingly mild relative to previous experience, so that central banks have not had to raise short-term interest rates to reduce inflationary pressures. Partly as a result, growth in oil-importing countries has been relatively unaffected, implying that trade balances may take longer to adjust; set against this, for net debtors, relatively lower interest payments on external debt have reduced any negative impact on current accounts.[23]

To examine the potential impact of these various factors on the adjustment of global imbalances, IMF staff undertook two simulations using the IMF's MULTIMOD model.[24] The first scenario assumes rapid adjustment in oil exporters, as compared to the WEO baseline where their existing current account surpluses continue into the medium term. Specifically, the scenario assumes that imports by oil exporters increase by $150 billion in 2006 (about ⅓ of their aggregate 2005 current account surplus, or ⅓ percent of world GDP), and $350 billion (about ¾ of their current surplus) by 2010. This more rapid pace of expenditure shrinks the U.S. current account deficit, by almost ¾ percent of GDP by 2010, and also leads to some real dollar appreciation (Table 2.5). The decline in global savings results in an increase in real and nominal interest rates in oil importers, amounting to up to 40 basis points. There is little net impact on growth in advanced economies.

In the second scenario, it is assumed that the low level of pass-through into core inflation cannot be sustained and that pass-through picks up in 2006, although its magnitude is still only half of what would have been expected based on his-

---

[23]In addition, historical experience may prove misleading in illustrating the potential impact of any large future oil price shock, if there are important nonlinearities in the effects of such shocks.

[24]For a description of MULTIMOD, see Laxton and others (1998); see Hunt, Isard, and Laxton (2001) for the specific version employed here. MULTIMOD does not have a separate "oil exporters" group. The estimates reported aggregate all those countries whose trade surplus increases in response to an oil price increase. This includes Canada, the United Kingdom, the "small industrial economies" group, and a group of high-income developing economies that are mainly oil exporters.

Table 2.5. Impact of Oil Price Shock: Greater Spending by Fuel Exporters
(Relative to baseline)

	2006	2007	2008	2009	2010
Current account balance (in percent of GDP)					
United States	0.4	0.4	0.5	0.6	0.7
Japan	0.5	0.7	0.9	1.0	1.1
Euro area	0.5	0.7	0.9	1.0	1.1
Core inflation (in percentage points)					
United States	0.1	0.1	—	—	0.1
Japan	0.1	0.1	0.1	0.1	0.1
Euro area	0.2	0.2	0.1	—	0.1
Real short-term interest rate (in percentage points)					
United States	0.3	0.3	0.3	0.3	0.3
Japan	0.4	0.4	0.3	0.3	0.4
Euro area	0.5	0.5	0.3	0.3	0.4
Nominal short-term interest rate (in percentage points)					
United States	0.4	0.4	0.4	0.3	0.4
Japan	0.5	0.5	0.4	0.4	0.4
Euro area	0.6	0.6	0.4	0.4	0.4
GDP (in percent)					
United States	0.5	0.1	−0.4	−0.2	−0.1
Japan	0.5	0.2	−0.4	−0.3	−0.1
Euro area	0.7	0.2	−0.5	−0.3	−0.1
Real effective exchange rate (in percent)					
United States	−0.8	−0.7	−0.6	−0.6	−0.6
Japan	0.7	0.7	0.7	0.6	0.6
Euro area	−0.3	−0.3	−0.4	−0.4	−0.4

Source: IMF staff calculations.

Table 2.6. Impact of Oil Price Shock: Delayed Pass-Through to Core Inflation
(Relative to baseline)

	2006	2007	2008	2009	2010
Current account balance (in percent of GDP)					
United States	—	—	−0.1	−0.1	−0.1
Japan	—	0.1	0.2	0.2	0.1
Euro area	—	—	—	—	—
Core inflation (in percentage points)					
United States	0.1	0.3	0.1	0.1	—
Japan	0.1	0.3	0.1	—	—
Euro area	0.1	0.2	0.1	—	—
Real short-term interest rate (in percentage points)					
United States	0.2	0.6	0.4	0.3	0.2
Japan	0.2	0.5	0.3	0.2	0.1
Euro area	0.2	0.5	0.2	0.1	—
Nominal short-term interest rate (in percentage points)					
United States	0.3	0.7	0.6	0.3	0.2
Japan	0.3	0.6	0.4	0.2	0.1
Euro area	0.2	0.6	0.3	0.1	—
GDP (in percent)					
United States	−0.3	−0.8	−0.7	−0.5	−0.4
Japan	−0.2	−0.6	−0.6	−0.4	−0.3
Euro area	−0.2	−0.5	−0.5	−0.3	−0.2
Real effective exchange rate (in percent)					
United States	0.1	0.3	0.3	0.2	0.1
Japan	—	0.1	—	0.1	0.1
Euro area	−0.1	−0.4	−0.3	−0.2	−0.2

Source: IMF staff calculations.

torical experience through 2003. As core inflation increases, central banks respond by increasing nominal interest rates significantly (by about 70 basis points for the United States in 2007, relative to the baseline), so as to contain the inflationary impact of the increase in energy prices (Table 2.6). In turn, higher interest rates act to depress demand and output, with some positive effects on the trade balance. Higher interest rates also increase the interest burden

on the U.S. stock of net foreign liabilities, which tends to raise both the U.S. current account deficit and the Japanese current account surplus.[25] Nevertheless, as long as monetary policy responds promptly to the inflationary pressures, the effects on both output and, especially, the current account are relatively mild. If the monetary policy response were instead delayed, the eventual effects would prove much more sizable.[26]

---

[25]The impact on net foreign assets, however, would be mitigated by valuation effects working in favor of the United States but not present in the model.

[26]For technical reasons, all scenarios assume that the oil price is driven only by oil supply shocks. This tends to overestimate the positive impact of lower oil prices on real GDP in oil-consuming countries. However, there is no a priori reason why the assumption should affect results for either scenario relative to the baseline. In addition, all scenarios assume full and immediate pass-through of the world oil price into domestic oil prices. Incomplete pass-through would result in slower adjustment.

Box 2.3. The Impact of Petrodollars on U.S. and Emerging Market Bond Yields

How does the recycling of oil-export revenues affect global financial markets? To the extent that higher oil prices increase world net savings, and that saved petrodollars are used to purchase given securities, the outcome would be an increase in the price of (or, equivalently, a lower interest rate on) such securities. In turn, this could lead to a second-round effect on the price of other, similar securities. This box analyzes the issue by focusing on the link between oil prices and interest rates on U.S. and emerging market bonds.

Examining first the United States, direct evidence of a link between petrodollars, capital inflows, and interest rates is not available, in large part because many oil exporters tend to purchase U.S. securities through third-country intermediaries. Such third-country trades confound the country attribution of U.S. capital flows data. The estimation here therefore proceeds more indirectly. As a first step, following Warnock and Warnock (2006), there is evidence that capital flows to the United States do put downward pressure on U.S. interest rates (see the first table, column 1). Foreign flows into U.S. government securities in the 12-month period through May 2005 depressed U.S. 10-year yields by 86 basis points,[1] controlling for factors such as inflation expectations and the federal funds rate. On this basis, if one assumed that fuel exporters used one half of their current account surplus to finance investments in the United States, the increase in oil prices over the last two years would have reduced U.S. yields by about ⅓ percentage point (holding constant all other capital flows).

To investigate the issue further, the Warnock and Warnock regression analysis was extended by disaggregating total capital flows into the United States into two components: those attributable to East Asian countries, which are unlikely to directly reflect oil-export revenues;

The Impact of Oil Revenues on U.S. Interest Rates[1]

	Nominal 10-Year Treasury Yield		
	(1)	(2)	(3)
Foreign capital inflows[2,3]	−0.24*	. . .	. . .
East Asian flows	. . .	−0.42*	−0.35*
Other flows	. . .	−0.14*	. . .
Oil-related	. . .	. . .	−0.12
Residual	. . .	. . .	−0.13*
Inflation expectations, 10-year ahead	0.63*	0.67*	0.65*
Interest rate risk premium	1.88*	3.16*	0.90*
Federal funds rate	0.36*	0.33*	0.35*
Structural budget deficit[2]	0.25*	0.23*	0.22*
R^2	0.90	0.90	0.85

Source: Authors' calculations.

[1]The sample is monthly, from August 1987 to May 2005. Yields are measured in percentage points. Asterisks denote statistical significance at the 1 percent level. The following variables are included but not reported: expected real GDP growth; the difference between 1-year ahead and 10-year ahead inflation expectations; and a constant.

[2]Scaled by lagged GDP.

[3]Twelve-month benchmark-consistent foreign official flows into U.S. treasury and agency bonds.

and all others ("Other Flows").[2] Perhaps surprisingly, East Asian inflows were found to have a relatively greater dollar-for-dollar impact on U.S. yields, although Other Flows have recently been somewhat larger in absolute terms (see the first table, column 2). Among possible explanations, East Asian purchases may have been concentrated on more thinly traded, longer-maturity portions of the yield curve, where purchases have a greater impact. In addition, interventions by Asian central banks may have been interpreted as a signal that they were likely to continue buying dollars in the future.[3] Overall, the regression attributes 52 basis points of the total

Note: The main authors of this box are Laura Kodres and Frank Warnock.

[1]Calculated as 12-month inflows, amounting to 3.65 (percent of lagged GDP), times the estimated coefficient, −0.236.

[2]For the purpose of this box, East Asia consists of China, Hong Kong SAR, Japan, Korea, and Taiwan Province of China—countries and territories whose governments have recently accumulated substantial positions in U.S. government securities.

[3]On a more technical note, "Other Flows" may also contain private flows that are related to other variables in the regression. In contrast, East Asian flows are primarily official flows, and may more reasonably be treated as exogenous.

Box 2.3 *(concluded)*

yield reduction between June 2004 and May 2005 to East Asian flows, but only 34 basis points to Other Flows.

Of course, Other Flows cannot be entirely assumed to reflect oil-export revenues—they have many potential sources. To isolate the effect of oil revenues, Other Flows were explicitly regressed on oil prices.[4] In this regression, however, oil prices have very little explanatory power. Further, the part of Other Flows that is related to oil prices does not help explain lower U.S. rates, even though non-oil-related Other Flows do have a statistically significant impact (see the first table, column 3).[5]

Summing up, while one might expect higher oil prices and the consequent recycling of petrodollars to exert downward pressure on U.S. interest rates, such an effect is hard to detect statistically among all the competing influences on U.S. yields. This may well reflect the relatively limited magnitude of petrodollar flows. Two caveats should, however, be stressed. First, these negative findings in part likely reflect the lack of direct data on capital inflows from fuel-exporting countries. Second, the above analysis treats U.S. interest rates as being determined separately from global interest rates. In an integrated world capital market, oil prices may also affect U.S. rates indirectly, through the impact of recycled petrodollars on interest rates in other countries. That said, the regressions failed to find a statistically significant impact of interest rate differentials or exchange rates on U.S. yields.[6]

[4]Allowing for 24 monthly lags, and deflating by nominal GDP. An alternative specification also included oil-export revenues, as proxied by oil prices times fuel exporters' total petroleum output, but these did not prove significant.

[5]Over selected subperiods (e.g., starting in January 1999), there is a relationship between Other Flows and oil prices. However, the portion of Other Flows attributable to oil prices over such subperiods still does not help explain U.S. rates.

[6]Their effect may already be picked up through other included variables, such as inflationary expectations or output. In a similar vein, purchases of U.S. corporate securities by oil exporters might impact U.S. interest rates; this effect is again not explicitly modeled.

Determinants of Emerging Market Bond Spreads

Explanatory Variable	Coefficient[1]
Oil price[2]	0.005
Non-fuel commodity prices[2]	−1.096*
World industrial production[2]	−1.173
Predicted credit ratings and outlooks[3]	0.237*
Federal funds three-month future rate	0.076*
R^2	Within = 0.49; Between = 0.73; Overall = 0.64

Sources: Bloomberg, L.P.; The PRS Group; J.P. Morgan; Bloomberg; and authors' calculations.

[1]Fixed-effects panel regression using 2,345 monthly observations on 29 countries, from January 1991 to May 2005. The dependent variable is the log of Emerging Market Bond Spreads, measured in basis points, using the J.P. Morgan Emerging Market Bond Indices (EMBI) relative to the U.S. 10-year treasury bond. All countries for which EMBI are available are included, except that Algeria and Côte d'Ivoire are excluded owing to lack of other data; Russia and Venezuela are excluded owing to significant oil exports; Nigeria is excluded on both grounds; and Argentina is excluded owing to its crisis-related spreads in 2001. Asterisks denote statistical significance at the 1 percent level. The following variables are included but not reported: expectations of federal funds rate (FF) increase; expectations of FF decrease; volatility of FF futures; volatility of FF futures × expectations of FF increase; volatility of FF futures × expectations of FF decrease; volatility of S&P 500 options; a constant; and a time trend.

[2]In logs.

[3]Predicted value for default risk, from a separate first-stage regression.

Even if petrodollars have only a limited effect on the large U.S. bond market, they might have a more sizable impact on the smaller market for emerging market debt. This hypothesis is explored next, using a model of emerging market bond spreads that controls for the impact of country-specific and global macroeconomic fundamentals and of variables related to U.S. financial markets. Specifically, the model recognizes that oil prices (as well as nonfuel commodity prices, global industrial production, and U.S. interest rates) influence emerging market bond spreads through two separate channels. First, oil prices affect emerging market "fundamentals," as proxied by their credit ratings and outlooks, which in turn affect their spreads. In particular, for oil importers, higher oil prices may negatively affect the current account, one of the variables used to establish credit ratings.

Second, as discussed above, if a significant share of oil exporters' revenues is used to purchase emerging market debt , then higher oil prices may be associated with lower emerging market spreads. However, even after controlling for fundamentals, estimates suggest that any link between higher oil prices and lower emerging market spreads becomes statistically insignificant when industrial production is also included in the regressions (see the second table). Oil prices and industrial production both move in sync with the global economic cycle, making their independent influence on spreads difficult to disentangle. Interestingly, nonfuel commodity prices do have a statistically significant, negative impact on spreads. Either their positive influence on fundamentals in those nonfuel commodity exporters included in the sample (such as Chile) is not sufficiently captured by credit ratings, or the associated export revenues are being used to purchase emerging market debt.

Conclusions

Global imbalances had emerged long before the current oil price shock began. Nevertheless, some of these imbalances have clearly been exacerbated by higher energy prices. In particular, the increase in oil prices since 2003 has directly worsened the U.S. current account deficit by over 1 percent of GDP; at the same time, higher oil prices have tended to reduce surpluses in non-oil-exporting developing countries, notably in Asia. To the extent that higher net savings by oil exporters have driven down global interest rates, and that these lower rates have boosted demand in economies with market-based financial systems, such as the United States, the oil price shock may also have had an additional indirect negative effect on the U.S. external position. Since it is neither feasible nor desirable for oil exporters to spend their newfound revenues immediately, global current account imbalances are likely to remain at elevated levels for longer than would otherwise have been the case, heightening the risk of a sudden, disorderly adjustment.

In the past, current accounts have tended to adjust relatively quickly to oil shocks, as higher energy prices led to a rise in interest rates, a slowdown in growth and domestic demand, and changes in exchange rates and asset prices. This time, in part because of improved monetary frameworks and credibility, the impact on short-term interest rates, growth, and inflation has been smaller than before, while deeper financial integration may facilitate the persistence of deficits. Further, authorities in fuel-exporting countries are being somewhat more cautious in increasing spending, even though market expectations indicate that the current energy price shock is likely to prove more persistent than in the 1970s. All this suggests that current accounts may adjust more slowly now than in the past.

As with any terms-of-trade shock, much of the adjustment must take place in the private sector, but policies can also play an important supporting role. For consuming countries, this requires full pass-through of world oil prices into domestic energy prices, accompanied by a monetary stance that guards against potential spillovers into core inflation. For producers, most of which are developing countries, the rise in oil revenues represents a major development opportunity. While the pace at which oil earnings can be usefully spent will vary by country, measures to boost expenditures in areas where returns are high (as well as structural reforms to boost domestic supply, particularly of nontradables) would be highly desirable both from a domestic perspective and to help reduce global imbalances.

Appendix 2.1. Oil Prices and Global Imbalances: Methodology, Data, and Further Results

The authors of this appendix are Alessandro Rebucci and Nikola Spatafora.

This appendix describes more fully the empirical evidence, presented earlier in this chapter, regarding the effects of oil price shocks on external imbalances and the associated adjustment process. Specifically, the appendix describes the econometric models and data used and the identification of the oil price shocks. It also reports additional results underlying the aggregate responses depicted in Figure 2.7.

The Econometric Models

The econometric models used to analyze the response to oil price shocks of the current account or net foreign assets (NFA) are standard VARs, which include one lag of the following endogenous variables:[27]

- The real oil price, defined as the average annual nominal oil price deflated by the U.S. CPI, in first-difference form; and

- The current account (in the first VAR), or NFA as estimated by Lane and Milesi-Ferretti (2006) (in the second VAR), both as a share of world GDP.

The model also includes the following exogenous variables (as well as a constant and a time trend):

- World growth and world consumer price inflation.[28]

- A measure of the change in world oil supply due to events that are exogenous to the oil market, from Kilian (2006).

The model is estimated for the following countries and country groups: the United States; fuel exporters, as defined earlier; China; other advanced economies;[29] and other developing economies.[30] The current account and NFA of each country group are constructed as the sum of the values for individual countries.[31]

The econometric model used to analyze the broader macroeconomic adjustment process is instead the global, multiregion VAR (GVAR) estimated by Dees and others (forthcoming).[32] In this GVAR, country-specific VARs are first estimated for 33 countries (see below for model details and sample), under the assumption that foreign variables are weakly exogenous. Then, the country-specific VARs are combined to solve for a global model in which world variables and country-specific variables are jointly determined. Each country-specific model embeds a set of co-integrating relations derived from a standard, New-Keynesian small open economy model.[33] Hence, the GVAR may be interpreted as the empirical counterpart to a simplified, global, dynamic general equilibrium model.[34]

Each of the underlying country-specific VARs incorporates the following variables, subject to data availability: the level of real GDP; consumer price inflation; the real bilateral exchange rate versus the U.S. dollar; short and long nominal interest rates; real equity prices; and the foreign counterparts of these variables. The (nominal) oil price is endogenous in the VAR for the

---

[27]Data frequency is annual, and the sample period is 1972–2004.

[28]We treat these variables as exogenous because, while they are likely to affect oil prices quickly, it may take significant time for oil prices to affect them; and endogenizing world growth and inflation would use up a needed degree of freedom.

[29]Consisting of Australia, Canada, Cyprus, Denmark, euro area, Iceland, Israel, Japan, New Zealand, Sweden, Switzerland, and the United Kingdom.

[30]Consisting of all other countries in the Lane and Milesi-Ferretti (2006) data set.

[31]Inclusion of the global discrepancy in the empirical analysis does not change the results.

[32]Data frequency is quarterly, and the sample period is 1979:Q2–2003:Q4. On GVAR modeling, see also Pesaran, Schuermann, and Weiner (2004).

[33]For each country, these restrictions are first tested using an unrestricted model; if not rejected, they are then imposed on the data.

[34]Technically, it may also be seen as an approximation to a global common factor model.

United States and hence in the GVAR, but weakly exogenous in all other country-specific VARs (see Dees and others, forthcoming, for more details on all these variables). Lag length is selected at the level of the country-specific VARs, using standard selection criteria.

After estimating the responses of individual countries, weighted averages of these individual responses (with weights given by PPP-adjusted GDP) are used to construct aggregate responses for the following country groups: fuel exporters, both advanced and developing;[35] other advanced economies, consisting of Japan, available euro area economies[36] and other small advanced economies;[37] and other developing economies, consisting of East Asia,[38] Latin America,[39] and others.[40]

Description and Identification of Oil Price Shocks

Figure 2.6 reports the generalized impulse responses (GIRs) to a permanent shock to the real oil price.[41] The magnitude of the shock is normalized to $10 per barrel at constant 2005 prices. The GIRs are rescaled to show the impact on current account and NFA in terms of own GDP, although the models are estimated using current account and NFA as a share of *world* GDP.

The VARs for external positions control separately for those changes in world oil supply that are due to exogenous events, such as wars, domestic political instability, or other geopolitical events. Hence, the oil price shock should be viewed as that part of the change in real oil prices that is *not* due to such geopolitical events. The rationale for discarding such events is that, while wars, revolutions, and the consequent disruption of economic activity will undoubtedly be associated with changes in current accounts and NFA, the relevant channels (at least in the case of the directly affected countries) may go well beyond changes in oil prices, and hence have little to do with those economic mechanisms that are the focus of this chapter.

As a result, the oil price shock being analyzed embodies a mixture of demand and supply factors (for instance, expected future market tightness, long production lags, or discoveries of new oil reserves). And there is no a priori reason to expect that the responses to pure demand and supply shocks would be the same. No attempt is made to separate demand from supply shocks, since no generally accepted procedure for doing so exists.

Figure 2.7 reports the GIR to a permanent shock to the nominal oil price. The magnitude of the shock is again normalized to $10 per barrel at constant 2005 prices, for greater ease of comparison.[42]

Additional Details on GVAR Results

Figure 2.7 only reports the GIR to a permanent oil price shock for selected countries and country groups—specifically, the United States, China, all fuel exporters, all other advanced economies, and all other developing economies. Figure 2.8 presents more disaggregated

[35]Advanced economy fuel exporters are Canada, Norway, and the United Kingdom. Developing economy fuel exporters are Indonesia, Mexico, and Saudi Arabia.

[36]Austria, Belgium, Finland, France, Germany, Italy, the Netherlands, and Spain.

[37]Australia, New Zealand, Sweden, and Switzerland.

[38]Korea, Malaysia, the Philippines, Singapore, and Thailand.

[39]Argentina, Brazil, Chile, and Peru.

[40]India, South Africa, and Turkey.

[41]Also shown are two-standard-deviation error bands, computed analytically. GIRs illustrate the effects of changes in observed variables (such as oil prices) on the evolution of other variables in the system, taking into account the historical correlations between shocks to all variables in the system. The use of GIRs allows the computation of impulse responses without the large number of arguably arbitrary identification assumptions typically needed to orthogonalize shocks. The disadvantage is that the shocks are not structural and are therefore harder to interpret as supply or demand shocks.

[42]Since the GVAR is estimated using quarterly data, the distinction between real and nominal oil prices makes little difference to the results. Also shown are error bands, computed using bootstrap simulation, which contain 95 percent of the simulated distribution.

Figure 2.8. Additional Results: Adjustment to Oil Price Shocks, 1979:Q2–2003:Q4[1]

(Percent unless otherwise indicated, x-axis in quarters)

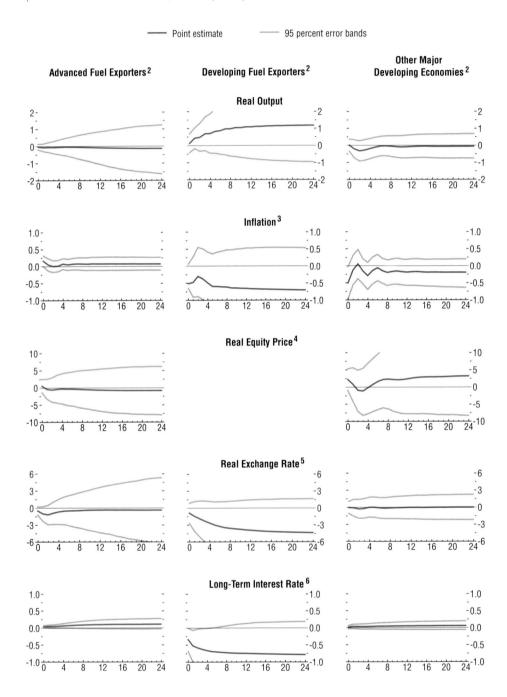

Figure 2.8 *(concluded)*

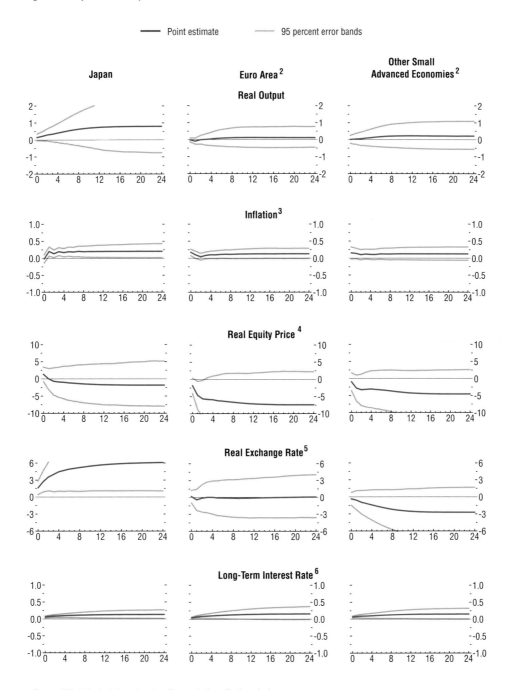

Source: IMF staff calculations, based on Dees and others (forthcoming).
[1]Response to a $10 a barrel annual average increase in oil prices (measured in constant 2005 U.S. dollars).
[2]Groups described in Appendix 2.1.
[3]Y-axis in percentage points at a quarterly rate. Developing fuel exporters and Turkey partially out of scale.
[4]Insufficient data available for developing fuel exporters. For other major developing countries, only India and South Africa shown. Euro area and other major developing countries partially out of scale.
[5]CPI-based real bilateral exchange vis-à-vis the United States shown. Developing fuel exporters and Japan partially out of scale.
[6]Y-axis in percentage points at a quarterly rate. For developing fuel exporters, short-term interest rates for Indonesia and Mexico shown. For other major developing countries, only South Africa shown.

responses; all groups referenced therein are defined as discussed above. Estimated responses for short-term interest rates are also available, although not reported.

References

Bank for International Settlements (BIS), 2005, *75th Annual Report,* Chapter 2. Available via the Internet: http://www.bis.org/publ/arpdf/ar2005e2.htm.

Cashin, Paul, and C. John McDermott, 2003, "Intertemporal Substitution and Terms of Trade Shocks," *Review of International Economics,* Vol. 11 (September), pp. 604–18.

Dees, Stephane, Filippo di Mauro, M. Hashem Pesaran, and Vanessa Smith, forthcoming, "Exploring the International Linkages of the Euro Area: A Global VAR Analysis," *Journal of Applied Econometrics.*

Hamilton, James D., 2005, "Oil and the Macro-economy" (La Jolla, California: University of California, San Diego). Available via the Internet: http://dss.ucsd.edu/~jhamilto/JDH_palgrave_oil.pdf.

Hunt, Ben, Peter Isard, and Douglas Laxton, 2001, "The Macroeconomic Effects of Higher Oil Prices," IMF Working Paper 01/14 (Washington: International Monetary Fund).

International Monetary Fund, 2000, "The Impact of Higher Oil Prices on the Global Economy" (Washington). Available via the Internet: http://www.imf.org/external/pubs/ft/oil/2000/oilrep.pdf

———, 2005, "Regional Economic Outlook: Middle East and Central Asia" (Washington). Available via the Internet: http://www.imf.org/external/pubs/ft/reo/2005/eng/meca0905.pdf.

———, 2006, *Global Financial Stability Report,* April, World Economic and Financial Surveys (Washington).

Kilian, Lutz, 2006, "Exogenous Oil Supply Shocks: How Big Are They and How Much Do They Matter for the U.S. Economy?" (Ann Arbor, Michigan: University of Michigan). Available via the Internet: http://www-personal.umich.edu/~lkilian/oil1jan01_06.pdf.

Lane, Philip, and Gian Maria Milesi-Ferretti, 2006, "The External Wealth of Nations Mark II: Revised and Extended Estimates of Foreign Assets and Liabilities, 1970–2004," IMF Working Paper 06/69 (Washington: International Monetary Fund).

Laxton, Douglas, Peter Isard, Hamid Faruqee, Eswar Prasad, and Bart Turtelboom, 1998, *MULTIMOD Mark III: The Core Dynamic and Steady-State Models,* IMF Occasional Paper No. 164 (Washington: International Monetary Fund).

Ostry, Jonathan D., and Carmen M. Reinhart, 1992, "Private Savings and Terms of Trade Shocks: Evidence from Developing Countries," *IMF Staff Papers,* International Monetary Fund, Vol. 39 (September), pp. 495–517.

Pesaran, M. Hashem, Til Schuermann, and Scott Weiner, 2004, "Modeling Regional Interdependencies Using a Global Error-Correcting Macro-econometric Mode," *Journal of Business and Economics Statistics,* Vol. 22, pp. 129–62.

Warnock, Francis E., and Veronica Cacdac Warnock, 2006, "International Capital Flows and U.S. Interest Rates" (Charlottesville: University of Virginia). Available via the Internet: http://www.faculty.darden.virginia.edu/warnockf/research.htm.

CHAPTER III HOW HAS GLOBALIZATION AFFECTED INFLATION?

Inflation in advanced and many emerging market economies has remained remarkably subdued over the past two years despite a significant rise in commodity prices, strong growth, and a broadly accommodating monetary policy stance in the major currency areas. Is this situation sustainable or does it foreshadow unwelcome inflation surprises in the near future? Some analysts have argued that low and stable inflation reflects more intense global competition, which prevents firms from raising prices and puts downward pressures on wages in many sectors.[1] If so, and given that lower-cost producers in emerging markets and developing countries will continue to integrate into the global trading system, these forces are likely to ensure low inflation in the foreseeable future, reminiscent of the secular deflation associated with broad productivity increases during the classical gold standard in the late nineteenth century. However, such views are not universally shared. Other analysts have offered alternative explanations for the recent inflation performance, including improved monetary policy credibility, broad productivity gains of uncertain duration, or cyclical conditions.[2]

Looking forward, the issue of whether or not globalization has indeed been a factor driving recent inflation behavior has important implications for the conduct of monetary policy. For example, if it could be established that the tailwind from declining prices of many internationally traded goods matters for inflation and is likely to continue, monetary policy would likely have to be less restrictive to meet a certain inflation target than it would have to be otherwise. If the magnitudes and duration of the tailwind were overestimated, however, monetary policy may risk being too expansionary.

Against this background, this chapter explores the relationship between globalization and inflation, using both aggregate and sectoral analysis. The chapter seeks to address the following questions.

- How has globalization affected inflation over the past 15 years or so?
- How has globalization affected prices and costs at the sectoral level?
- Will globalization put downward pressure on inflation in the future, and, if so, what are the implications for monetary policy?

Two points should be noted at the outset.

- The chapter will take the now firmly entrenched goals of low and stable inflation as given.
- As usual, one needs to be specific in delineating the scope of globalization. For the purposes of the chapter, globalization is defined broadly as the acceleration in the pace of growth of international trade in goods, services, and financial assets relative to the rate of growth in domestic trade.[3] At the global level, this encompasses the growth spurts in key emerging market economies—notably China and, to a lesser extent, India. Globalization has also overlapped with economic and financial deregulation in many countries and with the information technology revolution. While an attempt is made to distinguish between these phenomena, this is often difficult to accomplish in practice.

The main authors of this chapter are Thomas Helbling, Florence Jaumotte, and Martin Sommer, with consultancy support from Laurence Ball. Angela Espiritu provided research assistance.

[1]See, among others, BIS (2005); Greenspan (2005); or Fisher (2006).
[2]See, among others, Ball and Moffitt (2001); Kamin, Marazzi, and Schindler (2004); or Buiter (2000).
[3]See Chapter III of the April 2005 *World Economic Outlook*.

Figure 3.1. Inflation
(Distribution of five-year averages of year-on-year CPI inflation across countries)

Inflation declined significantly during the 1980s and 1990s in industrial countries and, with a lag, major emerging markets.

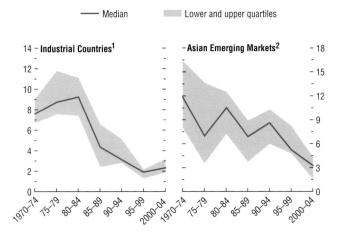

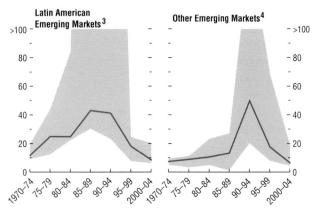

Source: IMF staff calculations.
[1]Australia, Austria, Belgium, Canada, Denmark, Finland, France, Germany, Greece, Iceland, Ireland, Italy, Japan, Luxembourg, the Netherlands, Norway, Portugal, Spain, Sweden, Switzerland, the United Kingdom, and the United States.
[2]China, India, Indonesia, Korea, Malaysia, the Philippines, and Thailand.
[3]Argentina, Brazil, Chile, Colombia, Dominican Republic, Ecuador, Mexico, Peru, and Venezuela.
[4]Czech Republic, Egypt, Hungary, Poland, Romania, Russia, South Africa, and Turkey.

The chapter is organized as follows. The next section provides an overview of salient features of recent inflation developments. The chapter then discusses the broad channels through which globalization affects inflation. The fourth section looks at the relationship between inflation and globalization at the aggregate level. The focus is on how globalization affects inflation variability over the cycle and how large declines in relative import prices influence aggregate inflation. The ensuing section then analyzes the relationship at the sectoral level, focusing on the impact of globalization on domestic (relative) producer prices. The last section provides a summary and policy conclusions.

Recent Inflation Developments

For a meaningful analysis of globalization and inflation in recent years, the relationship needs to be seen against the background of recent inflation developments. Following current central bank practice, aggregate inflation is measured by changes in consumer price indices. The picture would be broadly similar if other aggregate price measures were used.

- *Average inflation in industrial countries has been low since the early 1990s,* reflecting success in stabilizing inflation after the 1970s and early 1980s (Figure 3.1). Specifically, inflation rates have fluctuated around an average of 2–3 percent, with very little dispersion across countries. In contrast, the average was about 9 percent in the early 1980s and dispersion was wider. The low, roughly constant average inflation rates since the early 1990s closely match the central banks' explicit or implicit inflation targets.

- *Inflation in industrial countries has also become less volatile.* Magnitudes of inflation fluctuations around the average are thus smaller, reflecting in part the determined policy efforts in keeping inflation close to targets (Figure 3.2). As a result, expected deviations from an inflation target will now be smaller, everything else being equal.

- *The relationship between current and past inflation in industrial countries has weakened.* This decline in the so-called persistence means that deviations of actual inflation from its average are shorter-lived, and that the impact of disturbances to inflation has declined.[4]

- *The declines in inflation and inflation volatility in the major emerging market economies have lagged the declines in industrial countries.* High inflation remained a problem in many major emerging market economies, notably in Latin America, until the early 1990s. Since then, however, progress in stabilizing inflation at single-digit levels has been remarkable. In the emerging market economies of Asia, inflation typically was close to levels observed in the industrial countries.

- *Prices of services in industrial countries have typically increased faster than those for goods.* This has reflected generally faster productivity growth and higher trade openness in goods production but also the increasing expenditure shares on services associated with rising per capita incomes (Figure 3.3).[5] That said, the differential between services and goods price inflation has recently narrowed in a number of countries and for a number services that have been subject to increased competition, especially in business services (see below).

Understanding Globalization and Inflation: A Broad Framework

There is widespread agreement that globalization has accelerated since the early 1990s. In particular, cross-border trade in financial instruments has skyrocketed, both in advanced and

[4]The extent of the decline remains subject to debate and partly depends on the underlying methodology and data. See, among others, Pivetta and Reis (2004); O'Reilly and Whelan (2005); or Stock (2002).

[5]This trend is documented for the major industrial countries in Clark (2004) and Gagnon, Sabourin, and Lavoie (2004). For similar reasons, broad indices of domestically produced goods and services have usually risen faster than broad price indices for imports, which remain determined mainly by goods price developments.

Figure 3.2. Inflation Volatility
(Standard deviations of rolling five-year windows of year-on-year CPI inflation; distribution across countries)

With declining average rates, inflation volatility has also declined significantly.

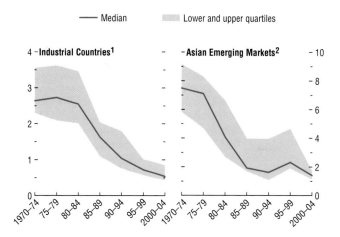

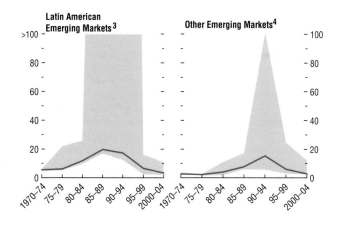

Source: IMF staff calculations.
[1]Australia, Austria, Belgium, Canada, Denmark, Finland, France, Germany, Greece, Iceland, Ireland, Italy, Japan, Luxembourg, the Netherlands, Norway, Portugal, Spain, Sweden, Switzerland, the United Kingdom, and the United States.
[2]China, India, Indonesia, Korea, Malaysia, the Philippines, and Thailand.
[3]Argentina, Brazil, Chile, Colombia, Dominican Republic, Ecuador, Mexico, Peru, and Venezuela.
[4]Czech Republic, Egypt, Hungary, Poland, Romania, Russia, South Africa, and Turkey.

Figure 3.3. Prices of Goods and Services

Price increases in services have typically exceeded those in goods prices, reflecting both supply and demand factors.

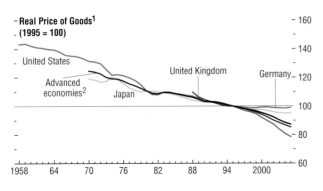

Real Price of Goods[1]
(1995 = 100)

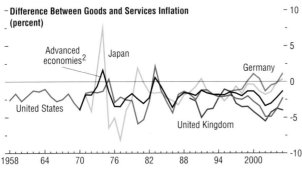

Difference Between Goods and Services Inflation (percent)

Sources: Eurostat; Haver Analytics; national authorities; and IMF staff calculations.
[1]Ratio of consumer prices of goods to overall CPI.
[2]The group of advanced economies includes Australia, Canada, France, Germany, Italy, Japan, the United Kingdom, and the United States.

major emerging market economies (Figure 3.4). In international trade, the locational fragmentation in the production of manufactured goods and the growing importance of emerging market economies in world trade have reshaped many markets and industries. Measures of trade and financial integration obviously are highly correlated, and in the subsequent analysis, trade openness is used to quantify the exposure to globalization.

How have such globalization-related changes affected inflation? As a first step toward answering this question, it is useful to review the main broad channels through which globalization affects national inflation.

- *Policy incentives.* Determined monetary policy efforts aimed at reaching and maintaining low inflation have been a major factor in the global decline in inflation and inflation volatility during the 1980s and 1990s documented earlier. These efforts have reflected a number of factors. Policymakers have learned from the mistakes of the 1970s. Financial deepening, improved fiscal policies, and smaller disturbances have also played a role.[6] Globalization may have played a subtle role in the strengthened conduct of monetary policy by changing the incentives of policymakers (e.g., Rogoff, 2003). In particular, globalization may reduce their ability to temporarily stimulate output (e.g., Romer, 1993) and/or may increase the costs of imprudent macroeconomic policies through the adverse response of international capital flows (e.g., Fischer, 1997; or Tytell and Wei, 2004). Central banks in industrial countries are unlikely to lower their inflation targets further despite continued globalization. This is because of concerns about the adverse consequences of targets that are too close to zero at times of weak aggregate demand conditions. However, in many developing and emerging market countries, globalization is

[6]See, among, others Sims (1999); Romer and Romer (2002); Sargent (1999); Cogley and Sargent (2002 and 2005); Stock (2002); Goodfriend and King (2005); and Sargent, Williams, and Zha (2005).

likely to continue to affect inflation through its impact on central banks' inflation objectives (Box 3.1, "Globalization and Inflation in Emerging Markets").

- *Trade integration and price level declines.* Globalization and the associated rise in trade integration have reduced the barriers to market access by foreign producers. This tends to bolster price competition in domestic markets and increase imports. It has also led to the relocation of production of many internationally traded goods and, to a much smaller extent, of services to the most cost-efficient firms in the countries with a comparative advantage. As a result, the prices of affected goods or services typically decline compared to the general price level—in other words, their relative price declines. A case in point is the observed fall in the relative prices of many manufactured goods, such as textiles, that has accompanied the rapid integration of emerging market economies into the world trade system. Because such goods prices are a component of consumer prices (and other aggregate prices), their fall has, to some extent, contributed to low overall inflation. In addition to such direct effects, increased competition may also have indirect effects by moderating domestic producer prices, input prices, and markups in some industries more generally, given the availability of close substitutes produced abroad.

- *Productivity growth, aggregate supply, and relative prices.* Globalization can raise productivity growth, reflecting increased pressures to innovate and other forms of nonprice competition. By increasing aggregate supply, such productivity gains typically lower prices, which may affect aggregate inflation, along the lines discussed above, with the effects possibly amplified by positive feedback from low inflation to productivity growth. Clearly, globalization-related productivity increases have overlapped with increases due to other factors, including the information technology revolution.

- *Inflation response to domestic output fluctuations.* Globalization may have affected the strength

Figure 3.4. Trade and Financial Openness
(Percent of GDP)

In the early 1990s, international trade and financial openness increased for both industrial and emerging market economies, reflecting an acceleration in globalization.

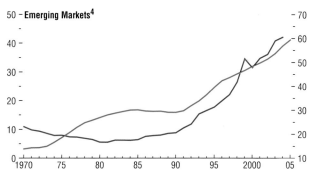

Sources: Lane and Milesi-Ferretti (2006); and IMF staff calculations.
[1]Measured as the sum of exports and imports in percent of GDP (five-year moving average).
[2]Measured as the sum of the stocks of external assets and liabilities of foreign direct investment and portfolio investment in percent of GDP.
[3]Australia, Austria, Belgium, Canada, Denmark, Finland, France, Germany, Greece, Iceland, Ireland, Italy, Japan, Luxembourg, the Netherlands, Norway, Portugal, Spain, Sweden, Switzerland, the United Kingdom, and the United States.
[4]Argentina, Brazil, Chile, China, Colombia, Czech Republic, Dominican Republic, Ecuador, Egypt, Hungary, India, Indonesia, Korea, Malaysia, Mexico, Peru, the Philippines, Poland, Romania, Russia, South Africa, Thailand, Turkey, and Venezuela.

Box 3.1. Globalization and Inflation in Emerging Markets

Average inflation in emerging market economies has declined dramatically since the early 1990s—in many cases from double- and triple-digit levels—to about 5 percent at the present time. This decline in inflation, which has now been sustained for more than half a decade, is impressive compared with the experience from the mid-1970s to the mid-1990s when recurring episodes of loose fiscal and monetary policies, combined with commodity price shocks, kept inflation high (see figure).[1]

The inflation performance has reflected policymakers' increasing preference for low and stable inflation. This policy shift in part resulted from the earlier experience with high and variable inflation in both emerging markets and advanced economies. In the early 1980s, the perceived costs of double-digit inflation increased, as high inflation coincided with low growth and rising unemployment.[2] Governments in the advanced economies responded first by strengthening institutional and policy frameworks to foster monetary stability.[3] The combination of falling external inflation, learning from successful policies elsewhere, and public dissatisfaction with inflation explain much of the subsequent shift to low-inflation policies in emerging markets. Moreover, the gradual deepening of domestic financial markets and greater central bank independence have made inflationary financing of fiscal deficits less common.

Aside from these factors, globalization may also have strengthened policymakers' incentives to conduct prudent monetary policy. Rogoff (1985 and 2003) and Romer (1993) noted that in open economies, policymakers benefit less

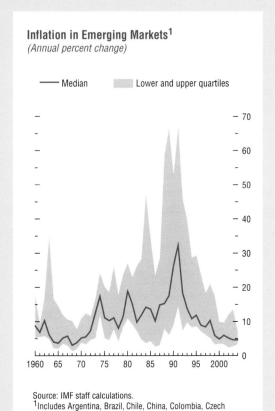

Inflation in Emerging Markets[1]
(Annual percent change)

—— Median   Lower and upper quartiles

Source: IMF staff calculations.
[1]Includes Argentina, Brazil, Chile, China, Colombia, Czech Republic, Dominican Republic, Ecuador, Egypt, Hungary, India, Indonesia, Korea, Malaysia, Mexico, Peru, the Philippines, Poland, Romania, Russia, South Africa, Thailand, Turkey, and Venezuela.

Note: The main author of this box is Martin Sommer.
[1]In the Central and Eastern European countries, inflation spikes were associated with the initial stage of economic transformation.
[2]See the May 2001 issue of the *World Economic Outlook* for a detailed review of inflation developments in emerging markets.
[3]For example, by boosting the central bank transparency and independence and—in some countries— adopting an explicit inflation target (see the September 2005 issue of the *World Economic Outlook*).

from accommodative policies because monetary expansion has a smaller impact on domestic output than in closed economies.[4] In addition, rising trade and financial integration tends to weaken the co-movement between domestic consumption and production, which increases the welfare costs of inflation variability (Razin and Loungani, 2005). Finally, international capital markets may have a disciplining effect on monetary policy, including through the risk of a reduction in foreign investment (see, for example, Tytell and Wei, 2004).

[4]For the recent empirical analysis of links between trade openness and inflation, see Gruben and McLeod (2004). The early research includes Triffin and Grubel (1962) and Iyoha (1977).

Inflation in Emerging Markets: Probit Estimates

	Dependent Variable: Probability of Achieving Low Inflation[1]			
	(1)	(2)	(3)	(4)
Openness[2]	0.39***	0.76***	0.45**	0.30**
Fiscal balance[3]	1.17***	2.48***	1.36***	2.55***
Inflation in advanced economies[4]	−2.95***	−6.12***	. . .	−4.42***
Depth of financial sector[5]	0.94***	1.04**	1.05**	−0.35
Pegged exchange rate regime[6]	. . .	36.46***	. . .	. . .
Central bank independence[7]	. . .	−10.30**	. . .	. . .
Other	. . .	. . .	Time dummies	Country dummies
Sample	1960–2004	1975–2004	1960–2004	1960–2004
Number of observations	815	484	815	804

Sources: IMF, *International Financial Statistics*; Reinhart and Rogoff (2002); World Bank, *World Development Indicators*; *World Economic Outlook;* and IMF staff calculations.

[1]Low inflation is defined as annual inflation below 10 percent. The probability is scaled between 0 and 100. All explanatory variables are lagged by one year. *** denotes statistical significance at the 1 percent level; and ** at the 5 percent level.

[2]Trade in percent of GDP.

[3]Central government balance in percent of GDP.

[4]Expressed as a percentage. The group of advanced economies consists of Australia, Canada, France, Germany, Italy, Japan, the United Kingdom, and the United States.

[5]Money in percent of GDP.

[6]The dummy takes value of 1 (peg) or 0 (otherwise) and is calculated from the Reinhart-Rogoff (2002) data set.

[7]Proxied by the central bank governor's turnover. Higher turnover may be associated with lower central bank independence.

How much has globalization contributed to the decline of inflation in emerging market economies? To answer this question, IMF staff estimated an econometric model that links the likelihood of good inflation performance—defined as annual inflation below 10 percent—to the factors discussed above.[5] Specifically, the model specification includes trade openness, inflation in advanced economies, the depth of the domestic financial sector, and the fiscal balance. In addition, the model also controls for monetary policy credibility and conduct—as measured by central bank independence—and the exchange rate regime (see table).[6] The results suggest that more open economies tend to experience lower inflation rates, even after accounting for the other inflation determinants. Coefficient estimates vary across specifications, but, on average, a country whose trade-to-GDP ratio is 25 percentage points higher than in another country[7] is over 10 percentage points more likely to achieve single-digit inflation. Moreover, since average openness in the sample increased from approximately 30 to 60 percent over the past four decades, globalization has increased the probability of low inflation by about 10 percent in the whole group of emerging markets.[8]

While growing openness may have boosted incentives for the prudent conduct of monetary policy and thus helped to reduce inflation, the model confirms that the other policy determinants discussed above have played a key role. The model attributes a significant weight to

[5]The probit model is estimated for 24 emerging market economies over 1960–2004 (see figure footnote for the complete list).

[6]See Catão and Terrones (2005) and the May 2001 *World Economic Outlook* for analysis of the relationship between fiscal deficits and inflation. Alesina and Summers (1993) document the broad correlation between measures of central bank independence and average inflation. Boschen and Weise (2003) find that U.S. inflation is a useful predictor of inflation spurts in the OECD countries. Ghosh and others (1997) provide evidence that the fixed exchange rate regime can

help reduce inflation, although in the long term, the currency peg may incur large output and inflation costs if it is not supported by appropriate policies and breaks down (Mishkin, 1999).

[7]This figure roughly corresponds to 1 standard deviation of trade openness across countries in the sample.

[8]These calculations are based on specifications (3) and (4) in the table.

Box 3.1 *(concluded)*

the inflation performance in advanced economies. The disinflation that took place there in the early 1980s is estimated to have increased the likelihood of low inflation in emerging markets by 30 percentage points or more. Fiscal policy—a traditional source of inflation pressure—is also identified as an important determinant of inflation. In general, a 10 percent budget deficit relative to GDP increases the likelihood of high inflation by up to 25 percentage points. Moreover, countries that had a high turnover of central bank governors—which tends to be associated with low central bank independence—were less likely to achieve low inflation. Finally, a fixed exchange rate regime on average improved chances of attaining low inflation, although sustaining currency pegs in emerging markets have proven difficult in the long term.[9]

Will low inflation in emerging markets prove to be durable? With price stability abroad and domestic budget positions strengthened, the risk of a sustained increase in inflation rates at present appears small. Should fiscal deficits rise significantly in the future, they could again put pressure on the monetary authorities to inflate, especially in the countries with shallow financial markets. However, the ability of governments to obtain inflationary financing from the central bank and reduce the real value of their debts has increasingly been constrained by greater central bank independence. More generally, the stronger institutional and policy frameworks for monetary policy,[10] deepening financial systems, and policy incentives provided by globalization are all important factors that may help to prevent inflation in emerging markets from returning to high levels.

[9]See the September 2004 issue of the *World Economic Outlook* for a discussion of recent developments in exchange rate regimes in emerging markets.

[10]The September 2005 issue of the *World Economic Outlook* analyzes the benefits and costs of adopting inflation targeting in emerging markets.

of the cyclical response of inflation to output fluctuations for a number of reasons. For example, prices of many items that are produced or consumed at home are increasingly determined by foreign demand and supply factors rather than local factors. This is reinforced by the effects of financial integration, which allows for larger trade balance deficits or surpluses and, thereby, weakens the relationship between domestic output and demand. While it is widely thought that globalization has reduced the sensitivity to fluctuations in domestic production, some aspects of globalization may actually have increased it, as elaborated below.

An important question that naturally arises is that of whether the effects of globalization on aggregate inflation are likely to be lasting or only temporary. There is broad agreement among macroeconomists that in the long run inflation is determined by the nominal anchor, the nominal target variable for monetary policy. If credibly and effectively pursued, this anchor will determine expected and actual inflation in the medium term. Accordingly, to the extent that globalization has contributed to changing nominal anchors through its impact on policy incentives, it may have had permanent effects—most recently primarily in emerging market economies, as noted above.[7] In contrast, to the

[7]On empirical grounds, it would be difficult to argue that globalization has had an impact on the medium-term level of inflation targeted by central banks in advanced economies over the past decade or so. During the 1990s, formal inflation targets were introduced in many advanced economies and have been held largely unchanged since. That said, greater openness may have further strengthened policymakers' resolve to keep inflation close to the targets over the cycle or over their forward-looking policy horizon.

extent that it may have primarily affected relative prices or the cyclical behavior of inflation, the effects may have been substantial over short- to medium-term horizons, but are unlikely to be lasting in the sense of affecting long-run average inflation.

Globalization and Inflation: An Aggregate Perspective

This section analyzes the relationship between inflation and globalization at the aggregate level, focusing on two of the broad channels discussed earlier. The first issue of interest is whether globalization and the associated increase in trade flows have reduced the sensitivity of prices to domestic economic conditions. The second issue is the impact of large declines in the relative import prices of some goods on aggregate inflation.

Inflation over the Business Cycle

How might globalization influence the sensitivity of prices to domestic economic conditions? With the growing share of international trade, prices of many items that are produced or consumed at home are increasingly determined by foreign demand and supply factors. Similarly, stronger foreign competition may reduce the pricing power of domestic corporations, limiting their ability to raise prices during booms.[8] Consequently, prices become less sensitive to the domestic cycle, and the business-cycle volatility of inflation decreases.

Of course, openness is not the only factor that could have weakened the co-movement of output and inflation. The strengthened conduct of monetary policy over the past two decades is

likely to have contributed as well for at least two reasons. First, in a low-inflation environment, firms re-price their production less often (Ball, Mankiw, and Romer, 1988). Second, increasing policy credibility increases the weight that price setters put on expected inflation or inflation targets when they set their prices (Bayoumi and Sgherri, 2004).

However, certain factors related to globalization and the associated push for structural reforms may have acted in the opposite direction, effectively raising the sensitivity of inflation to output. In highly competitive markets with very low margins, producers respond faster to changes in their cost structure and may become more sensitive to demand fluctuations if production costs vary with volumes over the cycle. Co-movements between output and inflation could therefore increase when economies become less regulated, more competitive, and more flexible.[9] Which of the competing factors have so far been most important for the output-inflation relationship needs to be determined empirically.

Figure 3.5 illustrates the behavior of headline and core inflation in selected countries over past business cycles. While the figure can be no substitute for a model that takes into account various determinants of inflation, it seems that over the past two decades, inflation has become less responsive to output gap fluctuations. This has occurred against the background of rising trade openness, greater monetary policy credibility, and more flexible wage-setting mechanisms in some countries (see Figure 3.6).

To examine the issue in more detail, IMF staff constructed a model of inflation for selected advanced economies (see Appendix 3.1 for details).[10] The model is an extension of the tra-

---

[8]See, for example, Kohn (2005). Razin and Loungani (2005) point out that financial integration weakens the link between output and domestic demand by allowing for greater variation in net exports. This can also reduce the consumer price response to domestic output fluctuations.

[9]Cournède, Janovskaia, and van den Noord (2005) find that inflation responds more weakly to economic downturns in economies with greater labor and product market rigidities. Nunziata and Bowdler (2005) present evidence that a high degree of labor market coordination dampens the effect of unemployment movements and other shocks on inflation. By contrast, high unionization rates amplify the inflation response to shocks.

[10]The sample consists of Australia, Canada, France, Germany, Italy, Japan, the United Kingdom, and the United States, and spans 1960–2004.

Figure 3.5. Inflation over the Business Cycle, 1961–2003[1]

(Annual percent change for inflation; percentage points for output gap)

In many countries, the sensitivity of headline and core inflation to the business cycle seems to have diminished.

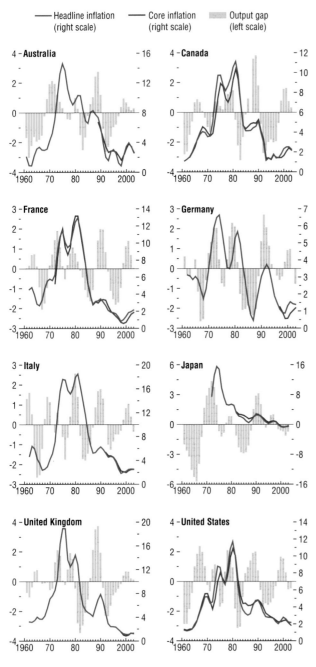

Sources: Eurostat; Haver Analytics; national authorities; and IMF staff calculations.
[1]Output gap is defined as the percent deviation of real GDP from its long-term trend. Core inflation refers to headline CPI excluding food and energy. All variables are expressed as three-year centered moving averages. See Appendix 3.1 for details.

ditional Phillips curve framework, which relates wage inflation to the rate of unemployment or, alternatively, the inflation rate to the degree of spare capacity in the economy. For each country in the panel data set, annual inflation is related to its own lag (to capture the persistence in inflation outcomes, which can reflect policies, structural rigidities, and the importance of past inflation in the formation of expectations) and a measure of spare capacity in the economy. The inflation response to output is allowed to vary across countries and over time, as it is interacted with the various factors discussed above. The basic version of the model also contains oil price changes to account for one particularly important source of large relative price changes with a potentially broad price impact. To control for shifts in policymakers' inflation objectives and expectations about monetary policy behavior, the regressions include either time dummies or a measure of monetary policy credibility.[11] The econometric analysis suggests that the sensitivity of prices to domestic economic conditions has indeed been falling over the past couple of decades (Table 3.1). Currently, the estimated average inflation-output elasticity implies that if a country's output rises above its long-term trend by 2 percentage points for a year,[12] inflation would be higher by 0.4 percentage points in the first year, instead of 0.6 percentage points a couple of decades ago.

Trade openness appears to be the key factor behind the reduced sensitivity of prices to output. The coefficient on openness remains negative (therefore reducing the inflation sensitivity) and statistically significant in most modifications of the basic model. Reduction in labor market rigidities (as measured by an index of centraliza-

[11]One additional point is worth mentioning here. Since the model residuals include, in addition to the modeling error, also the impact of external environment on domestic prices—which is to some extent shared across countries—the panel model is estimated using the Seemingly Unrelated Regression method. This method exploits correlation in the residuals across countries to obtain more precise estimates of the model parameters (Zellner, 1962).

[12]This figure roughly corresponds to 1 standard deviation of output gaps in the sample over 1983–2004.

Table 3.1. Estimates of Output-Inflation Sensitivity and Inflation Persistence in Advanced Economies[1]

Inflation-output elasticity	
1960	0.3
1983	0.3
2004	0.2
Inflation persistence	
1960	0.6
1983	0.7
2004	0.6

Source: IMF staff calculations.

[1]The underlying inflation model relates current inflation to past inflation, a measure of cyclical slack in the economy and other variables. The model coefficients vary across countries and time, and depend on the various factors discussed in the main text. Inflation persistence refers to the effective coefficient on past inflation, and inflation-output elasticity refers to the effective coefficient on the measure of business cycle. The reported coefficients are PPP-weighted average of estimates for Australia, Canada, Germany, France, Italy, Japan, the United Kingdom, and the United States. See Appendix 3.1 for a detailed specification of the inflation model and its variants.

tion and coordination in wage bargaining) in some countries has partly offset the effects of openness by raising the price sensitivity, but this effect tends to be small.[13]

The estimation results also confirm that the strengthened conduct of monetary policy over the past two decades has reduced inflation persistence, as measured by the effective coefficient on the inflation lag, which partly depends on a measure of monetary policy credibility.[14] As policy credibility has improved, the estimated coefficient on the first lag of inflation has declined from over 0.7 in the early 1980s to less than 0.6

[13]For example, the fall in the extent of economy-wide wage bargaining centralization and coordination is estimated to have raised the sensitivity of inflation to output by about 0.025 in Australia and 0.05 in the United Kingdom. It needs to be noted, however, that due to their qualitative nature, the available measures of wage bargaining may be imprecise.

[14]It should be noted that the credibility measure, which was developed by Laxton and N'Diaye (2002), is based on government bonds yields (see Appendix 3.1). It encompasses many of the factors underlying the credibility of monetary policy. While one would expect the measure to reflect primarily expectations about future inflation, such expectations partly depend on the record of previous macroeconomic policies, including past fiscal policies, and institutional arrangements governing these policies, including central bank independence, transparency, and any specific commitment mechanisms to low budget deficits or public debt.

Figure 3.6. Selected Structural Indicators

Trade openness has been rising in most advanced economies. Credibility of monetary policy strengthened substantially during the past two decades, and recovered from the earlier period of monetary instability. Wage-setting mechanisms vary widely across countries but tend to be highly persistent over time.

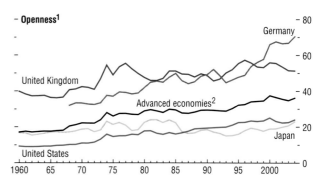

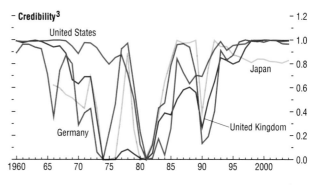

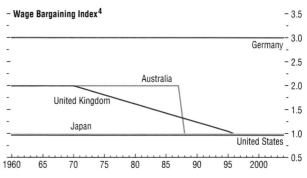

Sources: Elmeskov, Martin, and Scarpetta (1998); Laxton and N'Diaye (2002); Nicoletti and others (2001); and IMF staff calculations.
[1]Share of non-oil trade in GDP.
[2]The group of advanced economies includes Australia, Canada, France, Germany, Italy, Japan, the United Kingdom, and the United States.
[3]Measure of Laxton and N'Diaye (2002). The minimum score for the indicator is zero, the maximum is one. See Appendix 3.1 for details.
[4]Summary index of wage-setting centralization and coordination by Elmeskov, Martin, and Scarpetta (1998), as updated by Nicoletti and others (2001). The wage bargaining index ranges from one (low) to three (high). See Appendix 3.1 for details.

Figure 3.7. Import Prices

Real prices of internationally traded commodities have been on a trend decline. However, import prices are highly volatile, reflecting various factors such as oil price fluctuations and exchange rate movements. In the United States, relative prices of imported consumer and capital goods continue to fall, though on the whole, import prices are now contributing to inflation.

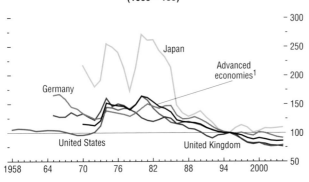

Real Price of Imports in Advanced Economies
(1995 = 100)

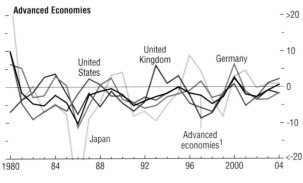

Real Import Price Changes
(percent)

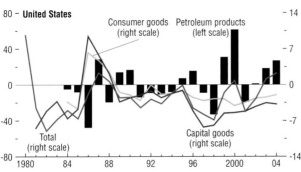

Sources: Haver Analytics; and IMF staff calculations.
[1]The group of advanced economies includes Australia, Canada, France, Germany, Italy, Japan, the United Kingdom, and the United States.

for the last observation.[15] This lowers the extent to which disturbances propagate over time. Continuing with the earlier example, the second-year impact of a temporary 2 percentage point output increase would now almost be to raise inflation in that year by 0.22 percentage points, instead of 0.45 percentage points some 20 years ago. By the third year, that same output disturbance would now almost cease to affect inflation, while earlier, half of its cumulative effect would still be forthcoming. Overall, the analysis suggests that openness contributed over half of the decline in the sensitivity of prices to domestic output, while improved monetary policy credibility and the low inflation environment account for the remainder.[16]

The Impact of Import Price Changes

Trade integration, notably with developing countries and emerging markets, has been accompanied by a rapid decline in the prices of certain goods and services. From the aggregate perspective, this has been reflected in falling real import prices (that is, import prices relative to broad price indices that include prices of domestically produced goods and services) in the advanced economies over the past two decades (Figure 3.7) and was supportive of the declines in the real prices of goods noted earlier.[17] The question of interest is whether the various relative price changes associated with globalization have had a significant impact on inflation in advanced economies and how persistent these effects have been. Clearly, if recent inflation developments in the advanced econo-

---

[15]The estimation results indicate that together with persistence, the implied average annual inflation declined as well—from a peak of about 10 percent in 1981 to roughly 2 percent in 2004.

[16]Loungani, Razin, and Yuen (2001) examined the impact of financial integration on the output–inflation sensitivity and made a similar finding. In their empirical specification, countries with stricter capital controls had a steeper Phillips curve.

[17]Real goods prices would generally be falling on average even in a closed economy because productivity in the goods-producing sectors tends to grow faster than in the services sectors.

mies had reflected tailwinds from globalization, import prices would need to have played a significant role in the process.

A brief look at Figure 3.7 suggests that, in general, the role of import prices in keeping inflation low has likely been limited. The downward trend in relative import prices started before the acceleration in globalization, and the recent fluctuations in these prices do not appear unusual in either magnitude or persistence. On the contrary, they appear to broadly reflect fluctuations in global economic activity, as before. Specifically, during the past decade, relative import prices in advanced economies declined during 1997–98 (in parallel with the Asian crisis when currencies of advanced economies appreciated and prices of many manufactures and commodities fell), increased during the ensuing recovery in Asia and with strong global growth, and then declined again during the 2001–02 downturn. To give a sense of the magnitudes, in the sample of eight advanced economies analyzed in this section, real import prices fell on average by 3.8 percent a year during 1997–98, compared to an average decline of 1 percent a year during 1960–2004.[18] With import shares in the sample ranging from 10 to 35 percent, the immediate direct impact on inflation of import price movements of a few percentage points is likely small.

To examine the impact of relative import prices on inflation more formally, one of the model specifications from the previous subsection explicitly includes import prices (Appendix 3.1 provides details).[19] The estimation results corroborate the intuition—on average, only about one-tenth of an import price decline relative to the long-term trend passes through into inflation during the first year (Table 3.2). Moreover, the effects of an import price decline almost disappear from headline inflation after two years in all countries in the sample.

Table 3.2. The Cumulative Impact of a 1 Percent Decrease in Real Import Prices on Inflation
(Percentage points)

	Impact on Inflation			
	First year	Second year	Third year	Import Share[1]
Australia	−0.10	−0.07	−0.03	0.21
Canada	0.08	−0.07	−0.03	0.34
France	−0.07	−0.01	0.01	0.26
Germany	−0.07	−0.01	—	0.33
Italy	−0.01	−0.05	−0.02	0.26
Japan	−0.08	—	—	0.11
United Kingdom	0.19	−0.07	−0.03	0.28
United States	−0.15	−0.12	−0.06	0.15
Advanced economies[2]	−0.08	−0.07	−0.03	0.20

Source: IMF staff calculations.
[1]Share of imports in GDP.
[2]PPP-weighted average of the sample countries.

What do the estimates above mean in practice? Figure 3.8 presents simulations of the path of inflation under the assumption that real import prices during 1997–2005 were evolving in line with their historical trend. In the first simulation, real import prices during 1997–2005 fall on average at the rate of one percent a year (Scenario A in the figure). The results suggest that the large fall in real import prices in recent years has contributed importantly to inflation developments in the short term. On average, import prices contributed about ½ percentage point to the reduction in inflation in both 1998 and 1999, and over ¼ percentage point in 2002. For some countries, the calculations point to a stronger impact—especially in those cases where the broad decline in prices of internationally traded commodities were accompanied by real appreciation. In the United States, for example, the contribution of import prices to disinflation was 1¼ percentage point in 1998 and over ¾ percentage point in 2002. Excluding the direct impact of oil prices (Scenario B), these magnitudes are reduced by up to ¼–½ percent-

---

[18]The cross-country differences in the broad trend of real import prices are not large and can often be related to the real exchange rate movements. See Clark (2004) for a detailed analysis of country-specific fluctuations in the real goods prices.

[19]The specification includes real import price changes weighted by the import share. The model therefore allows for a time-varying response of inflation to import price changes. The persistence of the effects of import price changes also varies over time because of their dependence on the coefficient on lagged inflation, which evolves in line with monetary policy credibility, as described earlier.

Figure 3.8. The Impact of Import Prices on CPI Inflation
(Annual percent change)

Had import prices evolved during 1997–2005 in line with historical trends, inflation in the advanced economies would—until recently—have been higher. Import prices contributed to disinflation, especially in the late 1990s after the Asian currency crisis (½ percentage point on average in advanced economies and more than 1 percentage point in the United States). Import prices also helped temporarily reduce inflation during the global slowdown in 2001–02.

—— Headline inflation
—— Headline inflation assuming trend import prices (scenario A)[1]
—— Headline inflation assuming trend non-oil import prices (scenario B)[2]

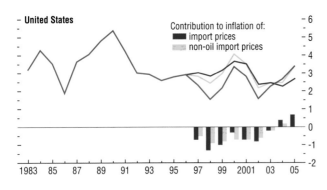

Sources: Eurostat; Haver Analytics; national authorities; and IMF staff calculations.
[1]Scenario A assumes that during 1997–2005, real import prices fell at the historical average rate of about 1 percent a year.
[2]To capture the impact of globalization on inflation more precisely, scenario B removes the impact of oil prices from scenario A. Real import price changes are first decomposed into the contribution of oil prices and non-oil commodities. The scenario then assumes that the contribution of oil prices to import price changes was the same as the actual values during 1997–2005 but the contribution of non-oil commodities was at the historical average rate of about 1.6 percent a year.
[3]The group of advanced economies includes Australia, Canada, France, Germany, Italy, Japan, the United Kingdom, and the United States.

age point, which suggests that the disinflation pressures that can be directly associated with globalization in the production of goods may have been somewhat less.

The simulations also show that during 2003–05, there was almost no globalization-related impact on inflation. The differences between actual and simulated inflation were almost entirely due to oil price increases. Overall, the results suggest that while the initial effects of substantial import price changes can be sizable in times of low inflation—up to the order of 40–60 percent of average inflation—the cumulative effects tend to be small. In both episodes with above-average import price declines, inflation tended to return to its average level within a period of two years in all countries.

When interpreting this finding, it is useful to realize that the effects of price declines generated by foreign competition—such as the falling prices of textiles and other consumer goods—are very similar in their nature to the effects of other, perhaps more "traditional," kinds of so-called price shocks, such as swings in the prices of food or energy. These reflect fluctuations in the equilibrium price of specific products or commodities (relative to prices of other products) because of changes in demand or supply conditions. If policymakers do not change their monetary policy objectives (such as the inflation or monetary target) in the aftermath of the shock and keep policy rates at levels consistent with those objectives, the impact of the disturbances will only be temporary and inflation will return to the range desired by policymakers.[20] In such an environment, the falling prices in the sectors most affected by globalization will simply be offset by rising prices elsewhere, partly because consumers will use the related increase in purchasing power to boost their spending on other goods, including on other imports. Hence, large changes in the import price of some goods need not result in large increases or decreases in broad price indices.

[20]See Hooker (2002) for a recent study on the inflation impact of oil price shocks.

A number of conclusions emerge from this analysis.

- Concerns about the risks of ongoing deflation due to globalization clearly need to be reconsidered. The main reason for the secular deflation in the last era of accelerated globalization—the period 1880–96 under the classical gold standard—was that a roughly constant gold stock did not allow the accommodation of the increased demand for money due to high, productivity-driven growth (Box 3.2, "Globalization and Low Inflation in a Historical Perspective"). In today's environment, with a determined monetary policy response to downward deviations of inflation from the medium-term target at times of large declines in import prices, such risks generally seem small, especially at the current juncture.

- While the results do not suggest a strong persistent effect of falling import prices on aggregate inflation in the advanced economies,[21] the sizable effects found for one- to two-year periods may offer opportunities for disinflation. Under such circumstances, policymakers may permanently lower their target for average inflation while avoiding the output losses that would have been incurred in the absence of such favorable external conditions.[22]

- At the current juncture, with the global economy expanding strongly, there is no noticeable impact of globalization on inflation in the advanced economies. This highlights that in the short term, there are both upside and downside risks to the inflation impact of globalization. The possible upside risks are reinforced by the recent increases in commodity prices, which have been associated with the very same force that has put pressure on prices of manufactures, namely the rising integration of major emerging market economies into the world trade system.[23]

- Since import prices are partly determined by exchange rate fluctuations, the evidence of low persistence in imported inflation is also consistent with the literature on diminishing pass-through of exchange rate changes to inflation (see Box 3.3, "Exchange Rate Pass-Through to Import Prices").

A Sectoral Perspective on Globalization and Prices

This section examines differences in producer price changes across sectors and investigates how they might be related to globalization. The sectoral perspective complements the aggregate perspective and can deepen the understanding of the relationship between globalization and changes in relative prices. In particular, since the extent of globalization differs across sectors, a sectoral approach might help in better identifying the indirect effects of globalization on domestic relative prices—through the competitive effects associated with the increased availability of close substitutes produced abroad—in addition to the direct effect through relative import prices.

Globalization in the sense of more market access for foreign producers fosters competition by increasing the price elasticity of demand, which may force producers to lower margins while rents in factors of production may decrease (Chen, Imbs, and Scott, 2004). In addition, the exit of inefficient firms may lower the average costs of production. The predicted negative relationship between globalization and sectoral inflation, which will be

---

[21]This is consistent with other studies. Kamin, Marazzi, and Schindler (2004) find that China's exports to the United States have only had a marginal impact on import and producer prices in the United States. Similarly, Feyzioglu and Willard (2006) suggest that prices in China have a fairly small and temporary impact on inflation in the U.S. and Japan, although they find evidence of stronger price linkages in some sectors.

[22]See Orphanides and Wilcox (2002) for a discussion of such an "opportunistic approach to disinflation." It should be noted that the role of globalization in disinflation in this case differs from that discussed earlier, as it affects decisions through its impact on the policy environment rather than policy incentives.

[23]See, for example, Chapter IV of the April 2005 *World Economic Outlook* on the long-run oil market outlook.

Box. 3.2. Globalization and Low Inflation in a Historical Perspective

The present era of globalization and low infla-tion has an important precedent: 1880–1914, the era of the classical gold standard. In the context of this chapter, the most noteworthy feature of this precedent is the coincidence of globalization with secular deflation from 1880–96. Given current views that lower cost producers are "exporting deflation," a reexami-nation of the deflation experience under the classical gold standard clearly is of interest. This box documents the extent of deflation, exam-ines the underlying forces, assesses the impact of deflation on economic activity, and discusses implications for today.

Today, it is widely believed that the deflation of 1880–96 reflected the interaction of favorable supply disturbances—productivity growth shifted the aggregate supply curve to the right—and the nominal anchor, the classical gold standard. The latter prevailed from 1880 to 1914, when the majority of countries adhered to the rule of fixing the prices of their currencies in terms of gold (Bordo, 1999). The world price level was determined by the demand and supply of mone-tary gold, which depended on gold production on the one hand and the relative demands on gold for monetary and nonmonetary (e.g., jew-elry, industrial use) purposes on the other (Barro, 1979). In the long run, global prices were anchored by the (roughly constant) mar-ginal cost of producing gold.

In this setup, disturbances to the demand and supply of gold could lead to persistent, but not necessarily permanent, changes in the price level because the stock of monetary gold was exogenous in the short to medium term. In the case of global disturbances, the global price level would change. For example, the increased global income associated with a global produc-tivity boom would boost the demand for mone-tary gold, which, with an unchanged stock of monetary gold, would lead to deflation initially. Over time, however, the stock of monetary gold would adjust because of the implied changes in

the real price of gold (the nominal price of gold divided by the price level). Under deflation, the rise in the real price would encourage gold pro-duction and the search for new sources, as well as the conversion of nonmonetary gold into monetary gold (see, among others, Rockoff, 1984). The resulting increase in the world mon-etary gold stock would generate inflation and thereby offset the price level effects of the ear-lier deflation.

Reflecting this mechanism, the gold standard era was characterized by alternating episodes of inflation and deflation. The top panel of the fig-ure shows the movements in the world gold stock and the world monetary gold stock. Gold production remained fairly stable until the 1890s. Then the combination of the develop-ment of the cyanide process for extracting gold from low-grade ore and the discovery of low-grade deposits in South Africa led to a dramatic expansion in world gold production.

The middle panel of the figure documents the price level behavior during 1880–1914 era in the four core countries of the era—the United Kingdom, France, Germany, and the United States. The broad picture is one of deflation fol-lowed by inflation. Prices fell in all countries between 1880 and 1896 but rose subsequently. The lower panel shows growth in the four coun-tries. While somewhat slower during the defla-tion phase, the sustained growth during the era does not seem consistent with the proposition that this was the period of the "great depres-sion" in the United Kingdom or the "longue stagnation" in France, as economic historians used to classify the years 1880–96 (e.g., Craig and Fisher, 2000).

What were the effects of the secular deflation on economic activity during the first era of glob-alization? Bordo, Landon Lane, and Redish (2004 and 2005) addressed this issue for the 1880–1914 experience of the four core countries using a structural vector-autoregressive model. Specifically, they decompose fluctuations in prices, output, and the money stock in each country into the effects of a gold stock shock, a domestic aggregate supply shock, and a domestic

Note: The main author of this box is Michael Bordo.

Gold, Prices, and Growth Under the Classical Gold Standard

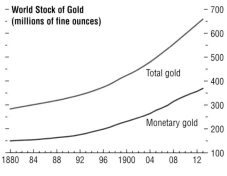

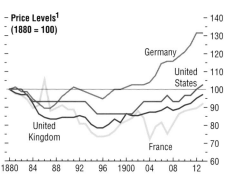

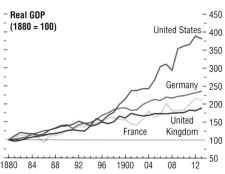

Sources: Bordo and others (2005); and IMF staff calculations.
[1]Implicit GDP deflator.

aggregate demand shock. The key presumption underlying the analysis is that the impact of deflation depends on the underlying disturbance. Deflation owing to shocks to aggregate supply is likely to be different in its interaction with economic activity than deflation due to, say, stagnant gold production or a banking panic.

The results show that in European economies, output movements were mainly driven by supply shocks, while price level fluctuations were dominated by gold stock shocks. In the United States, deflation was driven by positive supply shocks, but also by adverse gold stock shocks (which helped induce serious banking panics) in the mid-1890s, which had real effects. Overall, the evidence suggests that the deflation experience in the nineteenth century was benign, reflecting the prevalence of favorable supply shocks—for example, the second industrial revolution—that were rapidly reflected in real income gains, as there were virtually no nominal rigidities. The latter may not be the case today. Moreover, while pre-1914 deflation seemed benign in its impact, contemporaries did not feel good about it. The common perception was that deflation was depressing. This may have reflected the fact that deflation was largely unanticipated by certain groups affected by its redistribution effects or money illusion.

Overall, the experience with the classical gold standard suggests that the risks of deflation are clearly different today, given that positive inflation targets allow for the more immediate accommodation of increased money demand with strong growth. However, with regard to the credibility of the nominal anchor, the experience of the gold standard still seems relevant. If the nominal anchor is credible, and if agents expect inflation to be anchored at a low level, then temporary disturbances (business cycles)—including, as discussed in the chapter, a large fall in import prices—will lead to temporary departures of inflation from the long-run average. Indeed, under the gold standard, the expected inflation rate hovered around zero and long-run price level uncertainty was low, which is consistent with the observed mean-reversion in price levels (Klein, 1975; Borio and Filardo, 2004; and Bordo and Filardo, 2005). Moreover, the persistence of price level changes was low and symmetric. These features are akin to key characteristics of today's inflation behavior.

Box 3.3. Exchange Rate Pass-Through to Import Prices

Exchange rate pass-through measures the extent to which movements in the nominal exchange rate affect either domestic import prices (first stage) or the consumer price level (second stage). Empirical evidence suggests that the rate of exchange rate pass-through (first and second) varies widely across countries, reflecting their ability to influence import prices in an increasingly global setting, but in general tends to be less than complete.[1] Moreover, the degree of exchange rate pass-through in advanced economies appears to have declined significantly since the 1980s (see the figure). Lower exchange rate pass-through implies that larger movements in the exchange rate are necessary to reduce current account imbalances or influence growth via the import/exchange rate channel. On the other hand, lower exchange rate pass-through may also enhance the performance of monetary policy by limiting the impact of exogenous exchange rate fluctuations on the domestic price level and output.

A number of competing arguments have been offered for the decline in exchange rate pass-through, a subset of which includes:

- *Lower headline inflation.* Exchange rate pass-through is linked explicitly to the level of inflation and, indirectly, to domestic monetary conditions (positive association). In contrast to the standard literature on the determinants of exchange rate pass-through, which emphasizes market structure and the elasticity of demand, Taylor (2000) argues that in a stable, low inflation environment supported by a credible inflation-targeting regime, firms reduce the extent to which they pass on exchange-related cost increases because the

Response of Import Prices to Nominal Effective Exchange Rate Movements
(Percentage decline: 1990–2002 over 1975–89)

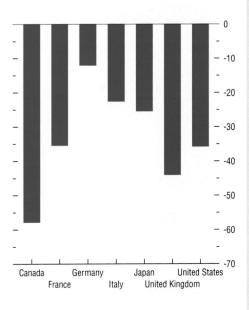

Source: IMF staff calculations.

Note: The authors of this box are Kornélia Krajnyák and Sam Ouliaris.

[1]See Goldberg and Knetter (1997) for an extensive review of the empirical literature on exchange rate pass-through. In the case of the United States, they conclude that the median estimate of exchange rate pass-through is approximately 0.5. More recent studies (e.g., Marazzi, Sheets, and Vigfusson, 2005) suggest that the first stage exchange rate pass-through coefficient has declined to 0.2.

latter are likely to be perceived as temporary in such an environment. Others link exchange rate pass-through to inflation by arguing that the costs of maintaining fixed prices (namely, forgone profits) are much greater than the costs of changing prices. Numerous empirical papers have obtained support for Taylor's (2000) hypothesis by including the level and variability of inflation in standard empirical models of exchange rate pass-through (e.g., Choudhri and Hakura, 2001).

- *Changes in import composition.* Campa and Goldberg (2002) question the macroeconomic/monetary explanation for the decline in exchange rate pass-through exposited in Taylor (2000). In particular, they argue that the decline in exchange rate pass-through is better explained in terms of a shift in the import bundle away from energy and raw materials toward manufactured goods, which have lower estimated pass-through rates. While Campa and Goldberg (2002) confirm that countries with lower inflation have lower exchange rate pass-through coefficients, they conclude that the decline in exchange rate pass-through is due more to a change in the composition of imports rather than lower inflation. This view is largely endorsed by Marazzi, Sheets, and Vigfusson (2005) for the United States, but the authors also emphasize the role of China's increasing presence in the U.S. market.

- *Structural reforms.* Since the early 1980s, a number of industrial countries have implemented structural reforms that have resulted in substantial gains in multifactor productivity, lower unit costs, and greater choice to consumers (see Rogoff, 2003; and Chen, Imbs, and Scott, 2004). As a result, firms now operate in a more competitive environment relative to the 1980s, thereby reducing their ability to pass on cost increases. Moreover, by lowering unit costs of production, multifactor productivity gains increase the capacity of firms to absorb exchange rate losses, possibly lowering exchange rate pass-through. Of course, the validity of the structural reform argument relies on the presence of imperfect competition and excessive "quasi-rents" (or "abnormal" markups) to monopolistic firms prior to the introduction of the reforms. Exchange rate pass-through could rise once these

markups decline to more normal levels—for instance, as the level of competition approaches what is prevalent in energy and commodity markets. Evidence in favor of the "structural reform" hypothesis is reported in Ouliaris (2006), who finds that the decline in exchange rate pass-through can be better explained using structural reform indicators rather than the average rate of inflation or other proxies for monetary conditions. Moreover, the decline in pass-through is evident only in the short-run/business cycle components of the data, and is therefore likely to be *temporary* in nature.

Has exchange rate pass-through declined permanently? If structural reforms or the changing composition of international trade are the main driving factors, then the decline is likely to be temporary. Rationalizing lower pass-through by appealing to "lower cost producers" or "decreasing importer's willingness to increase domestic prices" relies on the existence of significant markups over costs or "quasi-rents" that are likely to be eventually eroded in a heightened competitive environment. The tighter margins will naturally limit the ability of competitive firms to absorb nominal exchange rate movements, placing upward pressure on the degree of exchange rate pass-through to import prices. However, the eventual impact on final goods prices will be influenced by the conduct and credibility of monetary policy, particularly in an inflation-targeting setting.

referred to as the "global competition hypothesis," has several implications at the sectoral level. For example, if increased exposure to foreign competition has helped to contain inflation, one would expect smaller price increases in manufacturing than in services, as the former

sector has long been, and continues to be, more open than the latter.

Patterns in overall producer price inflation are very similar to those for consumer price inflation discussed earlier.[24] After declining in the late 1980s and early 1990s, producer price

---

[24]The analysis is based on sectoral producer prices and their components from the OECD's Structural Analysis (STAN) Database. For consistency, much of the analysis is performed for the advanced economies, with the most complete data coverage for the period 1987–2003 (Austria, Denmark, Finland, France, Germany, Italy, Japan, Korea, Luxembourg, Norway, and the United States). Unless mentioned otherwise, sectoral averages are simple averages of the country data. See Appendix 3.2 for a description of the data.

Figure 3.9. Inflation in Manufacturing and Business Services in Selected Industrial Countries[1]
(Annual percent change)

While inflation in manufacturing has been consistently below overall inflation, business services have also significantly contributed to the decline in inflation.

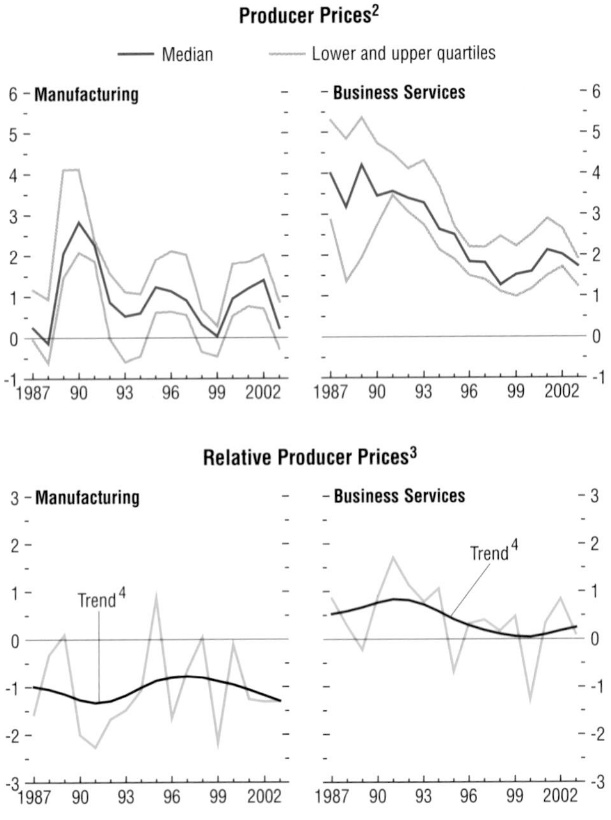

Producer Prices[2]

——— Median   ——— Lower and upper quartiles

Relative Producer Prices[3]

Sources: OECD, STAN database; and IMF staff calculations.
[1] Sample includes Austria, Denmark, Finland, France, Germany, Italy, Japan, Korea, Luxembourg, Norway, and the United States.
[2] Three-year moving average.
[3] Difference between sectoral producer price inflation and producer price inflation in all sectors.
[4] Trend derived using Hodrick-Prescott filter.

inflation has been about stable from the mid-1990s. Comparing manufacturing and business services—the two largest sectors that have been most exposed to globalization-related changes over the past decade or so—shows that in the former, producer price increases have consistently been below those registered in overall prices (Figure 3.9).[25]

In contrast, while changes in producer prices in business services used to exceed overall producer price inflation, they have fallen at a faster rate than overall inflation since the mid-1990s, thereby contributing at least as much as manufacturing to the decline in overall producer price inflation.[26] A possible explanation for this finding could be the substantial extent of deregulation in important business services sectors, including, for example, telecommunications, although improvements in the measurement of prices of services may also have played a role.[27]

Within manufacturing, relative prices have, on average, declined less in low-tech sectors than in high-tech sectors (the distinction is based on a measure of spending on research and development). Since the mid-1990s, however, both low- and high-tech sectors have experienced a similar trend of disinflation (Figure 3.10).[28] Likewise,

---

[25] Together, manufacturing and business services sectors account for some 70 percent of a typical industrial country economy in the sample. The other sectors are agriculture, mining, construction, utilities, and community, social and personal services (including government). Details on the sectors and the subsectors therein are provided in Appendix 3.2.

[26] Other sectors' contributions are smaller in part because their weights in the overall economy are smaller.

[27] Output volumes (and hence prices) are notoriously difficult to measure in services due to the complexity of the products. As a result, part of the productivity increases or quality enhancements are recorded as price increases instead of volume increases. To the extent that measurement may have improved over the last 15 years, this could partly explain a decrease in measured business services inflation.

[28] It should be noted that sectoral price changes are often expressed relative to the aggregate rate of producer price inflation in order to eliminate fluctuations in inflation that are common to all sectors. An example would be fluctuations due to monetary policy, which in itself tends to affect all sectoral prices equally in the longer run.

price increases in high-skill sectors (based on average education levels of the labor force) have, on average, been lower than in low-skill sectors, both in manufacturing and in the overall economy.[29]

Overall, the most important recent changes in broad patterns of sectoral producer price developments appear to have occurred in some services and high-skill, high-tech manufacturing sectors. At first glance, these results are difficult to reconcile with a narrow version of the global competition hypothesis that views most of the competitive pressure arising from the integration of developing and emerging market countries into the world trade system as being in low-tech and low-skill sectors. The results are, however, consistent with a broader notion of the hypothesis that views trade integration more generally, including in high-end manufacturing, as the driving force behind increasing global competition. China, for example, exports a large and increasing set of products that may be classified as high-tech or high-skill.[30] The findings may also reflect the impact of the information technology revolution, which has led to sharp declines in the relative prices of high-tech and high-skill electronics goods. Finally, it is worth noting that the data also suggest that increased competition may have begun to affect price developments in the business services sectors.

How Has Globalization Affected Prices in Different Sectors of the Economy?

How do these sectoral patterns in inflation relate to globalization? To analyze this, changes in relative producer prices in a sector were related to changes in the sector's exposure to globalization, as measured by its import-to-production ratio (Chen, Imbs, and Scott, 2004).

[29]Agriculture, mining, refined petroleum, and community, social, and personal services are excluded from both the low-skill and high-skill aggregates.

[30]According to Rodrik (2006), the implied income level in China's export basket is much higher than its actual (PPP-adjusted) income.

Figure 3.10. Relative Producer Price Inflation by Technological and Skill Intensity[1]
(Annual percent change)

Interestingly, inflation has been higher in low-tech sectors than in high-tech sectors. In the overall economy, low-skill sectors also have had higher inflation than sectors classified as high-skill.

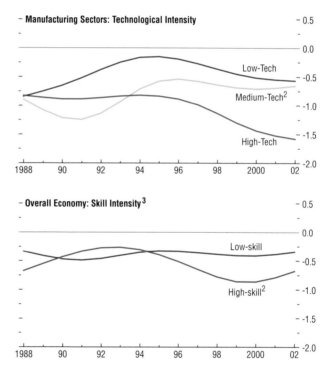

Sources: OECD, STAN database; and IMF staff calculations.
[1]Growth in the ratio of sectoral producer price indices and the producer price index in all sectors. See Appendix 3.2 for the list of sectors included within each grouping.
[2]Excludes refined petroleum products.
[3]Excludes agriculture, mining, and community, social, and personal services sectors.

The expectation is that the relationship is negative; faster increases in trade openness in a sector would be associated with smaller producer price increases. Simple correlations confirm this expectation, as the relationship between changes in the relative producer price and changes in the import ratio is indeed negative (Figure 3.11). In particular, in textiles, telecoms, and electrical and optical equipment, the strong increases in openness are clearly associated with negative changes in relative prices.[31]

Econometric analysis supports this broad finding (details of the econometric analysis can be found in Appendix 3.2). The analysis is performed both for the manufacturing sectors, for which trade data are more readily available and are of better quality, and for the manufacturing and business services sectors together.

The results show that changes in the import ratio and changes in relative producer prices are negatively and significantly related (Table 3.3). According to the central estimates for the manufacturing sector, a 1 percent increase in the import ratio reduces the relative producer price by about 0.1 percent. The results also suggest that the effect tends to be the same for manufacturing and business services sectors, as simple tests for a differential impact yield insignificant results. Changes in labor productivity also have a significant impact on changes in relative producer prices, with a 1 percent increase in labor productivity also reducing relative producer prices by about 0.1 percent.[32] As shown in Appendix 3.2, the impact of globalization on producer prices is robust and does not depend on a specific model or a specific variable to measure globalization, even when allowing for reverse causality (including for productivity growth).

Figure 3.11. Producer Price Inflation and Openness
(1987–2003; annual percent change)

Changes in trade openness and relative producer prices are negatively correlated.

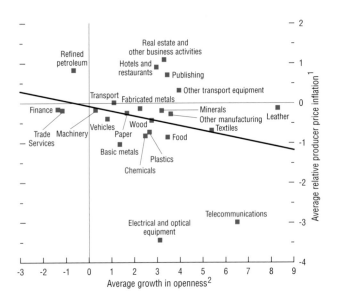

Sources: OECD, STAN database; and IMF staff calculations.
[1]Growth in the ratio of sectoral producer price indices and the producer price index in all sectors.
[2]Growth in a sector's import-to-production ratio.

---

[31]A similar picture emerges for the simple correlation between the relative unit labor cost growth and the import ratio growth.

[32]Increased productivity growth does, to some extent, result from increased competitive pressures due to globalization, but this indirect effect of globalization on inflation is very small, as detailed in the next subsection.

Table 3.3. Impact of Trade Openness on Relative Producer Price Inflation[1]

| | Dependent Variable: Changes in Relative Producer Prices | | |
| | Manufacturing[2] (16 sectors) | | Manufacturing and business services[2] (22 sectors) |
Explanatory Variables	1977–2003 (all countries available)	1988–2003 (core countries)[3]	1977–2003 (all countries available)
Change in import share	–0.11**	–0.12***	–0.12**
Difference for services[4]	. . .	. . .	–0.01
Change in labor productivity	–0.10***	–0.09***	–0.10***
Difference for services[4]	. . .	. . .	–0.08

Source: IMF staff calculations.

[1]All variables are in natural logarithms. The equations are estimated by two-step feasible generalized method of moments treating changes in import shares as an endogenous variable. Control variables include the dollar exchange rate interacted with sectoral dummies (effect through cost of intermediates), and sectoral and country dummies. *** denotes statistical significance at the 1 percent level; ** at the 5 percent level.

[2]The refined petroleum sector is excluded from the regressions because its behavior is strongly affected by oil price developments.

[3]Restricted to countries used in the descriptive analysis of sectoral inflation patterns.

[4]Variables interacted with a dummy variable indicating a business services sector.

Put another way, the increase in openness explains about 30 percent of the 1 percent inflation differential between manufacturing and the overall economy during 1987–2003 while labor productivity growth accounts for about 40 percent of this differential (Figure 3.12). Increased openness has played a particularly important role in Japan and the United States, where the manufacturing sectors appear to have opened relatively more during the past 15 years than in other countries.

Within manufacturing, increased openness contributed about twice as much to lower inflation in low-tech sectors than in high-tech sectors, in line with what conventional wisdom would have predicted.[33] Interestingly, changes in openness were roughly similar between high-skill and low-skill manufacturing sectors, and the differ-

[33]Part of the difference in relative price changes between high-tech and low-tech sectors remains unexplained: the model underpredicts the fall in relative prices of high-tech sectors while it overpredicts the fall in low-tech sector prices.

Figure 3.12. Contributions to Declines in Relative Producer Prices[1]

(Percent; annual average)

Increased openness contributed approximately 0.3 percentage point to the average decline in relative producer prices in manufacturing.

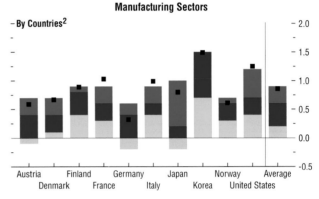

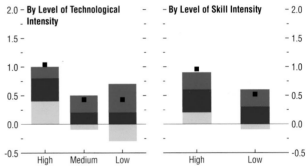

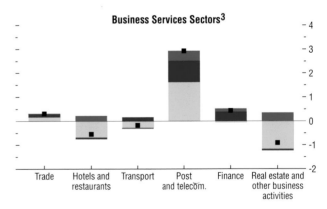

Sources: OECD, STAN database; and IMF staff calculations.

[1]Based on estimates of the global competition hypothesis reported in column two of Table 3.3. Positive values reflect contributions to decreases in relative producer prices while negative values reflect contributions to increases in relative producer prices.

[2]Averages are for the period 1987–2003 except for France (1987–2002), Germany (1991–2003), and Korea (1995–2003).

[3]Averages are for the period 1992–2002.

Figure 3.13. Producer Price Inflation by Cost Components
(Annual percent change)

The decline in unit labor cost increases appears to be greater than the decline in producer price inflation (PPI). On the other hand, changes in other cost components, such as unit gross operating surplus, have been moving relatively closely with PPI.

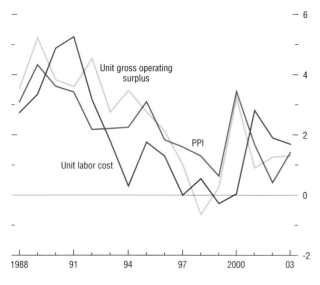

Sources: OECD, STAN database; and IMF staff calculations.

ences in relative inflation rates between these two types of sectors appear to be primarily due to higher labor productivity growth in high-skill sectors. Looking at business services, the contribution of globalization to lower inflation was as strong as in manufacturing in a number of sub-sectors, especially telecoms, other business activities, and hotels and restaurants (the latter category includes some tourism services). In finance and telecoms, sizable productivity increases also had a moderating effect on sectoral producer prices.

The impact of globalization in the manufacturing sectors in most countries has increased in recent years. While openness explained only one-quarter of the decline in relative prices of manufacturing over the period 1987–94, it accounted for about 40 percent of the decline over the more recent period. This acceleration of globalization was visible at all levels of technological intensity, but more so in low-skill than high-skill activities.

Finally, if trade integration in business services sectors were to reach the levels currently seen in manufacturing—which would mean that the average import ratio in business services would quadruple[34]—the relative producer prices for these services would, on average, decline by slightly less than 20 percent. This clearly illustrates the substantial impact that further trade integration in services could have. Clearly, such an increase in openness would occur gradually, and the year-on-year declines in relative prices of business services would thus be smaller.

Overall, therefore, the analysis provides robust support for the global competition hypothesis, with differences in the openness explaining about one-third of the differences in relative producer prices. That said, in terms of the actual

[34]This illustrates how despite strong opening in some services sectors in recent years, levels of openness in business services remain low on average compared to manufacturing, even when the provision of services through foreign affiliates is taken into account (considered to be imports).

Table 3.4. Producer Price Inflation by Cost Components[1]
(Average deviations from changes in the overall economy in percent)

	Manufacturing and Business Services		Manufacturing				
	Manufacturing	Business services	High-tech	Medium-tech[2]	Low-tech	High-skill[2]	Low-skill
Changes in producer prices and costs[3]							
Producer prices	**−1.0*****	0.4	**−0.9****	−0.6	−0.4	**−0.9****	−0.6
Unit labor costs	**−1.2*****	−0.1	**−1.5****	−0.7	−0.6	**−1.4****	−0.7
Nominal labor compensation	**0.6*****	−0.2	**0.7****	0.2	0.3	**0.7****	0.3
Real productivity	**1.8*****	−0.1	**2.7*****	1.1	1.0	**2.6*****	1.2
Unit intermediate costs	**−1.0*****	1.1	−0.8	−0.6	−0.5	−0.9	−0.6
Unit gross operating surplus[4]	−0.8	−0.2	2.7	−0.7	1.2	4.0	0.2
Contribution to producer price inflation by cost components[5]							
Unit labor costs	**−0.4*****	—	**−0.5****	−0.2	−0.3	**−0.4***	−0.3
Unit intermediate costs	**−0.2*****	0.2	−0.2	−0.1	0.1	**−0.3+**	0.0
Unit gross operating surplus[4]	**−0.4*****	0.2	−0.3	−0.3	−0.2	−0.2	−0.3

Source: IMF staff calculations.

[1]A bold entry indicates that the deviation from the country average is significant at the 5 percent level. Significant differences between sectors (e.g., high-tech versus medium-tech and low-tech) are marked by *** (1 percent confidence level); ** (5 percent confidence level); * (10 percent confidence level); or + (15 percent confidence level).

[2]The refined petroleum sector is excluded from medium-tech and high-skill because its behavior is strongly impacted by oil price changes.

[3]The entry "−1.0" for changes in producer prices in manufacturing means that annual inflation in manufacturing was on average (across countries and years) 1 percentage point lower than inflation in the overall economy.

[4]The sample size is somewhat smaller for the unit gross operating surplus.

[5]A contribution of unit labor costs to producer price inflation in manufacturing of −0.4 means that changes in unit labor costs imply that annual producer price inflation should be on average −0.4 percentage points below overall producer price inflation.

moderation of domestic producer prices, the estimated magnitudes of the globalization effects are relatively small. On average, the increased trade openness has reduced relative producer prices in manufacturing by about 0.3 percentage point a year over the past 15 years.

A Cost Perspective on the Moderation in Sectoral Producer Prices

How has the moderation in sectoral producer prices been mirrored in producer's cost components, especially unit labor costs? By definition, changes in producer prices must be reflected in changes in at least one of the following components: unit labor cost, unit intermediate cost, unit gross operating surplus (or loss), and unit net taxes. As discussed in Appendix 3.2, the change in producer prices is just the weighted average of changes in its components, with weights given by the cost shares.

At the economy-wide level, the most noticeable feature of cost developments is the greater decline in unit labor cost increases compared to producer price inflation during the mid- to late 1990s (Figure 3.13). In contrast, changes in other cost components appear to have closely followed changes in overall producer prices. As a result, the labor share declined during the 1990s.[35]

Differences in unit labor costs also appear to explain most of the differences in cost developments between manufacturing and business services and within manufacturing (Table 3.4). Labor compensation in manufacturing increased in nominal terms at a faster rate and in business services at a slower rate than in the overall economy. However, in manufacturing, the faster rise in nominal compensation was more than offset by strong labor productivity growth, so that unit labor costs increased at a rate below that in the overall economy. Similarly, within manufactur-

[35]The labor share is the ratio of the unit labor cost over the unit producer price.

Table 3.5. Impact of Trade Openness on Productivity, Labor Compensation, and Unit Labor Costs[1]
(Manufacturing subsectors relative to the overall economy)[2]

Explanatory Variables	Dependent Variable		
	Change in relative productivity	Change in relative labor compensation	Change in relative unit labor cost
Change in import share	0.12**	−0.10***	−0.09***
Change in relative labor productivity	. . .	0.63***	−0.71***
Interacted with import share	. . .	−0.18*	. . .

Source: IMF staff calculations.
[1]All variables are in natural logarithms. The equations are estimated by two-step feasible generalized method of moments treating changes in import shares and changes in relative labor productivity as endogenous variables. Other control variables include sectoral and country dummy variables. *** denotes statistical significance at the 1 percent level; ** at the 5 percent level; and * at the 10 percent level.
[2]The sample covers the period 1977–2003, the maximum number of countries, and 16 manufacturing subsectors. The refined petroleum sector is excluded from the regressions because its behavior is strongly affected by oil price developments.

ing, much stronger productivity growth, not fully compensated by stronger increases in nominal labor compensation, accounted for the smaller increase in unit labor costs in high-tech sectors compared to the medium- or low-tech sectors, and in high-skill sectors compared to low-skill sectors.

Regarding other costs, relative declines in unit intermediate costs appear to have contributed to lower relative producer price inflation in manufacturing, but not in business services, where these costs actually rose faster than in the overall economy. Finally, the rate of change in the gross operating surplus—which includes both the cost of capital and profits—has declined broadly in line with overall producer price inflation. While there is some evidence that the surplus has increased relatively less in manufacturing than in business services, the difference appears not to be significant.

Econometric analysis confirms that sectoral differences in openness partly explain these pat-

terns in unit labor costs and labor compensation. An increase in openness is found to reduce the response of nominal labor compensation to productivity changes, both directly, as a 1 percent increase in the import ratio of a sector reduces its relative compensation by about 0.1 percent for a given level of productivity growth, and indirectly through a reduction in the response of compensation to productivity growth (Table 3.5). The effects of openness on labor compensation remain negative even if the significant, small positive relationship between openness and productivity (and, therefore, labor compensation) is considered; a 1 percent increase in sectoral openness raises sectoral productivity by 0.1 percent, after controlling for the overall level of productivity in the economy.[36] Unit labor costs are affected in a similar way by openness.[37]

Overall, therefore, the empirical evidence appears to support the proposition that the moderating effects of globalization on domestic producer prices are restraining unit labor costs and labor compensation. In addition, a fall in relative unit intermediate costs appears to have played some role in explaining the faster decline in relative prices in manufacturing. This could reflect outsourcing, which, in turn, could in part explain the behavior of unit labor costs. Evidence for the gross operating surplus is less conclusive. Finally, the analysis also highlights the important role that productivity differentials play in explaining differences in unit labor cost and wage behavior across sectors.

Summary and Policy Conclusions

This chapter has examined the proposition that globalization has been an important factor behind low and steady inflation in recent years. The main points arising from the chapter are as follows.

---

[36]The relationship between openness and productivity might actually be stronger but data limitations prevent obtaining better estimates by controlling for more determinants of sectoral productivity (such as spending on research and development).

[37]The effect of labor productivity on unit labor costs is negative but smaller than minus one (about −0.7) because productivity increases are partly absorbed by compensation gains.

- Over the medium term, the prevailing nominal anchor—such as the central bank's inflation target—determines inflation. Therefore, the impact of globalization on inflation will be temporary unless it changes the overarching objectives of monetary policy. This is unlikely in industrial countries given the already low single-digit inflation targets (explicit or implicit). In emerging market and developing countries, however, greater openness appears to have been—and is likely to remain—an important factor behind the sustained improvement in inflation.

- The direct effect of globalization on inflation through import prices has in general been small in the industrial economies. That said, when global spare capacity increases—such as during the 1997–98 Asian financial crises and the 2001–02 global slowdown—import price declines have had sizable effects on inflation over one- to two-year periods, shaving more than 1 percentage point off actual inflation in some advanced economies. With low average inflation, such effects are economically significant. This lends support to the view that inflation targets should not be set too close to zero—otherwise shocks of this size could result in periods of deflation.

- Globalization has contributed to reducing the sensitivity of inflation to domestic capacity constraints in advanced economies over the past couple of decades—for example, through the impact on the labor markets and wages. As global economic developments have become increasingly important for domestic inflation, they will require closer monitoring by monetary policymakers in the years ahead.

- Globalization has had a significant effect on relative prices in industrial economies. Sectors that have become more exposed to foreign competition have seen the largest relative price declines in recent years. Nevertheless, globalization is not the only factor driving relative price changes. While openness has been important, particularly in low-tech and low-skill sectors, productivity growth has also contributed significantly to relative price changes, particularly in the high-tech manufacturing and services sectors. Indeed, while price increases in the manufacturing sector have consistently been below those in services, the decline in inflation in some services sectors since the mid-1990s has been more pronounced, contributing as much to the decline in overall producer price inflation as the manufacturing sector.

Against this background, the immediate policy concern is judging how globalization may impact inflation in the future. Globalization has undoubtedly provided some break on inflation in the industrial economies in recent years and has allowed for a more measured monetary policy tightening to date. Ongoing trade integration will continue to put downward pressure on prices in many industries in the foreseeable future, although the extent of these pressures will vary with the economic cycle. The experience with earlier episodes of rapid integration, such as those of Japan from the mid-1950s, suggests that China's share in world trade may double over the next 10 years or so.[38] Moreover, international trade in services is also likely to accelerate, leading to declining relative prices in the concerned sectors.

Notwithstanding these developments, however, globalization cannot be relied upon to keep a lid on inflationary pressures in present circumstances. Strong global growth and diminishing economic slack have reduced the restraining impact of declining import prices on inflation, and with strong global growth expected to continue, the primary risk is that a further upturn in import prices could result in stronger inflationary pressures going forward, particularly in countries that are well advanced in the economic cycle. The possibility of further, partly globalization-related, commodity price increases

---

[38]See Chapter II in the April 2004 *World Economic Outlook*.

Table 3.6. Inflation in Advanced Economies: SUR Estimates

Estimated Equation: $\pi_{it} = c_i(1 + \phi Credib_{it}) + \alpha_i(1 + \theta Credib_{it})\pi_{it-1} + \beta_i(1 + \gamma Open_{it}^{DV} + \lambda Credib_{it}^{DV} + \delta\overline{\pi}_{it}^{DV} + \chi Bargain_{it}^{DV})y_{it} + \varepsilon_{it}$

Model	(1)	(2)	(3)	(4)	(5)
c_i (average)	0.010***	0.013***	0.011***	0.010***	0.012***
ϕ	−0.091	. . .	−0.309*	−0.105	−0.098
α_i (average)	0.768***	0.641***	0.774***	0.763***	0.748***
θ	−0.243***	. . .	−0.232***	−0.241***	−0.275***
β_i (average)	0.223***	0.312***	0.217***	0.237***	0.201***
γ	−2.711***	−1.719*	−1.915*	−2.517***	−1.737+
λ	−0.309	−0.154	. . .	−0.225	. . .
δ	. . .	. . .	0.481	. . .	. . .
χ	. . .	. . .	. . .	−0.233	. . .
Oil price					
Current (average)	0.032***	. . .	0.026***	0.032***	. . .
Lagged (average)	0.020***	. . .	0.021***	0.020***	. . .
Import prices × import share					
Current (average)	. . .	. . .	. . .	. . .	0.224***
Lagged (average)	. . .	. . .	. . .	. . .	0.122*
Time dummies	No	Yes	No	No	No
Memorandum:					
Inflation-output elasticity[1]					
1960	0.26	0.31	0.35	0.27	. . .
1983	0.27	0.31	0.24	0.27	0.19
2004	0.17	0.24	0.19	0.17	0.16
Adjusted R^2 (average)	0.823	. . .	0.812	0.817	0.726
Sample	1960–2004	1960–2004	1960–2004	1960–2004	1970–2004
Number of observations	333	333	284	333	278

Source: IMF staff calculations.

Notes: The inflation model was estimated for Australia, Canada, Germany, France, Italy, Japan, the United Kingdom, and the United States using the Seemingly Unrelated Regressions estimator. *Credib* stands for the monetary policy credibility measure of Laxton and N'Diaye (2002); *Open* denotes a country's openness to trade; $\overline{\pi}$ is the average inflation level; and *Bargain* is the wage bargaining index of Elmeskov, Martin, and Scarpetta (1998) and Nicoletti and others (2001). The variables labeled *DV* are expressed as deviations from the sample mean. *Average* refers to the simple average of country-specific coefficients or regression statistics. *** denotes statistical significance at the 1 percent level; ** at the 5 percent level; * at the 10 percent level; and + at the 15 percent level.

[1]PPP-weighted average of the sample countries.

adds to these upside risks from the external sector. Monetary policymakers must therefore remain vigilant for any signs of a pickup in inflation in the period ahead.

Appendix 3.1. Sample Composition, Data Sources, and Methods

The main author of this appendix is Martin Sommer.

This appendix provides further details on the sample composition, the data and their sources, and the empirical strategies used in the analysis of inflation in the chapter.

Inflation Model

The inflation model presented in Table 3.6 consists of eight equations, one for each country in the sample: Australia, Canada, France, Germany, Italy, Japan, the United Kingdom, and the United States. Most parameters of the model are allowed to vary across countries (constant, average persistence, and average slope of the output-inflation relationship). However, it is assumed that changes in openness, credibility, average inflation, and wage-bargaining index influence these country-specific parameters similarly, through multiplicative terms.[39] To capture changes in inflation persistence over time, the

[39]Variables labeled *DV* denote deviations from the sample mean. The equation also contains contemporaneous and lagged oil price changes to control for large inflation shocks or, alternatively, import prices.

constant term and the coefficient on past inflation depends on a measure of monetary policy credibility detailed below.

$$\pi_{it} = c_i (1 + \phi Credib_{it}) + \alpha_i (1 + \theta Credib_{it})\pi_{it-1}$$
$$+ \beta_i (1 + \gamma Open_{it}^{DV} + \lambda Credib_{it}^{DV} + \delta\overline{\pi_{it}^{DV}}$$
$$+ \chi Bargain_{it}^{DV}) y_{it} + \varepsilon_{it}.$$

The model is estimated over 1960–2004 using an iterative Seemingly Unrelated Regressions estimator. The starting values for the iterative estimation are Least-Squares estimates of the system.[40] The inflation-output elasticity and inflation persistence in Table 3.1 were calculated for each country separately from specification (4) in Table 3.6, using the country-specific coefficient estimates and actual values of openness, credibility, and other relevant variables. The advanced country average is computed on the basis of purchasing-power-parity (PPP) weights.

The counterfactual simulations in Figure 3.8 indicate what inflation might have been in the advanced economies if import prices evolved over 1997–2005 in line with their historical trend. The counterfactual simulations have two versions. In Scenario A, real import prices are assumed to be falling during 1997–2005 at the sample average rate for each country—the advanced economy average rate would be about 1 percent a year. The simulated inflation paths are averaged into an advanced economy aggregate using PPP weights. In an attempt to capture the impact of globalization on inflation more precisely, Scenario B removes the impact of oil prices from Scenario A. Real import prices are first decomposed into the contribution of oil prices and non-oil commodities. The scenario then assumes that the contribution of oil prices to import price changes was the same as actual values over 1997–2005 but the contribution of non-oil commodities was at its historical average rate for each country—or about 1.6 percent a year for the advanced economy group average.

Variable Definitions and Data Sources

The variables of the inflation model are defined below. The data sources are listed in parentheses.

- Inflation, π, is defined as the change in the natural logarithm of annual consumer price index (Eurostat; Haver Analytics; national authorities, and *World Economic Outlook*).
- Output gap, y, is defined as the difference between the natural logarithm of annual GDP and the natural logarithm of its trend, calculated by the Hodrick-Prescott filter with the smoothing parameter of 100 (Haver Analytics; *World Economic Outlook;* and IMF staff calculations). These estimates of the output gap are similar to the data published by, for example, the OECD.
- Openness, *Open*, is defined as the share of nominal non-oil exports and non-oil imports in GDP (World Bank's *World Development Indicators*). The data on crude oil imports and exports are from the database of International Energy Agency.
- Monetary policy credibility, *Credib*, is calculated using the formula of Laxton and N'Diaye (2002):

$$Credib_{it} = \frac{(R_{it} - R_i^{High})^2}{(R_{it} - R_i^{High})^2 + (R_{it} - R_i^{Low})^2},$$

where R_{it} denotes yield of long-term government bonds in country i at time t (Haver Analytics; IMF's *International Financial Statistics*; and IMF staff calculations); R_i^{High} denotes the maximum yield in country i over the sample period; and R_i^{Low} is calibrated at 5 percent in line with Laxton and N'Diaye (2002). Since the credibility measure is calculated from bond yields, it captures a variety of factors. First, the bond yields reflect expectations about future inflation, and therefore also the record of previous stabilization policies and various institutional arrange-

---

[40]The estimation results are qualitatively similar when lagged output gap instead of its contemporaneous value is used as a regressor or when the measures of openness and credibility enter the model with a lag, or as a moving average of their historical values.

ments, including central bank independence, transparency, and accountability. Second, the risk premiums in the bond yields are related to the fiscal performance and any institutional commitment to low deficits or debt. In the sample of advanced economies analyzed here, it is likely that the credibility measure mostly reflects behavior of inflation expectations.

- Average inflation, $\bar{\pi}$, is calculated as the simple average of actual inflation rates over $t - 2, \ldots, t - 12$.

- Oil price is expressed as the change in the natural logarithm of the simple average of the spot prices of the Brent, Dubai, and West Texas Intermediate crude oil varieties (Source: IMF's *Commodity Price System* database).

- Import prices are measured using the import price deflator (*World Economic Outlook*). The inflation model incorporates this variable as the change in the natural logarithm of the real import price.[41] The change in the real import price is weighted by the import share (including oil) to allow for time-varying contemporaneous impact of import prices on inflation. Effectively, the persistence of import price shocks is also allowed to vary over time—to the extent that the coefficient on the inflation lag depends on the credibility of policymakers.

- Index of wage bargaining, *Bargain*, is a summary measure of wage-setting centralization and coordination by Elmeskov, Martin, and Scarpetta (1998). The index reflects the proportion of workers who are members of a trade union, the level at which wages are negotiated (aggregate, sectoral, or firm level), and the degree of coordination between employers and trade unions. The index ranges from one (low) to three (high). The original data set of Elmeskov, Martin, and Scarpetta was updated by Nicoletti and others (2001). Values of the index are assumed unchanged during 2001–04.

Appendix 3.2. A Sectoral Perspective on Globalization and Inflation

The main author of this appendix is Florence Jaumotte.

This appendix provides further details on the data and their sources and the empirical strategy used in the analysis of the relationship between globalization and sectoral prices.

Variables and Their Sources

Most data used in the section are from the OECD's Structural Analysis (STAN) database. The following are the main variables (from STAN unless otherwise noted).

- *Relative producer prices.* The relative producer price of a sector is the producer price of the sector scaled by the overall producer price. Producer prices are defined by the ratio of the value of production at current prices and the volume of production in a sector. The value of production includes the cost of intermediate inputs.

- *Import ratio.* This variable is the ratio of the import value to the value of production in a sector. The imports referred to are those produced by foreign producers in the same sector and not the imports of intermediates by domestic producers in the sector. For services, import data are from the OECD's *Statistics of International Trade in Services* and include, in addition to traditional measures of imports, the services performed by foreign affiliates established and temporary workers posted in the country when available.

- *Labor productivity.* This variable is defined as a ratio of the volume of production in a sector to the number of employees. When data on the number of employees were incomplete, they were spliced using growth rates from total employment (including self-employed and unpaid family workers).

- *Components of unit costs.* The nominal value of production by definition equals the sum of the

---

[41]Using real rather than nominal changes is consistent with the theoretical literature (e.g., Ball and Mankiw, 1995). However, estimation results are similar when the nominal changes are used.

Table 3.7. Classification of Sectors by Technological and Skill Intensity

	High-Skill	Low-Skill	Not Classified
Manufacturing			
High-tech	Chemicals Electrical and optical equipment Other transport equipment	Machinery Motor vehicles	
Medium-tech	Refined petroleum	Plastics Minerals Basic metals Fabricated metals	
Low-tech	Publishing	Food Textile Leather Wood Paper	Other manufacturing
Business services	Trade Telecoms Finance Other business activities	Hotels and restaurants Transport	
Other sectors	Utilities	Construction	

Sources: OECD; and IMF staff estimates.

costs of intermediates, costs of labor, gross operating surplus and net taxes.[42]

$$PY = P_{IM}IM + P_L L + GOS + TAXN,$$

where P denotes the producer price and Y the production volume; P_{IM} is the price of intermediates and IM is the volume of intermediates; P_L is the nominal compensation per employee and L is the number of employees; and GOS is the gross operating surplus and $TAXN$ represents the net taxes. Accordingly, the producer price equals the sum of the unit intermediate cost, the unit labor cost, the unit gross operating surplus, and the unit net tax.

$$P = P_{IM}(IM/Y) + P_L(L/Y) + GOS/Y + TAXN/Y$$
$$= UIC + ULC + UGOS + UTAXN.$$

- *Changes in unit costs.* The change in producer prices is by definition a weighted average of the changes in the various cost components, where the weights are the shares of the respective unit cost components in the producer price.

$$dP/P = (dUIC/UIC)(UIC/P)$$
$$+ (dULC/ULC)(ULC/P)$$
$$+ (dUGOS/UGOS)(UGOS/P)$$
$$+ (dUTAXN/UTAXN)(UTAXN/P).$$

In Table 3.4, the contribution of unit cost components to producer price inflation is defined as the product of the change in the unit cost component and its share in total unit costs.

The *sectoral classification* is based on the *International Standard Industrial Classification* (ISIC), Revision 3. Most of the econometric analysis uses a disaggregation of the sectors at the two-digit level for manufacturing (depending on data availability) and at the single-digit level for business services. The descriptive analysis, on the other hand, distinguishes various broad aggregate sectors (Table 3.7).

- *Manufacturing* versus *business services.*
- *High-tech, medium-tech,* and *low-tech.* This distinction is based on the intensity of R&D in the sector and follows the OECD classification. For technical reasons, the definition of the

[42]The net tax is a partial measure calculated as the difference between the value of production and the sum of the cost of intermediates, the cost of labor, and the gross operating surplus (which includes the consumption of fixed capital). When data for the gross operating surplus were not available, the variable was calculated using tax adjustment factors prepared by the OECD.

high-tech category used in this chapter includes both high-tech and medium high-tech sectors while medium-tech refers to medium low-tech sectors.

- *High-skill* and *low-skill*. This distinction is based on the fraction of skilled labor in the employment of a sector, where a person is considered skilled if he or she has at least upper secondary education. Data on the average fraction of skilled labor in each sector (across 16 OECD countries from 1994 to 1998) are taken from Jean and Nicoletti (2002). The threshold between high-skill and low-skill sectors was put at 20 percent of skilled employment in order to achieve a rough balance between the number of observations in high-skill and low-skill sectors in the overall economy (40 percent versus 60 percent).

Advanced economies with coverage from 1987 to 2003 include Austria, Denmark, Finland, France, Germany, Italy, Japan, Korea, Luxembourg, Norway, and the United States. Data are also available for shorter periods of time for Belgium and Greece. The descriptive analysis is based on the 11 countries for which coverage over time is similar.

Econometric Analysis

This part of the appendix provides details on the specification of the various equations reported in the main text and the econometric methodology. It also presents additional results on the relationship between sectoral inflation and sectoral import prices, as well as on the effect of trade openness on cost components other than unit labor costs.

Sectoral Inflation and Globalization

The econometric analysis of the relationship between inflation and globalization at the sec-

toral level is based on the following variant of Chen, Imbs, and Scott (2004),

$$p_{ijt} - p_{it} = \alpha(my)_{ijt} + \beta(yl)_{ijt} + \gamma_j(\$xr)_{it} + \eta_i + \mu_j + \zeta_i t + \xi_j t + \varepsilon_{ijt}, \quad (1)$$

where the subscript j denotes the sector; the subscript i the country; and the subscript t the time period. The variables are defined as follows: p is the logarithm of the producer price; my represents the logarithm of the import-to-production ratio; yl is the logarithm of average real productivity per employee; $\$xr$ represents the nominal local currency to U.S. dollar exchange rate; η are the country fixed effects and μ are sector fixed effects. Sectoral price levels are scaled by the overall producer price to account for the influence of monetary policy and the fact that in the long-run price levels are determined by monetary policy. The relative price of a sector is allowed to depend on the sectoral import ratio, sectoral labor productivity, and an interaction term between a sectoral dummy and the local currency to U.S. dollar exchange rate. The latter captures the impact that exchange rate fluctuations exert on sectoral producer prices through the price of imported intermediates in the sector. This effect is allowed to vary across sectors because the share of imported intermediates differs across sectors. Finally, the specification controls for country and sector fixed effects and time trends. Among other things, sector fixed effects control for important sectoral differences in technological intensity, skill intensity, and degree of differentiation of products.

The equation is estimated in first differences using a two-step feasible generalized method of moments estimator instrumenting for the changes in the import ratio given concerns about their endogeneity.[43] The list of instruments used is as follows:

- A measure of how close (geographically) the country is from the large producers in a sector

---

[43]There are two sources of possible bias in the estimates. On the one hand, high producer price inflation in a sector lowers competitiveness and increases the import ratio, inducing an upward bias in the estimates. On the other hand, high producer price inflation in a sector could trigger stronger protectionism, thereby reducing the import ratio and imparting a downward bias on the estimates.

at a point in time: for each country, this variable is constructed as a weighted sum of the shares of the other countries in the "world" production of a sector (excluding the country's production), where the weights are the inverse distances between the country and the other producers.

- The nominal effective exchange rate, which captures the countrywide evolution in import prices and competitiveness and affects directly each sector's import-to-production ratio.

A relevant and valid set of instruments comprising various lags of the difference and level of these two variables was identified based on the Anderson likelihood-ratio test of relevance of the instruments and the Hansen-Sargan test of validity of the instruments (as implemented in Stata, a data processing software).

Equation (1) is estimated first for 16 manufacturing subsectors and then for all 16 manufacturing sectors jointly with six business services sectors.[44] Two different samples of countries and years are used: one with the maximum number of countries and years available, and another one restricted to the countries and years included in the descriptive analysis of sectoral inflation patterns. The maximum sample covers the period 1977–2003 and the following 11 OECD countries: Austria, Belgium, Denmark, Finland, France, Greece, Italy, Japan, Norway, the United Kingdom, and the United States (Germany does not report production volumes and Korea does not provide labor productivity data for most of the two-digit level subsectors of manufacturing).[45] The results are robust when the sample excludes Belgium and Greece and is restricted to the period 1988–2003 to match the sample used in the descriptive analysis. Results are reported in Table 3.3. Variables have the expected sign and are significant, generally at the 5 percent level.[46] The magnitude of the coefficients is also broadly similar to that found by comparable studies.[47]

IMF staff also explored the relationship between changes in relative producer prices and changes in the price of imported goods in that sector. This relationship is the price dual of the relationship between sectoral relative prices and quantities of imported goods in the sector (Gamber and Hung, 2001). Sectoral import prices, which are only available for manufacturing sectors, are based on unit values of imports of products classified under the sector.[48] The specification is the same as equation (1) except that changes in the sectoral import ratio are replaced by changes in sectoral import prices. An equation including both changes in the sectoral import ratio and changes in sectoral import prices is also estimated. The estimation method and the samples are the same as before and the instrumental variables are again chosen based on validity and relevance. Results reported in Table 3.8 show that changes in relative producer prices are positively and significantly related to import price inflation, confirming that import price developments constrain the ability of domestic producers to raise prices. Specifically, a 1 percent change in import prices is associated with a 0.15 percent change in producer prices. These estimates are close to those found by Gamber and Hung (2001) for the United States. Finally, the model that includes both changes in the import ratio and import price inflation lead to coefficients that are similar in

---

[44]As in the descriptive analysis, the refined petroleum sector is excluded because its behavior is strongly influenced by oil price developments.

[45]The period covered varies across sectors and countries depending on data availability, and the panel data set is thus not balanced.

[46]Although not reported, the results are also robust when IT sectors such as electrical and optical equipment and telecommunication services are excluded. Allowing for endogenous labor productivity growth in the estimation yields similar results, although the negative effect of productivity growth on sectoral price changes becomes somewhat larger in magnitude.

[47]See, for example, Chen, Imbs, and Scott (2004) for the effect of the import ratio and labor productivity on sectoral inflation in a sample of European countries.

[48]This measure does not control for composition changes within lines of products and quality improvements, but it is a widely used proxy measure. The main source is the United Nations' Comtrade database.

Table 3.8. Impact of Changes in Import Prices on Relative Producer Price Inflation[1]

	Dependent Variable: Changes in Relative Producer Prices in Manufacturing Sectors (16)[2]			
	Price version		Price and quantity version	
	1981–2003 (all countries available)	1988–2003 (core countries)[3]	1981–2003 (all countries available)	1988–2003 (core countries)[3]
Change in import prices	0.16***	0.15***	0.12***	0.25***
Change in import share	. . .	. . .	–0.12**	–0.19**
Change in labor productivity	–0.08***	–0.09***	–0.11***	–0.13***

Source: IMF staff calculations.

[1]All variables are in natural logarithms. The equations are estimated by two-step feasible generalized method of moments instrumenting for changes in import prices and changes in the import share. Other control variables include the dollar exchange rate interacted with sectoral dummies (effect through cost of intermediates), and sectoral and country dummies. *** denotes statistical significance at the 1 percent level; ** at the 5 percent level.

[2]The refined petroleum sector is excluded from the regressions because its behavior is strongly affected by oil price developments.

[3]Restricted to countries used in the descriptive analysis of sectoral inflation patterns.

magnitudes and significance. Overall, therefore, the impact of globalization on producer price does not depend on a specific model or a specific variable to measure globalization.

Sectoral Unit Labor Cost Changes and Globalization

The econometric analysis of the relationship between globalization and unit labor cost (denoted as *ulc* below) changes at the sectoral level is based on a similar specification as equation (1), except for the exchange rate term, which is not needed:

$$dulc_{ijt} - dulc_{it} = \alpha(dmy)_{ijt} + \beta(dyl_{ijt} - dyl_{it}) \\ + \zeta_i + \xi_j + \varepsilon_{ijt} - \varepsilon_{ijt-1}. \quad (2)$$

In order to gain a better understanding of the effects at work, similar equations are estimated for the two components of unit labor cost changes, namely changes in labor compensation per employee (*plab*) and changes in productivity per employee (labor productivity, denoted as *yl*),

$$dplab_{ijt} - dplab_{it} = \alpha(dmy)_{ijt} \\ + (\beta + \gamma M_{ijt})(dyl_{ijt} - dyl_{it}) \\ + \zeta_i + \xi_j + \varepsilon_{ijt} - \varepsilon_{ijt-1} \quad (3)$$

$$dyl_{ijt} - dyl_{it} = \alpha(dmy)_{ijt} + \zeta_i + \xi_j + \varepsilon_{ijt} - \varepsilon_{ijt-1}. \quad (4)$$

These equations allow one to estimate separately the direct effect of the import ratio on labor compensation (or unit labor costs)—controlling for labor productivity—and its indirect effect through labor productivity. Equation (3) also allows the elasticity of the relative price of labor to the relative productivity to depend on the level of the import ratio (denoted as M_{ijt}) in order to test whether globalization affects the extent to which productivity changes are translated into labor compensation changes.

Equations (2), (3), and (4) are estimated using a two-step feasible generalized method of moments estimator instrumenting for the changes in the import ratio and, in equations (2) and (3), for the changes in relative productivity. The instrumental variables used are the same as before and the specific lags included were selected using tests of the relevance and validity of the instruments.[49] Results of the estimation are reported in Table 3.5 and are robust to restricting the sample to countries covered in the descriptive analysis and reducing the period covered to 1987 onwards.

Finally, it is also of interest to examine the effect of globalization, as measured by increases in the import ratio, on changes in unit intermediate costs (*uic*) and changes in the unit gross operating surplus (*ugos*). The following two

[49]For equation (3), the lagged relative productivity growth was used as an additional instrument.

Table 3.9. Impact of Trade Openness on Cost Components[1]
(Manufacturing subsectors relative to the overall economy)[2]

	Dependent Variable[2]					
	Change in relative unit labor cost		Change in relative unit intermediate cost		Change in relative unit gross operating surplus	
	1977–2003 (all available countries)	1988–2003 (core countries)[3]	1977–2003 (all available countries)	1988–2003 (core countries)[3]	1977–2003 (all available countries)	1988–2003 (core countries)[3]
Change in import share	−0.13***	−0.16***	−0.12***	−0.19***	—	0.30

Source: IMF staff calculations.

[1]All variables are in natural logarithms. The equations are estimated by two-step feasible generalized method of moments instrumenting for changes in import prices and changes in the import share. Other control variables include the dollar exchange rate interacted with sectoral dummies (effect through cost of intermediates), and sectoral and country dummies. *** denotes statistical significance at the 1 percent level.

[2]The refined petroleum sector is excluded from the regressions because its behavior is strongly affected by oil price developments.

[3]Restricted to countries used in the descriptive analysis of sectoral inflation patterns.

equations are estimated using the same estimation and instrumentation methods as above:

$$duic_{ijt} - duic_{it} = \alpha(dmy)_{ijt} + \gamma_j(d\$xr)_{it}$$
$$+ \zeta_i + \xi_j + \varepsilon_{ijt} - \varepsilon_{ijt-1}$$

$$dugos_{ijt} - dugos_{it} = \alpha(dmy)_{ijt} + \zeta_i + \xi_j + \varepsilon_{ijt} - \varepsilon_{ijt-1}.$$

The results reported in Table 3.9 suggest that increases in trade openness also contributed to reduce increases in unit intermediate costs, while the effect on changes in the unit gross operating surplus is not significantly estimated.

References

Alesina, Alberto, and Larry H. Summers, 1993, "Central Bank Independence and Macroeconomic Performance: Some Comparative Evidence," *Journal of Money, Credit and Banking*, Vol. 25 (May), pp. 151–62.

Ball, Laurence, and Gregory Mankiw, 1995, "Relative-Price Changes as Aggregate Supply Shocks," *Quarterly Journal of Economics*, Vol. 110 (February), pp. 161–93.

———, and David Romer, 1988, "The New Keynesian Economics and the Output-Inflation Trade-Off," *Brookings Papers on Economic Activity: 1*, Brookings Institution.

Ball, Laurence, and Robert Moffitt, 2001, "Productivity Growth and the Phillips Curve," NBER Working Paper No. 8421 (Cambridge, Massachusetts: National Bureau of Economic Research).

Bank for International Settlements, 2005, *Annual Report 2005* (Basel).

Barro, Robert, 1979, "Money and the Price Level Under the Gold Standard," *Economic Journal*, Vol. 89 (March), pp. 13–33.

Bayoumi, Tamim, and Silvia Sgherri, 2004, "Deconstructing the Art of Central Banking," IMF Working Paper 04/195 (Washington: International Monetary Fund).

Bordo, Michael, 1999, *The Gold Standard and Related Regimes* (New York: Cambridge University Press).

———, and Andrew Filardo, 2005, "Deflation and Monetary Policy in a Historical Perspective: Remembering the Past or Being Condemned to Repeat It?" *Economic Policy*, Vol. 20 (October), pp. 801–44.

Bordo, Michael, John Landon Lane, and Angela Redish, 2004, "Good Versus Bad Deflation: Lessons from the Gold Standard Era," NBER Working Paper No. 10329 (Cambridge, Massachusetts: National Bureau of Economic Research).

———, 2005, "Deflation, Productivity Shocks and Gold: Evidence from the 1880–1914 Period," (unpublished; Rutgers University, Department of Economics).

Borio, Claudio, and Andrew Filardo, 2004, "Back to the Future? Assessing the Deflation Record," BIS Working Paper No. 152 (Basel: Bank for International Settlements).

Boschen, John F., and Charles L. Weise, 2003, "What Starts Inflation: Evidence From The OECD Countries," *Journal of Money, Credit and Banking*, Vol. 35 (June), pp. 323–49.

Buiter, Willem H., 2000, "Monetary Misconceptions," CEPR Discussion Paper No. 2365 (London: Centre for Economic Policy Research).

Campa, Jose M., and Linda S. Goldberg, 2002, "Exchange Rate Pass-Through into Import Prices: A Macro or Micro Phenomenon," NBER Working Paper No. 8934 (Cambridge, Massachusetts: National Bureau of Economic Research).

Catão, Luis A.V., and Marco E. Terrones, 2005, "Fiscal Deficits and Inflation," *Journal of Monetary Economics,* Vol. 52 (April), pp. 529–54.

Chen, Natalie, Jean Imbs, and Andrew Scott, 2004, "Competition, Globalization and the Decline of Inflation," CEPR Discussion Paper No. 4695 (London: Centre for Economic Policy Research).

Choudhri, Ehsan U., and Dalia Hakura, 2001, "Exchange Rate Pass-Through to Domestic Prices: Does the Inflationary Environment Matter?" IMF Working Paper 01/194 (Washington: International Monetary Fund).

Clark, Todd E., 2004, "An Evaluation of the Decline in Goods Inflation," *Economic Review,* Federal Reserve Bank of Kansas City (first quarter), pp. 19–51.

Cogley, Timothy, and Thomas Sargent, 2002, "Evolving Post-World War II U.S. Inflation Dynamics," Chapter 6 in *NBER Macroeconomics Annual 2001,* ed. by Ben S. Bernanke and Kenneth Rogoff (Cambridge and London: MIT Press).

———, 2005, "The Conquest of US Inflation: Learning and Robustness to Model Uncertainty," *Review of Economic Dynamics,* Vol. 8 (April), pp. 528–63.

Cournède, Boris, Alexandra Janovskaia, and Paul van den Noord, 2005, "Sources of Inflation Persistence in the Euro Area," OECD Economic Department Working Paper No. 435 (Paris: Organization for Economic Cooperation and Development).

Craig, Lee A., and Douglas Fisher, 2000, *The European Macroeconomy: Growth, Integration, and Cycles 1500–1913* (Northampton, Massachusetts: Edward Elgar Publishing).

Elmeskov, Jørgen, John P. Martin, and Stefano Scarpetta, 1998, "Key Lessons for Labor Market Reforms: Evidence from OECD Countries' Experiences," *Swedish Economic Policy Review,* Vol. 5, No. 2, pp. 205–52.

Feyzioglu, Tarhan, and Luke Willard, 2006, "Does Inflation in China Affect the United States and Japan?" IMF Working Paper 06/36 (Washington: International Monetary Fund).

Fischer, Stanley, 1997, "Capital Account Liberalization and the Role of the IMF," speech at the IMF seminar on Asia and the IMF, Hong Kong SAR, September 19. Available via the Internet: http://www.imf.org/external/np/speeches/1997/091997.htm.

Fisher, Richard W., 2006, "Coping with Globalization's Impact on Monetary Policy," remarks for the National Association for Business Economics Panel

Discussion at the 2006 Allied Social Science Associations Meetings, Boston, January 6.

Gagnon, Edith, Patrick Sabourin, and Sébastien Lavoie, 2004, "The Comparative Growth of Goods and Services Prices," *Bank of Canada Review* (Winter), pp. 3–10.

Gamber, Edward, and Juann H. Hung, 2001, "Has the Rise in Globalization Reduced U.S. Inflation in the 1990s?" *Economic Inquiry,* Vol. 39 (January), pp. 58–73.

Ghosh, Atish R., Anne-Marie Gulde, Jonathan D. Ostry, and Holger C. Wolf, 1997, "Does the Nominal Exchange Rate Regime Matter?" NBER Working Paper No. 5874 (Cambridge, Massachusetts: National Bureau of Economic Research).

Goldberg, P. K., and Michael Knetter, 1997, "Goods Prices and Exchange Rates: What Have We Learned?" *Journal of Economic Literature,* Vol. 35 (September), pp. 1243–72.

Goodfriend, Marvin, and Robert King, 2005, "The Incredible Volcker Disinflation," NBER Working Paper No. 11562 (Cambridge, Massachusetts: National Bureau of Economic Research).

Greenspan, Alan, 2005, "Economic Outlook," testimony before the Joint Economic Committee, U.S. Congress, November 3.

Gruben, William C., and Darryl McLeod, 2004, "The Openness-Inflation Puzzle Revisited," *Applied Economics Letters,* Vol. 11 (June 15), pp. 465–68.

Hooker, Mark A., 2002, "Are Oil Shocks Inflationary? Asymmetric and Nonlinear Specifications versus Changes in Regime," *Journal of Money, Credit and Banking,* Vol. 34 (May), pp. 540–61.

Iyoha, Milton A., 1977, "Inflation and 'Openness' in Less Developed Economies: A Cross-Country Analysis," *Economic Development and Structural Change,* Vol. 26, No. 1, pp. 153–55.

Jean, Sébastien, and Giuseppe Nicoletti, 2002, "Product Market Regulation and Wage Premia in Europe and North America: An Empirical Investigation," OECD Economics Department Working Paper No. 318 (Paris: Organization for Economic Cooperation and Development).

Kamin, Steven B., Mario Marazzi, and J. W. Schindler, 2004, "Is China 'Exporting Deflation'?" International Finance Discussion Papers No. 791 (Washington: Board of Governors of the Federal Reserve System).

Klein, Benjamin, 1975, "Our Monetary Standard: The Measurement and Effects of Price Uncertainty, 1880–1973," UCLA Economics Working Paper

No. 062. Available via the Internet: http://www.econ.ucla.edu/workingpapers/wp062.pdf.

Kohn, Donald L., 2005, "Globalization, Inflation, and Monetary Policy," remarks at the James R. Wilson Lecture Series, The College of Wooster, Wooster, Ohio, October 11.

Lane, Philip R., and Gian Maria Milesi-Ferretti, 2006, "The External Wealth of Nations Mark II: Revised and Extended Estimates of Foreign Assets and Liabilities, 1970–2004," IMF Working Paper 06/69 (Washington: International Monetary Fund).

Laxton, Douglas, and Papa N'Diaye, 2002, "Monetary Policy Credibility and the Unemployment-Inflation Trade-Off: Some Evidence from 17 Industrial Countries," IMF Working Paper 02/220 (Washington: International Monetary Fund).

Loungani, Prakash, Assaf Razin, and Chi-Wa Yuen, 2001, "Capital Mobility and the Output–Inflation Tradeoff," *Journal of Development Economics*, Vol. 64 (February), pp. 255–74.

Marazzi, Mario, Nathan Sheets, and Robert Vigfusson, 2005, "Exchange Rate Pass-Through to U.S. Import Prices: Some New Evidence," International Finance Discussion Paper No. 833 (Washington: Board of Governors of the Federal Reserve System).

Mishkin, Frederic S., 1999, "International Experiences with Different Monetary Policy Regimes," *Journal of Monetary Economics*, Vol. 43 (June), pp. 576–606.

Nicoletti, Giuseppe, Andrea Bassanini, Ekkehard Ernst, Sébastian Jean, Paulo Santiago, and Paul Swaim, 2001, "Product and Labor Markets Interactions in OECD Countries," OECD Economics Department Working Paper No. 312 (Paris: Organization for Economic Cooperation and Development).

Nunziata, Luca, and Christopher Bowdler, 2005, "Inflation Adjustment and Labor Market Structures: Evidence from a Multi-Country Study," IZA Discussion Paper No. 1510 (Bonn, Germany: Institute for the Study of Labor).

O'Reilly, Gerard, and Karl Whelan, 2005, "Has Euro-Area Inflation Persistence Changed Over Time?" *The Review of Economics and Statistics*, Vol. 87 (November), pp. 709–20.

Orphanides, Athanasios, and David W. Wilcox, 2002, "The Opportunistic Approach to Disinflation," *International Finance*, Vol. 5 (Spring), pp. 47–71.

Ouliaris, Sam, 2006, "Exchange Rate Pass-Through: Structural Reforms versus Macro Conditions"

(unpublished; Washington: International Monetary Fund).

Pivetta, Frederic, and Ricardo Reis, 2004, "The Persistence of Inflation in the United States" (unpublished; Harvard University).

Razin, Assaf, and Prakash Loungani, 2005, "Globalization and Disinflation: The Efficiency Channel," CEPR Discussion Paper No. 4895 (London: Centre for Economic Policy Research).

Reinhart, Carmen M., and Kenneth S. Rogoff, 2002, "The Modern History of Exchange Rate Arrangements: A Reinterpretation," NBER Working Paper No. 8963 (Cambridge, Massachusetts: National Bureau of Economic Research).

Rockoff, Hugh, 1984, "Some Evidence on the Real Price of Gold, Its Costs of Production, and Commodity Prices," in *A Retrospective on the Classical Gold Standard, 1821–1931*, ed. by Michael Bordo and Anna Schwartz (Chicago: University of Chicago Press).

Rodrik, Dani, 2006, "What's So Special About China's Exports?" NBER Working Paper No. 11947 (Cambridge, Massachusetts: National Bureau of Economic Research).

Rogoff, Kenneth, 1985, "Can International Monetary Policy Cooperation Be Counterproductive?" *Journal of International Economics*, Vol. 18 (May), pp. 199–217.

———, 2003, "Globalization and Global Disinflation," paper prepared for the Federal Reserve Bank of Kansas City conference on "Monetary Policy and Uncertainty: Adapting to a Changing Economy," Jackson Hole, Wyoming, August 29.

Romer, Christina, and David Romer, 2002, "The Evolution of Economic Understanding and Postwar Stabilization Policy," NBER Working Paper No. 9274 (Cambridge, Massachusetts: National Bureau of Economic Research).

Romer, David, 1993, "Openness and Inflation: Theory and Evidence," *The Quarterly Journal of Economics*, Vol. 107 (November), pp. 869–903.

Sargent, Thomas J., 1999, *The Conquest of American Inflation* (Princeton, New Jersey: Princeton University Press).

———, Noah Williams, and Tao Zha, 2005, "Shocks and Government Beliefs: The Rise and Fall of American Inflation" (unpublished; New York: New York University, Department of Economics).

Sims, Christopher A., 1999, "Drift and Breaks in Monetary Policy" (unpublished: Princeton, New Jersey: Princeton University, Department of Economics).

Stock, James H., 2002, "Evolving Post-World War II U.S. Inflation Dynamics: Comment," in *NBER*

Macroeconomics Annual 2001, ed. by Ben S. Bernanke and Kenneth Rogoff (Cambridge and London: MIT Press).

Taylor, John B., 2000, "Low Inflation, Pass-Through, and the Pricing Power of Firms," *European Economic Review,* Vol. 44, No. 7, pp. 1195–1408.

Triffin, Robert, and Herbert Grubel, 1962, "The Adjustment Mechanism to Differential Rates of Monetary Expansion Among the Countries of the European Economic Community," *The Review of Economics and Statistics,* Vol. 44 (November), pp. 486–91.

Tytell, Irina, and Shang-Jin Wei, 2004, "Does Financial Globalization Induce Better Macroeconomic Policies?" IMF Working Paper 04/84 (Washington: International Monetary Fund).

Zellner, Arnold, 1962, "An Efficient Method of Estimating Seemingly Unrelated Regressions and Tests for Aggregation Bias," *Journal of the American Statistical Association,* Vol. 57 (June), pp. 348–68.

CHAPTER IV

AWASH WITH CASH: WHY ARE CORPORATE SAVINGS SO HIGH?

Companies, which normally borrow other folks' savings in order to invest, have turned thrifty. Even companies enjoying strong profits and cash flow are building cash hoards, reducing debt and buying back their own shares—instead of making investment bets.

—David Wessel, *Wall Street Journal*, July 21, 2005

Two striking changes have taken place in the global financial landscape in recent years. First, reflecting a combination of low investment and—more recently—strong revenues from oil exports, emerging market and oil-exporting countries have become substantial net savers. As a consequence, capital is flowing from emerging markets to industrial countries (notably the United States), the opposite of what would be predicted by economic theory (see Chapter II of the September 2005 *World Economic Outlook*). Second, since the bursting of the equity market bubble in the early 2000s, companies in many industrial countries have moved from their traditional position of borrowing funds to finance their capital expenditures to running financial surpluses that they are now lending to other sectors of the economy.

The large current account surplus in emerging market (and, more recently, oil-producing) countries has been labeled a global "savings glut," and advanced as a reason why the United States has been able to finance a record high current account deficit at low interest rates (Bernanke, 2005). Yet, the $1.3 trillion of corporate excess saving (undistributed profits less capital spending) in the Group of Seven (G-7) countries in 2003–04 was more than twice the size of the accumulated current account surpluses of emerging market and developing countries during those two years. The recent behavior of the corporate sector—which until recently has received much less attention—could therefore be an equally important contributor to the relatively low level of global long-term interest rates at a time of a ballooning U.S. current account deficit (J.P. Morgan, 2005).

Against this background, this chapter assesses the recent behavior of the corporate sector in the G-7 countries. It asks why the strong increase in profits has been used by nonfinancial corporates to acquire financial assets—including a substantial amount of liquid assets ("cash" for short) during 2003–04—or to repay debt, rather than to finance new capital investments or to increase distributions to shareholders through dividends.[1] Specifically, three questions are considered:

- What has been driving the recent increase in excess saving of companies in industrial countries?
- Are there significant cross-country differences in corporate behavior?
- Is the increase in excess saving a temporary or more permanent phenomenon?

In addressing these questions, the chapter explicitly looks at the interaction between real

---

The main authors of this chapter are Roberto Cardarelli and Kenichi Ueda, with support from Vojislav Maksimovic. Ben Sutton provided research assistance.

[1]In the chapter, "cash" refers to currency and deposits plus short-term securities (including treasury bills, commercial paper, and certificates of deposits). Data availability does not allow for the inclusion of bank lines of credit, which can be a viable liquidity alternative to cash, especially for profitable firms (Sufi, 2006).

Figure 4.1. Group of Seven (G-7), Excluding Germany: Gross Saving, Capital Spending, and Net Lending/Borrowing[1]

(Percent of total GDP)

Total corporate net lending was at a historical high on average during 2002–04, driven by the turnaround in the position of nonfinancial corporates.

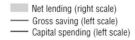

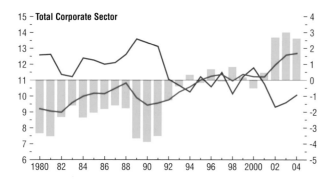

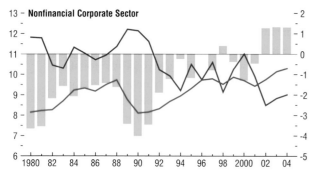

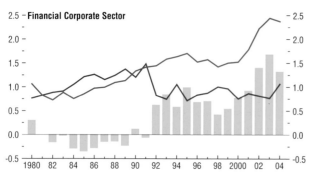

Sources: Eurostat; national authorities; and IMF staff calculations.
[1]GDP-weighted averages using GDP in U.S. dollars at market exchange rates.

and financial decisions of the corporate sector. For example, are recent financial surpluses simply a residual decision, left after firms have made their capital spending plans, or have they been shaped by balance sheet considerations (e.g., the need to reduce high debt levels) or other factors (including a firm's desire to insure against the increased volatility it may face in an increasingly globalized corporate environment)?

What Has Been Driving the Increase in Corporate Excess Saving?

Since the 1980s, the corporate sector of the G-7 economies has swung from being a large net borrower of funds from other sectors of the economy to a net lender of funds. Indeed, on average over 2002–04, the excess saving (or "net lending") of the corporate sector—defined as the difference between undistributed profits (gross saving) and capital spending—was at a historic high of 2½ percent of GDP in the G-7 countries (Figure 4.1). This behavior has been widespread, taking place in economies that have experienced strong economic growth (Canada, the United Kingdom, and the United States) and in those where growth has been relatively weak (Europe and, until recently, Japan). Most of these economies, however, were affected by the boom-and-bust cycle in equity valuations in the late 1990s–early 2000s, which left corporations with high debt levels.

In all of the G-7 countries, higher corporate excess saving (or lower net borrowing in France and Italy) in recent years has partly offset—and in some cases more than balanced—the increase in net borrowing by other sectors of the economy. In the United States—where the current account deficit has widened further in recent years—higher corporate excess saving has offset one-half of the increase in government and household net borrowing, thereby helping to mitigate the impact on the external deficit (see Box 4.1 for a discussion of the link between corporate and household saving).

A number of factors have driven this change from net borrower to net lender status:

Box 4.1. Drawing the Line Between Personal and Corporate Savings

In stark contrast to the secular decline in household saving, corporate saving in the G-7 countries has increased strongly over the last decade, and now accounts for about 70 percent of total private (household plus corporate) saving, compared to 50 percent in the early 1990s (first figure). The strong increase in corporate saving at a time of historically low household saving is a reminder that household and corporate saving decisions are inherently linked. This box discusses this link from two perspectives:

- From economic theory, since households own corporations and should adjust their saving plans—or "pierce the corporate veil"—to offset the saving done by corporates on their behalf (Poterba, 1987; and Auerbach and Hassett, 1991).
- From a definitional standpoint, because there are several questions about the demarcation between household and corporate saving in the national accounts, and several alternatives are available that could be more relevant and appropriate for economic analysis (Gale and Sabelhaus, 1999).

Do Households Pierce the Corporate Veil?

The argument that households may offset changes in corporate saving can be illustrated with a simple example. Suppose a corporation decides to increase its saving—that is, to retain earnings rather than distribute them as dividends—sophisticated shareholders should understand that their net worth has increased (through the increase in the market value of equity) and reduce their savings to re-establish their optimal life-cycle consumption.

However, a variety of factors related to constraints on consumer and corporate financial behavior may in practice lead to the imperfect substitutability between personal and corporate saving (Bernheim, 2002). In particular:

- Consumers may have a lower marginal propensity to save out of an increase in wealth rather than out of disposable income (which

Note: The main author of this box is Roberto Cardarelli.

Private, Corporate, and Household Gross Saving Ratios in the G-7[1]
(Percent of GDP)

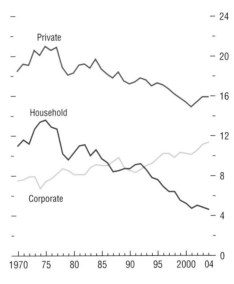

Sources: OECD; Eurostat; and national authorities.
[1] GDP-weighted averages using GDP in U.S. dollars at market exchange rates.

would increase if retained earnings were distributed as dividends). For example, they may be liquidity constrained, or they may tend to perceive capital gains as transitory.

- Even in the absence of liquidity constraints and myopic behavior, and with individuals successfully piercing the corporate veil, exogenous shocks that redistribute wealth from individuals to corporations may increase aggregate savings if shareholders have a higher propensity to save than do other consumers.
- The value of the firm may not change dollar-to-dollar with retained earnings, reflecting problems in corporate governance and imperfect observability of new investment projects. For example, if managers invest retained earnings in projects yielding below-market returns, then share values will grow by less than the increase in retained earnings (Jensen, 1986).

Box 4.1 *(concluded)*

The opposite would happen if retained earnings were to be invested in high-yielding projects that would have been more difficult or costly to finance through financial markets, due to asymmetry of information.

Ultimately, the degree of substitutability between corporate and household saving is an empirical question. The few empirical analyses available tend to show that the "piercing of the corporate veil" is incomplete, which is consistent with the declining trend in private savings shown in the first figure (i.e., corporate saving has not risen sufficiently to completely offset the decline in household saving in recent years). As an example, Poterba (1987) finds that for the United States a $1 increase in corporate saving is likely to increase total private saving by about $0.25–0.50, as households reduce their saving by $0.50–0.75.[1]

The Definition of Corporate Savings in the National Accounts

Turning to the definition of corporate saving in the national accounts, two adjustments need to be considered to make the data more economically meaningful. First, retained earnings do not include inflationary gains on nominal debt, which were large during the high inflation decades of the 1970s and 1980s. In particular, as part of nominal interest payments is effectively a repayment of principal (reflecting the inflation-driven erosion of the real value of interest bearing assets), it could be argued that this should be included in corporate saving (Auerbach, 1982; and Poterba, 1987). Making such an adjustment eliminates the upward trend in the G-7 gross corporate saving ratio and cuts the average net borrowing by the G-5 (excluding Germany and

[1]Auerbach and Hassett (1991) show that *predictable* changes in dividends and other forms of capital income do not affect consumption, suggesting that no corporate veil exists. However, they also find that wealth-neutral transfers from corporations to individuals would increase aggregate consumption via distributional effects, owing to the heterogeneity in consumption behavior and a lower marginal propensity to consume out of changes in wealth.

Group of Seven (G-7), Excluding Germany and Italy: Nonfinancial Corporate Sector[1]
(Percent of GDP)

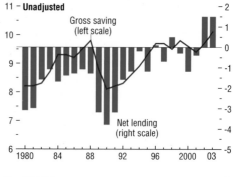

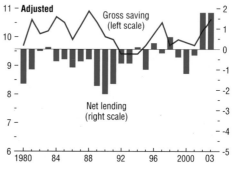

Sources: Eurostat; national authorities; and IMF staff calculations.
[1]GDP-weighted averages using GDP in U.S. dollars at market exchange rates.

Italy) nonfinancial corporations in the 1980s by about one-half (second figure). As discussed in the main text, however, even with this adjustment, nonfinancial corporate sector (NFCS) excess saving in these countries has still been at a historical high during the last two years.

A second adjustment concerns the treatment of pension plans. In the national accounts, all employer-sponsored pension funds are classified as the property of households, so that employer contributions and the interest and dividend earnings are counted as part of household income and thus savings in the year in which they occur. While this treatment seems reasonable for defined contribution plans, it may not be appropriate for defined benefit plans, as employees do not have the right to all funds that accrue to these plans, but only to the stream of pension benefits deriving from a formula that typically depends on salaries and years of service.

This treatment of pension plans appears to have been particularly important in the 1990s when a strong stock market and high interest rates reduced the contributions companies needed to make in order to meet their defined benefit pension obligations. This contributed negatively to household savings and positively to corporate savings, with Lusardi, Skinner, and Venti (2003) estimating that around 40 percent of the 5 percentage points of GDP fall in the U.S. household saving rate between 1988 and 2000 is explained by the accounting of pension inflows and outflows. More recently, though, the acceleration of employer pension contributions after the decline in the stock market in the early

2000s suggests that defined benefit pension schemes may have been adding to personal saving and subtracting from corporate saving.

Finally, there is one last definitional issue to be considered. While both dividend payments and share repurchases involve channeling funds from the corporate to the household sector, only the former is considered as a form of corporate "dissaving" in the national accounts. The reason is that, consistent with economic theory, transactions that involve exchanging one asset for another (cash against equity) do not alter the amount of income that is available to fund capital accumulation—that is, saving. Still, in the presence of liquidity constraints and/or agency issues discussed above, which prevent households from completely "piercing the corporate veil," any channeling of resources to the household sector may increase personal consumption and reduce private sector saving.

- First, financial corporations have been registering positive and increasing excess-saving positions since the early 1990s. The developments in the financial sector are related to structural factors that are specific to financial institutions and are thus likely to be part of a longer-term trend (see Box 4.2).
- Second, the nonfinancial corporate sector (NFCS) has turned around more recently to become a net lender (and has largely driven the recent behavior of the overall corporate sector). Part of this turnaround reflects the decline in interest payments that has taken place as nominal interest rates have fallen with inflation. Even after adjusting for inflation, however, the excess-saving position of the NFCS in the G-7 countries in recent years stands out as an unusual phenomenon from a historic perspective.

Given the importance of the NFCS in driving the behavior of the overall corporate sector, and because the behavior of the financial sector appears to be driven by factors specific to that sector, the rest of the chapter focuses on the NFCS.

The aggregate trends in the NFCS in the G-7 countries do mask differences across countries (Figure 4.2). While NFCS excess saving has recently reached a historic high in Canada, the United Kingdom, and the United States (and Germany and Japan, when large one-off capital transfers from the government to the nonfinancial corporate sector in 1995 and 1998 are excluded), the nonfinancial corporate sectors in France and Italy have remained net borrowers.[2]

A range of complex and interrelated factors have likely driven recent NFCS behavior, and

[2]For Germany, the massive capital transfer reflected the assumption by the federal government of the debt of the *Treuhandanstalt*, the trust fund created to privatize some 8,500 state-owned enterprises in the former German Democratic Republic (East Germany). For Japan, the capital transfer derived from the assumption by the central government of the debt of the Japan Railway Settlement Corporation before its privatization.

Figure 4.2. Nonfinancial Corporate Sector: Gross Saving, Capital Spending, and Net Lending/Borrowing
(Percent of GDP)

Over the recent past, net lending has been especially high in the United States, the United Kingdom, Canada, and in Japan and Germany (excluding the official capital transfers in 1998 and 1995, respectively). Nonfinancial corporates in France and Italy were still in a net borrowing position.

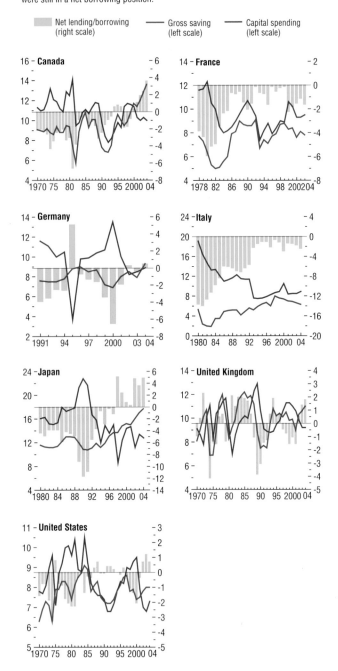

Sources: Eurostat; national authorities; and IMF staff calculations.

these have not only differed in importance over time and between countries, but have also varied between companies and sectors in the same country. The remainder of this section discusses some of the broad factors that appear to explain the recent increase in NFCS net lending, including whether it has largely been driven by real sector developments—profitability and investment decisions—or by financial considerations, such as the desire to repay debt.

A Sustainable Increase in Profits?

One factor behind the increase in NFCS excess saving since 2000 has been the strong rise in profitability (earnings after interest and tax, as a percent of GDP) that has underpinned higher corporate saving despite an increase in dividends paid (Table 4.1). This increase has been particularly striking in Germany and Japan. In Italy, however, profits have declined sharply—indeed, corporate saving has declined in both France and Italy, in the former due to a rise in dividend payments. A closer examination reveals that the increase in profits is mainly due to lower tax and interest payments and, in some countries, to higher profits received from foreign operations, rather than to a rise in gross operating surplus.[3] Indeed, gross operating surplus has fallen in France, Italy, and the United Kingdom, while in Japan and the United States—where the NFCS gross operating surplus as a share of GDP has risen sharply over the recent past—the increase does not appear to be out of line with previous cyclical episodes (Figure 4.3). Only in Germany has operating profitability reached a high over the sample period (which starts from the 1990s), reflecting the restructuring that has

---

[3]The decline of corporate tax payments since 2000 may be partly the consequence of the economic cycle (tax receipts may have also been reduced by corporates carrying forward the losses from the economic downturn in 2001) but it is also the effect of the general decline in statutory corporate income tax rates in the G-7 economies over the last decade (KPMG, various issues; and European Commission, 2005).

Table 4.1. Nonfinancial Corporate Sector: Change in Selected Variables
(Percent of GDP)

	Gross Operating Surplus (adjusted)[1] (1)	Property Income[2] (2)	Net Interest Paid (3)	Taxes (4)	Profits After Net Interest and Taxes (5 = 1 + 2 − 3 − 4)	Dividends Paid (6)	Gross Savings (7 = 5 − 6)	Capital Spending[3] (8)	Net Lending (9 = 7 − 8)
				2004 less 2000					
Canada	. . .	. . .	. . .	. . .	. . .	. . .	1.8	−1.5	3.3
France	−0.2	0.9	−0.1	−0.3	1.1	1.6	−0.5	−1.1	0.6
Germany	1.6	−0.5	−0.4	−0.7	2.2	−0.2	2.5	−4.6	7.1
Italy	−1.5	−0.5	−0.2	0.4	−2.1	−0.9	−1.1	−1.7	0.5
Japan	1.7	0.4	−1.3	—	3.4	0.9	2.5	−1.6	4.1
United Kingdom	−1.2	1.1	—	−0.5	0.4	−0.7	1.1	−1.8	2.9
United States	0.3	−0.1	−0.5	−0.3	1.1	0.4	0.7	−2.1	2.8
G-7[4]	0.4	0.3	−0.6	−0.3	1.6	0.9	0.8	−2.2	3.0
				2004 less mid-1990s[5]					
Canada	. . .	. . .	. . .	. . .	. . .	. . .	3.6	0.6	2.9
France	−0.3	2.6	−1.5	0.3	3.5	3.1	0.4	1.2	−0.8
Germany	3.3	0.3	−0.6	0.1	4.0	3.3	0.8	−1.4	2.2
Italy	−1.6	—	−1.5	−0.4	0.3	0.3	−0.1	1.2	−1.3
Japan	1.8	0.4	−3.8	−0.5	6.5	1.0	5.6	−0.7	6.3
United Kingdom	−2.1	1.3	0.4	−0.4	−0.8	−1.3	0.5	−0.2	0.7
United States	−0.4	0.3	−0.1	−0.5	0.5	0.6	−0.1	−0.8	0.7
G-7[4]	−0.3	0.7	−1.3	−0.4	2.1	1.3	1.0	−0.9	1.9

Sources: Eurostat; national statistical sources; and IMF staff calculations.

[1]Gross operating surplus is defined as gross value added less compensation of employees and taxes on production and imports, net of subsidies. Adjusted gross operating surplus adds net rents and current transfers to gross value added, and includes social benefits other than social transfers in kind less social contributions received in compensation of employees.

[2]Property income includes net reinvested earnings on direct foreign investment, dividends received, and property income attributed to insurance policyholders, and subtracts the adjustment for the change in net equity of households in pension fund reserves.

[3]Includes gross fixed capital formation, change in inventories, capital transfers, and acquisition of nonfinancial nonproduced assets.

[4]GDP-weighted average.

[5]Mid-1990s is average of 1994, 1995, and 1996 values. Germany data on capital spending were corrected for the 1995 capital transfer referred to in footnote 2.

occurred in the corporate sector mainly through a sharp reduction in wage costs (Schumacher, 2005).[4]

Declining Capital Spending: A "Real" Story?

While higher profits explain part of the rise in NFCS excess saving in recent years, the decline in nominal capital spending explains around three-quarters of the increase in NFCS net lending since 2000 in the G-7 countries. Simply put, firms have been investing a smaller share of their profits in upgrading and expanding their capital stock. A key question in trying to understand corporate behavior is whether this decline in investment spending is simply a short-term reaction to the high corporate debt levels of the early 2000s.

Empirical evidence certainly suggests that high-leverage positions may have a substantial negative impact on investment activity, with a financial accelerator mechanism crimping investment through the decline in firms' net worth and collateral.[5] Nevertheless, there has

[4]This does not preclude the possibility that structural factors could boost NFCS operating surpluses going forward in other countries, particularly if strong productivity growth (especially in the United States) and subdued wage developments (especially in European countries) continue to compress unit labor costs (which were flat on average in 2002–04 in the G-7 economies, compared to an average 1½ percent growth rate over the previous seven years).

[5]See "When Bubbles Burst," Chapter II in the April 2003 *World Economic Outlook*; and Jaeger (2003). At least in some countries, increased caution on capital spending and heavier reliance on internal resources may also reflect the fallout for the cost of capital and market confidence from the corporate accounting and governance scandals of the early 2000s.

Figure 4.3. Nonfinancial Corporate Sector: Gross Operating Surplus and Profits
(Percent of GDP)

While profits (after taxes and interest) were on an upward trend in almost all G-7 countries, gross operating surplus as a share of GDP has increased only in Germany over the last decade.

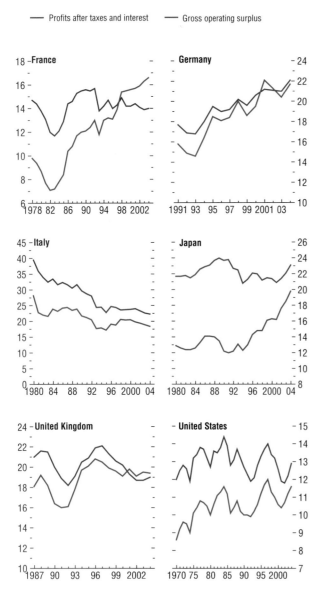

Sources: Eurostat; national authorities; and IMF staff calculations.

also been a longer-term downward trend in the relative price of capital goods. Firms now have to invest less in nominal terms to achieve a given real investment rate. Indeed, while capital spending measured in current prices has declined in all the G-7 countries since 2000, in real terms the trends have been more variable. The real capital spending of the NFCS has increased in Canada, remained broadly constant in the United Kingdom, and picked up strongly over the last two years in France, Japan, and Italy, where it is almost back to the levels in 2000. Germany and the United States are exceptions, as the fall in the NFCS real investment ratio in these two countries has been more pronounced.[6] For the G-7 as a whole, about one-half of the decline in the nominal investment ratio is due to the decline in relative prices of capital goods.

Overall, therefore, the subdued level of NFCS nominal capital spending may not simply be a reaction to the "excesses" of the late 1990s.[7] Indeed, IMF staff estimates suggest that the behavior of real investment ratios in the industrial countries in recent years is relatively well explained by a set of basic economic fundamentals, although real investment ratios are still currently below what an econometric model would

[6]This could be due to the relatively higher indebtedness of German and U.S. nonfinancial corporates at the time of the equity market decline in the early 2000s—between 1995 and 2001 leverage ratios (net debt over internal funds) increased more sharply in Germany and the United States than in the other G-7 economies (with the exception of the United Kingdom). However, the fall in NFCS real investment in these two countries also reflects structural factors: in Germany, the weak profitability of small and medium enterprises that account for most of the domestic investment (IMF, 2006a); in the United States, the 30-year secular decline of investment in structures (in 2004, real investment in equipment and software of the total private sector was back at its 2000 level).

[7]Desai and Goolsbee (2004) show that U.S. firms and sectors that were holding back investment plans in 2004 were not the same as those that invested the most in the late 1990s, suggesting that the cyclical weakness of U.S. business investment does not reflect a capital overhang from the late 1990s.

Box 4.2. Trends in the Financial Sector's Profits and Savings

The financial corporate sector (FCS) in the G-7 countries has been in a financial surplus (i.e., undistributed profits have exceeded capital expenditure) since the early 1990s and, driven by a strong acceleration in undistributed profits, this surplus reached a two-decade high in 2004. Although financial corporations accounted for only one-fourth of the increase in the excess savings of the total (nonfinancial plus financial) G-7 corporate sector between 2000 and 2004, it is important to understand what has been driving the behavior of this sector, given the differences with the nonfinancial corporate sector (see the main text).

As FCS investment levels have been relatively stable in most G-7 countries during the last decade (first figure)—with the exceptions of Canada and Germany where capital spending has declined markedly since the late 1990s— excess saving has primarily been driven by changes in undistributed profits. In turn, with dividends paid by financial corporations relatively flat, or increasing modestly, in most G-7 economies, the main source of the increase in FCS undistributed profits is found in after-tax profits (which accounted for around three-fourths of the increase between 2000 and 2004).[1]

This box examines the main factors that underlie the evolution of financial sector profitability in the G-7 countries from the perspective of national accounts data.[2] At the outset, it should be kept in mind that the financial corporate sector comprises several different types of institutions (primarily banks, pension funds, and insurance companies)

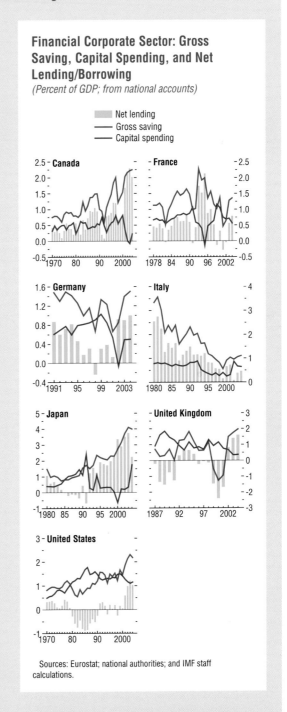

Financial Corporate Sector: Gross Saving, Capital Spending, and Net Lending/Borrowing
(Percent of GDP; from national accounts)

Sources: Eurostat; national authorities; and IMF staff calculations.

Note: The main authors of this box are Roberto Cardarelli, Daniel Hardy, and Miguel Segoviano.
[1]The only exception is France, where undistributed profits have trended downward since the mid-1990s because of the strong increase in dividends paid by financial corporations.
[2]The national account concepts differ from those used in commercial accounting and in particular they do not take into account valuation changes, such as gains and losses on securities held on investment accounts and credit write-offs.

whose behavior is driven by different factors which need to be disentangled to explain sector-wide trends.

Box 4.2 *(concluded)*

A Longer-Term Perspective

Even though some general patterns are evident in the financial industry at a global level—including the shift to consumer-driven financial products, within industry consolidation, and a growing demand for asset management and private banking services—there have been considerable differences across G-7 countries in the behavior of financial sector profits over the past two decades. In particular, in France, Japan, and the United States, profits have been on a rising trend, while in Italy they have been falling; while exhibiting some cyclicality, neither Germany nor the United Kingdom shows any clear trend. This cross-country variation may reflect differences in regulatory frameworks and in macroeconomic conditions that have affected both the intensity and the timing with which global patterns have impacted national financial systems.

Among the most important factors explaining FCS developments at the national level are the following:

• The upward trend in Japan FCS profits has been driven mainly by public financial institutions—which have intermediated an increasing volume of funds over the 1990s (Bank of Japan, 2005)—and, to a lesser extent, domestic banks. The high profitability of the public financial institutions is partly explained by the competitive advantage they have enjoyed—including an implicit government guarantee on borrowing and exemptions from paying corporate tax and deposit insurance premiums (Callen and Ostry, 2003). For the domestic banks, the observed upward trend in financial corporate profits in the national accounts appears at odds with the past weakness of the Japanese banking sector, which has been severely affected by credit costs and losses on large equity holdings following the asset prices boom-bust cycle of the late 1980s (IMF, 2005). However, excluding losses from financial operations and provisions against bad loans—as the national accounts statistics do—Japanese banks' profits have been on a modest upward trend since the early 1990s, mainly reflecting falling operating expenses as banks have inten-

Net Income Before Provisions of Banks in Selected G-7 Countries
(Percent of GDP; from financial statements of banks)

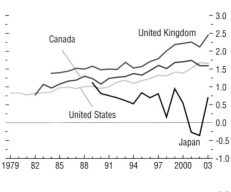

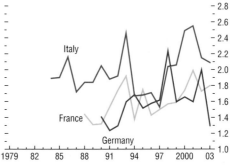

Sources: OECD, *Bank Profitability Database*; and IMF staff calculations.

sified their administrative cost-cutting efforts, particularly in the personnel area.

• The upward trend in the U.S. FCS profits is attributable to banks and especially finance companies, the major suppliers of credit to consumers and businesses (second figure).[3] This trend may in part be explained by advances in financial technology, such as

---

[3]Finance companies are nonbank financial institutions that provide credit to households—including loans and leases to finance the purchase of consumer goods, such as automobiles, furniture, and household appliances—and businesses—including short- and intermediate-term credit for the purpose of purchasing equipment and motor vehicles and the financing of inventories.

credit scoring systems, and increased borrowing by households in recent years.

- Profits of financial corporations in European countries were generally flat or falling over the 1990s. This, however, seems primarily attributable to developments among nonbank financial institutions (such as the pension and insurance sector) where increased competition compressed margins. On the other hand, bank profitability has been rising relative to GDP since the early 1990s, especially in the United Kingdom. The negative long-term trends may also be related to declining inflation.

More Recent Developments

In all countries, profits of the financial corporate sector have accelerated strongly since the early 2000s. Part of the reason is cyclical as net income tends to rise during upswings, reflecting a pickup in lending—which increases both inter-

est and noninterest income, mainly from fees associated with the origination, sales, and servicing of financial products—and the steep yield curve in the initial stages of recovery that allows banks to increase their net interest income.[4] In addition, there has been a tendency to distribute a smaller share of these profits through dividends (particularly in European countries), partly reflecting greater pressure from markets for financial institutions to improve their ratings by strengthening their capital bases (see IMF, 2006b).

[4]This effect has been less important for Japan, where the yield curve has remained relatively flat since 2000. Moreover, in several of the G-7 countries the yield curve has been flattening since early 2004, suggesting that this effect is not going to play a role going forward. It should also be noted that changes in the yield curve may have now a more muted impact on banks' profitability compared to the past, as financial innovation has reduced banks' reliance on interest margins.

predict.[8] This result seems inconsistent with the view that there has been a regime change in the underlying capital accumulation process of industrial countries in recent years, and it also suggests that at least some of the reduction in nominal capital spending is unlikely to be reversed.[9]

Paying Down Debt

Faced with unexpectedly high debt ratios after the fall of equity valuations in the early 2000s, some firms have clearly made an explicit decision to use profits to repay debt (bank loans and corporate bonds) rather than reinvest them in their

businesses or distribute them to shareholders as dividends. In addition, concerns about the vulnerability to changes in financial market conditions and about the access to credit in an adverse economic environment have induced firms to reduce their dependence on external financing and to rely more on internally generated funds.

Net borrowing by the NFCS has declined in all the G-7 countries since the late 1990s although only in Japan and, more recently, in France and Germany have companies, in aggregate, actually been repaying debt (Figure 4.4). Indeed, only in Canada and Japan is corporate leverage substantially below its late 1990s levels, although firms

[8]Estimated on annual data. The set of explanatory variables includes the first lag of the gross fixed investment ratio; real per capita output growth; the cost of capital, measured as the ratio of the real interest rate to the relative price of capital; and the elderly and youth dependency ratios. The dynamic panel model was estimated using the Generalized Method of Moments estimator with robust errors. See "Global Imbalances: A Saving and Investment Perspective," Chapter II in the September 2005 *World Economic Outlook,* for a more detailed description.

[9]Technological progress will likely continue to lower the prices of capital goods, especially in information technology (IT) capital, and this in turn will help to boost the volume of capital spending. However, as the IT industry has matured—and most companies now need to upgrade their existing stock of IT technology rather than building it from scratch—the response of corporate spending on IT capital for a given change in prices is likely to be more muted compared to the 1990s (Doms, 2005). This suggests that nominal spending on IT capital may not increase as quickly as it did in the late 1990s, and that real spending in IT goods may also grow at more modest rates.

Figure 4.4. Nonfinancial Corporate Sector: Financial Accounts, Selected Variables
(Percent of gross saving)

Net borrowing has fallen sharply in almost all G-7 countries since the early 2000s. The accumulation of equities has been on an upward trend in several G-7 economies since the early 1990s, while cash holdings have accelerated more recently, especially in the United States, the United Kingdom, and Canada.

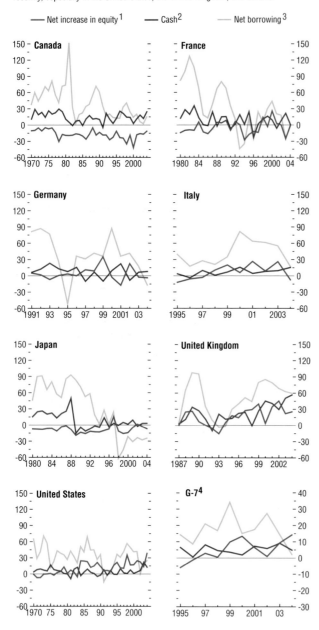

Sources: Eurostat; national authorities; and IMF staff calculations.
[1]Net shares and other equity (change in assets minus change in liabilities).
[2]Net currency and deposits plus short-term securities other than shares (change in assets minus change in liabilities).
[3]Net loans and long-term securities other than shares (change in liabilities minus change in assets).
[4]GDP-weighted averages using GDP in U.S. dollars at market exchange rates.

in a number of G-7 countries have taken advantage of low interest rates to lengthen the maturity profile of their debt, and the share of the short-term to total NFCS debt has declined noticeably in almost all of the G-7 countries.[10] Debt repayment, however, has not been the primary reason for companies' excess savings. Rather, for the G-7 as a group, nonfinancial corporations have tended to invest their excess cash flow primarily into equities and cash, rather than repaying debt (Figure 4.5).

Accumulating Equities

In Italy (until 2004), the United Kingdom, and the United States, the nonfinancial corporate sector has been accumulating substantial amounts of equity in recent years. This equity accumulation reflects higher (net) direct investment abroad and/or the repurchase of equities from the household and government sectors. While the lack of sufficiently detailed flow of funds data for all the G-7 countries prevents drawing broad conclusions, some insights on the relative importance on these two types of financial transactions can be drawn for the United Kingdom and the United States where data is available.

- Share repurchasing has been very important in the United States, in particular, where nonfinancial corporates have retired an extraordinary amount of equity since the late 1990s, both in cash-financed mergers and through share repurchase programs.[11]

[10]At the same time, firm-level data discussed in the next section show that, over the recent past, at least some firms have financed "cash hoarding" with external financing, as they took advantage of favorable financial market conditions (low interest rates, tight credit spreads, and rising equity prices) to accumulate cash buffers.
[11]Share repurchasing can be interpreted as a more tax-effective way of transferring resources to the household sector, as it subjects individual investors to capital gains taxes that are usually lower than dividend taxes. Surveys of U.S. financial executives, however, suggest that managers believe investors have a strong preference for dividends and tend to repurchase shares when facing temporary earning increases or lack of good investment opportunities, rather than as an alternative to dividend payments (Brav and others, 2003). The increased reliance

- The (net) purchase of equities from the rest of the world shows that nonfinancial corporations in the United Kingdom and the United States have been pursuing a strategy of expansion through acquiring assets abroad, including in emerging markets. Rather than financing new investment at home, part of the internal funds available to nonfinancial corporations in these two countries has been used to purchase existing capital equipment abroad. For the United States, if net direct investment abroad by nonfinancial corporations is added to their domestic capital spending, nominal total NFCS capital spending in 2004 is broadly at the same level as in the late 1990s. This suggests that one factor behind the relative weakness of domestic capital spending by nonfinancial corporations in the United States in recent years is their increased financial investment overseas.

Why Are Firms Accumulating So Much Cash?

Companies in Canada, Japan, the United States, and, particularly, the United Kingdom have increased their cash holdings in recent years. This cash accumulation is more difficult to rationalize than either debt repayment or equity accumulation: why would firms want to hold so much cash on their balance sheets? Firm-level data for listed, nonfinancial companies in the G-7 countries provide the following insights into this cash accumulation.[12]

---

on share repurchasing in the United States may also reflect the record number of stock options issued in the 1990s, which provided managers with a strong incentive to repurchase their firm's shares in order to maintain high stock prices (Weisbenner, 2000).

[12]The sample of firms is from the Worldscope database and covers about 10,000 nonfinancial listed companies in the G-7 countries in 2004. Differences in accounting principles and in sample coverage prevent an exact mapping between the trends in the national accounts and firm-level data. However, aggregating cash and saving at the firm level obtains broadly the same patterns shown by national accounts—specifically, a sharp increase in undistributed profits as a share of revenues from sales, and of cash accumulation as a share of undistributed profits over the recent past, particularly in Canada, the United Kingdom, and the United States.

Figure 4.5. Financial Transactions: Nonfinancial Corporate Sector of the G-7 Countries[1]
(Average, percent of GDP)

Nonfinancial corporates primarily invested in equities and cash on average during the 2001–04 period.

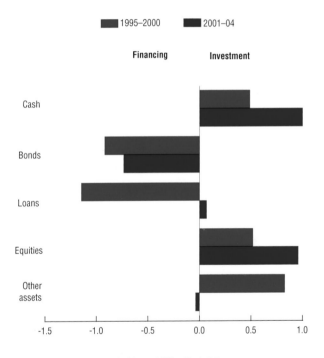

Sources: Eurostat; national authorities; and IMF staff calculations.
[1]GDP-weighted averages using GDP in U.S. dollars at market exchange rates.

Figure 4.6. Cash Accumulation in the G-7 Countries by Industry[1]
(Percent of total assets)

Cash accumulation has been particularly strong in the information technology (IT) sector in recent years. In 2004, only the IT and resource sectors have significantly accelerated the accumulation of cash holdings.

- Change from 2003–04
- Average for the period 1996–2000
- Average for the period 2001–04

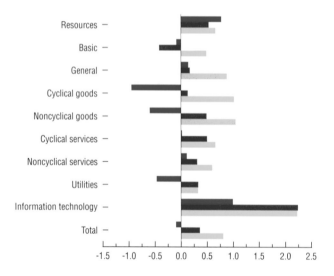

Sources: Thomson Worldscope database; and IMF staff calculations.
[1] Industry averages calculated as the sum of cash accumulation for the stated period divided by the sum of total assets for the same period.

- Cash accumulation (as a share of total assets) was more than twice as high during 2001–04 than 1996–2000, with all sectors increasing their cash accumulation (Figure 4.6). However, aggregate corporate cash accumulation declined modestly in 2004 as continued increases in the information technology (IT) and resources sectors were more than offset by declines in other sectors, particularly utilities and cyclical goods. This suggests that while there were common factors behind the increase in corporate cash holdings in the early 2000s, recent behavior has been driven by industry-specific factors, particularly stronger profits in resource companies following the upsurge in commodity prices (which likely continued in 2005).

- As well as differences across industries, the distribution of cash accumulation across firms is very unequal in dollar terms, with the median increase in cash among the largest firms being eight times larger than among the mid-size firms in the sample (Table 4.2). Further, the accumulation of cash is far from universal—about 40 percent of the firms in the sample actually reduced their cash balances during 2001–04. Nevertheless, while the biggest 100 firms in the sample accounted for about 40 percent of total cash accumulation on average between 2001 and 2004, they also accounted for 40 percent of total sales, indicating that cash accumulation has been relatively evenly distributed once firm size is accounted for. This stands in contrast to the 1996–2000 period when cash accumulation was driven primarily by the smallest firms, suggesting that some of the factors underlying cash accumulation may have changed over these two periods.

The economics literature, summarized in Opler and others (1999), presents two views on corporate cash holdings. The first is that cash holdings are simply a sideshow—they change mechanically with a firm's excess cash flow (retained earnings less capital expenditure). The alternative view is that, in an attempt to maximize shareholder wealth, cash holdings are set at

Table 4.2. Group of Seven (G-7) Countries: Cash Accumulation, by Size of Firm's Sales

Range of Sales (Billions of U.S. dollars)[1]	Number of Firms	Share of Total Change in Cash (Percent)	Median Change in Cash (Millions of U.S. dollars)	90th Percentile Change in Cash (Mllions of U.S. dollars)
Average 1996–2000				
0.0–3.1	3,075	75.8	0	29
3.2–9.3	302	11.9	3	224
9.4–19.6	119	20.7	10	517
20.4–48.0	52	14.8	44	1,016
49.6–172.0	19	−23.0	123	2,708
Average 2001–2004				
0.0–3.1	5,044	23.5	1	36
3.1–10.0	508	19.4	14	303
10.0–24.8	184	14.0	34	713
24.8–57.3	76	19.7	208	1,895
59.3–252.5	27	23.3	371	5,766

Source: IMF staff calculations based on Worldscope data.

[1]Groups are obtained by ranking each firm in the G-7 by their sales every year, and then dividing total yearly sales by 5. The top (fifth) group is thus formed by the biggest N firms that together account for one-fifth of total sales, the fourth group by those immediately smallest N firms that accounted for another fifth of total sales, and so on.

a level that equates the marginal cost and benefit. While the cost of holding liquidity is the lower expected return, the benefits derive from the reduced probability of being short of financing if profits fail to meet expectations, and, therefore, being forced to cut investment plans and/or dividend payments or having to raise costly external finance.

The accumulation of cash in recent years may therefore be related to strong profit growth, but also reflects factors that have changed the expected benefits or costs of cash holdings, including lower interest rates; higher sales (and profit) volatility as firms are now operating in a more uncertain environment (Figure 4.7);[13] and the larger share of intangible assets in corporate balance sheets (firms with more intangible assets are likely to hold more cash given the higher cost of external finance for these type of uncolla-

terized and more volatile assets; see Passov, 2003).

Indeed, firms that have accumulated more cash relative to their total assets (those in the top quartile of the increase in cash over total assets distribution) tend to have more volatile sales, a higher share of intangible assets, and higher Tobin's q (which proxies for higher expected profitable investment opportunities; see Appendix 4.1). At the same time, however, cash-rich firms are also the ones with larger excess cash flow (the difference between gross savings and capital spending), suggesting that strong profitability has also played a role.[14] If cash accumulation has been driven by changes in the marginal cost and benefits of holding liquid assets rather than simply excess cash flows, the variables described earlier should be able to explain a significant share of the increase in

[13]Comin and Philippon (2006) show an increase in firm volatility in the United States since the mid 1950s, and attribute it to increased competition spurred by globalization.

[14]Firms with the highest increase in cash relative to their total assets also had relatively higher access to external financing, lending some support to the view that at least some firms may have been taking advantage of temporarily advantageous conditions for external financing to accumulate cash holdings that will be used as a buffer when external capital is more expensive (Greenwood, 2005). Also, on average over 2001–04, cash-rich firms tend to have smaller net assets from acquisitions, contrary to the view that associates the recent increase in cash accumulation with the resurgence of mergers and acquisition ventures. A possible explanation is that if the threat of takeovers increases with a firm's liquidity position, companies that operate in sectors with relatively strong mergers and acquisition activity have an incentive to hold less, not more, cash.

Figure 4.7. Sales Volatility and Intangible Assets in the G-7 Countries

Over the last decade, sales volatility and the share of intangible assets have increased in the sample of firms considered.

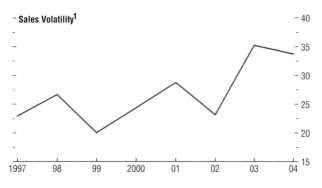

Sales Volatility[1]

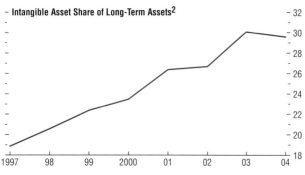

Intangible Asset Share of Long-Term Assets[2]

Sources: Thomson Analytics Worldscope database; and IMF staff calculations.
[1]Market capitalization-weighted average of five-year rolling standard deviation of growth rate of firms' sales.
[2]Market capitalization-weighted average of the stock of intangible assets in percent of long-term assets (defined as total assets minus assets with maturity of one year or less).

cash holdings over the recent period. The econometric analysis—shown in Appendix 4.1—indicates that:[15]

• On average for the 2001–04 period, the coefficients of industry sales volatility, the industry share of intangibles assets, and industry Tobin's q all have the expected signs and are statistically significant determinants of changes in cash relative to total assets among G-7 firms.

• A 1 percent increase in the intangible asset share of a company or a 1 standard deviation increase in sales volatility would induce a 5 percent increase in the share of savings invested in cash.[16] Together, these two variables explain around one-third of the increase in cash over total assets on average in 2001–04.

• The regression covering the whole period, 1996–2004, also shows that the accumulation of cash balances accelerated especially in those sectors with higher volatility of sales.

All in all, the econometric results provide some important insights into why corporates have increased their cash holdings in recent years, yet a good deal of the buildup remains unexplained, suggesting that country- and firm-specific factors have played an important role.

One commonly cited factor, for example, is that some companies have large unfunded pension liabilities. The plunge in equity valuations in the early 2000s and declining interest rates have caused the funded status of corporate-sponsored defined benefit pension plans to deteriorate significantly. In the United States, defined benefit pension plans sponsored by the S&P 500 firms moved from a $200 billion surplus in 2000 to a $200 billion deficit at end-2004 (see Zion

[15]The econometric analysis is based on a cross-section regression, which explains the average relationship between the increase in cash over total assets and the explanatory variables in the most recent period, 2001–04; and a panel regression, which captures the possible changes in this relationship over the whole sample period, 1996–2004.
[16]The impact on the share of retained earnings invested in cash is derived from the regression coefficients using the average ratio between retained earnings and total assets in the G-7 countries over 2001–04.

Table 4.3. Defined Benefits Corporate Pension Plans: Assets Over Liabilities[1]

	1999	2002	2003	2004
Canada	...	...	0.86	0.83
France	...	...	...	0.47
Germany	...	...	0.36	0.51
Japan	...	...	0.58	0.59
United Kingdom	...	...	0.77	0.80
United States	1.31	0.82	0.89	0.90

Sources: Watson Wyatt, 2006; and Watson Wyatt *Insider*, various issues.

[1]Pension liabilities are defined as the actuarial present value of benefit obligations. A ratio higher than 1 means that the pension schemes are overfunded. Positions are as of December 31 of each year.

and Carcache, 2005). Recent estimates (Watson Wyatt, 2006) suggest that corporate defined benefit pension plans are significantly underfunded in all the G-7 countries, but particularly in Europe (Table 4.3).[17] Firms in these countries may therefore be building up cash holdings as a precaution against the need to contribute larger-than-anticipated amounts into their pension plans—for example, by purchasing long-term assets.[18] Unfortunately, company-specific data is not available to test this within the econometric framework.

Are Current Trends in Corporate Excess Saving Sustainable?

As discussed in the previous section, excess saving in corporate sectors of G-7 countries has been at a historic high in recent years. This has helped offset some of the decline in household and government saving, and has contributed to the relatively low level of long-term interest rates. A key question going forward is whether this increase in excess saving is largely a temporary phenomenon, and therefore likely to be reversed over the next few years, or whether it represents a more fundamental change in corporate behavior. Some of the factors that will determine this are discussed below.

- *The profit outlook.* It is difficult to argue that there has been a significant and permanent increase in the profitability of the nonfinancial corporate sector in all the G-7 countries in recent years. Rather, NFCS profits have greatly benefited from current low interest rates and reductions in corporate tax payments. Both of these are likely to reverse to some degree. Monetary policy will likely tighten going forward, raising interest payments, although the decreased reliance on short-term debt and the decline in debt ratios should help limit the increase. Further, earlier corporate tax cuts, at least in some countries, may need to be withdrawn under increasing pressures on government budget positions (although cross-country tax competition may limit this).

- *Will domestic investment pick up?* With capacity utilization increasing in some countries, it seems reasonable to expect that investment will strengthen going forward. Nevertheless, the ongoing decline in the relative price of capital goods means that nominal investment ratios are likely to remain below those seen in previous cycles.[19]

[17]This does not mean that European countries have a more serious problem of underfunding, however, as company-sponsored defined benefit pension plans play a more limited role in the overall pension systems of these countries compared to the other G-7 countries (see IMF, 2004).

[18]In the United Kingdom—where NFCS cash holdings have increased the most over the recent past—changes in the minimum funding requirement for occupational defined benefit pension plans were introduced in 2005 that aim at eliminating the underfunding over a 10-year time span. Based on estimates from the U.K. Pension Regulator, this will require £130 billion additional contributions into company pension schemes, imposing a substantial burden on the pension contribution paid by employers, which has already increased sharply over the last four years—in 2004 they stood at approximately £38 billion, almost doubling the £21 billion paid in 2000.

[19]Legislative and regulatory measures recently implemented in several industrial countries to improve corporate governance may have a positive effect on corporate and investor confidence and, therefore, capital spending. These measures, however, may also reduce the valuation discount that shareholders apply to firms with high cash balances and lower dividend payouts, as stronger corporate governance reduces the risk of overinvestment in negative yield projects or outright stealing from entrenched managers (see Kalcheva and Lins, 2005).

Figure 4.8. Nonfinancial Corporate Sector Debt[1]
(Percent of gross saving)

Only in Japan and Canada is corporate debt (as a ratio to internal funds)
significantly below its mid-1990s level.

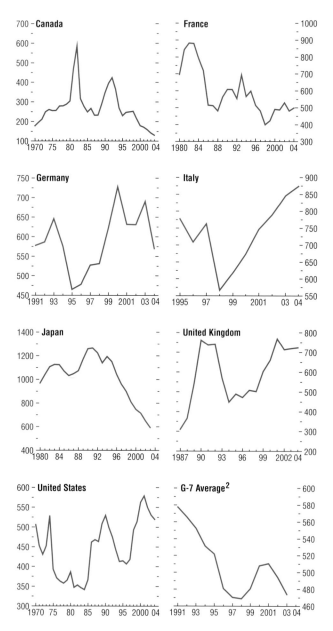

Sources: Eurostat; national authorities; and IMF staff calculations.
[1]Net loans and long-term securities other than shares (liabilities minus assets).
[2]GDP-weighted averages using GDP in U.S. dollars at market exchange rates.

• *Has the process of deleveraging been completed?* It
is clearly difficult to know whether the
deleveraging process has ended. Substantial
progress has been made in reducing corporate debt in some countries, and an international survey by Merrill Lynch Global Fund
Managers shows that investors have become
much less worried about companies leverage ratios. Indeed, only 18 percent of the
investors questioned in the most recent survey
wanted companies to improve their balance
sheets, compared to 31 percent at the end of
2003 and 55 percent at the end of 2002.
Nevertheless, even if low interest rates have
helped nonfinancial corporations to extend
their average debt maturity, only in Canada
and Japan is the ratio of debt to undistributed
profits (internal funds) below the levels seen
in the late 1990s (Figure 4.8). At the same
time, the lack of comprehensive data on off-
balance-sheet liabilities makes it impossible to
assess the complete corporate credit picture.
In particular, unfunded pension liabilities are
excluded from reported balance sheet leverage, and consequently debt ratios could be
severely understated.

• *Investment in equities is here to stay.* There is no
reason to expect the accumulation of equities
by corporates—through either share repurchasing or investing abroad—to come to a
halt. Indeed, given ongoing globalization and
the opportunities that companies in industrial
countries enjoy in emerging markets, the pace
of overseas asset acquisition may actually
increase.

• *Will firms want to continue to hold cash?* While
the upward trend in both sales volatility and
the share of intangible assets at the firm level
may have increased the desired amount of
cash balances, these two trends can only partially explain the increase in cash holdings
over the last four years. Other factors suggest
this is a relatively temporary phenomenon. In
particular, the fact that cash accumulation
during 2004 increased solely in the IT and
resources sectors—where profits were strong—
suggests this process may now be tailing off.

In sum, while it is clearly very difficult to predict the behavior of the corporate sector going forward, the most likely scenario is that excess savings will decline from current levels over the next few years if investment picks up, some of the factors that have driven recent profits wane, or investors put less pressure on corporations to reduce their debt levels. Nevertheless, a number of structural changes—including increased volatility in the operating environment, a desire to increase investment overseas, and the need to finance off-balance-sheet liabilities—means that corporate excess saving may remain more elevated than during the 1990s.

Conclusions

The corporate sector in the G-7 countries has moved from being a net borrower to a substantial net saver in recent years. This has followed the earlier move by emerging market countries to a net saver status following the financial crises of the late 1990s. Taken together, these developments have substantially altered the financial landscape of the global economy—two sectors that have traditionally been sources of demand for financing are now lending to other countries/sectors. These changes in behavior are one factor behind the relatively low level of global long-term interest rates at present.

With regard to the nonfinancial corporate sector, one commonly held view is that the recent increase in net lending is mainly a reaction to the excess debt and physical capital that was accumulated in the 1990s, and it is therefore temporary. Once these excesses have been worked out, the corporate sector will again become a net borrower, and as this occurs, it will put upward pressure on long-term interest rates. This chapter, however, has suggested that the story is not as simple as this—indeed, only in Canada and Japan has the reduction in corporate debt been substantial enough to be consistent with this story. Other factors, some cyclical and some structural, have also played a role, although their importance has differed across countries. In particular:

- Profits have been strong, primarily because of low interest rates and a generalized reduction of corporate tax payments, while operating profits do not appear to be abnormally high, despite their recent acceleration in a few countries. If companies view these factors as unlikely to be sustained going forward, they may hold back on investment plans and instead boost their savings;
- Ongoing technological change has reduced the relative price of capital goods, and reduced the nominal spending needed to achieve a given *volume* of capital;
- Companies have increased their purchases of assets abroad, shifting resources from domestic capital accumulation; and
- Companies have increased their desired cash holdings, partly as a reaction to the more uncertain operating environment they face, the increasing role of intangible assets in the knowledge-based economy, and possibly the uncertainties associated with how they will be asked to meet currently unfunded pension liabilities.

Judging the relative weight of all these factors in explaining the current high level of corporate excess saving is clearly a difficult task. It does, however, seem reasonable to conclude that the corporate sector in industrial countries will not return to the large negative financing positions of the past—paralleling to some degree the behavior of emerging market economies, where current account surpluses have proved more long-lasting than originally projected. Nevertheless, excess savings are also unlikely to be sustained at current record levels going forward, particularly if the degree of slack in the advanced economies continues to narrow—thereby encouraging stronger investment spending—or corporate profitability weakens. Thus, high corporate saving should not be relied on to keep longer-term interest rates low in the future. Indeed, without some increase in household and government saving in the coming years, changing corporate behavior will likely start to put upward pressure on interest rates, and could exacerbate the current pattern of global imbalances if it lowered total private saving in deficit countries.

Appendix 4.1. Econometric Methodology

The main authors of this appendix are Roberto Cardarelli and Kenichi Ueda.

To investigate the accumulation of liquid assets (or "cash") of nonfinancial corporations in the G-7 economies, firm-level data were used from the Worldscope database.[20] After screening for outliers, the sample covered about 10,000 nonfinancial listed companies in the G-7 countries in 2004. About 4,000 of these are from the United States, 3,000 from Japan, 1,000 from the United Kingdom, 700 from Canada, 500 from France, 400 from Germany, and 200 from Italy. Each country's share of total (G-7) revenues from sales is approximately equal to its share of total GDP, suggesting that each country is adequately represented in the sample. While data are available since the 1980s, only for the United States is there a sufficiently large number of firms before the mid-1990s. Therefore, this chapter restricts the analysis to the 1996–2004 period (in 1996, the sample contains about 3,500 firms).

Using firm-level data, the chapter relates cash accumulation to a series of variables that are generally believed to affect the marginal costs and benefits of holding cash (the expected sign of the causality direction is indicated in parenthesis):[21]

- Size/age of firms (−/+); bigger/older firms should have easier or cheaper access to external financing, so they should hold less cash. However, if cash accumulation is simply a residual, larger and mature firms should have more cash as they are more likely to generate cash flow in excess of profitable investment opportunities.

- Volatility of sales (+); firms with more uncertain sales revenues (e.g., those in a more competitive industry) should invest more in liquidity because (all other things being equal) they are more likely to suffer from cash shortages.

- Tobin's q (+); firms with a higher Tobin's q (more profitable investment opportunities) should accumulate more cash, as cash shortages would mean these firms have to forgo high-return projects.

- Intangible asset share of total fixed assets (+); firms characterized by a larger share of intangible assets (e.g., patents and goodwill) should hold more cash, given the higher cost of external finance for these type of uncollaterizable assets.

- Net assets from acquisition (−/+); firms that operate in sectors and countries with a relatively high level of merger and acquisition activity should hold more cash, as cash-rich firms are more likely to make acquisitions. However, if the threat of takeovers increases with a firm's liquidity position, this could have a negative effect on cash holdings.

In investigating these determinants empirically, both descriptive statistics and regression analysis are used in the chapter.

First, firms that have invested in cash the most, on average over 2001–04 (those in the top quartile of the distribution of the change in cash—Increase in Cash and Short-Term Investments in Worldscope (WS), with code 04851—relative to firm's total assets, WS 02999) are compared to those that invested in cash the least (those in the bottom quartile of the same distribution), in order to uncover systematic relations between cash accumulation and key firms' characteristics. In particular, the following variables were considered:

- Firm size, captured by the logarithm of revenues from sales (WS 01001) and logarithm of total assets.

---

[20]Income and balance sheet information are entered in Worldscope for each listed stock. As the same firm may be listed in several markets and it may have several types of listed stocks in the same market, information on the same firm may be entered several times. To avoid duplications, only balance sheet information associated with the most widely traded stock listed in the major home stock exchange is picked for each company. Liquid assets or "cash" is here defined as cash and short-term investments, including treasury bills, commercial paper, and certificates of deposits.

[21]See, for example, Opler and others (1999); and Almeida, Campello, and Weisbach (2002).

- Excess cash flows, defined as saving (net income, WS 04001, plus depreciation, WS 04051, less dividends paid, WS 04551) less capital expenditure (WS 04601), divided by total assets.
- Volatility of sales, defined as the five-year rolling standard deviation of sales growth.
- Tobin's q, defined as (market capitalization, WS 08001 + book value of total debt, WS 03255) divided by total assets.
- Intangible assets (WS 02649) divided by long-term assets (total assets less short-term assets—that is, assets expected to be realized, sold, or consumed within a year, WS 02201).
- Net assets from acquisition (WS 04355, from the cash flow statement) divided by total sources of cash (cash from operating activities, external financing, and decrease of investments).
- Net cash flow from financing (WS 04890) divided by total assets.
- Stock of cash (WS 02001) divided by total assets.

Both the univariate comparison of firms' characteristics by quartiles of cash accumulation and the regression analysis below are restricted to firms with positive net income, as the relationship between cash holdings and the explanatory factors listed above would be irrelevant for firms that do not have a chance to save.

For all firms with increases in cash over total assets in the same quartile, Table 4.4 shows the weighted averages, median, and 90th percentile of the variables described above. The last column reports the *p*-value of a *t*-test on the difference of averages of the first and fourth quartiles. The table shows that firms in the top quartile of the cash distribution significantly differ from those in the lowest quartile because they tend to be relatively smaller, have more volatile sales (although in median only), a higher share of

intangible assets, and higher Tobin's q. All these results accord well with the predictions of the trade-off model of cash holdings (Opler and others, 1999; and Almeida, Campello, and Weisbach, 2002), as it is especially for these types of firms that the cost of accessing external funds or having to cut down investment plans—and thus the benefit of holding additional cash—is larger. However, the table also shows that cash-rich firms tend to be those with the largest excess cash flows, consistent with the view that cash holdings are the side effect of higher earnings and lower capital spending.[22] The table also shows that cash-rich firms tend to have smaller net assets from acquisitions (on average, as the zero median reflects the relatively scarce number of firms reporting this type of investment), a relatively higher access to external financing (net cash flow from financing for the 90th percentile is monotonically increasing with cash accumulation), and relatively larger stocks of liquidity (relative to total assets).

Second, a formal regression analysis was conducted to examine the determinants of cash accumulation by G-7 firms. Specifically, changes in cash relative to firm's total assets at firm level were regressed on:

- Firm-level variables, including firm size (defined as logarithm of sales) and firm age (the number of years since the firm was founded, WS 18272, or incorporated, WS 18273).[23]
- Industry-level variables, including volatility of sales, the intangible share of long-term assets, Tobin's q, net assets from acquisition as a share of total sources of cash, and industry dummies.
- Country-level variables, including the yield spread (difference between long-term and short-term interest rates; source, IMF, *International Financial Statistics*, or IFS); general gov-

---

[22]This is what the pecking-order model of financing choice would predict. Based on this model, firms try avoiding issuing equity since information asymmetries make it too expensive, and thus accumulate cash—or pay back debt—when faced with a surplus of internal funds. When they have a deficit of internal resources, firms first decrease their cash balances and only eventually raise debt.

[23]If both are available for a company, the larger number is used.

Table 4.4. Weighted Average, Median, and 90th Percentile of Selected Series, by Change in Cash to Total Assets by Quartile, 2001–04[1]

Variable	First Quartile	Second Quartile	Third Quartile	Fourth Quartile	t-Test of Means First and Fourth Quartile
Change in cash in percent of total assets[2]	−3.3 [−3.1] (−1.2)	−0.1 [0.0] (0.4)	1.9 [1.9] (3.4)	8.0 [8.2] (22.3)	105.1
Saving less capital expenditure in percent of total assets[2]	1.9 [1.7] (10.1)	1.9 [2.5] (9.3)	2.8 [3.6] (10.8)	6.3 [8.0] (19.7)	29.9
Log of sales[3]	13.0 [13.0] (15.3)	13.4 [13.4] (15.9)	13.3 [13.3] (15.6)	12.4 [12.4] (14.8)	−19.2
Log of total assets[3]	13.0 [13.0] (15.3)	13.4 [13.4] (16.1)	13.2 [13.3] (15.7)	12.3 [12.3] (14.8)	−21.9
Volatility of sales[4]	37.6 [11.7] (41.4)	21.7 [11.0] (40.4)	21.3 [11.0] (36.8)	21.1 [15.1] (52.2)	−0.3
Tobin's q[4]	2.4 [1.0] (2.5)	1.7 [0.9] (2.0)	2.0 [1.0] (2.3)	3.4 [1.4] (3.9)	41.8
Intangible assets in percent of long-term assets[4]	24.8 [9.4] (73.1)	26.9 [11.2] (71.9)	26.8 [13.4] (71.8)	28.4 [18.5] (77.5)	7.4
Net assets from acquisition in percent of total sources of cash[5]	6.4 [0.0] (34.3)	5.9 [0.0] (28.7)	5.7 [0.0] (25.6)	3.6 [0.0] (13.7)	−9.0
Net cash flow from financing in percent of total assets[2]	−3.8 [−3.5] (4.1)	−2.9 [−2.6] (6.4)	−1.3 [−1.9] (6.2)	−1.0 [−0.6] (17.9)	14.5
Stock of cash in percent of total assets[2]	9.6 [8.6] (32.8)	5.0 [2.5] (16.3)	9.6 [8.2] (25.9)	20.4 [21.8] (53.3)	43.7
Memorandum Range of change in cash in percent of total assets	−87 to −0.93	−0.93 to 0.61	0.61 to 3.93	3.93 to 100	
Observations	4,330	4,330	4,330	4,329	

Sources: Worldscope; and IMF staff calculations.
[1]Median values in brackets, 90th percentile values in parentheses.
[2]Firm ratios weighted by total assets of firm.
[3]Simple average of firm ratios.
[4]Firm ratios weighted by market capitalization.
[5]Firm ratios weighted by total sources of cash.

ernment balance as a ratio to GDP (source: IFS); and country dummies.

Industry-level variables were obtained as market capitalization weighted averages of variables at firm level. Seventy-three nonfinancial industries were considered, based on the two-digit U.S. Standard Industrial Classification (SIC) from Worldscope (WS 07021).

The industry-level variables were constructed based only on U.S. data, on the assumption that the underlying feature of an industry can be measured only in the most competitive environment (see Rajan and Zingales, 1998, for a similar methodology). However, the degree to which an industry is exposed to a competitive environment differs among countries, and so the list of regressors also includes differences (at an aggregate level) between each country and the United States for all industry characteristics.[24] As an example, the volatility of revenues from sales of the textile sector in France is proxied by the volatility of sales of the U.S. textile industry and the difference between the aggregate volatility of sales in France and that in the United States. An important motivation for this regression strategy is also that the United States is the only country for which there is a sufficiently large number of firms in every industry in the early years of the sample. Hence, the U.S. industry variables are less likely to be affected by sample biases.

On the set of macroeconomic variables at the country level, the yield spread was included to capture the opportunity cost of holding cash, considering that cash includes short-term interest-bearing securities. The general government-balance-to-GDP ratio was introduced, as it may affect availability of external financing and also to capture the possible offset between corporate and government saving.

Two estimation methods were adopted. First, a cross-section regression was run based on 2001–04 averages. Second, a time series dimension was added by running a panel regression with three periods (the three-year averages: 1996–98, 1999–2001, and 2002–04) so as to assess whether there have been changes in cash accumulation since the mid-1990s. Time dummies were also introduced in the panel regression. The regressions were estimated using weighted ordinary least squares (OLS), with each firm weighted by its (own country) relative market capitalization at the beginning of the period. This gives large firms more weight in the regression, consistent with the objective of explaining the aggregate trends in cash accumulation. At the same time, the within-country market capitalization weighting gives each country the same influence in the regression.

Table 4.5. Regression Results: Dependent Variable—Change in Cash and Short-Term Investments[1]
(In percent of total assets)

	Weighted Cross-Section	Weighted Panel
Size of firm	−1.310 (0.034)**	−2.425 (0.001)***
Age of firm	0.003 (0.533)	0.001 (0.913)
Volatility of sales by SIC2 industry	0.165 (0.040)**	0.147 (0.009)***
Intangible asset share of long-term assets by SIC2 industry	0.171 (0.037)**	−0.117 (0.285)
Tobin's q by SIC2 industry	2.581 (0.012)**	0.015 (0.969)
Net assets from acquisitions in percent of total sources of cash by SIC2 industry	0.013 (0.794)	0.073 (0.211)
Volatility of sales by country	−0.001 (0.945)	−0.019 (0.143)
Intangible asset share of long-term assets by country	0.075 (0.311)	0.062 (0.318)
Net assets from acquisitions in percent of total sources of cash by country	0.268 (0.17)	0.292 (0.12)
Yield spread of interest rates, in percent	−0.466 (0.435)	0.215 (0.814)
General government balance, in percent of GDP	−0.348 (0.589)	−0.432 (0.312)
Observations	6,084	12,436
R-squared	0.568	0.552

Sources: Datastream Worldscope database; and IMF staff calculations.
[1]Robust p-values in parentheses; ** significant at 5 percent; *** significant at 1 percent.

The results of the analysis are presented in Table 4.5. In particular:
- In the cross-section, the coefficients on firm size, industry sales volatility, Tobin's q, and the industry share of intangible assets all have the expected signs and are significant. None of the country variables is statistically different than zero.
- In the panel regression, only firm size and industry sales volatility have coefficients statis-

---

[24]The exception is Tobin's q, which is considered only at the industry level. This is because cross-country variations of Tobin's q are sensitive to differences in market conditions (e.g., interest rates) and accounting systems, and are thus unlikely to reflect cross-country differences in growth opportunities for firms.

tically different than zero. This implies that, over the sample period, cash accumulation has accelerated in industries with higher sales volatility and that the increases in sales volatility have boosted cash accumulation over time.

- In both the cross-section and panel regressions the industry dummies substantially improve the goodness of fit, and are thus included in the final specification (however, they are not reported in Table 4.5). On the contrary, time and country effects are excluded as they are not statistically significant and fail to improve the goodness of fit, implying that both the cross-country and time variations of cash holdings are largely captured by the regressors.

References

Almeida, Heitor, Murillo Campello, Michael S. Weisbach, 2002, "Corporate Demand for Liquidity," NBER Working Paper No. 9253 (Cambridge, Massachusetts: National Bureau of Economic Research).

Auerbach, Alan, 1982, "Issues in the Measurement and Determinants of Business Saving," NBER Working Paper No. 1024 (Cambridge, Massachusetts: National Bureau of Economic Research).

———, and Kevin Hassett, 1991, "Corporate Savings and Shareholder Consumption," NBER Working Paper No. 2994 (Cambridge, Massachusetts: National Bureau of Economic Research).

Bank of Japan, 2005, "Japan's Financial Structure Since the 1980s—In View of the Flow of Funds Accounts," Bank of Japan Research Paper. Available via the Internet: http://www.boj.or.jp/en/ronbun/05/data/ron0503a.pdf.

Bernanke, Ben, 2005, "The Global Saving Glut and the U.S. Current Account Deficit," remarks by Governor Ben S. Bernanke at the Homer Jones Lecture, St. Louis, Missouri, April 14.

Bernheim, B. Douglas, 2002, "Taxation and Saving," Chapter 18 in *Handbook of Public Economics*, Volume 3, ed. by Alan J. Auerbach and Martin Feldstein (New York: North Holland).

Brav, Alon, John R. Graham, Campbell R. Harvey, and Roni Michaely, 2003, "Payout Policy in the 21st Century," NBER Working Paper No. 9657 (Cambridge, Massachusetts: National Bureau of Economic Research).

Callen, Tim, and Jonathan Ostry, 2003, *Japan's Lost Decade: Policies for Economic Revival* (Washington: International Monetary Fund).

Comin, Diego, and Thomas Philippon, 2006, "The Rise in Firm-Level Volatility: Causes and Consequences," in *NBER Macroeconomics Annual 2005*, ed. by Mark Gertler and Kenneth Rogoff (Cambridge, Massachusetts: MIT Press). Available via the Internet at: http://www.nber.org/books/macro20/index.html.

Desai, Mihir, and Austan Goolsbee, 2004, "Investment, Overhang, and Tax Policy," *Brookings Papers on Economic Activity: 2*, Brookings Institution.

Doms, Mark, 2005, "IT Investment: Will the Glory Days Ever Return?" Economic Letter No. 2005-13 (San Francisco: Federal Reserve Bank of San Francisco).

European Commission, 2005, "Structures of the Taxation Systems in the European Union" (Luxembourg). Available via the Internet: http://europa.eu.int/comm/taxation_customs/resources/documents/taxation/gen_info/economic_analysis/tax_structures/Structures2005.pdf.

Gale, William G., and John Sabelhaus, 1999, "Perspectives on the Household Saving Rate," *Brookings Papers on Economic Activity: 1*, Brookings Institution.

Greenwood, Robin, 2005, "Aggregate Corporate Liquidity and Stock Returns," Harvard Business School Working Paper No. 05-014 (Cambridge, Massachusetts: Harvard Business School).

International Monetary Fund, 2004, *Global Financial Stability Report*, September, World Economic and Financial Surveys (Washington).

———, 2005, "Why Is Japanese Banking Sector Profitability So Low?" in IMF Country Report No. 05/272 (Washington).

———, 2006a, "The Performance of Germany's Nonfinancial Corporate Sector: An International Perspective," in *Germany: Selected Issues*, IMF Country Report No. 06/17 (Washington).

———, 2006b, *Global Financial Stability Report*, April, World Economic and Financial Surveys (Washington: International Monetary Fund).

Jaeger, Albert, 2003, "Corporate Balance Sheet Restructuring and Investment in the Euro Area," IMF Working Paper 03/117 (Washington: International Monetary Fund).

Jensen, Michael, 1986, "Agency Costs of Free Cash Flow, Corporate Finance and Takeovers," *American Economic Review*, Vol. 76 (May), pp. 323–29.

J.P. Morgan Chase & Co., 2005, "The Corporate Saving Glut," June 24.

KPMG, *Corporate Tax Rates Survey*, various issues.

Kalcheva, Ivalina, and Karl V. Lins, 2005, "International Evidence on Cash Holdings and Expected Managerial Agency Problems" (unpublished; Salt Lake City: University of Utah, David Eccles School of Business).

Lusardi, Annamaria, Jonathan Skinner, and Steven Venti, 2003, "Saving Puzzles and Saving Policies in the United States," *Oxford Review of Economic Policy*, Vol. 17 (Spring), pp. 95–115.

Opler, Tim, Lee Pinkowitz, René Stulz, and Rohan Williamson, 1999, "The Determinants and Implications of Corporate Cash Holdings," *Journal of Financial Economics*, Vol. 52 (April), pp. 3–46.

Passov, Richard, 2003, "How Much Cash Does Your Company Need?" *Harvard Business Review*, Harvard School of Business (November).

Poterba, James, 1987, "Tax Policy and Corporate Saving," in *Brookings Papers on Economic Activity: 2*, Brookings Institution.

Rajan, Raghuram, and Luizi Zingales, 1998, "Financial Dependence and Growth," *The American Economic Review*, Vol. 88 (June), pp. 559–86.

Schumacher, Dirk, 2005, "Germany Profits from Restructuring," Goldman Sachs Global Economics Paper No. 122.

Sufi, Amir, 2006, "Bank Lines of Credit in Corporate Finance: An Empirical Analysis," CFR Working Paper No. 2006-01 (Washington: Federal Deposit Insurance Corporation, Center for Financial Research).

Watson Wyatt, 2006, "2005 Global Survey of Accounting Assumptions for Defined Benefit Plans,"

———, *Insider*, various issues.

Weisbenner, Scott, 2000, "Corporate Share Repurchases in the 1990s: What Role Do Stock Options Play?" Finance and Economics Discussion Paper No. 2000-29 (Washington: Board of Governors of the Federal Reserve System).

Zion, David, and Bill Carcache, 2005, "Pension Update: Pension Plans Getting Weaker This Year," Credit Suisse First Boston, Equity Research.

IMF EXECUTIVE BOARD DISCUSSION OF THE OUTLOOK, MARCH 2006

The following remarks by the Acting Chair were made at the conclusion of the Executive Board's discussion of the World Economic Outlook *on March 31, 2006.*

Executive Directors welcomed the continued strong expansion of the global economy, which has exceeded expectations at the time of their last discussion of the *World Economic Outlook* in August 2005. Despite higher oil prices and a number of natural disasters, economic activity in the second half of last year and early 2006 was strong, and inflationary pressures remain subdued. The economic expansion has also become more broadly based. While the United States is still the main engine of growth among industrial countries, it is increasingly supported by the ongoing expansion in Japan and signs of a sustained recovery in the euro area. Among emerging markets and developing countries, growth remains strong, with particularly buoyant activity in China, India, and Russia. Directors emphasized that, despite these broadly favorable developments, key vulnerabilities—most notably global current account imbalances—have still not been addressed, raising the risks to the world economy.

Looking ahead, Directors expected that global economic conditions would remain favorable, with a gradual pickup in investment helping to weather the continued headwinds from high oil prices. At the same time, Directors identified a number of uncertainties facing the world economy, and felt that the balance of risks remains slanted to the downside. On the upside, Directors acknowledged that, if growth in some emerging market countries continues to exceed expectations, or the corporate sector in the advanced economies runs down its financial surpluses more rapidly than expected—either through higher investment or increased wages and dividends—the growth outlook could be

more positive. On the downside, with the oil market remaining vulnerable to shocks given limited excess production capacity, and with prices increasingly driven by supply side concerns, many Directors felt that the adverse impact of high oil prices on global growth could well be greater going forward than it has been in the recent past. Other risks identified by Directors are an abrupt tightening in financial market conditions and a possible avian flu pandemic.

Of most concern to Directors, however, was the further widening of global imbalances. The U.S. current account deficit has widened further to record levels, which is being matched by large surpluses in oil exporters, a number of small industrialized countries, Japan, China, and a number of other emerging Asian countries. While noting that financing of the U.S. deficit has not been a problem so far, Directors were of the view that these imbalances pose increasing risks over time to the global growth outlook. Directors generally believed that the probability of a disorderly unwinding of imbalances remains low. However, such an outcome, should it occur, could have sizable negative effects for the global economy and the international financial system. Directors considered that this assessment calls for actions aimed at reducing these vulnerabilities, whose implementation should be facilitated by the current favorable environment. Directors believed that a progressive narrowing of imbalances will need to be based on both a significant rebalancing of demand across countries, and adjustments in exchange rates.

Directors emphasized that, while the private sector will play a key role in the resolution of global imbalances, a purely market-driven adjustment carries significant risks. This underscores the importance of more rapid implementation of the agreed policy strategy to address imbalances, including raising national saving in the United States—with measures to reduce the budget deficit and spur private saving; allowing currencies in surplus countries—including in parts of Asia and a number of oil producers—to appreciate; and implementing structural and other reforms to boost domestic demand in countries with large current account surpluses. In this context, the importance of achieving a better balance between externally and domestically led growth and undertaking reforms of domestic financial systems to help boost domestic demand was also noted. Given economic interlinkages, all countries and regions will play a role in the adjustment of imbalances, and countries should therefore increase the flexibility of their domestic economies to adapt better to changing global patterns of domestic and external demand.

Elaborating on the required policy actions in surplus countries, Directors welcomed the staff analysis on the relationship between oil prices and global imbalances. They urged oil exporters to take advantage of the current conjuncture to undertake structural reforms and boost expenditures to support long-term growth, which would also have beneficial effects for reducing global imbalances. Some Directors pointed out that the scope for such spending increases in oil-exporting countries would vary, depending on country-specific circumstances. With regard to exchange rate adjustment as well, a number of Directors observed that the need for, and size of, any exchange rate appreciation would have to be assessed on a case-by-case basis, taking into account the economic fundamentals in individual countries. Some Directors noted that structural measures aimed at improving market flexibility and enhancing economic productivity should complement exchange rate adjustment in these countries in bringing about an effective correction of global imbalances.

Directors considered that the Fund continues to have a central role to play in promoting a coordinated, multilateral, medium-term solution for reducing global imbalances. With the broad strategy espoused by the Fund generally agreed, the challenge now is to work out the precise modalities and accelerate implementation. Directors also underscored the importance of the Fund's advice in urging countries to resist protectionist pressures and in helping them to exploit comparative advantages through deeper integration.

Directors reiterated their concerns regarding two other long-standing policy challenges facing the global economy.

- *First, unsustainable medium-term fiscal positions remain a key risk.* Among the major industrial countries, underlying fiscal positions—outside Japan—have improved only modestly since 2003, and Directors noted that in many countries little further improvement is projected over the next two years. They underscored the importance of more ambitious fiscal consolidation in order to limit upward pressure on interest rates, reduce risks to macroeconomic stability, and improve the scope for a fiscal response to future shocks.

- *Second, more ambitious efforts are needed to put in place the preconditions for taking advantage of the opportunities from globalization and for supporting growth.* In this context, Directors reiterated the need to resist protectionist pressures that have been rising in a number of countries, while ensuring an ambitious outcome to the Doha Round. Directors regretted the limited flexibility in country positions displayed so far under the trade negotiations and warned of the risks to the global economy and the multilateral trading system from a disappointing outcome of the Doha Round. Directors agreed that, at the national level, advancing the structural reform agenda remains key to removing the impediments to long-run growth.

Another critical question is whether inflation will remain moderate in the face of rapid global growth. In this context, Directors welcomed the staff analysis of the relationship between globalization and inflation, which they noted makes a valuable contribution to the quantification of the effects of globalization. While emphasizing that the impact of globalization on inflation will be temporary unless it changes the objectives of monetary policy, they observed that import price declines have had sizable effects on inflation in industrial countries over one- to two-year periods, particularly when there has been considerable global spare capacity. Directors also noted that globalization has had a significant impact on relative prices, with important implications for some sectors of the economy. Directors agreed, however, that globalization cannot be relied upon to prevent a pickup in inflation and that central banks must remain vigilant for signs of inflationary pressures. Some Directors pointed to the recent rise in producer prices and in non-oil commodity prices, which could feed into higher consumer prices.

Conditions in global financial markets remain very favorable, characterized by unusually low risk premia and volatility. Directors noted that high corporate saving is one factor that has contributed to the low global interest rate environment during the current expansion, and they welcomed the staff's analysis of corporate saving behavior in the G-7 countries. Most Directors agreed with the staff's assessment that corporate excess saving will decline from current high levels over the next few years as investment increases, and that this will likely put upward pressure on long-term interest rates going forward.

Industrial Countries

Directors welcomed the continued strong expansion in the *United States* despite the temporary slowdown in the fourth quarter of 2005. They viewed risks as being broadly balanced in the short term, but slanted to the downside further out. With corporate profits expanding robustly, business investment and employment could be stronger than expected. On the downside, however, the large current account deficit makes the United States vulnerable to a swing in investor sentiment, while a sharp weakening of the housing market and higher energy prices

could slow consumption. With core inflation well contained, financial markets expect that the current tightening cycle in the United States is nearly complete, although Directors emphasized the need for vigilance for signs of inflationary pressures as spare capacity diminishes. While welcoming the marked improvement in the federal budget deficit in FY2005, most Directors believed that a much more ambitious fiscal adjustment is needed in FY2006 and beyond, with the aim of achieving broad budget balance (excluding Social Security) by 2010, based on further spending discipline and consideration of revenue enhancements. In this context, a few Directors noted that a rapid decline in the U.S. fiscal deficit could slow U.S. and global growth in the absence of increased domestic demand elsewhere.

Directors were encouraged by the signs of a stronger recovery in the *euro area,* while cautioning that it remains unduly vulnerable to external factors, particularly oil prices and world demand. Against the background of limited underlying inflationary pressures and still fragile domestic demand, most Directors observed that monetary policy needs to remain appropriately supportive of the recovery, with some Directors suggesting that further increases in interest rates should await clear signs of a self sustaining recovery in domestic demand. Directors noted with concern the lack of progress in reducing area-wide budget deficits, and shared the view that most countries should aim for a broadly balanced fiscal position by the end of the decade. With rising fiscal pressures from an aging population, Directors attached particular importance to the need to reform Europe's social systems in line with the objectives of the Lisbon Agenda, and a few expressed concern about the rising resistance to reforms in some countries. Directors noted that examples of successful social policies within Europe could be a useful guide in reforming social models in other countries, but cautioned that reforms will have to take into account important country specific differences. More generally, Directors reiterated the importance of continued structural reforms for enhancing the region's low potential growth rate.

Directors welcomed the increasingly well established economic recovery in *Japan*. They noted that the expansion is being driven by domestic demand, and underpinned by rising employment, buoyant corporate profits, and a turnaround in bank credit growth. Directors expected the positive growth momentum to continue, with potential risks to the upside from stronger-than-anticipated private consumption in response to rising employment and labor income. Directors welcomed that core CPI inflation has turned slightly positive, and that the Bank of Japan has been able to move away from its quantitative easing framework, but they emphasized that interest rates should be kept at zero until deflation is decisively beaten. Directors acknowledged the reduction in the general government budget deficit, but called for more rapid progress in improving the fiscal position going forward, in order to stabilize public debt and accommodate the budgetary pressures from an aging population. Directors underscored the need to complete the remaining agenda of structural reforms to boost productivity, particularly in the nontraded sector, and to complete financial and corporate restructuring.

Emerging Market and Developing Countries

Directors welcomed the continued rapid growth in *emerging Asia*. With global economic conditions—now supported by the ongoing recovery in domestic demand in Japan—expected to remain favorable, Directors expected the expansion to maintain momentum in 2006, once again led by China and India. Directors emphasized the need for more balanced growth in the region, and encouraged policymakers to strengthen the pace of structural reforms, emphasizing the key objectives of increasing household consumption in China and domestic investment in much of the rest of the region. Most Directors also considered that

exchange rates would need to be allowed to appreciate in the surplus countries in the region.

Directors expected the robust economic expansion in *Latin America* to continue in 2006, with external demand continuing to remain an important driver of growth. While welcoming the disciplined fiscal policies in much of the region, many Directors called for further progress in debt reduction in a number of these countries. Directors accordingly called on policymakers in these countries to focus on further reducing these vulnerabilities through continued tight fiscal policies—which could be challenging in some countries given the electoral schedule—and structural reforms that raise the long-term growth potential, including steps to improve the business climate in order to attract greater investment.

In *emerging Europe*, growth is expected to remain firm, although Directors cautioned that the expansion will depend on the strength of the recovery of demand in the euro area. Directors saw downside risks to the outlook arising mainly from the region's large current account deficits, and the rapid expansion of credit growth in a number of countries. Directors urged increased fiscal consolidation in central Europe to reduce external deficits, while in the Baltics and southern Europe, several Directors saw a role for policies to reduce the rapid pace of credit expansion.

In the *Commonwealth of Independent States*, real GDP growth slowed noticeably, reflecting primarily the sharp slowdown in Ukraine, but also more moderate growth elsewhere. Looking forward, Directors emphasized that monetary policy will need to play a more active role in containing inflation, including through allowing greater nominal exchange rate appreciation where necessary. While countries benefiting from higher oil revenues have scope to raise productive spending, Directors cautioned that such spending should be consistent with broader macroeconomic objectives and cyclical considerations. They stressed the need for structural reforms to strengthen the role of the private sector and deepen market institutions.

Directors welcomed the robust economic expansion in *sub-Saharan Africa,* and expected that growth in the region would strengthen in 2006 to its strongest pace in three decades, underpinned by high commodity prices, improved macroeconomic policies, and structural reforms. They stressed that maintaining high long-term growth rates will be crucial to reducing the incidence of poverty in the region and making progress toward the Millennium Development Goals. In this regard, Directors underscored the importance of continued reforms to improve the institutional environment, along with structural reforms designed to encourage greater private investment and make economies less dependent on global commodity cycles. Directors also called on the international community to support Africa's reform efforts, including by following through on commit-ments for greater resource flows and improved market access.

In the *Middle East,* led by substantially higher export earnings among oil-exporting countries, growth remains robust. Despite a strengthening in domestic demand, inflation has remained subdued as countries have saved a larger proportion of the increase in oil revenues compared with previous oil cycles. Some Directors expressed concern about the rise in property and stock market prices in the region, underscoring the need for careful monitoring of potential risks from any abrupt market corrections. Directors emphasized that with a significant proportion of higher oil revenues expected to be permanent, increased consideration should be given to carefully planned expenditures to raise potential growth in both the oil and non-oil economy and provide increased employment opportunities for the growing working-age population.

STATISTICAL APPENDIX

The statistical appendix presents historical data, as well as projections. It comprises five sections: Assumptions, What's New, Data and Conventions, Classification of Countries, and Statistical Tables.

The assumptions underlying the estimates and projections for 2006–07 and the medium-term scenario for 2008–11 are summarized in the first section. The second section presents a brief description of changes to the database and statistical tables. The third section provides a general description of the data, and of the conventions used for calculating country group composites. The classification of countries in the various groups presented in the *World Economic Outlook* is summarized in the fourth section.

The last, and main, section comprises the statistical tables. Data in these tables have been compiled on the basis of information available through early April 2006. The figures for 2006 and beyond are shown with the same degree of precision as the historical figures solely for convenience; since they are projections, the same degree of accuracy is not to be inferred.

Assumptions

Real effective *exchange rates* for the advanced economies are assumed to remain constant at their average levels during the period February 9 to March 9, 2006. For 2006 and 2007, these assumptions imply average U.S. dollar/SDR conversion rates of 1.438 and 1.441, U.S. dollar/euro conversion rate of 1.19 and 1.20, and yen/U.S. dollar conversion rates of 116.9 and 115.9, respectively.

It is assumed that the *price of oil* will average $61.25 a barrel in 2006 and $63.00 a barrel in 2007.

Established *policies* of national authorities are assumed to be maintained. The more specific policy assumptions underlying the projections for selected advanced economies are described in Box A1.

With regard to *interest rates*, it is assumed that the London interbank offered rate (LIBOR) on six-month U.S. dollar deposits will average 5.0 percent in 2006 and 5.1 percent in 2007, that three-month euro deposits will average 3.0 percent in 2006 and 3.4 percent in 2007, and that six-month Japanese yen deposits will average 0.3 percent in 2006 and 0.9 percent in 2007.

With respect to *introduction of the euro*, on December 31, 1998, the Council of the European Union decided that, effective January 1, 1999, the irrevocably fixed conversion rates between the euro and currencies of the member states adopting the euro are as follows.

1 euro =	13.7603	Austrian schillings
=	40.3399	Belgian francs
=	1.95583	Deutsche mark
=	5.94573	Finnish markkaa
=	6.55957	French francs
=	340.750	Greek drachma[1]
=	0.787564	Irish pound
=	1,936.27	Italian lire
=	40.3399	Luxembourg francs
=	2.20371	Netherlands guilders
=	200.482	Portuguese escudos
=	166.386	Spanish pesetas

See Box 5.4 in the October 1998 *World Economic Outlook* for details on how the conversion rates were established.

What's New

The country composition of the fuel-exporting group has been revised to reflect the peri-

---

[1]The conversion rate for Greece was established prior to inclusion in the euro area on January 1, 2001.

Box A1. Economic Policy Assumptions Underlying the Projections for Selected Advanced Economies

The short-term *fiscal policy assumptions* used in the *World Economic Outlook* are based on officially announced budgets, adjusted for differences between the national authorities and the IMF staff regarding macroeconomic assumptions and projected fiscal outturns. The medium-term fiscal projections incorporate policy measures that are judged likely to be implemented. In cases where the IMF staff has insufficient information to assess the authorities' budget intentions and prospects for policy implementation, an unchanged structural primary balance is assumed, unless otherwise indicated. Specific assumptions used in some of the advanced economies follow (see also Tables 12–14 in the Statistical Appendix for data on fiscal and structural balances).[1]

United States. The fiscal projections are based on the Administration's FY2007 Budget (February 6, 2006), adjusted to take into account differences in macroeconomic projections as well as staff assumptions about (1) additional defense spending based on analysis by the Congressional Budget Office; (2) slower compression in the growth rate of discretionary spending; (3) government spending for the clean-up and reconstruction in areas damaged by Hurricane Katrina; and (4) alternative minimum tax (AMT) reform beyond FY2007.

Japan. The medium-term fiscal projections assume that expenditure and revenue of the general government (excluding social security) are adjusted in line

with the current government target to achieve a primary fiscal balance by the early 2010s.

Germany. Official estimates were used for 2005. For 2006–2011, the *World Economic Outlook* projections reflect measures as announced in the new government's coalition agreement. These aim to reduce the overall fiscal balance to below 3 percent of GDP in 2007, centered around a 3 percent increase in the value added tax, or VAT (as of January 2007).

France. The projections for 2006 are based on the initial budget adjusted for the IMF staff's macroeconomic assumptions. For 2007–09, the projections are based on the intentions underlying the 2007–09 Stability Program Update adjusted for the IMF staff's macroeconomic assumptions, lower projections for nontax revenue, unchanged tax policy beyond 2007, and a less sharp deceleration in spending growth than projected by the authorities beyond 2007. For 2010–11, the IMF staff assumes unchanged tax policies and real expenditure growth as in the 2009 projection.

Italy. Fiscal projections from 2007 onward are based on a technical assumption of a constant primary structural balance net of one-off measures. They do not incorporate measures that would be adopted in the 2007 budget.

United Kingdom. The fiscal projections are based on information provided in the 2006 Budget Report. Additionally, the projections incorporate the most recent statistical releases from the Office for National Statistics, including provisional budgetary outturns through 2005:Q4. The computation of the structural fiscal balance is based on staff projections of the output gap.

Canada. Projections are based on costing of the new government's program provided during the recent election campaign, which were examined for accuracy by Canada's Conference Board (http://www.conservative.ca/media/20060113-FiscalPlan.pdf).

Australia. The fiscal projections through the fiscal year 2008/09 are based on the 2005–06 Mid-Year Economic and Fiscal Outlook published in December 2005. For the remainder of the projection period, the IMF staff assumes unchanged policies.

---

[1]The output gap is actual less potential output, as a percent of potential output. Structural balances are expressed as a percent of potential output. The structural budget balance is the budgetary position that would be observed if the level of actual output coincided with potential output. Changes in the structural budget balance consequently include effects of temporary fiscal measures, the impact of fluctuations in interest rates and debt-service costs, and other noncyclical fluctuations in the budget balance. The computations of structural budget balances are based on IMF staff estimates of potential GDP and revenue and expenditure elasticities (see the October 1993 *World Economic Outlook*, Annex I). Net debt is defined as gross debt less financial assets of the general government, which include assets held by the social security insurance system. Estimates of the output gap and of the structural balance are subject to significant margins of uncertainty.

Austria. Fiscal figures for 2005 are based on the authorities' estimated outturn. Projections for 2006 are based on this year's budget. Projections for 2007–08 are based on the Austrian Stability Program. For 2009–11, projections assume unchanged overall and structural balances from those in 2008.

Belgium. The projections for 2006 are based on the 2006 budget adjusted for the IMF staff's macroeconomic assumptions and an assumed lower yield of some specific items. For 2007–11, the projections assume unchanged tax policies and real primary expenditure growth as in the recent past.

Denmark. Estimates for 2005 are aligned with the latest official projections and budget, adjusted for the IMF staff macroeconomic projections. For 2006–11, projections are in line with the authorities' medium-term framework—adjusted for the IMF staff macroeconomic projections—targeting an average budget surplus of 1.5–2.5 percent of GDP, supported by a ceiling on real public consumption growth.

Greece. Projections are based on the 2006 budget, adjusted for IMF staff projections for economic growth. For 2007 and beyond, tax revenues as a percent of GDP are assumed constant, while social insurance contributions are assumed to continue their trend increase and EU transfers are assumed to decline. Total expenditure is assumed to remain broadly constant as a percent of GDP.

Korea. Estimates for 2005 are based on the initial budget adjusted for the latest official estimates of some components. Projections for 2006 are based on the authorities' budget. For 2007–09, projections are in line with the authorities' National Fiscal Management Plan. For 2010–11, IMF staff assumes unchanged revenue and expenditure growth from the 2007–09 projections.

Netherlands. The fiscal projections for 2006 and beyond build on the 2006 budget, the latest Stability Program, and other forecasts provided by the authorities, adjusted for the IMF staff's macroeconomic assumptions.

New Zealand. The fiscal projections through the fiscal year 2009/10 are based on the 2005 Half Year Economic and Fiscal Update published in December 2005. For the remainder of the projection period, the IMF staff assumes unchanged policies.

Portugal. Fiscal projections for 2006 build on the authorities' budget. Projections for 2007 and beyond are based on the current Stability and Growth Program by the authorities.

Spain. Fiscal projections through 2008 are based on the policies outlined in the national authorities' updated Stability Program of December 2005. These projections have been adjusted for the IMF staff's macroeconomic scenario. In subsequent years, the fiscal projections assume no significant changes in these policies.

Sweden. The fiscal projections are based on information provided in the budget, presented on September 20, 2005. Additionally, the projections incorporate the most recent statistical releases from Statistics Sweden, including provisional budgetary outturns through December 2005.

Switzerland. Estimates for 2005 and projections for 2006–11 are based on IMF staff calculations, which incorporate measures to restore balance in the Federal accounts and strengthen the social security finances.

Monetary policy assumptions are based on the established policy framework in each country. In most cases, this implies a nonaccommodative stance over the business cycle: official interest rates will therefore increase when economic indicators suggest that prospective inflation will rise above its acceptable rate or range, and they will decrease when indicators suggest that prospective inflation will not exceed the acceptable rate or range, that prospective output growth is below its potential rate, and that the margin of slack in the economy is significant. On this basis, the LIBOR on six-month U.S. dollar deposits is assumed to average 5.0 percent in 2006 and 5.1 percent in 2007. The projected path for U.S. dollar short-term interest rates reflects the assumption implicit in prevailing forward rates. The rate on three-month euro deposits is assumed to average 3.0 percent in 2006 and 3.4 percent in 2007. The interest rate on six-month Japanese yen deposits is assumed to average 0.3 percent in 2006 and 0.9 percent in 2007. Changes in interest rate assumptions compared with the September 2005 *World Economic Outlook* are summarized in Table 1.1.

odic update of the classification criteria; and the purchasing-power-parity (PPP) weights have been updated to reflect the most up-to-date PPP conversion factor provided by the World Bank.

Data and Conventions

Data and projections for 175 countries form the statistical basis for the *World Economic Outlook* (the World Economic Outlook database). The data are maintained jointly by the IMF's Research Department and area departments, with the latter regularly updating country projections based on consistent global assumptions.

Although national statistical agencies are the ultimate providers of historical data and definitions, international organizations are also involved in statistical issues, with the objective of harmonizing methodologies for the national compilation of statistics, including the analytical frameworks, concepts, definitions, classifications, and valuation procedures used in the production of economic statistics. The World Economic Outlook database reflects information from both national source agencies and international organizations.

The comprehensive revision of the standardized *System of National Accounts 1993 (SNA)*, the IMF's *Balance of Payments Manual, Fifth Edition (BPM5), the Monetary and Financial Statistics Manual (MFSM)*, and the *Government Finance Statistics Manual 2001 (GFSM 2001)* represented important improvements in the standards of economic statistics and analysis.[2] The IMF was actively involved in all these projects, particularly the new *Balance of Payments Manual*, which reflects the IMF's special interest in countries' external positions. Key changes introduced with the new *Manual* were summarized in

Box 13 of the May 1994 *World Economic Outlook*. The process of adapting country balance of payments data to the definitions of the new *BPM5* began with the May 1995 *World Economic Outlook*. However, full concordance with the *BPM5* is ultimately dependent on the provision by national statistical compilers of revised country data, and hence the *World Economic Outlook* estimates are still only partially adapted to the *BPM5*.

In line with recent improvements in standards of reporting economic statistics, several countries have phased out their traditional *fixed base-year* method of calculating real macroeconomic variables levels and growth by switching to a *chain-weighted* method of computing aggregate growth. Recent dramatic changes in the structure of these economies have obliged these countries to revise the way in which they measure real GDP levels and growth. Switching to the chain-weighted method of computing aggregate growth, which uses current price information, allows countries to measure GDP growth more accurately by eliminating upward biases in new data.[3] Currently, real macroeconomic data for Australia, Austria, Azerbaijan, Canada, Czech Republic, euro area, Germany, Greece, Iceland, Ireland, Italy, Japan, Luxembourg, the Netherlands, New Zealand, Portugal, Spain, Sweden, the United Kingdom, and the United States are based on chain-weighted methodology. However, data before 1988 (Austria), 2000 (Azerbaijan), 1995 (Czech Republic), 1995 (euro area), 1991 (Germany), 2000 (Greece), 1990 (Iceland), 1997 (Ireland), 2001 (Italy), 1994 (Japan), 1995 (Luxembourg), 2001 (the Netherlands), 1995 (Portugal), and 1995 (Spain) are based on unrevised national accounts and subject to revision in the future.

---

[2]Commission of the European Communities, International Monetary Fund, Organization for Economic Cooperation and Development, United Nations, and World Bank, *System of National Accounts 1993* (Brussels/Luxembourg, New York, Paris, and Washington, 1993); International Monetary Fund, *Balance of Payments Manual, Fifth Edition* (Washington, 1993); International Monetary Fund, *Monetary and Financial Statistics Manual* (Washington, 2000); and International Monetary Fund, *Government Finance Statistics Manual* (Washington, 2001).

[3]Charles Steindel, 1995, "Chain-Weighting: The New Approach to Measuring GDP," *Current Issues in Economics and Finance* (Federal Reserve Bank of New York), Vol. 1 (December).

The members of the European Union have adopted a harmonized system for the compilation of the national accounts, referred to as ESA 1995. All national accounts data from 1995 onward are presented on the basis of the new system. Revision by national authorities of data prior to 1995 to conform to the new system has progressed, but has in some cases not been completed. In such cases, historical *World Economic Outlook* data have been carefully adjusted to avoid breaks in the series. Users of EU national accounts data prior to 1995 should nevertheless exercise caution until such time as the revision of historical data by national statistical agencies has been fully completed. See Box 1.2, "Revisions in National Accounts Methodologies," in the May 2000 *World Economic Outlook.*

Composite data for country groups in the *World Economic Outlook* are either sums or weighted averages of data for individual countries. Unless otherwise indicated, multiyear averages of growth rates are expressed as compound annual rates of change. Arithmetically weighted averages are used for all data except inflation and money growth for the other emerging market and developing country group, for which geometric averages are used. The following conventions apply.

- Country group composites for exchange rates, interest rates, and the growth rates of monetary aggregates are weighted by GDP converted to U.S. dollars at market exchange rates (averaged over the preceding three years) as a share of group GDP.
- Composites for other data relating to the domestic economy, whether growth rates or ratios, are weighted by GDP valued at purchasing power parities (PPPs) as a share of total world or group GDP.[4]

- Composites for data relating to the domestic economy for the euro area (12 member countries throughout the entire period unless otherwise noted) are aggregates of national source data using weights based on 1995 ECU exchange rates.
- Composite unemployment rates and employment growth are weighted by labor force as a share of group labor force.
- Composites relating to the external economy are sums of individual country data after conversion to U.S. dollars at the average market exchange rates in the years indicated for balance of payments data and at end-of-year market exchange rates for debt denominated in currencies other than U.S. dollars. Composites of changes in foreign trade volumes and prices, however, are arithmetic averages of percentage changes for individual countries weighted by the U.S. dollar value of exports or imports as a share of total world or group exports or imports (in the preceding year).

For central and eastern European countries, external transactions in nonconvertible currencies (through 1990) are converted to U.S. dollars at the implicit U.S. dollar/ruble conversion rates obtained from each country's national currency exchange rate for the U.S. dollar and for the ruble.

Classification of Countries

Summary of the Country Classification

The country classification in the *World Economic Outlook* divides the world into two major groups: advanced economies, and other emerging market and developing countries.[5] Rather than being based on strict criteria, economic or otherwise, this classification has

---

[4]See Box A2 of the April 2004 *World Economic Outlook* for a summary of the revised PPP-based weights and Annex IV of the May 1993 *World Economic Outlook.* See also Anne-Marie Gulde and Marianne Schulze-Ghattas, "Purchasing Power Parity Based Weights for the *World Economic Outlook,*" in *Staff Studies for the World Economic Outlook* (International Monetary Fund, December 1993), pp. 106–23.

[5]As used here, the term "country" does not in all cases refer to a territorial entity that is a state as understood by international law and practice. It also covers some territorial entities that are not states, but for which statistical data are maintained on a separate and independent basis.

Table A. Classification by World Economic Outlook Groups and Their Shares in Aggregate GDP, Exports of Goods and Services, and Population, 2005[1]

(Percent of total for group or world)

	Number of Countries	GDP		Exports of Goods and Services		Population	
		Advanced economies	World	Advanced economies	World	Advanced economies	World
Advanced economies	**29**	**100.0**	**52.3**	**100.0**	**68.9**	**100.0**	**15.3**
United States		38.4	20.1	14.6	10.1	30.6	4.7
Euro area	12	28.3	14.8	42.9	29.5	32.1	4.9
Germany		7.9	4.1	13.0	9.0	8.5	1.3
France		5.7	3.0	6.4	4.4	6.4	1.0
Italy		5.2	2.7	5.3	3.6	6.0	0.9
Spain		3.4	1.8	3.3	2.2	4.3	0.7
Japan		12.2	6.4	7.8	5.3	13.2	2.0
United Kingdom		5.7	3.0	6.6	4.5	6.2	0.9
Canada		3.5	1.8	4.9	3.4	3.3	0.5
Other advanced economies	13	11.9	6.2	23.3	16.1	14.6	2.2
Memorandum							
Major advanced economies	7	78.7	41.2	58.6	40.4	74.3	11.3
Newly industrialized Asian economies	4	6.2	3.2	13.6	9.4	8.5	1.3

	Number of Countries	GDP		Exports of Goods and Services		Population	
		Other emerging market and developing countries	World	Other emerging market and developing countries	World	Other emerging market and developing countries	World
Other emerging market and developing countries	**146**	**100.0**	**47.7**	**100.0**	**30.8**	**100.0**	**84.7**
Regional groups							
Africa	48	6.9	3.3	7.9	2.4	15.0	12.7
Sub-Sahara	45	5.4	2.6	5.8	1.8	13.7	11.6
Excluding Nigeria and South Africa	43	2.8	1.3	2.8	0.9	10.1	8.5
Central and eastern Europe	15	6.9	3.3	14.1	4.4	3.4	2.9
Commonwealth of Independent States[2]	13	7.9	3.8	9.8	3.0	5.2	4.4
Russia		5.4	2.6	6.8	2.1	2.7	2.2
Developing Asia	23	56.7	27.1	38.9	12.1	61.5	52.1
China		32.3	15.4	21.5	6.7	24.3	20.6
India		12.5	5.9	4.0	1.3	20.2	17.1
Excluding China and India	21	12.0	5.7	13.4	4.2	17.0	14.4
Middle East	14	5.9	2.8	14.8	4.6	4.8	4.1
Western Hemisphere	33	15.5	7.4	14.5	4.5	10.0	8.5
Brazil		5.4	2.6	3.4	1.1	3.4	2.9
Mexico		3.7	1.8	3.9	1.2	2.0	1.7
Analytical groups							
By source of export earnings							
Fuel	24	13.2	6.3	26.6	8.3	11.4	9.6
Nonfuel	122	86.8	41.4	73.4	22.8	88.6	75.1
of which, primary products	23	2.1	1.0	2.3	0.7	5.3	4.5
By external financing source							
Net debtor countries	126	53.9	25.7	49.9	15.5	67.7	57.4
of which, official financing	50	12.7	6.0	8.8	2.7	22.5	19.0
Net debtor countries by debt-servicing experience							
Countries with arrears and/or rescheduling during 1999–2003	56	12.2	5.8	11.1	3.5	23.9	20.2
Other net debtor countries	70	41.7	19.9	38.8	12.1	43.8	37.1
Other groups							
Heavily indebted poor countries	29	1.9	0.9	1.2	0.4	8.0	6.7
Middle East and North Africa	20	7.8	3.7	17.1	5.3	6.9	5.9

[1]The GDP shares are based on the purchasing-power-parity (PPP) valuation of country GDPs. The number of countries comprising each group reflects those for which data are included in the group aggregates.

[2]Mongolia, which is not a member of the Commonwealth of Independent States, is included in this group for reasons of geography and similarities in economic structure.

Table B. Advanced Economies by Subgroup

Major Currency Areas	Other Subgroups					
	Euro area		Newly industrialized Asian economies	Major advanced economies	Other advanced economies	
United States	Austria	Ireland	Hong Kong SAR[1]	Canada	Australia	Korea
Euro area	Belgium	Italy	Korea	France	Cyprus	New Zealand
Japan	Finland	Luxembourg	Singapore	Germany	Denmark	Norway
	France	Netherlands	Taiwan Province	Italy	Hong Kong SAR[1]	Singapore
	Germany	Portugal	of China	Japan	Iceland	Sweden
	Greece	Spain		United Kingdom	Israel	Switzerland
				United States		Taiwan Province
						of China

[1]On July 1, 1997, Hong Kong was returned to the People's Republic of China and became a Special Administrative Region of China.

evolved over time with the objective of facilitating analysis by providing a reasonably meaningful organization of data. A few countries are presently not included in these groups, either because they are not IMF members and their economies are not monitored by the IMF, or because databases have not yet been fully developed. Because of data limitations, group composites do not reflect the following countries: The Islamic Republic of Afghanistan, Bosnia and Herzegovina, Brunei Darussalam, Eritrea, Liberia, Serbia and Montenegro, Somalia, and Timor-Leste. Cuba and the Democratic People's Republic of Korea are examples of countries that are not IMF members, whereas San Marino, among the advanced economies, and Aruba, among the developing countries, are examples of economies for which databases have not been completed.

Each of the two main country groups is further divided into a number of subgroups. Among the advanced economies, the seven largest in terms of GDP, collectively referred to as the major advanced countries, are distinguished as a subgroup, and so are the 12 members of the euro area and the four newly industrialized Asian economies. The other emerging market and developing countries are classified by region, as well as into a number of analytical groups. Table A provides an overview of these standard groups in the *World Economic Outlook*, showing the number of countries in each group and the average 2005 shares of groups in aggregate PPP-valued GDP, total exports of goods and services, and population.

General Features and Composition of Groups in the *World Economic Outlook* Classification

Advanced Economies

The 29 advanced economies are listed in Table B. The seven largest in terms of GDP—the United States, Japan, Germany, France, Italy, the United Kingdom, and Canada—constitute the subgroup of *major advanced economies,* often referred to as the Group of Seven (G-7) countries. The euro area (12 countries) and the *newly industrialized Asian economies* are also distinguished as subgroups. Composite data shown in the tables for the euro area cover the current members for all years, even though the membership has increased over time.

In 1991 and subsequent years, data for *Germany* refer to west Germany *and* the eastern Länder (i.e., the former German Democratic Republic). Before 1991, economic data are not available on a unified basis or in a consistent manner. Hence, in tables featuring data expressed as annual percent change, these apply to west Germany in years up to and including 1991, but to unified Germany from 1992 onward. In general, data on national accounts and domestic economic and financial activity through 1990 cover west Germany only, whereas data for the central government and balance of

Table C. European Union

Austria	France	Latvia	Portugal
Belgium	Germany	Lithuania	Slovak Republic
Cyprus	Greece	Luxembourg	Slovenia
Czech Republic	Hungary	Malta	Spain
Denmark	Ireland	Netherlands	Sweden
Estonia	Italy	Poland	United Kingdom
Finland			

payments apply to west Germany through June 1990 and to unified Germany thereafter.

Table C lists the member countries of the European Union, not all of which are classified as advanced economies in the *World Economic Outlook*.

Other Emerging Market and Developing Countries

The group of other emerging market and developing countries (146 countries) includes all countries that are not classified as advanced economies.

The *regional breakdowns* of other emerging market and developing countries—*Africa, central and eastern Europe, Commonwealth of Independent States, developing Asia, Middle East, and Western Hemisphere*—largely conform to the regional breakdowns in the IMF's *International Financial Statistics*. In both classifications, Egypt and the Libyan Arab Jamahiriya are included in the *Middle East* region rather than in Africa. In addition, the *World Economic Outlook* sometimes refers to the regional group of Middle East and North Africa countries, also referred to as the MENA countries, whose composition straddles the Africa and Middle East regions. This group is defined as the Arab League countries plus the Islamic Republic of Iran (see Table D).

Other emerging market and developing countries are also classified according to *analytical criteria*.

Table D. Middle East and North Africa Countries

Algeria	Iraq	Mauritania	Sudan
Bahrain	Jordan	Morocco	Syrian Arab Republic
Djibouti	Kuwait	Oman	Tunisia
Egypt	Lebanon	Qatar	United Arab Emirates
Iran, I.R. of	Libya	Saudi Arabia	Yemen

Table E. Other Emerging Market and Developing Countries by Region and Main Source of Export Earnings

	Fuel	Nonfuel, of Which Primary Products
Africa	Algeria Angola Congo, Rep. of Equatorial Guinea Gabon Nigeria Sudan	Botswana Burkina Faso Burundi Chad Congo, Dem. Rep. of Côte d'Ivoire Ghana Guinea Guinea-Bissau Malawi Mauritania Namibia Niger Sierra Leone Uganda Zambia Zimbabwe
Commonwealth of Independent States	Azerbaijan Russia Turkmenistan	Tajikistan Uzbekistan
Developing Asia		Papua New Guinea Solomon Islands
Middle East	Bahrain Iran, I.R. of Iraq Kuwait Libya Oman Qatar Saudi Arabia Syrian Arab Republic United Arab Emirates Yemen	
Western Hemisphere	Ecuador Trinidad and Tobago Venezuela	Chile Suriname

teria. The analytical criteria reflect countries' composition of export earnings and other income from abroad, exchange rate arrangements, a distinction between net creditor and net debtor countries, and, for the net debtor countries, financial criteria based on external financing source and experience with external debt servicing. The detailed composition of other emerging market and developing countries in the regional and analytical groups is shown in Tables E and F.

Table F. Other Emerging Market and Developing Countries by Region, Net External Position, and Heavily Indebted Poor Countries

Africa	Net creditor	Net debtor[1]	Heavily Indebted Poor Countries
Maghreb			
Algeria	★		
Morocco		★	
Tunisia		★	
Sub-Sahara			
South Africa	★		
Horn of Africa			
Djibouti		•	
Ethiopia		•	★
Sudan	★		
Great Lakes			
Burundi		•	★
Congo, Dem. Rep. of		•	★
Kenya		•	
Rwanda		•	★
Tanzania		•	★
Uganda	★		★
Southern Africa			
Angola		★	
Botswana	★		
Comoros		•	
Lesotho		★	
Madagascar		•	★
Malawi		•	★
Mauritius		★	
Mozambique, Rep. of		★	★
Namibia	★		
Seychelles		★	
Swaziland		★	
Zambia		•	★
Zimbabwe		★	
West and Central Africa			
Cape Verde		★	
Gambia, The		★	★
Ghana		•	★
Guinea		•	★
Mauritania		★	★
Nigeria		★	
São Tomé and Príncipe		★	★
Sierra Leone		•	★
CFA franc zone			
Benin		•	★
Burkina Faso		•	★
Cameroon		★	★
Central African Republic		•	
Chad		•	★
Congo, Rep. of		•	★
Côte d'Ivoire		•	
Equatorial Guinea		★	
Gabon		•	
Guinea-Bissau		•	★
Mali		•	★
Niger		•	★
Senegal		★	★
Togo		•	

Central and eastern Europe	Net creditor	Net debtor[1]	Heavily Indebted Poor Countries
Albania		★	
Bulgaria	★		
Croatia		★	
Czech Republic		★	
Estonia		★	
Hungary		★	
Latvia		★	
Lithuania		★	
Macedonia, FYR		★	
Malta		★	
Poland		★	
Romania		★	
Slovak Republic		★	
Slovenia	★		
Turkey		★	
Commonwealth of Independent States[2]			
Armenia		★	
Azerbaijan		★	
Belarus		★	
Georgia		★	
Kazakhstan		★	
Kyrgyz Republic		•	
Moldova		★	
Mongolia		•	
Russia	★		
Tajikistan		★	
Turkmenistan	★		
Ukraine	★		
Uzbekistan		★	
Developing Asia			
Bhutan		•	
Cambodia		•	
China	★		
Fiji		★	
Indonesia		•	
Kiribati	★		
Lao PDR		★	
Malaysia	★		
Myanmar		★	
Papua New Guinea		•	
Philippines		★	
Samoa		★	
Solomon Islands		•	
Thailand		★	
Tonga		★	
Vanuatu		★	
Vietnam		•	
South Asia			
Bangladesh		•	
India		★	
Maldives		★	
Nepal		•	
Pakistan		•	
Sri Lanka		•	

Table F *(concluded)*

	Net External Position		Heavily Indebted Poor Countries
	Net creditor	Net debtor[1]	
Middle East			
Bahrain		*	
Iran, I.R. of	*		
Iraq		*	
Kuwait	*		
Libya	*		
Oman	*		
Qatar	*		
Saudi Arabia	*		
United Arab Emirates	*		
Yemen	*		
Mashreq			
Egypt		*	
Jordan		*	
Lebanon		•	
Syrian Arab Republic		*	
Western Hemisphere			
Mercosur			
Argentina		•	
Bolivia (associate member)		•	*
Brazil		*	
Chile (associate member)		*	
Paraguay		•	
Uruguay		•	
Andean region			
Colombia		•	
Ecuador		*	
Peru		*	
Venezuela	*		

	Net External Position		Heavily Indebted Poor Countries
	Net creditor	Net debtor[1]	
Mexico, Central America, and Caribbean			
Mexico		*	
Central America			
Costa Rica		*	
El Salvador		•	
Guatemala		*	
Honduras		•	*
Nicaragua		*	*
Panama		*	
Caribbean			
Antigua and Barbuda		*	
Bahamas, The		*	
Barbados		*	
Belize		*	
Dominica		*	
Dominican Republic		•	
Grenada		•	
Guyana		*	*
Haiti		•	
Jamaica		*	
Netherlands Antilles		*	
St. Kitts and Nevis		*	
St. Lucia		•	
St. Vincent and the Grenadines		*	
Suriname		*	
Trinidad and Tobago		*	

[1]Dot instead of star indicates that the net debtor's main external finance source is official financing.

[2]Mongolia, which is not a member of the Commonwealth of Independent States, is included in this group for reasons of geography and similarities in economic structure.

The analytical criterion, by *source of export earnings*, distinguishes between categories: *fuel* (Standard International Trade Classification— SITC 3) and *nonfuel* and then focuses on *nonfuel primary products* (SITC 0, 1, 2, 4, and 68).

The financial criteria focus on *net creditor, net debtor countries, and heavily indebted poor countries (HIPCs)*. Net debtor countries are further differentiated on the basis of two additional financial criteria: by *official external financing* and by *experience with debt servicing*.[6] The HIPC group comprises the countries considered by the IMF and the World Bank for their debt initiative, known as the HIPC Initiative, with the aim of reducing the external debt burdens of all the eligible HIPCs to a "sustainable" level in a reasonably short period of time.[7]

[6]During 1999–2003, 56 countries incurred external payments arrears or entered into official or commercial bank debt-rescheduling agreements. This group of countries is referred to as *countries with arrears and/or rescheduling during 1999–2003.*

[7]See David Andrews, Anthony R. Boote, Syed S. Rizavi, and Sukwinder Singh, *Debt Relief for Low-Income Countries: The Enhanced HIPC Initiative*, IMF Pamphlet Series, No. 51 (Washington: International Monetary Fund, November 1999)

Output

Inflation

Financial Policies

Foreign Trade

Current Account Transactions

Table 1. Summary of World Output[1]
(Annual percent change)

	Ten-Year Averages		1998	1999	2000	2001	2002	2003	2004	2005	2006	2007
	1988–97	1998–2007										
World	**3.4**	**4.1**	**2.8**	**3.7**	**4.8**	**2.6**	**3.1**	**4.1**	**5.3**	**4.8**	**4.9**	**4.7**
Advanced economies	**2.9**	**2.6**	**2.6**	**3.4**	**3.9**	**1.2**	**1.6**	**2.0**	**3.3**	**2.7**	**3.0**	**2.8**
United States	3.0	3.2	4.2	4.4	3.7	0.8	1.6	2.7	4.2	3.5	3.4	3.3
Euro area	. . .	2.0	2.8	2.9	3.8	1.9	0.9	0.7	2.1	1.3	2.0	1.9
Japan	2.9	1.3	−1.8	−0.2	2.9	0.4	0.1	1.8	2.3	2.7	2.8	2.1
Other advanced economies[2]	3.6	3.3	2.0	4.7	5.3	1.7	3.2	2.5	3.9	3.1	3.5	3.3
Other emerging market and developing countries	**4.1**	**5.8**	**3.1**	**4.1**	**6.1**	**4.4**	**5.1**	**6.7**	**7.6**	**7.2**	**6.9**	**6.6**
Regional groups												
Africa	2.3	4.3	2.8	2.6	3.1	4.2	3.6	4.6	5.5	5.2	5.7	5.5
Central and eastern Europe	0.9	4.0	2.9	0.6	5.0	0.3	4.4	4.7	6.5	5.3	5.2	4.8
Commonwealth of Independent States[3]	. . .	5.7	−3.5	5.2	9.0	6.3	5.3	7.9	8.4	6.5	6.0	6.1
Developing Asia	7.9	7.3	4.3	6.3	7.0	6.1	7.0	8.4	8.8	8.6	8.2	8.0
Middle East	3.7	4.8	3.9	2.0	5.4	3.2	4.3	6.6	5.4	5.9	5.7	5.4
Western Hemisphere	2.9	2.7	2.3	0.5	3.9	0.5	—	2.2	5.6	4.3	4.3	3.6
Memorandum												
European Union	2.3	2.3	3.0	3.0	3.9	2.0	1.3	1.3	2.5	1.8	2.4	2.3
Analytical groups												
By source of export earnings												
Fuel	−0.1	5.2	−0.2	3.1	7.1	4.4	4.2	6.9	7.1	6.7	6.5	6.1
Nonfuel	4.8	5.9	3.6	4.3	5.9	4.4	5.2	6.7	7.7	7.2	7.0	6.7
of which, primary products	3.1	3.5	2.9	1.0	1.6	2.8	2.9	3.2	5.6	4.9	5.2	5.0
By external financing source												
Net debtor countries	3.6	4.3	2.0	2.9	4.7	2.5	3.2	4.9	6.3	5.8	5.7	5.5
of which, official financing	4.5	3.6	−0.8	1.0	3.3	2.3	1.7	5.2	6.2	6.3	5.6	5.5
Net debtor countries by debt-servicing experience												
Countries with arrears and/or rescheduling during 1999–2003	4.0	4.0	−0.9	1.6	3.7	3.1	2.3	5.7	6.4	6.6	6.2	5.9
Memorandum												
Median growth rate												
Advanced economies	3.0	2.9	3.6	4.0	4.1	1.5	1.8	2.0	3.6	2.7	3.1	2.7
Other emerging market and developing countries	3.3	4.3	3.7	3.4	4.2	3.7	3.6	4.4	5.2	5.1	5.0	4.8
Output per capita												
Advanced economies	2.2	2.1	2.0	2.8	3.3	0.6	1.0	1.4	2.7	2.2	2.4	2.3
Other emerging market and developing countries	2.3	4.4	1.6	2.7	4.7	3.0	3.8	5.4	6.4	5.9	5.7	5.4
World growth based on market exchange rates	**2.6**	**3.0**	**2.1**	**3.1**	**4.1**	**1.5**	**1.8**	**2.7**	**4.0**	**3.4**	**3.6**	**3.4**
Value of world output in billions of U.S. dollars												
At market exchange rates	25,120	37,495	29,656	30,760	31,624	31,461	32,729	36,758	41,253	44,433	46,718	49,557
At purchasing power parities	30,643	53,049	40,193	42,252	45,216	47,465	49,749	52,797	57,010	61,078	65,174	69,553

[1]Real GDP.
[2]In this table, "other advanced economies" means advanced economies excluding the United States, euro area countries, and Japan.
[3]Mongolia, which is not a member of the Commonwealth of Independent States, is included in this group for reasons of geography and similarities in economic structure.

Table 2. Advanced Economies: Real GDP and Total Domestic Demand
(Annual percent change)

	Ten-Year Averages		1998	1999	2000	2001	2002	2003	2004	2005	2006	2007	Fourth Quarter[1]		
	1988–97	1998–2007											2005	2006	2007
Real GDP															
Advanced economies	**2.9**	**2.6**	**2.6**	**3.4**	**3.9**	**1.2**	**1.6**	**2.0**	**3.3**	**2.7**	**3.0**	**2.8**	. . .	. . .	. . .
United States	3.0	3.2	4.2	4.4	3.7	0.8	1.6	2.7	4.2	3.5	3.4	3.3	3.2	3.7	3.3
Euro area	. . .	2.0	2.8	2.9	3.8	1.9	0.9	0.7	2.1	1.3	2.0	1.9	1.7	2.3	1.7
Germany	2.7	1.3	2.0	1.9	3.1	1.2	0.1	−0.2	1.6	0.9	1.3	1.0	1.6	2.0	0.8
France	2.0	2.2	3.4	3.2	4.1	2.1	1.3	0.9	2.1	1.4	2.0	2.1	1.5	2.3	1.9
Italy	1.8	1.2	1.8	1.7	3.0	1.8	0.3	0.1	0.9	0.1	1.2	1.4	0.5	1.4	1.7
Spain	2.9	3.7	4.5	4.7	5.0	3.5	2.7	3.0	3.1	3.4	3.3	3.2	3.5	3.2	3.2
Netherlands	2.9	2.1	4.3	4.0	3.5	1.4	0.1	−0.1	1.7	1.1	2.5	2.4	2.1	2.0	2.5
Belgium	2.6	2.1	1.9	3.1	3.7	1.2	1.5	0.9	2.4	1.5	2.1	2.4	1.3	2.3	2.3
Austria	2.5	2.2	3.6	3.3	3.4	0.8	1.0	1.4	2.4	1.9	2.2	2.1	1.9	1.9	2.2
Finland	1.5	3.1	5.0	3.4	5.0	1.0	2.2	2.4	3.6	2.1	3.5	2.7	2.3	3.4	2.3
Greece	2.0	3.9	3.4	3.4	4.5	4.6	3.8	4.6	4.7	3.7	3.3	3.2	3.7	3.3	2.6
Portugal	3.7	1.8	4.8	3.9	3.9	2.0	0.8	−1.1	1.1	0.3	0.8	1.5	0.7	1.3	1.7
Ireland	5.9	6.4	8.5	10.7	9.2	6.2	6.1	4.4	4.5	4.7	5.0	5.2	5.5	5.0	5.0
Luxembourg	5.5	4.7	6.9	7.8	9.0	1.5	2.5	2.9	4.5	4.3	4.0	3.8	. . .	. . .	. . .
Japan	2.9	1.3	−1.8	−0.2	2.9	0.4	0.1	1.8	2.3	2.7	2.8	2.1	4.3	2.1	2.1
United Kingdom	2.2	2.7	3.2	3.0	4.0	2.2	2.0	2.5	3.1	1.8	2.5	2.7	1.8	2.6	2.8
Canada	2.2	3.4	4.1	5.5	5.2	1.8	3.1	2.0	2.9	2.9	3.1	3.0	2.9	3.1	3.0
Korea	7.7	4.3	−6.9	9.5	8.5	3.8	7.0	3.1	4.6	4.0	5.5	4.5	5.4	4.5	4.6
Australia	3.3	3.4	5.0	4.4	3.3	2.2	4.1	3.1	3.6	2.5	2.9	3.2	2.7	3.1	3.6
Taiwan Province of China	7.0	4.0	4.5	5.7	5.8	−2.2	4.2	3.4	6.1	4.1	4.5	4.5	6.4	3.2	5.1
Sweden	1.5	3.0	3.7	4.5	4.3	1.1	2.0	1.7	3.7	2.7	3.5	2.4	3.4	3.2	2.3
Switzerland	1.4	1.7	2.8	1.3	3.6	1.0	0.3	−0.3	2.1	1.8	2.2	1.7	2.8	1.9	1.7
Hong Kong SAR	5.2	3.9	−5.5	4.0	10.0	0.6	1.8	3.2	8.6	7.3	5.5	4.5	7.7	4.8	4.3
Denmark	2.0	2.0	2.2	2.6	3.5	0.7	0.5	0.7	1.9	3.4	2.7	2.3	3.8	2.4	2.2
Norway	3.3	2.3	2.6	2.1	2.8	2.7	1.1	1.1	3.1	2.3	2.2	2.6	2.5	2.0	3.2
Israel	5.2	3.2	3.7	2.3	7.7	−0.3	−1.2	1.7	4.4	5.2	4.2	4.2	5.0	3.4	4.7
Singapore	9.1	4.5	−1.4	7.2	10.0	−2.3	4.0	2.9	8.7	6.4	5.5	4.5	8.7	1.6	6.5
New Zealand	2.1	2.8	−0.1	4.4	3.4	3.0	4.8	3.4	4.4	2.2	0.9	2.1	1.8	1.1	2.8
Cyprus	5.3	3.9	5.0	4.8	5.0	4.1	2.1	1.9	3.9	3.7	4.0	4.0	. . .	. . .	. . .
Iceland	1.2	4.1	5.8	4.3	4.1	3.8	−1.0	3.0	8.2	5.5	5.5	2.3	. . .	. . .	. . .
Memorandum															
Major advanced economies	2.7	2.5	2.6	3.1	3.6	1.1	1.2	1.9	3.1	2.6	2.8	2.6	2.8	2.9	2.6
Newly industrialized Asian economies	7.2	4.2	−2.4	7.4	7.9	1.1	5.3	3.2	5.8	4.6	5.2	4.5	6.2	4.0	4.8
Real total domestic demand															
Advanced economies	**2.9**	**2.8**	**3.0**	**4.0**	**3.9**	**1.1**	**1.7**	**2.2**	**3.4**	**2.8**	**2.9**	**2.6**	. . .	. . .	. . .
United States	2.9	3.6	5.3	5.3	4.4	0.9	2.2	3.0	4.7	3.6	3.4	3.1	3.2	3.4	3.0
Euro area	. . .	2.1	3.6	3.6	3.3	1.2	0.4	1.3	2.0	1.5	2.1	1.9	1.6	2.3	1.6
Germany	2.5	0.8	2.3	2.7	2.2	−0.5	−1.9	0.6	0.5	0.3	1.2	0.6	0.8	1.5	0.2
France	1.6	2.7	4.0	3.6	4.4	2.0	1.3	1.8	3.1	2.4	2.5	2.4	2.3	2.4	2.3
Italy	1.5	1.6	3.1	3.2	2.3	1.4	1.7	0.9	0.7	0.3	1.2	1.3	0.4	1.2	1.4
Spain	2.9	4.7	6.2	6.5	5.4	3.6	3.3	3.8	5.0	5.3	4.5	3.8	5.0	3.7	3.9
Japan	2.9	1.0	−2.2	−0.1	2.5	1.2	−0.6	1.2	1.5	2.6	2.3	2.1	3.6	2.2	2.1
United Kingdom	2.3	3.2	4.9	4.1	4.1	2.8	3.2	2.7	3.8	1.9	2.5	2.7	1.3	2.7	2.8
Canada	2.0	3.6	2.5	4.2	4.7	1.2	3.5	4.7	4.0	4.6	3.5	3.0	3.4	3.4	3.0
Other advanced economies	5.1	2.9	−1.3	5.4	5.3	0.4	3.5	1.3	4.2	3.0	3.6	3.3	. . .	. . .	. . .
Memorandum															
Major advanced economies	2.6	2.7	3.3	3.8	3.7	1.1	1.4	2.3	3.3	2.7	2.7	2.5	2.7	2.7	2.4
Newly industrialized Asian economies	8.2	2.5	−7.7	7.8	7.6	−0.1	4.1	—	4.3	2.2	3.9	3.9	1.6	3.7	4.1

[1]From fourth quarter of preceding year.

Table 3. Advanced Economies: Components of Real GDP

(Annual percent change)

	Ten-Year Averages		1998	1999	2000	2001	2002	2003	2004	2005	2006	2007
	1988–97	1998–2007										
Private consumer expenditure												
Advanced economies	**2.9**	**2.8**	**2.9**	**4.1**	**3.9**	**2.2**	**2.2**	**1.9**	**2.9**	**2.6**	**2.5**	**2.4**
United States	2.9	3.6	5.0	5.1	4.7	2.5	2.7	2.9	3.9	3.6	2.8	2.7
Euro area	. . .	1.9	3.1	3.4	3.2	1.9	0.9	1.0	1.5	1.3	1.6	1.6
Germany	2.6	0.9	1.5	3.0	2.4	1.9	−0.5	0.1	0.6	—	0.6	—
France	1.4	2.6	3.6	3.3	3.5	2.5	2.4	1.6	2.2	2.1	2.4	2.4
Italy	1.9	1.4	3.2	2.6	2.7	0.8	0.2	1.0	0.5	0.1	1.2	1.5
Spain	2.5	4.0	4.8	5.3	4.9	3.2	2.9	2.6	4.4	4.4	3.7	3.6
Japan	2.9	1.3	−0.8	1.1	1.1	1.4	1.1	0.6	1.9	2.2	2.5	2.1
United Kingdom	2.6	3.2	4.0	4.4	4.6	3.0	3.5	2.6	3.5	1.7	2.5	2.6
Canada	2.3	3.3	2.8	3.8	4.0	2.3	3.7	3.1	3.4	4.0	3.3	2.6
Other advanced economies	5.0	3.1	−0.8	5.8	5.4	2.6	3.7	1.1	3.2	3.1	3.6	3.3
Memorandum												
Major advanced economies	2.6	2.7	3.3	3.8	3.6	2.2	2.0	2.0	2.8	2.5	2.4	2.2
Newly industrialized Asian economies	7.8	3.1	−5.2	8.2	7.3	3.2	4.9	−0.4	2.2	3.1	4.2	3.9
Public consumption												
Advanced economies	**1.9**	**2.3**	**1.7**	**2.8**	**2.5**	**2.8**	**3.5**	**2.5**	**1.9**	**1.7**	**2.1**	**1.9**
United States	1.1	2.5	1.6	3.1	1.7	3.1	4.3	3.0	2.1	1.5	2.2	2.6
Euro area	. . .	1.8	1.4	2.0	2.2	2.2	2.6	1.7	1.1	1.4	1.8	1.2
Germany	1.8	0.4	1.8	1.2	1.4	0.5	1.4	0.1	−1.6	0.1	−0.4	—
France	2.2	1.9	−0.2	1.9	2.2	1.9	2.9	2.1	2.7	1.5	2.3	2.1
Italy	0.7	1.4	0.3	1.4	1.7	3.8	2.2	2.1	0.6	1.2	—	0.3
Spain	3.8	4.5	3.5	4.0	5.3	3.9	4.5	4.8	6.0	4.5	5.1	3.8
Japan	3.0	2.4	1.8	4.1	4.3	3.0	2.4	2.3	2.0	1.7	1.0	1.0
United Kingdom	0.9	3.1	1.1	4.0	3.7	1.7	4.4	4.5	3.1	2.9	3.2	2.5
Canada	1.1	2.8	3.2	2.1	3.1	3.9	2.6	2.9	2.7	2.8	2.5	2.2
Other advanced economies	4.3	2.4	2.7	1.8	2.1	3.3	3.6	2.0	1.6	2.3	2.7	2.2
Memorandum												
Major advanced economies	1.5	2.2	1.5	2.9	2.3	2.7	3.4	2.6	1.8	1.6	1.7	1.9
Newly industrialized Asian economies	6.2	2.5	3.0	0.7	2.4	3.7	4.3	2.3	1.3	2.3	2.4	2.2
Gross fixed capital formation												
Advanced economies	**3.6**	**3.3**	**5.0**	**5.5**	**5.1**	**−0.8**	**−1.7**	**2.1**	**5.3**	**4.7**	**4.3**	**3.8**
United States	3.9	4.6	9.1	8.2	6.1	−1.7	−3.5	3.3	8.4	7.3	5.3	4.5
Euro area	. . .	2.7	5.7	6.1	4.9	0.5	−1.5	0.8	2.3	2.1	3.4	3.3
Germany	2.9	0.7	4.0	4.7	3.0	−3.7	−6.1	−0.8	−0.2	−0.2	3.3	3.3
France	1.4	3.7	6.9	7.9	7.5	2.3	−1.6	2.7	2.1	3.4	3.4	2.9
Italy	1.4	2.6	4.0	5.0	6.9	1.9	4.0	−1.5	1.9	−0.4	2.0	2.4
Spain	3.4	6.4	11.1	10.3	6.5	4.6	3.4	5.8	4.9	7.3	5.8	4.4
Japan	2.8	−0.2	−6.5	−0.7	1.2	−0.9	−5.0	0.3	1.1	3.3	3.0	2.9
United Kingdom	2.8	3.7	13.0	2.1	3.5	2.4	3.0	—	5.1	3.2	2.5	3.1
Canada	2.4	4.9	2.4	7.3	4.7	4.0	1.7	5.9	6.6	6.6	5.9	4.3
Other advanced economies	6.7	2.9	−1.1	2.8	6.8	−4.4	3.4	2.6	6.9	4.0	4.6	3.9
Memorandum												
Major advanced economies	3.2	3.2	5.4	5.7	4.9	−0.7	−2.7	1.9	5.2	4.8	4.2	3.8
Newly industrialized Asian economies	10.5	1.8	−9.0	2.8	10.8	−6.5	1.9	1.6	7.6	1.5	3.8	4.7

Table 3 *(concluded)*

| | Ten-Year Averages | | 1998 | 1999 | 2000 | 2001 | 2002 | 2003 | 2004 | 2005 | 2006 | 2007 |
	1988–97	1998–2007										
Final domestic demand												
Advanced economies	**2.9**	**2.8**	**3.0**	**4.1**	**3.9**	**1.6**	**1.6**	**2.1**	**3.2**	**2.9**	**2.8**	**2.6**
United States	2.8	3.6	5.3	5.4	4.5	1.8	1.8	3.0	4.4	3.9	3.2	3.0
Euro area	. . .	2.0	3.2	3.7	3.1	1.7	0.6	1.2	1.4	1.5	2.0	2.0
Germany	2.4	0.7	2.4	2.7	2.2	–0.5	–1.9	0.6	0.6	0.3	0.7	0.7
France	1.6	2.6	3.3	3.8	4.0	2.3	1.7	1.9	2.3	2.2	2.6	2.4
Italy	1.5	1.6	2.8	2.9	3.4	1.6	1.4	0.6	0.8	0.2	1.1	1.5
Spain	3.0	4.7	6.0	6.3	5.4	3.7	3.3	3.8	4.8	5.2	4.5	3.8
Japan	2.9	1.1	–2.0	1.1	1.6	1.1	–0.2	0.8	1.8	2.4	2.4	2.1
United Kingdom	2.3	3.3	4.8	3.9	4.2	2.7	3.6	2.5	3.7	2.2	2.6	2.7
Canada	2.0	3.5	2.8	4.2	4.0	2.9	3.0	3.6	3.9	4.3	3.7	2.9
Other advanced economies	5.7	2.9	–1.1	4.3	5.4	1.0	3.8	1.6	3.8	3.1	3.7	3.3
Memorandum												
Major advanced economies	2.5	2.7	3.3	4.0	3.6	1.6	1.2	2.2	3.1	2.8	2.6	2.5
Newly industrialized Asian economies	8.3	2.6	–5.7	5.4	7.6	0.7	4.0	0.6	3.3	2.6	3.9	3.9
Stock building[1]												
Advanced economies	**—**	**—**	**—**	**—**	**0.1**	**–0.5**	**—**	**0.1**	**0.3**	**–0.1**	**0.1**	**—**
United States	0.1	—	—	—	–0.1	–0.9	0.4	0.1	0.4	–0.3	0.2	0.1
Euro area	. . .	0.1	0.4	–0.1	0.2	–0.5	–0.2	0.1	0.6	0.1	0.1	–0.1
Germany	—	—	0.4	–0.2	–0.1	–0.9	–0.6	0.6	0.5	0.3	0.1	—
France	—	0.1	0.7	–0.2	0.5	–0.3	–0.4	–0.1	0.8	0.2	–0.1	—
Italy	–0.1	—	0.3	0.3	–1.1	–0.1	0.3	0.2	–0.1	0.1	—	–0.2
Spain	—	0.1	0.2	0.3	—	–0.1	—	—	0.2	0.2	—	—
Japan	0.1	—	–0.2	–1.1	0.8	0.2	–0.4	0.3	–0.2	0.2	—	—
United Kingdom	—	—	0.1	0.2	–0.1	0.1	–0.3	0.2	0.1	–0.3	–0.1	—
Canada	0.1	—	–0.3	0.1	0.8	–1.7	0.4	0.9	—	0.3	–0.2	0.1
Other advanced economies	—	—	–0.8	1.2	—	–0.5	–0.1	–0.2	0.5	–0.2	—	—
Memorandum												
Major advanced economies	—	—	0.1	–0.2	0.1	–0.6	0.1	0.2	0.3	–0.1	0.1	—
Newly industrialized Asian economies	—	–0.1	–1.9	2.1	–0.1	–0.7	0.1	–0.5	0.9	–0.4	—	—
Foreign balance[1]												
Advanced economies	**0.1**	**–0.1**	**–0.3**	**–0.6**	**—**	**0.1**	**–0.1**	**–0.2**	**–0.2**	**–0.1**	**0.1**	**0.1**
United States	0.1	–0.5	–1.2	–1.0	–0.9	–0.2	–0.7	–0.5	–0.7	–0.3	–0.1	0.1
Euro area	. . .	—	–0.6	–0.6	0.6	0.6	0.5	–0.6	0.1	–0.2	—	0.1
Germany	0.2	0.5	–0.4	–0.8	1.0	1.7	1.9	–0.8	1.1	0.6	0.2	0.4
France	0.4	–0.5	–0.5	–0.4	–0.3	0.1	—	–0.9	–1.1	–1.0	–0.5	–0.3
Italy	0.4	–0.4	–1.2	–1.4	0.8	–0.4	–1.0	–0.8	0.1	–0.3	0.4	0.1
Spain	–0.3	–1.3	–1.7	–1.9	–0.5	–0.2	–0.7	–0.9	–2.2	–2.2	–1.5	–1.0
Japan	—	0.3	0.4	–0.2	0.5	–0.8	0.7	0.6	0.8	0.2	0.5	—
United Kingdom	—	–0.6	–1.4	–0.9	–0.1	–0.6	–1.2	–0.2	–0.8	–0.1	–0.1	–0.1
Canada	0.1	–0.1	1.7	1.4	0.6	0.7	–0.2	–2.4	–0.9	–1.5	–0.3	0.2
Other advanced economies	–0.3	1.0	2.8	0.3	0.7	0.9	0.4	1.4	0.8	1.0	0.9	0.7
Memorandum												
Major advanced economies	0.1	–0.3	–0.7	–0.7	–0.2	–0.1	–0.2	–0.4	–0.3	–0.2	—	0.1
Newly industrialized Asian economies	–0.9	2.0	5.6	0.4	0.5	1.1	1.2	3.2	2.2	2.6	1.7	1.1

[1]Changes expressed as percent of GDP in the preceding period.

Table 4. Advanced Economies: Unemployment, Employment, and Real Per Capita GDP
(Percent)

| | Ten-Year Averages[1] | | 1998 | 1999 | 2000 | 2001 | 2002 | 2003 | 2004 | 2005 | 2006 | 2007 |
	1988–97	1998–2007										
Unemployment rate												
Advanced economies	**6.8**	**6.1**	**6.7**	**6.3**	**5.8**	**5.8**	**6.3**	**6.6**	**6.3**	**6.0**	**5.8**	**5.8**
United States[2]	6.0	5.0	4.5	4.2	4.0	4.7	5.8	6.0	5.5	5.1	4.9	5.1
Euro area	...	8.6	10.0	9.2	8.2	7.8	8.3	8.7	8.9	8.6	8.3	8.1
Germany	7.0	8.2	8.1	7.5	6.9	6.9	7.7	8.8	9.2	9.1	8.7	8.8
France	10.5	9.5	11.1	10.5	9.1	8.4	8.9	9.5	9.5	9.6	9.6	9.1
Italy	11.3	9.3	11.8	11.4	10.6	9.5	9.0	8.2	8.3	8.1	7.8	7.6
Spain	20.0	11.9	18.6	15.6	13.9	10.6	11.5	11.5	11.0	9.2	8.6	8.5
Netherlands	6.2	3.7	3.8	3.2	2.8	2.2	2.8	3.7	4.6	4.9	4.5	4.3
Belgium	8.3	8.0	9.3	8.6	6.9	6.6	7.5	8.2	8.4	8.4	8.3	8.2
Austria	3.5	4.3	4.5	3.9	3.6	3.6	4.2	4.3	4.8	5.2	4.8	4.5
Finland	10.5	9.2	11.4	10.2	9.8	9.1	9.1	9.0	8.8	8.4	7.9	7.8
Greece	8.6	10.5	11.2	12.1	11.4	10.8	10.3	9.7	10.5	9.9	9.5	9.5
Portugal	5.8	5.8	5.0	4.4	3.9	4.0	5.0	6.3	6.7	7.6	7.7	7.6
Ireland	13.9	4.7	7.6	5.6	4.3	3.9	4.4	4.7	4.5	4.3	4.1	4.0
Luxembourg	2.2	3.4	3.0	2.9	2.5	2.3	2.6	3.5	3.9	4.2	4.5	4.7
Japan	2.6	4.6	4.1	4.7	4.7	5.0	5.4	5.3	4.7	4.4	4.1	4.0
United Kingdom	8.6	5.2	6.3	6.0	5.5	5.1	5.2	5.0	4.8	4.8	4.9	4.8
Canada	9.5	7.2	8.3	7.6	6.8	7.2	7.6	7.6	7.2	6.8	6.6	6.6
Korea	2.5	4.3	7.0	6.6	4.4	4.0	3.3	3.6	3.7	3.7	3.5	3.3
Australia	8.5	6.1	7.7	6.9	6.3	6.8	6.4	6.1	5.5	5.1	5.2	5.2
Taiwan Province of China	1.8	4.0	2.7	2.9	3.0	4.6	5.2	5.0	4.4	4.1	4.0	3.9
Sweden	5.3	4.9	6.5	5.6	4.7	4.0	4.0	4.9	5.5	5.6	4.5	4.2
Switzerland	2.5	2.8	3.4	2.4	1.7	1.6	2.3	3.4	3.5	3.4	3.3	3.3
Hong Kong SAR	2.0	5.8	4.4	6.3	5.1	4.9	7.2	7.9	6.9	5.7	4.5	4.5
Denmark	10.2	5.7	6.6	5.7	5.4	5.2	5.2	6.2	6.4	5.7	5.1	5.3
Norway	5.1	3.9	3.2	3.2	3.4	3.5	3.9	4.5	4.5	4.6	4.1	4.0
Israel	8.6	9.3	8.5	8.9	8.7	9.3	10.3	10.7	10.3	9.0	8.5	8.2
Singapore	2.3	3.0	2.5	2.8	2.7	2.7	3.6	4.0	3.4	3.0	2.9	2.9
New Zealand	7.8	5.2	7.4	6.8	6.0	5.3	5.2	4.7	3.9	3.7	4.1	4.6
Cyprus	2.6	3.3	3.4	3.6	3.4	2.9	3.2	3.5	3.6	3.3	3.0	3.0
Iceland	3.1	2.2	2.8	1.9	1.3	1.4	2.5	3.4	3.1	2.1	1.9	2.0
Memorandum												
Major advanced economies	6.5	6.1	6.2	6.0	5.6	5.8	6.4	6.6	6.3	6.0	5.9	5.8
Newly industrialized Asian economies	2.2	4.3	5.4	5.4	4.0	4.2	4.2	4.4	4.2	4.0	3.7	3.5
Growth in employment												
Advanced economies	**1.1**	**1.0**	**1.1**	**1.4**	**2.1**	**0.7**	**0.3**	**0.6**	**1.0**	**1.2**	**1.2**	**0.9**
United States	1.4	1.2	1.5	1.5	2.5	—	−0.3	0.9	1.1	1.8	1.8	1.2
Euro area	...	1.2	1.9	1.8	2.7	1.5	0.6	0.2	0.7	1.0	1.0	0.9
Germany	0.4	0.4	1.2	1.4	1.9	0.4	−0.6	−0.9	0.4	−0.2	0.5	0.4
France	0.3	1.0	1.5	2.0	2.7	1.7	0.7	−0.1	0.1	0.2	0.4	0.6
Italy	−0.3	1.1	1.1	1.3	1.9	2.1	1.5	1.9	0.7	0.2	0.3	0.3
Spain	2.3	3.4	4.5	4.6	5.1	3.2	2.4	2.6	2.6	3.6	3.2	2.7
Japan	1.0	−0.3	−0.7	−0.8	−0.2	−0.5	−1.3	−0.3	0.2	0.4	0.1	—
United Kingdom	0.5	0.9	1.0	1.4	1.2	0.8	0.8	1.0	1.0	1.0	0.4	0.6
Canada	1.1	1.9	2.5	2.6	2.5	1.2	2.4	2.4	1.8	1.4	1.2	0.9
Other advanced economies	1.7	1.3	−1.0	1.6	2.9	1.1	1.6	0.5	1.6	1.5	1.4	1.4
Memorandum												
Major advanced economies	0.9	0.8	1.0	1.1	1.8	0.4	−0.1	0.5	0.8	1.0	1.0	0.7
Newly industrialized Asian economies	2.3	1.2	−3.0	1.5	3.6	0.8	2.0	0.3	1.9	1.2	1.7	1.8

Table 4 *(concluded)*

	Ten-Year Averages[1]		1998	1999	2000	2001	2002	2003	2004	2005	2006	2007
	1988–97	1998–2007										
Growth in real per capita GDP												
Advanced economies	**2.2**	**2.1**	**2.0**	**2.8**	**3.3**	**0.6**	**1.0**	**1.4**	**2.7**	**2.2**	**2.4**	**2.3**
United States	1.8	2.1	3.0	3.3	2.5	–0.3	0.6	1.7	3.2	2.6	2.4	2.3
Euro area	. . .	1.7	2.6	2.6	3.3	1.5	0.4	0.2	1.5	0.8	1.7	1.6
Germany	1.9	1.2	2.0	1.9	3.0	1.1	–0.1	–0.3	1.6	0.9	1.3	0.9
France	1.5	1.7	3.0	2.7	3.5	1.4	0.7	0.3	1.4	1.0	1.6	1.7
Italy	1.7	1.1	1.7	1.6	3.0	1.8	0.4	0.2	—	–0.1	1.1	1.3
Spain	2.7	3.0	4.2	4.3	3.8	2.9	2.0	2.4	2.5	2.8	2.8	2.7
Japan	2.5	1.2	–2.0	–0.4	2.7	0.1	–0.1	1.6	2.2	2.7	2.7	2.1
United Kingdom	2.0	2.3	3.0	2.7	3.7	1.8	1.6	2.1	2.6	1.3	2.0	2.2
Canada	1.0	2.4	3.2	4.7	4.3	0.7	1.9	1.0	1.9	2.0	2.0	2.1
Other advanced economies	3.6	2.8	–0.3	4.5	5.0	0.6	3.0	1.8	3.9	3.0	3.4	3.1
Memorandum												
Major advanced economies	2.0	1.9	2.0	2.5	3.0	0.5	0.6	1.3	2.6	2.1	2.3	2.1
Newly industrialized Asian economies	6.1	3.5	–3.4	6.5	7.0	0.4	4.7	2.6	5.3	4.0	4.7	4.0

[1]Compound annual rate of change for employment and per capita GDP; arithmetic average for unemployment rate.
[2]The projections for unemployment have been adjusted to reflect the survey techniques adopted by the U.S. Bureau of Labor Statistics in January 1994.

Table 5. Other Emerging Market and Developing Countries: Real GDP
(Annual percent change)

	Ten-Year Averages		1998	1999	2000	2001	2002	2003	2004	2005	2006	2007
	1988–97	1998–2007										
Other emerging market and developing countries	**4.1**	**5.8**	**3.1**	**4.1**	**6.1**	**4.4**	**5.1**	**6.7**	**7.6**	**7.2**	**6.9**	**6.6**
Regional groups												
Africa	2.3	4.3	2.8	2.6	3.1	4.2	3.6	4.6	5.5	5.2	5.7	5.5
Sub-Sahara	2.3	4.2	1.9	2.6	3.4	4.2	3.6	4.2	5.6	5.5	5.8	5.7
Excluding Nigeria and South Africa	2.3	4.7	3.2	3.0	2.4	5.5	4.0	3.6	6.3	5.6	6.9	6.8
Central and eastern Europe	0.9	4.0	2.9	0.6	5.0	0.3	4.4	4.7	6.5	5.3	5.2	4.8
Commonwealth of Independent States[1]	. . .	5.7	−3.5	5.2	9.0	6.3	5.3	7.9	8.4	6.5	6.0	6.1
Russia	. . .	5.3	−5.3	6.3	10.0	5.1	4.7	7.3	7.2	6.4	6.0	5.8
Excluding Russia	. . .	6.4	0.6	2.3	6.6	9.1	6.6	9.1	11.1	6.7	6.0	6.6
Developing Asia	7.9	7.3	4.3	6.3	7.0	6.1	7.0	8.4	8.8	8.6	8.2	8.0
China	9.9	8.9	7.8	7.1	8.4	8.3	9.1	10.0	10.1	9.9	9.5	9.0
India	5.9	6.5	6.0	7.0	5.3	4.1	4.2	7.2	8.1	8.3	7.3	7.0
Excluding China and India	6.3	4.1	−4.7	3.7	5.7	3.2	4.8	5.8	6.0	5.6	5.4	5.9
Middle East	3.7	4.8	3.9	2.0	5.4	3.2	4.3	6.6	5.4	5.9	5.7	5.4
Western Hemisphere	2.9	2.7	2.3	0.5	3.9	0.5	—	2.2	5.6	4.3	4.3	3.6
Brazil	2.0	2.3	0.1	0.8	4.4	1.3	1.9	0.5	4.9	2.3	3.5	3.5
Mexico	3.0	3.1	5.0	3.8	6.6	—	0.8	1.4	4.2	3.0	3.5	3.1
Analytical groups												
By source of export earnings												
Fuel	−0.1	5.2	−0.2	3.1	7.1	4.4	4.2	6.9	7.1	6.7	6.5	6.1
Nonfuel	4.8	5.9	3.6	4.3	5.9	4.4	5.2	6.7	7.7	7.2	7.0	6.7
of which, primary products	3.1	3.5	2.9	1.0	1.6	2.8	2.9	3.2	5.6	4.9	5.2	5.0
By external financing source												
Net debtor countries	3.6	4.3	2.0	2.9	4.7	2.5	3.2	4.9	6.3	5.8	5.7	5.5
of which, official financing	4.5	3.6	−0.8	1.0	3.3	2.3	1.7	5.2	6.2	6.3	5.6	5.5
Net debtor countries by debt-servicing experience												
Countries with arrears and/or rescheduling during 1999–2003	4.0	4.0	−0.9	1.6	3.7	3.1	2.3	5.7	6.4	6.6	6.2	5.9
Other groups												
Heavily indebted poor countries	1.7	4.6	3.3	3.6	2.8	5.0	3.6	4.3	6.5	5.6	5.6	5.7
Middle East and north Africa	3.3	4.8	4.3	2.2	4.9	3.5	4.2	6.5	5.3	5.6	5.9	5.6
Memorandum												
Real per capita GDP												
Other emerging market and developing countries	2.3	4.4	1.6	2.7	4.7	3.0	3.8	5.4	6.4	5.9	5.7	5.4
Africa	−0.4	2.0	0.4	0.3	0.8	2.0	1.4	2.4	3.3	3.0	3.5	3.4
Central and eastern Europe	0.3	3.5	2.4	0.2	4.6	−0.1	4.0	4.2	6.1	4.9	4.8	4.4
Commonwealth of Independent States[1]	. . .	5.9	−3.4	5.4	9.2	6.5	5.6	8.2	8.7	6.7	6.2	6.3
Developing Asia	6.2	6.0	2.9	4.9	5.7	4.9	5.8	7.2	7.6	7.5	7.1	6.8
Middle East	1.1	2.7	1.7	−0.1	3.3	1.2	2.2	4.5	3.4	3.9	3.6	3.4
Western Hemisphere	1.1	1.2	0.7	−1.1	2.4	−1.0	−1.4	0.7	4.2	2.9	2.9	2.3

[1]Mongolia, which is not a member of the Commonwealth of Independent States, is included in this group for reasons of geography and similarities in economic structure.

Table 6. Other Emerging Market and Developing Countries—by Country: Real GDP[1]

(Annual percent change)

	Average 1988–97	1998	1999	2000	2001	2002	2003	2004	2005	2006	2007
Africa	**2.3**	**2.8**	**2.6**	**3.1**	**4.2**	**3.6**	**4.6**	**5.5**	**5.2**	**5.7**	**5.5**
Algeria	1.0	5.1	3.2	2.2	2.6	4.7	6.9	5.2	5.3	4.9	5.0
Angola	0.9	—	3.2	3.0	3.1	14.4	3.4	11.1	15.7	26.0	20.2
Benin	4.0	4.0	5.3	4.9	6.2	4.5	3.9	3.1	3.5	4.0	5.1
Botswana	7.0	5.9	5.5	7.6	5.1	5.0	6.6	4.9	3.8	3.5	3.5
Burkina Faso	5.7	8.4	4.1	3.3	6.7	5.2	7.9	5.5	7.5	4.2	6.3
Burundi	−1.0	4.8	−1.0	−0.9	2.1	4.4	−1.2	4.8	0.9	6.3	5.8
Cameroon[2]	−1.6	5.0	4.4	4.2	4.5	4.0	4.1	3.6	2.6	4.2	4.3
Cape Verde	5.3	8.4	11.9	7.3	6.1	5.3	4.7	4.4	6.3	7.0	6.5
Central African Republic	—	3.9	3.6	1.8	0.3	−0.6	−7.6	1.3	2.2	3.2	3.8
Chad	3.5	7.0	−0.7	−0.4	10.4	8.4	14.9	29.5	5.6	3.0	3.0
Comoros	1.1	1.2	1.9	2.4	2.3	2.3	2.1	1.9	2.0	3.0	4.1
Congo, Dem. Rep. of	−5.1	−1.7	−4.3	−6.9	−2.1	3.5	6.0	6.9	6.5	7.0	7.2
Congo, Rep. of	4.7	3.7	−3.0	8.2	3.6	5.4	0.3	3.6	9.2	5.2	2.2
Côte d'Ivoire	3.4	4.7	1.5	−3.3	—	−1.4	−1.5	1.8	0.5	2.4	2.6
Djibouti	−1.6	0.1	4.1	0.4	2.0	2.6	3.2	3.0	3.2	4.2	5.0
Equatorial Guinea	23.5	25.7	24.3	14.1	78.3	21.3	14.1	32.4	6.0	−1.1	9.4
Eritrea	...	1.8	—	−13.1	9.2	0.7	3.0	2.8	4.8	1.5	1.3
Ethiopia	2.3	−4.3	6.6	5.4	7.9	—	−3.1	12.3	8.7	5.3	5.7
Gabon	4.8	3.5	−8.9	−1.9	2.1	−0.3	2.4	1.4	2.9	2.9	3.0
Gambia, The	3.6	6.5	6.4	6.4	5.8	−3.2	6.9	5.1	5.0	4.5	5.0
Ghana	4.6	4.7	4.4	3.7	4.2	4.5	5.2	5.8	5.8	6.0	6.0
Guinea	4.4	4.8	4.7	1.9	4.0	4.2	1.2	2.7	3.0	5.0	5.4
Guinea-Bissau	3.6	−27.2	7.6	7.5	0.2	−7.1	−0.6	2.2	2.0	2.6	2.9
Kenya	2.6	3.3	2.4	0.6	4.7	0.3	2.8	4.3	4.7	3.3	4.9
Lesotho	6.0	−3.5	−0.6	1.6	2.8	3.2	3.3	2.0	−0.7	2.3	2.0
Madagascar	1.5	3.9	4.7	4.7	6.0	−12.7	9.8	5.3	4.6	5.7	6.3
Malawi	3.9	1.1	3.5	0.8	−4.1	2.1	3.9	5.1	1.9	8.3	5.6
Mali	5.1	8.4	3.0	−3.2	12.1	4.3	7.2	2.3	5.4	5.4	6.1
Mauritania	3.1	3.9	7.8	6.7	3.6	2.3	6.4	6.2	5.5	18.4	13.6
Mauritius	6.4	5.9	4.4	6.0	6.0	2.5	2.9	4.2	3.5	2.7	2.9
Morocco	3.1	7.7	−0.1	1.0	6.3	3.2	5.5	4.2	1.8	5.4	4.4
Mozambique, Rep. of	4.6	12.6	7.5	1.9	13.1	8.2	7.9	7.5	7.7	7.9	7.0
Namibia	3.4	3.3	3.4	3.5	2.4	6.7	3.5	5.9	3.5	4.5	4.5
Niger	1.6	10.4	−0.6	−1.4	7.1	3.0	5.3	—	7.0	3.6	4.2
Nigeria	4.3	0.3	1.5	5.4	3.1	1.5	10.7	6.0	6.9	6.2	5.2
Rwanda	−2.6	8.9	7.6	6.0	6.7	9.4	0.9	4.0	5.0	4.0	4.3
São Tomé and Príncipe	1.3	2.5	2.5	3.0	4.0	4.1	4.0	3.8	3.8	4.5	5.5
Senegal	2.3	4.5	6.2	3.0	4.7	1.1	6.5	6.2	6.2	5.0	5.1
Seychelles	6.0	2.5	1.9	4.3	−2.2	1.3	−6.3	−2.0	−2.3	−1.4	−1.5
Sierra Leone	−6.3	−0.8	−8.1	3.8	18.2	27.5	9.3	7.4	7.2	7.4	6.5
South Africa	1.7	0.5	2.4	4.2	2.7	3.7	3.0	4.5	4.9	4.3	4.1
Sudan	2.6	4.3	3.1	8.4	6.1	6.4	5.6	5.2	8.0	13.0	10.3
Swaziland	4.6	2.8	3.5	2.6	1.6	2.9	2.4	2.1	2.2	1.2	1.0
Tanzania	3.4	3.7	3.5	5.1	6.2	7.2	7.1	6.7	6.9	5.8	7.0
Togo	2.7	−2.3	2.4	−1.6	2.9	4.1	1.9	3.0	0.8	4.2	4.5
Tunisia	4.1	4.8	6.1	4.7	4.9	1.7	5.6	6.0	4.2	5.8	6.0
Uganda	6.6	3.6	8.3	5.3	4.8	6.9	4.4	5.6	5.6	6.2	6.1
Zambia	−0.1	−1.9	2.2	3.6	4.9	3.3	5.1	5.4	5.1	6.0	6.0
Zimbabwe	3.6	0.1	−3.6	−7.3	−2.7	−4.4	−10.4	−3.8	−6.5	−4.7	−4.1

Table 6 *(continued)*

	Average 1988–97	1998	1999	2000	2001	2002	2003	2004	2005	2006	2007
Central and eastern Europe³	**0.9**	**2.9**	**0.6**	**5.0**	**0.3**	**4.4**	**4.7**	**6.5**	**5.3**	**5.2**	**4.8**
Albania	−1.8	12.7	10.1	7.3	7.0	2.9	5.7	5.9	5.5	5.0	6.0
Bosnia and Herzegovina	...	17.6	9.5	5.4	4.3	5.3	4.4	6.2	5.0	5.0	5.2
Bulgaria	−5.8	4.0	2.3	5.4	4.1	4.9	4.5	5.7	5.5	5.6	5.8
Croatia	...	2.5	−0.9	2.9	4.4	5.2	4.3	3.8	4.1	4.1	4.5
Czech Republic	...	−1.1	1.2	3.9	2.6	1.5	3.2	4.7	6.0	5.5	4.5
Estonia	...	4.4	0.3	7.9	6.5	7.2	6.7	7.8	9.8	7.9	7.1
Hungary	−0.9	4.9	4.2	5.2	4.3	3.8	3.4	4.6	4.1	4.4	4.2
Latvia	...	4.7	3.3	8.4	8.0	6.5	7.2	8.5	10.2	9.0	7.0
Lithuania	...	7.3	−1.7	4.7	6.4	6.8	10.5	7.0	7.3	6.5	6.0
Macedonia, FYR	...	3.4	4.4	4.5	−4.5	0.9	2.8	4.1	3.8	4.0	4.5
Malta	5.8	3.4	4.1	9.9	−0.4	1.0	−1.9	1.0	1.0	1.3	1.5
Serbia and Montenegro	...	2.5	−18.0	5.0	5.5	4.3	2.4	8.8	4.7	4.9	4.9
Poland	2.3	5.0	4.5	4.2	1.1	1.4	3.8	5.3	3.2	4.2	3.8
Romania	−2.5	−4.8	−1.2	2.1	5.7	5.1	5.2	8.4	4.1	5.2	5.6
Slovak Republic	...	4.2	1.5	2.0	3.8	4.6	4.5	5.5	6.0	6.3	6.7
Slovenia	...	3.9	5.4	4.1	2.7	3.5	2.7	4.2	3.9	4.0	4.0
Turkey	4.2	3.1	−4.7	7.4	−7.5	7.9	5.8	8.9	7.4	6.0	5.0
Commonwealth of Independent States³,⁴	**...**	**−3.5**	**5.2**	**9.0**	**6.3**	**5.3**	**7.9**	**8.4**	**6.5**	**6.0**	**6.1**
Russia	...	−5.3	6.3	10.0	5.1	4.7	7.3	7.2	6.4	6.0	5.8
Excluding Russia	...	0.6	2.3	6.6	9.1	6.6	9.1	11.1	6.7	6.0	6.6
Armenia	...	7.3	3.3	6.0	9.6	13.2	13.9	10.1	13.9	7.5	6.0
Azerbaijan	...	6.0	11.4	6.2	6.5	8.1	10.4	10.2	24.3	26.2	22.9
Belarus	...	8.4	3.4	5.8	4.7	5.0	7.0	11.4	9.2	5.5	4.0
Georgia	...	2.9	3.0	1.9	4.7	5.5	11.1	6.2	7.7	6.4	5.0
Kazakhstan	...	−1.9	2.7	9.8	13.5	9.8	9.3	9.6	9.4	8.0	8.3
Kyrgyz Republic	...	2.1	3.7	5.4	5.3	—	7.0	7.0	−0.6	5.0	5.5
Moldova	...	−6.5	−3.4	2.1	6.1	7.8	6.6	7.3	7.0	6.0	5.0
Mongolia	−0.1	3.5	3.2	1.1	1.0	4.0	5.6	10.7	6.2	6.5	6.0
Tajikistan	...	5.2	3.7	8.3	10.2	9.1	10.2	10.6	6.7	8.0	6.0
Turkmenistan	...	6.7	16.5	18.6	20.4	15.8	17.1	17.2	9.6	6.5	6.0
Ukraine	...	−1.9	−0.2	5.9	9.2	5.2	9.6	12.1	2.6	2.3	4.3
Uzbekistan	...	2.1	3.4	3.3	4.1	3.1	1.5	7.4	7.0	7.2	5.0

Table 6 *(continued)*

	Average 1988–97	1998	1999	2000	2001	2002	2003	2004	2005	2006	2007
Developing Asia	**7.9**	**4.3**	**6.3**	**7.0**	**6.1**	**7.0**	**8.4**	**8.8**	**8.6**	**8.2**	**8.0**
Afghanistan, I.S. of	...	...	...	...	...	28.6	15.7	8.0	13.8	11.7	10.6
Bangladesh	4.4	5.0	5.4	5.6	4.8	4.8	5.8	5.9	5.8	6.0	6.3
Bhutan	4.3	5.8	7.7	9.5	8.6	7.1	6.8	8.7	6.5	13.2	11.5
Brunei Darussalam	...	−4.0	2.6	2.8	3.1	2.8	3.8	1.7	3.0	2.2	2.3
Cambodia	...	5.0	12.6	8.4	5.7	5.5	7.1	7.7	7.0	6.0	6.0
China	9.9	7.8	7.1	8.4	8.3	9.1	10.0	10.1	9.9	9.5	9.0
Fiji	4.1	1.2	9.2	−2.8	2.7	4.3	3.0	4.1	2.1	2.6	1.8
India	5.9	6.0	7.0	5.3	4.1	4.2	7.2	8.1	8.3	7.3	7.0
Indonesia	6.9	−13.1	0.8	5.4	3.8	4.4	4.7	5.1	5.6	5.0	6.0
Kiribati	3.6	12.6	9.5	6.9	5.0	2.2	−1.4	−3.7	0.3	0.8	0.8
Lao PDR	6.0	4.0	7.3	5.8	5.8	5.8	6.1	6.4	7.0	7.1	6.0
Malaysia	9.3	−7.4	6.1	8.9	0.3	4.4	5.4	7.1	5.3	5.5	5.8
Maldives	7.7	9.8	7.2	4.8	3.5	6.5	8.5	8.8	−3.6	8.0	4.0
Myanmar	3.5	5.8	10.9	13.7	11.3	12.0	13.8	3.0	5.0	3.5	3.5
Nepal	5.3	2.9	4.5	6.1	5.6	−0.6	3.3	3.8	2.7	3.0	3.0
Pakistan	4.4	3.1	4.0	3.0	2.5	4.1	5.7	7.1	7.0	6.4	6.3
Papua New Guinea	4.0	4.7	1.9	−2.5	−0.1	−0.2	2.9	2.9	3.0	3.5	3.5
Philippines	3.8	−0.6	3.4	6.0	1.8	4.4	4.5	6.0	5.1	5.0	5.6
Samoa	2.6	1.1	2.1	3.7	7.1	4.4	1.8	2.8	5.6	4.5	3.5
Solomon Islands	4.7	1.8	−0.5	−14.3	−9.0	−2.4	5.6	5.5	5.2	4.8	4.5
Sri Lanka	4.8	4.7	4.3	6.0	−1.5	4.0	6.0	5.4	5.9	5.6	6.2
Thailand	8.4	−10.5	4.4	4.8	2.2	5.3	7.0	6.2	4.4	5.0	5.4
Timor-Leste, Dem. Rep. of	...	...	...	15.4	16.6	−6.7	−6.2	1.8	3.2	5.0	4.6
Tonga	1.0	3.6	2.3	5.6	1.8	2.1	2.9	1.5	2.5	2.8	2.9
Vanuatu	4.3	4.5	−3.2	2.7	−2.7	−4.6	2.4	4.0	3.0	3.0	2.8
Vietnam	7.6	5.8	·4.8	6.8	6.9	7.1	7.3	7.7	7.5	7.4	7.4
Middle East	**3.7**	**3.9**	**2.0**	**5.4**	**3.2**	**4.3**	**6.6**	**5.4**	**5.9**	**5.7**	**5.4**
Bahrain	4.9	4.8	4.2	5.3	4.6	5.2	7.2	5.4	6.9	7.1	6.3
Egypt	3.4	7.5	6.1	5.4	3.5	3.2	3.1	4.1	5.0	5.2	5.2
Iran, I.R. of	3.6	2.7	1.9	5.1	3.7	7.5	6.7	5.6	5.9	5.3	5.0
Iraq	...	...	...	...	...	...	...	...	...	...	...
Jordan	2.6	3.0	3.4	4.3	5.3	5.7	4.1	7.7	7.2	5.0	5.0
Kuwait	1.2	3.7	−1.8	4.7	0.7	5.1	13.4	6.2	8.5	6.2	4.7
Lebanon	−3.6	2.3	−1.2	1.2	4.2	2.9	5.0	6.0	1.0	3.0	3.4
Libya	0.3	−0.4	0.3	1.1	4.5	3.3	9.1	4.6	3.5	5.0	4.6
Oman	5.5	2.7	−0.2	5.5	7.5	2.3	1.9	4.5	3.8	6.2	6.0
Qatar	4.0	11.7	4.5	9.1	4.5	7.3	8.6	9.3	5.5	7.1	5.3
Saudi Arabia	3.7	2.8	−0.7	4.9	0.5	0.1	7.7	5.2	6.5	6.3	6.4
Syrian Arab Republic	5.7	5.5	−3.6	0.6	3.6	4.1	1.3	2.5	3.5	3.6	3.6
United Arab Emirates	6.3	0.1	3.1	12.4	1.7	2.6	11.6	7.8	8.0	6.5	5.2
Yemen	...	5.3	3.5	4.4	4.6	3.9	3.1	2.6	3.8	3.9	3.0

Table 6 *(concluded)*

	Average 1988–97	1998	1999	2000	2001	2002	2003	2004	2005	2006	2007
Western Hemisphere	**2.9**	**2.3**	**0.5**	**3.9**	**0.5**	**—**	**2.2**	**5.6**	**4.3**	**4.3**	**3.6**
Antigua and Barbuda	3.6	4.9	4.9	3.3	1.5	2.0	4.3	5.2	3.0	4.0	4.3
Argentina	3.2	3.9	–3.4	–0.8	–4.4	–10.9	8.8	9.0	9.2	7.3	4.0
Bahamas, The	1.1	6.8	4.0	1.9	0.8	1.4	1.9	3.0	3.4	3.6	4.0
Barbados	0.9	6.2	0.5	2.3	–2.6	0.5	1.9	4.8	4.2	4.2	4.5
Belize	5.9	3.7	8.7	13.0	4.6	4.7	9.2	4.6	2.2	2.7	4.0
Bolivia	4.1	5.0	0.4	2.5	1.7	2.4	2.8	3.6	3.9	4.1	3.9
Brazil	2.0	0.1	0.8	4.4	1.3	1.9	0.5	4.9	2.3	3.5	3.5
Chile	7.9	3.2	–0.8	4.5	3.4	2.2	3.7	6.1	6.3	5.5	5.2
Colombia	4.0	0.6	–4.2	2.9	1.5	1.9	3.9	4.8	5.1	4.5	4.0
Costa Rica	4.6	8.4	8.2	1.8	1.1	2.9	6.4	4.1	4.1	3.6	3.0
Dominica	2.6	3.0	1.6	1.3	–4.2	–5.1	0.1	3.6	2.4	3.0	3.0
Dominican Republic	3.7	7.4	8.1	8.1	3.6	4.4	–1.9	2.0	9.0	5.4	5.0
Ecuador	3.7	2.1	–6.3	2.8	5.1	3.3	2.7	6.9	3.3	3.0	2.2
El Salvador	4.4	3.7	3.4	2.2	1.7	2.2	1.8	1.5	2.8	3.5	3.5
Grenada	3.0	7.9	7.3	7.0	–4.4	0.8	5.8	–3.0	1.5	6.5	5.0
Guatemala	4.0	5.0	3.8	3.6	2.3	2.2	2.1	2.7	3.2	4.1	4.0
Guyana	3.8	–1.7	3.0	–1.3	2.3	1.1	–0.7	1.6	–2.8	4.2	3.8
Haiti	–0.6	2.2	2.7	0.9	–1.0	–0.5	0.5	–3.8	1.5	2.5	4.0
Honduras	3.5	2.9	–1.9	5.7	2.6	2.7	3.5	4.6	4.2	4.3	4.5
Jamaica	0.9	–0.6	1.1	0.8	1.0	1.9	2.0	2.5	0.7	3.7	3.0
Mexico	3.0	5.0	3.8	6.6	—	0.8	1.4	4.2	3.0	3.5	3.1
Netherlands Antilles	3.0	–3.1	–1.8	–2.0	1.4	0.4	1.4	1.0	0.7	1.8	2.7
Nicaragua	0.5	3.7	7.0	4.1	3.0	0.8	2.3	5.1	4.0	3.7	4.3
Panama	3.6	7.3	3.9	2.7	0.6	2.2	4.2	7.6	5.5	4.5	4.0
Paraguay	3.7	0.6	–1.5	–3.3	2.1	—	3.8	4.1	3.0	3.5	4.0
Peru	0.6	–0.7	0.9	2.9	0.2	4.9	4.0	4.8	6.7	5.0	4.5
St. Kitts and Nevis	5.2	1.0	3.9	6.5	1.7	–0.3	–0.9	6.4	4.9	3.7	4.4
St. Lucia	4.5	3.3	3.9	–0.3	–4.1	0.1	2.9	4.0	5.1	5.8	2.4
St. Vincent and the Grenadines	4.2	4.6	4.1	1.8	–0.1	3.2	3.4	4.3	4.9	4.3	4.1
Suriname	1.7	1.6	–0.9	–0.1	4.5	3.0	5.3	7.8	5.1	4.5	4.4
Trinidad and Tobago	1.8	8.1	8.0	6.9	4.2	7.4	13.7	6.6	7.0	10.4	4.9
Uruguay	3.3	4.5	–2.8	–1.4	–3.4	–11.0	2.2	12.3	6.0	4.0	3.5
Venezuela	2.6	0.3	–6.0	3.7	3.4	–8.9	–7.7	17.9	9.3	6.0	3.0

[1]For many countries, figures for recent years are IMF staff estimates. Data for some countries are for fiscal years.
[2]The percent changes in 2002 are calculated over a period of 18 months, reflecting a change in the fiscal year cycle (from July–June to January–December).
[3]Data for some countries refer to real net material product (NMP) or are estimates based on NMP. For many countries, figures for recent years are IMF staff estimates. The figures should be interpreted only as indicative of broad orders of magnitude because reliable, comparable data are not generally available. In particular, the growth of output of new private enterprises of the informal economy is not fully reflected in the recent figures.
[4]Mongolia, which is not a member of the Commonwealth of Independent States, is included in this group for reasons of geography and similarities in economic structure.

Table 7. Summary of Inflation
(Percent)

	Ten-Year Averages		1998	1999	2000	2001	2002	2003	2004	2005	2006	2007
	1988–97	1998–2007										
GDP deflators												
Advanced economies	**3.1**	**1.6**	**1.3**	**0.9**	**1.5**	**2.1**	**1.6**	**1.6**	**1.8**	**1.8**	**1.9**	**1.9**
United States	2.7	2.1	1.1	1.4	2.2	2.4	1.7	2.0	2.6	2.8	2.4	2.0
Euro area	...	1.9	1.6	0.9	1.5	3.1	2.6	2.0	1.9	1.7	1.9	2.2
Japan	0.9	−1.0	−0.1	−1.3	−1.7	−1.2	−1.6	−1.6	−1.2	−1.3	—	0.4
Other advanced economies[1]	4.3	1.9	2.0	1.0	2.0	2.0	1.7	1.9	1.9	1.9	2.2	2.0
Consumer prices												
Advanced economies	**3.4**	**1.9**	**1.5**	**1.4**	**2.2**	**2.1**	**1.5**	**1.8**	**2.0**	**2.3**	**2.3**	**2.1**
United States	3.5	2.6	1.5	2.2	3.4	2.8	1.6	2.3	2.7	3.4	3.2	2.5
Euro area[2]	...	2.0	1.1	1.1	2.1	2.3	2.2	2.1	2.1	2.2	2.1	2.2
Japan	1.5	−0.2	0.6	−0.3	−0.9	−0.7	−0.9	−0.3	—	−0.3	0.3	0.6
Other advanced economies	4.2	1.9	2.2	1.1	1.8	2.1	1.7	1.8	1.7	2.1	2.0	2.1
Other emerging market and developing countries	**53.5**	**6.8**	**11.1**	**10.1**	**7.1**	**6.6**	**5.8**	**5.8**	**5.7**	**5.4**	**5.4**	**4.8**
Regional groups												
Africa	29.1	10.1	9.3	11.9	13.6	12.7	9.9	10.8	8.1	8.5	9.1	7.3
Central and eastern Europe	65.4	13.6	32.7	23.0	22.8	19.4	14.7	9.2	6.1	4.8	4.1	3.4
Commonwealth of Independent States[3]	...	19.7	23.9	69.6	24.6	20.3	13.8	12.0	10.3	12.3	10.4	9.7
Developing Asia	10.5	3.4	7.7	2.4	1.8	2.6	2.0	2.5	4.2	3.6	3.9	3.5
Middle East	14.1	7.6	8.3	8.4	5.9	5.5	6.3	7.1	8.4	8.4	8.7	8.5
Western Hemisphere	162.8	7.4	9.0	8.2	7.6	6.1	8.9	10.5	6.5	6.3	5.8	5.6
Memorandum												
European Union	9.3	2.2	2.1	1.7	2.5	2.5	2.2	2.0	2.2	2.2	2.1	2.2
Analytical groups												
By source of export earnings												
Fuel	73.7	14.5	18.4	37.2	14.8	14.3	12.1	11.7	10.0	10.3	9.6	9.1
Nonfuel	50.6	5.6	10.0	6.5	5.9	5.5	4.8	5.0	5.1	4.7	4.7	4.2
of which, primary products	65.9	19.2	12.9	25.4	31.4	28.4	15.7	18.9	14.0	16.1	17.9	13.3
By external financing source												
Net debtor countries	61.1	8.4	15.5	10.6	9.1	8.4	8.4	7.6	6.0	6.6	6.6	5.5
of which, official financing	37.6	9.2	18.9	10.3	6.3	7.5	9.6	7.5	6.9	8.9	9.6	7.0
Net debtor countries by debt-servicing experience												
Countries with arrears and/or rescheduling during 1999–2003	45.9	12.4	21.5	13.8	10.0	11.3	13.7	11.1	9.5	11.4	13.0	9.7
Memorandum												
Median inflation rate												
Advanced economies	3.3	2.0	1.6	1.4	2.6	2.5	2.1	2.1	1.9	2.1	2.0	2.0
Other emerging market and developing countries	10.7	4.7	6.6	4.0	4.3	4.8	3.4	4.2	4.6	5.9	5.1	4.5

[1]In this table, "other advanced economies" means advanced economies excluding the United States, euro area countries, and Japan.
[2]Based on Eurostat's harmonized index of consumer prices.
[3]Mongolia, which is not a member of the Commonwealth of Independent States, is included in this group for reasons of geography and similarities in economic structure.

Table 8. Advanced Economies: GDP Deflators and Consumer Prices
(Annual percent change)

	Ten-Year Averages		1998	1999	2000	2001	2002	2003	2004	2005	2006	2007	Fourth Quarter[1]		
	1988–97	1998–2007											2005	2006	2007
GDP deflators															
Advanced economies	**3.1**	**1.6**	**1.3**	**0.9**	**1.5**	**2.1**	**1.6**	**1.6**	**1.8**	**1.8**	**1.9**	**1.9**	...	...	...
United States	2.7	2.1	1.1	1.4	2.2	2.4	1.7	2.0	2.6	2.8	2.4	2.0	3.1	2.0	2.0
Euro area	...	1.9	1.6	0.9	1.5	3.1	2.6	2.0	1.9	1.7	1.9	2.2	2.2	1.8	2.2
Germany	3.5	0.9	0.6	0.4	−0.6	1.2	1.4	1.1	0.8	0.5	1.2	2.4	0.5	1.6	2.8
France	2.1	1.4	1.1	−0.1	1.5	1.8	2.2	1.4	1.6	1.3	1.5	1.6	1.3	1.5	1.7
Italy	5.4	2.7	2.7	1.6	2.2	5.2	3.4	3.1	2.9	2.1	2.1	2.2	1.7	2.4	1.9
Spain	5.2	3.6	2.5	2.6	3.5	4.2	4.4	4.0	4.1	4.4	3.6	3.1	4.4	3.1	3.0
Netherlands	1.9	2.9	1.7	1.6	3.9	9.7	3.8	2.5	0.9	1.6	1.6	2.2	1.6	1.6	2.6
Belgium	2.6	1.8	1.8	0.7	1.7	1.8	1.8	1.7	2.3	2.4	2.4	1.8	3.5	1.2	2.2
Austria	2.7	1.5	0.3	0.6	1.8	1.8	1.3	1.4	1.9	2.0	1.8	1.7	1.8	1.8	1.6
Finland	3.5	1.4	3.7	−0.3	3.0	3.2	1.0	−0.3	0.5	1.6	0.7	1.0	1.7	0.6	1.3
Greece	13.5	3.6	5.2	3.0	3.4	3.5	4.0	3.5	3.6	3.2	3.3	3.0	2.4	2.0	3.6
Portugal	7.9	3.0	3.7	3.3	3.0	3.7	3.9	2.7	2.8	2.7	2.3	2.3	2.8	2.5	2.1
Ireland	3.2	4.0	6.5	4.0	5.5	5.7	5.0	2.0	2.2	3.1	3.1	2.7	3.7	2.4	2.9
Luxembourg	3.1	2.4	2.7	2.2	4.2	1.9	1.1	2.1	2.5	2.5	2.5	2.5	...	...	...
Japan	0.9	−1.0	−0.1	−1.3	−1.7	−1.2	−1.6	−1.6	−1.2	−1.3	—	0.4	−1.7	1.2	−0.3
United Kingdom	4.5	2.4	2.8	2.1	1.2	2.3	3.1	2.9	2.1	2.0	2.7	2.5	1.7	2.7	2.4
Canada	2.4	2.2	−0.4	1.7	4.1	1.1	1.0	3.3	3.1	3.1	3.0	1.7	4.1	1.6	1.8
Korea	7.3	2.1	5.8	−0.1	0.7	3.5	2.8	2.7	2.7	0.4	1.0	1.7	—	1.6	1.8
Australia	3.1	2.9	0.5	0.5	4.1	4.0	2.6	3.2	3.4	4.5	3.5	2.5	4.9	2.2	3.0
Taiwan Province of China	2.7	−0.4	2.6	−1.3	−1.6	0.5	−0.8	−2.1	−1.6	−0.7	−0.1	1.4	—	0.5	1.5
Sweden	4.4	1.5	0.6	0.9	1.4	2.1	1.6	2.0	0.8	1.1	2.1	2.2	1.8	2.3	2.2
Switzerland	2.3	0.8	−0.3	0.7	0.8	0.6	1.6	1.2	0.5	0.6	1.0	1.1	0.1	1.0	1.1
Hong Kong SAR	7.7	−2.6	0.2	−5.8	−5.6	−1.8	−3.5	−6.3	−3.6	−0.3	−0.2	1.3	0.4	−0.8	2.5
Denmark	2.5	2.2	1.2	1.7	3.0	2.5	2.3	1.9	2.2	2.5	2.7	1.8	1.4	3.8	0.5
Norway	2.8	4.6	−0.7	6.6	15.9	1.1	−1.6	2.6	5.6	8.5	6.0	3.4	9.0	4.1	2.9
Israel	14.3	2.5	6.5	6.5	1.5	1.9	4.4	—	−0.2	0.6	1.7	2.0	2.6	1.6	2.0
Singapore	3.2	0.2	−1.7	−5.3	3.7	−1.8	−0.7	−0.9	3.5	0.6	2.5	2.3	−0.2	2.5	2.3
New Zealand	3.0	2.3	1.8	0.6	2.9	3.9	0.3	2.2	3.8	2.3	2.9	2.4	1.3	2.9	2.1
Cyprus	4.2	2.8	2.4	2.3	3.7	3.2	2.2	5.0	2.4	2.6	2.0	2.0	...	...	...
Iceland	8.3	3.9	5.0	3.2	3.6	8.6	5.6	0.5	2.3	2.9	6.0	1.8	...	...	...
Memorandum															
Major advanced economies	2.8	1.5	1.0	0.8	1.2	1.8	1.4	1.5	1.8	1.7	1.9	1.8	1.8	1.9	1.7
Newly industrialized Asian economies	5.7	0.6	3.6	−1.5	−0.6	1.6	0.7	−0.1	0.6	—	0.6	1.6	0.1	1.1	1.9
Consumer prices															
Advanced economies	**3.4**	**1.9**	**1.5**	**1.4**	**2.2**	**2.1**	**1.5**	**1.8**	**2.0**	**2.3**	**2.3**	**2.1**	...	...	...
United States	3.5	2.6	1.5	2.2	3.4	2.8	1.6	2.3	2.7	3.4	3.2	2.5	3.7	2.6	2.5
Euro area[2]	...	2.0	1.1	1.1	2.1	2.3	2.2	2.1	2.1	2.2	2.1	2.2	2.2	1.9	1.9
Germany	2.7	1.5	0.6	0.7	1.4	1.8	1.4	1.0	1.8	1.9	1.8	2.5	2.2	1.6	2.6
France	2.4	1.7	0.7	0.6	1.8	1.8	1.9	2.2	2.3	1.9	1.7	1.8	1.8	1.9	1.4
Italy	4.9	2.3	2.0	1.7	2.6	2.3	2.6	2.8	2.3	2.3	2.5	2.1	2.7	2.2	2.0
Spain	5.1	3.0	1.8	2.2	3.5	2.8	3.6	3.1	3.1	3.4	3.4	3.1	3.5	3.3	3.0
Japan	1.5	−0.2	0.6	−0.3	−0.9	−0.7	−0.9	−0.3	—	−0.3	0.3	0.6	−0.5	0.6	0.7
United Kingdom[2]	4.0	1.5	1.6	1.4	0.8	1.2	1.3	1.4	1.3	2.1	1.9	1.9	2.1	1.9	2.0
Canada	2.8	2.1	1.0	1.7	2.7	2.5	2.3	2.7	1.8	2.2	1.8	2.0	2.3	1.7	2.0
Other advanced economies	4.8	2.0	2.9	0.9	2.0	2.4	1.7	1.8	1.9	2.1	2.2	2.3	...	...	...
Memorandum															
Major advanced economies	3.1	1.8	1.2	1.4	2.1	1.9	1.3	1.7	2.0	2.3	2.3	2.1	2.5	2.0	2.1
Newly industrialized Asian economies	5.3	1.9	4.4	—	1.1	1.9	0.9	1.4	2.4	2.2	2.2	2.3	2.3	2.5	2.2

[1]From fourth quarter of preceding year.
[2]Based on Eurostat's harmonized index of consumer prices.

Table 9. Advanced Economies: Hourly Earnings, Productivity, and Unit Labor Costs in Manufacturing

(Annual percent change)

	Ten-Year Averages		1998	1999	2000	2001	2002	2003	2004	2005	2006	2007
	1988–97	1998–2007										
Hourly earnings												
Advanced economies	**4.7**	**3.8**	**3.3**	**3.1**	**5.4**	**3.0**	**4.4**	**5.0**	**2.5**	**4.3**	**3.6**	**3.9**
United States	3.3	5.3	5.8	3.9	9.0	2.4	7.3	8.3	2.2	6.6	3.5	4.0
Euro area	. . .	3.5	2.8	5.2	5.2	4.4	3.3	2.6	3.1	2.6	2.9	3.1
Germany	5.4	2.4	1.3	2.5	3.6	3.5	2.4	2.5	0.7	1.9	3.0	3.0
France	3.7	3.0	0.6	1.0	3.8	1.2	4.1	4.1	3.5	3.6	3.9	4.5
Italy	6.5	2.4	–1.4	2.3	3.1	3.3	2.3	3.0	3.5	2.9	2.7	2.6
Spain	6.4	3.3	3.3	2.7	2.8	4.1	4.4	4.2	3.0	2.7	2.7	2.7
Japan	3.9	0.7	0.8	–0.7	–0.1	1.0	–1.3	1.0	0.4	1.2	2.6	2.5
United Kingdom	6.4	4.1	4.6	4.0	4.7	4.3	3.5	3.6	3.7	3.6	4.7	4.1
Canada	3.8	3.5	2.7	1.2	2.0	2.3	4.7	0.9	2.3	4.9	5.9	8.6
Other advanced economies	8.4	5.0	2.8	6.4	6.2	6.3	4.5	4.9	5.3	3.6	5.0	5.0
Memorandum												
Major advanced economies	4.2	3.7	3.4	2.6	5.6	2.4	4.4	5.2	2.0	4.5	3.5	3.8
Newly industrialized Asian economies	12.9	6.5	1.7	9.6	7.7	8.2	5.9	7.1	7.6	4.1	6.4	6.3
Productivity[1]												
Advanced economies	**3.1**	**3.5**	**2.3**	**3.8**	**5.3**	**0.9**	**4.1**	**3.9**	**4.7**	**3.5**	**3.1**	**3.1**
United States	2.9	4.4	4.9	3.6	4.6	2.1	6.6	5.6	5.4	4.8	3.3	3.0
Euro area	. . .	3.2	3.8	5.3	6.6	2.4	1.5	1.1	3.9	2.5	2.5	2.6
Germany	3.6	3.2	0.3	2.6	5.4	3.0	1.1	4.3	4.9	5.4	2.8	2.8
France	4.3	3.6	5.5	2.9	6.9	0.9	3.8	0.1	4.0	3.0	4.5	5.0
Italy	2.6	0.3	–0.6	1.5	3.8	–0.8	–2.0	–0.8	–0.3	–0.1	0.9	1.1
Spain	3.0	1.7	1.4	1.4	0.4	—	1.4	3.4	2.4	2.2	2.2	2.2
Japan	2.7	2.5	–3.6	3.2	6.8	–3.0	3.7	5.3	5.3	1.8	3.2	2.7
United Kingdom	3.0	3.7	1.3	4.3	6.3	3.4	1.5	4.5	6.2	2.5	3.3	4.1
Canada	2.6	3.3	3.1	4.1	4.5	–2.4	4.0	–1.5	3.8	5.1	5.2	8.0
Other advanced economies	3.7	3.8	0.9	7.9	7.1	0.1	4.3	3.6	5.0	3.0	3.5	3.2
Memorandum												
Major advanced economies	3.1	3.5	2.3	3.3	5.3	1.0	4.3	4.2	4.8	3.8	3.3	3.3
Newly industrialized Asian economies	6.0	5.8	–0.8	13.0	11.9	–0.5	6.1	5.5	7.8	5.5	5.6	5.0
Unit labor costs												
Advanced economies	**1.6**	**0.4**	**1.1**	**–0.7**	**0.1**	**2.1**	**0.3**	**1.0**	**–2.1**	**0.7**	**0.4**	**0.7**
United States	0.3	0.9	0.9	0.3	4.2	0.3	0.6	2.5	–3.1	1.8	0.2	1.0
Euro area	. . .	0.3	–1.0	–0.2	–1.3	1.9	1.8	1.4	–0.8	0.1	0.5	0.6
Germany	1.7	–0.8	1.0	–0.1	–1.7	0.5	1.3	–1.7	–4.0	–3.3	0.2	0.2
France	–0.5	–0.6	–4.6	–1.8	–2.9	0.2	0.3	4.0	–0.5	0.5	–0.6	–0.5
Italy	3.8	2.1	–0.8	0.8	–0.7	4.1	4.3	3.9	3.7	3.0	1.7	1.5
Spain	3.3	1.5	1.9	1.2	2.3	4.1	2.9	0.9	0.6	0.5	0.5	0.5
Japan	1.1	–1.7	4.6	–3.8	–6.5	4.0	–4.8	–4.1	–4.7	–0.6	–0.6	–0.2
United Kingdom[2]	3.4	0.3	3.3	–0.3	–1.5	0.8	1.9	–0.9	–2.4	1.1	1.3	—
Canada	1.2	0.2	–0.4	–2.8	–2.4	4.8	0.7	2.5	–1.4	–0.1	0.6	0.5
Other advanced economies	4.6	1.0	2.3	–1.3	–1.0	6.0	—	0.8	–0.1	0.4	1.3	1.5
Memorandum												
Major advanced economies	1.1	0.2	1.1	–0.7	0.3	1.4	0.2	1.0	–2.6	0.8	0.2	0.6
Newly industrialized Asian economies	6.4	0.3	3.2	–2.7	–3.9	8.0	–0.5	0.8	–1.0	–1.6	0.4	1.0

[1]Refers to labor productivity, measured as the ratio of hourly compensation to unit labor costs.
[2]Data refer to unit wage cost.

Table 10. Other Emerging Market and Developing Countries: Consumer Prices
(Annual percent change)

	Ten-Year Averages		1998	1999	2000	2001	2002	2003	2004	2005	2006	2007
	1988–97	1998–2007										
Other emerging market and developing countries	**53.5**	**6.8**	**11.1**	**10.1**	**7.1**	**6.6**	**5.8**	**5.8**	**5.7**	**5.4**	**5.4**	**4.8**
Regional groups												
Africa	29.1	10.1	9.3	11.9	13.6	12.7	9.9	10.8	8.1	8.5	9.1	7.3
Sub-Sahara	34.6	12.4	10.9	15.0	17.4	15.7	12.3	13.4	9.7	10.6	10.7	8.3
Excluding Nigeria and South Africa	55.1	17.9	14.1	24.4	29.6	23.0	14.3	19.1	14.7	14.4	15.4	11.0
Central and eastern Europe	65.4	13.6	32.7	23.0	22.8	19.4	14.7	9.2	6.1	4.8	4.1	3.4
Commonwealth of Independent States[1]	...	19.7	23.9	69.6	24.6	20.3	13.8	12.0	10.3	12.3	10.4	9.7
Russia	...	21.3	27.7	85.7	20.8	21.5	15.8	13.7	10.9	12.6	10.4	9.5
Excluding Russia	...	16.0	15.9	37.0	34.3	17.6	9.3	8.3	9.1	11.7	10.5	10.2
Developing Asia	10.5	3.4	7.7	2.4	1.8	2.6	2.0	2.5	4.2	3.6	3.9	3.5
China	11.4	0.9	−0.8	−1.4	0.4	0.7	−0.8	1.2	3.9	1.8	2.0	2.2
India	9.3	5.1	13.2	4.7	4.0	3.8	4.3	3.8	3.8	4.2	4.8	4.9
Excluding China and India	10.0	7.7	21.7	8.8	2.7	6.0	6.5	4.6	5.4	8.0	8.7	5.8
Middle East	14.1	7.6	8.3	8.4	5.9	5.5	6.3	7.1	8.4	8.4	8.7	8.5
Western Hemisphere	162.8	7.4	9.0	8.2	7.6	6.1	8.9	10.5	6.5	6.3	5.8	5.6
Brazil	576.3	6.8	3.2	4.9	7.1	6.8	8.4	14.8	6.6	6.9	4.9	4.4
Mexico	28.0	7.2	15.9	16.6	9.5	6.4	5.0	4.5	4.7	4.0	3.5	3.0
Analytical groups												
By source of export earnings												
Fuel	73.7	14.5	18.4	37.2	14.8	14.3	12.1	11.7	10.0	10.3	9.6	9.1
Nonfuel	50.6	5.6	10.0	6.5	5.9	5.5	4.8	5.0	5.1	4.7	4.7	4.2
of which, primary products	65.9	19.2	12.9	25.4	31.4	28.4	15.7	18.9	14.0	16.1	17.9	13.3
By external financing source												
Net debtor countries	61.1	8.4	15.5	10.6	9.1	8.4	8.4	7.6	6.0	6.6	6.6	5.5
of which, official financing	37.6	9.2	18.9	10.3	6.3	7.5	9.6	7.5	6.9	8.9	9.6	7.0
Net debtor countries by debt-servicing experience												
Countries with arrears and/or rescheduling during 1999–2003	45.9	12.4	21.5	13.8	10.0	11.3	13.7	11.1	9.5	11.4	13.0	9.7
Other groups												
Heavily indebted poor countries	64.6	11.8	10.6	19.5	26.6	20.4	6.1	8.5	6.6	9.9	7.0	5.0
Middle East and north Africa	15.3	6.6	7.7	7.3	5.0	4.9	5.5	6.1	7.3	7.0	7.6	7.4
Memorandum												
Median												
Other emerging market and developing countries	10.7	4.7	6.6	4.0	4.3	4.8	3.4	4.2	4.6	5.9	5.1	4.5
Africa	10.3	5.1	6.0	4.1	5.7	5.0	4.1	5.4	4.1	6.5	5.0	4.9
Central and eastern Europe	51.6	4.1	8.2	3.3	6.2	5.5	3.3	2.3	3.5	3.1	3.2	2.7
Commonwealth of Independent States[1]	...	10.6	10.5	23.5	18.7	9.8	5.6	5.6	7.1	10.3	7.9	6.5
Developing Asia	8.7	5.0	8.6	4.0	2.2	3.7	3.8	3.5	6.0	7.0	6.0	5.0
Middle East	7.0	2.7	3.0	2.1	1.0	1.6	1.4	2.0	4.0	3.7	3.9	4.0
Western Hemisphere	12.7	4.4	5.1	3.5	4.6	3.6	4.2	4.5	4.4	5.4	4.7	4.2

[1]Mongolia, which is not a member of the Commonwealth of Independent States, is included in this group for reasons of geography and similarities in economic structure.

Table 11. Other Emerging Market and Developing Countries—by Country: Consumer Prices[1]

(Annual percent change)

	Average 1988–97	1998	1999	2000	2001	2002	2003	2004	2005	2006	2007
Africa	**29.1**	**9.3**	**11.9**	**13.6**	**12.7**	**9.9**	**10.8**	**8.1**	**8.5**	**9.1**	**7.3**
Algeria	18.2	5.0	2.6	0.3	4.2	1.4	2.6	3.6	1.6	5.0	5.5
Angola	363.6	107.4	248.2	325.0	152.6	108.9	98.3	43.6	23.0	13.0	8.3
Benin	6.9	5.8	0.3	4.2	4.0	2.4	1.5	0.9	5.5	3.0	2.5
Botswana	11.5	6.5	7.8	8.5	6.6	8.0	9.3	6.9	8.6	8.9	5.8
Burkina Faso	4.3	5.0	−1.1	−0.3	4.7	2.3	2.0	−0.4	6.3	2.1	2.0
Burundi	13.6	12.5	3.4	24.3	9.3	−1.3	10.7	8.0	13.6	3.1	5.5
Cameroon[2]	4.6	3.9	2.9	0.8	2.8	6.3	0.6	0.3	2.0	2.6	1.0
Cape Verde	7.2	4.4	4.3	−2.4	3.7	1.9	1.2	−1.9	0.4	2.1	2.0
Central African Republic	3.5	−1.9	−1.4	3.2	3.8	2.3	4.4	−2.2	3.0	2.3	2.1
Chad	5.6	4.3	−8.4	3.8	12.4	5.2	−1.8	−5.4	7.9	3.0	3.0
Comoros	2.8	1.2	1.1	5.9	5.6	3.5	3.8	4.5	4.9	4.4	3.5
Congo, Dem. Rep. of	821.6	29.1	284.9	550.0	357.3	25.3	12.8	4.0	21.4	9.3	6.4
Congo, Rep. of	4.2	1.8	3.1	0.4	0.8	3.1	1.5	3.6	2.0	2.5	2.2
Côte d'Ivoire	6.0	4.5	0.7	2.5	4.4	3.1	3.3	1.5	3.9	2.8	3.0
Djibouti	4.9	2.2	0.2	1.6	1.8	0.6	2.0	3.1	3.1	2.2	2.0
Equatorial Guinea	6.2	7.9	0.4	4.8	8.8	7.6	7.8	3.8	6.8	5.5	5.0
Eritrea	...	9.5	8.4	19.9	14.6	16.9	22.7	25.1	12.4	10.9	10.0
Ethiopia	7.5	3.6	4.8	6.2	−5.2	−7.2	15.1	8.6	6.8	10.8	6.0
Gabon	4.4	2.3	−0.7	0.5	2.1	0.2	2.1	0.4	0.1	1.0	1.0
Gambia, The	6.8	1.1	3.8	0.9	4.5	8.6	17.0	14.2	4.3	4.0	3.7
Ghana	29.4	19.2	12.4	25.2	32.9	14.8	26.7	12.6	15.1	8.8	7.1
Guinea	5.2	5.1	4.6	6.8	5.4	3.0	12.9	17.5	31.4	24.1	9.5
Guinea-Bissau	49.9	8.0	−2.1	8.6	3.3	3.3	−3.5	0.8	3.4	3.1	2.5
Kenya	16.0	6.7	5.8	10.0	5.8	2.0	9.8	11.6	10.3	11.5	2.8
Lesotho	12.1	7.8	8.6	6.1	6.9	11.6	7.7	5.2	3.7	5.0	5.0
Madagascar	18.5	6.2	8.1	10.7	6.9	16.2	−1.1	14.0	18.4	9.5	7.0
Malawi	26.2	29.8	44.8	29.6	27.2	14.9	9.6	11.6	12.3	9.0	7.0
Mali	4.4	4.1	−1.2	−0.7	5.2	5.0	−1.3	−2.8	5.0	−1.5	2.5
Mauritania	6.5	8.5	9.3	4.5	4.8	6.4	4.6	10.4	12.1	6.5	4.7
Mauritius	8.2	6.1	6.9	5.5	4.8	6.3	5.1	4.1	5.6	7.1	6.2
Morocco	4.7	2.7	0.7	1.9	0.6	2.8	1.2	1.5	1.0	2.0	2.0
Mozambique, Rep. of	42.5	0.6	2.9	12.7	9.1	16.8	13.4	12.6	7.2	7.5	6.5
Namibia	11.5	6.2	8.6	9.3	9.3	11.3	7.2	4.1	2.4	5.1	5.0
Niger	4.2	4.5	−2.3	2.9	4.0	2.7	−1.8	0.4	7.8	0.3	2.0
Nigeria	35.7	10.0	6.6	6.9	18.0	13.7	14.0	15.0	17.9	9.4	6.5
Rwanda	16.3	6.8	−2.4	3.9	3.4	2.0	7.4	12.0	9.2	5.5	5.0
São Tomé and Príncipe	43.0	42.1	11.0	11.0	9.5	9.2	9.6	12.8	16.2	14.8	11.1
Senegal	3.7	1.1	0.8	0.7	3.0	2.3	—	0.5	1.8	2.6	1.7
Seychelles	1.5	2.7	6.3	6.3	6.0	0.2	3.2	3.9	1.0	−0.7	1.7
Sierra Leone	45.0	36.0	34.1	−0.9	2.6	−3.7	7.5	14.2	12.5	11.7	9.0
South Africa	11.4	6.9	5.2	5.4	5.7	9.2	5.8	1.4	3.4	4.5	4.9
Sudan	87.6	17.1	16.0	8.0	4.9	8.3	7.7	8.4	8.5	7.5	5.0
Swaziland	10.9	7.5	5.9	7.2	7.5	11.7	7.4	3.4	4.8	5.1	5.6
Tanzania	25.8	13.2	9.0	6.2	5.2	4.6	4.5	4.3	4.6	5.2	5.0
Togo	5.8	1.0	−0.1	1.9	3.9	3.1	−0.9	0.4	6.8	2.9	2.7
Tunisia	5.8	3.1	2.7	3.0	1.9	2.8	2.8	3.6	2.0	3.0	2.0
Uganda	38.6	5.8	0.2	5.8	4.5	−2.0	5.7	5.0	8.0	6.5	4.0
Zambia	82.4	24.5	26.8	26.1	21.7	22.2	21.4	18.0	18.3	13.3	7.5
Zimbabwe	21.4	31.3	58.0	55.6	73.4	133.2	365.0	350.0	237.8	850.4	584.2

Table 11 *(continued)*

	Average 1988–97	1998	1999	2000	2001	2002	2003	2004	2005	2006	2007
Central and eastern Europe[3]	**65.4**	**32.7**	**23.0**	**22.8**	**19.4**	**14.7**	**9.2**	**6.1**	**4.8**	**4.1**	**3.4**
Albania	32.0	20.9	0.4	—	3.1	5.2	2.4	2.9	2.5	2.5	3.0
Bosnia and Herzegovina	. . .	−0.4	3.0	5.1	3.2	0.3	0.6	0.3	2.8	5.0	2.5
Bulgaria	108.0	18.8	2.6	10.4	7.5	5.8	2.3	6.1	5.0	7.2	4.1
Croatia	. . .	5.7	4.1	6.2	4.9	1.7	1.8	2.1	3.3	3.2	2.5
Czech Republic	. . .	10.6	2.1	3.9	4.7	1.8	0.1	2.8	1.8	2.8	3.0
Estonia	. . .	8.2	3.3	4.0	5.8	3.6	1.3	3.0	4.1	3.6	3.2
Hungary	22.9	14.2	10.0	9.8	9.2	5.2	4.7	6.7	3.5	2.0	2.7
Latvia	. . .	4.6	2.4	2.6	2.5	1.9	2.9	6.3	6.7	6.4	5.5
Lithuania	. . .	5.1	0.7	1.0	1.3	0.3	−1.2	1.2	2.6	3.2	2.7
Macedonia, FYR	. . .	−0.1	−2.0	6.2	5.3	2.4	1.2	−0.3	0.5	1.8	2.0
Malta	2.7	3.8	2.2	3.1	2.5	2.7	1.9	2.7	3.1	2.8	2.4
Poland	76.7	11.8	7.3	10.1	5.5	1.9	0.8	3.5	2.1	1.3	2.3
Romania	94.0	59.1	45.8	45.7	34.5	22.5	15.3	11.9	9.0	7.9	4.8
Serbia and Montenegro	. . .	29.5	42.1	69.9	91.1	21.2	11.3	9.5	16.3	11.4	8.2
Slovak Republic	. . .	6.7	10.7	12.0	7.3	3.3	8.5	7.5	2.8	3.6	2.5
Slovenia	. . .	8.0	6.2	8.8	8.4	7.5	5.6	3.6	2.5	2.4	2.4
Turkey	75.8	83.6	63.5	54.3	53.9	44.8	25.2	8.6	8.2	6.5	4.4
Commonwealth of Independent States[3,4]	. . .	**23.9**	**69.6**	**24.6**	**20.3**	**13.8**	**12.0**	**10.3**	**12.3**	**10.4**	**9.7**
Russia	. . .	27.7	85.7	20.8	21.5	15.8	13.7	10.9	12.6	10.4	9.5
Excluding Russia	. . .	15.9	37.0	34.3	17.6	9.3	8.3	9.1	11.7	10.5	10.2
Armenia	. . .	8.7	0.6	−0.8	3.1	1.1	4.7	7.0	0.6	3.0	3.0
Azerbaijan	. . .	−0.8	−8.5	1.8	1.5	2.8	2.2	6.7	9.7	8.6	11.8
Belarus	. . .	73.0	293.7	168.6	61.1	42.6	28.4	18.1	10.3	10.4	13.3
Georgia	. . .	3.6	19.1	4.0	4.7	5.6	4.8	5.7	8.3	5.3	4.0
Kazakhstan	. . .	7.3	8.4	13.3	8.4	5.9	6.4	6.9	7.6	7.5	7.5
Kyrgyz Republic	. . .	10.5	35.9	18.7	6.9	2.1	3.1	4.1	4.3	5.7	4.5
Moldova	. . .	7.7	39.3	31.3	9.8	5.3	11.7	12.5	11.9	9.4	8.7
Mongolia	. . .	9.4	7.6	11.6	6.3	0.9	5.1	7.9	12.5	5.5	5.0
Tajikistan	. . .	43.2	27.5	32.9	38.6	12.2	16.4	7.1	7.1	7.8	5.0
Turkmenistan	. . .	16.8	23.5	8.0	11.6	8.8	5.6	5.9	10.8	7.9	5.0
Ukraine	. . .	10.6	22.7	28.2	12.0	0.8	5.2	9.0	13.5	13.0	12.5
Uzbekistan	. . .	16.7	44.7	49.5	47.5	44.3	14.8	8.8	21.0	11.3	6.5

Table 11 *(continued)*

	Average 1988–97	1998	1999	2000	2001	2002	2003	2004	2005	2006	2007
Developing Asia	**10.5**	**7.7**	**2.4**	**1.8**	**2.6**	**2.0**	**2.5**	**4.2**	**3.6**	**3.9**	**3.5**
Afghanistan, I.S. of	. . .	. . .	. . .	. . .	. . .	. . .	35.8	13.1	12.9	8.9	5.0
Bangladesh	6.8	8.6	6.2	2.2	1.5	3.8	5.4	6.1	7.0	6.1	5.6
Bhutan	10.0	10.6	6.8	4.0	3.4	2.5	2.1	4.6	5.2	6.0	6.0
Brunei Darussalam	. . .	−0.4	—	1.2	0.6	−2.3	0.3	0.9	1.0	1.0	1.0
Cambodia	. . .	13.3	−0.5	−0.8	0.7	3.3	1.2	3.9	5.8	4.1	3.2
China	11.4	−0.8	−1.4	0.4	0.7	−0.8	1.2	3.9	1.8	2.0	2.2
Fiji	5.1	5.9	2.0	1.1	4.3	0.8	4.2	2.8	3.7	4.2	3.2
India	9.3	13.2	4.7	4.0	3.8	4.3	3.8	3.8	4.2	4.8	4.9
Indonesia	8.0	58.0	20.7	3.8	11.5	11.8	6.8	6.1	10.5	14.2	6.6
Kiribati	3.7	4.7	0.4	1.0	7.3	1.1	−1.6	−0.6	—	1.6	2.5
Lao PDR	12.5	90.1	128.4	23.2	7.8	10.6	15.5	10.5	7.2	6.8	5.0
Malaysia	3.4	5.1	2.8	1.6	1.4	1.8	1.1	1.4	3.0	3.1	2.7
Maldives	9.7	−1.4	3.0	−1.2	0.7	0.9	−2.9	6.4	5.7	7.0	6.0
Myanmar	25.9	49.1	10.9	−1.7	34.5	58.1	24.9	4.2	17.7	27.5	32.5
Nepal	9.8	11.4	3.4	2.4	2.9	4.7	4.0	4.5	9.1	5.3	5.5
Pakistan	10.3	6.5	4.1	4.4	3.1	3.2	2.9	7.4	9.1	8.4	6.9
Papua New Guinea	6.8	13.6	14.9	15.6	9.3	11.8	14.7	7.4	6.0	4.5	3.0
Philippines	10.4	9.7	6.7	4.3	6.1	2.9	3.5	6.0	7.6	7.4	4.7
Samoa	5.3	5.4	0.8	−0.2	1.9	7.4	4.3	7.9	7.8	3.0	3.0
Solomon Islands	11.8	12.3	8.0	6.9	7.6	9.4	10.1	6.9	7.3	7.2	7.7
Sri Lanka	12.3	9.4	4.0	1.5	12.1	10.2	2.6	7.9	10.6	8.0	7.0
Thailand	5.1	8.1	0.3	1.6	1.7	0.6	1.8	2.8	4.5	3.6	2.2
Timor-Leste, Dem. Rep. of	. . .	. . .	. . .	63.6	3.6	4.8	7.1	3.3	0.9	2.0	2.5
Tonga	5.1	2.9	3.9	4.9	7.3	10.0	10.7	11.8	11.2	9.0	5.0
Vanuatu	4.3	3.3	2.2	2.5	3.7	2.0	3.0	1.4	1.0	2.3	2.4
Vietnam	47.2	7.7	4.2	−1.7	−0.4	4.0	3.2	7.7	8.0	7.0	6.0
Middle East	**14.1**	**8.3**	**8.4**	**5.9**	**5.5**	**6.3**	**7.1**	**8.4**	**8.4**	**8.7**	**8.5**
Bahrain	1.2	−0.4	−1.3	−3.6	−1.2	−0.5	1.7	2.3	2.6	2.0	2.1
Egypt[5]	13.4	4.7	3.7	2.8	2.4	2.4	3.2	10.3	11.4	4.4	4.5
Iran, I.R. of[5]	24.4	18.1	20.1	12.6	11.4	15.8	15.6	15.2	13.0	17.0	17.0
Iraq	. . .	. . .	. . .	. . .	. . .	. . .	. . .	. . .	. . .	. . .	. . .
Jordan	7.7	3.1	0.6	0.7	1.8	1.8	1.6	3.4	3.5	6.9	5.8
Kuwait	3.1	0.6	3.1	1.6	1.4	0.8	1.0	1.3	3.9	3.5	3.0
Lebanon	44.2	4.5	0.2	−0.4	−0.4	1.8	1.3	3.0	0.3	2.5	2.0
Libya	7.1	3.7	2.6	−2.9	−8.8	−9.9	−2.1	−2.2	2.5	3.0	3.5
Oman	1.8	0.4	0.5	−1.2	−0.8	−0.2	0.2	0.8	1.9	1.1	1.2
Qatar	3.2	2.9	2.2	1.7	1.4	1.0	2.3	6.8	3.0	2.7	2.5
Saudi Arabia	1.5	−0.2	−1.3	−0.6	−0.8	0.2	0.6	0.3	0.4	1.0	1.0
Syrian Arab Republic	12.1	−1.0	−3.7	−3.9	5.6	−2.3	5.9	4.6	7.2	7.2	5.0
United Arab Emirates	3.9	2.0	2.1	1.4	2.8	2.9	3.1	4.6	6.0	5.5	5.0
Yemen	37.2	11.5	8.0	10.9	11.9	12.2	10.8	12.5	11.8	15.5	12.0

Table 11 *(concluded)*

	Average 1988–97	1998	1999	2000	2001	2002	2003	2004	2005	2006	2007
Western Hemisphere	**162.8**	**9.0**	**8.2**	**7.6**	**6.1**	**8.9**	**10.5**	**6.5**	**6.3**	**5.8**	**5.6**
Antigua and Barbuda	4.0	3.8	0.6	−0.6	−0.4	1.8	2.8	1.3	1.2	4.1	2.0
Argentina	159.4	0.9	−1.2	−0.9	−1.1	25.9	13.4	4.4	9.6	12.9	15.0
Bahamas, The	3.5	1.3	1.3	1.6	2.0	2.2	3.0	0.8	2.0	1.2	2.0
Barbados	4.0	−1.3	1.6	2.4	2.8	0.2	1.6	1.4	5.9	6.2	4.7
Belize	2.7	−0.9	−1.2	0.6	1.2	2.2	2.6	3.1	3.5	1.9	3.6
Bolivia	12.5	7.7	2.2	4.6	1.6	0.9	3.3	4.4	5.4	3.4	3.1
Brazil	576.3	3.2	4.9	7.1	6.8	8.4	14.8	6.6	6.9	4.9	4.4
Chile	13.9	5.1	3.3	3.8	3.6	2.5	2.8	1.1	3.1	3.8	3.0
Colombia	24.5	18.7	10.9	9.2	8.0	6.3	7.1	5.9	5.0	4.7	4.2
Costa Rica	18.3	11.7	10.0	11.0	11.3	9.2	9.4	11.5	13.6	13.1	11.0
Dominica	3.1	1.0	1.2	0.9	1.6	0.1	1.6	2.4	1.6	1.5	1.5
Dominican Republic	21.2	4.8	6.5	7.7	8.9	5.2	27.4	51.5	4.2	8.5	5.0
Ecuador	42.7	36.1	52.2	96.1	37.7	12.6	7.9	2.7	2.4	3.4	3.0
El Salvador	13.9	2.5	−1.0	4.3	1.4	2.8	2.5	5.4	4.0	4.0	2.5
Grenada	3.0	1.4	0.5	2.2	1.7	1.1	2.2	2.5	6.0	2.0	2.0
Guatemala	15.9	6.6	5.2	6.0	7.3	8.1	5.6	7.6	9.1	6.9	5.4
Guyana	33.2	4.7	7.4	6.1	2.7	5.4	6.0	4.7	7.1	6.9	4.4
Haiti	19.6	13.5	8.0	11.0	16.7	9.6	26.7	28.3	16.8	13.1	8.9
Honduras	18.3	13.7	11.6	11.0	9.7	7.7	7.7	8.1	8.8	6.8	5.7
Jamaica	27.2	8.1	6.3	7.7	8.0	6.5	12.9	12.8	16.5	11.3	10.2
Mexico	28.0	15.9	16.6	9.5	6.4	5.0	4.5	4.7	4.0	3.5	3.0
Netherlands Antilles	2.6	1.4	0.8	4.4	1.6	0.4	1.9	1.6	3.2	2.8	2.5
Nicaragua	269.4	18.5	7.2	9.9	4.7	4.0	5.2	8.5	9.6	8.8	6.1
Panama	1.0	0.6	1.3	1.4	0.3	1.0	0.6	0.5	2.9	2.2	1.5
Paraguay	19.3	11.6	6.8	9.0	7.3	10.5	14.2	4.3	6.8	7.4	4.4
Peru	267.1	7.3	3.5	3.8	2.0	0.2	2.3	3.7	1.6	2.7	2.2
St. Kitts and Nevis	3.3	3.7	3.4	2.1	2.1	2.1	2.3	2.1	1.8	2.0	2.0
St. Lucia	3.0	2.8	3.5	3.6	2.1	−0.3	1.0	1.5	3.0	4.0	4.0
St. Vincent and the Grenadines	3.1	2.1	1.0	0.2	0.8	1.3	0.2	3.0	2.6	1.9	1.7
Suriname	58.0	19.1	98.7	58.6	39.8	15.5	23.0	9.1	9.9	14.8	7.0
Trinidad and Tobago	6.9	5.3	3.4	3.6	5.5	4.2	3.8	3.8	6.9	7.8	7.5
Uruguay	59.0	10.8	5.7	4.8	4.4	25.9	10.2	7.6	5.9	5.5	4.9
Venezuela	51.4	35.8	23.6	16.2	12.5	22.4	31.1	21.7	15.9	11.7	17.3

[1]In accordance with standard practice in the *World Economic Outlook*, movements in consumer prices are indicated as annual averages rather than as December/December changes, as is the practice in some countries. For many countries, figures for recent years are IMF staff estimates. Data for some countries are for fiscal years.

[2]The percent changes in 2002 are calculated over a period of 18 months, reflecting a change in the fiscal year cycle (from July–June to January–December).

[3]For many countries, inflation for the earlier years is measured on the basis of a retail price index. Consumer price indices with a broader and more up-to-date coverage are typically used for more recent years.

[4]Mongolia, which is not a member of the Commonwealth of Independent States, is included in this group for reasons of geography and similarities in economic structure.

[5]Data refer to fiscal years.

Table 12. Summary Financial Indicators

(Percent)

	1998	1999	2000	2001	2002	2003	2004	2005	2006	2007
Advanced economies										
Central government fiscal balance[1]										
Advanced economies	−1.0	−1.0	0.1	−0.9	−2.4	−3.0	−2.8	−2.4	−2.4	−2.4
United States	0.5	1.2	2.0	0.5	−2.4	−3.5	−3.5	−3.0	−3.2	−3.1
Euro area	−2.4	−1.6	−0.4	−1.6	−2.1	−2.3	−2.3	−1.9	−1.8	−1.7
Japan	−3.5	−8.2	−6.7	−6.1	−6.7	−6.8	−5.8	−5.4	−5.4	−5.3
Other advanced economies[2]	—	0.5	1.4	0.6	−0.1	−0.6	−0.2	−0.1	—	—
General government fiscal balance[1]										
Advanced economies	−1.5	−1.1	−0.2	−1.6	−3.5	−4.1	−3.6	−3.1	−3.1	−3.0
United States	0.1	0.6	1.3	−0.7	−4.0	−5.0	−4.7	−4.1	−4.3	−4.0
Euro area	−2.3	−1.3	−1.0	−1.9	−2.6	−3.0	−2.7	−2.3	−2.3	−2.1
Japan	−5.6	−7.5	−7.7	−6.4	−8.2	−8.1	−6.6	−5.8	−5.7	−5.4
Other advanced economies[2]	−0.2	0.6	1.8	0.2	−0.9	−1.2	−0.6	−0.2	−0.2	−0.1
General government structural balance[3]										
Advanced economies	−1.6	−1.4	−1.3	−1.9	−3.3	−3.6	−3.4	−3.0	−3.1	−2.9
Growth of broad money[4]										
Advanced economies	6.8	5.9	4.9	8.1	5.7	5.5	5.3	5.5	. . .	. . .
United States	8.7	6.0	6.1	10.5	6.4	4.8	5.6	3.9	. . .	. . .
Euro area	5.0	5.7	4.1	8.0	6.9	7.1	6.6	7.3	. . .	. . .
Japan	4.0	2.7	1.9	3.3	1.8	1.6	1.8	2.0	. . .	. . .
Other advanced economies[2]	9.4	9.2	6.7	8.2	6.2	8.3	5.4	8.8	. . .	. . .
Short-term interest rates[5]										
United States	4.9	4.8	6.0	3.5	1.6	1.0	1.4	3.2	4.9	5.1
Euro area	3.7	3.0	4.4	4.3	3.3	2.3	2.1	2.2	3.0	3.4
Japan	0.2	0.0	0.2	0.0	0.0	0.0	0.0	0.0	0.3	0.9
LIBOR	5.6	5.5	6.6	3.7	1.9	1.2	1.8	3.8	5.0	5.1
Other emerging market and developing countries										
Central government fiscal balance[1]										
Weighted average	−3.7	−3.8	−2.9	−3.1	−3.4	−2.7	−1.6	−0.8	−0.9	−0.8
Median	−2.8	−3.1	−2.6	−3.6	−3.6	−3.1	−2.6	−2.2	−2.4	−1.7
General government fiscal balance[1]										
Weighted average	−4.7	−4.7	−3.4	−3.9	−4.3	−3.4	−2.1	−1.3	−1.2	−1.0
Median	−3.4	−3.3	−2.7	−3.2	−3.6	−2.9	−2.4	−1.9	−2.0	−1.6
Growth of broad money										
Weighted average	18.5	17.7	16.5	15.0	16.7	16.3	17.6	18.8	15.1	13.0
Median	11.3	13.2	14.1	13.7	13.2	13.0	13.9	13.4	11.9	10.3

[1]Percent of GDP.
[2]In this table, "other advanced economies" means advanced economies excluding the United States, euro area countries, and Japan.
[3]Percent of potential GDP.
[4]M2, defined as M1 plus quasi-money, except for Japan, for which the data are based on M2 plus certificates of deposit (CDs). Quasi-money is essentially private term deposits and other notice deposits. The United States also includes money market mutual fund balances, money market deposit accounts, overnight repurchase agreements, and overnight Eurodollars issued to U.S. residents by foreign branches of U.S. banks. For the euro area, M3 is composed of M2 plus marketable instruments held by euro-area residents, which comprise repurchase agreements, money market fund shares/units, money market paper, and debt securities up to two years.
[5]Annual data are period average. For the United States, three-month treasury bills; for Japan, three-month certificates of deposit; for the euro area, the three-month EURIBOR; and for LIBOR, London interbank offered rate on six-month U.S. dollar deposits.

Table 13. Advanced Economies: General and Central Government Fiscal Balances and Balances Excluding Social Security Transactions[1]

(Percent of GDP)

	1998	1999	2000	2001	2002	2003	2004	2005	2006	2007
General government fiscal balance										
Advanced economies	**−1.5**	**−1.1**	**−0.2**	**−1.6**	**−3.5**	**−4.1**	**−3.6**	**−3.1**	**−3.1**	**−3.0**
United States	0.1	0.6	1.3	−0.7	−4.0	−5.0	−4.7	−4.1	−4.3	−4.0
Euro area	−2.3	−1.3	−1.0	−1.9	−2.6	−3.0	−2.7	−2.3	−2.3	−2.1
Germany	−2.2	−1.5	1.3	−2.8	−3.7	−4.0	−3.7	−3.3	−3.3	−2.4
France[2]	−2.6	−2.5	−1.5	−1.5	−3.1	−4.2	−3.7	−2.9	−2.9	−3.0
Italy	−2.8	−1.7	−0.8	−3.1	−2.7	−3.4	−3.4	−4.1	−4.0	−4.3
Spain	−3.0	−1.1	−0.9	−0.5	−0.3	—	−0.1	1.1	0.9	0.7
Netherlands	−0.8	0.7	2.2	−0.3	−2.0	−3.2	−2.1	−0.6	−1.0	−0.7
Belgium	−0.8	−0.5	0.1	0.6	—	0.1	—	—	−0.4	−1.1
Austria[3]	−2.4	−2.3	−1.6	—	−0.6	−1.3	−1.1	−1.8	−1.8	−0.9
Finland	1.6	2.2	7.1	5.2	4.2	2.3	1.9	2.4	2.5	2.4
Greece	−4.3	−3.5	−4.1	−6.1	−4.9	−5.7	−6.6	−4.6	−2.8	−3.2
Portugal	−2.4	−2.7	−2.7	−4.2	−2.9	−2.9	−3.2	−6.0	−4.6	−3.8
Ireland[4]	2.5	2.4	4.4	0.7	−0.5	0.2	1.5	0.3	−0.3	−0.5
Luxembourg	3.3	3.5	6.1	6.1	2.1	0.2	−1.2	−2.3	−2.2	−2.1
Japan	−5.6	−7.5	−7.7	−6.4	−8.2	−8.1	−6.6	−5.8	−5.7	−5.4
United Kingdom	—	1.1	1.5	0.9	−1.5	−3.2	−3.2	−3.6	−3.1	−2.8
Canada	0.1	1.6	2.9	0.7	−0.1	—	0.7	1.7	1.3	1.1
Korea[5]	−3.9	−2.5	1.1	0.6	2.3	2.7	2.3	1.9	1.5	1.7
Australia[6]	0.8	1.7	1.4	0.1	0.3	1.1	1.1	0.8	0.6	0.6
Taiwan Province of China	−3.2	−5.7	−4.5	−6.4	−4.3	−2.8	−2.9	−2.5	−1.7	−1.7
Sweden	1.9	2.3	5.0	2.6	−0.5	−0.1	1.0	1.4	0.7	1.1
Switzerland	−1.5	−0.6	2.2	0.1	−1.2	−1.6	−1.2	−1.1	−1.0	−0.9
Hong Kong SAR	−1.8	0.8	−0.6	−4.9	−4.8	−3.3	−0.3	0.3	0.6	0.7
Denmark	—	1.4	2.3	1.2	0.2	−0.1	1.7	2.5	2.4	2.2
Norway	3.6	6.2	15.6	13.6	9.3	7.5	11.7	15.8	16.3	16.5
Israel	−3.7	−4.2	−2.0	−3.9	−4.2	−6.5	−5.1	−2.5	−3.5	−3.5
Singapore	3.6	4.6	7.9	4.8	4.0	5.7	6.0	6.0	4.3	4.4
New Zealand[7]	2.1	1.5	1.2	1.6	1.7	3.4	4.6	3.8	3.6	3.0
Cyprus	−4.2	−4.4	−2.4	−2.3	−4.5	−6.3	−4.1	−2.7	−2.1	−1.9
Iceland	0.5	2.3	2.4	0.2	−0.8	−2.0	−0.1	1.5	2.2	—
Memorandum										
Major advanced economies	−1.5	−1.3	−0.4	−1.9	−4.1	−4.9	−4.4	−3.9	−3.9	−3.7
Newly industrialized Asian economies	−2.1	−3.0	−2.1	−4.7	−3.4	−1.9	−1.2	−0.8	−0.4	−0.4
Fiscal balance excluding social security transactions										
United States	−0.6	−0.4	0.2	−1.5	−4.4	−5.3	−5.2	−4.7	−4.8	−4.7
Japan	−7.0	−8.5	−8.2	−6.5	−7.9	−8.2	−6.9	−5.7	−5.5	−5.3
Germany	−2.3	−1.7	1.3	−2.6	−3.4	−3.6	−3.6	−2.9	−2.8	−1.5
France	−2.9	−3.1	−2.0	−1.7	−2.9	−3.8	−2.7	−2.4	−2.8	−2.9
Italy	1.3	2.7	3.3	0.8	1.4	0.7	0.8	0.1	0.6	0.4
Canada	2.7	3.9	4.8	2.4	1.4	1.4	2.1	3.3	2.8	2.6

Table 13 *(concluded)*

	1998	1999	2000	2001	2002	2003	2004	2005	2006	2007
Central government fiscal balance										
Advanced economies	**−1.0**	**−1.0**	**0.1**	**−0.9**	**−2.4**	**−3.0**	**−2.8**	**−2.4**	**−2.4**	**−2.4**
United States[8]	0.5	1.2	2.0	0.5	−2.4	−3.5	−3.5	−3.0	−3.2	−3.1
Euro area	−2.4	−1.6	−0.4	−1.6	−2.1	−2.3	−2.3	−1.9	−1.8	−1.7
Germany[9]	−1.8	−1.5	1.4	−1.3	−1.7	−1.8	−2.3	−2.5	−2.2	−1.8
France	−3.7	−2.5	−2.4	−2.2	−3.8	−3.9	−3.2	−3.1	−2.7	−2.8
Italy	−2.7	−1.5	−1.1	−2.9	−2.8	−2.6	−2.6	−2.9	−2.9	−3.0
Spain	−2.3	−1.0	−1.0	−0.6	−0.5	−0.3	−1.2	0.4	0.1	0.1
Japan[10]	−3.5	−8.2	−6.7	−6.1	−6.7	−6.8	−5.8	−5.4	−5.4	−5.3
United Kingdom	0.1	1.2	1.6	0.9	−1.7	−3.5	−3.2	−3.4	−3.1	−2.9
Canada	0.8	0.9	1.9	1.1	0.8	0.1	0.6	0.4	0.3	0.2
Other advanced economies	−0.4	—	1.2	0.4	0.5	0.6	1.2	1.4	1.4	1.4
Memorandum										
Major advanced economies	−1.0	−1.1	—	−1.1	−2.9	−3.7	−3.5	−3.2	−3.2	−3.1
Newly industrialized Asian economies	−1.1	−0.8	0.2	−0.7	0.3	0.4	0.7	0.5	0.6	0.7

[1]On a national income accounts basis except as indicated in footnotes. See Box A1 for a summary of the policy assumptions underlying the projections.
[2]Adjusted for valuation changes of the foreign exchange stabilization fund.
[3]Based on ESA95 methodology, according to which swap income is not included.
[4]Data include the impact of discharging future pension liabilities of the formerly state-owned telecommunications company at a cost of 1.8 percent of GDP in 1999.
[5]Data cover the consolidated central government including the social security funds but excluding privatization.
[6]Cash basis, underlying balance.
[7]Government balance is revenue minus expenditure plus balance of state-owned enterprises, excluding privatization receipts.
[8]Data are on a budget basis.
[9]Data are on an administrative basis and exclude social security transactions.
[10]Data are on a national income basis and exclude social security transactions.

Table 14. Advanced Economies: General Government Structural Balances[1]
(Percent of potential GDP)

	1998	1999	2000	2001	2002	2003	2004	2005	2006	2007
Structural balance										
Advanced economies	**−1.6**	**−1.4**	**−1.3**	**−1.9**	**−3.3**	**−3.6**	**−3.4**	**−3.0**	**−3.1**	**−2.9**
United States	−0.7	−0.6	0.1	−1.1	−3.7	−4.4	−4.4	−3.9	−4.0	−3.9
Euro area[2,3]	−1.9	−1.5	−1.6	−2.3	−2.6	−2.5	−2.2	−1.8	−1.7	−1.5
Germany[2]	−1.4	−1.0	−1.2	−2.7	−3.2	−3.0	−3.2	−2.6	−2.8	−1.6
France[2]	−1.8	−2.2	−2.1	−2.1	−3.1	−3.4	−2.7	−2.1	−1.6	−1.9
Italy[2]	−3.1	−2.0	−2.8	−3.9	−3.4	−2.9	−3.2	−3.3	−3.1	−3.3
Spain[2]	−2.8	−1.4	−1.6	−1.2	−0.3	0.1	0.9	1.1	0.9	0.7
Netherlands[2]	−1.4	−0.7	−0.2	−1.2	−2.3	−2.4	−1.2	−0.2	−0.1	0.2
Belgium[2]	−0.6	−1.0	−1.5	−0.7	−0.4	−1.3	0.3	0.6	0.2	−0.7
Austria[2]	−2.6	−2.7	−3.4	−0.8	−0.4	−0.2	−0.8	−1.6	−1.7	−0.8
Finland	1.5	1.6	5.9	4.8	4.2	2.6	2.0	2.9	2.6	2.4
Greece	−2.5	−2.0	−3.8	−6.2	−5.1	−6.1	−7.5	−5.4	−3.4	−3.7
Portugal[2]	−2.9	−3.7	−4.6	−5.6	−5.5	−4.7	−4.6	−5.1	−3.6	−2.8
Ireland[2]	1.9	0.8	2.6	−0.6	−1.2	0.4	1.7	0.2	−0.6	−1.0
Japan	−4.9	−6.3	−7.2	−5.6	−6.9	−7.0	−5.8	−5.4	−5.6	−5.5
United Kingdom	—	1.2	1.3	0.3	−1.8	−3.2	−3.4	−3.7	−3.0	−2.6
Canada	0.5	1.3	2.0	0.4	−0.2	0.3	0.9	1.9	1.3	1.1
Other advanced economies	−0.2	0.4	1.3	0.6	—	0.2	0.6	0.6	0.4	0.4
Australia[4]	0.7	1.5	1.3	0.1	0.3	1.1	0.9	0.8	0.7	0.7
Sweden	2.7	1.9	4.5	3.2	0.6	1.2	1.9	2.1	1.0	1.1
Denmark	−1.4	−0.9	0.7	0.3	0.2	0.4	1.1	1.3	1.4	2.2
Norway[5]	−4.5	−3.7	−2.4	−1.1	−3.8	−5.7	−4.4	−4.3	−4.4	−5.2
New Zealand[6]	1.8	0.9	1.3	2.1	3.2	4.2	4.8	4.4	3.7	3.3
Memorandum										
Major advanced economies	−1.7	−1.6	−1.4	−2.1	−3.8	−4.2	−4.0	−3.6	−3.6	−3.4

[1]On a national income accounts basis. The structural budget position is defined as the actual budget deficit (or surplus) less the effects of cyclical deviations of output from potential output. Because of the margin of uncertainty that attaches to estimates of cyclical gaps and to tax and expenditure elasticities with respect to national income, indicators of structural budget positions should be interpreted as broad orders of magnitude. Moreover, it is important to note that changes in structural budget balances are not necessarily attributable to policy changes but may reflect the built-in momentum of existing expenditure programs. In the period beyond that for which specific consolidation programs exist, it is assumed that the structural deficit remains unchanged.

[2]Excludes one-off receipts from the sale of mobile telephone licenses equivalent to 2.5 percent of GDP in 2000 for Germany, 0.1 percent of GDP in 2001 and 2002 for France, 1.2 percent of GDP in 2000 for Italy, 0.1 percent of GDP in 2000 for Spain, 0.7 percent of GDP in 2000 for the Netherlands, and 0.2 percent of GDP in 2001 for Belgium, 0.4 percent of GDP in 2000 for Austria, 0.3 percent of GDP in 2000 for Portugal, and 0.2 percent of GDP in 2002 for Ireland. Also excludes one-off receipts from sizable asset transactions, in particular 0.5 percent of GDP for France in 2005.

[3]Excludes Luxembourg.

[4]Excludes commonwealth government privatization receipts.

[5]Excludes oil.

[6]Government balance is revenue minus expenditure plus balance of state-owned enterprises, excluding privatization receipts.

Table 15. Advanced Economies: Monetary Aggregates[1]

(Annual percent change)

	1998	1999	2000	2001	2002	2003	2004	2005
Narrow money[2]								
Advanced economies	**5.7**	**8.4**	**2.0**	**9.4**	**9.1**	**8.1**	**6.4**	**5.1**
United States	2.1	2.6	−3.2	8.7	3.1	7.0	5.2	−0.2
Euro area[3]	10.5	10.6	5.3	6.0	9.9	10.6	8.9	11.3
Japan	5.0	11.7	3.5	13.7	23.5	4.5	4.0	5.6
United Kingdom	6.0	11.4	4.6	7.6	6.4	7.4	5.7	4.7
Canada[4]	8.7	8.9	14.4	15.3	4.6	10.8	11.9	11.2
Memorandum								
Newly industrialized Asian economies	0.9	19.9	4.6	11.4	13.4	13.9	9.2	1.6
Broad money[5]								
Advanced economies	**6.8**	**5.9**	**4.9**	**8.1**	**5.7**	**5.5**	**5.3**	**5.5**
United States	8.7	6.0	6.1	10.5	6.4	4.8	5.6	3.9
Euro area[3]	5.0	5.7	4.1	8.0	6.9	7.1	6.6	7.3
Japan	4.0	2.7	1.9	3.3	1.8	1.6	1.8	2.0
United Kingdom	8.4	4.1	8.4	6.7	7.0	7.2	8.8	12.6
Canada[4]	0.8	5.1	6.6	6.0	5.1	6.1	6.3	5.4
Memorandum								
Newly industrialized Asian economies	20.0	17.3	14.5	7.3	5.7	6.8	3.4	3.7

[1]End-of-period based on monthly data.

[2]M1 except for the United Kingdom, where M0 is used here as a measure of narrow money; it comprises notes in circulation plus bankers' operational deposits. M1 is generally currency in circulation plus private demand deposits. In addition, the United States includes traveler's checks of nonbank issues and other checkable deposits and excludes private sector float and demand deposits of banks. Canada excludes private sector float.

[3]Excludes Greece prior to 2001.

[4]Average of Wednesdays.

[5]M2, defined as M1 plus quasi-money, except for Japan, and the United Kingdom, for which the data are based on M2 plus certificates of deposit (CDs), and M4, respectively. Quasi-money is essentially private term deposits and other notice deposits. The United States also includes money market mutual fund balances, money market deposit accounts, overnight repurchase agreements, and overnight Eurodollars issued to U.S. residents by foreign branches of U.S. banks. For the United Kingdom, M4 is composed of non-interest-bearing M1, private sector interest-bearing sterling sight bank deposits, private sector sterling time bank deposits, private sector holdings of sterling bank CDs, private sector holdings of building society shares and deposits, and sterling CDs less building society of banks deposits and bank CDs and notes and coins. For the euro area, M3 is composed of M2 plus marketable instruments held by euro-area residents, which comprise repurchase agreements, money market fund shares/units, money market paper, and debt securities up to two years.

Table 16. Advanced Economies: Interest Rates
(Percent a year)

	1998	1999	2000	2001	2002	2003	2004	2005	March 2006
Policy-related interest rate[1]									
United States	4.7	5.3	6.4	1.8	1.2	1.0	2.2	4.2	4.5
Euro area[2]	...	3.0	4.8	3.3	2.8	2.0	2.0	2.3	2.5
Japan	0.3	0.0	0.2	0.0	0.0	0.0	0.0	0.0	0.0
United Kingdom	6.3	5.5	6.0	4.0	4.0	3.8	4.8	4.5	4.5
Canada	5.0	4.8	5.8	2.3	2.8	2.8	2.5	3.3	3.8
Short-term interest rate[2]									
Advanced economies	**4.0**	**3.4**	**4.4**	**3.2**	**2.1**	**1.6**	**1.7**	**2.5**	**3.4**
United States	4.9	4.8	6.0	3.5	1.6	1.0	1.4	3.2	4.5
Euro area	3.7	3.0	4.4	4.3	3.3	2.3	2.1	2.2	2.7
Japan	0.2	0.0	0.2	0.0	0.0	0.0	0.0	0.0	0.0
United Kingdom	7.4	5.5	6.1	5.0	4.0	3.7	4.6	4.7	4.6
Canada	4.7	4.7	5.5	3.9	2.6	2.9	2.2	2.7	3.9
Memorandum									
Newly industrialized Asian economies	10.6	4.6	4.6	3.7	2.7	2.3	2.2	2.5	3.8
Long-term interest rate[3]									
Advanced economies	**4.5**	**4.6**	**5.1**	**4.4**	**4.1**	**3.6**	**3.8**	**3.7**	**3.9**
United States	5.3	5.6	6.0	5.0	4.6	4.0	4.3	4.3	4.6
Euro area	4.7	4.6	5.5	5.0	4.9	4.0	3.9	3.7	3.6
Japan	1.3	1.7	1.7	1.3	1.3	1.0	1.5	1.4	1.8
United Kingdom	5.1	5.2	5.0	5.0	4.8	4.5	4.8	4.3	4.1
Canada	5.3	5.6	5.9	5.5	5.3	4.8	4.6	4.1	4.2
Memorandum									
Newly industrialized Asian economies	9.6	7.3	7.0	5.5	5.0	3.9	3.8	4.0	5.3

[1]Annual data are end of period. For the United States, federal funds rate; for Japan, overnight call rate; for the euro area, main refinancing rate; for the United Kingdom, base lending rate; and for Canada, target rate for overnight money market financing.

[2]Annual data are period average. For the United States, three-month treasury bill market bid yield at constant maturity; for Japan, three-month bond yield with repurchase agreement; for the euro area, three-month EURIBOR; for the United Kingdom, three-month interbank offered rate; for the Canada, three-month treasury bill yield.

[3]Annual data are period average. For the United States, 10-year treasury bond yield at constant maturity; for Japan, 10-year government bond yield; for the euro area, a weighted average of national 10-year government bond yields through 1998 and 10-year euro bond yield thereafter; for the United Kingdom, 10-year government bond yield; and for Canada, 10-year government bond yield.

Table 17. Advanced Economies: Exchange Rates

	1998	1999	2000	2001	2002	2003	2004	2005	Exchange Rate Assumption 2006
	U.S. dollars per national currency unit								
U.S. dollar nominal exchange rates									
Euro	. . .	1.067	0.924	0.896	0.944	1.131	1.243	1.246	1.195
Pound sterling	1.656	1.618	1.516	1.440	1.501	1.634	1.832	1.820	1.751
	National currency units per U.S. dollar								
Japanese yen	130.4	113.5	107.7	121.5	125.2	115.8	108.1	110.0	116.9
Canadian dollar	1.482	1.486	1.485	1.548	1.569	1.397	1.299	1.211	1.154
Swedish krona	7.948	8.257	9.132	10.314	9.707	8.068	7.338	7.450	7.859
Danish krone	6.691	6.967	8.060	8.317	7.870	6.577	5.985	5.987	6.230
Swiss franc	1.447	1.500	1.687	1.686	1.554	1.346	1.242	1.243	1.308
Norwegian krone	7.544	7.797	8.782	8.989	7.932	7.074	6.730	6.439	6.765
Israeli new sheqel	3.786	4.138	4.077	4.205	4.735	4.548	4.481	4.485	4.755
Icelandic krona	70.94	72.30	78.28	96.84	91.19	76.64	70.07	62.94	66.26
Cyprus pound	0.517	0.542	0.621	0.643	0.609	0.517	0.468	0.464	0.481
Korean won	1,401.4	1,188.8	1,131.0	1,291.0	1,251.1	1,191.6	1,145.3	1,024.1	970.0
Australian dollar	1.589	1.550	1.717	1.932	1.839	1.534	1.358	1.309	1.354
New Taiwan dollar	33.434	32.263	31.216	33.787	34.571	34.441	33.418	32.156	32.243
Hong Kong dollar	7.745	7.757	7.791	7.799	7.799	7.787	7.788	7.777	7.758
Singapore dollar	1.674	1.695	1.724	1.792	1.791	1.742	1.690	1.664	1.639
			Index, 2000 = 100						*Percent change from previous assumption[2]*
Real effective exchange rates[1]									
United States	90.5	90.3	100.0	102.4	102.5	93.8	85.9	85.3	−1.0
Euro area[3]	118.1	113.4	100.0	101.8	107.5	121.3	127.5	126.6	0.1
Germany	105.0	104.8	100.0	101.5	101.7	105.4	104.4	102.8	—
France	112.6	107.6	100.0	97.9	99.8	104.1	104.5	102.9	—
Italy	106.7	106.7	100.0	100.7	107.3	116.4	123.6	126.9	—
Spain	101.0	100.2	100.0	102.1	104.9	109.1	112.6	112.5	—
Netherlands	105.6	103.9	100.0	102.9	108.5	117.8	119.7	117.3	—
Belgium	106.1	106.5	100.0	102.0	103.0	107.5	110.9	110.9	0.1
Austria	116.0	110.5	100.0	96.4	97.4	100.4	101.5	100.0	—
Finland	114.7	110.3	100.0	105.2	104.8	109.9	113.8	112.9	—
Greece	103.8	104.6	100.0	99.4	102.6	107.5	115.4	118.3	−0.1
Portugal	97.8	99.8	100.0	102.4	105.3	109.7	113.4	112.6	—
Ireland	130.9	117.8	100.0	98.8	93.6	101.1	109.0	109.2	0.1
Luxembourg	103.9	104.7	100.0	101.8	102.2	105.3	108.2	108.3	—
Japan	87.9	97.5	100.0	92.8	83.9	80.2	79.9	74.8	−0.1
United Kingdom	97.6	97.9	100.0	97.1	100.2	94.9	98.7	97.9	−0.6
Canada	106.6	103.9	100.0	101.5	99.0	108.6	113.9	120.5	1.1
Korea	90.4	94.2	100.0	92.9	96.7	94.9	97.7	115.7	4.7
Australia	100.9	103.4	100.0	94.3	99.6	111.6	124.4	130.9	−0.7
Taiwan Province of China	90.0	96.2	100.0	106.0	94.1	86.3	82.5	83.9	2.0
Sweden	110.8	103.4	100.0	96.9	92.6	95.2	99.2	97.8	0.6
Switzerland	101.6	101.1	100.0	105.5	111.6	113.5	114.8	113.9	−0.8
Hong Kong SAR	108.2	102.9	100.0	103.4	98.5	86.1	77.3	73.0	−0.8
Denmark	106.5	105.2	100.0	101.3	103.7	108.1	113.9	113.6	−0.1
Norway	98.0	99.3	100.0	102.3	116.1	116.4	113.0	116.7	−1.1
Israel	91.9	89.5	100.0	101.6	89.3	82.4	83.2	85.9	−2.5
Singapore	112.7	98.7	100.0	104.7	102.1	97.8	99.7	100.0	2.1
New Zealand	115.7	113.1	100.0	96.3	105.3	120.1	131.4	138.2	−4.2

[1]Defined as the ratio, in common currency, of the unit labor costs in the manufacturing sector to the weighted average of those of its industrial country trading partners, using 1999–2001 trade weights.

[2]In nominal effective terms. Average December 2–30, 2005 rates compared with February 9–March 9, 2006 rates.

[3]A synthetic euro for the period prior to January 1, 1999 is used in the calculation of real effective exchange rates for the euro. See Box 5.5 in the *World Economic Outlook*, October 1998.

Table 18. Other Emerging Market and Developing Countries: Central Government Fiscal Balances
(Percent of GDP)

	1998	1999	2000	2001	2002	2003	2004	2005	2006	2007
Other emerging market and developing countries	**−3.7**	**−3.8**	**−2.9**	**−3.1**	**−3.4**	**−2.7**	**−1.6**	**−0.8**	**−0.9**	**−0.8**
Regional groups										
Africa	−3.8	−3.5	−1.3	−2.1	−2.3	−1.4	−0.1	1.3	1.8	1.9
Sub-Sahara	−3.7	−3.8	−2.4	−2.6	−2.4	−2.4	−0.6	0.2	0.9	1.0
Excluding Nigeria and South Africa	−3.4	−4.9	−4.4	−2.8	−2.9	−2.9	−1.7	−1.2	−1.1	−0.7
Central and eastern Europe	−4.1	−5.4	−5.0	−7.3	−8.0	−6.3	−5.1	−3.1	−3.4	−2.6
Commonwealth of Independent States[1]	−5.2	−4.0	0.3	1.8	1.0	1.1	2.7	5.4	5.1	4.3
Russia	−6.0	−4.2	0.8	2.7	1.3	1.6	4.3	7.4	7.6	6.5
Excluding Russia	−3.1	−3.2	−1.5	−0.9	0.3	−0.1	−1.8	−0.1	−1.8	−1.8
Developing Asia	−3.4	−4.2	−4.3	−3.9	−3.7	−3.2	−2.3	−2.0	−2.0	−1.7
China	−2.8	−3.7	−3.3	−2.7	−3.0	−2.4	−1.5	−1.3	−1.1	−1.0
India	−5.3	−6.5	−7.1	−6.6	−6.1	−5.3	−4.4	−4.1	−4.2	−3.7
Excluding China and India	−2.8	−2.9	−3.9	−3.7	−3.2	−2.8	−2.3	−2.0	−2.1	−1.8
Middle East	−5.1	−1.8	4.2	−0.5	−3.4	−1.1	1.3	5.9	4.7	3.9
Western Hemisphere	−3.3	−2.9	−2.3	−2.6	−3.0	−3.0	−1.4	−2.1	−1.9	−1.6
Brazil	−5.4	−2.7	−2.3	−2.1	−0.8	−4.0	−1.5	−3.8	−2.8	−2.1
Mexico	−2.3	−2.2	−1.6	−1.3	−1.5	−1.6	—	−0.5	−1.1	−1.1
Analytical groups										
By source of export earnings										
Fuel	−5.7	−3.0	3.7	1.2	−0.3	1.4	4.1	8.2	8.2	7.4
Nonfuel	−3.4	−3.9	−3.9	−3.8	−3.9	−3.4	−2.4	−2.2	−2.2	−1.9
of which, primary products	−2.3	−4.0	−4.7	−3.0	−3.1	−2.6	−1.4	0.3	0.2	−0.4
By external financing source										
Net debtor countries	−3.8	−4.1	−4.1	−4.2	−4.3	−3.8	−2.8	−2.5	−2.5	−2.2
of which, official financing	−3.2	−3.5	−4.1	−4.0	−4.5	−3.0	−2.6	−2.4	−2.6	−2.3
Net debtor countries by debt-servicing experience										
Countries with arrears and/or rescheduling during 1999–2003	−2.9	−3.1	−3.1	−3.3	−3.8	−2.4	−1.4	−1.1	−0.8	−0.4
Other groups										
Heavily indebted poor countries	−3.6	−4.4	−4.9	−4.0	−4.3	−3.9	−3.0	−2.3	−2.6	−2.4
Middle East and north Africa	−4.7	−1.8	3.6	−0.6	−2.8	−0.4	1.4	5.4	4.5	3.9
Memorandum										
Median										
Other emerging market and developing countries	−2.8	−3.1	−2.6	−3.6	−3.6	−3.1	−2.6	−2.2	−2.4	−1.7
Africa	−3.2	−3.4	−2.7	−3.4	−3.8	−3.1	−2.7	−2.1	−2.0	−1.7
Central and eastern Europe	−2.8	−2.9	−2.5	−4.2	−5.3	−3.9	−3.3	−2.3	−2.7	−1.6
Commonwealth of Independent States[1]	−5.0	−4.2	−1.2	−1.4	−0.4	−0.9	−0.2	−0.6	−1.7	−2.1
Developing Asia	−2.2	−3.3	−3.8	−4.4	−4.1	−3.1	−2.6	−3.1	−3.3	−2.7
Middle East	−5.7	−1.3	5.2	0.8	−0.8	−0.2	−0.2	2.1	1.2	0.6
Western Hemisphere	−2.3	−2.9	−2.3	−4.2	−4.6	−3.8	−2.9	−2.3	−2.4	−1.5

[1]Mongolia, which is not a member of the Commonwealth of Independent States, is included in this group for reasons of geography and similarities in economic structure.

Table 19. Other Emerging Market and Developing Countries: Broad Money Aggregates
(Annual percent change)

	1998	1999	2000	2001	2002	2003	2004	2005	2006	2007
Other emerging market and developing countries	**18.5**	**17.7**	**16.5**	**15.0**	**16.7**	**16.3**	**17.6**	**18.8**	**15.1**	**13.0**
Regional groups										
Africa	18.0	19.3	19.8	20.8	21.1	21.4	18.9	23.0	16.7	13.6
Sub-Sahara	16.4	21.4	22.4	21.9	24.3	24.7	21.9	27.0	18.0	14.4
Central and eastern Europe	36.9	37.2	24.0	37.8	10.9	10.4	15.7	15.3	12.0	11.3
Commonwealth of Independent States[1]	44.1	53.2	57.5	37.9	34.0	38.7	34.7	35.3	29.2	23.2
Russia	50.2	48.1	57.2	35.7	33.9	39.4	33.7	35.5	30.0	24.0
Excluding Russia	24.8	70.3	58.2	43.2	34.2	36.8	37.5	35.0	26.7	20.6
Developing Asia	18.6	14.3	12.2	13.1	15.6	16.3	14.8	16.6	16.0	13.6
China	14.8	14.7	12.3	14.8	19.7	19.6	14.9	17.6	16.0	13.0
India	20.2	18.6	16.2	13.9	15.1	15.9	18.3	18.4	18.1	17.3
Excluding China and India	22.2	11.5	9.7	9.6	8.5	10.4	12.1	13.2	14.6	12.1
Middle East	8.6	10.7	12.6	14.0	17.1	13.9	19.2	19.7	17.6	14.3
Western Hemisphere	10.3	10.2	12.0	6.0	15.7	13.5	17.4	17.5	8.8	8.2
Brazil	4.1	6.9	15.5	12.6	23.2	3.7	18.6	18.9	0.5	8.2
Mexico	24.6	22.8	16.2	13.7	12.6	11.7	13.5	14.9	12.8	6.0
Analytical groups										
By source of export earnings										
Fuel	25.3	24.8	29.3	21.2	22.2	24.3	25.9	27.3	22.4	18.4
Nonfuel	17.1	16.3	14.2	13.8	15.6	14.7	15.9	17.0	13.4	11.6
of which, primary products	17.0	20.5	22.5	21.5	21.5	25.3	30.4	31.4	19.4	14.6
By external financing source										
Net debtor countries	17.8	16.8	15.2	13.9	14.8	13.2	16.4	16.8	12.8	11.3
of which, official financing	21.9	10.6	9.5	—	13.7	19.1	15.6	15.5	15.7	12.3
Net debtor countries by debt-servicing experience										
Countries with arrears and/or rescheduling during 1999–2003	23.6	12.5	14.2	2.7	18.2	24.4	20.4	21.9	19.5	16.0
Other groups										
Heavily indebted poor countries	18.0	23.8	30.4	19.3	19.9	16.2	16.4	15.3	15.3	12.2
Middle East and north Africa	11.1	11.2	12.7	14.7	16.4	13.9	18.0	18.8	17.0	13.9
Memorandum										
Median										
Other emerging market and developing countries	11.3	13.2	14.1	13.7	13.2	13.0	13.9	13.4	11.9	10.3
Africa	8.6	12.6	13.6	15.2	17.7	15.3	14.1	13.0	14.1	12.3
Central and eastern Europe	13.0	14.2	16.5	21.4	9.5	10.9	13.9	11.3	11.9	9.2
Commonwealth of Independent States[1]	25.3	32.1	40.1	35.7	34.1	30.7	32.3	26.4	23.6	15.8
Developing Asia	11.7	14.7	12.3	11.7	13.3	13.4	14.9	12.8	11.9	11.0
Middle East	8.3	11.0	10.4	13.4	12.8	10.9	12.2	15.9	13.9	11.4
Western Hemisphere	12.6	10.8	9.0	8.9	8.5	9.6	12.0	9.8	8.3	6.1

[1]Mongolia, which is not a member of the Commonwealth of Independent States, is included in this group for reasons of geography and similarities in economic structure.

Table 20. Summary of World Trade Volumes and Prices
(Annual percent change)

	Ten-Year Averages		1998	1999	2000	2001	2002	2003	2004	2005	2006	2007
	1988–97	1998–2007										
Trade in goods and services												
World trade[1]												
Volume	7.0	6.4	4.6	5.7	12.1	0.3	3.4	5.4	10.4	7.3	8.0	7.5
Price deflator												
In U.S. dollars	1.4	1.5	−5.7	−1.6	−0.4	−3.5	1.2	10.4	9.7	5.2	0.7	0.4
In SDRs	0.8	1.1	−4.4	−2.3	3.3	—	−0.6	2.1	3.8	5.5	3.5	0.2
Volume of trade												
Exports												
Advanced economies	7.1	5.2	4.3	5.6	11.7	−0.6	2.2	3.3	8.5	5.3	6.6	6.1
Other emerging market and developing countries	7.6	9.0	5.5	3.4	13.3	3.1	7.0	10.6	14.6	11.5	10.9	10.3
Imports												
Advanced economies	6.7	5.8	6.0	8.1	11.6	−0.5	2.5	4.1	8.9	5.8	6.2	5.6
Other emerging market and developing countries	7.3	8.6	−0.1	0.1	14.5	3.4	6.3	10.3	15.8	12.4	12.9	11.9
Terms of trade												
Advanced economies	−0.1	−0.1	1.3	−0.3	−2.6	0.5	0.8	1.1	−0.1	−1.3	−0.9	0.2
Other emerging market and developing countries	−0.8	1.1	−6.7	4.5	6.9	−2.7	0.7	0.6	2.2	5.0	1.5	−0.1
Trade in goods												
World trade[1]												
Volume	7.2	6.5	4.8	5.4	12.9	−0.3	3.7	6.0	10.7	7.2	8.0	7.5
Price deflator												
In U.S. dollars	1.3	1.6	−6.7	−1.0	0.2	−3.8	0.6	10.3	9.9	6.1	1.2	0.4
In SDRs	0.7	1.1	−5.3	−1.8	3.9	−0.3	−1.2	2.0	4.0	6.3	4.0	0.2
World trade prices in U.S. dollars[2]												
Manufactures	1.4	1.3	−4.1	−2.5	−5.9	−3.7	2.4	14.4	9.6	4.5	−1.4	1.2
Oil	0.6	12.6	−32.1	37.5	57.0	−13.8	2.5	15.8	30.7	41.3	14.8	2.9
Nonfuel primary commodities	1.3	1.6	−14.3	−7.2	4.8	−4.9	1.7	6.9	18.5	10.3	10.2	−5.5
World trade prices in SDRs[2]												
Manufactures	0.8	0.8	−2.7	−3.3	−2.4	−0.2	0.6	5.8	3.7	4.7	1.4	0.9
Oil	—	12.1	−31.2	36.4	62.8	−10.7	0.8	7.1	23.6	41.6	18.0	2.6
Nonfuel primary commodities	0.7	1.1	−13.1	−7.9	8.6	−1.5	—	−1.2	12.1	10.5	13.2	−5.7
World trade prices in euros[2]												
Manufactures	1.6	0.7	−2.9	2.4	8.7	−0.7	−2.9	−4.5	−0.3	4.3	2.8	1.2
Oil	0.7	12.0	−31.3	44.4	81.3	−11.1	−2.8	−3.3	18.9	41.0	19.7	2.8
Nonfuel primary commodities	1.5	1.1	−13.3	−2.6	20.9	−1.9	−3.5	−10.8	7.8	10.0	14.9	−5.5

Table 20 *(concluded)*

| | Ten-Year Averages | | | | | | | | | | | |
	1988–97	1998–2007	1998	1999	2000	2001	2002	2003	2004	2005	2006	2007
Trade in goods												
Volume of trade												
Exports												
Advanced economies	7.2	5.2	4.5	5.1	12.6	−1.3	2.3	3.4	8.5	5.1	6.6	6.1
Other emerging market and developing countries	7.6	8.9	5.7	2.6	14.2	2.8	7.4	11.4	14.4	10.8	10.1	10.0
Fuel exporters	4.4	5.0	1.6	−1.8	8.4	1.7	3.1	9.1	9.9	6.0	6.6	5.3
Nonfuel exporters	8.9	10.2	7.1	3.8	16.0	3.1	8.9	12.1	16.0	12.5	11.6	12.0
Imports												
Advanced economies	7.0	5.9	6.0	8.5	12.3	−1.5	2.9	4.7	9.4	5.9	6.3	5.5
Other emerging market and developing countries	7.4	8.9	1.3	−1.2	14.9	3.5	6.6	11.5	16.6	12.1	12.9	12.4
Fuel exporters	1.3	9.0	−2.4	−8.2	13.5	15.3	8.9	6.4	14.4	19.4	16.2	10.3
Nonfuel exporters	9.5	8.9	2.2	0.3	15.2	1.4	6.1	12.6	17.1	10.7	12.3	12.8
Price deflators in SDRs												
Exports												
Advanced economies	0.5	0.5	−4.0	−3.0	0.4	−0.3	−0.9	3.0	3.3	3.9	2.4	0.5
Other emerging market and developing countries	1.4	3.5	−10.8	5.4	14.4	−1.2	−0.2	1.9	6.9	13.4	7.8	—
Fuel exporters	1.0	8.5	−23.5	24.2	41.4	−7.2	0.5	5.3	14.0	31.1	13.5	0.8
Nonfuel exporters	1.7	1.7	−6.4	0.3	5.8	1.2	−0.5	0.7	4.5	7.0	5.5	−0.3
Imports												
Advanced economies	0.3	0.6	−5.1	−3.0	3.7	−0.6	−1.8	1.5	3.3	5.6	3.1	0.2
Other emerging market and developing countries	2.3	1.9	−4.8	−0.4	6.3	1.5	−0.8	1.1	4.3	6.7	5.4	—
Fuel exporters	2.5	1.0	−3.0	−3.0	1.1	1.6	−0.1	2.6	2.4	4.8	4.0	0.5
Nonfuel exporters	2.1	2.0	−5.2	0.1	7.3	1.5	−1.0	0.8	4.7	7.1	5.7	−0.1
Terms of trade												
Advanced economies	0.2	−0.1	1.2	—	−3.1	0.4	0.9	1.5	—	−1.7	−0.7	0.3
Other emerging market and developing countries	−0.9	1.6	−6.3	5.8	7.6	−2.7	0.6	0.8	2.5	6.2	2.3	0.1
Fuel exporters	−1.5	7.4	−21.2	28.1	39.8	−8.7	0.6	2.7	11.3	25.2	9.2	0.3
Nonfuel exporters	−0.4	−0.3	−1.3	0.2	−1.4	−0.3	0.5	−0.1	−0.2	−0.1	−0.2	−0.2
Memorandum												
World exports in billions of U.S. dollars												
Goods and services	5,039	9,884	6,789	7,046	7,835	7,572	7,944	9,254	11,196	12,641	13,731	14,829
Goods	4,026	7,919	5,381	5,584	6,295	6,031	6,304	7,375	8,952	10,171	11,103	11,990

[1]Average of annual percent change for world exports and imports.
[2]As represented, respectively, by the export unit value index for the manufactures of the advanced economies; the average of U.K. Brent, Dubai, and West Texas Intermediate crude oil spot prices; and the average of world market prices for nonfuel primary commodities weighted by their 1995–97 shares in world commodity exports.

Table 21. Nonfuel Commodity Prices[1]
(Annual percent change; U.S. dollar terms)

| | Ten-Year Averages | | 1998 | 1999 | 2000 | 2001 | 2002 | 2003 | 2004 | 2005 | 2006 | 2007 |
	1988–97	1998–2007										
Nonfuel primary commodities	**1.3**	**1.6**	**−14.3**	**−7.2**	**4.8**	**−4.9**	**1.7**	**6.9**	**18.5**	**10.3**	**10.2**	**−5.5**
Food	0.7	−0.1	−11.1	−12.6	2.5	0.2	3.4	5.2	14.3	−0.3	2.7	−2.5
Beverages	1.8	−3.2	−13.2	−21.3	−15.1	−16.1	16.5	4.9	3.0	21.0	1.6	−3.8
Agricultural raw materials	2.6	−0.4	−16.7	1.2	4.4	−4.9	1.8	3.7	5.5	1.6	6.1	−4.8
Metals	1.3	5.5	−17.7	−1.1	12.2	−9.8	−2.7	12.2	36.1	26.4	20.0	−8.3
Advanced economies	**1.5**	**2.1**	**−15.8**	**−6.0**	**5.6**	**−6.1**	**1.9**	**8.1**	**20.6**	**12.2**	**12.8**	**−6.3**
Other emerging market and developing countries	**1.6**	**1.7**	**−16.1**	**−7.3**	**4.5**	**−7.0**	**2.2**	**8.4**	**20.8**	**12.3**	**12.1**	**−6.6**
Regional groups												
Africa	1.2	1.4	−14.7	−6.9	2.6	−6.9	4.4	8.1	14.7	10.8	11.6	−5.0
Sub-Sahara	1.2	1.5	−14.8	−6.7	2.6	−7.2	4.5	8.3	14.7	11.2	12.0	−5.0
Central and eastern Europe	1.6	2.7	−16.6	−4.6	6.5	−7.1	1.0	8.4	23.4	15.4	14.1	−7.1
Commonwealth of Independent States[2]	...	4.1	−17.9	−2.6	9.9	−8.5	−0.7	10.6	29.8	20.7	17.9	−8.2
Developing Asia	1.6	1.0	−13.6	−7.5	2.3	−6.3	2.8	6.7	16.6	9.1	9.6	−5.6
Middle East	1.3	2.4	−15.4	−7.1	6.4	−7.2	0.9	9.8	21.8	13.7	13.2	−6.2
Western Hemisphere	1.9	1.2	−18.4	−10.0	4.6	−7.1	2.5	9.2	22.8	11.1	11.3	−7.0
Analytical groups												
By source of export earnings												
Fuel	1.3	3.4	−17.0	−4.6	8.3	−8.4	−0.4	10.8	26.6	18.3	15.9	−7.0
Nonfuel	1.7	1.7	−16.1	−7.4	4.4	−7.0	2.3	8.3	20.7	12.1	12.0	−6.6
of which, primary products	1.2	2.4	−16.8	−7.7	4.6	−7.6	4.1	9.3	23.6	15.1	15.4	−8.9
By source of external financing												
Net debtor countries	1.7	1.5	−16.1	−8.1	3.9	−6.9	2.6	8.3	20.1	11.6	11.6	−6.4
of which, official financing	1.1	1.1	−12.9	−10.1	0.4	−7.1	4.5	8.1	15.7	10.9	10.8	−4.8
Net debtor countries by debt-servicing experience												
Countries with arrears and/or rescheduling during 1999–2003	1.5	1.3	−15.4	−9.6	2.6	−7.3	3.6	8.8	18.9	11.1	11.1	−5.7
Other groups												
Heavily indebted poor countries	0.6	0.8	−13.7	−12.4	−2.5	−7.6	9.7	9.5	12.3	10.0	10.8	−3.3
Middle East and north Africa	1.3	1.9	−14.9	−7.7	5.5	−6.3	1.6	8.9	19.7	11.6	11.8	−5.7
Memorandum												
Average oil spot price[3]	0.6	12.6	−32.1	37.5	57.0	−13.8	2.5	15.8	30.7	41.3	14.8	2.9
In U.S. dollars a barrel	18.36	35.28	13.08	17.98	28.24	24.33	24.95	28.89	37.76	53.35	61.25	63.00
Export unit value of manufactures[4]	1.4	1.3	−4.1	−2.5	−5.9	−3.7	2.4	14.4	9.6	4.5	−1.4	1.2

[1]Averages of world market prices for individual commodities weighted by 1995–97 exports as a share of world commodity exports and total commodity exports for the indicated country group, respectively.
[2]Mongolia, which is not a member of the Commonwealth of Independent States, is included in this group for reasons of geography and similarities in economic structure.
[3]Average of U.K. Brent, Dubai, and West Texas Intermediate crude oil spot prices.
[4]For the manufactures exported by the advanced economies.

Table 22. Advanced Economies: Export Volumes, Import Volumes, and Terms of Trade in Goods and Services

(Annual percent change)

| | Ten-Year Averages | | 1998 | 1999 | 2000 | 2001 | 2002 | 2003 | 2004 | 2005 | 2006 | 2007 |
	1988–97	1998–2007										
Export volume												
Advanced economies	**7.1**	**5.2**	**4.3**	**5.6**	**11.7**	**−0.6**	**2.2**	**3.3**	**8.5**	**5.3**	**6.6**	**6.1**
United States	9.2	4.1	2.4	4.3	8.7	−5.4	−2.3	1.8	8.4	7.0	8.2	9.0
Euro area	6.5	5.1	7.4	5.2	12.0	3.6	1.5	1.3	6.1	3.7	5.5	5.5
Germany	6.0	6.7	8.0	5.9	13.5	6.4	4.2	2.4	9.3	6.3	6.0	5.3
France	6.5	4.6	7.7	3.9	13.0	2.6	1.5	−1.8	2.2	3.2	6.5	7.5
Italy	6.4	2.4	3.4	0.1	9.7	6.8	−4.0	−2.2	2.5	0.7	4.0	4.1
Spain	8.6	4.5	8.0	7.4	10.3	4.0	1.8	3.6	3.3	1.0	2.1	3.7
Japan	5.4	5.6	−2.3	1.5	12.2	−6.7	7.5	9.0	13.9	6.9	10.4	5.4
United Kingdom	5.4	4.1	3.1	4.3	9.1	2.9	0.2	1.2	4.6	5.6	5.7	4.8
Canada	6.9	4.1	9.1	10.7	8.9	−3.0	1.0	−2.1	5.0	2.3	5.1	4.8
Other advanced economies	8.3	7.1	2.4	8.5	14.7	−1.9	6.2	8.1	13.1	7.2	6.9	6.4
Memorandum												
Major advanced economies	6.8	4.7	4.0	4.3	10.7	−0.6	1.0	1.7	7.4	5.3	6.9	6.3
Newly industrialized Asian economies	10.8	8.9	1.2	9.4	17.1	−3.8	10.0	13.4	17.7	9.3	9.0	7.6
Import volume												
Advanced economies	**6.7**	**5.8**	**6.0**	**8.1**	**11.6**	**−0.5**	**2.5**	**4.1**	**8.9**	**5.8**	**6.2**	**5.6**
United States	6.9	6.9	11.6	11.5	13.1	−2.7	3.4	4.6	10.7	6.4	6.0	5.4
Euro area	5.7	5.5	9.9	7.6	11.0	2.1	0.2	2.8	6.2	4.6	5.7	5.5
Germany	5.5	5.6	9.4	8.6	10.2	1.2	−1.4	5.1	7.0	5.3	6.2	4.9
France	4.5	6.4	10.6	5.9	14.9	2.4	1.5	1.3	6.1	6.5	7.6	7.9
Italy	5.1	4.0	8.9	5.6	7.1	8.5	−0.5	1.0	1.9	1.8	2.5	3.7
Spain	9.3	8.0	14.8	13.6	10.8	4.2	3.9	6.0	9.3	7.1	5.8	5.4
Japan	7.3	4.0	−6.7	3.6	8.5	1.0	0.8	4.0	8.5	6.2	8.6	6.9
United Kingdom	5.6	5.9	9.3	7.9	9.0	4.8	4.5	1.8	6.7	5.3	5.3	4.7
Canada	6.8	4.7	5.1	7.8	8.1	−5.1	1.5	4.1	8.1	7.0	6.5	5.0
Other advanced economies	8.8	6.1	−2.1	7.1	14.1	−3.7	6.2	7.2	13.8	7.2	6.8	6.2
Memorandum												
Major advanced economies	6.1	5.8	7.7	8.3	11.0	0.3	1.8	3.6	8.0	5.7	6.2	5.5
Newly industrialized Asian economies	12.6	6.7	−8.2	8.4	17.6	−5.7	8.8	9.7	16.8	7.2	7.9	7.5
Terms of trade												
Advanced economies	**−0.1**	**−0.1**	**1.3**	**−0.3**	**−2.6**	**0.5**	**0.8**	**1.1**	**−0.1**	**−1.3**	**−0.9**	**0.2**
United States	0.4	−0.3	3.4	−1.2	−2.1	2.3	0.6	−0.9	−1.3	−2.6	−1.6	0.4
Euro area	−0.6	—	1.2	0.1	−3.9	1.0	1.2	1.1	−0.1	−1.1	−0.5	0.5
Germany	−1.8	−0.1	1.3	0.4	−4.6	0.2	1.5	1.7	0.2	−1.5	−1.0	1.2
France	−0.7	−0.1	1.2	0.3	−3.7	1.2	0.6	0.8	0.4	−0.9	−0.9	0.2
Italy	0.2	0.1	2.0	0.3	−7.2	3.3	1.9	2.3	−0.1	−1.7	−0.2	0.6
Spain	0.9	0.7	2.5	−0.1	−2.8	2.4	3.1	1.3	0.1	−0.2	1.0	—
Japan	−0.5	−2.0	3.4	−0.2	−5.3	—	−0.6	−1.8	−3.6	−5.7	−5.6	−0.6
United Kingdom	0.7	0.4	2.1	0.6	−0.8	−0.6	2.8	1.1	—	−1.7	0.4	−0.1
Canada	—	1.4	−3.9	1.4	4.0	−1.6	−2.4	5.9	3.9	3.9	3.9	−0.7
Other advanced economies	0.3	−0.2	−0.3	−0.9	−0.8	−0.4	0.3	—	—	—	—	−0.1
Memorandum												
Major advanced economies	−0.3	−0.2	1.9	−0.1	−3.2	0.7	0.9	1.6	—	−2.0	−1.6	0.3
Newly industrialized Asian economies	0.2	−1.4	0.3	−2.4	−3.2	−0.6	—	−1.7	−2.0	−2.5	−1.5	−0.3
Memorandum												
Trade in goods												
Advanced economies												
Export volume	7.2	5.2	4.5	5.1	12.6	−1.3	2.3	3.4	8.5	5.1	6.6	6.1
Import volume	7.0	5.9	6.0	8.5	12.3	−1.5	2.9	4.7	9.4	5.9	6.3	5.5
Terms of trade	0.2	−0.1	1.2	—	−3.1	0.4	0.9	1.5	—	−1.7	−0.7	0.3

Table 23. Other Emerging Market and Developing Countries—by Region: Total Trade in Goods
(Annual percent change)

| | Ten-Year Averages | | 1998 | 1999 | 2000 | 2001 | 2002 | 2003 | 2004 | 2005 | 2006 | 2007 |
	1988–97	1998–2007										
Other emerging market and developing countries												
Value in U.S. dollars												
Exports	9.0	12.8	−7.0	7.8	25.4	−2.0	8.7	22.5	28.9	24.7	15.3	10.1
Imports	9.6	11.3	−4.7	−1.7	17.7	1.3	7.6	21.7	28.5	19.3	15.7	12.4
Volume												
Exports	7.6	8.9	5.7	2.6	14.2	2.8	7.4	11.4	14.4	10.8	10.1	10.0
Imports	7.4	8.9	1.3	−1.2	14.9	3.5	6.6	11.5	16.6	12.1	12.9	12.4
Unit value in U.S. dollars												
Exports	2.0	4.0	−12.1	6.2	10.3	−4.7	1.5	10.2	13.0	13.1	4.9	0.3
Imports	2.9	2.3	−6.1	0.3	2.5	−2.0	0.9	9.3	10.3	6.5	2.5	0.2
Terms of trade	−0.9	1.6	−6.3	5.8	7.6	−2.7	0.6	0.8	2.5	6.2	2.3	0.1
Memorandum												
Real GDP growth in developing country trading partners	3.5	3.3	1.8	3.5	4.9	1.6	2.3	3.0	4.5	3.8	3.8	3.5
Market prices of nonfuel commodities exported by other emerging market and developing countries	1.6	1.7	−16.1	−7.3	4.5	−7.0	2.2	8.4	20.8	12.3	12.1	−6.6
Regional groups												
Africa												
Value in U.S. dollars												
Exports	4.9	11.6	−13.9	7.7	28.0	−6.4	2.7	25.7	29.0	27.2	16.4	9.4
Imports	5.5	9.5	−2.4	0.5	3.5	1.5	9.7	22.5	26.4	17.0	11.3	8.3
Volume												
Exports	4.5	5.3	2.2	1.4	10.6	1.4	1.9	6.6	6.9	5.2	8.9	8.0
Imports	4.5	6.6	4.1	1.9	2.3	6.6	8.3	7.1	9.4	8.7	9.9	8.2
Unit value in U.S. dollars												
Exports	0.6	6.2	−15.8	6.8	15.6	−7.7	0.9	18.1	20.7	21.0	7.2	1.5
Imports	1.5	3.0	−6.1	−1.2	1.9	−4.7	1.4	16.2	15.6	7.8	1.5	—
Terms of trade	−0.9	3.1	−10.3	8.1	13.4	−3.2	−0.5	1.7	4.4	12.2	5.6	1.5
Sub-Sahara												
Value in U.S. dollars												
Exports	4.5	11.5	−14.2	6.5	25.5	−6.5	3.1	26.4	30.1	26.4	16.6	10.4
Imports	5.4	9.2	−4.9	−0.5	3.3	1.3	9.0	25.2	26.4	19.9	9.7	7.6
Volume												
Exports	4.7	5.4	1.5	−0.8	12.0	1.3	0.9	7.3	7.6	5.2	10.8	9.5
Imports	4.5	6.3	2.0	1.3	1.8	5.6	8.5	8.5	9.7	10.2	8.6	7.3
Unit value in U.S. dollars												
Exports	−0.1	5.8	−15.5	7.9	11.8	−7.7	2.3	18.2	21.0	20.4	5.4	1.1
Imports	1.3	3.2	−6.7	−1.7	2.5	−3.9	0.7	18.0	15.2	9.0	1.2	0.2
Terms of trade	−1.4	2.6	−9.4	9.8	9.1	−3.9	1.6	0.2	5.0	10.4	4.1	0.9

Table 23 *(continued)*

	Ten-Year Averages		1998	1999	2000	2001	2002	2003	2004	2005	2006	2007
	1988–97	1998–2007										
Central and eastern Europe												
Value in U.S. dollars												
Exports	7.0	13.5	6.4	−2.3	13.2	10.8	13.7	28.9	31.4	16.5	9.8	10.1
Imports	9.6	12.3	5.9	−4.2	16.0	−0.4	13.5	29.6	31.6	15.8	10.4	9.6
Volume												
Exports	5.5	9.9	9.7	0.2	14.8	10.9	8.1	11.8	16.4	9.4	9.0	9.5
Imports	9.5	8.7	11.9	−3.0	14.9	2.1	8.4	11.4	17.3	8.0	8.1	8.9
Unit value in U.S. dollars												
Exports	2.3	3.4	−3.1	−2.5	−1.5	0.6	5.3	15.7	13.2	6.6	0.7	0.5
Imports	2.4	3.5	−5.3	−1.1	1.0	−2.3	5.0	16.7	12.4	7.4	2.2	0.6
Terms of trade	−0.1	−0.1	2.4	−1.4	−2.5	2.9	0.3	−0.8	0.7	−0.7	−1.4	−0.1
Commonwealth of Independent States[1]												
Value in U.S. dollars												
Exports	...	13.0	−14.0	0.1	37.0	−0.9	6.3	26.8	36.7	28.9	16.0	5.7
Imports	...	8.9	−15.9	−25.8	14.6	15.0	9.6	26.5	29.5	23.6	15.6	11.0
Volume												
Exports	...	5.4	—	−1.4	9.9	3.8	7.0	10.8	13.4	1.4	4.4	6.0
Imports	...	6.8	−12.3	−21.5	14.2	17.9	8.4	14.8	16.0	16.5	12.1	10.9
Unit value in U.S. dollars												
Exports	...	7.2	−13.4	1.2	23.9	−4.6	−0.7	14.6	20.9	27.3	11.1	−0.5
Imports	...	2.0	−4.4	−5.5	0.4	−2.3	1.6	10.3	11.8	6.2	3.3	0.3
Terms of trade	...	5.1	−9.4	7.1	23.4	−2.4	−2.3	3.9	8.2	19.8	7.5	−0.8
Developing Asia												
Value in U.S. dollars												
Exports	15.7	14.2	−2.4	8.5	22.3	−1.7	14.0	23.3	28.0	22.5	17.1	15.3
Imports	14.2	14.0	−13.7	9.1	26.9	−0.6	12.8	26.8	31.5	20.1	19.2	16.0
Volume												
Exports	13.3	12.8	7.3	5.6	21.3	0.5	13.4	16.3	18.8	16.7	14.9	15.1
Imports	11.8	11.5	−5.3	5.6	20.7	1.5	12.8	18.7	19.2	12.6	15.5	16.6
Unit value in U.S. dollars												
Exports	2.3	1.6	−8.8	4.7	0.8	−2.2	0.6	6.1	8.0	5.1	2.1	0.3
Imports	2.5	2.6	−9.0	6.2	5.5	−1.9	—	6.9	10.4	6.5	3.3	−0.3
Terms of trade	−0.2	−1.0	0.2	−1.5	−4.4	−0.3	0.6	−0.8	−2.1	−1.3	−1.2	0.6
Excluding China and India												
Value in U.S. dollars												
Exports	14.9	8.0	−4.2	10.3	18.9	−9.3	6.1	11.7	18.3	14.1	9.8	7.6
Imports	15.4	7.0	−23.3	6.2	22.8	−6.8	6.2	13.4	23.5	17.6	10.8	8.6
Volume												
Exports	12.2	6.0	9.5	3.7	17.6	−6.7	5.7	4.6	7.4	7.3	6.5	6.1
Imports	12.6	4.6	−14.6	−0.5	20.4	−6.6	6.7	7.2	12.8	9.8	8.1	7.4
Unit value in U.S. dollars												
Exports	2.6	2.3	−12.3	9.9	1.1	−2.8	0.5	7.0	10.4	6.4	3.1	1.5
Imports	2.9	2.8	−10.3	12.1	2.1	−0.1	−0.4	5.8	9.8	7.0	2.5	1.2
Terms of trade	−0.3	−0.5	−2.2	−2.0	−1.0	−2.7	0.9	1.1	0.6	−0.6	0.6	0.3

Table 23 *(concluded)*

	Ten-Year Averages		1998	1999	2000	2001	2002	2003	2004	2005	2006	2007
	1988–97	1998–2007										
Middle East												
Value in U.S. dollars												
Exports	7.1	14.1	−25.9	31.6	45.3	−8.3	6.1	23.6	28.9	37.1	17.2	5.9
Imports	5.2	10.8	−0.9	−1.5	9.3	8.8	9.0	15.4	20.8	21.1	16.7	11.6
Volume												
Exports	8.1	5.4	1.5	0.6	7.3	3.4	3.6	9.8	9.1	7.7	7.3	4.5
Imports	3.3	9.4	3.0	1.5	12.1	11.0	7.7	5.1	13.8	17.1	14.9	9.4
Unit value in U.S. dollars												
Exports	−0.5	8.5	−26.4	30.7	35.2	−11.2	3.7	12.1	18.5	27.9	9.2	1.4
Imports	2.0	1.2	−3.7	−2.9	−2.3	−2.0	1.1	9.9	6.3	3.6	1.2	1.3
Terms of trade	−2.5	7.2	−23.6	34.5	38.4	−9.3	2.6	2.0	11.5	23.4	7.9	0.1
Western Hemisphere												
Value in U.S. dollars												
Exports	10.6	8.6	−3.9	4.0	19.6	−3.7	0.5	11.3	24.4	22.1	12.1	4.2
Imports	13.9	6.6	4.6	−6.9	14.7	−1.4	−8.6	4.3	22.9	19.3	13.9	8.3
Volume												
Exports	8.6	5.4	7.7	2.1	7.8	2.1	0.3	3.4	10.9	8.4	5.9	6.1
Imports	11.2	5.3	8.8	−4.4	12.4	−0.3	−7.6	0.5	15.0	12.0	11.9	7.9
Unit value in U.S. dollars												
Exports	3.2	3.2	−10.9	3.3	11.0	−5.7	0.4	7.7	12.0	12.6	6.0	−1.7
Imports	3.6	1.3	−3.8	−2.5	2.2	−1.1	−1.2	4.0	7.0	6.6	1.8	0.5
Terms of trade	−0.3	1.9	−7.4	6.0	8.6	−4.7	1.6	3.6	4.7	5.7	4.2	−2.2

[1]Mongolia, which is not a member of the Commonwealth of Independent States, is included in this group for reasons of geography and similarities in economic structure.

Table 24. Other Emerging Market and Developing Countries—by Source of Export Earnings: Total Trade in Goods
(Annual percent change)

	Ten-Year Averages		1998	1999	2000	2001	2002	2003	2004	2005	2006	2007
	1988–97	1998–2007										
Fuel												
Value in U.S. dollars												
Exports	5.5	14.1	−23.7	22.3	48.3	−8.9	4.6	24.6	32.1	38.2	17.6	6.4
Imports	3.8	10.7	−6.5	−10.1	10.5	13.1	10.4	17.7	23.6	24.5	17.6	11.4
Volume												
Exports	4.4	5.0	1.6	−1.8	8.4	1.7	3.1	9.1	9.9	6.0	6.6	5.3
Imports	1.3	9.0	−2.4	−8.2	13.5	15.3	8.9	6.4	14.4	19.4	16.2	10.3
Unit value in U.S. dollars												
Exports	1.6	9.0	−24.6	25.2	36.4	−10.5	2.3	13.9	20.5	30.8	10.5	1.0
Imports	3.1	1.5	−4.3	−2.3	−2.5	−2.0	1.6	10.9	8.3	4.5	1.2	0.7
Terms of trade	−1.5	7.4	−21.2	28.1	39.8	−8.7	0.6	2.7	11.3	25.2	9.2	0.3
Nonfuel												
Value in U.S. dollars												
Exports	10.6	12.4	−1.3	4.0	18.3	0.7	10.2	21.8	27.8	19.9	14.3	11.7
Imports	11.5	11.4	−4.3	0.1	19.1	−0.8	7.0	22.5	29.5	18.3	15.3	12.6
Volume												
Exports	8.9	10.2	7.1	3.8	16.0	3.1	8.9	12.1	16.0	12.5	11.6	12.0
Imports	9.5	8.9	2.2	0.3	15.2	1.4	6.1	12.6	17.1	10.7	12.3	12.8
Unit value in U.S. dollars												
Exports	2.3	2.2	−7.7	1.1	2.1	−2.4	1.2	8.9	10.5	6.8	2.6	−0.1
Imports	2.7	2.5	−6.5	0.9	3.5	−2.0	0.8	9.0	10.7	6.8	2.8	0.1
Terms of trade	−0.4	−0.3	−1.3	0.2	−1.4	−0.3	0.5	−0.1	−0.2	−0.1	−0.2	−0.2
Primary products												
Value in U.S. dollars												
Exports	5.3	7.4	−9.7	2.2	4.6	−5.0	2.6	18.4	37.3	16.5	14.9	0.1
Imports	5.8	5.9	−6.7	−12.1	5.1	−0.8	2.1	14.2	26.1	20.5	10.6	5.9
Volume												
Exports	6.0	4.4	1.8	5.8	2.2	3.8	0.8	4.3	14.2	1.8	2.4	7.3
Imports	4.8	5.1	2.9	−8.8	3.4	4.2	3.4	6.1	12.6	12.5	9.7	6.2
Unit value in U.S. dollars												
Exports	0.9	3.0	−11.1	−3.3	2.3	−8.3	1.9	13.5	19.7	14.8	12.1	−6.4
Imports	1.5	1.2	−9.3	−3.5	2.3	−4.7	−1.3	9.6	12.2	7.4	1.0	−0.2
Terms of trade	−0.6	1.8	−2.0	0.2	—	−3.8	3.3	3.5	6.6	6.8	11.0	−6.2

Table 25. Summary of Payments Balances on Current Account
(Billions of U.S. dollars)

	1998	1999	2000	2001	2002	2003	2004	2005	2006	2007
Advanced economies	**18.1**	**−116.5**	**−268.4**	**−219.8**	**−237.4**	**−217.2**	**−283.9**	**−510.7**	**−602.7**	**−615.7**
United States	−214.1	−300.1	−416.0	−389.5	−475.2	−519.7	−668.1	−805.0	−864.2	−899.4
Euro area[1]	50.3	25.6	−41.9	0.2	37.5	31.2	75.2	2.5	−23.8	−1.4
Japan	119.1	114.5	119.6	87.8	112.6	136.2	172.1	163.9	140.2	133.6
Other advanced economies[2]	62.8	43.5	69.9	81.6	87.7	135.1	136.9	127.8	145.1	151.4
Memorandum										
Newly industrialized Asian economies	64.6	57.5	38.8	47.8	55.3	80.0	88.8	85.5	88.6	93.9
Other emerging market and developing countries	**−113.1**	**−13.0**	**91.1**	**44.2**	**84.5**	**148.5**	**219.8**	**423.3**	**486.7**	**473.2**
Regional groups										
Africa	−19.4	−15.0	7.2	0.5	−7.5	−2.5	0.9	15.2	23.5	25.9
Central and eastern Europe	−19.3	−26.4	−32.4	−16.2	−24.0	−37.1	−59.2	−63.1	−72.2	−77.0
Commonwealth of Independent States[3]	−7.4	23.7	48.3	33.1	30.2	35.8	62.4	90.3	112.4	109.4
Developing Asia	49.3	48.4	46.1	40.6	72.2	86.3	94.7	155.4	159.5	171.9
Middle East	−25.7	12.9	70.0	39.8	29.5	59.0	103.4	196.0	240.9	235.6
Western Hemisphere	−90.6	−56.7	−48.1	−53.6	−16.0	7.1	17.7	29.6	22.7	7.5
Memorandum										
European Union	35.8	−21.6	−87.0	−32.5	11.3	12.4	26.9	−54.0	−91.2	−76.8
Analytical groups										
By source of export earnings										
Fuel	−36.4	37.0	148.8	84.3	63.8	109.2	188.8	347.4	423.7	423.8
Nonfuel	−76.7	−50.0	−57.7	−40.0	20.7	39.4	31.1	75.9	63.1	49.5
of which, primary products	−7.4	−2.5	−2.7	−3.7	−3.7	−3.1	0.6	−2.1	0.1	−2.7
By external financing source										
Net debtor countries	−129.0	−85.0	−76.4	−65.0	−32.7	−26.1	−57.4	−88.8	−103.3	−120.1
of which, official financing	−32.9	−17.7	−11.6	−6.9	9.2	9.6	−4.6	−11.5	−17.3	−21.9
Net debtor countries by debt-servicing experience										
Countries with arrears and/or rescheduling during 1999–2003	−35.2	−22.3	−1.7	−6.0	2.4	5.6	−2.2	−0.9	3.5	4.1
Total[1]	**−95.0**	**−129.5**	**−177.3**	**−175.6**	**−152.9**	**−68.6**	**−64.1**	**−87.5**	**−116.0**	**−142.5**
Memorandum										
In percent of total world current account transactions	−0.7	−0.9	−1.1	−1.1	−1.0	−0.4	−0.3	−0.3	−0.4	−0.5
In percent of world GDP	−0.3	−0.4	−0.6	−0.6	−0.5	−0.2	−0.2	−0.2	−0.2	−0.3

[1]Reflects errors, omissions, and asymmetries in balance of payments statistics on current account, as well as the exclusion of data for international organizations and a limited number of countries. Calculated as the sum of the balance of individual euro area countries. See "Classification of Countries" in the introduction to this Statistical Appendix.
[2]In this table, "other advanced economies" means advanced economies excluding the United States, euro area countries, and Japan.
[3]Mongolia, which is not a member of the Commonwealth of Independent States, is included in this group for reasons of geography and similarities in economic structure.

Table 26. Advanced Economies: Balance of Payments on Current Account

	1998	1999	2000	2001	2002	2003	2004	2005	2006	2007
					Billions of U.S. dollars					
Advanced economies	**18.1**	**−116.5**	**−268.4**	**−219.8**	**−237.4**	**−217.2**	**−283.9**	**−510.7**	**−602.7**	**−615.7**
United States	−214.1	−300.1	−416.0	−389.5	−475.2	−519.7	−668.1	−805.0	−864.2	−899.4
Euro area[1]	50.3	25.6	−41.9	0.2	37.5	31.2	75.2	2.5	−23.8	−1.4
Germany	−17.5	−26.8	−32.5	0.4	40.8	45.5	101.7	114.8	98.3	122.7
France	38.6	42.0	18.0	21.5	14.5	7.9	−8.4	−27.6	−40.6	−44.8
Italy	20.0	8.1	−5.8	−0.7	−9.4	−19.4	−15.1	−26.6	−18.5	−11.9
Spain	−7.0	−18.1	−23.2	−23.6	−22.5	−31.6	−55.3	−85.9	−93.7	−104.3
Netherlands	13.0	15.6	7.2	9.8	10.9	29.4	54.2	40.0	43.1	51.4
Belgium	13.3	20.1	9.4	7.9	11.7	12.7	11.8	16.6	17.9	18.6
Austria	−5.2	−6.8	−4.9	−3.7	0.7	−0.5	0.7	2.0	2.9	3.0
Finland	7.3	7.8	9.2	8.6	8.9	7.0	9.4	4.7	5.4	5.4
Greece	−5.9	−8.6	−9.9	−9.5	−9.7	−12.5	−13.0	−17.5	−17.9	−19.1
Portugal	−8.5	−10.4	−11.7	−11.7	−9.9	−9.2	−13.0	−16.8	−17.2	−17.7
Ireland	0.8	0.3	−0.3	−0.6	−1.2	—	−1.5	−3.8	−6.0	−7.4
Luxembourg	1.6	2.3	2.7	1.8	2.5	1.9	3.5	2.7	2.6	2.7
Japan	119.1	114.5	119.6	87.8	112.6	136.2	172.1	163.9	140.2	133.6
United Kingdom	−6.6	−39.3	−37.0	−31.9	−24.8	−26.1	−43.2	−58.1	−61.3	−66.2
Canada	−7.7	1.7	19.7	16.2	13.5	13.2	22.2	25.0	39.3	38.3
Korea	40.4	24.5	12.3	8.0	5.4	11.9	28.2	16.6	16.4	16.2
Australia	−18.4	−22.4	−15.2	−7.8	−16.2	−29.5	−40.2	−42.2	−40.8	−41.8
Taiwan Province of China	3.4	8.4	8.9	18.2	25.6	29.3	18.5	16.4	18.8	20.7
Sweden	9.7	10.6	9.9	9.8	12.5	22.4	24.0	21.8	18.2	16.7
Switzerland	26.1	29.4	30.7	20.0	23.0	43.0	52.4	50.7	49.4	48.0
Hong Kong SAR	2.5	10.3	7.0	9.8	12.4	16.5	15.9	19.0	18.9	20.0
Denmark	−1.4	3.3	2.3	5.1	4.1	6.7	5.1	6.1	6.4	7.3
Norway	0.1	8.5	26.1	26.2	24.4	28.9	34.6	49.7	56.9	63.2
Israel	−1.1	−1.6	−1.2	−1.6	−1.3	0.8	1.8	2.4	1.2	2.7
Singapore	18.3	14.4	10.7	11.8	11.9	22.3	26.3	33.6	34.5	37.0
New Zealand	−2.1	−3.5	−2.7	−1.4	−2.4	−3.4	−6.5	−9.6	−9.5	−8.4
Cyprus	0.3	−0.2	−0.5	−0.3	−0.5	−0.3	−0.9	−0.8	−1.0	−0.8
Iceland	−0.6	−0.6	−0.9	−0.4	0.1	−0.5	−1.2	−2.6	−2.3	−1.5
Memorandum										
Major advanced economies	−68.3	−199.7	−334.0	−296.1	−328.0	−362.3	−438.8	−613.6	−706.9	−727.7
Euro area[2]	23.0	−34.6	−90.2	−17.7	54.3	38.2	56.8	−34.6	−4.0	19.3
Newly industrialized Asian economies	64.6	57.5	38.8	47.8	55.3	80.0	88.8	85.5	88.6	93.9

Table 26 *(concluded)*

	1998	1999	2000	2001	2002	2003	2004	2005	2006	2007
					Percent of GDP					
Advanced economies	**0.1**	**−0.5**	**−1.1**	**−0.9**	**−0.9**	**−0.7**	**−0.9**	**−1.5**	**−1.7**	**−1.7**
United States	−2.4	−3.2	−4.2	−3.8	−4.5	−4.7	−5.7	−6.4	−6.5	−6.5
Euro area[1]	0.7	0.4	−0.7	—	0.5	0.4	0.8	—	−0.2	—
Germany	−0.8	−1.2	−1.7	—	2.0	1.9	3.7	4.1	3.6	4.3
France	2.6	2.9	1.3	1.6	1.0	0.4	−0.4	−1.3	−1.9	−2.1
Italy	1.7	0.7	−0.5	−0.1	−0.8	−1.3	−0.9	−1.5	−1.1	−0.7
Spain	−1.2	−2.9	−4.0	−3.9	−3.3	−3.6	−5.3	−7.6	−8.1	−8.5
Netherlands	3.3	3.9	2.0	2.4	2.5	5.5	8.9	6.4	6.9	7.9
Belgium	5.2	7.9	4.0	3.4	4.6	4.1	3.3	4.5	4.8	4.8
Austria	−2.4	−3.2	−2.5	−1.9	0.3	−0.2	0.2	0.7	0.9	0.9
Finland	5.6	6.0	7.6	7.0	6.7	4.3	5.0	2.4	2.8	2.7
Greece	−4.9	−6.9	−8.7	−8.0	−7.2	−7.2	−6.3	−7.9	−7.9	−7.9
Portugal	−7.2	−8.6	−10.4	−10.1	−7.8	−5.9	−7.3	−9.2	−9.5	−9.4
Ireland	0.9	0.3	−0.4	−0.6	−1.0	—	−0.8	−1.9	−2.9	−3.3
Luxembourg	8.7	11.4	13.7	9.0	11.6	6.8	11.1	7.9	7.3	7.3
Japan	3.1	2.6	2.6	2.1	2.9	3.2	3.8	3.6	3.2	2.9
United Kingdom	−0.5	−2.7	−2.6	−2.2	−1.6	−1.4	−2.0	−2.6	−2.7	−2.8
Canada	−1.2	0.3	2.7	2.3	1.8	1.5	2.2	2.2	3.1	2.9
Korea	11.7	5.5	2.4	1.7	1.0	2.0	4.1	2.1	1.8	1.7
Australia	−4.9	−5.6	−3.9	−2.1	−3.9	−5.6	−6.3	−6.0	−5.6	−5.5
Taiwan Province of China	1.2	2.8	2.8	6.2	8.7	9.8	5.7	4.7	5.4	5.5
Sweden	3.9	4.2	4.1	4.4	5.1	7.3	6.8	6.1	5.1	4.5
Switzerland	9.7	11.1	12.4	8.0	8.3	13.3	14.6	13.8	13.7	13.1
Hong Kong SAR	1.5	6.3	4.1	5.9	7.6	10.4	9.6	10.7	10.1	10.1
Denmark	−0.8	1.9	1.4	3.2	2.3	3.1	2.1	2.4	2.4	2.6
Norway	—	5.4	15.6	15.4	12.8	13.0	13.6	16.8	18.6	19.9
Israel	−1.1	−1.5	−1.1	−1.4	−1.2	0.7	1.6	1.9	1.0	2.1
Singapore	22.2	17.4	11.6	13.8	13.4	24.1	24.5	28.5	26.7	26.3
New Zealand	−3.9	−6.2	−5.2	−2.8	−4.0	−4.3	−6.6	−8.8	−8.9	−7.6
Cyprus	3.1	−1.8	−5.3	−3.3	−4.5	−2.5	−5.7	−5.1	−5.6	−4.6
Iceland	−6.9	−6.9	−10.3	−4.4	1.5	−5.0	−9.4	−16.6	−13.8	−8.6
Memorandum										
Major advanced economies	−0.4	−1.0	−1.6	−1.4	−1.5	−1.5	−1.7	−2.3	−2.5	−2.5
Euro area[2]	0.3	−0.5	−1.5	−0.3	0.8	0.5	0.6	−0.3	—	0.2
Newly industrialized Asian economies	7.4	5.8	3.5	4.7	5.1	6.9	7.0	6.0	5.7	5.6

[1]Calculated as the sum of the balances of individual euro area countries.
[2]Corrected for reporting discrepancies in intra-area transactions.

Table 27. Advanced Economies: Current Account Transactions
(Billions of U.S. dollars)

	1998	1999	2000	2001	2002	2003	2004	2005	2006	2007
Exports	4,187.1	4,296.2	4,679.8	4,448.9	4,584.3	5,267.2	6,234.8	6,783.8	7,198.7	7,690.1
Imports	4,130.6	4,377.3	4,913.4	4,645.1	4,771.7	5,479.6	6,542.8	7,299.6	7,784.3	8,246.6
Trade balance	56.6	−81.1	−233.6	−196.1	−187.4	−212.4	−308.0	−515.9	−585.6	−556.5
Services, credits	1,137.3	1,200.5	1,253.8	1,249.7	1,327.6	1,523.2	1,791.9	1,929.5	2,008.5	2,143.9
Services, debits	1,060.1	1,121.1	1,179.5	1,188.2	1,250.1	1,427.9	1,667.1	1,776.6	1,860.0	1,983.9
Balance on services	77.2	79.3	74.3	61.5	77.5	95.4	124.8	152.8	148.6	160.0
Balance on goods and services	133.7	−1.7	−159.3	−134.6	−109.9	−117.0	−183.2	−363.0	−437.1	−396.5
Income, net	15.1	15.9	30.1	43.3	18.6	78.7	107.0	74.2	37.1	−7.1
Current transfers, net	−130.8	−130.7	−139.2	−128.5	−146.1	−178.8	−207.6	−221.9	−202.8	−212.2
Current account balance	**18.1**	**−116.5**	**−268.4**	**−219.8**	**−237.4**	**−217.2**	**−283.9**	**−510.7**	**−602.7**	**−615.7**
Balance on goods and services										
Advanced economies	**133.7**	**−1.7**	**−159.3**	**−134.6**	**−109.9**	**−117.0**	**−183.2**	**−363.0**	**−437.1**	**−396.5**
United States	−165.0	−263.4	−378.3	−362.7	−421.2	−494.8	−617.6	−723.6	−786.2	−771.3
Euro area[1]	139.8	99.2	35.4	89.2	155.4	175.7	203.3	147.7	125.9	154.1
Germany	24.4	11.7	1.0	34.2	83.7	95.4	136.1	140.1	130.9	156.1
France	42.3	36.3	16.5	21.4	24.7	19.1	4.9	−18.1	−30.2	−33.9
Italy	39.8	24.5	10.5	15.5	10.7	8.9	12.6	0.4	6.3	11.6
Spain	−1.7	−11.5	−17.7	−14.0	−13.1	−18.7	−38.2	−60.7	−70.1	−79.7
Japan	73.2	69.2	69.0	26.5	51.7	72.5	94.2	69.0	44.8	33.2
United Kingdom	−13.2	−24.9	−29.2	−38.8	−47.4	−50.6	−71.5	−85.4	−83.8	−88.4
Canada	11.8	23.8	41.3	40.6	31.6	33.1	41.1	44.0	60.6	58.8
Other advanced economies	87.1	94.4	102.5	110.7	119.9	147.2	167.3	185.3	201.6	217.1
Memorandum										
Major advanced economies	13.3	−122.9	−269.1	−263.4	−266.2	−316.5	−400.1	−573.6	−657.6	−633.9
Newly industrialized Asian economies	63.6	57.9	41.3	45.7	56.2	77.7	84.1	87.7	90.3	96.5
Income, net										
Advanced economies	**15.1**	**15.9**	**30.1**	**43.3**	**18.6**	**78.7**	**107.0**	**74.2**	**37.1**	**−7.1**
United States	4.3	13.9	21.1	25.2	10.0	46.3	30.4	1.6	−18.5	−65.4
Euro area[1]	−39.1	−26.0	−30.4	−40.1	−67.7	−76.8	−49.9	−60.1	−62.1	−64.2
Germany	−11.8	−12.2	−7.8	−9.8	−17.0	−18.0	0.8	10.8	3.2	3.6
France	8.7	19.0	15.5	15.0	4.0	8.0	8.5	10.5	10.5	10.9
Italy	−12.3	−11.1	−12.0	−10.3	−14.6	−20.2	−18.2	−17.0	−14.9	−13.2
Spain	−8.6	−9.6	−6.8	−11.2	−11.6	−13.1	−17.0	−22.6	−19.7	−20.8
Japan	54.7	57.4	60.4	69.2	65.8	71.2	85.7	103.3	104.2	109.2
United Kingdom	20.4	−2.4	6.9	16.4	35.5	40.9	48.4	49.9	45.2	46.3
Canada	−20.0	−22.6	−22.3	−25.4	−18.7	−20.0	−19.2	−18.8	−21.2	−20.4
Other advanced economies	−5.1	−4.4	−5.6	−2.0	−6.3	17.1	11.5	−1.6	−10.4	−12.6
Memorandum										
Major advanced economies	43.9	42.0	61.7	80.2	65.0	108.1	136.4	140.3	108.5	70.9
Newly industrialized Asian economies	2.0	2.6	2.4	8.2	6.3	10.9	14.1	8.7	10.4	10.0

[1]Calculated as the sum of the individual euro area countries.

Table 28. Other Emerging Market and Developing Countries: Payments Balances on Current Account

	1998	1999	2000	2001	2002	2003	2004	2005	2006	2007
					Billions of U.S. dollars					
Other emerging market and developing countries	**−113.1**	**−13.0**	**91.1**	**44.2**	**84.5**	**148.5**	**219.8**	**423.3**	**486.7**	**473.2**
Regional groups										
Africa	−19.4	−15.0	7.2	0.5	−7.5	−2.5	0.9	15.2	23.5	25.9
Sub-Sahara	−17.7	−14.4	−0.7	−7.4	−12.6	−12.2	−10.8	−6.6	2.2	5.9
Excluding Nigeria and South Africa	−12.4	−10.6	−5.8	−9.7	−7.9	−8.4	−6.7	−9.0	−4.4	−4.0
Central and eastern Europe	−19.3	−26.4	−32.4	−16.2	−24.0	−37.1	−59.2	−63.1	−72.2	−77.0
Commonwealth of Independent States[1]	−7.4	23.7	48.3	33.1	30.2	35.8	62.4	90.3	112.4	109.4
Russia	0.2	24.6	46.8	33.9	29.1	35.4	58.6	86.6	106.0	99.0
Excluding Russia	−7.6	−0.9	1.4	−0.8	1.1	0.4	3.8	3.7	6.4	10.4
Developing Asia	49.3	48.4	46.1	40.6	72.2	86.3	94.7	155.4	159.5	171.9
China	31.6	15.7	20.5	17.4	35.4	45.9	68.7	158.6	173.3	189.6
India	−6.9	−3.2	−4.6	1.4	7.1	8.8	1.4	−19.0	−26.1	−28.7
Excluding China and India	24.6	36.0	30.2	21.8	29.7	31.6	24.6	15.8	12.3	11.0
Middle East	−25.7	12.9	70.0	39.8	29.5	59.0	103.4	196.0	240.9	235.6
Western Hemisphere	−90.6	−56.7	−48.1	−53.6	−16.0	7.1	17.7	29.6	22.7	7.5
Brazil	−33.4	−25.3	−24.2	−23.2	−7.6	4.2	11.7	14.2	10.5	2.6
Mexico	−16.0	−13.9	−18.6	−17.6	−13.5	−8.6	−7.2	−5.7	−5.5	−6.8
Analytical groups										
By source of export earnings										
Fuel	−36.4	37.0	148.8	84.3	63.8	109.2	188.8	347.4	423.7	423.8
Nonfuel	−76.7	−50.0	−57.7	−40.0	20.7	39.4	31.1	75.9	63.1	49.5
of which, primary products	−7.4	−2.5	−2.7	−3.7	−3.7	−3.1	0.6	−2.1	0.1	−2.7
By external financing source										
Net debtor countries	−129.0	−85.0	−76.4	−65.0	−32.7	−26.1	−57.4	−88.8	−103.3	−120.1
of which, official financing	−32.9	−17.7	−11.6	−6.9	9.2	9.6	−4.6	−11.5	−17.3	−21.9
Net debtor countries by debt-servicing experience										
Countries with arrears and/or rescheduling during 1999–2003	−35.2	−22.3	−1.7	−6.0	2.4	5.6	−2.2	−0.9	3.5	4.1
Other groups										
Heavily indebted poor countries	−7.8	−9.2	−7.1	−7.2	−8.7	−7.3	−7.6	−8.2	−8.6	−8.9
Middle East and north Africa	−29.2	10.6	75.8	45.5	33.1	67.1	113.1	214.1	259.8	253.3

Table 28 *(concluded)*

	Ten-Year Averages		1998	1999	2000	2001	2002	2003	2004	2005	2006	2007
	1988–97	1998–2007										
	Percent of exports of goods and services											
Other emerging market and developing countries	**−7.5**	**4.7**	**−7.7**	**−0.8**	**4.8**	**2.4**	**4.2**	**6.0**	**6.9**	**10.8**	**10.8**	**9.5**
Regional groups												
Africa	−8.1	−1.1	−16.2	−11.7	4.6	0.3	−4.9	−1.3	0.3	4.9	6.6	6.6
Sub-Sahara	−9.4	−6.8	−19.6	−15.0	−0.6	−6.7	−11.2	−8.5	−5.9	−2.9	0.8	2.0
Excluding Nigeria and South Africa	−20.9	−12.7	−27.6	−22.0	−10.8	−18.2	−13.8	−12.3	−7.6	−8.4	−3.3	−2.7
Central and eastern Europe	−2.4	−10.6	−8.5	−12.4	−13.3	−6.2	−8.3	−10.1	−12.5	−11.4	−11.9	−11.6
Commonwealth of Independent States[1]	...	18.8	−5.8	19.2	29.3	20.0	16.9	16.0	20.6	23.4	25.3	23.3
Russia	...	27.4	0.3	29.1	40.9	29.9	24.1	23.3	28.8	32.3	34.3	30.9
Excluding Russia	...	0.1	−19.0	−2.3	2.8	−1.6	1.9	0.6	3.8	3.2	4.7	6.9
Developing Asia	−7.3	8.3	9.2	8.4	6.6	5.9	9.2	9.1	7.6	10.2	8.8	8.2
China	4.6	11.6	15.2	7.1	7.3	5.8	9.7	9.5	10.5	18.8	16.9	15.4
India	−19.4	−4.3	−15.1	−6.3	−7.7	2.3	10.0	10.3	1.2	−12.0	−13.2	−12.2
Excluding China and India	−11.3	6.4	8.6	11.7	8.5	6.6	8.5	8.3	5.3	3.0	2.1	1.8
Middle East	−7.5	18.4	−16.2	6.4	24.9	15.2	10.6	17.3	23.8	33.6	35.5	32.8
Western Hemisphere	−14.5	−6.8	−30.9	−18.7	−13.4	−15.5	−4.6	1.8	3.8	5.2	3.6	1.1
Brazil	−12.2	−15.0	−56.6	−45.9	−37.5	−34.4	−10.9	5.0	10.7	10.6	7.1	1.7
Mexico	−26.7	−9.9	−18.5	−14.3	−15.8	−15.5	−11.8	−7.3	−5.4	−3.7	−3.2	−3.6
Analytical groups												
By source of export earnings												
Fuel	−2.8	20.5	−12.9	11.0	30.7	18.8	13.5	18.6	24.6	33.2	34.5	32.5
Nonfuel	−9.1	−0.7	−6.5	−4.1	−4.1	−2.8	1.3	2.1	1.3	2.6	1.9	1.3
of which, primary products	−12.2	−5.1	−15.8	−5.3	−5.5	−7.7	−7.5	−5.4	0.8	−2.4	0.1	−2.6
By external financing source												
Net debtor countries	−12.1	−6.0	−14.4	−9.3	−7.2	−6.1	−2.9	−2.0	−3.5	−4.5	−4.7	−5.0
of which, official financing	−16.4	−4.1	−17.1	−9.3	−5.3	−3.3	4.2	4.0	−1.5	−3.3	−4.5	−5.3
Net debtor countries by debt-servicing experience												
Countries with arrears and/or rescheduling during 1999–2003	−16.4	−2.8	−17.9	−10.8	−0.7	−2.5	0.9	1.9	−0.6	−0.2	0.7	0.7
Other groups												
Heavily indebted poor countries	−29.6	−25.1	−32.7	−39.5	−28.1	−27.4	−32.0	−22.9	−18.7	−17.4	−16.3	−16.1
Middle East and north Africa	−7.9	17.3	−15.4	4.5	23.3	14.9	10.3	16.9	22.5	32.0	33.3	30.5
Memorandum												
Median												
Other emerging market and developing countries	−12.6	−10.1	−15.7	−10.8	−9.8	−10.3	−9.5	−7.9	−7.9	−10.1	−9.4	−9.5

[1]Mongolia, which is not a member of the Commonwealth of Independent States, is included in this group for reasons of geography and similarities in economic structure.

Table 29. Other Emerging Market and Developing Countries—by Region: Current Account Transactions
(Billions of U.S. dollars)

	1998	1999	2000	2001	2002	2003	2004	2005	2006	2007
Other emerging market and developing countries										
Exports	1,194.1	1,287.4	1,614.8	1,581.8	1,720.1	2,107.7	2,717.0	3,387.5	3,904.5	4,299.8
Imports	1,213.2	1,193.1	1,404.6	1,423.0	1,530.6	1,862.7	2,394.0	2,855.3	3,304.0	3,713.8
Trade balance	−19.1	94.3	210.3	158.8	189.5	245.1	323.0	532.1	600.6	586.0
Services, net	−46.5	−48.2	−59.7	−64.3	−63.9	−69.3	−71.5	−87.0	−101.3	−100.7
Balance on goods and services	−65.6	46.1	150.6	94.5	125.6	175.7	251.5	445.1	499.3	485.2
Income, net	−97.0	−113.0	−118.3	−117.9	−125.0	−145.8	−170.6	−185.4	−186.0	−183.2
Current transfers, net	49.6	53.9	58.8	67.6	83.9	118.7	138.9	163.5	173.4	171.2
Current account balance	**−113.1**	**−13.0**	**91.1**	**44.2**	**84.5**	**148.5**	**219.8**	**423.3**	**486.7**	**473.2**
Memorandum										
Exports of goods and services	1,464.3	1,548.9	1,901.0	1,873.6	2,032.2	2,463.1	3,169.4	3,927.4	4,523.5	4,995.5
Interest payments	134.6	134.7	130.4	126.8	119.5	132.8	141.3	166.8	183.3	196.0
Oil trade balance	102.5	153.2	240.6	201.7	208.3	257.9	327.3	455.4	515.1	518.5
Regional groups										
Africa										
Exports	98.1	105.7	135.3	126.7	130.1	163.5	210.9	268.3	312.4	341.8
Imports	100.9	101.4	105.0	106.6	116.9	143.2	181.1	211.9	235.8	255.3
Trade balance	−2.8	4.3	30.3	20.1	13.2	20.3	29.8	56.4	76.7	86.5
Services, net	−11.6	−11.1	−11.3	−11.8	−12.2	−13.2	−16.8	−24.9	−31.6	−37.1
Balance on goods and services	−14.4	−6.8	19.0	8.3	1.1	7.1	13.0	31.6	45.1	49.4
Income, net	−16.2	−18.2	−23.3	−20.8	−22.7	−27.9	−34.8	−41.5	−47.1	−49.7
Current transfers, net	11.1	10.0	11.5	13.0	14.1	18.3	22.7	25.1	25.5	26.1
Current account balance	**−19.4**	**−15.0**	**7.2**	**0.5**	**−7.5**	**−2.5**	**0.9**	**15.2**	**23.5**	**25.9**
Memorandum										
Exports of goods and services	119.6	128.0	157.5	149.9	154.4	194.2	247.7	309.3	357.6	389.3
Interest payments	14.8	14.3	13.6	11.9	10.7	11.4	11.8	13.0	12.8	13.2
Oil trade balance	18.4	25.7	45.8	38.7	38.1	53.8	74.2	110.7	139.0	155.8
Central and eastern Europe										
Exports	161.5	157.7	178.5	197.9	225.0	290.1	381.1	443.9	487.4	536.6
Imports	208.8	200.1	232.2	231.3	262.6	340.3	447.8	518.3	572.3	627.1
Trade balance	−47.4	−42.4	−53.7	−33.5	−37.6	−50.3	−66.7	−74.4	−84.9	−90.6
Services, net	21.6	11.3	16.6	14.1	12.4	15.0	19.2	22.6	24.5	25.9
Balance on goods and services	−25.8	−31.1	−37.1	−19.4	−25.2	−35.2	−47.4	−51.9	−60.4	−64.7
Income, net	−6.4	−6.6	−7.1	−8.0	−11.0	−15.4	−28.0	−31.4	−36.1	−38.3
Current transfers, net	12.9	11.3	11.8	11.2	12.3	13.5	16.3	20.2	24.3	26.0
Current account balance	**−19.3**	**−26.4**	**−32.4**	**−16.2**	**−24.0**	**−37.1**	**−59.2**	**−63.1**	**−72.2**	**−77.0**
Memorandum										
Exports of goods and services	227.6	213.8	242.7	259.9	288.5	367.8	474.5	553.1	605.9	664.9
Interest payments	11.5	11.8	12.7	13.8	13.8	16.6	25.9	28.6	34.7	37.4
Oil trade balance	−12.9	−14.4	−22.6	−21.0	−21.6	−26.7	−33.4	−46.4	−53.5	−55.9

Table 29 *(concluded)*

	1998	1999	2000	2001	2002	2003	2004	2005	2006	2007
Commonwealth of Independent States[1]										
Exports	107.5	107.5	147.3	145.9	155.1	196.7	268.7	346.5	401.8	424.8
Imports	99.4	73.8	84.6	97.3	106.7	135.0	174.8	216.0	249.6	276.9
Trade balance	8.0	33.7	62.7	48.6	48.4	61.7	94.0	130.5	152.2	147.8
Services, net	−3.8	−3.9	−7.0	−10.8	−11.8	−13.1	−17.6	−22.2	−23.3	−24.7
Balance on goods and services	4.2	29.8	55.7	37.8	36.7	48.6	76.3	108.4	128.9	123.1
Income, net	−13.1	−8.5	−9.8	−6.9	−9.1	−16.1	−17.5	−22.6	−21.7	−20.0
Current transfers, net	1.4	2.4	2.4	2.1	2.6	3.4	3.6	4.5	5.2	6.3
Current account balance	**−7.4**	**23.7**	**48.3**	**33.1**	**30.2**	**35.8**	**62.4**	**90.3**	**112.4**	**109.4**
Memorandum										
Exports of goods and services	127.2	123.6	164.7	165.9	178.6	224.0	302.3	385.0	444.6	470.6
Interest payments	17.4	13.1	13.3	12.4	13.4	25.1	23.8	35.5	35.3	38.5
Oil trade balance	13.6	19.7	38.5	36.8	43.3	57.4	84.9	129.5	157.7	174.3
Developing Asia										
Exports	455.3	493.8	604.1	593.6	676.7	834.1	1,067.5	1,307.6	1,531.1	1,764.8
Imports	388.2	423.3	537.2	533.8	602.3	764.0	1,004.3	1,205.7	1,437.2	1,667.3
Trade balance	67.1	70.5	66.9	59.8	74.4	70.1	63.2	101.9	93.9	97.5
Services, net	−12.3	−8.1	−14.1	−13.8	−10.1	−15.6	−8.9	−4.0	5.6	23.0
Balance on goods and services	54.8	62.4	52.8	46.0	64.3	54.5	54.3	97.9	99.5	120.5
Income, net	−27.3	−39.6	−36.6	−39.3	−34.7	−32.6	−29.6	−24.1	−23.6	−23.6
Current transfers, net	21.8	25.7	29.9	33.9	42.6	64.4	70.0	81.6	83.5	75.0
Current account balance	**49.3**	**48.4**	**46.1**	**40.6**	**72.2**	**86.3**	**94.7**	**155.4**	**159.5**	**171.9**
Memorandum										
Exports of goods and services	538.2	578.9	696.9	689.9	786.2	953.2	1,240.3	1,528.8	1,802.5	2,088.1
Interest payments	33.2	33.2	25.1	25.6	23.7	23.7	23.7	31.2	36.8	41.3
Oil trade balance	−13.7	−23.7	−49.5	−43.1	−49.8	−68.5	−114.4	−190.4	−255.1	−304.2
Middle East										
Exports	130.8	172.1	250.0	229.3	243.2	300.7	387.4	531.2	622.6	659.5
Imports	132.8	130.7	142.9	155.4	169.3	195.5	236.1	285.9	333.6	372.2
Trade balance	−2.0	41.4	107.1	73.9	73.9	105.2	151.3	245.2	289.0	287.3
Services, net	−25.0	−24.6	−31.4	−27.5	−32.7	−33.9	−38.6	−44.1	−55.4	−63.8
Balance on goods and services	−27.0	16.9	75.7	46.4	41.2	71.2	112.7	201.1	233.6	223.5
Income, net	17.0	12.3	13.1	12.5	6.3	5.3	7.7	12.8	25.6	31.6
Current transfers, net	−15.7	−16.3	−18.9	−19.0	−17.9	−17.6	−16.9	−17.9	−18.3	−19.5
Current account balance	**−25.7**	**12.9**	**70.0**	**39.8**	**29.5**	**59.0**	**103.4**	**196.0**	**240.9**	**235.6**
Memorandum										
Exports of goods and services	158.7	201.8	281.1	262.3	278.5	341.6	435.1	583.1	678.3	719.2
Interest payments	6.7	6.4	6.9	6.6	6.9	5.3	5.4	6.3	7.5	8.1
Oil trade balance	81.1	121.1	188.8	160.5	165.9	205.8	268.2	381.1	444.1	464.9
Western Hemisphere										
Exports	241.0	250.6	299.5	288.4	289.9	322.7	401.3	490.0	549.2	572.3
Imports	283.2	263.8	302.7	298.5	272.8	284.7	349.9	417.6	475.5	514.9
Trade balance	−42.2	−13.2	−3.1	−10.1	17.1	38.0	51.4	72.4	73.7	57.4
Services, net	−15.4	−11.8	−12.5	−14.5	−9.5	−8.5	−8.8	−14.3	−21.0	−24.0
Balance on goods and services	−57.5	−25.0	−15.6	−24.7	7.6	29.5	42.6	58.1	52.7	33.4
Income, net	−51.2	−52.3	−54.6	−55.4	−53.8	−59.1	−68.2	−78.5	−83.1	−83.2
Current transfers, net	18.1	20.6	22.1	26.4	30.3	36.7	43.3	50.0	53.1	57.3
Current account balance	**−90.6**	**−56.7**	**−48.1**	**−53.6**	**−16.0**	**7.1**	**17.7**	**29.6**	**22.7**	**7.5**
Memorandum										
Exports of goods and services	293.0	302.8	358.1	345.6	346.0	382.2	469.4	568.1	634.5	663.4
Interest payments	51.1	56.0	58.7	56.5	51.0	50.7	50.8	52.4	56.2	57.4
Oil trade balance	16.1	24.8	39.6	29.7	32.4	36.1	47.9	70.8	83.0	83.7

[1]Mongolia, which is not a member of the Commonwealth of Independent States, is included in this group for reasons of geography and similarities in economic structure.

Table 30. Other Emerging Market and Developing Countries—by Analytical Criteria: Current Account Transactions
(Billions of U.S. dollars)

	1998	1999	2000	2001	2002	2003	2004	2005	2006	2007
By source of export earnings										
Fuel										
Exports	251.1	307.1	455.3	414.7	434.0	540.9	714.4	986.9	1,160.9	1,235.3
Imports	214.2	192.7	212.9	240.8	265.8	312.9	386.8	481.5	566.3	630.6
Trade balance	36.9	114.4	242.4	174.0	168.2	228.0	327.5	505.4	594.6	604.7
Services, net	−45.7	−47.9	−57.5	−57.2	−62.7	−68.7	−84.1	−101.4	−120.8	−137.0
Balance on goods and services	−8.8	66.5	184.9	116.8	105.5	159.3	243.4	404.0	473.9	467.7
Income, net	−8.1	−9.4	−12.9	−8.3	−19.0	−29.3	−35.3	−37.2	−29.6	−22.7
Current transfers, net	−19.5	−20.1	−23.2	−24.1	−22.7	−20.8	−19.3	−19.3	−20.6	−21.2
Current account balance	**−36.4**	**37.0**	**148.8**	**84.3**	**63.8**	**109.2**	**188.8**	**347.4**	**423.7**	**423.8**
Memorandum										
Exports of goods and services	282.3	335.1	485.1	448.1	472.3	586.3	767.4	1,046.2	1,227.1	1,305.8
Interest payments	31.0	26.8	27.4	25.0	25.3	35.6	34.6	47.6	49.3	52.5
Oil trade balance	133.6	193.4	315.0	271.4	281.8	353.2	476.6	690.2	816.2	871.6
Nonfuel exports										
Exports	943.0	980.4	1,159.5	1,167.1	1,286.1	1,566.8	2,002.6	2,400.5	2,743.6	3,064.5
Imports	999.0	1,000.4	1,191.6	1,182.2	1,264.8	1,549.7	2,007.1	2,373.8	2,737.7	3,083.2
Trade balance	−56.0	−20.1	−32.1	−15.1	21.3	17.1	−4.5	26.7	5.9	−18.7
Services, net	−0.8	−0.3	−2.2	−7.1	−1.2	−0.6	12.6	14.5	19.5	36.3
Balance on goods and services	−56.8	−20.4	−34.3	−22.2	20.0	16.4	8.1	41.2	25.4	17.6
Income, net	−88.9	−103.6	−105.4	−109.5	−106.0	−116.5	−135.3	−148.1	−156.4	−160.6
Current transfers, net	69.1	73.9	82.0	91.7	106.7	139.4	158.2	182.8	194.0	192.5
Current account balance	**−76.7**	**−50.0**	**−57.7**	**−40.0**	**20.7**	**39.4**	**31.1**	**75.9**	**63.1**	**49.5**
Memorandum										
Exports of goods and services	1,182.0	1,213.8	1,415.9	1,425.4	1,559.9	1,876.8	2,402.0	2,881.1	3,296.4	3,689.7
Interest payments	103.6	107.9	102.9	101.8	94.2	97.2	106.7	119.3	134.0	143.4
Oil trade balance	−31.1	−40.1	−74.4	−69.6	−73.5	−95.3	−149.3	−234.8	−301.1	−353.1
Nonfuel primary products										
Exports	39.3	40.2	42.0	39.9	40.9	48.5	66.5	77.5	89.1	89.2
Imports	40.9	35.9	37.8	37.5	38.3	43.7	55.1	66.4	73.4	77.8
Trade balance	−1.6	4.2	4.2	2.4	2.7	4.8	11.4	11.2	15.7	11.4
Services, net	−4.0	−4.0	−3.8	−3.7	−4.2	−4.4	−5.2	−5.6	−7.0	−5.6
Balance on goods and services	−5.6	0.2	0.4	−1.3	−1.6	0.4	6.3	5.6	8.6	5.8
Income, net	−4.9	−5.7	−6.4	−6.0	−6.4	−8.8	−12.9	−16.5	−17.2	−17.5
Current transfers, net	3.1	3.0	3.2	3.7	4.3	5.2	7.3	8.7	8.7	8.9
Current account balance	**−7.4**	**−2.5**	**−2.7**	**−3.7**	**−3.7**	**−3.1**	**0.6**	**−2.1**	**0.1**	**−2.7**
Memorandum										
Exports of goods and services	47.1	47.8	49.6	47.8	49.2	58.1	77.9	90.1	102.5	104.3
Interest payments	4.0	3.8	4.1	3.8	3.5	3.2	3.3	3.4	4.1	4.0
Oil trade balance	−1.7	−2.0	−3.1	−3.2	−4.2	−3.9	−3.7	−4.5	−3.8	−3.9

Table 30 *(continued)*

	1998	1999	2000	2001	2002	2003	2004	2005	2006	2007
By external financing source										
Net debtor countries										
Exports	693.7	723.0	856.6	850.1	901.8	1,065.6	1,333.5	1,588.1	1,784.3	1,933.7
Imports	808.7	788.5	909.9	895.3	928.4	1,095.0	1,388.8	1,664.7	1,872.1	2,044.3
Trade balance	−115.0	−65.4	−53.4	−45.2	−26.6	−29.4	−55.3	−76.5	−87.7	−110.6
Services, net	−5.7	−1.7	−2.9	−9.3	−5.4	−3.4	6.4	—	−4.3	−1.1
Balance on goods and services	−120.7	−67.1	−56.2	−54.5	−32.0	−32.8	−48.9	−76.5	−92.0	−111.7
Income, net	−75.4	−86.5	−94.6	−92.8	−95.5	−116.4	−147.2	−174.4	−188.2	−196.0
Current transfers, net	67.1	68.5	74.5	82.3	94.7	123.1	138.7	162.1	176.9	187.5
Current account balance	**−129.0**	**−85.0**	**−76.4**	**−65.0**	**−32.7**	**−26.1**	**−57.4**	**−88.8**	**−103.3**	**−120.1**
Memorandum										
Exports of goods and services	893.7	915.6	1,066.0	1,057.8	1,117.2	1,310.5	1,646.8	1,961.4	2,207.3	2,401.4
Interest payments	99.0	103.6	98.9	95.4	86.9	89.9	98.0	107.4	117.2	123.7
Oil trade balance	−0.1	10.1	18.2	12.7	13.4	19.3	18.0	22.5	38.3	53.5
Official financing										
Exports	156.7	154.8	182.0	172.1	176.6	200.4	237.2	279.7	313.0	333.6
Imports	168.4	154.9	171.7	162.2	155.7	179.6	227.3	277.4	313.8	339.3
Trade balance	−11.7	−0.1	10.3	9.8	21.0	20.8	9.9	2.3	−0.9	−5.7
Services, net	−22.2	−12.7	−17.6	−16.6	−14.7	−17.3	−18.9	−22.6	−28.4	−29.7
Balance on goods and services	−33.9	−12.8	−7.3	−6.8	6.3	3.6	−9.0	−20.4	−29.3	−35.4
Income, net	−17.6	−26.0	−28.4	−27.3	−28.4	−30.5	−37.1	−38.2	−38.8	−40.2
Current transfers, net	18.7	21.1	24.1	27.2	31.3	36.5	41.5	47.1	50.7	53.8
Current account balance	**−32.9**	**−17.7**	**−11.6**	**−6.9**	**9.2**	**9.6**	**−4.6**	**−11.5**	**−17.3**	**−21.9**
Memorandum										
Exports of goods and services	192.3	190.4	219.5	211.3	216.4	242.6	298.2	346.4	384.3	409.0
Interest payments	29.5	30.5	24.3	23.7	21.2	21.0	21.3	22.3	23.0	23.5
Oil trade balance	3.3	4.2	5.2	1.8	0.7	1.3	−0.5	−4.1	−4.1	−5.7
Net debtor countries by debt-servicing experience										
Countries with arrears and/or rescheduling during 1999–2003										
Exports	163.2	173.4	221.5	209.2	215.9	249.6	302.9	372.7	428.9	468.2
Imports	166.2	161.7	180.8	177.5	181.3	210.8	262.3	323.5	363.9	394.9
Trade balance	−2.9	11.7	40.7	31.7	34.5	38.9	40.6	49.2	65.0	73.3
Services, net	−26.7	−17.9	−23.2	−24.4	−21.9	−25.9	−29.8	−40.8	−52.0	−57.9
Balance on goods and services	−29.6	−6.2	17.6	7.4	12.7	13.0	10.8	8.4	12.9	15.4
Income, net	−22.2	−31.9	−37.4	−33.9	−36.5	−40.1	−50.8	−53.1	−56.6	−60.6
Current transfers, net	16.7	15.8	18.2	20.5	26.2	32.7	37.8	43.9	47.2	49.2
Current account balance	**−35.2**	**−22.3**	**−1.7**	**−6.0**	**2.4**	**5.6**	**−2.2**	**−0.9**	**3.5**	**4.1**
Memorandum										
Exports of goods and services	196.9	206.1	256.7	244.9	253.6	289.5	360.9	437.1	499.4	543.0
Interest payments	32.7	34.0	27.5	26.0	22.6	22.5	22.6	23.7	23.2	23.7
Oil trade balance	20.3	32.0	52.5	47.1	46.1	57.1	72.8	94.6	117.3	134.3

Table 30 *(concluded)*

	1998	1999	2000	2001	2002	2003	2004	2005	2006	2007
Other groups										
Heavily indebted poor countries										
Exports	18.2	17.2	18.9	19.7	20.2	24.0	31.1	36.3	41.2	43.1
Imports	24.1	24.9	25.2	26.3	29.1	32.4	39.9	46.4	51.3	54.1
Trade balance	−5.9	−7.7	−6.2	−6.6	−8.9	−8.4	−8.8	−10.1	−10.1	−10.9
Services, net	−3.9	−3.4	−3.2	−3.5	−3.6	−4.1	−4.6	−5.1	−6.1	−6.0
Balance on goods and services	−9.8	−11.2	−9.4	−10.0	−12.5	−12.5	−13.4	−15.2	−16.2	−16.9
Income, net	−2.8	−3.0	−3.5	−4.0	−3.6	−3.9	−5.2	−6.1	−6.2	−6.4
Current transfers, net	4.9	5.1	5.9	6.9	7.4	9.1	11.0	13.1	13.8	14.4
Current account balance	**−7.8**	**−9.2**	**−7.1**	**−7.2**	**−8.7**	**−7.3**	**−7.6**	**−8.2**	**−8.6**	**−8.9**
Memorandum										
Exports of goods and services	23.7	23.2	25.2	26.2	27.1	31.9	40.7	46.8	52.6	55.3
Interest payments	3.6	3.2	3.1	2.9	2.8	2.8	2.9	3.0	3.0	3.0
Oil trade balance	−0.2	−0.4	—	−0.9	−1.7	−0.9	0.4	1.0	1.4	0.9
Middle East and north Africa										
Exports	154.8	198.9	287.2	264.3	278.9	344.8	443.5	603.9	710.4	755.0
Imports	161.0	159.6	173.2	186.7	204.0	235.6	287.4	343.8	401.1	447.2
Trade balance	−6.2	39.3	113.9	77.6	74.9	109.3	156.1	260.0	309.3	307.8
Services, net	−24.1	−23.8	−30.7	−26.3	−31.4	−32.2	−36.8	−42.1	−54.8	−64.0
Balance on goods and services	−30.3	15.5	83.2	51.3	43.5	77.1	119.3	217.9	254.5	243.9
Income, net	11.9	6.8	6.8	7.4	1.1	−0.6	0.5	3.2	12.8	17.7
Current transfers, net	−10.7	−11.7	−14.2	−13.2	−11.5	−9.4	−6.7	−7.1	−7.5	−8.2
Current account balance	**−29.2**	**10.6**	**75.8**	**45.5**	**33.1**	**67.1**	**113.1**	**214.1**	**259.8**	**253.3**
Memorandum										
Exports of goods and services	189.2	235.6	325.1	305.3	322.7	395.9	503.4	670.0	781.3	830.9
Interest payments	−11.4	−11.0	−11.4	−10.4	−10.1	−8.3	−8.6	−9.3	−10.5	−11.2
Oil trade balance	89.7	131.8	209.1	178.3	183.4	229.2	299.4	425.7	501.1	527.4

Table 31. Other Emerging Market and Developing Countries—by Country: Balance of Payments on Current Account

(Percent of GDP)

	1998	1999	2000	2001	2002	2003	2004	2005	2006	2007
Africa	**−4.5**	**−3.5**	**1.6**	**0.1**	**−1.6**	**−0.4**	**0.1**	**1.9**	**2.6**	**2.7**
Algeria	−1.9	—	16.7	12.8	7.6	13.0	13.1	21.3	18.9	16.5
Angola	−28.8	−27.5	8.7	−14.8	−2.9	−5.2	4.2	8.2	11.3	12.0
Benin	−5.4	−7.3	−7.7	−6.4	−8.4	−8.3	−7.2	−6.4	−8.8	−6.1
Botswana	4.1	12.3	10.4	11.5	3.6	6.0	9.5	8.9	4.8	3.5
Burkina Faso	−8.4	−10.6	−12.2	−11.0	−10.0	−8.6	−7.8	−9.2	−9.2	−10.2
Burundi	−7.5	−6.1	−9.9	−5.8	−5.2	−4.8	−7.2	−4.4	−8.1	−11.2
Cameroon	−2.2	−3.8	−1.5	−3.6	−6.1	−2.1	−3.4	−1.5	−1.6	−1.8
Cape Verde	−11.0	−12.4	−11.2	−10.1	−11.4	−9.5	−6.7	−4.3	−10.7	−11.9
Central African Republic	−6.1	−1.6	−3.0	−2.5	−3.4	−4.7	−4.5	−4.1	−3.9	−3.7
Chad	−8.1	−11.3	−15.4	−33.9	−101.0	−48.4	−6.6	2.2	8.2	7.2
Comoros	−8.4	−6.8	1.7	3.0	−0.6	−4.3	−2.6	−4.3	−3.8	−1.9
Congo, Dem. Rep. of	−9.0	−2.6	−4.6	−4.9	−3.2	−1.8	−5.7	−4.8	−2.6	−2.1
Congo, Rep. of	−20.6	−17.1	7.9	−3.2	−0.3	1.0	2.2	13.9	13.6	10.3
Côte d'Ivoire	−2.7	−1.4	−2.8	−1.1	6.4	1.8	2.7	0.7	1.9	1.9
Djibouti	−1.3	2.0	−3.4	2.7	4.5	5.5	−0.8	−4.2	−3.6	−5.4
Equatorial Guinea	−89.3	−29.9	−16.4	−49.0	−13.5	−43.8	−24.2	−13.3	−5.8	−4.8
Eritrea	−23.8	−18.0	0.5	4.2	3.6	5.2	5.8	—	−1.1	−1.2
Ethiopia	−1.4	−6.7	−4.3	−3.0	−4.7	−2.2	−5.1	−9.1	−7.5	−4.3
Gabon	−13.8	8.4	19.7	11.0	6.8	12.0	9.9	15.7	19.6	20.3
Gambia, The	−2.4	−2.8	−3.1	−2.6	−2.8	−5.1	−11.8	−13.1	−11.5	−7.1
Ghana	−5.0	−11.6	−8.4	−5.3	0.5	1.7	−2.7	−6.6	−7.8	−5.3
Guinea	−8.5	−6.9	−6.4	−2.7	−4.3	−3.4	−5.6	−3.4	−3.4	−4.7
Guinea-Bissau	−14.3	−13.3	−5.6	−22.1	−10.7	−2.8	0.7	−1.5	−19.6	−17.7
Kenya	−4.0	−1.8	−2.3	−3.1	2.2	−0.2	−2.5	−7.6	−4.4	−5.9
Lesotho	−25.0	−22.7	−18.8	−14.1	−17.9	−10.7	−2.8	−14.7	−15.9	−15.6
Madagascar	−7.5	−5.6	−5.6	−1.3	−6.0	−4.9	−10.8	−12.8	−10.4	−9.9
Malawi	−0.4	−8.3	−5.3	−6.8	−11.2	−7.6	−9.3	−7.7	−4.6	−6.0
Mali	−6.6	−8.5	−10.0	−10.4	−3.1	−6.2	−7.9	−9.2	−7.5	−7.5
Mauritania	−2.7	−0.2	−13.7	−10.7	−3.7	−18.3	−36.8	−35.5	3.3	2.3
Mauritius	−2.8	−1.6	−1.5	3.4	5.5	2.4	0.8	−3.5	−2.5	−2.8
Morocco	−0.4	−0.5	−1.4	4.8	4.1	3.6	2.2	0.9	−0.8	−0.9
Mozambique, Rep. of	−14.4	−21.9	−17.6	−19.2	−18.9	−14.8	−8.4	−11.6	−10.4	−13.5
Namibia	2.8	7.3	10.9	3.2	5.4	5.1	10.2	5.7	6.6	5.4
Niger	−6.9	−6.5	−6.2	−4.8	−6.5	−5.6	−6.5	−6.1	−7.2	−5.0
Nigeria	−8.9	−8.4	11.7	4.5	−11.7	−2.7	4.6	12.6	14.2	15.3
Rwanda	−9.6	−7.7	−5.0	−5.9	−6.7	−7.8	−3.1	−3.9	−9.9	−7.0
São Tomé and Príncipe	−30.8	−32.8	−31.4	−22.3	−24.1	−22.3	−20.1	−33.1	−28.4	−29.4
Senegal	−4.1	−5.1	−6.8	−4.7	−6.0	−6.6	−6.7	−7.9	−8.2	−7.9
Seychelles	−16.5	−19.8	−7.3	−23.5	−16.3	6.4	5.3	−14.6	−1.8	−5.0
Sierra Leone	−2.6	−11.1	−15.2	−16.2	−4.8	−7.6	−4.9	−8.5	−6.4	−6.7
South Africa	−1.8	−0.5	−0.1	0.1	0.6	−1.3	−3.4	−4.2	−3.9	−3.6
Sudan	−15.3	−15.9	−14.9	−15.8	−9.8	−7.7	−6.3	−10.7	−6.9	−5.4
Swaziland	−6.9	−2.6	−5.4	−4.5	4.8	1.9	1.7	−1.4	−1.3	−1.8
Tanzania	−11.0	−9.9	−5.3	−4.7	−3.8	−2.4	−1.6	−2.6	−7.6	−8.7
Togo	−8.8	−8.1	−11.8	−12.7	−9.5	−9.4	−8.3	−11.6	−10.3	−8.7
Tunisia	−3.4	−2.2	−4.2	−4.2	−3.5	−2.9	−2.0	−1.3	−1.4	−1.1
Uganda	−7.5	−9.4	−7.0	−3.8	−4.9	−5.8	−1.7	−1.2	−3.9	−4.2
Zambia	−16.7	−13.7	−18.2	−20.0	−15.4	−15.2	−10.3	−10.2	−9.3	−7.6
Zimbabwe	−4.7	2.5	0.4	−0.3	−0.6	−2.9	−8.3	−11.1	1.7	−15.0

Table 31 *(continued)*

	1998	1999	2000	2001	2002	2003	2004	2005	2006	2007
Central and eastern Europe	**−3.1**	**−4.4**	**−5.3**	**−2.7**	**−3.5**	**−4.3**	**−5.7**	**−5.2**	**−5.5**	**−5.4**
Albania	−3.6	2.3	−3.6	−2.8	−7.1	−5.5	−3.8	−5.6	−6.7	−5.9
Bosnia and Herzegovina	−8.4	−9.1	−17.5	−20.0	−26.5	−22.4	−24.4	−26.4	−23.0	−23.0
Bulgaria	−0.5	−5.0	−5.6	−7.3	−5.6	−9.2	−5.8	−11.8	−10.2	−9.1
Croatia	−6.7	−7.0	−2.6	−3.7	−8.4	−6.3	−5.6	−6.0	−5.9	−5.9
Czech Republic	−2.0	−2.5	−4.9	−5.4	−5.6	−6.3	−6.0	−2.1	−2.3	−2.3
Estonia	−8.7	−4.4	−5.5	−5.6	−10.2	−12.1	−12.7	−10.5	−10.1	−9.6
Hungary	−7.2	−7.9	−8.5	−6.2	−7.1	−8.7	−8.8	−7.9	−8.2	−7.5
Latvia	−9.0	−9.0	−4.8	−7.6	−6.6	−8.1	−12.9	−12.5	−12.8	−12.0
Lithuania	−11.7	−11.0	−5.9	−4.7	−5.2	−6.9	−7.7	−7.5	−7.5	−7.3
Macedonia, FYR	−7.5	−0.9	−2.0	−5.7	−8.4	−3.4	−7.6	−0.8	−3.7	−4.3
Malta	−6.2	−3.4	−12.6	−4.4	0.3	−5.8	−10.4	−6.7	−6.5	−6.3
Poland	−4.0	−7.4	−5.8	−2.8	−2.5	−2.1	−4.1	−1.6	−2.5	−3.1
Romania	−7.1	−4.1	−3.7	−5.5	−3.3	−5.8	−8.4	−8.7	−8.3	−8.1
Serbia and Montenegro	−4.8	−7.5	−3.9	−4.6	−8.9	−9.7	−12.5	−8.8	−9.5	−8.3
Slovak Republic	−9.6	−4.8	−3.5	−8.4	−8.0	−0.9	−3.5	−7.2	−6.4	−5.5
Slovenia	−0.5	−3.2	−2.8	0.2	1.4	−0.4	−2.1	−0.9	−0.3	0.1
Turkey	1.0	−0.7	−5.0	2.4	−0.8	−3.3	−5.2	−6.3	−6.5	−6.1
Commonwealth of Independent States[1]	**−1.9**	**8.2**	**13.6**	**8.0**	**6.5**	**6.3**	**8.1**	**9.1**	**9.6**	**8.1**
Russia	0.1	12.6	18.0	11.1	8.4	8.2	9.9	11.3	11.8	9.5
Excluding Russia	−6.8	−0.9	1.5	−0.8	1.0	0.3	2.1	1.6	2.4	3.4
Armenia	−22.1	−16.6	−14.6	−9.5	−6.2	−6.8	−4.6	−3.3	−3.9	−4.3
Azerbaijan	−30.7	−13.1	−3.5	−0.9	−12.3	−27.8	−30.0	−5.2	17.7	40.0
Belarus	−6.7	−1.7	−2.6	−3.2	−2.1	−2.4	−5.3	1.2	−0.8	−2.0
Georgia	−12.8	−10.0	−6.0	−6.5	−5.9	−7.3	−8.3	−7.4	−7.1	−5.5
Kazakhstan	−5.5	−0.2	3.0	−5.4	−4.1	−0.9	1.2	1.8	2.3	2.4
Kyrgyz Republic	−22.3	−14.8	−4.3	−1.5	−5.0	−4.1	−3.4	−8.1	−6.8	−5.6
Moldova	−19.7	−6.7	−8.4	−2.5	−4.4	−6.8	−2.7	−5.5	−5.2	−5.3
Mongolia	−7.8	−6.7	−5.7	−7.6	−9.6	−7.7	1.1	4.5	2.9	−1.7
Tajikistan	−7.3	−5.6	−6.0	−4.9	−3.5	−1.3	−4.0	−3.4	−4.2	−4.8
Turkmenistan	−32.7	−14.8	8.2	1.7	6.7	2.7	0.6	2.8	1.4	1.1
Ukraine	−3.1	5.3	4.7	3.7	7.5	5.8	10.5	2.7	1.2	−2.1
Uzbekistan	−0.7	−1.0	1.7	−1.0	1.2	8.7	10.0	10.8	9.6	9.2

Table 31 *(continued)*

	1998	1999	2000	2001	2002	2003	2004	2005	2006	2007
Developing Asia	**2.5**	**2.3**	**2.0**	**1.7**	**2.7**	**2.9**	**2.7**	**3.9**	**3.6**	**3.5**
Afghanistan, I.S. of	...	...	...	...	−3.5	3.1	1.8	0.6	−1.3	−2.4
Bangladesh	−1.1	−0.9	−1.4	−0.8	0.3	0.2	−0.3	−0.9	−1.0	−1.1
Bhutan	9.8	2.2	−9.4	−5.3	−9.1	−11.3	−7.9	−23.1	−9.6	2.2
Brunei Darussalam	44.7	34.9	68.2	69.7	59.3	68.0	68.2	72.8	67.0	64.0
Cambodia	−5.9	−5.2	−3.0	−1.2	−1.0	−3.1	−3.4	−3.9	−5.5	−5.0
China	3.1	1.4	1.7	1.3	2.4	2.8	3.6	7.1	6.9	6.7
Fiji	−0.3	−3.8	−5.8	−3.3	−1.6	−4.7	−5.0	−4.5	−4.2	−3.4
India	−1.7	−0.7	−1.0	0.3	1.4	1.5	0.2	−2.5	−3.1	−3.1
Indonesia	3.8	3.7	4.8	4.2	3.9	3.4	1.2	1.1	0.4	—
Kiribati	35.2	13.3	12.6	1.9	−1.8	6.5	−11.1	−21.1	−16.5	−15.5
Lao PDR	−4.6	−4.0	−10.5	−8.3	−7.2	−8.1	−14.4	−16.4	−12.7	−14.7
Malaysia	13.2	15.9	9.4	8.3	8.4	12.7	12.6	15.6	14.9	14.7
Maldives	−4.1	−13.4	−8.2	−9.4	−5.6	−4.6	−16.1	−36.5	−38.5	−21.6
Myanmar	−11.7	−6.8	4.6	−4.4	2.3	0.3	2.9	4.8	5.1	4.5
Nepal	−1.0	4.3	3.2	4.8	4.5	2.6	3.0	5.5	4.0	3.7
Pakistan	−2.6	−2.3	−1.6	0.3	3.7	3.4	0.2	−2.4	−3.2	−3.0
Papua New Guinea	0.6	2.8	8.5	6.5	−1.0	4.4	2.1	4.2	4.6	−2.0
Philippines	2.3	9.5	8.2	1.9	5.7	1.8	2.7	3.0	2.1	1.6
Samoa	9.5	2.0	1.0	0.1	−1.1	5.8	8.3	14.1	−3.8	−3.4
Solomon Islands	−1.6	3.1	−10.6	−12.5	−7.2	1.3	12.5	−7.9	−10.5	−7.5
Sri Lanka	−1.4	−3.6	−6.5	−1.1	−1.4	−0.4	−3.0	−2.4	−5.3	−4.4
Thailand	12.8	10.2	7.6	5.4	5.5	5.6	4.2	−2.3	−2.0	−2.1
Timor-Leste, Dem. Rep. of	...	2.1	11.8	12.5	7.6	5.0	38.0	77.8	101.0	156.6
Tonga	−10.5	−0.6	−5.9	−9.2	4.9	−3.0	4.0	−2.2	−1.1	−1.2
Vanuatu	2.5	−4.9	2.0	2.0	−9.0	−10.2	−9.5	−7.1	−8.8	−7.7
Vietnam	−3.9	4.5	2.1	2.1	−1.2	−4.9	−3.8	−4.4	−4.0	−4.0
Middle East	**−5.0**	**2.3**	**11.1**	**6.2**	**4.6**	**8.1**	**12.4**	**19.1**	**20.4**	**18.1**
Bahrain	−12.6	−0.3	10.6	3.0	−0.4	2.3	4.0	5.8	7.3	5.3
Egypt	−2.9	−1.9	−1.2	—	0.7	2.4	4.3	2.8	1.3	−0.4
Iran, I.R. of	−2.2	6.3	13.0	5.2	3.1	0.6	2.5	7.5	7.6	6.2
Iraq	...	...	...	...	...	...	...	...	...	...
Jordan	0.3	5.0	0.7	−0.1	5.6	11.6	−0.2	−17.8	−16.0	−14.4
Kuwait	8.5	16.8	38.9	23.9	11.2	20.4	31.1	43.3	49.9	48.7
Lebanon	−29.5	−18.8	−17.1	−19.2	−15.4	−15.2	−18.2	−12.7	−12.9	−12.1
Libya	−1.2	9.2	22.5	13.8	2.9	21.5	24.2	40.2	43.3	44.6
Oman	−22.3	−2.9	15.5	9.3	6.6	4.0	1.7	7.0	8.5	9.4
Qatar	−21.5	6.8	18.0	19.9	16.5	25.9	37.9	45.6	51.7	51.8
Saudi Arabia	−9.0	0.3	7.6	5.1	6.3	13.1	20.5	28.3	28.3	23.9
Syrian Arab Republic	0.5	1.6	5.3	4.0	4.6	3.2	−2.0	−5.5	−7.3	−8.6
United Arab Emirates	1.8	1.6	17.2	9.4	5.0	8.7	11.8	22.0	27.0	26.1
Yemen	−2.8	2.7	13.2	5.3	5.4	−0.1	1.9	2.6	−5.2	−9.6

Table 31 *(concluded)*

	1998	1999	2000	2001	2002	2003	2004	2005	2006	2007
Western Hemisphere	**−4.5**	**−3.2**	**−2.4**	**−2.8**	**−0.9**	**0.4**	**0.9**	**1.2**	**0.8**	**0.2**
Antigua and Barbuda	−7.5	−8.9	−9.7	−8.9	−15.7	−14.2	−10.8	−11.6	−13.7	−13.0
Argentina	−4.8	−4.2	−3.2	−1.2	8.9	6.3	2.2	1.8	1.2	0.5
Bahamas, The	−23.2	−5.1	−10.4	−11.4	−6.3	−8.0	−5.3	−12.3	−14.6	−14.2
Barbados	−2.3	−5.9	−5.6	−3.7	−7.5	−6.9	−11.9	−12.2	−11.7	−10.4
Belize	−6.0	−9.7	−18.7	−18.0	−20.2	−22.3	−17.7	−13.1	−8.6	−8.1
Bolivia	−7.8	−5.9	−5.3	−3.4	−4.1	0.6	3.2	2.6	1.7	1.0
Brazil	−4.2	−4.7	−4.0	−4.5	−1.7	0.8	1.9	1.8	1.0	0.2
Chile	−5.0	0.1	−1.2	−1.6	−0.9	−1.5	1.5	−0.4	0.5	−1.2
Colombia	−4.9	0.8	0.9	−1.3	−1.7	−1.2	−1.0	−1.7	−1.6	−2.7
Costa Rica	−3.5	−3.8	−4.3	−4.4	−5.6	−5.5	−4.3	−4.8	−4.6	−4.2
Dominica	−9.1	−13.0	−19.7	−18.7	−13.8	−13.0	−17.2	−26.3	−23.8	−23.1
Dominican Republic	−2.1	−2.4	−5.1	−3.4	−3.7	6.0	5.8	−1.0	−2.4	−3.0
Ecuador	−9.3	4.6	5.3	−3.3	−4.9	−1.7	−1.1	−0.9	0.2	0.4
El Salvador	−0.8	−1.6	−2.9	−0.9	−2.5	−4.3	−4.4	−4.0	−4.0	−4.0
Grenada	−23.5	−14.6	−21.5	−26.6	−32.0	−33.2	−13.5	−33.7	−33.2	−28.3
Guatemala	−5.3	−5.5	−5.4	−6.0	−5.3	−4.2	−4.4	−4.5	−4.2	−4.3
Guyana	−13.7	−11.4	−15.3	−19.2	−15.2	−11.8	−9.5	−24.2	−27.9	−20.8
Haiti	0.5	−1.0	−1.0	−2.0	−1.0	−0.1	0.4	0.4	−0.6	−0.4
Honduras	−2.5	−4.5	−3.9	−4.8	−3.6	−4.2	−5.6	−0.5	−3.4	−3.3
Jamaica	−2.0	−3.4	−4.9	−9.6	−15.2	−6.8	−6.1	−8.2	−12.8	−10.8
Mexico	−3.8	−2.9	−3.2	−2.8	−2.1	−1.3	−1.1	−0.7	−0.6	−0.8
Netherlands Antilles	−3.9	−5.1	—	−5.7	−1.8	−0.3	−3.2	−2.4	−2.3	−2.9
Nicaragua	−22.3	−28.2	−23.4	−19.4	−19.1	−18.1	−16.9	−16.9	−16.7	−16.0
Panama	−9.3	−10.1	−5.9	−1.5	−0.8	−3.9	−7.9	−5.4	−4.7	−4.6
Paraguay	−2.0	−2.3	−2.3	−4.1	1.8	2.4	0.2	−2.7	−1.7	−1.8
Peru	−6.4	−3.4	−2.8	−2.4	−2.0	−1.6	—	1.3	1.4	0.3
St. Kitts and Nevis	−16.5	−22.5	−21.0	−32.8	−37.9	−33.6	−23.7	−20.1	−18.3	−14.2
St. Lucia	−9.5	−16.6	−14.1	−16.2	−15.2	−20.3	−13.3	−16.7	−20.7	−8.0
St. Vincent and the Grenadines	−29.1	−20.9	−6.8	−10.5	−11.3	−19.9	−25.5	−27.6	−25.4	−23.1
Suriname	−14.3	−19.0	−3.8	−15.2	−6.3	−13.8	−5.1	−15.8	−11.9	−10.0
Trinidad and Tobago	−9.4	0.4	6.2	4.7	0.8	8.3	13.5	16.6	21.0	16.0
Uruguay	−2.1	−2.4	−2.8	−2.9	3.2	−0.5	−0.7	−2.4	−5.8	−2.5
Venezuela	−4.9	2.2	10.1	1.6	8.2	13.7	12.5	19.1	14.1	13.4

[1]Mongolia, which is not a member of the Commonwealth of Independent States, is included in this group for reasons of geography and similarities in economic structure.

Table 32. Summary of Balance of Payments, Capital Flows, and External Financing
(Billions of U.S. dollars)

	1998	1999	2000	2001	2002	2003	2004	2005	2006	2007
Other emerging market and developing countries										
Balance of payments[1]										
Balance on current account	−113.1	−13.0	91.1	44.2	84.5	148.5	219.8	423.3	486.7	473.2
Balance on goods and services	−65.6	46.1	150.6	94.5	125.6	175.7	251.5	445.1	499.3	485.2
Income, net	−97.0	−113.0	−118.3	−117.9	−125.0	−145.8	−170.6	−185.4	−186.0	−183.2
Current transfers, net	49.6	53.9	58.8	67.6	83.9	118.7	138.9	163.5	173.4	171.2
Balance on capital and financial account	154.0	68.5	−38.0	1.2	−26.8	−154.2	−245.7	−363.2	−456.5	−455.8
Balance on capital account[2]	6.4	9.5	22.8	4.1	1.6	10.8	17.6	16.0	23.3	22.1
Balance on financial account	147.6	59.0	−60.8	−2.9	−28.3	−164.9	−263.4	−379.2	−479.8	−477.9
Direct investment, net	158.4	158.0	150.1	169.7	155.1	145.4	192.0	206.2	216.1	213.6
Portfolio investment, net	28.8	25.5	−38.8	−45.9	−25.0	−31.0	0.5	−17.7	−121.8	−119.2
Other investment, net	−44.0	−80.1	−87.8	−27.1	−7.3	0.5	−21.4	−42.3	−40.8	−64.8
Reserve assets	4.4	−44.4	−84.2	−99.6	−151.1	−279.9	−434.4	−525.4	−533.3	−507.5
Errors and omissions, net	−40.9	−55.5	−53.1	−45.5	−57.7	5.6	25.9	−60.0	−30.2	−17.4
Capital flows										
Total capital flows, net[3]	143.2	103.4	23.5	96.7	122.8	115.0	171.0	146.2	53.4	29.6
Net official flows	50.8	44.4	−37.9	11.7	13.2	−47.2	−67.5	−123.5	−143.0	−143.8
Net private flows[4]	93.0	58.9	60.5	84.8	109.1	162.6	237.8	269.7	196.7	173.3
Direct investment, net	158.4	158.0	150.1	169.7	155.1	145.4	192.0	206.2	216.1	213.6
Private portfolio investment, net	23.0	11.7	−11.9	−36.1	−26.9	18.1	69.7	78.2	32.0	35.0
Other private flows, net	−88.4	−110.8	−77.7	−48.9	−19.1	−1.0	−23.9	−14.7	−51.4	−75.4
External financing[5]										
Net external financing[6]	285.4	247.8	247.9	188.6	195.0	281.1	449.5	512.1	518.5	489.6
Non-debt-creating flows	185.4	188.8	200.8	178.4	165.2	184.3	274.0	296.7	311.4	315.0
Capital transfers[7]	6.4	9.5	22.8	4.1	1.6	10.8	17.6	16.0	23.3	22.1
Foreign direct investment and equity security liabilities[8]	179.0	179.2	178.1	174.3	163.7	173.6	256.4	280.7	288.1	293.0
Net external borrowing[9]	100.0	59.0	47.1	10.2	29.8	96.8	175.5	215.3	207.1	174.5
Borrowing from official creditors[10]	44.7	30.6	−10.5	21.6	11.5	1.7	2.1	−27.6	10.7	10.5
of which, credit and loans from IMF[11]	14.0	−2.4	−10.9	19.0	13.4	1.7	−14.5	−39.9	. . .	. . .
Borrowing from banks[10]	8.5	−12.1	−10.8	−13.3	−13.6	9.1	34.6	36.7	43.4	30.8
Borrowing from other private creditors[10]	46.8	40.5	68.4	1.8	31.9	86.0	138.8	206.3	153.0	133.1
Memorandum										
Balance on goods and services in percent of GDP[12]	−1.1	0.8	2.4	1.5	1.9	2.3	2.9	4.3	4.2	3.7
Scheduled amortization of external debt	255.1	297.8	344.9	321.8	341.1	369.8	373.2	395.6	377.4	377.1
Gross external financing[13]	540.5	545.5	592.8	510.4	536.0	650.9	822.7	907.7	895.9	866.6
Gross external borrowing[14]	355.0	356.7	392.0	332.0	370.8	466.6	548.6	611.0	584.5	551.6
Exceptional external financing, net	42.0	28.4	9.7	30.3	58.7	35.1	20.4	−36.3	10.1	11.1
Of which,										
Arrears on debt service	21.8	8.2	−30.3	0.2	15.0	18.4	9.7	−24.1	. . .	. . .
Debt forgiveness	1.5	2.2	1.7	2.6	1.8	1.7	3.0	3.5	. . .	. . .
Rescheduling of debt service	7.8	14.6	3.1	7.7	10.4	5.9	8.7	3.7	. . .	. . .

[1]Standard presentation in accordance with the 5th edition of the International Monetary Fund's *Balance of Payments Manual* (1993).

[2]Comprises capital transfers—including debt forgiveness—and acquisition/disposal of nonproduced, nonfinancial assets.

[3]Comprise net direct investment, net portfolio investment, and other long- and short-term net investment flows, including official and private borrowing. In the standard balance of payments presentation above, total net capital flows are equal to the balance on financial account minus the change in reserve assets.

[4]Because of limitations on the data coverage for net official flows, the residually derived data for net private flows may include some official flows.

[5]As defined in the *World Economic Outlook* (see footnote 6). It should be noted that there is no generally accepted standard definition of external financing.

[6]Defined as the sum of—with opposite sign—the goods and services balance, net income and current transfers, direct investment abroad, the change in reserve assets, the net acquisition of other assets (such as recorded private portfolio assets, export credit, and the collateral for debt-reduction operations), and the net errors and omissions. Thus, net external financing, according to the definition adopted in the *World Economic Outlook*, measures the total amount required to finance the current account, direct investment outflows, net reserve transactions (often at the discretion of the monetary authorities), the net acquisition of nonreserve external assets, and the net transactions underlying the errors and omissions (not infrequently reflecting capital flight).

[7]Including other transactions on capital account.

[8]Debt-creating foreign direct investment liabilities are not included.

[9]Net disbursement of long- and short-term credits, including exceptional financing, by both official and private creditors.

[10]Changes in liabilities.

[11]Comprise use of IMF resources under the General Resources Account, Trust Fund, and Poverty Reduction and Growth Facility (PRGF). For further detail, see Table 36.

[12]This is often referred to as the "resource balance" and, with opposite sign, the "net resource transfer."

[13]Net external financing plus amortization due on external debt.

[14]Net external borrowing plus amortization due on external debt.

Table 33. Other Emerging Market and Developing Countries—by Region: Balance of Payments and External Financing[1]
(Billions of U.S. dollars)

	1998	1999	2000	2001	2002	2003	2004	2005	2006	2007
Africa										
Balance of payments										
Balance on current account	−19.4	−15.0	7.2	0.5	−7.5	−2.5	0.9	15.2	23.5	25.9
Balance on capital account	4.1	4.6	3.5	4.4	4.8	4.1	5.3	3.9	4.1	4.5
Balance on financial account	16.5	12.4	−10.0	−4.5	3.5	−3.2	−18.2	−18.3	−26.5	−29.4
Change in reserves (− = increase)	3.6	−0.4	−12.8	−9.8	−5.7	−11.4	−33.0	−42.1	−46.3	−54.7
Other official flows, net	5.3	3.8	2.7	−0.5	4.3	3.7	1.8	−6.6	3.2	4.2
Private flows, net	7.6	9.0	—	5.7	4.9	4.6	13.0	30.4	16.6	21.1
External financing										
Net external financing	27.5	30.1	15.1	19.5	19.4	22.9	28.7	29.1	33.3	35.2
Non-debt-creating inflows	20.1	23.0	15.6	23.4	17.1	21.5	30.1	35.1	33.9	34.6
Net external borrowing	7.4	7.1	−0.6	−3.9	2.2	1.4	−1.4	−5.9	−0.7	0.6
From official creditors	5.3	3.8	2.8	−0.4	4.3	3.6	1.8	−6.6	3.3	4.3
of which, credit and loans from IMF	−0.4	−0.2	−0.2	−0.4	−0.1	−0.8	−0.7	−1.0	. . .	. . .
From banks	−1.0	1.1	−1.0	−0.1	0.5	0.9	1.3	−1.4	0.7	−0.1
From other private creditors	3.0	2.2	−2.4	−3.4	−2.6	−3.1	−4.4	2.1	−4.6	−3.6
Memorandum										
Exceptional financing	8.8	8.5	6.4	5.2	18.5	6.7	6.5	−0.6	3.9	3.8
Sub-Sahara										
Balance of payments										
Balance on current account	−17.7	−14.4	−0.7	−7.4	−12.6	−12.2	−10.8	−6.6	2.2	5.9
Balance on capital account	4.0	4.2	3.4	4.2	4.6	4.0	5.2	3.8	4.0	4.4
Balance on financial account	15.5	10.8	−2.2	3.9	9.1	6.5	−6.1	2.9	−5.9	−10.2
Change in reserves (− = increase)	2.5	−0.8	−6.1	0.4	−1.4	−2.1	−21.1	−23.3	−25.3	−33.8
Other official flows, net	5.8	4.4	3.6	0.6	5.6	4.8	2.9	−6.2	3.7	4.6
Private flows, net	7.2	7.2	0.3	2.9	4.9	3.8	12.1	32.3	15.7	19.0
External financing										
Net external financing	26.0	27.4	14.0	15.9	18.2	21.8	27.2	29.8	30.9	31.6
Non-debt-creating inflows	18.5	21.0	14.0	18.8	14.7	18.0	27.2	31.3	30.7	31.3
Net external borrowing	7.6	6.4	−0.1	−2.9	3.5	3.9	—	−1.5	0.2	0.3
From official creditors	5.8	4.4	3.7	0.7	5.6	4.8	2.9	−6.1	3.7	4.7
of which, credit and loans from IMF	−0.3	−0.1	—	−0.2	0.2	−0.4	−0.3	−0.4	. . .	. . .
From banks	−1.0	−0.3	−1.3	−0.6	−0.3	0.1	0.9	−1.2	0.4	−0.3
From other private creditors	2.8	2.3	−2.4	−3.0	−1.8	−1.1	−3.9	5.9	−3.9	−4.0
Memorandum										
Exceptional financing	7.8	7.8	6.4	5.1	18.4	6.7	6.5	−0.6	3.9	3.8
Central and eastern Europe										
Balance of payments										
Balance on current account	−19.3	−26.4	−32.4	−16.2	−24.0	−37.1	−59.2	−63.1	−72.2	−77.0
Balance on capital account	0.4	0.4	3.0	4.2	5.2	5.3	13.0	18.7	20.9	19.4
Balance on financial account	18.8	22.4	34.9	13.0	25.4	34.6	50.0	58.7	66.5	69.1
Change in reserves (− = increase)	−9.3	−11.9	−6.6	−4.4	−20.3	−12.4	−14.3	−41.0	−25.5	−12.7
Other official flows, net	1.0	−2.6	1.8	5.9	−7.7	−5.3	−6.8	−8.5	−2.7	−2.6
Private flows, net	27.2	37.0	39.7	11.6	53.5	52.3	71.0	108.2	94.7	84.4
External financing										
Net external financing	34.0	47.1	54.8	31.1	49.6	60.9	108.6	132.8	127.9	115.4
Non-debt-creating inflows	21.2	21.5	26.9	28.7	30.8	24.4	52.1	70.5	70.1	65.7
Net external borrowing	12.8	25.6	27.8	2.4	18.8	36.5	56.5	62.3	57.8	49.8
From official creditors	1.0	−2.6	1.9	6.0	−7.6	−5.4	−6.7	−8.4	−2.7	−2.6
of which, credit and loans from IMF	−0.5	0.5	3.3	9.9	6.1	—	−3.8	−5.9	. . .	. . .
From banks	2.6	2.1	4.0	−7.5	3.1	11.3	13.9	16.6	15.7	15.2
From other private creditors	9.2	26.2	22.0	3.9	23.3	30.6	49.3	54.1	44.8	37.2
Memorandum										
Exceptional financing	0.2	1.1	4.8	11.0	7.0	−0.3	−3.6	−4.9	−2.9	−2.0

Table 33 *(continued)*

	1998	1999	2000	2001	2002	2003	2004	2005	2006	2007
Commonwealth of Independent States[2]										
Balance of payments										
Balance on current account	−7.4	23.7	48.3	33.1	30.2	35.8	62.4	90.3	112.4	109.4
Balance on capital account	−0.3	−0.4	10.7	−9.6	−12.5	−1.0	−1.6	−12.2	−6.7	−6.8
Balance on financial account	12.2	−21.3	−53.1	−11.6	−10.3	−24.0	−54.9	−65.7	−105.7	−102.5
Change in reserves (− = increase)	12.7	−6.2	−20.4	−12.9	−16.2	−31.7	−56.0	−75.2	−88.0	−76.8
Other official flows, net	1.7	−2.1	−6.3	−5.2	−10.7	−8.6	−7.7	−15.5	−3.7	−4.6
Private flows, net	−1.5	−13.1	−27.3	6.3	16.1	16.7	8.0	24.9	−13.7	−21.3
External financing										
Net external financing	15.8	1.1	−0.4	−3.7	0.3	38.6	55.0	72.1	62.2	67.0
Non-debt-creating inflows	5.6	4.6	14.2	−5.5	−7.7	8.6	15.4	8.4	10.7	12.9
Net external borrowing	10.3	−3.5	−14.6	1.9	8.0	30.1	39.6	63.7	51.5	54.0
From official creditors	1.4	−2.0	−5.9	−3.9	−10.4	−3.4	−2.7	−12.9	−1.2	−1.8
of which, credit and loans from IMF	5.8	−3.6	−4.1	−4.0	−1.8	−2.3	−2.1	−3.8	. . .	. . .
From banks	−2.1	2.7	1.2	1.9	−0.4	—	−1.1	−5.3	−2.9	−2.6
From other private creditors	10.9	−4.2	−10.0	3.8	18.8	33.4	43.4	81.9	55.6	58.4
Memorandum										
Exceptional financing	7.9	7.4	2.3	−0.1	−0.3	0.8	0.4	0.1	0.1	0.1
Developing Asia										
Balance of payments										
Balance on current account	49.3	48.4	46.1	40.6	72.2	86.3	94.7	155.4	159.5	171.9
Balance on capital account	1.0	0.8	0.9	0.9	0.9	1.2	1.0	1.6	2.1	1.8
Balance on financial account	−28.1	−27.2	−19.0	−32.2	−65.1	−95.2	−119.0	−135.3	−161.5	−173.7
Change in reserves (− = increase)	−21.1	−32.3	−10.6	−61.5	−104.4	−155.8	−259.5	−229.0	−253.7	−255.1
Other official flows, net	18.9	19.8	−3.8	−1.0	9.1	−1.2	17.1	23.9	20.8	12.1
Private flows, net	−25.9	−14.7	−4.6	30.3	30.2	61.8	123.4	69.8	71.4	69.3
External financing										
Net external financing	56.1	67.2	70.4	51.4	75.3	100.0	168.2	186.7	188.5	171.9
Non-debt-creating inflows	68.1	66.1	70.6	57.5	69.8	83.4	106.6	93.1	102.1	109.2
Net external borrowing	−12.0	1.1	−0.2	−6.0	5.5	16.7	61.6	93.6	86.4	62.7
From official creditors	18.9	19.8	−3.8	−1.0	9.1	−1.2	17.1	23.9	20.8	12.1
of which, credit and loans from IMF	6.6	1.7	0.9	−2.2	−2.7	−0.6	−1.9	−1.6	. . .	. . .
From banks	−12.4	−11.8	−13.2	−7.2	−3.2	2.2	23.7	24.7	23.8	16.3
From other private creditors	−18.5	−6.9	16.8	2.2	−0.4	15.7	20.9	45.0	41.8	34.3
Memorandum										
Exceptional financing	14.5	7.2	6.6	6.3	7.2	5.6	3.2	8.0	4.4	4.7
Excluding China and India										
Balance of payments										
Balance on current account	24.6	36.0	30.2	21.8	29.7	31.6	24.6	15.8	12.3	11.0
Balance on capital account	1.0	0.8	1.0	1.0	0.9	1.3	1.1	1.7	2.1	1.8
Balance on financial account	−20.0	−30.0	−14.7	−19.0	−15.1	−21.7	−21.4	−4.2	−14.4	−12.9
Change in reserves (− = increase)	−12.0	−17.7	6.0	−5.5	−10.0	−13.1	−29.5	−11.1	−27.6	−28.3
Other official flows, net	13.3	12.7	−3.3	−1.9	7.8	3.5	−0.7	1.1	0.9	−0.8
Private flows, net	−21.3	−25.0	−17.3	−11.6	−12.8	−12.1	8.8	5.8	12.3	16.3
External financing										
Net external financing	13.6	13.1	1.6	0.5	11.7	14.2	40.6	33.7	42.0	45.4
Non-debt-creating inflows	25.2	25.2	14.8	6.9	17.1	22.1	36.2	23.6	31.8	35.8
Net external borrowing	−11.6	−12.1	−13.2	−6.4	−5.5	−7.9	4.4	10.0	10.1	9.6
From official creditors	13.3	12.7	−3.3	−1.9	7.8	3.5	−0.7	1.1	0.9	−0.8
of which, credit and loans from IMF	7.0	2.1	0.9	−2.2	−2.7	−0.6	−1.9	−1.6	. . .	. . .
From banks	−15.4	−9.9	−6.9	−7.2	−5.3	−4.8	2.4	0.5	1.7	1.0
From other private creditors	−9.5	−14.9	−3.0	2.7	−8.0	−6.5	2.6	8.4	7.6	9.5
Memorandum										
Exceptional financing	14.5	7.2	6.6	6.3	7.2	5.6	3.2	8.0	4.4	4.7

Table 33 *(concluded)*

	1998	1999	2000	2001	2002	2003	2004	2005	2006	2007
Middle East										
Balance of payments										
Balance on current account	−25.7	12.9	70.0	39.8	29.5	59.0	103.4	196.0	240.9	235.6
Balance on capital account	−0.5	0.9	1.9	1.8	1.3	0.3	−1.1	2.4	2.3	2.4
Balance on financial account	34.4	13.7	−55.6	−19.0	4.0	−63.2	−95.8	−187.0	−228.7	−233.3
Change in reserves (− = increase)	10.2	−1.5	−31.2	−12.8	−2.2	−33.0	−47.4	−106.6	−70.5	−73.6
Other official flows, net	9.8	19.1	−27.2	−13.8	−0.2	−41.8	−64.7	−91.7	−151.4	−151.5
Private flows, net	14.4	−3.9	2.8	7.7	6.4	11.7	16.3	11.2	−6.9	−8.3
External financing										
Net external financing	30.0	5.6	32.8	4.6	19.5	15.9	49.1	48.3	41.7	29.7
Non-debt-creating inflows	6.7	6.1	2.3	6.6	6.9	8.5	14.8	20.9	31.0	30.2
Net external borrowing	23.3	−0.5	30.5	−2.0	12.6	7.5	34.3	27.4	10.7	−0.5
From official creditors	3.8	4.3	0.1	−3.0	−0.4	0.7	−0.1	−0.1	−0.5	−1.6
of which, credit and loans from IMF	0.1	0.1	−0.1	0.1	—	−0.1	0.3	−0.1	. . .	. . .
From banks	2.4	1.1	−0.1	—	−0.4	—	4.3	5.5	2.8	0.6
From other private creditors	17.1	−5.9	30.4	1.1	13.3	6.7	30.2	22.0	8.4	0.5
Memorandum										
Exceptional financing	0.4	0.2	0.3	0.3	0.6	2.5	0.3	0.4	0.3	0.2
Western Hemisphere										
Balance of payments										
Balance on current account	−90.6	−56.7	−48.1	−53.6	−16.0	7.1	17.7	29.6	22.7	7.5
Balance on capital account	1.7	3.4	2.9	2.4	1.9	0.9	1.1	1.5	0.7	0.8
Balance on financial account	93.7	59.0	42.0	51.4	14.2	−13.9	−25.4	−31.6	−23.9	−8.1
Change in reserves (− = increase)	8.4	7.9	−2.8	1.9	−2.2	−35.5	−24.3	−31.6	−49.2	−34.7
Other official flows, net	14.2	6.4	−5.2	26.3	18.5	6.1	−7.1	−25.2	−9.2	−1.5
Private flows, net	71.2	44.7	49.9	23.1	−2.1	15.5	6.0	25.2	34.6	28.1
External financing										
Net external financing	121.9	96.6	75.2	85.7	30.9	42.7	40.0	43.0	64.9	70.4
Non-debt-creating inflows	63.7	67.4	71.1	67.9	48.3	38.0	55.0	68.7	63.5	62.4
Net external borrowing	58.3	29.2	4.1	17.8	−17.4	4.7	−15.0	−25.7	1.4	8.0
From official creditors	14.4	7.4	−5.6	24.0	16.5	7.2	−7.2	−23.5	−8.9	0.1
of which, credit and loans from IMF	2.5	−0.9	−10.7	15.6	11.9	5.6	−6.3	−27.6	. . .	. . .
From banks	18.9	−7.2	−1.8	−0.3	−13.4	−5.2	−7.3	−3.5	3.3	1.5
From other private creditors	24.9	29.0	11.5	−5.8	−20.5	2.7	−0.5	1.3	7.0	6.4
Memorandum										
Exceptional financing	10.2	3.9	−10.8	7.7	25.7	19.8	13.5	−39.2	4.3	4.3

[1]For definitions, see footnotes to Table 32.
[2]Mongolia, which is not a member of the Commonwealth of Independent States, is included in this group for reasons of geography and similarities in economic structure.

Table 34. Other Emerging Market and Developing Countries—by Analytical Criteria: Balance of Payments and External Financing[1]

(Billions of U.S. dollars)

	1998	1999	2000	2001	2002	2003	2004	2005	2006	2007
By source of export earnings										
Fuel										
Balance of payments										
Balance on current account	−36.4	37.0	148.8	84.3	63.8	109.2	188.8	347.4	423.7	423.8
Balance on capital account	0.3	1.1	13.6	−6.1	−10.6	0.5	0.2	−12.3	−6.9	−7.1
Balance on financial account	49.9	−7.6	−139.4	−43.4	−13.6	−100.6	−184.6	−313.1	−401.6	−411.2
Change in reserves (− = increase)	28.8	−0.8	−67.6	−28.3	−16.1	−70.1	−121.5	−207.8	−197.0	−199.9
Other official flows, net	12.1	16.3	−29.8	−14.0	−8.6	−42.9	−69.3	−110.2	−151.5	−150.8
Private flows, net	9.7	−23.2	−42.9	−1.3	10.7	12.9	5.4	4.9	−52.8	−60.6
External financing										
Net external financing	54.7	12.4	34.2	3.3	14.3	46.2	75.8	73.0	82.0	77.6
Non-debt-creating inflows	18.2	13.6	23.6	10.5	6.9	27.2	41.5	37.3	47.5	50.3
Net external borrowing	36.6	−1.2	10.6	−7.2	7.4	19.1	34.3	35.7	34.5	27.3
From official creditors	5.4	1.0	−1.5	−3.2	−7.8	−0.1	−3.9	−18.6	−0.6	−0.9
of which, credit and loans from IMF	4.7	−4.1	−3.5	−4.1	−1.8	−2.4	−1.8	−4.3	. . .	. . .
From banks	−3.0	2.5	−0.8	0.1	−2.3	−1.4	−0.1	−3.1	−1.5	−3.3
From other private creditors	34.1	−4.7	13.0	−4.1	17.4	20.5	38.3	57.4	36.7	31.5
Memorandum										
Exceptional financing	14.8	12.7	4.6	2.2	2.6	3.3	2.7	−4.2	0.9	0.5
Nonfuel										
Balance of payments										
Balance on current account	−76.7	−50.0	−57.7	−40.0	20.7	39.4	31.1	75.9	63.1	49.5
Balance on capital account	6.1	8.5	9.1	10.2	12.1	10.3	17.5	28.3	30.2	29.2
Balance on financial account	97.7	66.6	78.6	40.5	−14.8	−64.3	−78.8	−66.1	−78.2	−66.7
Change in reserves (− = increase)	−24.4	−43.6	−16.7	−71.4	−135.0	−209.7	−313.0	−317.6	−336.3	−307.7
Other official flows, net	38.8	28.1	−8.1	25.7	21.8	−4.2	1.9	−13.3	8.5	7.0
Private flows, net	83.3	82.1	103.4	86.1	98.4	149.6	232.3	264.8	249.5	233.9
External financing										
Net external financing	230.7	235.3	213.7	185.3	180.7	234.9	373.7	439.1	436.5	411.9
Non-debt-creating inflows	167.3	175.2	177.3	167.9	158.3	157.2	232.6	259.4	263.9	264.8
Net external borrowing	63.4	60.2	36.4	17.4	22.4	77.7	141.2	179.7	172.5	147.2
From official creditors	39.3	29.5	−9.0	24.8	19.3	1.7	6.0	−9.0	11.4	11.4
of which, credit and loans from IMF	9.3	1.7	−7.4	23.1	15.2	4.1	−12.7	−35.6	. . .	. . .
From banks	11.5	−14.6	−10.0	−13.4	−11.4	10.6	34.8	39.8	44.9	34.2
From other private creditors	12.7	45.2	55.5	5.9	14.5	65.4	100.4	148.9	116.3	101.6
Memorandum										
Exceptional financing	27.2	15.7	5.1	28.1	56.1	31.8	17.7	−32.1	9.2	10.6
By external financing source										
Net debtor countries										
Balance of payments										
Balance on current account	−129.0	−85.0	−76.4	−65.0	−32.7	−26.1	−57.4	−88.8	−103.3	−120.1
Balance on capital account	6.7	9.2	9.4	10.5	12.6	10.6	19.3	27.8	30.0	28.7
Balance on financial account	127.4	86.5	87.4	61.4	43.1	23.2	34.1	86.9	86.7	101.6
Change in reserves (− = increase)	−13.0	−28.5	−14.0	−23.5	−52.6	−81.3	−94.5	−113.0	−120.2	−99.9
Other official flows, net	37.7	24.8	−2.7	25.4	21.1	3.3	−13.7	−40.9	−10.0	−4.1
Private flows, net	102.7	90.2	104.1	59.4	74.5	101.3	142.3	240.8	216.9	205.5
External financing										
Net external financing	213.4	196.5	152.6	140.7	121.2	160.1	237.5	300.6	301.5	297.8
Non-debt-creating inflows	119.4	137.4	119.1	130.0	109.2	105.3	163.6	208.5	208.7	207.6
Net external borrowing	94.1	59.1	33.4	10.7	12.0	54.8	73.9	92.2	92.8	90.2
From official creditors	38.2	26.2	−3.6	24.6	18.6	5.2	−12.6	−36.6	−7.2	0.3
of which, credit and loans from IMF	8.8	1.4	−6.9	23.3	15.5	4.3	−12.0	−35.1	. . .	. . .
From banks	6.3	−13.0	−3.7	−14.8	−13.5	3.9	13.1	14.7	25.5	21.6
From other private creditors	49.5	45.9	40.7	0.9	6.8	45.6	73.3	114.0	74.4	68.3
Memorandum										
Exceptional financing	32.9	20.6	7.1	30.5	59.1	34.5	20.0	−36.4	10.1	11.1

Table 34 *(continued)*

	1998	1999	2000	2001	2002	2003	2004	2005	2006	2007
Official financing										
Balance of payments										
Balance on current account	−32.9	−17.7	−11.6	−6.9	9.2	9.6	−4.6	−11.5	−17.3	−21.9
Balance on capital account	4.6	5.8	5.6	6.9	5.7	4.5	5.8	5.1	4.9	5.2
Balance on financial account	27.2	13.4	10.0	2.1	−1.5	1.9	3.3	14.9	12.4	17.3
Change in reserves (− = increase)	−6.1	−6.7	4.6	7.4	3.2	−12.9	−13.3	−16.2	−13.5	−17.8
Other official flows, net	12.6	20.6	4.2	13.9	17.6	15.0	2.5	2.3	−7.1	1.1
Private flows, net	20.7	−0.5	1.3	−19.3	−22.3	−0.2	14.2	28.8	33.0	33.9
External financing										
Net external financing	44.5	39.0	19.3	9.1	10.3	27.0	30.9	45.1	33.2	44.2
Non-debt-creating inflows	19.1	17.1	9.0	12.7	14.0	13.3	20.1	25.7	28.0	27.6
Net external borrowing	25.4	21.9	10.3	−3.6	−3.7	13.6	10.8	19.4	5.2	16.6
From official creditors	12.4	21.2	4.6	15.6	16.0	15.6	3.6	3.9	−6.8	2.8
of which, credit and loans from IMF	5.4	0.8	1.7	8.2	—	0.5	−3.3	−4.8	. . .	. . .
From banks	1.0	0.9	1.1	−3.9	−5.7	−1.3	1.5	−0.2	3.3	4.0
From other private creditors	12.0	−0.2	4.6	−15.2	−14.0	−0.6	5.7	15.8	8.7	9.8
Memorandum										
Exceptional financing	16.9	9.9	8.6	7.9	34.6	25.2	22.0	−6.9	10.6	10.9
Net debtor countries by debt-servicing experience										
Countries with arrears and/or rescheduling during 1999–2003										
Balance of payments										
Balance on current account	−35.2	−22.3	−1.7	−6.0	2.4	5.6	−2.2	−0.9	3.5	4.1
Balance on capital account	3.9	6.7	4.9	4.5	5.5	2.6	3.6	5.4	5.0	5.5
Balance on financial account	31.6	19.2	5.5	5.1	9.7	7.0	−0.3	2.0	−9.1	−9.7
Change in reserves (− = increase)	−5.5	−4.9	−3.0	5.3	3.5	−8.6	−23.8	−32.3	−32.4	−46.0
Other official flows, net	13.8	21.1	4.2	11.9	12.9	13.0	1.5	−7.5	−7.0	1.4
Private flows, net	23.2	3.1	4.3	−12.1	−6.7	2.6	22.0	41.8	30.3	34.8
External financing										
Net external financing	51.9	47.5	22.5	11.9	21.5	26.2	32.6	44.3	36.8	45.5
Non-debt-creating inflows	22.6	20.9	15.8	17.8	21.4	22.8	31.4	36.6	39.7	40.7
Net external borrowing	29.3	26.5	6.7	−5.9	0.1	3.4	1.2	7.7	−2.9	4.8
From official creditors	13.9	21.1	4.3	11.9	13.0	13.0	1.5	−7.5	−6.9	1.5
of which, credit and loans from IMF	5.3	1.1	1.9	8.1	−1.5	−0.2	−3.4	−5.4	. . .	. . .
From banks	−1.2	—	−0.2	−4.2	−5.1	−1.9	1.2	−0.8	4.3	3.5
From other private creditors	16.7	5.5	2.6	−13.7	−7.8	−7.8	−1.5	16.0	−0.2	−0.1
Memorandum										
Exceptional financing	23.3	16.2	12.1	12.4	40.1	27.8	27.0	−8.9	12.5	12.5
Other groups										
Heavily indebted poor countries										
Balance of payments										
Balance on current account	−7.8	−9.2	−7.1	−7.2	−8.7	−7.3	−7.6	−8.2	−8.6	−8.9
Balance on capital account	4.3	5.1	3.6	4.3	3.3	3.5	5.0	4.3	4.0	4.4
Balance on financial account	4.3	3.5	2.7	3.1	6.2	4.0	0.9	4.1	6.2	5.5
Change in reserves (− = increase)	0.5	−0.3	−0.4	−0.3	−2.1	−2.4	−2.9	−2.0	−0.6	−1.8
Other official flows, net	1.9	1.7	1.5	−0.3	4.1	4.4	2.7	−0.1	3.2	3.8
Private flows, net	2.0	2.1	1.7	3.7	4.2	1.9	1.1	6.2	3.6	3.5
External financing										
Net external financing	8.8	9.2	6.8	7.6	11.3	10.4	8.7	10.4	10.6	11.9
Non-debt-creating inflows	6.5	8.5	6.5	7.2	7.5	7.7	9.4	8.8	8.8	9.4
Net external borrowing	2.3	0.6	0.4	0.4	3.8	2.7	−0.7	1.6	1.8	2.6
From official creditors	1.9	1.7	1.6	−0.2	4.1	4.4	2.7	—	3.3	3.9
of which, credit and loans from IMF	0.2	0.3	0.2	—	0.2	−0.2	−0.1	−0.2	. . .	. . .
From banks	−0.1	—	−0.5	0.2	0.4	0.3	0.8	0.6	0.3	0.2
From other private creditors	0.5	−1.1	−0.7	0.5	−0.7	−2.0	−4.2	1.0	−1.8	−1.5
Memorandum										
Exceptional financing	2.1	2.8	2.7	2.8	13.6	3.5	4.9	4.3	2.6	2.3

Table 34 *(concluded)*

	1998	1999	2000	2001	2002	2003	2004	2005	2006	2007
Middle East and north Africa										
Balance of payments										
Balance on current account	−29.2	10.6	75.8	45.5	33.1	67.1	113.1	214.1	259.8	253.3
Balance on capital account	−0.4	1.1	1.9	1.9	1.4	0.3	−1.0	2.6	2.5	2.6
Balance on financial account	37.3	16.7	−62.0	−25.8	−0.6	−71.2	−106.4	−204.8	−246.2	−250.0
Change in reserves (− = increase)	11.2	−1.2	−37.8	−22.9	−6.7	−42.5	−59.9	−126.0	−92.1	−95.2
Other official flows, net	10.4	19.7	−26.9	−14.2	−0.9	−42.4	−65.2	−91.2	−150.9	−150.9
Private flows, net	15.6	−1.8	2.8	11.3	7.0	13.7	18.7	12.3	−3.2	−3.9
External financing										
Net external financing	33.2	9.7	35.3	9.6	21.8	18.7	53.0	51.3	47.7	36.4
Non-debt-creating inflows	9.1	8.3	4.2	11.8	10.0	13.2	19.5	27.5	37.0	36.1
Net external borrowing	24.2	1.4	31.1	−2.2	11.8	5.5	33.5	23.7	10.7	0.3
From official creditors	4.4	4.9	0.4	−3.4	−1.1	0.2	−0.6	0.4	—	−1.0
of which, credit and loans from IMF	−0.1	—	−0.3	−0.2	−0.3	−0.6	−0.1	−0.8	. . .	. . .
From banks	2.4	2.5	0.2	0.5	0.4	0.8	4.8	5.2	2.9	0.5
From other private creditors	17.3	−6.0	30.5	0.7	12.5	4.6	29.4	18.1	7.8	0.8
Memorandum										
Exceptional financing	2.8	2.3	1.8	1.4	1.5	3.2	1.0	1.1	1.0	0.6

[1]For definitions, see footnotes to Table 32.

Table 35. Other Emerging Market and Developing Countries: Reserves[1]

	1998	1999	2000	2001	2002	2003	2004	2005	2006	2007
					Billions of U.S. dollars					
Other emerging market and developing countries	**700.6**	**726.7**	**817.2**	**913.9**	**1,092.7**	**1,418.2**	**1,871.0**	**2,396.4**	**2,929.7**	**3,437.2**
Regional groups										
Africa	41.3	42.1	54.3	64.4	72.2	90.5	126.5	168.6	215.0	269.6
Sub-Sahara	27.9	29.3	35.3	35.6	36.2	40.3	62.6	85.9	111.1	144.9
Excluding Nigeria and South Africa	16.2	17.2	19.0	18.8	22.7	26.4	32.2	38.3	44.0	50.7
Central and eastern Europe	89.7	93.7	95.9	97.4	130.9	160.3	183.5	224.5	250.0	262.8
Commonwealth of Independent States[2]	15.1	16.5	33.2	44.2	58.3	92.8	149.0	224.2	312.2	389.0
Russia	8.5	9.1	24.8	33.1	44.6	73.8	121.5	186.4	266.2	338.9
Excluding Russia	6.6	7.4	8.4	11.0	13.7	19.0	27.6	37.8	46.0	50.2
Developing Asia	274.6	307.7	321.9	380.5	497.1	670.4	934.4	1163.4	1417.1	1672.1
China	149.8	158.3	168.9	216.3	292.0	409.2	615.5	824.0	1044.0	1264.0
India	27.9	33.2	38.4	46.4	68.2	99.5	127.2	136.7	142.8	149.5
Excluding China and India	96.8	116.2	114.6	117.8	136.9	161.8	191.7	202.7	230.3	258.6
Middle East	126.5	123.2	155.8	168.1	172.9	207.9	256.1	362.6	433.1	506.7
Western Hemisphere	153.4	143.4	156.1	159.2	161.3	196.2	221.4	253.0	302.3	336.9
Brazil	34.4	23.9	31.5	35.8	37.7	49.1	52.8	53.6	77.3	86.2
Mexico	31.8	31.8	35.5	44.8	50.6	59.0	64.1	71.3	77.4	84.7
Analytical groups										
By source of export earnings										
Fuel	139.2	135.4	200.1	225.0	239.3	315.8	437.8	645.5	842.5	1042.4
Nonfuel	561.3	591.3	617.0	688.9	853.4	1,102.5	1,433.2	1,750.9	2,087.2	2,394.8
of which, primary products	27.4	26.3	27.0	26.5	28.9	30.6	33.1	35.5	46.0	53.4
By external financing source										
Net debtor countries	404.3	420.9	444.4	468.9	548.5	666.5	777.3	890.2	1010.4	1110.3
of which, official financing	85.6	94.0	94.3	87.1	95.2	118.9	130.7	146.9	160.4	178.2
Net debtor countries by debt-servicing experience										
Countries with arrears and/or rescheduling during 1999–2003	84.7	92.6	100.5	93.7	99.1	115.2	137.5	169.7	202.2	248.2
Other groups										
Heavily indebted poor countries	8.4	9.3	9.9	10.7	13.2	15.9	18.9	20.9	21.5	23.3
Middle East and north Africa	140.3	136.5	175.3	197.4	209.7	259.6	322.0	447.9	540.0	635.2

Table 35 *(concluded)*

	1998	1999	2000	2001	2002	2003	2004	2005	2006	2007
	Ratio of reserves to imports of goods and services[3]									
Other emerging market and developing countries	**45.8**	**48.4**	**46.7**	**51.4**	**57.3**	**62.0**	**64.1**	**68.8**	**72.8**	**76.2**
Regional groups										
Africa	30.8	31.2	39.2	45.5	47.1	48.4	53.9	60.7	68.8	79.3
Sub-Sahara	27.2	28.6	33.6	33.2	31.4	28.1	34.9	39.5	45.9	55.3
Excluding Nigeria and South Africa	28.3	30.1	33.3	31.0	35.6	34.7	34.4	33.4	33.8	35.6
Central and eastern Europe	35.4	38.3	34.3	34.9	41.7	39.8	35.2	37.1	37.5	36.0
Commonwealth of Independent States[2]	12.3	17.6	30.5	34.5	41.1	52.9	65.9	81.0	98.9	111.9
Russia	11.5	17.2	40.6	44.6	52.9	71.5	92.7	112.7	142.1	162.2
Excluding Russia	13.5	18.2	17.5	20.6	23.8	26.3	29.0	34.0	35.8	36.2
Developing Asia	56.8	59.6	50.0	59.1	68.9	74.6	78.8	81.3	83.2	85.0
China	91.6	83.3	67.4	79.7	89.0	91.1	101.5	115.2	118.0	118.8
India	47.0	52.9	52.6	65.0	90.0	107.1	95.8	69.6	58.1	52.4
Excluding China and India	37.2	44.1	35.8	39.1	43.0	45.3	42.9	39.1	40.2	41.9
Middle East	68.1	66.6	75.9	77.9	72.8	76.9	79.4	94.9	97.4	102.2
Western Hemisphere	43.8	43.8	41.8	43.0	47.7	55.6	51.9	49.6	51.9	53.5
Brazil	45.4	37.6	43.5	49.2	61.1	77.2	65.9	54.8	68.3	68.6
Mexico	33.4	30.3	27.6	35.2	40.1	45.8	43.5	42.7	41.4	41.2
Analytical groups										
By source of export earnings										
Fuel	47.8	50.4	66.7	67.9	65.2	73.9	83.5	100.5	111.8	124.4
Nonfuel	45.3	47.9	42.5	47.6	55.4	59.3	59.9	61.7	63.8	65.2
of which, primary products	52.0	55.3	54.9	54.0	56.9	53.1	46.2	41.9	49.0	54.2
By external financing source										
Net debtor countries	39.9	42.8	39.6	42.2	47.7	49.6	45.8	43.7	43.9	44.2
of which, official financing	37.8	46.3	41.6	39.9	45.3	49.7	42.6	40.1	38.8	40.1
Net debtor countries by debt-servicing experience										
Countries with arrears and/or rescheduling during 1999–2003	37.4	43.6	42.0	39.4	41.1	41.7	39.3	39.6	41.6	47.0
Other groups										
Heavily indebted poor countries	25.1	27.0	28.7	29.4	33.2	35.8	35.0	33.7	31.3	32.3
Middle East and north Africa	63.9	62.0	72.5	77.7	75.1	81.4	83.8	99.1	102.5	108.2

[1]In this table, official holdings of gold are valued at SDR 35 an ounce. This convention results in a marked underestimate of reserves for countries that have substantial gold holdings.

[2]Mongolia, which is not a member of the Commonwealth of Independent States, is included in this group for reasons of geography and similarities in economic structure.

[3]Reserves at year-end in percent of imports of goods and services for the year indicated.

Table 36. Net Credit and Loans from IMF[1]
(Billions of U.S. dollars)

	1997	1998	1999	2000	2001	2002	2003	2004	2005
Advanced economies	**11.3**	**5.2**	**−10.3**	**—**	**−5.7**	**—**	**—**	**—**	**—**
Newly industrialized Asian economies	11.3	5.2	−10.3	—	−5.7	—	—	—	—
Other emerging market and developing countries	**3.3**	**14.0**	**−2.4**	**−10.9**	**19.0**	**13.4**	**1.7**	**−14.5**	**−39.9**
Regional groups									
Africa	−0.5	−0.4	−0.2	−0.2	−0.4	−0.1	−0.8	−0.7	−1.0
Sub-Sahara	−0.5	−0.3	−0.1	—	−0.2	0.2	−0.4	−0.3	−0.4
Excluding Nigeria and South Africa	−0.1	0.1	−0.1	—	−0.2	0.2	−0.4	−0.3	−0.4
Central and eastern Europe	0.4	−0.5	0.5	3.3	9.9	6.1	—	−3.8	−5.9
Commonwealth of Independent States[2]	2.1	5.8	−3.6	−4.1	−4.0	−1.8	−2.3	−2.1	−3.8
Russia	1.5	5.3	−3.6	−2.9	−3.8	−1.5	−1.9	−1.7	−3.4
Excluding Russia	0.5	0.5	—	−1.2	−0.2	−0.3	−0.4	−0.5	−0.4
Developing Asia	5.0	6.6	1.7	0.9	−2.2	−2.7	−0.6	−1.9	−1.6
China	—	—	—	—	—	—	—	—	—
India	−0.7	−0.4	−0.3	−0.1	—	—	—	—	—
Excluding China and India	5.7	7.0	2.1	0.9	−2.2	−2.7	−0.6	−1.9	−1.6
Middle East	0.2	0.1	0.1	−0.1	0.1	—	−0.1	0.3	−0.1
Western Hemisphere	−4.0	2.5	−0.9	−10.7	15.6	11.9	5.6	−6.3	−27.6
Brazil	—	4.6	4.1	−6.7	6.7	11.2	5.2	−4.4	−23.8
Mexico	−3.4	−1.1	−3.7	−4.3	—	—	—	—	—
Analytical groups									
By source of export earnings									
Fuel	1.4	4.7	−4.1	−3.5	−4.1	−1.8	−2.4	−1.8	−4.3
Nonfuel	1.9	9.3	1.7	−7.4	23.1	15.2	4.1	−12.7	−35.6
of which, primary products	−0.1	0.2	−0.1	−0.2	−0.2	0.1	−0.3	−0.3	−0.3
By external financing source									
Net debtor countries	1.3	8.8	1.4	−6.9	23.3	15.5	4.3	−12.0	−35.1
of which, official financing	2.6	5.4	0.8	1.7	8.2	—	0.5	−3.3	−4.8
Net debtor countries by debt-servicing experience									
Countries with arrears and/or rescheduling during 1999–2003	3.1	5.3	1.1	1.9	8.1	−1.5	−0.2	−3.4	−5.4
Other groups									
Heavily indebted poor countries	—	0.2	0.3	0.1	—	0.2	−0.2	−0.1	−0.2
Middle East and north Africa	0.3	−0.1	—	−0.3	−0.2	−0.3	−0.6	−0.1	−0.8
Memorandum									
Total									
Net credit provided under:									
General Resources Account	14.355	18.811	−12.856	−10.741	13.213	12.832	1.741	−14.276	−39.737
PRGF	0.179	0.374	0.194	−0.148	0.106	0.567	0.009	−0.179	−0.170
Disbursements at year-end under[3]									
General Resources Account	62.301	84.541	69.504	55.368	66.448	85.357	95.323	84.992	39.913
PRGF	8.037	8.775	8.749	8.159	7.974	9.222	10.108	10.421	9.516

[1]Includes net disbursements from programs under the General Resources Account and Poverty Reduction and Growth Facility (formerly ESAF-Enhanced Structural Adjustment Facility). The data are on a transactions basis, with conversion to U.S. dollar values at annual average exchange rates.
[2]Mongolia, which is not a member of the Commonwealth of Independent States, is included in this group for reasons of geography and similarities in economic structure.
[3]Data refer to disbursements at year-end correspond to the stock of outstanding credit, converted to U.S. dollar values at end-of-period exchange rates.

Table 37. Summary of External Debt and Debt Service

	1998	1999	2000	2001	2002	2003	2004	2005	2006	2007
					Billions of U.S. dollars					
External debt										
Other emerging market and developing countries	**2,550.5**	**2,597.0**	**2,523.6**	**2,519.5**	**2,612.6**	**2,852.5**	**3,083.9**	**3,224.3**	**3,410.1**	**3,575.2**
Regional groups										
Africa	282.7	281.3	269.9	258.5	271.1	294.6	305.8	282.1	265.4	265.3
Central and eastern Europe	269.8	286.7	309.9	316.0	368.2	460.5	553.8	604.6	656.5	706.2
Commonwealth of Independent States[1]	222.8	219.0	199.2	194.4	199.8	239.9	281.0	331.4	374.7	419.4
Developing Asia	695.0	693.1	656.5	661.2	665.2	697.7	751.0	828.0	909.6	967.5
Middle East	290.9	302.5	304.6	306.4	313.1	324.9	347.4	370.0	381.7	386.6
Western Hemisphere	789.4	814.5	783.4	782.9	795.3	834.7	844.7	808.4	822.3	830.4
Analytical groups										
By external financing source										
Net debtor countries	1,966.8	2,013.7	1,975.8	1,958.2	2,048.4	2,221.5	2,365.3	2,375.9	2,449.8	2,531.5
of which, official financing	587.3	594.9	583.2	578.8	599.9	651.4	680.6	663.4	676.9	693.8
Net debtor countries by debt-servicing experience										
Countries with arrears and/or rescheduling during 1999–2003	710.0	720.8	705.5	697.5	713.9	743.4	767.3	727.0	717.0	719.1
Debt-service payments[2]										
Other emerging market and developing countries	**377.8**	**408.6**	**462.4**	**443.1**	**427.3**	**488.1**	**488.3**	**581.1**	**540.1**	**564.1**
Regional groups										
Africa	25.5	25.3	26.3	26.2	21.3	25.6	28.4	34.6	25.0	26.1
Central and eastern Europe	55.0	58.0	64.2	74.1	77.2	96.4	104.2	123.0	138.5	145.6
Commonwealth of Independent States[1]	29.7	27.0	60.6	38.8	46.7	63.2	72.3	72.6	60.9	67.7
Developing Asia	99.4	94.0	97.6	105.3	115.1	113.6	98.4	107.6	119.1	127.0
Middle East	23.9	24.0	24.2	26.7	18.3	25.8	28.8	41.0	44.1	46.1
Western Hemisphere	144.3	180.3	189.3	172.0	148.6	163.6	156.2	202.3	152.6	151.4
Analytical groups										
By external financing source										
Net debtor countries	291.5	324.2	346.0	344.1	327.9	364.3	351.0	422.6	388.8	397.6
of which, official financing	82.0	77.1	87.7	94.7	76.6	81.9	69.3	88.4	73.6	63.4
Net debtor countries by debt-servicing experience										
Countries with arrears and/or rescheduling during 1999–2003	80.7	75.4	86.8	94.9	72.4	80.6	73.1	97.7	78.0	69.6

Table 37 *(concluded)*

	1998	1999	2000	2001	2002	2003	2004	2005	2006	2007
					Percent of exports of goods and services					
External debt[3]										
Other emerging market and developing countries	**174.2**	**167.7**	**132.8**	**134.5**	**128.6**	**115.8**	**97.3**	**82.1**	**75.4**	**71.6**
Regional groups										
Africa	236.3	219.7	171.4	172.5	175.6	151.7	123.5	91.2	74.2	68.1
Central and eastern Europe	118.6	134.1	127.7	121.6	127.6	125.2	116.7	109.3	108.4	106.2
Commonwealth of Independent States[1]	175.2	177.2	120.9	117.2	111.9	107.1	93.0	86.1	84.3	89.1
Developing Asia	129.1	119.7	94.2	95.8	84.6	73.2	60.6	54.2	50.5	46.3
Middle East	183.3	149.8	108.4	116.8	112.4	95.1	79.8	63.4	56.3	53.7
Western Hemisphere	269.4	269.0	218.8	226.5	229.9	218.4	179.9	142.3	129.6	125.2
Analytical groups										
By external financing source										
Net debtor countries	220.1	219.9	185.3	185.1	183.4	169.5	143.6	121.1	111.0	105.4
of which, official financing	305.4	312.4	265.6	274.0	277.3	268.5	228.3	191.5	176.1	169.6
Net debtor countries by debt-servicing experience										
Countries with arrears and/or rescheduling during 1999–2003	360.7	349.8	274.8	284.8	281.4	256.8	212.6	166.3	143.6	132.4
Debt-service payments										
Other emerging market and developing countries	**25.8**	**26.4**	**24.3**	**23.6**	**21.0**	**19.8**	**15.4**	**14.8**	**11.9**	**11.3**
Regional groups										
Africa	21.3	19.8	16.7	17.5	13.8	13.2	11.5	11.2	7.0	6.7
Central and eastern Europe	24.2	27.1	26.5	28.5	26.8	26.2	22.0	22.2	22.9	21.9
Commonwealth of Independent States[1]	23.3	21.9	36.8	23.4	26.2	28.2	23.9	18.9	13.7	14.4
Developing Asia	18.5	16.2	14.0	15.3	14.6	11.9	7.9	7.0	6.6	6.1
Middle East	15.0	11.9	8.6	10.2	6.6	7.6	6.6	7.0	6.5	6.4
Western Hemisphere	49.2	59.5	52.9	49.8	42.9	42.8	33.3	35.6	24.1	22.8
Analytical groups										
By external financing source										
Net debtor countries	32.6	35.4	32.5	32.5	29.4	27.8	21.3	21.5	17.6	16.6
of which, official financing	42.6	40.5	40.0	44.8	35.4	33.8	23.2	25.5	19.2	15.5
Net debtor countries by debt-servicing experience										
Countries with arrears and/or rescheduling during 1999–2003	41.0	36.6	33.8	38.7	28.5	27.9	20.2	22.4	15.6	12.8

[1]Mongolia, which is not a member of the Commonwealth of Independent States, is included in this group for reasons of geography and similarities in economic structure.
[2]Debt-service payments refer to actual payments of interest on total debt plus actual amortization payments on long-term debt. The projections incorporate the impact of exceptional financing items.
[3]Total debt at year-end in percent of exports of goods and services in year indicated.

Table 38. Other Emerging Market and Developing Countries—by Region: External Debt, by Maturity and Type of Creditor
(Billions of U.S. dollars)

	1998	1999	2000	2001	2002	2003	2004	2005	2006	2007
Other emerging market and developing countries										
Total debt	**2,550.5**	**2,597.0**	**2,523.6**	**2,519.5**	**2,612.6**	**2,852.5**	**3,083.9**	**3,224.3**	**3,410.1**	**3,575.2**
By maturity										
Short-term	357.4	332.8	311.9	333.4	323.0	399.7	482.0	564.3	629.3	672.8
Long-term	2,193.0	2,264.2	2,211.7	2,186.1	2,289.6	2,452.7	2,601.9	2,660.0	2,780.8	2,902.4
By type of creditor										
Official	1,020.4	1,023.4	987.7	999.0	1,033.7	1,088.3	1,093.4	1,046.0	1,036.4	1,042.6
Banks	718.7	717.3	669.0	644.5	650.2	676.0	757.7	799.8	866.3	944.1
Other private	811.4	856.3	866.9	876.0	928.7	1,088.2	1,232.8	1,378.5	1,507.5	1,588.5
Regional groups										
Africa										
Total debt	**282.7**	**281.3**	**269.9**	**258.5**	**271.1**	**294.6**	**305.8**	**282.1**	**265.4**	**265.3**
By maturity										
Short-term	34.9	36.3	15.8	13.9	17.5	18.5	20.4	17.2	16.0	14.8
Long-term	247.7	245.0	254.0	244.6	253.6	276.1	285.5	264.9	249.4	250.4
By type of creditor										
Official	207.5	204.6	201.4	199.1	213.1	229.6	235.0	211.8	192.4	192.0
Banks	47.7	46.8	41.8	38.7	36.9	41.6	44.1	41.5	42.9	43.7
Other private	27.4	29.9	26.7	20.7	21.1	23.4	26.7	28.7	30.1	29.6
Sub-Sahara										
Total debt	**220.0**	**221.4**	**215.1**	**208.3**	**218.9**	**238.2**	**251.1**	**233.8**	**218.1**	**219.2**
By maturity										
Short-term	33.1	34.5	14.0	12.1	15.1	16.2	17.6	13.0	12.7	11.8
Long-term	186.9	186.9	201.1	196.2	203.8	222.1	233.5	220.8	205.5	207.4
By type of creditor										
Official	161.0	160.7	160.8	161.6	172.8	185.6	192.2	174.6	156.0	157.1
Banks	36.7	34.7	30.4	27.8	25.9	29.3	32.2	30.5	31.9	32.6
Other private	22.3	26.1	23.9	18.9	20.3	23.4	26.7	28.7	30.1	29.6
Central and eastern Europe										
Total debt	**269.8**	**286.7**	**309.9**	**316.0**	**368.2**	**460.5**	**553.8**	**604.6**	**656.5**	**706.2**
By maturity										
Short-term	56.5	60.4	65.9	57.0	63.8	92.6	121.2	135.8	149.6	161.6
Long-term	213.3	226.3	244.1	259.1	304.4	367.9	432.6	468.8	506.9	544.6
By type of creditor										
Official	79.5	75.8	77.6	83.1	76.6	74.1	69.4	61.0	58.9	56.2
Banks	101.6	109.6	122.7	108.6	139.7	175.1	211.6	226.7	251.2	272.5
Other private	88.7	101.2	109.7	124.3	151.9	211.3	272.8	316.9	346.3	377.5
Commonwealth of Independent States[1]										
Total debt	**222.8**	**219.0**	**199.2**	**194.4**	**199.8**	**239.9**	**281.0**	**331.4**	**374.7**	**419.4**
By maturity										
Short-term	23.8	14.4	13.9	20.2	19.8	30.9	32.4	35.7	36.6	38.2
Long-term	199.1	204.6	185.3	174.2	179.9	209.0	248.6	295.7	338.0	381.1
By type of creditor										
Official	113.9	113.4	105.9	101.0	85.2	86.4	84.9	57.6	54.8	51.6
Banks	49.9	49.8	18.2	22.4	21.2	23.2	29.8	49.0	64.0	102.0
Other private	59.1	55.8	75.1	71.1	93.3	130.3	166.3	224.8	255.8	265.7

Table 38 *(concluded)*

	1998	1999	2000	2001	2002	2003	2004	2005	2006	2007
Developing Asia										
Total debt	**695.0**	**693.1**	**656.5**	**661.2**	**665.2**	**697.7**	**751.0**	**828.0**	**909.6**	**967.5**
By maturity										
Short-term	87.7	69.2	57.9	87.6	85.9	111.3	142.9	193.1	234.8	258.0
Long-term	607.3	623.9	598.6	573.6	579.3	586.5	608.1	634.9	674.8	709.5
By type of creditor										
Official	289.8	295.8	279.1	273.5	280.3	285.9	300.8	324.3	345.9	359.0
Banks	200.5	195.0	180.1	173.5	167.0	159.4	183.1	205.7	229.9	246.5
Other private	204.7	202.2	197.3	214.1	217.9	252.5	267.1	298.0	333.7	362.0
Middle East										
Total debt	**290.9**	**302.5**	**304.6**	**306.4**	**313.1**	**324.9**	**347.4**	**370.0**	**381.7**	**386.6**
By maturity										
Short-term	55.7	57.4	55.3	58.8	58.5	70.1	85.1	97.3	101.2	106.5
Long-term	235.1	245.0	249.3	247.6	254.6	254.8	262.3	272.7	280.5	280.0
By type of creditor										
Official	135.3	137.2	137.1	138.0	145.4	149.1	148.8	147.1	145.4	141.9
Banks	86.0	88.8	90.1	90.6	91.7	93.3	104.7	112.6	115.6	115.8
Other private	69.6	76.4	77.4	77.8	76.0	82.5	94.0	110.3	120.7	128.8
Western Hemisphere										
Total debt	**789.4**	**814.5**	**783.4**	**782.9**	**795.3**	**834.7**	**844.7**	**808.4**	**822.3**	**830.4**
By maturity										
Short-term	98.9	95.1	103.1	95.9	77.5	76.4	80.0	85.4	91.1	93.7
Long-term	690.4	719.5	680.4	687.0	717.8	758.3	764.7	723.0	731.2	736.7
By type of creditor										
Official	194.5	196.5	186.7	204.3	233.1	263.1	254.4	244.2	238.8	241.8
Banks	232.9	227.3	216.0	210.6	193.7	183.4	184.4	164.3	162.6	163.6
Other private	361.9	390.8	380.7	368.0	368.5	388.2	405.8	399.9	420.8	424.9

[1]Mongolia, which is not a member of the Commonwealth of Independent States, is included in this group for reasons of geography and similarities in economic structure.

Table 39. Other Emerging Market and Developing Countries—by Analytical Criteria: External Debt, by Maturity and Type of Creditor
(Billions of U.S. dollars)

	1998	1999	2000	2001	2002	2003	2004	2005	2006	2007
By source of export earnings										
Fuel										
Total debt	**584.0**	**587.3**	**560.3**	**552.8**	**560.8**	**605.5**	**653.6**	**700.7**	733.8	777.4
By maturity										
Short-term	83.7	75.7	53.9	62.0	60.5	78.9	93.1	102.8	106.0	108.5
Long-term	500.4	511.6	506.4	490.8	500.2	526.6	560.5	597.9	627.9	668.9
By type of creditor										
Official	287.4	286.7	282.0	279.0	276.3	285.1	284.1	237.9	219.1	214.2
Banks	141.4	142.7	110.8	113.8	111.0	113.8	128.5	152.2	168.7	205.9
Other private	155.3	157.8	167.5	160.0	173.5	206.6	240.9	310.6	346.0	357.3
Nonfuel										
Total debt	**1,966.4**	**2,009.7**	**1,963.3**	**1,966.6**	**2,051.9**	**2,247.0**	**2,430.3**	**2,523.6**	2,676.3	2,797.8
By maturity										
Short-term	273.8	257.1	258.0	271.4	262.5	320.9	388.9	461.5	523.3	564.3
Long-term	1,692.7	1,752.7	1,705.3	1,695.3	1,789.4	1,926.1	2,041.4	2,062.1	2,153.0	2,233.5
By type of creditor										
Official	733.0	736.7	705.7	720.0	757.5	803.2	809.2	808.0	817.2	828.3
Banks	577.3	574.6	558.2	530.7	539.2	562.1	629.3	647.7	697.6	738.3
Other private	656.2	698.5	699.4	716.0	755.2	881.6	991.8	1,067.9	1,161.5	1,231.2
Nonfuel primary products										
Total debt	**97.5**	**101.8**	**102.5**	**105.1**	**112.8**	**119.0**	**123.5**	**122.3**	118.4	116.8
By maturity										
Short-term	6.8	5.9	7.9	6.7	7.4	9.6	10.2	9.9	12.4	11.6
Long-term	90.7	96.0	94.7	98.4	105.3	109.4	113.3	112.4	106.0	105.2
By type of creditor										
Official	63.3	63.2	61.4	62.4	69.5	73.3	74.8	69.5	63.8	61.6
Banks	21.5	22.6	23.4	23.3	23.1	24.8	23.4	4.2	4.0	3.9
Other private	12.8	16.1	17.8	19.5	20.2	21.0	25.3	48.6	50.6	51.3
By external financing source										
Net debtor countries										
Total debt	**1,966.8**	**2,013.7**	**1,975.8**	**1,958.2**	**2,048.4**	**2,221.5**	**2,365.3**	**2,375.9**	2,449.8	2,531.5
By maturity										
Short-term	265.1	255.3	240.9	222.5	208.8	240.0	282.5	302.0	323.5	344.7
Long-term	1,701.7	1,758.3	1,735.0	1,735.7	1,839.5	1,981.5	2,082.8	2,073.9	2,126.3	2,186.8
By type of creditor										
Official	809.0	818.5	802.1	819.3	863.0	907.9	897.3	861.6	835.8	835.6
Banks	585.9	578.1	564.0	537.7	545.8	568.9	618.0	613.8	646.1	675.6
Other private	571.8	617.0	609.7	601.1	639.5	744.7	849.9	900.5	967.9	1020.3
Official financing										
Total debt	**587.3**	**594.9**	**583.2**	**578.8**	**599.9**	**651.4**	**680.6**	**663.4**	676.9	693.8
By maturity										
Short-term	69.4	66.4	69.0	65.4	51.8	58.5	68.9	72.9	75.2	79.1
Long-term	518.0	528.5	514.2	513.4	548.1	592.9	611.7	590.4	601.7	614.7
By type of creditor										
Official	280.3	290.0	284.7	296.4	321.4	359.5	360.6	358.6	349.9	356.8
Banks	97.9	95.7	89.9	88.6	82.3	82.2	87.7	86.0	89.9	93.6
Other private	209.2	209.2	208.5	193.9	196.2	209.6	232.4	218.8	237.0	243.4
Net debtor countries by debt-servicing experience										
Countries with arrears and/or rescheduling during 1999–2003										
Total debt	**710.0**	**720.8**	**705.5**	**697.5**	**713.9**	**743.4**	**767.3**	**727.0**	717.0	719.1
By maturity										
Short-term	64.2	62.0	41.8	34.8	26.8	29.6	34.3	30.4	30.1	29.5
Long-term	645.8	658.9	663.7	662.7	687.1	713.8	732.9	696.6	687.0	689.5
By type of creditor										
Official	404.3	418.6	415.5	420.8	434.0	456.0	458.0	437.7	409.7	409.6
Banks	139.3	138.5	131.3	134.1	128.3	127.6	132.4	126.9	132.1	135.3
Other private	166.5	163.7	158.7	142.6	151.5	159.8	176.9	162.5	175.2	174.1

Table 39 *(concluded)*

	1998	1999	2000	2001	2002	2003	2004	2005	2006	2007
Other groups										
Heavily indebted poor countries										
Total debt	**106.6**	**106.3**	**104.8**	**104.5**	**109.0**	**115.0**	**116.3**	**111.4**	**107.6**	**108.0**
By maturity										
Short-term	2.8	2.9	3.0	2.8	2.9	2.8	2.9	2.8	2.8	2.9
Long-term	103.8	103.4	101.8	101.6	106.0	112.2	113.4	108.6	104.8	105.1
By type of creditor										
Official	101.2	99.9	98.7	96.4	102.7	108.6	109.2	107.4	103.6	103.9
Banks	4.2	4.3	3.5	6.5	5.1	5.3	5.5	2.4	2.3	2.3
Other private	1.2	2.1	2.6	1.5	1.1	1.0	1.5	1.6	1.7	1.9
Middle East and north Africa										
Total debt	**378.2**	**387.4**	**381.7**	**379.9**	**391.0**	**409.4**	**430.6**	**447.8**	**460.4**	**466.0**
By maturity										
Short-term	57.7	59.2	57.1	60.7	60.8	72.4	87.9	101.4	104.5	109.5
Long-term	320.5	328.2	324.5	319.2	330.2	337.0	342.7	346.3	355.9	356.4
By type of creditor										
Official	201.0	200.9	196.6	195.2	207.6	217.1	215.8	209.6	208.6	205.4
Banks	101.3	105.0	104.1	104.3	105.6	109.1	120.0	127.0	130.1	130.7
Other private	75.9	81.5	80.9	80.4	77.7	83.2	94.7	111.3	121.7	129.9

Table 40. Other Emerging Market and Developing Countries: Ratio of External Debt to GDP[1]

	1998	1999	2000	2001	2002	2003	2004	2005	2006	2007
Other emerging market and developing countries	**43.0**	**44.7**	**39.8**	**39.1**	**39.5**	**38.1**	**34.9**	**30.9**	**28.8**	**27.5**
Regional groups										
Africa	65.5	64.9	60.5	58.3	57.7	51.6	44.3	35.2	29.9	27.6
Sub-Sahara	67.2	67.3	63.6	62.3	61.6	54.9	47.7	37.8	31.9	29.6
Central and eastern Europe	42.7	47.6	50.3	52.8	53.1	53.9	53.4	49.8	49.6	49.1
Commonwealth of Independent States[2]	58.2	75.2	56.0	47.0	43.2	42.0	36.4	33.3	32.1	30.9
Developing Asia	35.2	32.3	28.4	27.2	25.1	23.2	21.6	20.9	20.5	19.7
Middle East	57.1	54.1	48.1	47.5	48.3	44.8	41.5	36.1	32.3	29.8
Western Hemisphere	39.3	45.7	39.7	40.9	47.0	47.5	41.9	33.3	29.1	27.2
Analytical groups										
By source of export earnings										
Fuel	64.5	66.7	53.2	48.9	48.4	44.7	38.3	32.5	29.1	27.5
Nonfuel	39.1	40.7	37.2	37.0	37.6	36.6	34.1	30.5	28.7	27.5
of which, primary products	58.9	64.2	66.7	69.6	66.3	71.2	63.0	53.8	49.5	46.5
By external financing source										
Net debtor countries	49.5	52.8	48.6	49.2	51.4	49.6	45.8	39.2	35.9	34.1
of which, official financing	67.9	67.0	64.7	65.5	78.9	75.6	69.9	59.6	54.6	51.1
Net debtor countries by debt-servicing experience										
Countries with arrears and/or rescheduling during 1999–2003	90.7	88.2	82.5	80.9	92.4	84.9	77.6	63.4	55.4	50.5
Other groups										
Heavily indebted poor countries	103.0	102.8	104.3	101.2	99.9	92.5	82.2	69.7	62.6	58.5
Middle East and north Africa	60.4	57.3	50.6	49.4	50.1	46.5	42.1	36.2	32.3	29.8

[1]Debt at year-end in percent of GDP in year indicated.
[2]Mongolia, which is not a member of the Commonwealth of Independent States, is included in this group for reasons of geography and similarities in economic structure.

Table 41. Other Emerging Market and Developing Countries: Debt-Service Ratios[1]
(Percent of exports of goods and services)

	1998	1999	2000	2001	2002	2003	2004	2005	2006	2007
Interest payments[2]										
Other emerging market and developing countries	**9.5**	**8.8**	**7.5**	**7.5**	**6.2**	**5.7**	**4.6**	**4.4**	**4.1**	**4.0**
Regional groups										
Africa	8.1	7.6	5.9	6.2	4.2	4.0	3.4	3.0	2.2	2.2
Sub-Sahara	6.8	6.6	5.3	5.8	3.5	3.7	3.2	3.0	2.1	2.2
Central and eastern Europe	10.2	10.2	9.8	9.9	9.0	8.5	7.3	7.1	7.0	6.8
Commonwealth of Independent States[3]	13.3	10.3	8.2	7.5	7.5	11.2	7.9	9.2	7.9	8.1
Developing Asia	6.2	5.5	4.7	4.6	3.7	3.0	2.4	2.3	2.3	2.2
Middle East	3.9	3.2	2.5	2.3	1.9	1.6	1.2	1.3	1.4	1.4
Western Hemisphere	17.1	17.7	15.8	16.1	13.2	11.2	9.2	8.3	8.0	7.8
Analytical groups										
By source of export earnings										
Fuel	9.7	7.1	5.1	5.3	4.5	5.8	4.2	4.4	3.9	4.0
Nonfuel	9.5	9.2	8.4	8.2	6.7	5.7	4.7	4.4	4.2	4.0
of which, primary products	4.9	5.1	7.0	6.1	4.6	3.8	3.0	2.6	2.3	2.1
By external financing source										
Net debtor countries	11.6	11.3	10.3	10.3	8.4	7.4	6.1	5.7	5.4	5.2
of which, official financing	14.1	13.6	13.3	13.2	9.2	7.3	6.0	5.7	5.2	5.1
Net debtor countries by debt-servicing experience										
Countries with arrears and/or rescheduling during 1999–2003	13.7	12.6	11.4	11.9	7.3	6.0	4.9	4.7	4.0	3.8
Other groups										
Heavily indebted poor countries	7.4	6.6	7.7	6.5	4.5	4.3	4.7	3.9	3.0	3.1
Middle East and north Africa	5.2	4.2	3.1	2.9	2.5	2.0	1.6	1.5	1.5	1.5
Amortization[2]										
Other emerging market and developing countries	**16.3**	**17.6**	**16.8**	**16.1**	**14.8**	**14.1**	**10.8**	**10.4**	**7.8**	**7.3**
Regional groups										
Africa	13.2	12.2	10.8	11.3	9.6	9.2	8.1	8.2	4.7	4.5
Sub-Sahara	10.7	9.6	8.9	10.2	7.5	7.4	6.2	7.3	3.8	3.6
Central and eastern Europe	14.0	17.0	16.7	18.6	17.8	17.7	14.6	15.2	15.9	15.1
Commonwealth of Independent States[3]	10.0	11.6	28.6	15.9	18.7	17.0	16.1	9.7	5.8	6.3
Developing Asia	12.3	10.8	9.3	10.6	11.0	8.9	5.6	4.7	4.3	3.9
Middle East	11.1	8.7	6.2	7.9	4.7	5.9	5.4	5.7	5.1	5.0
Western Hemisphere	32.2	41.8	37.1	33.7	29.8	31.6	24.1	27.3	16.1	15.0
Analytical groups										
By source of export earnings										
Fuel	13.1	11.4	14.6	11.7	10.7	10.9	10.0	7.7	4.9	5.0
Nonfuel	17.0	19.3	17.6	17.5	16.1	15.0	11.1	11.3	8.9	8.1
of which, primary products	9.9	12.1	14.6	14.8	16.7	14.2	13.1	10.5	9.9	6.6
By external financing source										
Net debtor countries	21.0	24.1	22.1	22.2	21.0	20.4	15.2	15.8	12.2	11.4
of which, official financing	28.5	26.9	26.7	31.6	26.2	26.5	17.3	19.8	13.9	10.5
Net debtor countries by debt-servicing experience										
Countries with arrears and/or rescheduling during 1999–2003	27.3	24.0	22.4	26.8	21.2	21.9	15.4	17.6	11.6	9.0
Other groups										
Heavily indebted poor countries	15.6	11.8	13.2	14.7	9.7	7.5	6.8	5.8	5.7	5.0
Middle East and north Africa	12.6	10.3	7.4	8.7	6.1	7.0	6.4	6.3	5.4	5.2

[1]Excludes service payments to the International Monetary Fund.
[2]Interest payments on total debt and amortization on long-term debt. Estimates through 2005 reflect debt-service payments actually made. The estimates for 2006 and 2007 take into account projected exceptional financing items, including accumulation of arrears and rescheduling agreements. In some cases, amortization on account of debt-reduction operations is included.
[3]Mongolia, which is not a member of the Commonwealth of Independent States, is included in this group for reasons of geography and similarities in economic structure.

Table 42. IMF Charges and Repurchases to the IMF[1]
(Percent of exports of goods and services)

	1998	1999	2000	2001	2002	2003	2004	2005
Other emerging market and developing countries	**0.6**	**1.2**	**1.2**	**0.7**	**1.1**	**1.2**	**0.7**	**0.5**
Regional groups								
Africa	1.1	0.5	0.2	0.3	0.4	0.3	0.2	0.2
Sub-Sahara	0.8	0.2	0.1	0.1	0.2	—	0.1	—
Excluding Nigeria and South Africa	0.5	0.4	0.3	0.3	0.4	0.1	0.1	—
Central and eastern Europe	0.4	0.4	0.3	0.8	2.7	0.8	1.3	1.7
Commonwealth of Independent States[2]	1.7	4.9	3.2	3.1	1.2	1.1	0.7	0.9
Russia	1.9	5.9	3.1	3.8	1.4	1.3	0.9	1.3
Excluding Russia	1.2	2.9	3.4	1.4	0.7	0.6	0.5	—
Developing Asia	0.2	0.2	0.2	0.6	0.6	0.3	0.2	—
Excluding China and India	0.2	0.3	0.4	1.2	1.4	0.8	0.5	0.1
Middle East	—	0.1	0.1	0.1	—	—	—	—
Western Hemisphere	1.1	3.2	4.2	0.6	2.0	5.3	2.6	0.9
Analytical groups								
By source of export earnings								
Fuel	1.0	1.8	0.9	1.1	0.5	0.5	0.3	0.4
Nonfuel	0.5	1.0	1.3	0.6	1.3	1.4	0.9	0.5
By external financing source								
Net debtor countries	0.6	1.3	1.6	0.8	1.8	2.0	1.3	0.7
of which, official financing	0.7	0.9	1.1	1.9	2.2	3.6	2.9	1.4
Net debtor countries by debt-servicing experience								
Countries with arrears and/or rescheduling during 1999–2003	0.9	1.0	1.0	1.8	1.9	3.0	2.3	1.0
Other groups								
Heavily indebted poor countries	0.4	0.2	0.1	0.3	0.9	0.1	—	0.1
Middle East and north Africa	0.4	0.3	0.1	0.1	0.2	0.2	0.1	0.1
Memorandum								
Total, billions of U.S. dollars								
General Resources Account	8.809	18.531	22.863	13.849	22.352	29.425	23.578	18.983
Charges	2.510	2.829	2.846	2.638	2.806	3.020	3.384	3.216
Repurchases	6.300	15.702	20.017	11.211	19.546	26.405	20.193	17.225
PRGF[3]	0.881	0.855	0.835	1.042	1.214	1.225	1.432	0.520
Interest	0.040	0.042	0.038	0.038	0.040	0.046	0.050	0.048
Repayments	0.842	0.813	0.798	1.005	1.174	1.179	1.382	0.493

[1]Excludes advanced economies. Charges on, and repurchases (or repayments of principal) for, use of IMF credit.
[2]Mongolia, which is not a member of the Commonwealth of Independent States, is included in this group for reasons of geography and similarities in economic structure.
[3]Poverty Reduction and Growth Facility (formerly ESAF—Enhanced Structural Adjustment Facility).

Table 43. Summary of Sources and Uses of World Saving
(Percent of GDP)

	Averages 1984–91	Averages 1992–99	2000	2001	2002	2003	2004	2005	2006	2007	Average 2008–11
World											
Saving	22.9	22.0	22.3	21.2	20.4	20.7	21.4	22.0	22.5	22.8	23.2
Investment	23.7	22.5	22.4	21.4	20.7	21.0	21.7	22.2	22.8	23.1	23.6
Advanced economies											
Saving	22.4	21.6	21.6	20.4	19.1	19.1	19.4	19.4	19.6	19.8	20.2
Investment	22.9	21.8	22.1	20.8	19.8	19.9	20.5	20.9	21.3	21.5	21.9
Net lending	−0.5	−0.2	−0.5	−0.4	−0.7	−0.8	−1.0	−1.5	−1.7	−1.7	−1.6
Current transfers	−0.4	−0.5	−0.6	−0.5	−0.6	−0.6	−0.6	−0.7	−0.6	−0.6	−0.6
Factor income	−0.1	−0.2	0.7	0.6	0.3	0.2	0.2	0.2	0.1	—	−0.2
Resource balance	−0.1	0.5	−0.6	−0.5	−0.4	−0.4	−0.6	−1.1	−1.3	−1.1	−0.9
United States											
Saving	17.3	16.4	18.0	16.4	14.2	13.4	13.4	13.6	14.1	14.4	15.0
Investment	19.9	19.0	20.8	19.1	18.4	18.5	19.6	20.0	20.6	20.8	21.3
Net lending	−2.6	−2.6	−2.7	−2.8	−4.2	−5.0	−6.2	−6.5	−6.5	−6.5	−6.3
Current transfers	−0.4	−0.6	−0.6	−0.5	−0.6	−0.6	−0.7	−0.7	−0.4	−0.4	−0.5
Factor income	—	−0.6	1.7	1.3	0.5	0.1	−0.3	—	−0.1	−0.5	−1.0
Resource balance	−2.2	−1.5	−3.9	−3.6	−4.0	−4.5	−5.3	−5.8	−5.9	−5.5	−4.9
Euro area											
Saving	...	21.1	21.1	21.2	20.7	20.5	21.2	20.9	21.1	21.5	22.0
Investment	...	19.8	21.5	21.0	20.0	20.1	20.5	20.9	21.4	21.5	21.9
Net lending	...	1.3	−0.4	0.1	0.7	0.4	0.7	—	−0.3	—	0.1
Current transfers[1]	−0.5	−0.7	−0.8	−0.8	−0.7	−0.8	−0.8	−0.9	−0.9	−0.9	−0.9
Factor income[1]	−0.3	−0.4	−0.4	−0.5	−0.8	−0.9	−0.5	−0.6	−0.6	−0.6	−0.5
Resource balance[1]	1.2	1.6	0.6	1.4	2.3	2.1	2.1	1.5	1.3	1.5	1.5
Germany											
Saving	24.0	21.0	20.1	19.5	19.2	19.1	20.9	21.3	21.3	22.1	22.7
Investment	21.2	21.9	21.8	19.5	17.2	17.2	17.2	17.2	17.8	17.8	18.4
Net lending	2.8	−1.0	−1.7	—	2.0	1.9	3.7	4.1	3.6	4.3	4.3
Current transfers	−1.6	−1.5	−1.3	−1.3	−1.3	−1.3	−1.3	−1.3	−1.3	−1.3	−1.3
Factor income	0.8	—	−0.4	−0.5	−0.8	−0.7	—	0.4	0.1	0.1	0.1
Resource balance	3.5	0.5	0.1	1.8	4.1	3.9	4.9	5.0	4.8	5.5	5.5
France											
Saving	20.9	19.9	21.7	21.7	20.0	19.5	19.2	19.2	18.9	18.8	19.0
Investment	21.2	18.5	20.4	20.1	19.0	19.1	19.6	20.6	20.8	20.8	20.7
Net lending	−0.3	1.5	1.3	1.6	1.0	0.4	−0.4	−1.3	−1.9	−2.1	−1.7
Current transfers	−0.6	−0.7	−1.1	−1.1	−1.0	−1.1	−1.1	−1.0	−1.0	−1.0	−1.0
Factor income	−0.3	—	1.2	1.1	0.3	0.4	0.4	0.5	0.5	0.5	0.5
Resource balance	0.6	2.2	1.2	1.6	1.7	1.1	0.2	−0.9	−1.4	−1.6	−1.2
Italy											
Saving	21.0	20.2	19.7	20.5	20.3	19.4	19.8	19.4	20.4	20.7	21.6
Investment	22.5	19.2	20.2	20.6	21.1	20.7	20.7	20.9	21.5	21.4	21.6
Net lending	−1.6	1.0	−0.5	−0.1	−0.8	−1.3	−0.9	−1.5	−1.1	−0.7	—
Current transfers	−0.3	−0.6	−0.4	−0.5	−0.4	−0.5	−0.6	−0.6	−0.6	−0.6	−0.6
Factor income	−1.5	−1.6	−1.1	−0.9	−1.2	−1.3	−1.1	−1.0	−0.8	−0.7	−0.4
Resource balance	0.1	3.2	1.0	1.4	0.9	0.6	0.7	—	0.4	0.6	1.0
Japan											
Saving	33.0	30.6	27.8	26.9	25.9	26.2	26.4	26.8	26.9	26.9	26.8
Investment	30.3	28.1	25.2	24.8	23.0	23.0	22.7	23.2	23.7	24.0	23.9
Net lending	2.8	2.5	2.6	2.1	2.9	3.2	3.7	3.6	3.2	3.0	3.0
Current transfers	−0.1	−0.2	−0.2	−0.2	−0.1	−0.2	−0.2	−0.2	−0.2	−0.2	−0.2
Factor income	0.6	1.1	1.3	1.7	1.7	1.7	1.8	2.3	2.4	2.5	2.5
Resource balance	2.3	1.6	1.5	0.6	1.3	1.7	2.1	1.5	1.0	0.7	0.6
United Kingdom											
Saving	17.1	15.6	15.0	15.0	15.2	14.8	14.8	14.2	14.1	14.4	15.0
Investment	19.4	16.9	17.5	17.2	16.7	16.3	16.8	16.8	16.9	17.2	18.0
Net lending	−2.3	−1.3	−2.6	−2.2	−1.6	−1.4	−2.0	−2.6	−2.7	−2.8	−2.9
Current transfers	−0.7	−0.8	−1.0	−0.7	−0.8	−0.9	−0.9	−1.0	−1.0	−1.0	−1.0
Factor income	—	0.3	0.5	1.1	2.3	2.3	2.3	2.3	2.0	2.0	1.9
Resource balance	−1.6	−0.8	−2.0	−2.7	−3.0	−2.8	−3.4	−3.9	−3.8	−3.7	−3.8
Canada											
Saving	18.9	17.4	23.6	22.2	21.3	21.7	22.9	23.4	24.5	24.7	25.3
Investment	21.3	19.1	20.2	19.2	19.4	20.2	20.7	21.1	21.3	21.8	22.5
Net lending	−2.5	−1.7	3.4	3.0	1.8	1.5	2.2	2.2	3.1	2.9	2.7
Current transfers	−0.2	—	0.1	0.1	0.1	—	—	—	—	—	—
Factor income	−3.2	−3.6	−2.4	−2.8	−2.6	−2.3	−1.9	−1.7	−1.7	−1.6	−1.5
Resource balance	0.9	1.9	5.7	5.7	4.3	3.8	4.1	3.9	4.8	4.5	4.2

Table 43 *(continued)*

	Averages		2000	2001	2002	2003	2004	2005	2006	2007	Average 2008–11
	1984–91	1992–99									
Newly industrialized Asian economies											
Saving	35.1	33.8	31.9	29.9	29.6	31.4	33.0	31.8	31.7	31.7	31.3
Investment	28.7	31.1	28.4	25.3	24.6	24.5	26.0	25.7	26.0	26.1	25.9
Net lending	6.5	2.7	3.5	4.6	5.1	6.9	7.0	6.1	5.7	5.6	5.4
Current transfers	0.1	−0.2	−0.4	−0.6	−0.7	−0.7	−0.7	−0.8	−0.8	−0.8	−0.7
Factor income	1.0	0.7	0.2	0.8	0.6	0.9	1.1	0.8	0.7	0.6	0.5
Resource balance	5.3	2.2	3.8	4.5	5.1	6.7	6.6	6.1	5.8	5.8	5.5
Other emerging market and developing countries											
Saving	24.6	23.7	24.9	24.2	25.2	27.2	28.6	30.3	30.9	31.0	30.8
Investment	26.0	25.4	23.7	23.8	24.1	25.4	26.4	26.4	27.0	27.5	28.2
Net lending	−1.4	−1.7	1.2	0.4	1.1	1.8	2.3	3.9	3.9	3.5	2.6
Current transfers	0.3	0.8	0.9	1.0	1.3	1.6	1.6	1.6	1.5	1.3	1.2
Factor income	−1.7	−1.6	−2.1	−2.1	−2.1	−2.1	−2.2	−2.0	−1.7	−1.5	−1.1
Resource balance	−0.1	−0.9	2.4	1.5	1.9	2.3	2.9	4.3	4.2	3.7	2.6
Memorandum											
Acquisition of foreign assets	0.5	3.5	5.1	3.4	4.0	5.5	7.1	8.4	8.0	6.9	5.7
Change in reserves	—	1.1	1.3	1.5	2.3	3.7	4.9	5.0	4.5	3.9	3.1
Regional groups											
Africa											
Saving	18.6	17.1	21.0	20.1	18.5	20.5	21.7	23.4	24.5	24.8	24.4
Investment	21.2	20.0	19.3	20.0	19.0	20.6	21.6	21.1	22.0	22.4	22.7
Net lending	−2.6	−2.9	1.8	0.1	−0.5	−0.1	0.2	2.3	2.5	2.5	1.7
Current transfers	2.0	2.6	2.6	2.9	3.0	3.2	3.3	3.1	2.9	2.7	2.5
Factor income	−5.1	−4.2	−5.1	−4.6	−3.8	−4.5	−5.0	−4.7	−5.4	−5.4	−4.4
Resource balance	0.4	−1.2	4.3	1.9	0.2	1.2	1.9	3.9	5.1	5.1	3.6
Memorandum											
Acquisition of foreign assets	0.4	1.1	4.8	5.1	2.5	3.2	3.8	5.2	6.1	6.1	5.5
Change in reserves	0.3	0.4	2.9	2.2	1.2	2.0	4.8	5.3	5.2	5.7	5.2
Central and eastern Europe											
Saving	27.3	20.2	19.2	19.0	18.6	18.4	18.5	18.8	19.4	20.5	21.6
Investment	27.4	23.3	25.0	22.0	22.5	22.9	24.3	24.0	24.5	25.0	25.7
Net lending	−0.1	−3.1	−5.8	−3.0	−3.9	−4.6	−5.8	−5.2	−5.1	−4.5	−4.1
Current transfers	1.4	1.8	1.9	1.9	1.8	1.6	1.6	1.7	1.8	1.8	1.8
Factor income	−1.1	−1.9	−1.7	−1.6	−2.0	−2.0	−2.8	−2.6	−2.4	−1.8	−1.8
Resource balance	−0.4	−3.1	−6.0	−3.2	−3.6	−4.1	−4.6	−4.3	−4.6	−4.5	−4.1
Memorandum											
Acquisition of foreign assets	0.9	2.7	3.5	2.3	3.5	2.4	4.3	5.2	3.8	2.4	2.2
Change in reserves	−0.5	1.9	1.1	0.7	2.9	1.5	1.4	3.4	1.9	0.9	0.7
Commonwealth of Independent States[2]											
Saving	...	24.0	31.9	29.4	26.4	27.2	28.9	29.6	30.3	29.4	27.3
Investment	...	22.4	17.9	21.1	19.8	20.9	20.8	20.7	20.7	21.3	22.7
Net lending	...	1.6	14.0	8.3	6.6	6.2	8.1	8.9	9.6	8.1	4.6
Current transfers	...	0.8	0.7	0.5	0.6	0.6	0.5	0.5	0.4	0.5	0.4
Factor income	...	−1.1	−2.3	−1.4	−1.8	−2.9	−2.3	−2.5	−1.9	−1.5	−0.9
Resource balance	...	2.0	15.7	9.1	7.9	8.5	9.9	10.9	11.0	9.1	5.1
Memorandum											
Acquisition of foreign assets	...	4.0	12.6	6.5	5.8	11.4	14.0	14.4	13.3	11.6	7.9
Change in reserves	...	0.3	5.7	3.1	3.5	5.6	7.3	7.6	7.5	5.7	2.9

Table 43 *(continued)*

	Averages		2000	2001	2002	2003	2004	2005	2006	2007	Average 2008–11
	1984–91	1992–99									
Developing Asia											
Saving	26.8	31.8	30.3	30.6	32.3	34.9	36.0	38.2	39.2	39.9	40.4
Investment	29.2	32.3	28.2	28.9	29.7	31.9	33.4	34.3	35.6	36.4	37.1
Net lending	−2.4	−0.5	2.1	1.7	2.6	2.9	2.7	3.9	3.6	3.5	3.3
Current transfers	0.7	1.1	1.3	1.4	1.6	2.1	2.0	2.1	1.9	1.5	1.2
Factor income	−1.3	−1.3	−1.5	−1.6	−1.4	−1.0	−0.9	−0.6	−0.6	−0.5	−0.6
Resource balance	−1.8	−0.4	2.3	1.9	2.4	1.8	1.6	2.5	2.2	2.5	2.7
Memorandum											
Acquisition of foreign assets	1.2	6.2	4.8	3.4	5.3	6.1	7.4	8.3	7.6	6.7	5.5
Change in reserves	0.5	1.6	0.5	2.5	3.9	5.2	7.5	5.8	5.7	5.2	4.1
Middle East											
Saving	16.2	23.0	29.4	26.0	25.0	28.7	33.5	39.7	40.9	38.7	34.3
Investment	22.2	23.5	20.1	21.6	22.4	22.9	22.8	22.0	21.9	21.9	21.5
Net lending	−6.0	−0.6	9.3	4.4	2.5	5.8	10.8	17.7	19.0	16.8	12.8
Current transfers	−3.1	−3.1	−3.0	−3.0	−2.8	−2.4	−2.0	−1.8	−1.6	−1.5	−1.3
Factor income	0.1	3.2	0.3	0.2	−1.0	−1.6	−0.7	−0.2	0.8	1.1	2.1
Resource balance	−3.0	−0.6	12.0	7.2	6.3	9.8	13.5	19.6	19.8	17.2	12.0
Memorandum											
Acquisition of foreign assets	−1.6	1.7	16.1	7.0	7.7	11.1	17.8	23.5	23.5	20.0	16.3
Change in reserves	−1.0	0.7	4.9	2.0	0.3	4.6	5.7	10.4	6.0	5.7	5.5
Western Hemisphere											
Saving	19.8	18.1	18.5	17.1	18.5	20.0	21.3	21.8	21.6	21.2	20.8
Investment	20.6	21.3	21.1	20.1	19.4	19.6	20.6	20.7	21.0	21.1	21.4
Net lending	−0.8	−3.2	−2.7	−3.0	−0.9	0.4	0.7	1.1	0.6	0.1	−0.6
Current transfers	0.7	0.9	1.1	1.4	1.8	2.1	2.1	2.1	1.9	1.9	1.9
Factor income	−4.0	−2.7	−3.0	−3.1	−3.1	−3.4	−3.6	−3.4	−3.1	−2.8	−2.4
Resource balance	2.5	−1.4	−0.8	−1.3	0.4	1.7	2.1	2.4	1.9	1.1	−0.1
Memorandum											
Acquisition of foreign assets	0.7	1.9	1.0	1.5	0.6	2.4	2.2	2.4	2.7	2.2	1.6
Change in reserves	0.3	0.8	0.1	−0.1	0.1	2.0	1.2	1.3	1.7	1.1	0.7
Analytical groups											
By source of export earnings											
Fuel											
Saving	27.6	23.5	33.3	29.0	26.5	29.5	32.5	37.2	37.8	36.1	32.7
Investment	28.7	23.5	20.2	22.6	22.1	22.6	22.3	21.7	21.8	21.9	22.6
Net lending	−1.1	—	13.1	6.4	4.3	6.8	10.2	15.5	16.1	14.2	10.1
Current transfers	−1.3	−2.2	−2.2	−2.1	−2.0	−1.5	−1.1	−0.9	−0.8	−0.8	−0.6
Factor income	−0.4	−0.3	−2.3	−1.8	−2.8	−3.4	−2.9	−2.4	−1.9	−1.6	−0.5
Resource balance	0.6	2.5	17.6	10.3	9.1	11.8	14.3	18.8	18.8	16.5	11.2
Memorandum											
Acquisition of foreign assets	−0.1	2.4	16.8	7.5	6.3	10.9	14.5	18.2	18.9	16.6	12.9
Change in reserves	−0.4	0.1	6.4	2.5	1.4	5.2	7.1	9.6	7.8	7.1	5.4
Nonfuel											
Saving	23.1	23.7	23.2	23.2	25.0	26.7	27.7	28.5	29.1	29.6	30.3
Investment	24.7	25.8	24.4	24.1	24.6	26.1	27.4	27.7	28.4	29.0	29.8
Net lending	−1.6	−2.1	−1.2	−0.8	0.4	0.7	0.4	0.9	0.7	0.6	0.5
Current transfers	1.0	1.4	1.6	1.7	2.0	2.3	2.2	2.2	2.1	1.9	1.7
Factor income	−2.2	−1.8	−2.1	−2.2	−1.9	−1.9	−2.0	−1.8	−1.7	−1.5	−1.3
Resource balance	−0.4	−1.6	−0.6	−0.4	0.4	0.3	0.1	0.5	0.3	0.2	0.1
Memorandum											
Acquisition of foreign assets	0.7	3.7	2.7	2.5	3.5	4.3	5.3	5.9	5.1	4.3	3.5
Change in reserves	0.2	1.3	0.3	1.3	2.5	3.4	4.4	3.8	3.6	3.0	2.4

Table 43 *(concluded)*

	Averages		2000	2001	2002	2003	2004	2005	2006	2007	Average 2008–11
	1984–91	1992–99									
By external financing source											
Net debtor countries											
Saving	20.3	20.0	19.6	18.8	19.9	21.2	21.7	21.4	21.7	22.0	22.5
Investment	22.9	23.0	21.7	20.7	20.7	21.8	22.9	23.0	23.3	23.6	24.2
Net lending	−2.6	−2.9	−2.1	−1.8	−0.9	−0.6	−1.2	−1.5	−1.6	−1.6	−1.7
Current transfers	1.3	1.7	1.8	2.1	2.4	2.8	2.7	2.7	2.6	2.5	2.4
Factor income	−3.1	−3.1	−2.5	−2.5	−2.4	−2.6	−3.0	−3.0	−2.8	−2.6	−2.3
Resource balance	−0.7	−2.5	−1.4	−1.4	−0.8	−0.7	−0.9	−1.3	−1.3	−1.5	−1.8
Memorandum											
Acquisition of foreign assets	0.4	2.0	1.6	1.8	2.0	2.7	3.0	3.1	2.7	2.2	1.9
Change in reserves	0.1	1.0	0.3	0.6	1.3	1.8	1.8	1.9	1.8	1.3	1.1
Official financing											
Saving	16.6	19.4	17.2	17.3	19.9	21.9	20.5	19.8	19.9	20.2	20.7
Investment	21.1	23.0	18.9	18.5	18.6	20.9	21.1	20.8	21.3	21.8	22.4
Net lending	−4.5	−3.5	−1.7	−1.3	1.3	1.1	−0.5	−1.0	−1.4	−1.6	−1.7
Current transfers	1.6	2.0	2.7	3.1	4.1	4.2	4.3	4.2	4.1	4.0	3.6
Factor income	−4.3	−4.3	−3.5	−3.6	−3.6	−3.6	−3.9	−3.4	−3.1	−2.9	−2.5
Resource balance	−1.8	−3.3	−0.8	−0.8	0.8	0.4	−0.9	−1.8	−2.4	−2.6	−2.8
Memorandum											
Acquisition of foreign assets	0.6	2.2	0.7	0.1	2.5	4.4	2.8	2.8	1.5	1.8	1.2
Change in reserves	0.2	0.8	−0.5	−0.8	−0.4	1.5	1.4	1.5	1.1	1.3	0.9
Net debtor countries by debt-servicing experience											
Countries with arrears and/or rescheduling during 1999–2003											
Saving	15.4	19.1	18.3	17.6	19.2	21.7	20.9	20.9	21.4	21.7	21.9
Investment	20.6	23.1	19.4	19.0	18.4	21.0	21.2	20.7	21.2	21.6	22.0
Net lending	−5.2	−4.0	−1.1	−1.4	0.8	0.7	−0.3	0.2	0.2	0.2	−0.1
Current transfers	1.0	1.9	2.1	2.4	3.4	3.7	3.8	3.8	3.6	3.5	3.1
Factor income	−4.7	−4.7	−5.2	−4.6	−4.3	−4.6	−5.2	−4.3	−4.4	−4.4	−3.5
Resource balance	−1.5	−2.6	2.1	0.9	1.6	1.5	1.1	0.7	1.0	1.1	0.3
Memorandum											
Acquisition of foreign assets	−0.4	1.8	2.1	0.4	3.0	3.6	2.9	3.7	3.0	3.4	2.9
Change in reserves	0.4	0.7	0.3	−0.6	−0.5	1.0	2.4	2.8	2.5	3.2	2.9

Note: The estimates in this table are based on individual countries' national accounts and balance of payments statistics. Country group composites are calculated as the sum of the U.S dollar values for the relevant individual countries. This differs from the calculations in the April 2005 and earlier *World Economic Outlook*s, where the composites were weighted by GDP valued at purchasing power parities (PPPs) as a share of total world GDP. For many countries, the estimates of national saving are built up from national accounts data on gross domestic investment and from balance-of-payments-based data on net foreign investment. The latter, which is equivalent to the current account balance, comprises three components: current transfers, net factor income, and the resource balance. The mixing of data source, which is dictated by availability, implies that the estimates for national saving that are derived incorporate the statistical discrepancies. Furthermore, error omissions and asymmetries in balance of payments statistics affect the estimates for net lending; at the global level, net lending, which in theory would be zero, equals the world current account discrepancy. Notwithstanding these statistical shortcomings, flow of funds estimates, such as those presented in this tables, provide a useful framework for analyzing development in saving and investment, both over time and across regions and countries.

[1]Calculated from the data of individual euro area countries.

[2]Mongolia, which is not a member of the Commonwealth of Independent States, is included in this group for reasons of geography and similarities in economic structure.

Table 44. Summary of World Medium-Term Baseline Scenario

	Eight-Year Averages		Four-Year Average 2004–07	2004	2005	2006	2007	Four-Year Average 2008–11
	1988–95	1996–2003						
	Annual percent change unless otherwise noted							
World real GDP	**3.2**	**3.7**	**4.9**	**5.3**	**4.8**	**4.9**	**4.7**	**4.6**
Advanced economies	2.9	2.6	2.9	3.3	2.7	3.0	2.8	2.8
Other emerging market and developing countries	3.7	5.1	7.1	7.6	7.2	6.9	6.6	6.3
Memorandum								
Potential output								
Major advanced economies	2.6	2.6	2.6	2.6	2.6	2.5	2.5	2.5
World trade, volume[1]	**6.6**	**6.1**	**8.3**	**10.4**	**7.3**	**8.0**	**7.5**	**7.3**
Imports								
Advanced economies	6.4	5.9	6.6	8.9	5.8	6.2	5.6	5.7
Other emerging market and developing countries	6.5	6.9	13.2	15.8	12.4	12.9	11.9	11.0
Exports								
Advanced economies	6.8	5.3	6.6	8.5	5.3	6.6	6.1	5.8
Other emerging market and developing countries	6.9	7.9	11.8	14.6	11.5	10.9	10.3	10.1
Terms of trade								
Advanced economies	—	—	−0.5	−0.1	−1.3	−0.9	0.2	0.1
Other emerging market and developing countries	−1.2	0.6	2.1	2.2	5.0	1.5	−0.1	−0.5
World prices in U.S. dollars								
Manufactures	3.3	−1.6	3.4	9.6	4.5	−1.4	1.2	1.3
Oil	−0.7	6.7	21.5	30.7	41.3	14.8	2.9	−1.1
Nonfuel primary commodities	2.2	−2.4	8.0	18.5	10.3	10.2	−5.5	−4.4
Consumer prices								
Advanced economies	3.7	1.9	2.2	2.0	2.3	2.3	2.1	2.2
Other emerging market and developing countries	65.2	9.4	5.3	5.7	5.4	5.4	4.8	4.2
Interest rates (in percent)								
Real six-month LIBOR[2]	3.4	2.7	1.5	−0.8	1.0	2.6	3.1	3.1
World real long-term interest rate[3]	4.2	2.9	2.0	1.8	1.3	2.1	2.8	3.1
	Percent of GDP							
Balances on current account								
Advanced economies	−0.1	−0.4	−1.4	−0.9	−1.5	−1.7	−1.7	−1.7
Other emerging market and developing countries	−1.6	0.1	3.6	2.5	4.1	4.1	3.6	2.7
Total external debt								
Other emerging market and developing countries	34.1	39.9	30.5	34.9	30.9	28.8	27.5	24.7
Debt service								
Other emerging market and developing countries	4.5	6.4	5.0	5.5	5.6	4.6	4.3	3.9

[1]Data refer to trade in goods and services.
[2]London interbank offered rate on U.S. dollar deposits less percent change in U.S. GDP deflator.
[3]GDP-weighted average of 10-year (or nearest maturity) government bond rates for the United States, Japan, Germany, France, Italy, the United Kingdom, and Canada.

Table 45. Other Emerging Market and Developing Countries—Medium-Term Baseline Scenario: Selected Economic Indicators

	Eight-Year Averages		Four-Year Average 2004–07	2004	2005	2006	2007	Four-Year Average 2008–11
	1988–95	1996–2003						
	Annual percent change							
Other emerging market and developing countries								
Real GDP	3.7	5.1	7.1	7.6	7.2	6.9	6.6	6.3
Export volume[1]	6.9	7.9	11.8	14.6	11.5	10.9	10.3	10.1
Terms of trade[1]	−1.2	0.6	2.1	2.2	5.0	1.5	−0.1	−0.5
Import volume[1]	6.5	6.9	13.2	15.8	12.4	12.9	11.9	11.0
Regional groups								
Africa								
Real GDP	1.8	3.7	5.5	5.5	5.2	5.7	5.5	5.0
Export volume[1]	5.0	5.0	7.5	6.8	5.9	9.3	8.2	4.5
Terms of trade[1]	−2.6	1.8	5.1	3.8	11.1	5.0	0.9	−0.9
Import volume[1]	4.0	5.4	10.1	8.8	11.4	11.4	8.7	5.4
Central and eastern Europe								
Real GDP	—	3.4	5.5	6.5	5.3	5.2	4.8	4.6
Export volume[1]	5.0	9.1	10.2	14.8	9.2	8.6	8.5	7.8
Terms of trade[1]	0.7	−0.1	−0.3	0.2	0.2	−1.2	−0.2	0.1
Import volume[1]	7.3	9.5	10.0	15.3	8.7	7.9	8.1	7.6
Commonwealth of Independent States[2]								
Real GDP	...	3.3	6.8	8.4	6.5	6.0	6.1	5.5
Export volume[1]	...	4.9	7.0	13.6	2.1	6.1	6.5	5.1
Terms of trade[1]	...	2.5	6.8	7.6	18.4	4.7	−2.5	−2.5
Import volume[1]	...	5.0	12.8	16.6	16.3	10.0	8.6	6.6
Developing Asia								
Real GDP	8.0	6.8	8.4	8.8	8.6	8.2	8.0	7.5
Export volume[1]	13.0	10.9	17.6	20.2	17.7	16.5	15.9	14.7
Terms of trade[1]	0.1	−1.2	−1.3	−2.3	−1.8	−1.5	0.4	0.4
Import volume[1]	13.1	7.7	15.9	18.9	13.0	15.7	16.1	15.5
Middle East								
Real GDP	3.4	4.3	5.6	5.4	5.9	5.7	5.4	5.3
Export volume[1]	7.5	5.0	7.4	9.4	8.9	7.3	4.2	5.0
Terms of trade[1]	−4.0	4.8	9.5	10.1	20.7	7.3	0.8	−2.1
Import volume[1]	1.0	7.5	13.3	12.0	15.8	15.3	10.1	6.6
Western Hemisphere								
Real GDP	2.5	2.3	4.5	5.6	4.3	4.3	3.6	3.5
Export volume[1]	7.8	5.6	7.7	9.6	8.9	6.0	6.1	6.3
Terms of trade[1]	−0.6	0.3	2.3	5.6	3.2	2.4	−1.9	−1.4
Import volume[1]	9.8	4.3	11.0	14.4	11.1	10.9	7.8	7.0
Analytical groups								
Net debtor countries by debt-servicing experience								
Countries with arrears and/or rescheduling during 1999–2003								
Real GDP	3.6	3.3	6.3	6.4	6.6	6.2	5.9	5.7
Export volume[1]	6.3	6.7	8.5	7.1	7.6	10.5	8.7	5.6
Terms of trade[1]	−0.5	−0.9	1.8	2.0	5.0	0.9	−0.7	−1.1
Import volume[1]	4.5	3.6	10.8	11.2	14.1	10.5	7.4	5.7

Table 45 (concluded)

	1995	1999	2003	2004	2005	2006	2007	2011
	Percent of exports of goods and services							
Other emerging market and developing countries								
Current account balance	−7.3	−0.8	6.0	6.9	10.8	10.8	9.5	5.4
Total external debt	160.8	167.7	115.8	97.3	82.1	75.4	71.6	58.5
Debt-service payments[3]	20.7	26.4	19.8	15.4	14.8	11.9	11.3	9.0
Interest payments	8.1	8.8	5.7	4.6	4.4	4.1	4.0	3.2
Amortization	12.6	17.6	14.1	10.8	10.4	7.8	7.3	5.8
Regional groups								
Africa								
Current account balance	−13.1	−11.7	−1.3	0.3	4.9	6.6	6.6	3.5
Total external debt	247.3	219.7	151.7	123.5	91.2	74.2	68.1	64.5
Debt-service payments[3]	22.0	19.8	13.2	11.5	11.2	7.0	6.7	5.8
Interest payments	9.4	7.6	4.0	3.4	3.0	2.2	2.2	2.1
Amortization	12.6	12.2	9.2	8.1	8.2	4.7	4.5	3.7
Central and eastern Europe								
Current account balance	−3.8	−12.4	−10.1	−12.5	−11.4	−11.9	−11.6	−9.7
Total external debt	113.6	134.1	125.2	116.7	109.3	108.4	106.2	98.5
Debt-service payments[3]	19.3	27.1	26.2	22.0	22.2	22.9	21.9	20.6
Interest payments	6.0	10.2	8.5	7.3	7.1	7.0	6.8	5.8
Amortization	13.3	17.0	17.7	14.6	15.2	15.9	15.1	14.8
Commonwealth of Independent States								
Current account balance	2.9	19.2	16.0	20.6	23.4	25.3	23.3	12.0
Total external debt	118.0	177.2	107.1	93.0	86.1	84.3	89.1	119.2
Debt-service payments[3]	9.5	21.9	28.2	23.9	18.9	13.7	14.4	18.2
Interest payments	6.1	10.3	11.2	7.9	9.2	7.9	8.1	10.5
Amortization	3.4	11.6	17.0	16.1	9.7	5.8	6.3	7.7
Developing Asia								
Current account balance	−9.3	8.4	9.1	7.6	10.2	8.8	8.2	6.0
Total external debt	125.8	119.7	73.2	60.6	54.2	50.5	46.3	30.0
Debt-service payments[3]	16.3	16.2	11.9	7.9	7.0	6.6	6.1	4.0
Interest payments	6.2	5.5	3.0	2.4	2.3	2.3	2.2	1.4
Amortization	10.1	10.8	8.9	5.6	4.7	4.3	3.9	2.6
Middle East								
Current account balance	1.9	6.4	17.3	23.8	33.6	35.5	32.8	25.5
Total external debt	144.7	149.8	95.1	79.8	63.4	56.3	53.7	48.5
Debt-service payments[3]	13.0	11.9	7.6	6.6	7.0	6.5	6.4	5.1
Interest payments	3.3	3.2	1.6	1.2	1.3	1.4	1.4	1.4
Amortization	9.7	8.7	5.9	5.4	5.7	5.1	5.0	3.7
Western Hemisphere								
Current account balance	−15.0	−18.7	1.8	3.8	5.2	3.6	1.1	−4.2
Total external debt	252.5	269.0	218.4	179.9	142.3	129.6	125.2	107.3
Debt-service payments[3]	40.8	59.5	42.8	33.3	35.6	24.1	22.8	18.0
Interest payments	17.0	17.7	11.2	9.2	8.3	8.0	7.8	6.1
Amortization	23.8	41.8	31.6	24.1	27.3	16.1	15.0	11.8
Analytical groups								
Net debtor countries by debt-servicing experience								
Countries with arrears and/or rescheduling during 1999–2003								
Current account balance	−17.7	−10.8	1.9	−0.6	−0.2	0.7	0.7	−1.3
Total external debt	342.1	349.8	256.8	212.6	166.3	143.6	132.4	109.0
Debt-service payments[3]	30.1	36.6	27.9	20.2	22.4	15.6	12.8	10.6
Interest payments	11.8	12.6	6.0	4.9	4.7	4.0	3.8	3.2
Amortization	18.3	24.0	21.9	15.4	17.6	11.6	9.0	7.5

[1]Data refer to trade in goods and services.
[2]Mongolia, which is not a member of the Commonwealth of Independent States, is included in this group for reasons of geography and similarities in economic structure.
[3]Interest payments on total debt plus amortization payments on long-term debt only. Projections incorporate the impact of exceptional financing items. Excludes service payments to the International Monetary Fund.

WORLD ECONOMIC OUTLOOK AND STAFF STUDIES FOR THE WORLD ECONOMIC OUTLOOK, SELECTED TOPICS, 1995–2006

I. Methodology—Aggregation, Modeling, and Forecasting

II. Historical Surveys

III. Economic Growth—Sources and Patterns

IV. Inflation and Deflation; Commodity Markets

V. Fiscal Policy

VI. Monetary Policy; Financial Markets; Flow of Funds

VII. Labor Market Issues

IX. External Payments, Trade, Capital Movements, and Foreign Debt

X. Regional Issues

XI. Country-Specific Analyses

***Staff Studies for the
World Economic Outlook***